The Sphinx Mystery

THE SPHINX MYSTERY

The
Forgotten Origins
of the
Sanctuary of Anubis

Robert Temple
with Olivia Temple

Inner Traditions
Rochester, Vermont

Inner Traditions
One Park Street
Rochester, Vermont 05767
www.InnerTraditions.com

Library of Congress Cataloging-in-Publication Data
Temple, Robert K. G.
  The Sphinx mystery : the forgotten origins of the sanctuary of Anubis / Robert Temple with Olivia Temple.
    p. cm.
  Summary: "A book that verifies the existence of secret underground chambers beneath the Sphinx and demonstrates its origins as the Egyptian god of the dead, Anubis"—Provided by publisher.
  Includes bibliographical references and index.
  ISBN 978-1-59477-271-9
  1. Great Sphinx (Egypt) 2. Anubis (Egyptian deity) I. Temple, Olivia. II. Title.
  DT62.S7.T46 2009
  932—dc22

                                                                        2008045901

Printed and bound in Canada by Transcontinental Printing

10 9 8 7 6 5 4 3 2 1

Text design and layout by Jon Desautels
This book was typeset in Garamond Premier Pro with Novarese used as the display typeface

To send correspondence to the author of this book, mail a first-class letter to the author c/o Inner Traditions • Bear & Company, One Park Street, Rochester, VT 05767, and we will forward the communication.

To our friends
Mohamed Nazmy of Cairo
and
Stefano Greco, pianist and musicologist

◖◖ About the Illustrations ◗◗

All the illustrations in this book are presented as duotones to capture the flavor of the Egyptian landscape and to preserve the original reproduction quality of many of the historic photographs. We have framed these rare historic images in black to clearly separate them visually from the more modern photographs and the diagrams that comprise this book.

All the photographs originally taken in color may be seen in full color on the book's website, *www.sphinxmystery.info,* where other supplementary material and information is also available. The website is intended for use as a complement to the book, and though it does not accept e-mails or host discussion, we hope readers will find it a valuable, and graphically rich, information resource.

CONTENTS

was to become an *akh,* or immortal glorified spirit. One's mortal life was only to prepare for this end. So in some ways it simulates the Christian faith: we live on Earth as good citizens, acknowledging the divine and hoping after death to go to heaven.

In Egypt, it feels right to hail the symbolic power of the individual animal-headed gods who are so mysteriously carved onto the walls and crypts and painted on the ceilings and in the temples—a pagan worship, a giving thanks, and an awe of the skyward journey that brings the stars and sunbeams down to Earth. Not one almighty and vengeful God but many minor deities, each one vital in contributing to the whole, the Cosmic Order.

So, when we spent time, lots of time, on the Giza Plateau, wandering around for hours above- and belowground, in the Valley and Sphinx Temples, the Osiris Shaft, the Great Pyramid at night, and the Sphinx precincts, examining almost every stone and every inch, a new ray of recognition pierced our souls. Everyone who knows this place, who spends more than a casual amount of time in the sacred places of the ancient Egyptians, experiences a defining moment, an alchemical change, that creeps into your psyche like a drug.

Everyone has seen pictures of the Sphinx and the pyramids since childhood; they are stamped indelibly onto our memory bank. So, it was a big shock meeting the Sphinx face-to-face, walking the length of its scaffolding-clad body, seeing how deep down it sits in the sand, as if in a pit, and how it seems to smile graciously, offering up its secret if anyone will listen . . . Shhhh! . . . I am Anubis, can't you see? Oh! I see! The Sphinx is Anubis! Can't you see? That Mona Lisa smile, the elongated and huge body, the long front legs ready to spring into action when the starter gun pops, the strata stripes and weather-worn sides of the pit in which it sits, the solid hulk, marooned in the sand like a beached whale. There is a sense of water here, you can almost hear it; yes, the Sphinx has known a watery past.

Later, back in England, immersed in the early travelers' tales, when Cairo across the river was two hours from the pyramids along a palm-fringed lane, the water surrounding the Sphinx, the sense of it being an island with Anubis the Guardian, became more and more apparent.

For nearly two millennia, only the neck and head of the Sphinx were visible above the sand, with a vague spinal shape trailing behind it. There was no leonine creature, no Sphinx Temple, Valley Temple, or Chephren Causeway. Although Pliny describes the Sphinx in the first century AD, when it had been excavated and cleared of sand, as a burial place for a king, and the legend of a secret chamber was born, the desert sands did not take long to cover the colossus again. By the time of Napoleon's expedition in 1798, it was, once again, only the head and neck that showed above the ground. Time after time, excavators had unearthed the

INTRODUCTION

$\cdot\ \cdot\ \cdot\ \cdot\ \cdot\ \cdot\ \cdot\ \cdot\ \cdot\ \cdot\ \cdot\ \cdot\ \cdot\ \cdot\ \cdot\ \cdot\ \cdot\ \cdot\ \cdot$

OLIVIA TEMPLE

O Behold, I pass near you,
I have placed Anubis as your guardian,
I give you light.

THE VOICE OF THE SUN IN THE
ANCIENT EGYPTIAN TEXT
THE BOOK OF CAVERNS

I am not alone in dividing my life into two, an equivalent to BC and AD, which in my case is Before Egypt and After Egypt. Most people who spend time among the ancient places there find it becomes harder subsequently to visualize how life was *before* . . .

Since my first trip to Egypt many years ago, the meaning of life has become clearer. Questions and doubts, fears and shadows, have become mysteriously clarified as if I have suddenly found the key to a complicated coded message.

The most striking thing among the many that the ancient Egyptian world has revealed to me is that *there was no word in their language for religion.* It is only when you think about this for some time and have those words as a mantra in your subconscious as you explore the temples and tombs in Egypt that the enormity of this fact takes shape. Your own thought processes, the very foundations of your own culture and spirituality, are not so much questioned as reprogrammed. This brings to mind John Lennon's song *Imagine:* "Imagine there's no heaven . . . and no religion too . . ." All the things we imagined are suddenly not quite what they seem. One must always be aware of the fact that it was the afterlife that was the important part of life to the ancient Egyptians. Life itself was a big buildup and preparation for the ethereal journey to the otherworld. The ultimate goal

1

ACKNOWLEDGMENTS

We would like to thank Inner Traditions for their enthusiasm for this book and for their excellent work on its preparation and publication. In particular, we would like to thank Ehud Sperling, whose passion for ancient Egypt has continued unabated over the years and whose achievements as a publisher of esoteric and meaningful books for the English-speaking world has done so much to keep the spirit alive for the public in these days of rank commercialism and banality. Thanks also to Jon Graham for inspired work in the field of acquisitions, Jeanie Levitan for her competence as managing editor, Chanc VanWinkle as tireless project editor, Judy Stein and Elaine Cissi as sharp-eyed copy editors, Peri Ann Swan for the cover design, and Jon Desautels for the interior design and layout.

Daud Sutton's three wonderful drawings have been a magnificent contribution to the book, and we are all the more grateful in that they were given to us as a gesture of friendship, prepared with infinite patience during his busy schedule.

Michael Lee's tireless and cheerful contributions to the scanning, filing, archiving, and above all the meticulous cleaning of images have been peerless and crucial to the management of such a large number of illustrations as are found in this book.

Stefano Greco has been a good friend and determined researcher into the mysteries of the lost papers of Giambattista Caviglia in Italy, and in the course of this he discovered the unknown treatise of Annibale Brandi, which he has translated as an appendix for this book. Without his efforts, this priceless addition to our knowledge of the early excavation of the Sphinx would have remained unknown forever.

Eleonore Reed contributed so much of her time and energy toward assisting with translating the difficult article by Ludwig Borchardt that appears as an appendix to this book, and her friendship and efforts are greatly appreciated.

We wish to thank Mohamed Nazmy and his colleagues at Quest Travel for their extensive assistance in Egypt.

We wish to thank Robert and Rieki Rubinstein of Amsterdam for making possible the translation of the Dutch text of Edward Melton in part 2.

We are grateful to Terence du Quesne for materials and discussion about Anubis, a subject on which he is a leading expert in the field.

We wish to thank also Tom Rees for generously helping to understand some of the most obscure eighteenth-century French words and phrases, Ian Burlingham for his help with legal agreements, Professor Ioannis Liritzis for assisting with the inclinometer reading and other observations at the Sphinx Temple, and Professor Lal Gauri for answering numerous questions about his work on the Sphinx and about the limestone structure of the Giza Plateau.

Finally, we want to thank all our friends in England, whom we have neglected shamefully while focusing on life in ancient Egypt, for their patience in taking second place to the Sphinx for so long!

Sphinx, and time and again the sands drew a veil over it. When you walk or drive out into the deserts of Egypt it is quite a shock to discover how hilly and undulating, how ever-changing it is, shifting and stirring endlessly like a restless wind-blown ocean. Upon this furrowed surface you can find small pieces of petrified wood and occasionally a bit of iron from outer space. I saw a vivid mirage there on one of those long hot walks, a shimmering lake, complete with palm trees . . . illusion is never far from reality, and perhaps beyond was the Egyptian Eternity.

Before the hieroglyphs, before the mystifying and tantalizingly beautiful decorations of the temples etched with perfect exactitude and colored with rich pigments, before the high decoration of the Fifth Dynasty with its Pyramid Texts written on walls, the Sphinx was there, guardian, god, long before Jesus walked the earth. Our attempt at uncovering the mysteries of the Sphinx is perhaps only the beginning, and it will be for others who come after us to follow the trail and find more signs. But it is as if the Sphinx itself coauthors our offering, for he too wants his past to be revealed. He is our third collaborator, and no matter how many modern slabs of limestone cover him up and hide his origins, the Sphinx "Anubis" will continue to be the *ba,* or spiritual force that forever guards the pyramids.

> *From now on, O living matter, you are no more*
> *Than a lump of granite surrounded by a veil of terror,*
> *Dozing beneath the hazy Saharan sands.*
> *An ancient Sphinx unknown to the heedless world,*
> *Unmarked on the map, whose timid smile lights up*
> *Only when the sun goes down.*
>
> CHARLES BAUDELAIRE,
> "SPLEEN II" FROM *LES FLEURS DU MAI*
> TRANSLATED BY OLIVIA TEMPLE

In the evening she leads him to the graves of the elders

in the tradition of Lamenting, to the sibyls and the prophets.

But night comes on, so they go along more slowly, and soon

rising upwards and moonlit, stands he who watches over

all the funerary monuments. Brother to that of the Nile,

the sublime Sphinx—: for the sealed chamber, a

Countenance.

And they shudder at the kingly bedecked head, which for all time,

in silence, lays the human visage

upon the scale balance of the stars.

RAINER MARIA RILKE, *TENTH DUINO ELEGY* (71–80)
TRANSLATED BY ROBERT TEMPLE

INTRODUCTION

· · · · · · · · · · · · · · · · · · ·

ROBERT TEMPLE

The most important conclusion to be drawn from the strange odyssey of this book is that the Sphinx is not what we think it is. When Olivia and I first stood and looked at the Sphinx we both felt there was something wrong with it. Why was the head so ludicrously tiny? Why was the back flat? We thought it was supposed to be a lion, but that was no lion. And what was it doing down in that pit? Nothing seemed right, and it made us uncomfortable.

One of the things that most disturbs me is the phenomenon known as "consensus reality." That is what we all agree to believe. Often it is incorrect, but we go on believing it anyway, because we are too lazy to alter our views. Most people like to follow the line of least resistance in life, which means not having to bother to think too much. Thinking is wearisome, takes time and energy, and we have too little of both. So why not let somebody else do this painful task for us? Hence the popularity of "secondhand thinking," whereby we plug our brains into some remote service provider, like connecting our computers to the Internet, and allow other people's ideas to flood in and become our own. So easy! So convenient! Fast, clean, and efficient! Who needs to think of an idea when you can get an idea anytime from somewhere else and just click on "accept all changes" and it's done?

But I never accept anything unconditionally. I have to verify everything. If people say the light is switched off, I check anyway. If they say the sky is blue, I check. It might be gray; who knows? One reason why I do not believe that anyone is ever correct is that I do not believe it is possible to be correct. I certainly don't hold any of my opinions with certainty. I look upon *certainty* as a condition of the human species and precisely what is wrong with us. Everybody is certain, they are certain about this, certain about that. But they are all wrong. I refuse to be certain about anything. That is why I challenge conventional notions. I object to both the word *conventional* and the word *notion*.

So that is why I did not accept the Sphinx when I first saw it.

Having rejected the accepted consensus view of the Sphinx at first sight, we then had the problem of deciding what to do about it. If it wasn't what everybody knows, then what *was* it?

That's what this book is all about.

The first thing that seemed certain was that the Sphinx, whatever it was, was not a lion with a man's head. The second thing that seemed certain was that the head was not original, because it was out of proportion. Several people, I later discovered, had mentioned this over the years, and suggestions that the head had been recarved were not new, although they were still a minority opinion. The disproportionate size of the body to the head could not be seen prior to the excavation of the Sphinx in 1926, so that is why there were no earlier suggestions of the recarving of the head.

Those were good things to start with.

Then there was the question, which had nothing to do with what we were seeing, of whether there was a secret chamber under the Sphinx. This was a subject of feverish interest already, discussed in many popular books and articles and contemptuously rejected in various scholarly books and articles. From previous experience, I suspected that probably neither argument was right. In most cases where people argue violently with one another, they are all wrong.

And then yet again, there was the subject of "ancient rain." It was supposed to have rained at the Sphinx 12,500 years ago, various enthusiastic popular authors (all of whom I knew personally) insisted. That was where all the strange signs of what looked like water erosion came from. However, I knew enough about archaeology to know this wasn't possible, because it meant that seven thousand years or more of archaeological remains were missing. You can't just not have anything in the ground, because there is always something in the ground. So it had to be wrong. But clearly there *was* water erosion, and it is easy to see. So what was the answer to that, then?

There were plenty of enigmas to try and solve!

I have to admit that it has all been great fun. It has been a lot of hard work, but then nothing is fun if it is too easy. Sometimes I tell people I have been inside the Sphinx, and they think I am joking. Sometimes I tell them the Sphinx is not a lion with a man's head at all, and they think I am joking. Sometimes I tell them that the Sphinx once was a giant statue of Anubis, crouching as a guardian of the sacred necropolis at its entrance. They look surprised for a moment, and then they readily agree with me. Most people think it is obvious "once you think about it." And so our job was to think about it, so that everybody can see just how obvious it is. Take a look at figure 5.11 on page 206, and you will see what I mean.

This book has benefited from our special access to the Sphinx and the Valley Temples in front of the Sphinx, which was made possible because we were given permission by the Egyptian Supreme Council of Antiquities, along with a colleague from Greece, to do intensive studies of those two structures in connection with a dating project. As a result, I was able to make some fundamental observations relating to the Sphinx that would otherwise have been impossible. One study was the result of an idea I had while we were standing for hours on the floor of the Sphinx Temple (which is normally closed to all visitors). In a moment between other activities, I took a sighting with an inclinometer we happened to have with us, and the result was most astonishing; I describe it later on.

But the most important thing that resulted from that special access was something that I did not appreciate at the time at all. Because, as I described earlier, I always like to check everything personally, and I am so thorough about detail that everyone who is with me is exasperated by it, I meticulously took a very large number of photos of the passage between the two temples and especially of the base of the north wall of the Valley Temple. My attitude was "you never know when something is going to be useful one day." So I took a long series of photos of what most people would think was just a boring stone wall of no interest whatsoever. I had no idea at the time of the importance of the results. The wall was so uninteresting and unremarkable, in fact, that neither of the two excavators of the Sphinx Temple (Hassan and Ricke) nor the excavator of the Valley Temple (Hölscher) bothered to mention anything about it in their publications. In fact, there is no evidence they ever even bothered to look at it except in passing.

It later turned out that this series of photos of a stone wall, which no one else had ever looked at twice, was crucial evidence to support an astonishing conclusion about the Sphinx. These photos are all reproduced here, because as all the features shown in them have now been covered over with modern restoration stones and cement, they are the only surviving evidence.

Before a person can understand anything, he or she should study everything anybody else has ever said about it first. So we set about systematically collecting every account of the Sphinx since the first known one, by the Roman author Pliny in the first century AD. By the time we got to the year 1837 we were overcome by exhaustion and had to stop, as they were beginning to drown us. Most of the accounts were not in English, so those all had to be translated. Olivia translated all the French ones, I translated the German ones, and friends Robert and Reiki Rubinstein did the Dutch one. We did not collect every Arabic account, but we translated into English those Arabic accounts that had already been translated into French.

As a result of studying the early accounts of the Sphinx, I made the surprising discovery reported in chapter 3 of the survival of specific information through folklore for three thousand years, or seventy-five human generations! This in itself is a major insight into how information can survive without total degradation and loss of message across a length of time bordering on the inconceivable. If I had discovered nothing else, I would be proud of having brought that to light.

We are left now with a totally different Sphinx than the one with which we started. We started with a lion and we got a dog; we started with the face of either Cheops or Chephren and we got another pharaoh's face altogether, whom I have been able to identify precisely. We started with a dry Sphinx and we got a wet one. We started with a Sphinx that was not mentioned at all in the most ancient texts, the Pyramid Texts, and we ended with a Sphinx that was mentioned a great deal in the Pyramid Texts in the most specific way, even saying that it stood beside a causeway at Giza. We started with a Sphinx with nothing inside and we got an interior tunnel. We started with a Sphinx with no secret chamber and we got 281 years' worth of published eyewitness reports of the secret chamber beneath the Sphinx by people who even gave us its measurements and its precise location beneath the statue.

We have a new Sphinx now. Long live the Sphinx!

A Note on the Use of
⊘ Egyptian Words in This Book ⊘

The linguistic symbols used by Egyptologists to transliterate Egyptian words and names have not been used anywhere in this book, *including in quotations,* where we have spelled out whole words in common English spellings to facilitate the reading of these words and names. We hope that the quoted authors concerned will understand that we are trying to make their comments available to a wider public readership.

When Egyptological authors publish their works, they generally use hieroglyphs and other linguistic symbols or complex transliterations. The following passage that I have been translating from a text originally published in German by Erik Hornung is an example of Egyptian transliteration that uses recognizable letters but is nonetheless no more comprehensible for that.

". . . the *jpwt nt wnt nt Dhutj* . . . are from any point of view a mystery . . . King Cheops demands that Djedi fetches the *jpwt* for him, and moreover they are—an unknown number—inside a box of stone. Throughout, however, *jdt* seems to signify a box or chest . . . the mysterious box is described inside the secret chamber, so as in the Papyrus Westcar as a *fdt* in an *'t;* but this box does not contain a *jpwt* . . ."

The situation gets even worse when linguistic symbols other than normal letters (such as *ḫryw šsr.w=sn^n s3m=sn ḫfty.w R^c m-ḫt is 'p=f ḥr=sn*) are mixed in, as they always are. The use of these linguistic symbols or strings of consonants without vowels is intended to let professional readers know that the author is adhering to strict accuracy in transliteration. However, we have the responsibility of communicating with the general public, and having made this advance disclaimer, we hope that no misunderstandings will arise, or that any Egyptologist will in any way be blamed for our decision.

We have not bothered indicating these changes with brackets in order to avoid cluttering the content of the excerpted material. Anyone interested in seeing the original quoted excerpts will find source references in the notes or at the beginnings of the excerpts in part 2 and the appendices.

1

SPHINX OBSESSION

The Sphinx and the pyramids are the central attractions in Egypt. All tourists who visit Egypt go to Giza to see them (see figure 1.1). And we know they have always done so, for Greek and Roman graffiti have been found there in profusion. After Egypt opened up for the first time to foreigners in the sixth century BC, the Greeks poured in and arrived in such numbers that the Egyptian kings had to try to restrict them to special cities of their own on the Mediterranean coast. This was only partially successful. Eventually the Greeks ended up ruling Egypt under the Greek dynasty known as the Ptolemies. After the death of Cleopatra, who was the last Ptolemaic queen, rule of Egypt passed to Rome. And Roman tourists then arrived over many centuries in countless thousands.

The Sphinx is not mentioned by the Greeks in any surviving writing, presumably because it was covered in sand up to the neck, and the head alone could not readily be seen from the vicinity of the pyramids. The first mention of the Sphinx in any classical text is by the Roman author Pliny, in the first century AD, by which time the entire Sphinx had been excavated and was free of sand. And in that first surviving mention from classical literature, Pliny prominently insists that a king was buried "in the Sphinx." From that time, the beliefs that there was a chamber beneath the Sphinx and that a royal personage was buried there in such a chamber have grown into perennial obsessions.

But this has now, in our own time, turned into something more than just curiosity. Millions of people around the world today have become fixated on the Sphinx as an object that is at the center of conspiratorial acts of concealment, both ancient and modern. The interest is not really so much in the Sphinx itself. The question on people's minds is: Is there a chamber beneath the Sphinx? Or, better still, is there a *secret* chamber?

Many books have now been devoted to this subject, which apparently have

Figure 1.1. A view of the Sphinx that is never seen. I believe it has never been photographed from this precise angle. The Great Pyramid is in the background, and the white object at the base of its south face is the museum containing the ancient boat that was found buried in a pit at the foot of the pyramid. I took this photo leaning dangerously far over the southwestern corner of the roof of the Valley Temple, where no one is allowed to go today. (I had special permission from the Egyptian Supreme Council of Antiquities to do some work there.) On the other side of the fence in the foreground is the beginning of the Chephren Causeway, which extends up the hill to the Pyramid of Chephren, which is to the far left of the photo. (*Photo by Robert Temple*)

their origins in the clairvoyant perceptions of an American psychic named Edgar Cayce several decades ago. But despite all the talk, there has so far been a lack of ultimate or conclusive evidence that there is a chamber under the Sphinx, secret or not. Some soundings by high-technology gear have, as we shall see, suggested that there were cavities—many people prefer to call them chambers—in the rock beneath the Sphinx. The situation is complicated by the fact that the Giza Plateau is made of limestone and contains countless natural subterranean cavities in the rock.

In one "shallow seismic refraction" study, published in *The First International Symposium on the Great Sphinx, Book of Proceedings* in 1992, the conclusions about the "underground structure" surrounding the Sphinx are amazingly bland

Page 648. Vol.1.

Profile View of the Remains of the Sphinx near the Pyramids of Egypt.

Figure 1.2. This amusing view of the Sphinx's head sticking out of the sand was published by Dominique-Vivant Denon in his book of travels in Egypt published in 1810. It represents the Sphinx as it was in 1798 and 1799, at the time of the arrival of the Napoleonic expedition to Egypt, with which Denon traveled. The men seem to be measuring the height of the head above the ground. (*Collection of Robert Temple*)

Figure 1.3. The head of the Sphinx circa 1910, almost submerged again. (*Collection of Robert Temple*)

Figure 1.4. This evocative lithograph of the Sphinx dates from 1839 and was drawn by David Roberts, famous for his many artistic views of Egypt at that time. This view shows how the sand has once more engulfed the Sphinx after the excavations of Caviglia. (*Collection of Robert Temple*)

Figure 1.5. An old glass slide of unknown date, showing the Sphinx covered up to the shoulders in a sea of sand. Note the ragged edge of the left lappet of the Sphinx's headdress, which today is smoothed out with modern cement. (*Collection of Robert Temple*)

Figure 1.6. This photo is dated 1869. All we have is a sea of sand around the Sphinx, and of course the inevitable locals with nothing much to do that day. (*Collection of Robert Temple*)

Figure 1.7. This old photo is also dated 1869. We can see how both the Valley Temple and the Sphinx Temple were at this time so entirely buried under vast sand dunes (in the foreground) that there was no hint of their existence. (*Collection of Robert Temple*)

and essentially amount to this: "The underground Structure below the Sphinx area is composed of different layers of Limestone. . . . From all seismograms recorded, there is no indication of faulting."[1]

This is not very exciting.

In an earlier book, *Applications of Modern Sensing Techniques to Egyptology* (1977), we learn that the use of a magnetometer at the Sphinx, which was briefly used "in about an hour of working time," didn't find anything of interest. The authors conclude: "If anything interesting beneath the Sphinx exists, it is likely to be a shaft or cavity, probably now filled, which would have a very small magnetic anomaly. In fact, cavities or voids cannot normally be detected by a magnetometer if the cavity is much deeper than its own diameter."[2]

This is also pretty disappointing. However, a resistivity study (a study of the resistance to the flow of electricity through a material, and how this varies from place to place) at the Sphinx came up with some much more exciting findings, which the report describes as follows:

> Several anomalies were observed as a result of our resistivity survey at the Sphinx. . . . A very limited number of measurements were taken due to the time scheduling of the project. As a result of the survey, the team discovered five areas of interest.
>
> Behind the rear paws (northwest end) we ran two traverses. . . . Both traverses indicate an anomaly that could possibly be due to a tunnel aligned northwest to southeast.
>
> Another anomaly exists in the middle of the south side near a square cupola added apparently in Roman times. This anomaly was verified by two overlapping traverses. . . . When the electrodes were moved 2m away from the previous traverse, the anomaly decreased in value. This is typical of the behaviour expected from a vertical shaft. . . . There are two anomalies in front of the front paws of the Sphinx. The bedrock in front of the Sphinx is covered with Roman-era paving stones and poor electrical contact between the paving stones and bedrock gave somewhat noisy resistivity traverses. However, one anomaly occurs on large electrode spacings, suggesting a cavity or shaft as much as 10m deep. The cavity, if present, is probably filled with rubble. . . . We feel that a more detailed survey should be conducted.[3]

This report is not widely available, and copies are hard to find. I have been fortunate to obtain one. It is doubtless the lack of clarity and reporting of information on these matters that has encouraged a vast number of members of the reading public to become convinced that there is at present a vast and sinis-

Figure 1.8. A view of the Sphinx from the roof of the Valley Temple. Just behind the Sphinx's right shoulder are the two strange "boxes," the large one in front and the smaller not far behind it, that protrude from the Sphinx's body and are unexplained, and are certainly later in date than the Sphinx itself. Although the smaller one could easily have been a statue base, the larger one rises so high that any statue of comparable proportions would have acted as a serious distraction to the Sphinx itself, and besides, we have no fragments from excavations of such a gigantic statue. In this photo, the light allows us to see the strikingly different color of the recarved head from that of the main body. (*Photo by Robert Temple*)

ter conspiracy to cover up secret knowledge of underground chambers at the Sphinx.

But the problem is more a failure of communication, general vagueness, and lack of enthusiasm among the "conspirators." They are probably covering up little more than that they are themselves lacking any conclusive evidence and are unsure what to think.

This lack of conclusive evidence is surprising, so I am delighted to be able to produce some at last. Now, for the first time, I reveal some *real* reports of a Sphinx chamber from early travelers. There are clear eyewitness accounts from as early as 1678 that we will consider later, but my first knowledge of this evidence comes from an old book of a slightly later date, and we will start with that. This first report that I encountered is rather vague, but it set me off on a very long and

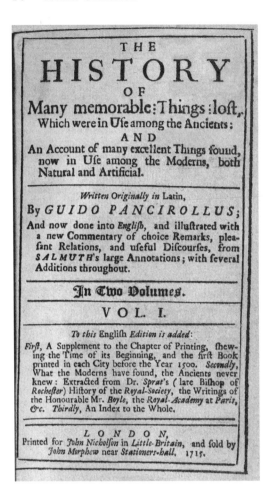

THE

HISTORY

OF

Many memorable Things loft,

Which were in Ufe among the Ancients:

AND

An Account of many excellent Things found, now in Ufe among the Moderns, both Natural and Artificial.

Written Originally in Latin,

By *GUIDO PANCIROLLUS*;

And now done into *Englifh*, and illuftrated with a new Commentary of choice Remarks, pleafant Relations, and ufeful Difcourfes, from *SALMUTH*'s large Annotations; with feveral Additions throughout.

In Two Volumes.

VOL. I.

To this Englifh *Edition is added*:

Firft, A Supplement to the Chapter of Printing, fhewing the Time of its Beginning, and the firft Book printed in each City before the Year 1500. *Secondly*, What the Moderns have found, the Ancients never knew: Extracted from Dr. *Sprat*'s (late Bifhop of *Rochefter*) Hiftory of the *Royal-Society*, the Writings of the Honourable Mr. *Boyle*, the *Royal-Academy* at *Paris*, &c. *Thirdly*, An Index to the Whole.

LONDON,

Printed for *John Nicholfon* in *Little-Britain*, and fold by *John Morphew* near *Stationers-hall*. 1715.

Figure 1.9. The title page of Guido Pancirollo's book *The History of Many Memorable Things Lost*, in its English translation (my own copy), London, 1715.

onerous search through all the early travelers' reports on the Sphinx to find more evidence, in which I was to be more successful than I had dared imagine.

Let us follow the process of discovery. When I first encountered this information, it appeared to be the only such account of a Sphinx chamber in existence. It was published in 1715, and for nearly three centuries no one had paid the slightest attention to it.

But eventually, everything somehow seems to come to light, and I came across this initial report while researching ancient optical technology for my book *The Crystal Sun*. At that time I looked at the report of the Sphinx only out of mild curiosity. In fact, I photocopied it and did not actually read that section of the photocopy for months, for my attention was elsewhere. The title page of the book, and the page about the Sphinx, are reproduced in figures 1.9 and 1.10.

But before we get into this account published in 1715 and begin to evaluate

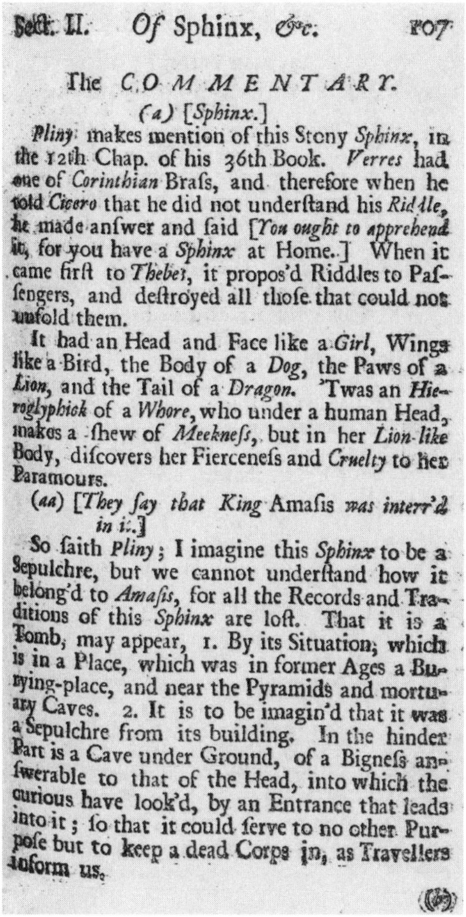

Figure 1.10. The page in Pancirollo's book that mentions the chamber beneath the Sphinx, which was the first pubished account of it I came across, although it was not the earliest, as I was to discover.

Sect. II.   *Of* Sphinx, *&c.*   107

The C O M M E N T A R Y.

(a) [*Sphinx*.]

Pliny makes mention of this Stony *Sphinx*, in the 12th Chap. of his 36th Book. *Verres* had one of *Corinthian* Brass, and therefore when he told *Cicero* that he did not understand his *Riddle*, he made answer and said [*You ought to apprehend it, for you have a Sphinx* at Home.] When it came first to *Thebes*, it propos'd Riddles to Passengers, and destroyed all those that could not unfold them.

It had an Head and Face like a *Girl*, Wings like a Bird, the Body of a *Dog*, the Paws of a *Lion*, and the Tail of a *Dragon*. 'Twas an *Hieroglyphick* of a *Whore*, who under a human Head, makes a shew of *Meekness*, but in her *Lion*-like Body, discovers her Fierceness and *Cruelty* to her Paramours.

(*aa*) [*They say that* King Amasis *was interr'd in it.*]

So saith *Pliny*; I imagine this *Sphinx* to be a Sepulchre, but we cannot understand how it belong'd to *Amasis*, for all the Records and Traditions of this *Sphinx* are lost. That it is a Tomb, may appear, 1. By its Situation; which is in a Place, which was in former Ages a Burying-place, and near the Pyramids and mortuary Caves. 2. It is to be imagin'd that it was a Sepulchre from its building. In the hinder Part is a Cave under Ground, of a Bigness answerable to that of the Head, into which the curious have look'd, by an Entrance that leads into it; so that it could serve to no other Purpose but to keep a dead Corps in, as Travellers inform us.

it, let me tell you about my own experience of entering a chamber beneath the Sphinx. This chamber is known by repute to everyone with a deep interest in the Sphinx; it is the bottom of the little tunnel beneath the Sphinx's rump. You can see the relatively tiny size of the tunnel in figures 1.11 to 1.13, and me crawling out of it in figure 1.14.

The rump tunnel, if that is not too rude a designation, has been entered by only a tiny handful of people. It is not at all easy to photograph the rump tunnel, because it is very narrow and cramped and there are not many features; and to demonstrate the scale, presumably someone should stand in the photo at the bottom of the tunnel, after first removing the accumulated rubbish. I have been unable to get the necessary lights or organize such a photo, and I am unaware of anyone else ever having done so. But some impression of the interior of the tunnel may be obtained from my flash photo in figure 1.15.

Figure 1.11. This tiny hole at the base of the rear end of the Sphinx of Giza shows the entrance to a passage that descends 20 feet. (*Photo by Robert Temple*)

Figure 1.12. A close-up photo of the entrance to the rump tunnel. All the flat limestone blocks are modern reconstruction stones, not part of the original Sphinx. The way the bedrock has been cut away in a circular shape may here be seen clearly. The top of an interior modern steel support may also be seen. Behind the reconstruction blocks, a bit of the original Sphinx stone may be glimpsed above the hole. The rough workmanship and clumsy hacking evident here demonstrate that this is an intruded shaft from a late period that never formed part of the original intention of the Sphinx. It takes a thin person to squeeze inside. (*Photo by Robert Temple*)

Figure 1.13. It's amazing how much there is to see when you look down below the Sphinx's bottom. (*Photo by Olivia Temple*)

Figure 1.14. Here I am emerging from the "rump tunnel" beneath the Sphinx or, to put it more bluntly, with my head sticking out of the Sphinx's ass. The original stone can be seen behind me underneath the layer of smooth modern restoration blocks. (*Photo by Olivia Temple*)

Figure 1.15. This is a photo looking directly downward inside the entrance of the little hole in the Sphinx's bottom. This shaft and pit have been excavated out of the bedrock. As may be seen, it is all littered with tourist rubbish. But the pieces of paper lying on the bottom help one get an accurate scale. The pit is about 15 feet down, has no sign of water, and would comfortably allow a single person to "incubate" overnight in search of a sacred dream. It is too small for a tomb. Because the shaft is so crudely cut out of the rock, showing no regularity or professionalism, it must be a late intruded shaft. It probably dates from the Ptolemaic Period and was used under the Greeks and Romans, at a high price to selected persons, for healing and inspiration purposes. Since it could be used only 365 times a year, by one person at a time, the number of clients was necessarily small. Alternatively, the hole may have been used for someone to sleep overnight to prepare him or her to deliver oracular prophecies through a speaking tube at dawn, when the crowds came to pray to the Sphinx. This shaft continues upward and curves around the southern side of the Sphinx. (*Photo by Robert Temple*)

Squeezing into the tiny opening at the base of the Sphinx's rump is a difficult business (see figure 1.13). As soon as you stick your head in, you can see that a metal ladder has been affixed inside, onto which you can cling, so that you can hoist yourself around and have something to hold on to. Then you can clamber into an upright position. Once you are standing, and not perilously poised over a hole, you can take the time to look around you. Naturally, you have to have a light in your hand or you cannot see a thing.

What you can see from the ladder is that a narrow tunnel about 15 feet deep has been dug out of the rock. At the bottom, the first thing you notice is a lot of rubbish that has blown in through the hole, as the Giza Plateau is covered with masses of rubbish dropped every day by tourists and visitors. As you peer intently to see just what is at the bottom, it becomes clear that the rock has been scooped to form a rounded hollow that is big enough for two people to stand in side by side.

What struck me about this hollow was that a lot of trouble seemed to have been taken to create it, and it did not resemble the effort of a treasure seeker. I had the impression that its real purpose was to enable a person to curl up in a bed and lie there comfortably overnight, or at least for some hours. My reaction to seeing this "cell," for that is what it reminded me of, was to assume that this is where special acts of incubation may have taken place. *Incubation* is the word used to describe the ancient practice, common among the Greeks, of sleeping in a temple overnight in order to have a sacred dream. The Greeks generally did this for medical reasons, in temples of their god of medicine, Asclepius. A typical example of such a temple is at Epidauros in the Pelopponese in Greece.

In Greek incubation, a sacred dream would come to the lucky person sleeping in the holy spot, and this dream would reveal the means of cure of the ailment. Other forms of incubation might have different aims: inspiration, prophecy, divine guidance, or communion with the divine might be sought instead of cures for disease. A classic book on this subject was written by Mary Hamilton, who says about Isis and "incubation":

> If the [account of Diodorus Siculus saying that the goddess Isis healed people in their sleep] were to be taken literally, it would mean that the activity of Isis as an iatromantic [medically prophesying] oracle reached far back into the obscurer centuries, and that incubation had been an Egyptian practice from early times. The importance of the role of Isis in medical science cannot be denied, but Welcker refuses to credit her with the position assigned by Diodorus. He considers that the priesthood established such a tradition at a late date in order to strengthen faith in the new practices of their health-oracles by fortifying

them with the assurance of antiquity. He believes that only under the Ptolemies [commencing in the late fourth century BC] did Isis begin to rank as a goddess of healing. . . . It may be that then, for the first time, the practice of incubation became general in Egypt, but as a healing goddess Isis had been honoured many centuries before.[4]

I am inclined to believe that the Sphinx rump tunnel, whatever its original date may be, was known and used during the period when we know that the Sphinx was cleared of sand under the Ptolemies, the period of Greek rule and Greek religious influence subsequent to the fourth century BC. Only the most special visitors, who were prepared to pay the priests a lot of money for the privilege, would have been allowed to sleep overnight beneath the rear of the Sphinx. After all, unlike the temples of Asclepius that could accommodate sometimes dozens of visitors at a time in incubation cells, the hollow beneath the Sphinx could hold only one person at a time. The Sphinx inspired a great deal of awe and at this late period was considered a sacred idol, who was called Harmachis; sacrifices were offered to it as a god, in front of the statue, where an altar existed between its paws (see figures 1.16 to 1.22). To be allowed to sleep beneath the Sphinx would have been a powerful and overwhelming experience, and by the power of autosuggestion alone, aside from any other factors, many clients would have been bound to have apocalyptic dreams. The word-of-mouth reputation would have created a vast waiting list of people wishing to have these experiences, just as there are thousands of tourists today who are prepared to pay extra fees to their tour groups for the privilege of standing between the paws of the Sphinx. People will always swarm to any place of healing, as Lourdes proves in our own day.

The vast stairway leading down to the Sphinx in Ptolemaic and Roman times is shown in figures 6.44 and 6.45, figure 6.45 being drawn shortly after its excavation in 1817. Not a stone of this stairway now remains, as it concealed a temple beneath, which has now been excavated (the Sphinx Temple). Indeed, this early drawing is apparently the only picture in existence of what the approach to the Sphinx looked like at that period of history. It was clearly designed for the use of large crowds, with smoking altars placed at intervals of the stairway as part of the crowd-management techniques in connection with the public ceremonies and mass access for offerings and worship. Countless offerings left both by the ordinary public and by dignitaries were dug up from around the Sphinx during the various excavations that took place between 1817 and 1937.

Figure 1.16. This old photo from 1896/1897 contains a contemporary inscription that gives us information that I have found nowhere else, namely that Colonel George Raum carried out excavations at the Sphinx in 1896. I don't believe there is any other surviving evidence that these excavations took place. Nor have I ever heard before of the "stone cap." The inscription reads: "Some successfull [sic] excavations at the foot of the Sphinx have recently been carried out by Col. Raum. In 1896 the stone cap was discovered—This discovery seems to have been of much advance by Dean Stanley who in his Travels wonders apropos of the colossal head of the Sphinx 'What a sight it must have been when on its head was the Royal Helmet of Egypt.'" (Note: The American colonel George Edward Raum, of San Francisco, arrived in Egypt in 1885. He found a portion of the "rock crown" of the Sphinx in an excavation between its forepaws on 26 February 1896.) (*Collection of Robert Temple*)

Figure 1.17. This mid- to late-nineteenth-century photo by a French photographer based at Port Said shows the north side of the Sphinx Moat (on the right in this photo) not only totally unexcavated but still containing late overlying structures protruding from the sand. Here, just above the left paw of the Sphinx, we can see the remains of a stone wall, for instance. At this period, the north side of the Sphinx Moat had not been clear since the time of the Roman Empire—in other words, for about 1,800 or 1,900 years. The small stones covering the toes of the Sphinx are reconstruction blocks dating from Roman times. (*Collection of Robert Temple*)

Figure 1.18. This stereoview was taken between 1926 and 1936, since it shows at far right the walls erected by Baraize in 1926 to hold back the sand on the north. The walls were demolished by Selim Hassan in 1936. (*Collection of Robert Temple*)

Figure 1.19. This photo shows very clearly the small altar between the paws of the Sphinx, at which offerings were burned during Roman times, when the Sphinx was thought to be a god named Harmachis. Farther back, between the paws and up against the chest of the Sphinx, stands the Dream Stela. This photo comes from Adolf Erman's book *Die Welt am Nil* (*The World on the Nile*), Leipzig, 1936, where it is Plate 13 opposite page 58. Erman credits Ludwig Borchardt. This photo probably dates from 1936, immediately after the lappets of the headdress had been "restored" by Selim Hassan, as the new concrete lower portions are still so fresh that they are far paler than the stone. Subsequently, the concrete darkened during curing, and this contrast was no longer so obvious.

Figure 1.20. This photo, probably dating from about 1850/1860, shows the limits of Caviglia's excavation of 1817. The little wall above the left foreleg of the Sphinx suggests that Caviglia never cleared the sand much farther than a few feet to the north of that foreleg. As for the south side of the Sphinx (its right, left of photo), the sand was right up to shoulder height. Nevertheless, we can see in the background that the rump is entirely clear. An Arab squats at the base of the Sphinx's neck on the north side. (*Collection of Robert Temple*)

Figure 1.21. I am inclined to suspect this glass slide is very early indeed. It shows the results of Caviglia having tried to make some clearance to the south, and just a bit at the north, of the Sphinx. The photo may be circa 1830, but I am just guessing. (*Collection of Robert Temple*)

Figure 1.22. This very strange photo shows the Sphinx acting as host to a visiting American baseball team! The photo was taken in 1889, and the baseball players were traveling with Albert Spalding; they were known as the Spalding National League. They went on a world tour "to bring baseball, and with it the American way, to the four corners of the earth," as it says in a book by Mark Lamster, *Spalding's World Tour*, New York, 2006. This photo gives a good view of the true condition of the paws of the Sphinx, as they were when still constituted of small stones dating from Roman times; today, these are completely covered in modern stones, and none of the Roman ones can be seen any longer beneath the present covering of white limestone blocks. (*Collection of Robert Temple*)

Figure 1.23. A photo circa 1870 showing a man standing on top of the Sphinx's forehead, his arm extended toward the east. Three figures stand on the back, just behind the head. This photo enables us to appreciate the scale of the sculpture, and even though the head is far too small for the body, it still utterly dwarfs the man. (*Collection of Robert Temple*)

Another interesting point is the connection of Isis with incubation, at least by Ptolemaic times. As may be seen in part 2, section 2, where I have gathered travelers' accounts of the Sphinx from Pliny up to the mid-nineteenth century, the tales of the Sphinx dating from the Middle Ages sometimes referred to the statue as "the Idol of Isis." This appears to be a survival of an old tradition that may refer to the association of incubation at the Sphinx with the patron goddess of such things, Isis. There was even a small Temple of Isis nearby during this period, just a short distance northwest of the Sphinx (see figures 1.24 to 1.27). This temple is mentioned by name in an enigmatic stela excavated at Giza that has come to be called the Inventory Stela (figures 5.12 and 5.13). The Inventory Stela is discussed in chapter 5.

The actual passage in Diodorus Siculus (circa 80–20 BC) is interesting to read. First I give it in the charming translation by Booth that was published in 1700, from one of my old leather-bound translation volumes: "The Egyptians report that Isis found out many medicines for the recovery of men's health, being very expert in the art of physick, and contriv'd many remedies for that purpose; and therefore even now when she is advanc'd to an immortal state, she takes pleasure in curing men's bodies, and to those that desire her assistance, in their sleep she clearly manifests her presence, and affords ready and effectual relief to them that stand in need of it."[5]

The modern translation, of which I give a greater portion, is less quaint:

As for Isis, the Egyptians say that she was the discoverer of many health-giving drugs and was greatly versed in the science of healing; consequently, now that she has attained immortality, she finds her greatest delight in the healing of mankind and gives aid in their sleep to those who call upon her, plainly manifesting both her very presence and her beneficence towards men who ask her help. In proof of this, as they say, they advance not legends, as the Greeks do, but manifest facts, for practically the entire inhabited world is their witness, in that it eagerly contributes to the honours of Isis, because she manifests herself in healings. For standing above the sick in their sleep she gives them aid for their diseases and works remarkable cures upon such as submit themselves to her; and many who have been despaired of by their physicians because of the difficult nature of their malady are restored to health by her, while numbers who have altogether lost the use of their eyes or of some other part of their body, whenever they turn for help to this goddess, are restored to their previous condition. Furthermore, she discovered also the drug which gives immortality.[6]

This explicit testimony from a writer of the first century BC makes it very clear that incubation at an Isis center was taking place in Egypt during Greek and Roman times. We can safely presume that this was happening at the Temple of Isis on the island of Philae, in the south of Egypt. However, the only Isis temple I know of in the north of Egypt is the one at Giza. It was so small that it is difficult to imagine incubation taking place there. I believe the evidence warrants the assumption that the cell beneath the rump of the Sphinx was used for incubation, and that the priests of the small Temple of Isis nearby were the ones who arranged this. As for Diodorus's reference to Isis becoming known all over the world for her healing abilities, this refers to the fact that during the Greek and Roman periods, Isis temples were founded all over the Mediterranean. Anyone who has visited Pompeii will have seen the one there, which is so well preserved. There was one in every Roman town of size. The Isis temple in Paris was outside the city walls of the Roman town

Figure 1.24. This is plate LIV (following p. 140) in Selim Hassan's report of his Sphinx excavations, *The Great Sphinx and Its Secrets: Historical Studies in the Light of Recent Excavations,* volume VIII of the series *Excavations at Giza,* in this case for the years 1936–37, Government Press, Cairo, 1953. This photo shows the chapel of the Temple of Isis at Giza that led into the inner sanctum. On Hassan's plan of the temple (see figure 1.25 below) this chapel is marked "H." This photo appears to have been taken facing north, from the inner sanctum itself looking outward through the chapel doorway. According to Hassan (p. 111), this temple was probably constructed during the Eighteenth Dynasty of the New Kingdom, as we know that King Ay, the successor of Tutankhamun, made an offering there, as did other New Kingdom personalities. After the reign of Rameses II, the temple seems to have experienced a decline, until it was revived in the Saite Period (664–525 BC), when it was once again very important up until the time of the Persian Conquest in 525 BC.

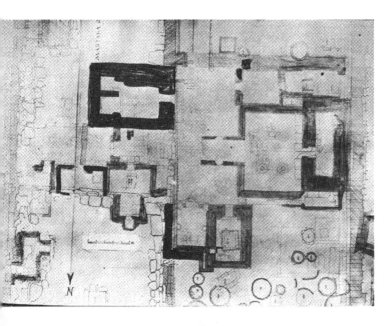

Figure 1.25. This is plate LII from Selim Hassan's book, *The Great Sphinx and Its Secrets,* Cairo, 1953. It shows Hassan's drawing of the plan of the ruined Temple of Isis, which lies at the foot of the Great Pyramid on the eastern side.

Figure 1.26. This photo is plate XLVIII in Selim Hassan's book, *The Great Sphinx and Its Secrets*, Cairo, 1953. It is of a limestone stela excavated in the Sphinx Pit showing the pharaoh Thutmosis (Thothmes) IV offering flowers to the goddess Isis, who holds a *uas* scepter in one hand and an ankh in the other. As we have already seen, a late Temple of Isis existed at Giza, though we do not know how far back her association with Giza extended. Clearly, in the New Kingdom, it was thought suitable to honor her in the Sphinx Pit, which was no longer a moat; it was completely dry.

THE TEMPLE OF ISIS BETWEEN THE THREE SMALL PYRAMIDS ON THE WEST AND A ROW OF LARGE MASTABAS ON THE EAST

Figure 1.27. A photo taken from the Great Pyramid, looking down on the remains of the Temple of Isis just to the east of the pyramid (the round column bases are part of it). This temple does not date from the time of the pyramids, but was a later edifice, built partially on top of one of the tombs dating from the reign of King Cheops. No one knows whether an earlier Temple of Isis existed at Giza, as claimed by the Inventory Stela, which may or may not draw on Old Kingdom texts. During the Middle Ages, the Sphinx was generally thought to be an image of the goddess Isis, because the *nemes* headdress worn by the pharaoh looked like a woman's bonnet, and people generally could not accept that it was the head of a man. This photo is plate LI in Selim Hassan's book, *The Great Sphinx and Its Secrets*, Cairo, 1953.

(known as Lutetia) and was on the site of the modern Church of Saint-Sulpice.

An alternative and possibly double use for the rump tunnel occurred to me when I was exploring it: during the worship of the Sphinx, it might have been consulted for oracular revelations. A priest might have lain concealed in the hollow beneath the Sphinx, which he would have entered under cover of darkness and where he would have remained until the following night, and during the daytime he could have spoken through a speaking tube to reply to inquirers' questions. People would have thought the Sphinx itself was speaking. Such tricks were played frequently in Ptolemaic times in Egypt, and trick chambers and passageways, holes for speaking tubes and so forth, can be seen in many surviving ruins of temples such as Kom Ombo and Edfu. The rump hollow is a cozy enough little cell to curl up in for a day or so, with your water jug and some food beside you, and a chamber pot nearby. Also, as we shall now see, there was a connecting tunnel to help enable such voice tricks to be relayed toward the front of the Sphinx. At the time I thought of this, I had not yet done my searches of the early travelers' reports of the Sphinx and was unaware that many of them had repeated the claims of the local population that someone concealed himself within the Sphinx in ancient times to deliver oracles. The fact that I thought of this idea independently and only later found it confirmed by countless early reports strengthens my conviction that there must be some truth in it. There is no hole in the mouth of the Sphinx by which oracles could be delivered, but as we will see later when we go into much more detail, there was another and better means of doing so.

So the rump hollow was probably either an incubation cell or an oracular hole, or perhaps it served as both. But there is more to it than just that. One's first suspicion is to think that perhaps the tunnel goes down farther, but this does not appear to be possible. I looked pretty carefully at the hollow, and the scooping away of the stone in a rounded fashion is clearly out of the bedrock. This tunnel does not go any farther down, nor was it ever intended to. There was no trace of water. The hole appeared perfectly dry, which is strange considering that water—supposedly from the rising water table—has been reported at *higher* levels elsewhere in association with the base of the Sphinx. The whole question of where water is and where it is not within the underground region of Giza is a complicated one, perhaps made more so by the fact that the limestone of the plateau is riddled with cavities like a Swiss cheese.

But what is very surprising indeed is that the Sphinx rump tunnel *does* continue—upward. After I had finished peering down, my attention was finally drawn to what was above my head. And then I had a great shock, for the tunnel beneath the Sphinx *continues upward into the body of the Sphinx.*

I was certainly not expecting this. The upward tunnel is not straight, and it

Figure 1.28. This is a photo looking upward inside the rump of the Sphinx. It shows the commencement of the tunnel that curves up inside the Sphinx from the top of the Sphinx's right hip until it comes to the point where Baraize filled it with cement in 1926. Before he did that, it certainly went at least as far as the crevice where the haunches had been broken off from the main body for centuries, until Baraize joined them again. That was the point where the shaft and burial chamber had been intruded into the Sphinx. The shaft and this tunnel would therefore once have intersected. Whether this tunnel ever continued beyond the shaft, farther forward to the front of the Sphinx's body, is entirely unknown to us now. Several wooden props have been placed here to support the Sphinx from inside, making it impossible for anyone to squeeze past them and crawl along this tunnel. (*Photo by Robert Temple*)

is rough-hewn. It curves around out of sight, and I was not able to see the end of it. All along the upward tunnel, wooden supports have been erected, as in a mine shaft, presumably to prevent the collapse of the rear of the Sphinx upon itself (see figure 1.28). These wooden props appeared to be very new, placed there at the time of the restoration of the Sphinx in the mid- to late 1990s, during the period when the Sphinx was covered with scaffolding. Although the upward tunnel was largely blocked by these struts, I was tempted nevertheless to crawl along at least sufficiently to have a look around the bend to see an end to the tunnel. But I decided against this idea when the very first wooden support by the ladder, against which I leaned slightly, moved! The possibility of dying inside the Sphinx, crushed by its collapsing rump, did not appeal to me, if only because I could not then make my report. So I was unable to form a personal impression of just how far this extraordinary interior tunnel in the Sphinx actually extended. It went both upward and along, curving up the rear haunch slightly toward the south and then heading around toward the east and disappearing out of sight in the direction of the Sphinx's waist.

It is immediately obvious that this interior tunnel provided a very convenient means in antiquity of conveying a crawling person who had slept overnight in the hollow, or alternatively of conveying his voice along a speaking tube to a forward part of the Sphinx, whether the area of the hips or beyond, so that oracular pronouncements could have been made and superstitious people would genuinely believe that the Sphinx had spoken to them with its voice. The actual location from which utterances might have emerged is something I will discuss later, but it was certainly not on the Sphinx's face or head. (There is a hole in the top of the head, but it was drilled for another purpose and does not connect with any other holes.)

Because I am a friend of the limestone expert Professor Lal Gauri, who worked for some years in the late 1970s with Zahi Hawass and Mark Lehner on the stone of the Sphinx, I sent him an e-mail asking him about this strange interior tunnel in the Sphinx. I knew that he too had been down the rump tunnel. He replied that he had also noticed the tunnel continuing upward and bending around out of sight, but he had not crawled along it or explored it either. He knew no more about it than I did.

If an expert who worked on the Sphinx for years does not know how far the tunnel goes, then the number of people who do must be very small indeed.

Perplexed, I talked to someone else about the matter. He had some familiarity with the tunnel. He told me the Sphinx tunnel "goes 6 meters down and 8 meters upwards." By that he meant that the hollow was 20 feet beneath the Sphinx base, and that the upward tunnel had a length of 26 feet, meaning that it went about twice as far as I could see. What happened then he didn't say clearly, except that it apparently came to an end of some kind. But unlike the hollow, which seems to stop at bedrock, one could presumably never be sure if something like an interior tunnel really ended naturally or had been blocked by a later repair. The hip area of the Sphinx has experienced a great deal of weakness and been repaired at various times throughout history. The question we have to keep firmly in mind is this: Why would anyone drive such a long tunnel along the length of the Sphinx if there was no purpose, or no objective at the end of it? It had to lead to *something*.

It was not until January 2001 that a colleague kindly gave me a photocopy of an article about the Sphinx Tunnel that had been published by Zahi Hawass and Mark Lehner in 1994 in a French Festschrift for the Egyptologist Jean Leclant.[7] This article gives a very full account of the rump tunnel. But previous to seeing this article, I had been puzzled at the lack of information available about it. Hawass published a booklet about the Sphinx four years later in which he gave relatively few details, and there was no indication in this later work that there was an earlier and fuller publication on the subject. In this brief booklet, *The Secrets of the Sphinx,* published in 1998, Hawass writes only this:

Tunnels under the Sphinx

Over the years, the Sphinx has revealed some of its secrets, though not all. In 1881 [sic; Vyse actually worked at the Sphinx in the 1830s] Henry Vyse found two tunnels inside the Sphinx, but his discovery was never published. In 1979, we opened these tunnels. [It was at this time that my friend Lal Gauri was working with Hawass on the Sphinx and went down the rump tunnel.]

The first tunnel is located behind the head of the Sphinx, cut into the mother rock about six meters. The second tunnel is located in the tail of the Sphinx. We learned of it from Sheikh Mohamed Abd al-Maugus, who in turn knew of it from his grandfather. It too is cut into the mother rock, about twelve meters. We found no significant artifacts inside the tunnel, but the evidence suggests that the tunnels were cut during the pharaonic period, I believe during the Twenty-sixth Dynasty [664–525 BC].

A third tunnel in the north side of the Sphinx, has not been opened since 1926, when Emile Baraize opened it. We have photographs showing two workmen inside it.[8] [These are the archive photos taken by Pierre Lacau in 1926, which I was not permitted to see, as I describe later.]

This was all he said, and it left me wondering: Why has no one explored the tunnel, which has been unopened since 1926? In figure 1.37 Olivia stands in front of this blocked doorway. It is so obvious that someone should remove some of those modern stones and have a look at what is behind them. Why has no one done that?

Another question I have is this: What evidence suggests that the rump tunnel dates from the Twenty-sixth Dynasty? If no "significant" artifacts were found inside the tunnel, what were the *insignificant* ones? In fact, I know what one was: Hawass told me he found an old pair of shoes at the bottom of the rump tunnel. But he did not say shoes of which period. Were they modern? Ptolemaic? Turkish? (They were evidently modern but not recent, as I later discovered.)

The 1994 article published in the French Festschrift is relatively little known. Leclant is a famous figure in Egyptology, and I met him in 2000. Presumably because he and Hawass have been friends since 1976, his Festschrift was chosen as the vehicle for this publication, but awareness of the article outside of professional Egyptological circles has been nil. For instance, it was obviously unknown to Paul Jordan, who wrote a book in 1998 that was entirely devoted to the Sphinx.[9]

When Jordan's book was published, I was overjoyed and rushed to order it. At last I would get some answers to the Sphinx tunnels, I hoped. But no, not at all. Sphinx tunnels are mentioned only twice, and we are told very little. On page 5, the author says, presumably drawing upon Hawass:

There are three passages into or under the Sphinx, two of them of obscure origin. The one of known cause is a short dead-end shaft behind the head

Figure 1.29. I lifted the lid and took this photo of the modern metal frame that has been inserted into the bedrock floor of the Sphinx Pit between the feet of the Sphinx. This is the entrance to the underground chamber in front of the Sphinx. Not only is the metal covering a modern one, but the chamber inside now contains modern bricks, put there by Henry Salt. A tunnel originally led off from this hole underground, but it was blocked in 1817 or 1818 by Henry Salt, according to an account left by Count Forbin, so we do not know where it led. This small chamber in the rock is probably where someone giving oracles sat and spoke through a tube to convince people that the Sphinx itself was speaking to them. I suggest that this happened not originally, but rather after the Sphinx was cleared of sand by King Thutmosis IV during the New Kingdom, and then again after the Sphinx was later cleared repeatedly during the Twenty-sixth Dynasty, the Ptolemaic Period, and the Roman period. During these later periods, the Sphinx was worshipped as an idol in a superstitious fashion. (*Photo by Robert Temple*)

drilled in the nineteenth century. No other tunnels or chambers in or under the Sphinx are known to exist. [This is demonstrably untrue; anyone can see the small chamber underground between the paws, for instance. A photo of the entrance to it may be seen in figure 1.29. And we shall see as we go along that the tunnels and chambers are more than we imagined.] A number of small holes in the Sphinx body may relate to scaffolding at the time of carving.

And on page 25, the same author adds:

Helferich [a sixteenth-century traveler, more correctly known as Johann Helffrich, or in Latin, Johannes Helfricus, who mentioned the Sphinx in his book of travels written in German in 1579,[10] to which Jordan gives no reference or title, however] adds a teasing detail that echoes down to our own day when he tells that "from afar, under the ground, through a narrow hidden passage, one can pass unseen. By this passage the heathen priests get inside the head and speak to the people out of it as if the statue itself had spoken."

That is all. But in our consideration of early descriptions of the Sphinx, as we shall see, there were many such accounts given by early travelers of secret passages and tunnels. Indeed, there are so many such accounts in my compilation of the earliest reports, which extends from Pliny until 1798, that they are rather overwhelming. (Later reports are in part 2, section 2, which presents early-nineteenth-century travelers' accounts.)

Although the 1994 article by Hawass and Lehner has received little or no attention, it is the definitive account of the rump tunnel, and we must see what it has to tell us. The story of the discovery of the rump tunnel in modern times is absolutely fascinating, not least because the existence of this tunnel was revealed by a man named Mohammed Fayed (not the father of Dodi Fayed, the late Princess Diana's boyfriend). I quote the beginning of the Hawass and Lehner article:

It is an age-old notion that the Sphinx conceals some sort of passage, tunnel, grotto, or chamber. The idea enjoys wide currency today in popular non-scientific publications about the Giza monuments.

During our work at the Sphinx, three elderly men in the employ of the Antiquities Organization at Giza told us of a passage under the rump of the Sphinx. They said that they saw the passage when Baraize revealed it in 1926 during his cleaning of the Sphinx, for which they worked as basket carriers. They said that the passage opened at floor level on the north side of the rump as it curves from the beginning of the tail. One of these men, Mohammed Abd al-Mawgud Fayed, recalled, some fifty-seven years after Baraize's excavation, that the opening of the passage was a round hole just under the masonry veneer. The passage descended to the water table under the Sphinx.

Like so much of Baraize's work, the passage went entirely undocumented and, since it was covered with masonry, it was nearly forgotten. Since the water table is a critical factor in the preservation of the Sphinx, and because such a passage would be an important part of the history of the statue, we decided to investigate these claims. Baraize covered the opening of the passage with stones and cement. It had been almost six decades since Mohammed Abd al-Mawgud had last seen the opening. Nevertheless, Mohammed was able to point to a specific brick-sized stone, bonded with modern cement, that could be removed to reveal the opening.

On October 16, 1980, we moved this single small slab to expose a grey cement packing characteristic of Baraize's repairs on the Sphinx. We forced a small hole through this packing and found that the bedrock floor dropped off into a cavity under the brick-sized veneer masonry that Baraize had replaced. Behind the brick-sized and cement/limestone packing Baraize had set a large limestone slab to bridge the opening of the passage. We moved the bridging slab to allow easier access. Behind it were two larger slabs set end to end to bridge the opening.[11]

It is good to have this candid tale on record, revealing how an attentive ear to the tales of the workmen can often result in the most significant discoveries in archaeology. We should also note that although the rump tunnel was discovered in 1980, it took fourteen years for an account of it to be published by its discoverers. Such are the delays of archaeological publication. That also explains why Lal Gauri was unaware of it, as no one bothered to send him a copy fourteen years later, and he does not read French Egyptological Festschrift volumes as a hobby, not being an Egyptologist.

The Hawass and Lehner article reveals the official measurements of the rump tunnel:

> The passage consists of an upper and lower part. . . . The lower part descends from a circular hole in the floor where it meets the rise of the bedrock core body. It slopes downward at a very steep angle towards the northeast, for a distance of 4 m. and a depth of 5 m. and terminates in a cul-de-sac in the natural rock. Just inside the entrance, the passage is 1.30 m. wide and narrows to 1.07 m. near the bottom. . . . The upper part of the passage rises to a height of 4 m. above the Sphinx floor and ends in a niche about 1 m. wide and 1.80 m. in height. It is about 1 m. wide at the lower end and measures 1.80 m. in width just before the niche.[12]

Hawass and Lehner give no measurement of the length of the upper part of the passage in their report, or of how far it actually extends into the body of the Sphinx. They mention only how high it goes (13 feet). Today, with the

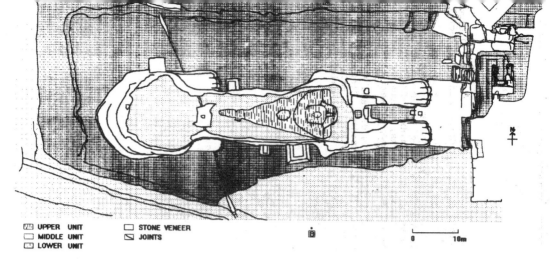

UPPER UNIT
MIDDLE UNIT
LOWER UNIT

STONE VENEER
JOINTS

0   10m

Figure 1.30. This is Professor Lal Gauri's plan of the Sphinx as seen from above. The huge blob of cement that Émile Baraize stuffed into the shaft at the haunches of the Sphinx may be seen here. And running across that blob diagonally, northwest to southeast, is the major fissure in the bedrock beneath the Sphinx that he found. This fissure goes directly across the point at which the subterranean burial chamber lies and was possibly caused by the shocks to the bedrock due to construction when that shaft and chamber were intruded, as they are most unlikely to have been original features of the Sphinx. The surviving description of the burial chamber as having walls covered in hieroglyphics would appear certainly to rule out any date prior to the Fifth Dynasty (hence excluding both Pharaohs Cheops and Chephren) and probably indicate an intruded shaft and chamber dating from Saite times (664–525 BC, ending with the Persian conquest of Egypt), which could even make Pliny's assertion that King Amasis was buried beneath the Sphinx absolutely correct. This drawing is reproduced from K. Lal Gauri, "Weathering and Preservation of the Sphinx Limestone," in *The First International Symposium on the Great Sphinx, Book of Proceedings*, Cairo, 1992, p. 54.

upper passage filled with wooden struts, it would be nearly impossible to make measurements of it or even to explore it. All the struts would first have to be removed, and whether that would be safe I cannot say, as their existence has not even been admitted by archaeologists, so we cannot draw any conclusions about their necessity.

As the reader may have gathered, the "restorations" by the French archaeologist Baraize were pretty drastic and heedless. Figure 1.31 is a particularly rare photo I found of the Sphinx taken circa 1920, before Baraize did the "restorations." This photo was used as the frontispiece to a book published in German by a Polish scientist, Klaus Kleppisch, in 1921, of which I believe no copy exists in Britain except for my own private copy, which I acquired from Switzerland through a German bookseller.[13] Certainly no copy is to be found in the British Library. The photo is taken from an unusual angle, on what we now know as the Chephren Causeway, and it is very revealing.

In the photo we can see that a huge fissure at that time existed in the region of the hips of the Sphinx, and that the entire rump of the Sphinx was effectively

Die Cheopspyramide mit Sphinx.

Aufnahme Photoglob., Zürich.

Figure 1.31. This photo, published in 1921, just a few years before Baraize filled it full of cement, shows clearly the cleft separating the main portion of the Sphinx from its rump. The rump had by this time split away due to the structural weakness in the stone caused by the hollow shaft that led down through the entire body of the Sphinx to the burial chamber beneath it at that point. The shaft was not original, but a later intrusion to enable a pharaoh to be buried in a chamber beneath the Sphinx, possibly a Saite pharaoh of the Twenty-sixth Dynasty, the last native Egyptian dynasty (664–525 BC). The Saites were obsessed by the Giza Plateau, and as part of their restoration efforts they may have partially or wholly cleared the Sphinx of sand, or at least cleared enough to give them ready access to the back so that they could make the shaft. By 1926, Baraize had entirely obliterated this evidence and permanently filled in the shaft with cement, thus making access to the subterranean chamber impossible. The rump tunnel inside the Sphinx also now terminates at this point, where Baraize's cement oozed into the tunnel and blocked it too. How far the lateral tunnel may have extended forward into the Sphinx's body, past the cleft and toward the chest, cannot now be determined. This photo appeared as a frontispiece in a rare volume that is not to be found in either the British Library or the Library of Congress, *Die Cheopspyramide: Ein Denkmal mathematischer Erkenntis* (*The Cheops Pyramid: A Monument of Mathematical Knowledge*), by the brilliant Austrian engineer Klaus Kleppisch, who lived in Warsaw. (*Verlag von R. Oldenbourg, Munich and Berlin, 1921; collection of Robert Temple*)

detached from the rest of the body. This is not just a minor detail! Because this now vanished feature is so important, I have spent some years collecting other photos that show it; see figures 1.32 to 1.34. These photos are taken from varying angles and help us evaluate the precise nature of the fissure as it existed prior to 1926.

Figure 1.32. A photo circa the 1860s, showing at extreme left a particularly good view of the "rump crack" of the Sphinx at the point of the shaft leading to the subterranean tomb chamber. At this period, the Valley Temple (on top of which the woman at right is standing) was still entirely covered in sand. The sand that had covered the back of the Sphinx during the 1830s, as seen in the earlier figure 1.4 has now been cleared away again. The low wall of small stones on which the man is seated has long vanished; it was of some late structure of which we know nothing and which probably had no archaeological importance. When tourists became more frequent in late Victorian times, sheds to cater to their needs were erected where these two people are seen, and they all had to be torn down at the beginning of the twentieth century to enable the Valley Temple to be excavated. (*Collection of Robert Temple*)

Figure 2.12 is my own photo of this region where the fissure once was, and a careful comparison of my photo with the earlier ones reveals the full extent of the massive infilling and "restoration" undertaken by Baraize. In figure 1.30, a drawing of the Sphinx seen from above, the area of infill can also be seen as a massive blob of restoration. And as we will see later in another early traveler's report, there was definitely once a rectangular entrance into the Sphinx here, measuring 4 feet by 2 feet, which restoration, either in the nineteenth century or in the 1920s, has completely sealed and obscured. The importance of this particular area is that it is the very area where the upper passage inside the Sphinx now terminates in a wall made with modern cement and placed there by Baraize.

In 1920 possibly, or certainly in the early nineteenth century, if one had been prepared to dig out large quantities of sand, one could have descended through the hip fissure of the Sphinx and presumably gained entry not only to the upper

Le Caire — Sphinx et Pyramide.
"The Tourist" opposite to Shepheard's Hotel.

Figure 1.33. This photo, from a postcard that was mailed from Cairo to France in 1909, shows clearly the split-off and detached rump of the Sphinx prior to 1926, just as does the photo seen in figure 1.31. In this photo, we also see that there was a vertical crack at the front of the Sphinx's body, not far behind the head. An Arab is standing on the Sphinx's right shoulder. The three specks along the Sphinx's flank, which look as if they might be holes, are, in fact, Arabs. (*Collection of Robert Temple*)

Below: Figure 1.34. An early photo of the Sphinx by W. Hammerschmidt, dated 1829. Just beside the rear of the horse on the left may be seen the large crack in the Sphinx's haunches leading to the shaft and the tomb below. (*Collection of Robert Temple*)

Grande Pyramide
de Ghyzeh, et Sphinx

passage but also to any continuation of it carried farther forward in the body of the Sphinx and now sealed and forgotten, as the rump tunnel itself was almost forgotten. And in fact, as we shall learn later on, it was in this region that entry to another very remarkable subterranean chamber was effected, descriptions of which from three successive centuries have turned up in my search of original source materials. But we have to leave the description of that until later, as we must first complete our study of the rump tunnel.

Let us see now how Hawass and Lehner describe the upper stage of the rump tunnel:

> The upper part of the passage runs along the curve of the bedrock profile of the statue but is covered by large Phase I restoration blocks. These blocks are covered in turn by the thinner Graeco-Roman (Phase III) and 1926 masonry [put there by Baraize]. Without these layers of masonry, the upper part of the passage would be an open trench in the Sphinx core body. . . . The top [that is, the termination] of the passage is sealed off by the Phase I blocks and a large patch of modern cement. Although it is difficult to know for sure, it seems most likely that the Phase I blocks do not entirely seal off the passage. The cement probably spilled down into the passage from the filling of the space between the Phase I slabs and the bedrock core on the ledge of the masonry at the upper part of the rump, about 3 m. above the passage.[14]

Figure 1 in the Hawass and Lehner article shows a drawing of the passage from above, and from this it is evident that the "cement fill" at the end of the upper part of the passage must extend for at least 6 to 10 feet. Such a massive filling of cement effectively destroyed the passage at that point and rendered examination of it nearly hopeless. What happened beyond that point is therefore unknown. There are no old Egyptian workmen left alive today who can shed any light on this, and 1926 was therefore the last time anyone was to have any opportunity to know the full story. Baraize really messed things up. And as we have already seen, it is only because of three old men in 1980 that the existence of the bottom part of this passage was ever known at all. If they had died earlier, the rump tunnel would have remained unknown forever. So near did we come to total ignorance. Instead, we are left today with only partial ignorance.

When we come to the evidence of 1715 and earlier, we will reconsider this matter of the tunnel that ends in a sea of cement, and whether in the period prior to its being blocked forever by Baraize the situation might have been rather different. Of course, we will have to keep an eye on just how much of the Sphinx was buried in sand at any given time. And because so much of it was buried for so long, the fact that the rump was effectively detached until 1926 is of particular importance, affording, as it may have done prior to 1926, a possible access route to the interior of the statue from above. And in connection with this idea, we have to keep in mind the proprietary interests of the inhabitants of Nazlet el-Samman, the Sphinx village, where a single family of local inhabitants may well have profited from this very route into the Sphinx, repeatedly covering and uncovering the entrance to the fissure when they had foreign customers who would pay for access. There are inhabitants of the same village today whose houses lie over important antiquities, such as Sabry Hatab, who, I am informed by local people, actually lives on top of the remains of the Valley Temple of Cheops! As he has no inclination to tear down his house, the temple remains officially unexcavated. It was discovered in recent years when a sewage system was installed for Giza. Perhaps Mr. Hatab will one day change his mind and decide to become a hero to archaeology.

We know about one end of the rump tunnel, although we can never properly know about the other. But what can we know about its origins? It is very interesting to learn that if the Phase I casing stones had not been laid over it, it would be an open channel. This means that the date of the Phase I casing stones takes on an even greater than usual importance. Whatever their date, they are later than the rump tunnel, since they are on top of it.

Hawass and Lehner are very clear about the Phase I casing stones. They say that there are two possibilities: either they date from the Fourth Dynasty of the Old Kingdom (circa 2500 BC) or they date from the Eighteenth Dynasty of the New Kingdom, a thousand years later. Hawass and Lehner are open to either possibility:

> We might consider the possibility that the lower casing blocks are part of an earlier, IVth Dynasty, casing that finished off the lion body of the Sphinx. The three courses of Phase I casing next to the bottom course are thicker than the blocks immediately above them. . . . In profile, the lower veneer of large blocks looks like the masonry casing on Old Kingdom mastabas at Giza. . . . The blocks above the lower three or four courses are thinner, but they also have the appearance of Old Kingdom casing; the range of their thickness is matched by that of slabs forming the walls of the Khafre causeway where it meets the Valley Temple. . . . As mentioned, it is clear that the natural Member II bedrock of the core body [of the Sphinx] was severely weathered before the application of Phase I casing. The major obstacle in assigning Phase I to the IVth Dynasty as the finish work for the Sphinx body, is the Phase I masonry fills in the deep recesses caused by the weathering away of the softest beds.

It is also clear from a detailed study of the Sphinx chapel, located between the forepaws, that the earliest phases of masonry on the statue, including

Figure 1.35. A close-up of some of the restoration on the Sphinx. The central limestone blocks are believed to be of Old Kingdom date, from the first repair job, but modern cement has been smeared into the cracks between them. Above them have been laid modern limestone pieces, carefully fitted to the surface, and below, larger limestone blocks have been cut and inserted into holes where older blocks had fallen out and been lost. (*Photo by Robert Temple*)

Phase I masonry on the chest and very large blocks behind the granite stela of Thutmose [Thutmosis] IV, are, in fact, XVIIIth Dynasty. At this time the Sphinx was excavated [having been covered up to its neck in sand for centuries], found in weathered condition, and its lion body reconstructed. The XVIIIth Dynasty restorers probably took the Phase I blocks from the Khafre causeway, in effect taking apart the monuments . . . to reconstruct the Sphinx as Horus-in-the-Horizon.[15]

Of course, if the Phase I casing blocks on the Sphinx were used to repair a weathered Sphinx body, as this report seems to indicate, and if those blocks were placed there in the Fourth Dynasty, then it means that the Sphinx is considerably older than the Fourth Dynasty. But at the moment, the orthodox view in Egytology is that the Sphinx was carved in the Fourth Dynasty and cannot possibly have needed repair of its weathering, since it was brand-new.

At the Eighth International Congress of Egyptologists in Cairo in March 2000, I attended a talk by Dr. Rainer Stadelmann, former director of the German Institute in Cairo. Dr. Stadelmann wished to discuss whether the Sphinx had been carved by Cheops or Chephren, which is a difference of only a few decades at most. Such intense passion was aroused by this apparently insignificant point that Dr. Zahi Hawass rushed up from the audience onto the podium to say into the microphone that he differed from Stadelmann! He then proceeded to give a mini-lecture of his own while the hapless Stadelmann stood beside him, pointing out that the pharaoh could not be the one Stadelmann preferred, and that Stadelmann was hopelessly wrong. Stadelmann preferred Cheops, but Hawass insisted on Chephren, which frankly seems too small a difference to matter very much. But certainly passions ran high, and voices were raised over this small matter. What, then, would be the reaction to the suggestion that the Sphinx was not carved by either pharaoh, but was really older? Please do not think that I am one of the people who believes that the Sphinx is twelve thousand years old! I am certain it is not. But surely it is possible to have a legitimate opinion, without being shouted at, that the Sphinx may be older than both Cheops and Chephren, indeed may have been repaired by one of them with the Phase I casing blocks, while still being of an age that is rational and does not require theories of Atlantis to explain it.

However, judging from the fact that one cannot even suggest the "pharaoh next door" as a builder at a supposedly sober international scholarly conference without having the microphone grabbed out of one's hand and being told one is wrong, and having an impassioned counter-speech made beside one, to make a bolder sugges-tion would seem to be more than one's life is worth in Egyptological circles.

Before we leave the Phase I casing blocks that cover the rump tunnel, I should give my own opinions and those of someone whom I regard as the leading expert. Figure 1.35 is a close-up photo I have taken of these blocks, from which it may be seen of what good quality they are. They are really the finest possible limestone masonry, expertly prepared and laid, and so superior to all other blocks (including the most recent) on the Sphinx as to put the others to shame. I have no doubt that these Phase I blocks are of Old Kingdom date, as no one later than that had the skill to produce and lay such stones, in my opinion. It was quite beyond the capabilities of the masons of the New Kingdom's Eighteenth Dynasty. One only has to look at the pathetic Eighteenth Dynasty temple remains beside the Sphinx (the small ruined temple at a high level, since the Sphinx Temple was buried in sand then and only excavated later in the New Kingdom) to see the stark con-trast in building capabilities. At least that is what I think. But I am not alone. I asked my friend Lal Gauri, the limestone expert who worked on the Sphinx with Hawass and Lehner, and he was inclined to believe that these stones were of Old Kingdom date, because of their remarkable quality of workmanship.

Now let us turn to the account of 1715 that reports entry into a chamber beneath the Sphinx. This is the first occasion in our times when documentary evi-dence has been presented that reports the discovery of such a chamber. In the next chapter, I reveal that many such reports have actually been published and discussed even up until 1953, but subsequently they have been systematically ignored because they did not fit the preconceived views of Egyptologists of the past half century, when consensus opinions have become far more ossified and intolerant than in the past, a sign of extreme decadence in the discipline of Egyptology as it exists today.

With all the books that have been written on the subject of the Sphinx since 1953, there has been no such evidence. Now at last we have real evidence, rather than merely the claims of a psychic in a trance, of the existence of an underground Sphinx chamber, and later we shall see that there is much more. Strangely enough, the evidence presented in this and the following chapter actually substantiates with a series of published eyewitness reports the "psychic reading" of Edgar Cayce concerning the Sphinx, at least insofar as he insisted on the basis of a psychic vision that there was an underground chamber there. We can now prove that he was correct about this general point. Although he "saw" a chamber in a different place at the Sphinx (and the existence of that one remains to be proved), he was correct in insisting on the existence of an underground chamber at the Sphinx. The mistake his followers have made subsequently was to not even attempt to search for the material that I have found. But that is presumably because followers of Edgar Cayce do not tend to be scholars and do not know how to do this sort of thing.

In any case, scholars are a vanishing species these days, and as they all die off, they are not really being replaced, due to the collapse of the Western educational systems (in contrast to that of China, which retains rigorous standards of excellence in education that perversely decadent Westerners have thrown overboard) and the impact of the information deluge, which has drowned out serious research and replaced it with the ludicrous substitutes of Google and Wikipedia. Those Internet sources, as with all such information sources based on nonrigorous data supply, are riddled with errors and misinformation and are often worse than worthless, since there are no safeguards against their being incomplete, misleading, and frankly wrong. Barely anyone is being trained these days to do real research in information that predates 1990 and depends on printed or manuscript materials, so that in twenty or thirty years' time, there may not be a genuine scholar left alive anywhere on the planet. Then, the lack of the ability to discover the truth about anything will be one of the main precipitating factors that will contribute to a total collapse of what humans have struggled for millennia to create: something fast vanishing called "civilization."

The first passage we will now examine occurs in the English translation of 1715 of a book written in Latin and first published in 1599. On further research, I discovered that the account did not appear in the original Latin text at all, so that it does not go back to 1599, but first appears in print in 1715. It was some information inserted by the English translator himself. To give him justice, he does freely state at the front that his translation contains such additional material. But we are handicapped by a major problem: he is anonymous, and we have no idea who he was!

The book concerned is a curious one, about which I have already had a lot to say in my earlier book *The Crystal Sun*. It was originally written by the Italian antiquarian and polymath Guido Pancirollo (in Latin, Pancirollus), but he died before it could be published, and so his close friend, a noted German antiquarian, Henry Salmuth, edited the work, added much material of his own, and saw it into print in 1599. It was published in the obscure Bavarian town of Amberg. Its title in Latin was *Rerum memorabilium iam olim deperditarum & contra recens atque ingeniose inventarum: Libri duo,* the translation of which was entitled *The History of Many Memorable Things Lost, Which Were in Use Among the Ancients: And an Account of Many Excellent Things Found, Now in Use Among the Moderns, Both Natural and Artificial,* and it was published at London in 1715 and reissued in 1727. I am fortunate to own a copy of this book in translation.

Since it is the translator of this book who tells us about the underground Sphinx chamber, as I shall describe in a moment, it is galling that he suffered from an overdose of modesty and refused to identify himself. That he was no humble clerk but rather an eminent and witty scholar is evident from his four-page "Preface of the Translator." This man regales us with his encounter with a pompous Oxford scholar whom he then lampoons. He heaps praise on the "genius" Robert Boyle and speaks of the contemporary scholar Mr. Glanville as if he were his equal. He then confidently says of Salmuth's annotations to the book: "I have par'd off the Excrescences of his luxuriant Style, and have pick'd out of his Notes the most pat Illustrations; to which I have added some Histories of my own, and some Observations and Remarks, such as I have met with in my slender Reading, and which I thought agreeable to the Argument in Hand."

These are not the comments of an unaccomplished man; they are the assurance of a man who knows his own worth in the scholarly field and seems to be a man of science of some kind. He must have been a person of note in his time. On the title page he further explains, or his publisher explains for him: "Now done into English, and illustrated with a new Commentary of choice Remarks, pleasant Relations, and useful Discourses, from Salmuth's large Annotations; with several Additions throughout." And further: "To this English Edition is added, First, A Supplement to the Chapter of Printing, shewing the Time of its Beginning, and the first Book printed in each City before the Year 1500. Secondly, What the Moderns have found, the Ancients never knew: Extracted from Dr. Sprat's (late Bishop of Rochester) History of the Royal-Society, the Writings of the Honourable Mr. Boyle, the Royal-Academy at Paris, &c."

Among the large "Additions throughout" are the comments on the Sphinx chamber, which appear to come from what the translator wittily calls his "slender Reading," which we can be sure was anything but slender. But alas, what could be the source on which he drew? It has never come to anyone else's attention. But, then, this book itself has never come to anyone's attention either. Not any modern person concerned with Sphinx chambers, I mean.

Here, then, is the brief and tantalizing description of an underground Sphinx chamber given by this 1715 translator:

> I imagine this Sphinx to be a Sepulchre, but we cannot understand how it belong'd to Amasis [the Greek name of a pharaoh whom he mentioned earlier, said by Pancirollo to have constructed the Sphinx], for all the Records and Traditions of this Sphinx are lost. That it is a Tomb, may appear, 1. By its Situation, which is in a Place, which was in former Ages a Burying-Place, and near the Pyramids and mortuary Caves. 2. It is to be imagin'd that it was a Sepulchre from its building. In the hinder Part is a Cave under Ground, of a Bigness answerable to [an eighteenth-century expression meaning "comparable to"] that of the Head, into which the curious have look'd, by an Entrance that leads into it; so that it could serve no other Purpose but to keep a dead Corps [*corpse*] in, as Travellers inform us. (page 107)

Earlier, Pancirollo (page 104) specifically states that the circumference of the head of the Sphinx is 102 feet. (Incidentally, he also says its body is not that of a lion but of a marmoset!)

Here we have a puzzle and several problems. The translator has not himself seen this Sphinx chamber, but has taken the description of it from "Travellers." There were indeed many accounts written by travelers prior to 1715, but which travelers? We are not told, and if they were the well-known ones, someone would have noticed an account of the chamber, surely. However, I realized that at least one such clear account must exist. I was certain that otherwise our translator would not have made this statement so confidently, especially as he does so not to impress us with the mysterious existence of a chamber, but to support his belief that the Sphinx contained a tomb. The translator does not give any indication that he thinks the existence of a Sphinx chamber anything at all unusual; to him it is merely another detail of the monument that he takes for granted, and his passing reference to it in the context of an argument gives us no reason to believe that he made this up. We are left, then, with the enigmatic description and must try to account for it.

The first thing that bothers us is that the size of the chamber is comparable to the size of the head, which the same book states to be 102 feet in circumference. The "den" at the end of the Sphinx's rump tunnel into which I crawled is hardly of that size! It may be perhaps 12 feet (4 meters) in circumference.

Then there is the problem of access. In the early nineteenth century, the

Sphinx was covered up to its neck in sand. So how did the travelers prior to 1715 get into anything at all at the rear of the Sphinx, much less a chamber? Here, however, we remember the fissure shown in figures 1.31 to 1.34 and the possibilities of entering the body of the Sphinx by squeezing down it prior to 1926, or at least prior to 1817, when Henry Salt began blocking up entrances into the Sphinx, as described later. Since the top of the Sphinx's back was easily reachable, if this upward tunnel prior to 1715 broke through to the surface, which is highly possible, "the curious" might have descended into it as a matter of course on their visits to the Sphinx. And this would take them inside the Sphinx's rump. This therefore leads us to the possibility that there may be another and larger chamber beneath the Sphinx's rump, perhaps farther forward, reachable from the upward tunnel by a different route that has long been blocked up and in modern times has not been unblocked. Even before the entire area was filled and thoroughly smeared with cement by Baraize in 1926, it is most likely that there was a concealment by some family of local tour guides, as I suggested a moment ago, of some special entrance into this fissure. For the extremely poor local inhabitants, to have even a single private trick to offer the discerning tourist might make the difference between eating for a week or going hungry. All of us who know Giza at all well know the truth of this. Any Giza taxi driver (and to call them loquacious is the understatement of the year) will explain to you in five minutes that if he loses a fare, his family cannot eat. Allowing for bravado and exaggeration—and there is plenty of that—the realities of life in Cairo are that if you are not rich, you are very, very poor. And being poor in Cairo is a form of desperation no Westerner would ever wish to experience, since such poverty in the West did not even exist in living memory and is incomprehensible to most people. I am talking about people who cannot afford shoes, who cannot buy soap, who can barely eat enough to live. When Olivia and I have given cheese sandwiches to beggar children at Giza, we have been horrified at the savage animal ferocity with which they crammed them into their mouths, not even chewing as they desperately gulped, with wild, staring eyes, anxiously worried that another child would try to grab a crumb from their very lips. In such a society, the possession of the secret of a single stone blocking an entrance to a single passage can mean the difference for an entire family between gnawing hunger and desperation and a feeling that life is worth living.

Apart from the rump tunnel and its upward annex to parts unknown, there are other Sphinx passages and entrances. Figures 1.36 and 1.37 are photos of the location of the entrance to a passage at the base of the Sphinx on its north side. The modern masonry was put there by Baraize, who walled up the passage in 1926. This one has not been unblocked, and we have absolutely no record of how far it extended, whether it went up or down, or anything at all other than the fact

Figure 1.36. This is the entrance to a tunnel entering the northern side of the Sphinx, which was blocked in 1926 by Baraize using stones that he found in the vicinity. No one has any idea what is inside. It would be an easy matter to pull out these stones and see what lies behind them. The height of this doorway can be judged from the photo in figure 1.37 below. This photo shows the full width. The exploration of this Sphinx tunnel should be a matter of the highest priority. (*Photo by Robert Temple*)

Figure 1.37. Olivia Temple stands against the modern blocks that seal the tunnel opening in the northern flank of the Sphinx. This tunnel was opened in 1926 by Baraize, who then sealed it again firmly with these cemented blocks. He did not bother to leave an account of what he found. No one has opened it since. This large and obvious opening clearly led into the interior of the Sphinx's body, but no one ever bothers to wonder what it led to or why. (*Photo by Robert Temple*)

that two men could stand inside, as there is a surviving photo in the possession of the archaeological authorities showing a workman inside it in 1926 before it was closed. Hawass and Lehner speak of this passage as follows:

> Several of the Archive Lacau photographs that document the excavations of the Sphinx during 1926–1928 show another spot where it appears that there might be a passage cut in and under the Sphinx. Arch. Lacau photos CI 17–20 show the north flank of the Sphinx when Baraize cleared the debris down to the floor level in 1925. The workers found a large number of Phase I–sized blocks toppled about in the debris at the base. CI 19 shows a close view of the base of the north belly where they found a large gap in the Phase I casing. A man is standing below the floor level in what may be a niche cut into the bedrock core body; another man stands on a small mound of sand just outside the gap. We identified this same spot on the basis of fissures showing in the core body above the casing. It is sealed off now by large stones, some of which are replaced Phase I slabs, sealed with grey cement [which is what Baraize used]. . . . It is possible that the passage in the north side of the Sphinx, like that at the rump, is ancient.[16]

It is interesting that this passage too had been covered by the early Phase I blocks, some of which Baraize put back in place and cemented, since this indicates an early date for this feature as well. The sealing of this passage has been accomplished so solidly that a major effort would have to be made to reopen it, and a decision was obviously made not to do so. Perhaps the passage will be reopened one day, especially in light of the information from the 1715 source, and the others to be discussed later, that there must be a chamber somewhere under the Sphinx, and any of the known passage entrances is a candidate for leading to it.

I tried very hard to locate the Lacau Archive photos mentioned by Hawass and Lehner, and it was with the greatest difficulty that I finally discovered where they were in Paris, in an obscure outlying facility of the Institut des Hautes Écoles called the Centre Golenischeff, which has a small Egyptological library. I made an appointment by telephone to go and see them, but when Olivia and I turned up at the library in Paris, we were refused access to the photos. We saw a door marked ARCHIVE in the library, but the girl would not admit us to it, although she let us look at books on the open shelves. She said her boss, Professor Christiane Zivie-Coche, wanted to know why we wanted to see the photos. Zivie-Coche has written a brief book about the history of the Sphinx.[17] The girl said the photos were "in boxes," but then most archive photos are in boxes! What else would they be in? The girl, Nathalie Toye, who was Zivie-Coche's student and writing a thesis on New Kingdom stela prayers, gave me Zivie-Coche's e-mail address and said

I would have to write to her to explain why I wanted to see the Lacau photos. When I complained that I had come from London with an appointment, she showed no concern that it was a wasted trip and that the appointment mutually agreed in advance had not been honored. There were drunks, who had mattresses and slept beneath the library, shouting beneath the windows, making the atmosphere even less pleasant in that not exactly thrilling part of Paris called Glacière. The library was actually housed in a student residence building, and to get to it from the street, you had to step around overflowing rubbish bins that stank. I sent an e-mail to Zivie-Coche when I returned to London, and she replied by e-mail dated 21 September 2007 refusing me access to the Lacau photos on the excuse that they were in boxes, but then going on to make clear that her real reason was that "we do not share the same way in analyzing the egyptological [sic] questions." She added: "I do not doubt that you worked on the question of the Great Sphinx so did I and so did Mark Lehner who is a [sic] excellent scholar and archaeologist with whom I worked on the spot." In other words, access to the Lacau photos was to be restricted to Lehner, Hawass, and Zivie-Coche, and to those who agree with or sympathize with them. My reply to her was as follows:

> Dear Madame, I am very disturbed by your email of 21 September. I am certain that Pierre Lacau would not have approved of your restricting access to his photos only to people who share your opinions. The Institut des Hautes Écoles would certainly not be in agreement with restricting public materials to private purposes. There is something called the community of scholars. Members of that community are meant to share information, not conceal it, especially information which was not originated by them.

No further reply was received. So, alas, I was unable to see the three Lacau photos showing the north side of the Sphinx during Baraize's excavations. Zivie-Coche, on the other hand, did not hesitate to reproduce seven of the Lacau photos in her own small book on the Sphinx, none of them with any copyright indicated, so they are all clearly in the public domain. The Lacau photos are therefore readily available for use by Zivie-Coche herself, but cannot even be looked at by anyone who "does not share the same way," to use her words, which presumably includes her theory recorded in her book: "I shall content myself with stating that the Sphinx was modeled as a gigantic image of Chephren."[18] As we shall see in chapter 4, the face of the Sphinx does not look anything like the face of Chephren (see figure 4.7) and is most definitely not "a gigantic image of Chephren." In chapter 4 I reveal which pharaoh's face it really is. Zivie-Coche and I therefore certainly do not "share the same way." Whether Zivie-Coche has abused her academic position by giving access to photos that are under her control to herself and her friends while denying access to those who disagree with her theories is for others to decide.

Hawass and Lehner also point out that there are old photos of 1925 (doubt-less further Lacau photos, though they do not specify this, and Zivie-Coche's refusal to allow me access to them means that I cannot check) showing evidence of "another large gap" near the base of the Sphinx masonry inside the large masonry box on the south side of the Sphinx. This may have been an opening to yet another Sphinx passage, but nobody can be sure today, for, as they say: "By the time of our work at the Sphinx in 1979, the gap was closed by limestone patching with modern mortar."[19] Baraize and his cement again! Indeed, one is tempted to view Baraize as a truly manic passage-sealer.

Hawass and Lehner do not mention the small underground chamber in front of the Sphinx, in which it is possible to crouch, and which is also sealed up, so we do not know whether it once led anywhere either. This little cell is now covered with a modern grille, and it is easy for anyone to see when you visit the paws of the Sphinx. The entrance hole to this cell is seen in figure 1.29. So what with all of these passages and entrances that lead nowhere today, one could be forgiven for being somewhat bewildered.

This brings us to the subject of the accessibility of the Sphinx and at what dates it was or was not covered by sand. In other words, if people were routinely entering a chamber beneath the rump of the Sphinx as reported in 1715, how were they doing this if there was too much sand to permit their reaching the base?

Other old photos of the Sphinx from my large collection, which are repro-duced as figures 1.31 to 1.34 also clearly show the exposed crack in the haunches at the rear through which entry to the passages could still have been possible prior to 1926.

This matter of the gap in the haunches is certainly an interesting conundrum. And it brings us back again to the question of the upward tunnel in the rump, for if that tunnel really does or did emerge at the top of the back, or if another simi-lar tunnel did emerge, then the underground chamber was reached not from the bedrock level but from a tunnel going down through the Sphinx's body from its back, and thus theoretically accessible for most of the period of the Sphinx's exis-tence. That local people informed Hawass of the existence of the rump tunnel is also suggestive: it clearly implies what I have said, that local guides kept as a trade secret the existence of that tunnel, its "den," and its associated upward tunnel. But how did they first learn of it? And what other such tunnels and chambers may not have been revealed to any archaeologist, contrary to the way this one was revealed to Hawass? If people were entering the underground chamber beneath the Sphinx prior to 1715, they were certainly paying some very good *baksheesh* to whoever had the secret of how to enter it.

What, then, of this matter of the sand covering the Sphinx? The fact is that we do not have reliable information about all the periods when the Sphinx has been freed or partially freed from sand. The first full and reliable accounts we have of this problem date from 1817, as I shall describe in a moment. The Sphinx was said to have been covered with sand to the level of the head in 1798 when the Napoleonic troops of France invaded Egypt. As is explained in the next chapter, there was actually a partial clearance before they arrived, a fact that was forgotten until I discovered the evidence of it in an unpublished manuscript source. It is normally assumed that the Sphinx had been untouched for centuries before the arrival of the French, and that is doubtless how the French would like the story to be told, because it enhances their glory, and the French are always very keen on *la gloire*. However, by bringing this correction to the historical record in the next chapter, I do not mean to disparage the achievements of the French. Napoleon sent a large group of scholars (known as the *savants,* or wise men) to Egypt with the troops, who spent many months carrying out detailed surveys and studies of all kinds, which were later published in Paris in a series of famous and massively illustrated volumes.[20] We know that they cleared some sand from the Sphinx, but apparently not much. Of this expedition, the British colonel Howard Vyse wrote in 1840: "The French are not supposed to have made any considerable excavations or discoveries about the Sphinx, which was opened by Mr. [Henry] Salt and M. [Captain Giovanni Battista] Caviglia in 1817; but it appears that when Dr. Whitman saw it [in 1801], some of the sand had been removed, as he describes the substructure, although he did not perceive the body of the image."[21]

In his book *Pyramid Facts and Fancies,* James Bonwick gives some information that makes the history of visibility of the Sphinx even more complicated. He has a short section about the Sphinx in which he points out that more of the Sphinx was visible in 1705 than in 1877, and presumably also more than was visible to Napoleon's scholars in 1798: "The head only appears above the sand at present [*1877*]. A picture in *Harris's Voyages,* about 1705, gives far more of the head than can now be distinguished. The wings, as they are called, behind the ears [he means the hanging folds of the nemes headdress, which are known as "lappets"], are very distinct, as well as the eyes, ears, and chin."[22]

In figure 1.46 we reproduce this illustration (which Harris had republished in 1705) in its original form, as it appeared in the 1611 book by George Sandys, which describes Sandys's visit to Egypt in 1610. The full text of Sandys's account of the Sphinx is given along with other early travelers' descriptions in part 2. The men riding on asses toward the Sphinx with harquebuses (old-fashioned

Figure 1.38. A nineteenth-century engraving by M. Kurz from a drawing done by A. Löffler showing the Sphinx largely buried in sand, which was prepared not for a book but as an engraving for separate sale in Germany at an unknown date. I purchased it from a German dealer; it is entitled "Sphinx und die Pyramiden." (*Collection of Robert Temple*)

Figure 1.39. The Sphinx in the middle of the nineteenth century, with only the desolate desert and sand dunes between it and the Pyramid of Chephren in the distance. The sand has already filled in again at the Sphinx's chest, following Caviglia's 1817 excavation of that area. The extreme erosion and poor condition of the left (north) side of the Sphinx is clear here. That has all now been covered over by "repairs." The great crack in front of the rump is seen here as a dark vertical streak in the side, as its top has been covered by windblown sand. The rear of the Sphinx, which was perfectly clear in 1827 (see figure 2.10 on page 95), has now been swallowed by sand again. (*Collection of Robert Temple*)

Figure 1.40. A Victorian photo of the Sphinx, showing the sand engulfing it on the north. In other Victorian photos, the sand is engulfing it from the south. (*Collection of Robert Temple*)

Figure 1.41. This old Victorian glass slide of the Sphinx shows that an ocean of sand has engulfed the south side of the Sphinx and that the mound on top of the Valley Temple has risen as high as the Sphinx's chin. After Caviglia cleared the space in front, this deluge of sand swallowed up the right leg again. (*Collection of Robert Temple*)

Figure 1.42. A Victorian glass slide, probably dating to the 1870s or 1880s, showing how the sand was reinvading the Sphinx after Caviglia's excavations. A man is sitting on top of the Sphinx's head, and another stands on top of the Dream Stela. It is clear from this photo how impossible it was to get an idea of the north side of the Sphinx (at right) prior to its excavation by Baraize in 1926. (*Collection of Robert Temple*)

Figure 1.43. Here is a Victorian glass slide of the Sphinx taken from the northeast and showing the height of the sand to the north of the statue. (*Collection of Robert Temple*)

Figure 1.44. This glass lantern slide from the latter half of the nineteenth century shows what was visible and accessible of the Sphinx at that time. Most of the clearance at the front, done in 1817, has now filled in again with sand. The ragged nature of the left lappet of the headdress is very evident here, in silhouette against the sky. This photo gives a clear indication of the severe crack behind the Sphinx's shoulder, which is filled in today with cement. The more serious crack at the rump is just visible at the edge of the photo. (*Collection of Robert Temple*)

Figure 1.45. A Victorian glass slide of the Sphinx from the southeast, taken from the mound that still covered the Valley Temple. The Great Pyramid is in the background. (*Collection of Robert Temple*)

Figure 1.46. This is how the Sphinx looked in 1610, just a head and neck sticking out of the sand (at left). This engraving appeared in the book by George Sandys, *A Relation of a Journey Begun An. Dom. 1610*, London, 1615. (*Collection of Robert Temple; I am descended from George's uncle Myles Sandys.*)

rifles) over their shoulders are Mameluke soldiers, sent to escort and protect the European visitors to Giza from the dangerous locals, who might attempt to rob them. At this time, no trace of the Sphinx's body was visible.

Figure 1.47 is a contemporary drawing of the Sphinx as it appeared during Caviglia's perilous and daring excavations, when many of his men were threatened daily with being engulfed with sand. The Sphinx emerges from its surrounding element rather like a whale coming up for air. A description of Caviglia's immense feats makes for interesting reading:

> He first began to open a deep trench on the left, or northern side, opposite the shoulder of the statue; and, though the sand was so loose, that the wind drove back frequently during the night more than half of what had been removed in the day, yet he managed by the aid of planks, arranged so as to support the sides, to dig down in a few days to the base. The trench, however, being no more than twenty feet across at the top, and not above three feet wide at the bottom, the workmen were evidently placed in a dangerous situation; for if any large body of sand had fallen in, it must have smothered those who were

Figure 1.47. This is Henry Salt's drawing of the Sphinx being excavated by Giambattista Caviglia in 1817. The most threatening mountain of sand was on the north side (to the right in this picture). In 1926, Baraize was so worried about the sand engulfing the monument from the north that he built the barrage walls seen in the aerial photo figure 6.50 on page 280. It was not until 1937, 120 years after the scene here, that the problem of the sand to the north of the Sphinx was solved by Selim Hassan, with his armies of laborers and rail carts (see figures 3.11 and 3.12). This illustration is from *Operations Carried On at the Pyramids of Gizeh in 1837* by Colonel Howard Vyse and John S. Perring, 3 vols., London, 1842, appendix volume III, opposite page 107. (*Collection of Robert Temple*)

employed below. It was, therefore, found necessary to abandon this part of the attempt. By what had been done, however, the height of the statue from the top of the head to the base was ascertained, and it was also found that the external surface of the body was composed of stones of various sizes, put together with much care. The form of the masonry was not very regular, but it consisted of three successive ledges, sufficiently broad for a man to stand upon, to represent the folds of a mantle or dress. It seemed to have been added by the Romans.

The result of the first operation not proving satisfactory, Captain Caviglia began a large excavation towards the front, in which he employed, from the beginning of March to the end of June, from sixty to a hundred labourers. Many interesting discoveries were now made. Among other fragments that were found, were portions of the beard of the Sphinx, and the head of a serpent. [This beard of the Sphinx was not original but was stuck on in the New Kingdom, as will be discussed later. These four fragments are seen in figure 3.1,

as drawn at the time by Henry Salt. As for the serpent, this was the head of the royal uraeus emblem (insignia of a serpent rearing its head) on the Sphinx's forehead.] Most of these lay in a small temple, ten feet long and five feet broad, which was immediately below the chin of the statue. . . . A large part of the left paw was uncovered, and the platform of masonry was found to extend beyond it. In the course of a fortnight Captain Caviglia had removed the sand from the paw, and from the outer walls of the temple, in front of which was an altar formed of granite. It is now in the British Museum, and has had at the angles projecting stones, which may be supposed to have been called the horns of the altar. This fragment still retains the marks of fire—the effects, probably, of burnt offerings.

Captain Caviglia succeeded in laying open the base of the Sphinx, and in clearing away the sand in front of it, to the extent of more than a hundred feet. Many short Greek inscriptions were indistinctly cut on the paws of the statue. [These can no longer be seen, as the paws have modern masonry covering them as a result of restoration efforts. Later, we shall see that an inscription carved into the middle toe of the left paw contained some important evidence about the original purpose of the Sphinx.] They prove that the image was held in high veneration. . . . It is scarcely possible for any person, unused to occupations of this kind, to form an idea of the difficulties which Captain Caviglia had to surmount when working at the depth of the base; for, in spite of all his precautions, the slightest breath of wind or concussion set the surrounding particles of sand in motion, so that the sloping side crumbled away, and mass after mass tumbled in, till the whole moving surface bore no unapt resemblance to a cascade of water. Even when the sides appeared most firm, if the labourers suspended their work only for an hour, they found that the greater part of their labour had to be renewed. This was particularly the case on the southern side of the right paw, where the people were employed for seven days without making any sensible advance, because the sand rolled down in one continued and regular torrent as fast as it was removed. He therefore only examined the end of the paw. . . . At the distance of about two feet to the southward of the right paw, the platform abruptly terminated. It was therefore supposed that the Sphinx was placed upon a pedestal; but, by extending the operations in front of the statue, the platform was found to be continued, and the steps were discovered. . . . Such was the result of Captain Caviglia's exertions in June, when, in consequence of exposing himself too much to the sun, he was unfortunately seized by an attack of ophthalmia [sunstroke], that compelled him to suspend his operations.[23]

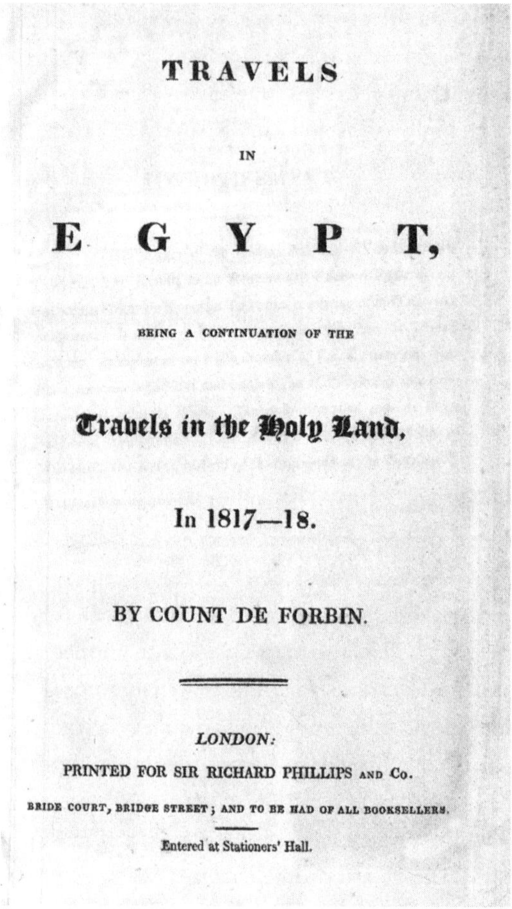

TRAVELS

IN

E G Y P T,

BEING A CONTINUATION OF THE

𝔗𝔯𝔞𝔳𝔢𝔩𝔰 𝔦𝔫 𝔱𝔥𝔢 𝔥𝔬𝔩𝔶 𝔏𝔞𝔫𝔡,

In 1817—18.

BY COUNT DE FORBIN.

LONDON:
PRINTED FOR SIR RICHARD PHILLIPS AND Co.
BRIDE COURT, BRIDGE STREET; AND TO BE HAD OF ALL BOOKSELLERS.

Entered at Stationers' Hall.

Figure 1.48. The title page of Count de Forbin's *Travels in Egypt, Being a Continuation of the Travels in the Holy Land, In 1817–18.*

These heroic exertions give us a vivid impression of just how difficult it was to clear the Sphinx so that its body could be seen at all. A contemporary visitor's account of this operation was written by the French Count de Forbin:

The colossal sphinx still rises thirty-eight feet above the sand that the winds from the desert are accumulating about it. My arrival was too late to avail myself of the labours of M. [Henry] Salt [British consul general at the time, who worked with Caviglia]. On clearing away about the base of this statue, he had found steps that communicated with the gates of a little temple erected between the feet of the sphinx. An unpardonable egotism led him to block up again objects which call for an active and vigorous investigation, which would throw great light on the history of the arts in ancient days, would bestow éclat on one of the most sublime monumental fictions to be found in ancient Egypt.[24]

This is a shocking eyewitness report that Henry Salt, through obstinacy and egotism, "block[ed] up" things at the Sphinx that should have been the subject of "an active and vigorous investigation." What does "block[ed] up" mean? It can only refer to openings and passages, and since the plural is clearly used, he must have done this to more than one. We are talking here of blockages made more than a century before Baraize. One of them certainly must be the blocked passage in the small underground chamber now covered with a metal grille beneath the face of the Sphinx. Since Count de Forbin is so adamant about it, we must presume that there was indeed an actual passage here that led away in some direction or other, which to us is unknown. Count de Forbin must have had an argument with Salt about it, insisting that someone should crawl along the passage and see where it went, but Salt couldn't be bothered and "dealt with the situation" in the manner of a diplomat, simply by sealing the damned thing off and settling the matter by brute force, a tactic of "block-and-run."

But as one of the blocked entrances may be identified, what could be another? Possibly Count de Forbin is referring to the one on the north side of the Sphinx that Baraize cemented over in the 1920s; Baraize may have opened it, had a look, and then resealed it as he did the rump tunnel. Or there may well be at least one completely different passage, of which we have no idea, or possibly several.

The blocked passage beneath the Sphinx's head is probably the answer to how the oracles were given by the Sphinx. The voice didn't actually come out of the head or mouth of the Sphinx, which was too high up to be heard easily, but out of the tiny chamber beneath the mouth at ground level, suitably obscured by a screen or even a cloth. The surviving little chamber is too cramped for a priest to crouch in for long, so he must have entered from the tunnel that Salt sealed up. But where was the entrance to this tunnel? Quite possibly it led from the northern side entrance sealed up by Baraize.

I have so far found one piece of evidence from an early traveler of the seventeenth century specifically mentioning a tunnel beneath the face of the Sphinx. There are many early travelers' reports, which we shall consider later on, that relate the local people's tradition that a tunnel led from the Sphinx to the Great Pyramid. But only one of these gives the additional detail that the tunnel of which this was claimed was, as the traveler puts it, "under the neck":

The upper part [of the Sphinx] remains above the sand; the lower part, on the contrary, is entirely covered. If it be true that the rest, or the lower part, is proportionate in size to the upper part, one must consider that it is one of the Seven Wonders of the World, for it seems to be cut from one piece of stone. Some people ask themselves if this stone colossus was cut from a natural rock in situ, or if it had been carried here from elsewhere. Plenty of people have wanted to examine it by excavation but they could not because of the sand. Others thought that this monster consisted of nothing more than half a body, for under the neck there is an opening of a stone tunnel which passes across the mountain of sand up to the pyramids, where it ends.[25]

This evidence from Father Antonius Gonzales, who visited the Sphinx in 1665, is highly specific. We need not accept the story that the tunnel went as far as the pyramids, but we must accept the likelihood that there was indeed an opening of a tunnel "under the neck" of the Sphinx, and this most probably is one of the things blocked up by Henry Salt that so enraged Count de Forbin.

At the very least, in light of this evidence, the blocked passage in the tiny chamber beneath the face of the Sphinx should be opened. This should not be very difficult. Salt is unlikely to have had the resources that Baraize had to enable him to pour vast quantities of cement into the Sphinx. Salt's blockage would probably be easy to unblock. And if this is ever done, we can thank Count de Forbin for the prompting that led us to rediscover whatever it is that may be found. Even if the passage leads only a short distance, it could provide the answer as to how the oracles were delivered at the Sphinx.

The clearance by Caviglia and Salt did not last long. A mere seventeen to eighteen years later, on December 31, 1835, the Sphinx was visited by John Lloyd Stephens, who recounted: "Next to the pyramids, probably as old, and hardly inferior in interest, is the celebrated Sphinx. Notwithstanding the great labors of Caviglia, it is now so covered with sand that it is difficult to realize the bulk of this gigantic monument. Its head, neck, shoulders, and breast are still uncovered; its face, though worn and broken, is mild, amiable, and intelligent, seeming, among the tombs around it, like a divinity guarding the dead."[26]

It is often difficult to construct a reliable picture of what portions of the Sphinx were exposed or accessible at which dates. Just as one thinks one knows what the status was at a certain period, an unexpected piece of evidence comes to light that gives one a shock. For instance, I had assumed that during the period when Napoleon's expedition was in Egypt commencing in 1798, the Sphinx was covered in sand up to its shoulders and nothing else was visible. However, I then unexpectedly came across a passing remark that stated that the French at that period had cleared only the back of the Sphinx. But I had not known that they had done that, and I don't believe anyone else today had realized it either. I found this in an anonymous article in the *Quarterly Review* for 1818: "The Arabs . . . told to Mr. Caviglia, that the French had discovered a door in the breast of the Sphinx, which opened into its body, and passed through it to the second pyramid.

The French never uncovered more than the back of the Sphinx."[27]

While still surprised at this, I then came across another account, published eight years earlier, which gave the French credit for doing much more:

> Upon the south-east side [of the Great Pyramid] is the gigantic statue of the Sphinx, the most colossal piece of sculpture which remains of all the works executed by the Antients. The French have uncovered all the pedestal of this statue, and all the cumbent [i.e., recumbent] or leonine parts of the figure; these were before entirely concealed by sand. Instead, however, of answering the expectations raised concerning the work upon which it was supposed to rest, the pedestal proves to be a wretched structure of brick-work, and small pieces of stone, put together like the most insignificant piece of modern masonry, and wholly out of character, both with respect to the prodigious labour bestowed upon the statue itself, and the gigantic appearance of the surrounding objects.[28]

This even more unexpected discovery appears to lead us to the conclusion that the French in about 1798/1799 may possibly have cleared the Sphinx entirely, and that less than two decades later it was all covered up again practically to the neck, so that in 1817 Caviglia had to clear the whole thing again. Although this at first seems unlikely, when we remember that Stephens tells us that less than two decades after Caviglia, the sand was back and the Sphinx was once more covered up to its shoulders, we see that the process merely repeated itself in the same length of time. It must have been an era of high winds!

In fact, the French clearing of the Sphinx must have been an incompetent effort, because a report by William Hamilton proves that the sand had blown back again within a period of between three and ten years. The French clearance of the monument was in 1798 or 1799, and William Hamilton first visited Egypt in 1801, the year the French left. His book *Aegyptiaca* was published in London in 1809, so it cannot describe anything later than 1808. Here is what he says in his book: "The French excavated the body of the lion; which they found uninjured: but the sands of the Desert very soon rendered their labour vain, and the last time I saw the sphinx, the head and neck alone were visible. These have been evidently painted all over, and many characters are to be traced upon the head-dress [*which are all gone today*]."[29]

It is important to try to figure out how much of the Sphinx was exposed at any given time when we evaluate the meaning of various travelers' reports about doorways and passages. If anyone says he saw a chamber, could he really have done so? Was there anything sufficiently exposed to enable him to have access to any chamber?

By going through the early reports, I have now found a sufficient number of accounts tallying with one another to put together a proper case, and we shall be considering it in detail as we progress. We will see clearly that we are not left relying upon a single account that may be either unreliable or a mere fantasy. Various patterns emerge in the accounts when one compares them. And these in turn can sometimes even be supplemented by genuinely ancient evidence. To give a single example of this, let us consider whether there is any ancient account that suggests that there might be a "door" or entrance in or near the Sphinx leading underground. As it happens, there is. This ancient text is cited by the famous excavator of the Sphinx, Dr. Selim Hassan. It comes from the *Book of the Dead.* At the time those funerary texts were written, the Sphinx was called Ruti. In chapter 41, line 2, we read: "O Atum, I was rendered shining before Ruti, the Great God, who opens the door of Geb."[30]

Geb is the god of the Earth. Consequently, we have here a genuinely ancient text that speaks of the Sphinx opening the door of the Earth.

In his translation of the *Book of the Dead,* Renouf does not use the proper name Ruti, but uses the word in its meaning of "lion"; he also gives the name of the Earth god in its variant form of Seb and Atum in its variant form of Tmu: "O Tmu, let me be glorified in presence of the god in Lion form, the great god; that he may open to me the gate of Seb."[31]

Sir Wallis Budge, in his translation of the text, also does not use the name Ruti, but in his case he assumes that Ruti is a "double-lion god," because of the old pictures showing a kind of double-lion facing each way (see figure 1.49 below), also known by the name of Aker, the double-form being known as the Akeru (which is plural). Budge also uses Seb instead of Geb and Tem instead of Atum: "Hail, Tem, I have become glorious (or a *Khu*) in the presence of the double Lion-god, the great god, therefore open thou unto me the gate of the god Seb. I smell

Figure 1.49. The double-headed lion facing both ways, symbol of the netherworld, which one enters by the eastern mouth as a corpse and leaves from the western mouth as a glorified spirit, called in Egyptian an *akh,* if one is lucky! (Many are the decapitated spirits of the damned that rumble forever in the stomach of this, the Earth Lion, screaming in agony as demons torment them in unspeakably vile ways.) This drawing comes from Selim Hassan's *Le Sphinx,* Cairo, 1951.

Figure 1.50. The Sphinx and the Pyramid of Chephren silhouetted at sunset, a view not seen by the public for a generation, as the Giza Plateau is locked long before this hour. (*Photo by Robert Temple*)

the earth. . . . I advance into the presence of the company of the gods who dwell with the beings who are in the underworld."[32]

So we see that this passage clearly refers to a door of the Earth god that leads into the underworld and that appears to be at the Sphinx. It is certainly suggestive, and in the following chapters we shall have plenty of opportunity to see just how much it may mean.

2

THE "SECRET CHAMBER" BENEATH THE SPHINX

The "secret chamber" beneath the Sphinx is not secret at all. It was known about for centuries, but forgotten in our own time. It was last described in print in 1953. Countless subsequent speculations about secret chambers beneath the Sphinx, and a book on the subject that was actually entitled *Secret Chamber,* have all been published without anyone having any recollection or knowledge of the many accounts of the *real* secret chamber that have appeared in print since 1672. Published accounts of the chamber beneath the Sphinx appeared several times during the 281 years that elapsed from the first to the last mention of it.

It certainly doesn't look very good that people have written so much about this subject without knowing anything about the plentiful evidence!

We shall see that the location and measurements of the shaft are known, along with the existence of an apparent burial chamber, which was entered by several people. But no one today who claims to be an expert on the Sphinx knows anything about it. Published reports on the subject that appeared over the course of more than two and a half centuries have therefore remained unknown, as if they had never been published.

I must make it clear that we are not here referring to the rump tunnel and the hollow in the rock at the bottom of it, all of which I have discussed at length in the first chapter. We are now considering instead the vertical shaft that was driven down into the Sphinx at about the point where the hips join the body—a shaft wholly filled with cement by Baraize in 1926, as I described in the previous chapter.

The first person to describe the shaft and burial chamber was the German traveler Johann Wansleben, often called Father Vansleb by the French and the English because the letter *W* in German is pronounced like a *V*. Sometimes his name has been misprinted *Vausleb*. A partial English translation of his account was published in London in 1678, with the title *The Present State of Egypt*. (I reproduce in figure 2.1 the title page of my own copy of the 1678 English edition of this book, where the author is called "F. Vansleb," the "F." standing for "Father." I also reproduce as figure 2.2 the relevant page of his book that contains his comments on the Sphinx.) I have also translated Wansleben's original account from German, as we shall see. The shaft and the chamber were next visited by an Englishman from Devonshire named Ellis Veryard in 1678, presumably stimulated by Wansleben's book, and Veryard then published his own account twenty-three years later, in 1701. In 1715, the anonymous translator of Pancirollo mentioned the subject in the book that was described in chapter 1. His description was lifted directly from Wansleben's book, as may be seen by a comparison of the wording. In 1721, the Englishman Thomas Shaw visited the Sphinx and mentioned the shaft and chamber in his published account in 1738. Five years before Shaw's book was published, in 1733, Charles Thompson visited the Sphinx and mentioned the shaft and chamber in his book of 1754. Meanwhile, in 1743, ten years after Thompson's visit but eleven years before his account was published, Richard Pococke described the shaft and chamber. They were mentioned again in 1757 by the Dane Friderik Norden. The entrance to the shaft then became inaccessible due to sand covering most of the back of the Sphinx, as Coutelle tells us in 1798. (Windblown sand covering the back of the Sphinx is clearly seen in figure 1.46.) But in the nineteenth century it was cleared first by Caviglia, whom we have already encountered. He entered and mapped the subterranean chambers, and then they were studied again by the archaeologist Auguste Mariette, whose account was published in 1855 (a translation of which may be found in appendix 1). Ludwig Borchardt mentioned the shaft and chamber in 1897 (in his pamphlet "On the Age of the Sphinx at Giza," translated here in its entirety, in appendix 2). And finally, Selim Hassan, excavator of the Sphinx, mentioned them again in his book of 1953. Incredibly, every one of these accounts has been overlooked until now. This shows that the state of scholarship in the Egyptological field has fallen to a very low level indeed—so perilously low, in fact, that it calls into question almost any assertion made today about anything in the entire field. The day of the Egyptological scholar appears to be gone. One of the problems is that professionals are too narrowly educated today, and too narrow also in their professional activities. Many of them would like to display wider interests, but they are cowed and intimidated by peer pressure into confining themselves to small areas

THE PRESENT

STATE

OF

EGYPT;

Or, A new

RELATION

OF A LATE

VOYAGE

INTO THAT

KINGDOM.

Performed in the Years 1672. and 1673.
By F. *VANSLEB*, R. D.

Wherein you have an exact and true Account of many Rare and Wonderful Particulars of that Ancient Kingdom.

Englifhed by *M. D.* B. D.

LONDON;
Printed by *R. E.* for *John Starkey*, at the Mi-
ter in *Fleet-ftreet*, near *Temple-Bar.* 1678.

Figure 2.1. This is the title page of the English translation published in 1678 of the book by "Father Vansleb," the German traveler Johann Wansleben. Wansleben visited Egypt twice, in 1664 and again in 1672. This translation does not contain all that he wrote, so I have translated further sections from the German original. The page of this translation discussing the Sphinx is also reproduced here, as figure 2.2. Wansleben describes seeing the chamber beneath the rear portion of the Sphinx, writing that it was of the same dimensions as the Sphinx's head. (*Collection of Robert Temple*)

of expertise. Anyone who dares to go against this bullying and "political correctness" run amok risks his or her career. So they keep their heads down and do not dare to challenge the Monitors of Narrowness. Thus, the public cannot obtain enlightenment, and a vacuum is created into which all sorts of "outsiders" enter. Then the Egyptologists complain because things are being written by "outsiders." But the Egyptologists themselves are largely to blame, by failing in their duties of communicating with the public themselves.

Anyone who has the intention of seriously discussing the Sphinx should as a first step collect all the existing textual evidence about the Sphinx that can be found. Sensing that it was my duty to find out what others had said about the Sphinx before I myself had the temerity to say anything at any length, I spent many months gathering all the reports of the Sphinx I could find. And I did this first, before I started writing what I myself might think. Many of the reports I found were in foreign languages, of course, so I translated or had translated every one that was not in English. My wife, Olivia, translated those that were in French,

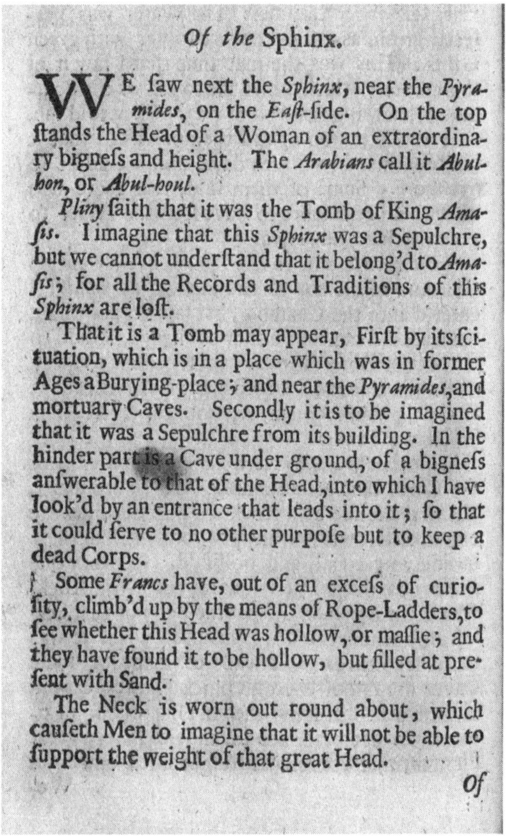

Figure 2.2. The page from the book by "Vansleb" (Wansleben) describing the Sphinx and the chamber beneath. (*Collection of Robert Temple*)

> *Of the* Sphinx.
>
> WE saw next the *Sphinx,* near the *Pyra-mides,* on the *East*-side.   On the top stands the Head of a Woman of an extraordinary bigness and height. The *Arabians* call it *Abul-hon,* or *Abul-houl.*
>
> *Pliny* saith that it was the Tomb of King *Ama-fis.* I imagine that this *Sphinx* was a Sepulchre, but we cannot understand that it belong'd to *Ama-fis;* for all the Records and Traditions of this *Sphinx* are lost.
>
> That it is a Tomb may appear, First by its sci-tuation, which is in a place which was in former Ages a Burying-place; and near the *Pyramides,* and mortuary Caves. Secondly it is to be imagined that it was a Sepulchre from its building. In the hinder part is a Cave under ground, of a bigness answerable to that of the Head, into which I have look'd by an entrance that leads into it; so that it could serve to no other purpose but to keep a dead Corps.
>
> Some *Francs* have, out of an excess of curio-fity, climb'd up by the means of Rope-Ladders, to fee whether this Head was hollow, or maffie; and they have found it to be hollow, but filled at pre-fent with Sand.
>
> The Neck is worn out round about, which caufeth Men to imagine that it will not be able to fupport the weight of that great Head.
>
> *Of*

I translated the ones that were in German (and some other German material was later translated with my colleague Eleonore Reed), and a friend translated one from the Dutch. The two in Latin were already published in English, and the Arabic ones that I was able to find were already published either in French or English translations. Doubtless I have missed some other Arabic texts, but I cannot read that language, and alas, this is one of my many failings and weaknesses. The Arabs are underrepresented, but with all their oil money, they ought to do more to make their own literature available to us infidels.

The result of these labors of mine and Olivia's was nearly sixty typed pages of descriptions of the Sphinx from the earliest times (Roman) until 1837 (see part 2 of this book), when we stopped trying to be comprehensive. These are very intriguing descriptions, and they reveal much.

Part 2 is intended as a standard reference source for everyone interested in the Sphinx in the future. There will be no need for anyone researching the Sphinx to go to libraries and dig it all out and translate it, as we have already done that for

Figure 2.3. A reconstruction of how the Giza Plateau would have looked in the reign of the pharaoh Chephren (Khafre) of the Fourth Dynasty, as envisaged in 1912. This drawing was published as the frontispiece to *Das Grabdenkmal des Königs Chephren* (*The Funerary Monument of King Chephren*), by Uvo Hölscher, Leipzig, 1912. The reconstruction was done by Hölscher and the artwork by Hölscher and A. Bollacher. The rectangular structure beside the Sphinx is the building that we now call the Valley Temple. It is linked by a covered causeway to the Pyramid of Chephren. The Great Pyramid is in the background, surrounded by many tombs of officials. What is missing from this reconstruction is the Sphinx Temple, situated directly in front of the Sphinx, which at this date was still entirely unknown because it was buried in a mound of sand. Instead, the area in front of the Sphinx in this view is shown simply as a flat expanse of sand. The Sphinx Pit, which had not yet been excavated, was not understood at this time either. Instead, in this view, the area to the left of the Sphinx is not bounded, but is open. Consequently, the vicinity of the Sphinx as shown here is falsely depicted. We now know that there was also a causeway in front of the Great Pyramid, but it is not depicted here at all. One interesting feature of this view is the distant hill on the horizon, with two pyramids sticking up

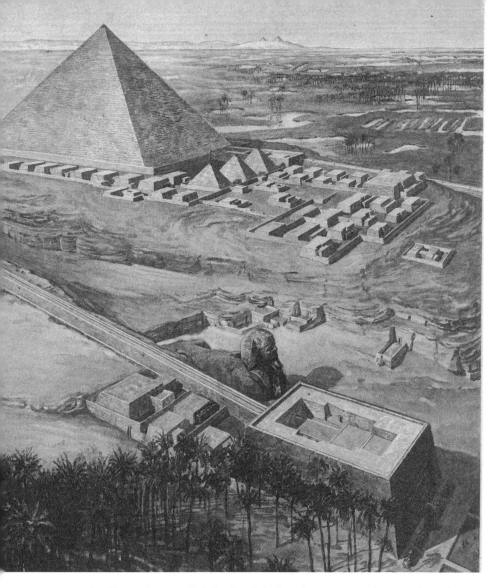

on top of it. This is the site called Abu Ruash. In fact, there is no conclusive evidence that any pyramid was ever fully constructed on that hill, much less two, though there is a gigantic hole in the ground on that hill that looks like the descending passage and chamber of what might have become a huge pyramid, if it had been finished. (Or it may have had another purpose; no one really knows.) It was at Abu Ruash that the small limestone female sphinx was found (see figures 4.3 to 4.6). It is a pity that more reconstruction drawings like this are not produced today, because even when they are wildly inaccurate, as this one is, they do give a vivid impression of the magnitude and grandeur of the Giza concept and help us visualize something of the general appearance of what ancient Egyptian monuments would have looked like when they were not ruins. As for the depiction of the Sphinx here, it is entirely incorrect and out of proportion. The body has been given a muscular, leonine form, and a gigantic head has been placed on the body, which the real Sphinx does not possess. When we look at the details of this picture, almost everything is wrong. But when we glimpse the totality, it still conveys an impression to us of the greatness of the Old Kingdom and its monuments.

them. Also, anyone reading this book who wants to check a reference has only to turn a few pages, rather than plan a visit to a major international library.

In the next chapter, I discuss one incredible piece of information recorded about the Sphinx in 1482, which I point out must have survived as folklore for approximately seventy-five generations—clearly a world record! There is no other explanation for that particular instance. But it does not relate to a chamber under the Sphinx, so it is left until later.

It is always simplest, and often best, to survey a series of descriptions chronologically as they occur. So this is what we shall do. The earliest apparent description of a shaft and chamber beneath the Sphinx that I found came from the seventeenth-century German traveler Johann Wansleben, so we will start with him. He actually visited Egypt twice, in 1664 and again in 1672. He wrote accounts of both journeys, but only the account of the second journey was translated and published in English, in 1678 under the title *The Present State of Egypt.*[1] Both of Wansleben's accounts were published together in German in 1794, and I have made my own translations from the two accounts in that edition.[2] First let us see what Wansleben wrote about the Sphinx in 1664, which does not mention any shaft or chamber:

Chapter 2. Concerning Abul-Haula, or the Sphinx

Near to the first pyramid, and below it, stands in the ground Abulhoula, or the Sphinx, as the French call it. It is an uncovered head and neck skillfully put together from stone; it is not hollow, but solid, and is 26 feet [Fuss] tall, as the Dutch Consul Johann Thyls has measured it. Nothing more protrudes above the earth; what is under the sand, I cannot say. The nose of the Sphinx has been chopped off and the moors tell a polite fiction about how that happened, which for the sake of brevity I omit.[3]

Now we shall see what Wansleben wrote about the Sphinx in 1672, when he studied it more closely, first taken from the English translation published in 1678, and then my own translation of the German original. Here is the version of the translation that was published in 1678:

We saw next the Sphinx, near the Pyramids, on the East-side. On the top stands the Head of a Woman of an extraordinary bigness and height. The Arabians call it Abul-hou, or Abul-houl.

Pliny saith that it was the Tomb of King Amasis. I imagine that this Sphinx was a Sepulchre, but we cannot understand that it belong'd to Amasis; for all the Records and Traditions of this Sphinx are lost.

That it is a Tomb may appear [old-fashioned way of saying "may be seen from the facts that"], First by its situation, which is in a place which was in former Ages a Burying-place; and near the Pyramides, and mortuary Caves. Secondly, it is to be imagined that it was a Sepulchre from its building [old-fashioned way of saying "its form"]. In the higher part [evidently the seventeenth-century publisher's error for "hinder part," the original German word being *hinterwärts,* which means "hinder part" or "rear part"] is a Cave under ground, of a bigness answerable to [old-fashioned way of saying "equivalent to"] that of the Head, into which I have look'd by an entrance that leads into it; so that it could serve no other purpose but to keep a dead Corps.

Some Francs [Frenchmen] have, out of an excess of curiosity, climb'd up by means of Rope-Ladders, to see whether this Head was hollow, or massie [solid]; and they have found it to be hollow, but filled at present with Sand.

The Neck is worn out round about, which causeth Men to imagine that it will not be able to support the weight of that great Head.[4]

It is important to note that the account of what the Frenchmen found on top of the head is recorded as hearsay, and is not Wansleben's eyewitness account. And we know that although there is a hole in the head, it is only a narrow drilled one that goes down a few feet, and was at that time filled with sand, so people thought it led to more than it did.

The original German text has one additional sentence that was not translated in the English edition, which merely says: "One can find the measurements of the Sphinx in Thévenot." This is a reference to Jean de Thévenot, who visited Egypt in 1655 and published a lengthy account of his travels in French in 1664–84, which was translated and published in English in 1687.[5]

I have translated the portion of Wansleben's second account more accurately, and here is the section that relates to the shaft and chamber: "It has a cavity under the ground there rearwards [*hinterwärts*], the width of which measures the same as the height of the head [which is 26 feet according to his 1664 account], into which I looked from an opening into it, and which can have served no other purpose than to have the corpse of a dead person put into it."[6]

If it were not for the existence of the many subsequent accounts, we might be inclined to assume that this description is somehow a confused account of looking down into the hollow at the bottom of the rump tunnel. But we must remember that the base of the back of the Sphinx was covered by sand at this time. So the reference must unquestionably be to something that Wansleben saw by descending into the shaft at the beginning of the Sphinx's hips. And although, as we have seen in the first chapter, he might have been able to crawl around to the rump tunnel from there, the hollow at the end of the rump tunnel is not of the size that Wansleben describes, nor is it large enough to have contained a corpse. Wansleben thus seems to have seen a different cavity beneath the Sphinx, which was considerably larger. And to confirm this, we must consider the subsequent accounts, which make the matter much clearer.

To understand how Wansleben was able to have such access to the Sphinx in 1672, it is useful to note what was stated about the sand level by a traveler who visited the Sphinx in 1614, Pietro della Valle. His testimony makes clear that in the seventeenth century, the sand level was not quite as high as we might have imagined. Although Wansleben says that only the head and neck protruded from the sand, more of the neck was probably visible, and hence more of the back, than we are used to seeing in the nineteenth-century photos of the head and neck protruding from the sand. According to Pietro della Valle, in 1614: "The country round there is very level and sandy, and the sand has increased in such a way that the Sphinx is buried there almost up to its shoulders."[7] We must thus probably understand Wansleben's "head and neck" as meaning that the tops of the shoulders were also visible, and that with such a sand level, more of the back was exposed than was the case in Victorian times.

Six years after the second visit to the Sphinx by Wansleben, and in the same year that Wansleben's account was published in English (1678), the Englishman Ellis Veryard, a medical doctor from Colyton in Devon, doubtless with a freshly printed copy of the Wansleben book in his eager hand, visited the Sphinx and saw the shaft and the chamber. But he did not actually publish his account until long afterward, in 1701. So what happened next in the chain of publications was something quite different. A bizarre book appeared in Dutch that purported to be by an Englishman named Edward Melton, who was said to have visited Egypt and the Sphinx in 1661, before Wansleben's first visit. For a long time I was puzzled by this book, in which the author is described specifically as "an English nobleman." I made extensive efforts to trace an Edward Melton, and even consulted a seventeenth-century manuscript pedigree of the Melton family in the British Library (MS. Egerton 3402, f. 119 verso), but there was no Edward mentioned anywhere in it.

The book by "Melton" was first published at Amsterdam in 1681 and was so successful that it was reprinted in 1702.[8] Strangely, for a book so successful in Dutch and supposedly written in English by an "English nobleman," no English edition ever appeared. After I had obtained a translation of the relevant passage from Dutch and could compare it to Wansleben's text, I realized that it was largely a paraphrase of Wansleben and Thévenot combined. It could not have been an original account by "Melton" as was claimed, because the very phrases themselves were copied from others. And when there were changes, they were apparently fraudulent, such as "Melton" claiming that he had climbed up on top of the Sphinx's head himself, in the way that Wansleben had said the Frenchmen had done. "Melton" refers to no shaft, but says the Sphinx sits above a basement which "has an entrance. This basement was without doubt used to bury the bodies of dead men."[9]

There seems little point in giving the full text from "Melton," as I became convinced that he never existed, and that the work and the author are equally spurious. Strangely, the existence of Melton has been uncritically accepted by several well-known Egyptologists over the years, not because they were interested in what he had to say about the Sphinx (there being no evidence that they ever read that bit), but because they were searching for early accounts of the two stone pyramids at Dashur, one of which is called the Red Pyramid and the other the Bent Pyramid because it changes the angle of its exterior slope in a very dramatic way. Those authors included Howard Vyse, Ahmed Fakhry, and Dietrich Wildung. However, a survey of the situation was published as an article by Kathleen M. Pickavance in *The Journal of Egyptian Archaeology* in 1981.[10] In her article, Pickavance struggles with the problem of Melton. She adds the information, possibly spurious, that he was "Born c. 1635 the second son of Sir John Melton, Kt. of London," and he studied at Oxford. I doubt this. I own my own copy of *Athenae Oxoniensis,* which surveys all Oxford men who became authors before 1721, and the only Melton who appears in the entire giant folio volume is a Wiliam de Melton of Yorkshire who died in 1528.[11] Pickavcance says of Melton's account of entering the Bent Pyramid at Dashur: "It is hardly to be believed. . . . The greatest obstacle to the belief that Melton entered the Bent Pyramid by the western entry rests in Perring's description of the state of the western passage as he had found it in 1837: 'The greater part of it was closed up with large blocks.' . . . We are then faced with the inconceivable possibility that the western passage was more or less open in 1661, and subsequently closed up again, with all the flush-fitting blocks in place, when Perring saw them in 1837. In fact, it is the archaeologists' findings which must surely prove that the belief that travelers entered a chamber in the Bent Pyramid from the west is untenable, and that any account which even suggests such a possibility is either misleading, false, or a misinterpretation." I would go so far as to say that the real reason why 'Melton' did not actually enter the Bent Pyramid as he claimed was that he did not really exist. The book attributed to him appears to have been a publishing hoax carried out for commercial motives. Some Dutchman must have pocketed a lot of money and laughed at the fools who were taken in by his tricks.

The next thing that happened in the succession of publications is that Ellis

Veryard's account of his journey to Egypt and other countries was finally published in 1701, twenty-three years after it had taken place.[12] Here is what he had to say about the Sphinx:

> About half a Mile from the Pyramids we saw an ancient Colossus representing the Sphinx, with a Woman's face, and the Body of a Beast. This Statue was in so great Veneration amongst the Egyptians heretofore, that they gave it the first place amongst their Gods, and received all their Oracles from it, which the Devil utter'd thro' the Mouth of this artificial monster. The Body is buried in the Sand, and only the Head and Breast remain above Ground; so that we may judge of the vast bulk of the whole by the Face, which is twenty four foot long. [Wansleben had said 26 feet, so Veryard must have taken his own measurements.] Pliny says it was the Tomb of King Amasis; but I am apt to think it was an Ornament placed on his Sepulchre; for behind it we found a Subterranean Vault cut out in the firm Rock, which in all likelihood was the Tomb.[13]

The phrasing is brief and vague, but as Veryard specifically says that he believed the Sphinx sat *on top of* the sepulchre, and then proceeds to say that the same sepulchre was "behind it," we must presume that he means behind the protruding head rather than behind the entire Sphinx. If he had meant to refer to a burial in the rocks a considerable distance behind the entire Sphinx, in the cliffs of Giza, this would have been in contradiction to his affirmation that the sepulchre was *beneath* the Sphinx. He must therefore be referring to the same chamber mentioned by Wansleben, which was *hinterwärts,* or to the rear of, but not behind and away from, the Sphinx. And once again we have specific testimony that the sand was too high for this to be the hollow at the base of the rump tunnel, as the opening at the base of the Sphinx was inaccessible.

The next publication mentioning the chamber beneath the Sphinx was fourteen years later, in 1715, when the English translation of Pancirollo appeared, the anonymous translator of which added the information, as I have described in the previous chapter.[14] However, the unattributed description by the anonymous translator was something I eventually tracked down when I discovered Wansleben's book, since the passage is taken directly from the 1678 English edition of Wansleben. And so that mystery, which had plagued me for many months, was solved. It was, after all, the Pancirollo book that I first encountered, and it was only by discovering the passage in it (which at first I assumed was translated from Pancirollo's original Latin work, until, having gone through all of its successive editions from 1599, I realized it was really an interpolation by the English translator) that I realized I had to find its source, which led to my discovering all the other references to the "secret chamber," and writing this chapter.

Here, then, is what the anonymous translator of Pancirollo inserted into Pancirollo's book in English in 1715 and which was reprinted in 1727, repeated so that the succession of relevant quotations may be complete:

> I imagine this Sphinx to be a Sepulchre, but we cannot understand how it belong'd to Amasis [the Greek name of a pharaoh whom he mentioned earlier, said by Pancirollo to have constructed the Sphinx], for all the Records and Traditions of this Sphinx are lost. That it is a Tomb, may appear, 1. By its Situation, which is in a Place, which was in former Ages a Burying-Place, and near the Pyramids and mortuary Caves. 2. It is to be imagin'd that it was a Sepulchre from its building. In the hinder Part is a Cave under Ground, of a Bigness answerable to [an eighteenth-century expression meaning "comparable to"] that of the Head, into which the curious have look'd, by an Entrance that leads into it; so that it could serve no other Purpose but to keep a dead Corps [corpse] in, as Travellers inform us.[15]

Notice that the translator specifically says this information comes from "travellers." So it is not a plagiarism in the style of "Melton." The question that I was confronted with for so long was: Who were the travelers? It is now clear that the travelers were Wansleben and Veryard. The text is more or less lifted directly from the English translation of Wansleben's book and adds nothing new. Mystery solved. But imagine how difficult it was to solve it, without any clues whatsoever and only a cutoff date of 1715 to go by. However, such are the perils of scholarship, and sometimes one succeeds, as I fortunately did here.

The next step along the road of published accounts about the Sphinx chamber came in 1721, when the famous English traveler Thomas Shaw visited Egypt. His account of his travels was published in 1738.[16] It is very well known, and ignorance of his comments on the shaft and chamber among Egyptologists is less excusable than it is for the preceding and highly obscure works that I have already cited.

Here, with Shaw, we finally get the specific and detailed information that we so greatly desire, frustrated as we have been with the vague and dreamy accounts of the previous visitors. For the satisfaction of readers, I shall give all of the comments on the Sphinx made by Shaw, commencing with some preliminary ones:

> The catacombs of Sakara, the Sphinx, and the Chambers, that are cut out of the natural rock, on the east and west side of these pyramids, do all of them

discover [i.e., display] the specific mark and characteristics of the pyramidal stones, and, as far as I could perceive, were not at all to be distinguished from them. The pyramidal stones, therefore, were, in all probability, taken from this neighbourhood; nay, perhaps they were those very stones, that had been dug away, to give the Sphinx, and the chambers I have mentioned, their proper views and elevations.[17]

A few pages later, Shaw returns to the Sphinx itself:

Of The Sphinx

Besides what has been already said of the Sphinx, we are to observe, that in July 1721, the sands were so far raised and accumulated about it, that we could only discover the back of it; upon which, over the rump, there was a square hole, about four feet long, and two broad, so closely filled with sand, that we could not lay it open enough to observe, whether it had been originally contrived for the admission of fresh air; or, like the well in the great pyramid, was intended for a stair-case. Upon the head of it there is another hole, of a round figure; which, I was told, for we could not get up to it, is five or six feet deep, and wide enough to receive a well-grown person. The stone, which this part of the head consists of, seems, from the colour, to be adventitious, and different from the rest of the figure, which is all of the same stone, and hewn out of the natural rock. [This is a very sharp observation, for we now know that the head was carved from a stratum of stronger limestone than the body and is indeed harder and "different," quite apart from the fact that it seems to have been cut down and recarved by a later pharaoh in his own image.] It must be left to future travellers to find out, whether these holes served only to transmit a succession of fresh air into the body of the sphinx, or whether they might not have had likewise a communication with the great pyramid, either by the well, or by the cavity or nich [niche] in the wall of the lower chamber [the Subterranean Chamber], that lies upon a level with it. Nay, it may some time appear, that there are chambers also in the two other pyramids [we now know this to be true]; and not only so, but that the eminence likewise, upon which they are both erected, is cut out into cryptae [crypts], narrow passages, and labyrinths, which may, all of them, communicate with the chambers of the priests, the artful contrivers of these adyta [adyta is plural of adytum, which means a restricted area at the back of a temple, reserved for the priests]; where their initiatory, as well as other mysterious rites and ceremonies, were to be carried on with the greater awe and solemnity.[18]

Here we have the first clear and detailed description of the entrance to the vertical shaft, together with careful measurements of its dimensions. Wansleben and Veryard had not bothered with such things. But in the forty-three years that had elapsed since the visit of Veryard, the shaft had become filled with sand again, so Shaw was unable to descend into the chamber below. The location of this carefully constructed entrance to a shaft confirms the information we have had from Wansleben and Veryard that it was at the rear of the Sphinx's body, associated with the haunches of the creature.

Anyone familiar with the way things have worked at Giza over the centuries, in terms of local families and their habit of earning their living from visiting foreigners' baksheesh, can well imagine what had transpired. Reading through all the travelers' reports over many centuries as I have done and as the reader may now do (since they are all collected and printed in this book), one finds a remarkable continuity of behavior on the part of the locals and their insatiable demands for baksheesh, as well as their devices for obtaining more. For instance, it is obvious that the local guides had measuring rods ready at hand for all the visitors, since they all make their own measurements of the Sphinx's head, and they cannot possibly all have come with their own rods! But trying to find a new angle to make more money in the middle of the seventeenth century, some enterprising man from the adjoining village now called Nazlett (but in Greek times known as Busiris, which is not to be confused with the other city called Busiris, which is far away in the Nile Delta; the old Egyptian name for Nazlett was Djedu, which means "ghosts") must have decided he could get more baksheesh if he cleared the sand from the vertical shaft in the haunches of the Sphinx. This must have caused him and his family and friends a great deal of trouble. But they were well rewarded in that they were able to expose a subterranean chamber, though from the surviving accounts, it appears that their clearance was not complete, since Wansleben and Veryard appear only to have peered into the chamber from the shaft. There is no evidence that they really were able to clamber into the chamber and inspect it fully. Probably the locals simply could not cope with clearing the chamber of all of its sand, and they thought that offering a glimpse to visitors prepared to thrust their heads inside would suffice. The encroaching sands kept pouring down the shaft, the man who initiated the clearance then presumably died during the forty-three years that intervened before Shaw's visit, and the locals were too lazy to keep the shaft open. However, the entrance remained exposed, and Shaw was able to measure it. It is interesting that Shaw found the sand that filled the shaft so compacted or intractable that he was unable to clear enough to examine the shaft as he wished to do.

The next traveler to describe the entrance to the shaft took much more

trouble than Shaw did over the matter. He was Charles Thompson, who visited Egypt in 1733 and published the account of his travels in 1754.[19] Since
Thompson's visit to the Sphinx took place five years before Shaw's book was
published, Thompson's investigation of the shaft entrance was independent, and
was not motivated by reading Shaw. In volume 2 of his lengthy work, Thompson
records this interesting information:

> Before I leave this Place [Giza], I must take some Notice of a Colossus, at least
> the Head of one, which stands about a Quarter of a Mile to the East of the sec-
> ond Pyramid. It is usually call'd a Sphinx, which is a fabulous Monster, having
> the Head and Breasts of a Woman, the Wings of a Bird, the Claws of a Lion,
> and the Body like a Dog. This figure, among the Egyptians, was a symbolical
> Representation of the rising of the Nile in the months of July and August,
> when the Sun passes through the Signs Leo and Virgo. They likewise made
> use of it in their Hieroglyphicks to represent a Harlot, intimating the Danger
> of being captivated by the Charms of a faithless Woman, whom the fond
> Lover in the End finds as cruel and rapacious as a Lion. Of this Sphinx how-
> ever, near the Pyramids, there is little to be discern'd but from the Shoulders
> upwards, being a monstrous Bust of a Woman, all cut out of the solid Rock,
> and never separated from it; except the upper Part of the Head, which seems
> to be adventitious [added on]. It is almost thirty Feet high, fifteen feet from
> the Ear to the Chin, and above thirty feet wide at the lower Part of the Neck
> or Beginning of the Breast. The sand is so accumulated about it, that one can
> but just discover the Top of the Back, in which there is a Hole about five Feet
> long, seventy-five [feet] from the hinder Part of the Neck, and thirty from the
> Tail. We could not get up to the Top of the Head, but those who have done it
> report, that there is a round Hole, by which a full-grown Person may descend
> into it, from whence it is supposed the artful Priests deliver'd their Oracles.
> Pliny makes mention of this Sphinx, and tells us that it was thought to be the
> Sepulchre of King Amasis. The Rock is dug away all round the Sphinx to a
> considerable Distance, and the Stone was undoubtedly employ'd in building
> the Pyramids, with which some Moderns have supposed it has a subterraneous
> Communication.[20]

Like all the visitors mentioned until now, Thompson persists in the view that
the head of the Sphinx is the head of a woman. This was obviously stressed by
all the guides and is a continuation of the long and persistent tradition that the
Sphinx represented the goddess Isis, although her name had long been forgotten
by this time, of course. (The sacred *nemes* headdress of the pharaoh, seen on the

Sphinx, was presumably interpreted as a woman's head scarf or bonnet of some kind, leading people to believe that the face was that of a woman, as no man would look like that. After the end of the Ptolemaic Period, native Egyptian traditions of the pharaoh were forgotten, and the existence of such a pharaonic headdress would no longer have been remembered.)

Thompson's attention was also drawn to the "hole in the top of the back," doubtless by the same guides whose fathers or grandfathers had once cleared the shaft of sand before it filled up again. By 1733, the sand had risen so much higher that Thompson only says he could "just discover" the hole. If we had had any doubts until now of the hole possibly being the one at the rear base, these are now wholly dispelled. This hole is in the top of the back. And just to be more specific, Thompson conveniently tells us precisely where in the top of the back it was, for he has the good sense to measure the distance of the hole from the head! It is 75 feet from the back of the head, and 30 feet from the tail. In other words, it is at the point where the hips commence, and precisely where the huge crack is shown in figure 1.31 to 1.34, which Baraize completely filled with modern cement.

Thompson must have made greater efforts than Shaw did to clear the sand away from this hole, because whereas Shaw described it as 4 feet long, Thompson was evidently able to clear enough sand away to reveal a greater length of the hole, and says it is about 5 feet long. Whether it was 4 feet or 5 feet, it was a pretty large and conspicuous shaft entrance, and its complete destruction in 1926 can only be called criminal damage.

We do not have to wait long for the next visitor to see the shaft entrance. The famous Irish bishop Richard Pococke turned up at the Sphinx only a few years later, in 1739, and published the account of his travels in two volumes over the period 1743–45.[21] Pococke was successively bishop of Ossory and of Meath in Ireland. Not only did I consult Pococke's published book, but I also consulted the twenty-one volumes of his unpublished manuscript travel diaries that are preserved in the British Library.[22] The manuscript of the published material is significantly not included among the original travel diaries, which indicates that the original copies of that material went to the publisher and were not returned to Pococke again afterward, which was apparently standard publishing practice. However, some further remarks about the Sphinx were made by Pococke in a letter to his mother, which I give here first: "I went to the Sphynx the head much worn by time, especially in the neck, one just sees the top of the back & either a tail or a thigh in a sitting posture;—the whole by the nicest examination I could make seems to be cut out of the rock;—went into some catacombs & round the second Pyramid. We dined together & returned."[23]

The main description of the Sphinx mentions the rear shaft, which he does not bother to mention in the letter, and considering how well Pococke's book is known, it is amazing to me that no Egyptologist has ever mentioned this before:

> Directly in front of the second pyramid, about a quarter of a mile to the east of it, is the famous sphinx H [a reference to his engraving, Figure XVI, where the Sphinx is marked H on a plan of the Giza Plateau] about half a quarter of a mile from the water when the Nile overflows, being on much lower ground than the pyramids. Here seems to have been the grand way up to these magnificent structures. . . . The rock seems to have been dug away all round the sphinx for a great way, and the stone was doubtless employ'd in building the pyramids, the sphinx being cut out of the solid rock; for what has been taken by some to be the joining of the stone, is only veins in the rock. This extraordinary monument is said to have been the sepulchre of Amasis, tho' I think it is mention'd by none of the antient authors, except Pliny [36.12]. [Pococke's footnote here states: "My account makes the sphinx one hundred and thirty feet long, that is about seventeen feet more than Pliny. He says it was sixty-three feet high, probably taking in a plinth that might be cut out under it; so that about thirty-six feet must be buried in the sand."] I found by the quadrant that it is about twenty-seven feet high, the neck and head only being above ground; the lower part of the neck, or the beginning of the breast, is thirty-three feet wide, and it is twenty feet from the fore part of the neck to the back, and thence to the hole in the back it is seventy-five feet, the hole being five feet long, from which to the tail, if I mistake not, it is thirty feet; which something exceeds Pliny's account, who says that it is a hundred and thirteen feet long. The sand is risen up in such a manner that the top of the back only is to be seen; some persons have lately got to the top of the head, where they found a hole, which probably served for the arts of the priests in uttering oracles; as that in the back might be to descend to the apartments beneath.[24]

Here we see that the entrance to the rear shaft, "the hole in the back," is described once again as 5 feet long. I suspect that Pococke took the measurements of the distance from the head and tail directly from Thompson, as his letter to his mother does not indicate that he spent sufficient time at the Sphinx to have taken personally all the measurements that he reports. He adds that the rear shaft was possibly intended "to descend to the apartments beneath," but these were as invisible in his day as they were in Thompson's.

Following Pococke, the Danish traveler Friderik Ludvig Norden, known in English as Frederick Lewis Norden, visited Egypt. He was a captain in the Danish navy. He wrote a book about his travels, which was published in French in Copenhagen in 1755. The English translation of his travels was published in 1757.[25] (A German translation followed in 1779.) Norden does not give much description of the Sphinx, merely saying that its "enormous size attracts your admiration, and at the same time you conceive a sort of indignation at those, who have had the brutality to disfigure strangely its nose." The reason I mention Norden is that he quotes the passage from Pococke that mentions the shaft opening, thus giving wider attention to the subject.[26] This wider attention was unproductive, however, as no one until now seems ever to have taken any notice of it whatever.

There seems to have been a kind of Curse of the Sphinx that made everyone blind, so that no matter how much was published about it, no one read it. Perhaps this book will break the spell at last.

That was the end of the early references to the shaft and chamber. Within decades, the sand had risen to such a height that even the entrance to the shaft had become invisible. Coutelle describes the Sphinx as it was during his visit in 1798 when he arrived with the Napoleonic expedition:

8. The Sphinx

It is in one of the faults of the Libyan hills, in the area which rises towards the west across the plain, that the sphinx has been cut; its height is about 13 metres [40 feet] above the actual ground, it remains like a witness and like a mass of stone raised up which has been superficially made to decorate this part of the hill. The rump, scarcely perceptible, seems only traced in the earth with a length of almost 22 metres; and the side which we wanted to discover in clearing away the sand which the winds had accumulated up to the level of the hill, presented no regular shape to us to a depth of approximately 9 or 10 metres [30 feet]: as to the hole which had been noticed on the [top of the] head, it is not deeper than 2 metres 924 mm [9 feet], of a conical and irregular shape.[27]

From this we learn that the Sphinx was hopelessly obscured by sand at this time. In fact, such was the deluge of sand over the monument that the French actually undertook an initial clearance in 1798, and although Coutelle mentions the clearing of one side to a depth of 30 feet, they later concentrated on exposing the rear (see figure 2.10 on page 95 for a drawing by Robert Hay of the cleared rump) so that they might arrive at a reliable measurement of the length of the Sphinx. This is described by Coutelle's contemporary Joseph Grobert:

Now we must leave the place far from the pyramids and go down towards the east. One follows the plateau; one passes in front of the meridional [north]

Der große Sphinx zur Zeit der französischen Expedition.

Figure 2.4. The Napoleonic Expedition

face of [the Pyramid of] Chephren, and one moves off as far as one can from it to the right. One goes down quite a gentle slope to find the Sphinx, almost entirely covered by sand, and of which the projecting head is concealed from the eye by the unevenness of the ground.

[Count Constantin-François de] Volney, the only author worth quoting when you want to recount a sound idea about this region, has rightly observed that the completely Ethiopian profile of the Sphinx bears witness, in an authentic way, that that nation has given the Egyptians its laws, its morals, and its religion. These last are no more than a colony descended from Sennahar and some vast regions which encompass Nubia; they have deteriorated by mixing with the Arabs. The foreigners who can stand the disgusting sight of the Hokheila [evidently a slave market] where Negroes are sold, will not find much there to resemble the profile of the Sphinx.

This monstrous statue, truly colossal, has been sculpted from a protruding piece of rock on which it sits. It is from a single piece. The quality of the stone perfectly resembles the rock itself despite being painted yellow, and the colour has been conserved up until our day in the places where it has not been damaged. Paintings found in Upper Egypt attest the talent of the Egyptians in composing colours and the influence of the dryness of the climate in preserving them.

The Sphinx is actually very dilapidated, much more than it was in 1738 when [Friderik] Norden drew it. I uncovered enough of its back to measure it. But there should be a very considerable excavation to uncover it entirely [this did not finally happen until 1926]. If one climbs onto the head, one sees a hole which is fifteen inches in diameter at its widest point, and about nine feet in depth. The direction is oblique. One sees that the depth has been diminished by stones which have been thrown down into it. It would be difficult to determine the use of this cavity, unless one presumes some underground passage which this passage leads to, and that the priests hidden in this place delivered their oracles from it. The Sphinx was definitely an idol, and the tutelary divinity of this cemetery. The placement of the surrounding sand makes one suspect that the plain, which is at the foot of the rock to the south, and which is more elevated than the usual flood level of the river, is equally strewn with tombs.—A little to the south-west is a tomb where a Turkish hermit lives, a chapel around which several trees have been planted.[28]

Two subsequent English travelers testified to the extent of the French clearance. The first was Edward Clarke, whose description is given in full on page 493, where he comments upon the "wretched structure of brick-work, and small pieces of stone."[29]

Clarke was obviously far more impressed by the French clearance than was the famous William Hamilton, who somewhat earlier had written:

A large and strong built causeway [the causeway of Chephren] has been carried from the entrances of each of these enclosures [the funerary temples in front of the Pyramids of Mycerinus and Chephren] to the celebrated sphinx, whose enigmatical meaning still continues to puzzle the antiquaries of Europe, and who has proved during a long lapse of ages the faithful depository of the mysteries which envelop every object round her. The French excavated the body of the lion; which they found uninjured: but the sands of the Desert very soon rendered their labour vain, and the last time I saw the sphinx, the head and neck alone were visible. These have been evidently painted all over, and many characters are to be traced upon the head-dress; but we could not ascertain whether they were the sacred or popular letters of Egypt [i.e., hieroglyphics or hieratic writing]; some indeed bore a resemblance to the Arabic. It is still a point of dispute among the learned, whether this combination of the human and the lion's form is typical of the rising of the Nile, the summer solstice, or the wisdom and power of the deity. Such a personification of human intelligence and brutal force might be the original of the Greek Minerva; and agreeably to this supposition, the sphinx is a very common ornament of this goddess on her statues and on her medals.[30]

ÉLÉVATION DU PLAN CI-DESSOUS.

LE SPHINX

J. Grobert Del.

Huot Sc.

PLAN DES PYRAMIDES DE GHIZE

Left: Figure 2.5. This is plate 1, a folding plate, from J. [Jacques-François-Louis] Grobert, *Description des Pyramides de Ghizé*, Paris, "An. IX" (i.e., 1801). The top view shows the three Giza pyramids, the Great Pyramid at right, the Pyramid of Chephren in the center, and the Pyramid of Mycerinus at the left. Below the left corner of the Pyramid of Chephren, the head and back of the Sphinx may be seen sticking out of the sand. This is a clear indication of the extent of the clearance of the Sphinx made by the Napoleonic Expedition, and is confirmed by the plan seen in the view below. The French obviously cleared the entire back to arrive at a reliable measurement of the length of the sculpture. On the plan below, the Sphinx is marked "T" (which can barely be seen in front of the Sphinx's head near the bottom of the plan) and sits alone in the sand, with no trace shown of either the Valley Temple or the Sphinx Temple. Behind and to the left of the Sphinx, marked "S" on the plan, are three old sycamore trees (still surviving in the nineteenth-century photo in figure 3.9) and a building that had vanished by Victorian times, which we know from written sources was the residence of a Muslim hermit. The plan shows cultivated fields at bottom right, reaching right up to the cliff edge, and these would have covered the site of the Cheops Valley Temple, which has never been excavated (but some carved blocks from which survive as reused blocks at the site of Lisht, farther south). Today, this unexcavated temple lies beneath a private house in Nazlet el-Samman. The plan also shows the contours very well, which indicate how the Nile's inundation waters (which even in Victorian times still covered those fields and went up to the cliff base) were able to approach the feet of the Sphinx, which had no cliff barrier like that barring the way to the Great Pyramid. It is interesting to see that in 1798/9, when this plan would have been drawn, one boat pit was known in front of the Great Pyramid. The Chephren Funerary Temple and Causeway were completely covered in sand. Not a single mastaba can be seen. The empty square shown behind the Sphinx, more or less directly in the path of the Chephren Causeway, seems too far back to be Campbell's Tomb, and may be a ruined superstructure that once stood on top of the causeway above the entrance to the so-called Osiris Shaft, which lies beneath the causeway. (My account of the Osiris Shaft is published in *Egyptian Dawn*.) (*Collection of Robert Temple*)

Figure 2.6. An engraving of the Pyramid of Chephren, center, and the Sphinx, bottom center of the picture, as seen in the seventeenth century. The small building to the left of the Sphinx beside some trees was a hermit's cell, which had vanished by the nineteenth century but is mentioned in the early travelers' accounts. At left in the engraving is the Pyramid of Mycerinus. This is the top portion of plate 1 from J. Grobert, *Description des pyramides de Ghize*, Paris, 1801 ("An. IX" of the Republic). (*Collection of Robert Temple*)

The only possible explanation for the conflicting statements of Hamilton and Clarke would seem to be that after Hamilton left in 1801, the French must have undertaken a second clearance before Clarke arrived. An unpublished manuscript by James Burton in the British Library reveals more interesting details about the various Sphinx clearance operations. Burton visited Giza in 1822, and his manuscripts show that he intended to publish an extensive account of his Egyptian travels, but he never did so. Perhaps because he was frustrated in this aim for some reason, all his papers were left to the British Library, where they have been carefully preserved but apparently rarely consulted. In fact, they are a priceless scholarly resource, full of wonderful information and illustrations. Burton was a scholar, and not just a casual visitor to Egypt. He was a serious student of the Arabic language and read a lot of Arabic histories. I have copied the following interesting remarks about the Sphinx from Burton's manuscript, but have omitted earlier ones, which include discussions of what various Arabic historians had said of it, what its Arabic name meant, a discussion of its original coloring, and quotations from Abdallatif and Denon:

> The statue was mutilated by a bigoted enthusiast [old-fashioned word for a fanatic], Sheckh [Sheikh] Mohammed, about year of the Hegira—? [Burton left a blank for the date.] It was probably when the nose was thus broken that the Asp [uraeus] and head dress were removed. There is little doubt that it carried these ornaments, from the hole now remaining in the top of the head, which the natives have at some time or other enlarged, in the hopes of finding in the interior some hidden treasure. The head however is solid stone, and they soon found their labour useless. I think I remember Mr. [Henry] Salt having told me, that he found in excavating the temple between its paws, part of an asp in bronze. This will have been that placed over the forehead.
>
> The rump was repaired with Mapara [?] stone probably by the Kornans [??]—their repairs were destroyed again by the late Defterdar in order to serve as building materials for one of his palaces.

Burton is obviously referring here to the Ottoman Turkish official called the Defterdar Bey. He acted as finance minister in Egypt and was directly appointed by the sultan in Istanbul. The Defterdar actually ranked higher than the bey (provincial governor). The office of Defterdar was abolished in 1837. The Defterdar's aims were to squeeze as much money as possible out of the subject populations and exploit any and all local resources to the fullest possible extent. It is shocking that he carried this so far that he stripped stones off the Sphinx. It is impossible to know whether this account refers to the actual rump and its casing stones or

Figure 2.7. This photo shows the socket between the eyes of the Sphinx where the nose was apparently reattached after the fanatical sheikh Mohammed struck it off as being offensive to Islam in the Middle Ages. (The story about the nose being shot off by soldiers is false.) (*Photo by Robert Temple*)

whether it might refer to stones that had been used to try to fill up the shaft at the haunches. If the latter is the case, then by removing stones from the shaft in a rough manner, he might have caused the huge crack to open and the haunches to split off, as we see in the various photos. In other words, this "rape of the Sphinx" by the Ottoman Defterdar may have split the Sphinx at the point of the shaft.

Burton's account continues: "Moorad Bey [Murad Bey, died 1801; see his portrait in figure 2.8] first uncovered the Sphinx but found nothing—he did not dig deep. The French then did it, and were equally unsuccessful. [Captain J.-B.] Caviglia finally succeeded, and the accompanying notice of the work is copied from the . . . " (here the text breaks off).[31]

The verso side of this manuscript leaf has Burton's copy of Henry Salt's plan of the paws and altar of the Sphinx (see figure 6.47 on page 278 for Salt's plan, as it appeared in the *Quarterly Review*, which is the reference Burton intended to insert), with identifying letters and specific descriptions. No succeeding leaf has been bound into this manuscript volume, and the subsequent leaves by Burton change subject.

Figure 2.8. A portrait of Murad Bey, who died in 1801. According to a manuscript report by James Burton, who went to Egypt twenty-one years after Murad Bey's death, it was this Egyptian ruler who carried out the first modern excavations of the Sphinx, "but found nothing—he did not dig deep." Not long afterward, Egypt was invaded by the French, and they also made excavations at the Sphinx, commencing in 1798, "and were equally unsuccessful." They did, however, find evidence of an opening between the paws, which was doubtless the "altar crypt," part of which is still visible through a metal grille in the rock today (see figure 1.29), and the rest of which was sealed up in two stages 120 years apart, first by Henry Salt and then by Professor Selim Hassan. Engraving by Sonnini de Manoncourt, made in 1799, two years before Murad Bey's death. (*Collection of Robert Temple*)

We learn here what I believe is recorded nowhere else, that the Turkish provincial governor of Egypt at the end of the 1700s, Murad Bey, had actually attempted to clear the Sphinx prior to its clearance by the French in 1798. Perhaps he even tried to repair some of the damage caused by the Defterdar many decades before. Burton's comment that both Murad Bey and the French had been unsuccessful must mean that the apparent second attempt by the French was also a failure. Indeed, it was not until Émile Baraize cleared the Sphinx to the bedrock in 1926 that the Sphinx had been fully exposed since Roman times. If a search were made of the Ottoman records in Istanbul, some record of the Turkish treatment of the Sphinx would doubtless be found, both the Defterdar's despoliations and sale of stones and Murad Bey's partial excavation and restoration attempts.

I have already had occasion to point out that Caviglia, an Italian who also wrote French and spoke but did not write English, did not leave his papers in what we would consider proper order. He gave many of them to the British consul Henry Salt, who had supplied some of the funds for the clearance, and as we have seen in the previous chapter, Salt published a lengthy account of Caviglia's excavation of the Sphinx in the *Quarterly Review* in London.[32] A few of Caviglia's papers are preserved in the British Library, and I have looked at all of these. But as we shall see in a moment, some of his crucial papers relating to the Sphinx made their way to Florence, where they were consulted in 1833 by an English Egyptologist, none of whose notes of them appears to survive. But it was these very papers that described not only his clearance of the vertical shaft, but also his actual entry into the subterranean chamber! Unfortunately, I have no idea where in Florence these papers of Caviglia's may have been deposited, or whether indeed they are still there. My friend Stefano Greco and I undertook some preliminary searching together in Florence, and Stefano has continued this search. One unexpected find was an account in Italian by one of Caviglia's friends, Annibale Brandi, in another Italian town. The section dealing with the Sphinx has been translated by Stefano and myself into English and is found in appendix 4. The information that it gives is discussed later on. In addition, we do have some further important information about Caviglia's activities preserved by Auguste Mariette, which is found in appendix 1, and that is discussed in a moment. And finally, as discussed later, some more material that had been "lost" since the Victorian era was recently published by the British Museum Press, having been found while moving offices. That Caviglia's work came to such an abrupt end because of his having a serious attack of sunstroke and being disabled meant that his reports were never finalized. He left Egypt suddenly, and apparently only returned to Giza to evacuate in the 1830s, more than fifteen years later.

That the Sphinx was cleared at the rear by the combined work of the French and remained so for a quarter of a century is shown in a rare rear-view drawing by the English artist Robert Hay in 1827, which I found in a manuscript in the British Library and reproduce in figure 2.8. This makes it clear that the rear portion of the Sphinx was entirely accessible for an investigation of the shaft and chamber beneath the haunches. And as we shall see, Caviglia fully cleared the shaft and the chamber in 1817 as well.

Caviglia spent ten months clearing the surrounding sand from the Sphinx, until he was incapacitated by sunstroke and had to stop, returning to his ship at Alexandria and resuming his life as a sea captain.[33] All this took place before Henry Salt published the account of Caviglia's work in the *Quarterly Review*. Caviglia's clearance and exploration of the shaft and chamber beneath the Sphinx must therefore also have taken place before Salt's publication. But why did Salt not mention it? Why, indeed, did Salt mention nothing whatever of the discoveries of tunnels and entrances relating to the Sphinx? Here we must recall the accusation made by Count de Forbin, as recounted in the first chapter, that Salt through arrogance and stupidity had blocked up some of these so that they could not be investigated further. Salt may have thought that as he was contributing to the funds that paid for the excavation, he had a right to interfere with it in this way. But what can have

Left: Figure 2.9. This is Henry Salt's drawing from 1817 of the cleared space beneath the chest of the Sphinx, between its front paws. The suspended object in the center top of the drawing is the remnants of the Sphinx's beard, which had been affixed to the recarved head of the Middle Kingdom pharaoh Amenemhet II, either by himself or later during the New Kingdom, when the Sphinx was excavated by Thutmosis IV. The large upright stela in the center of the scene is the Dream Stela, Henry Salt's separate drawing of which is shown in figure 3.7. (Modern photos of this stela are shown in figures 3.8 and 4.19.) At the time of its excavation by Caviglia, the inscription on the Dream Stela was intact, as I have discovered from an account in Italian left by a friend of Caviglia, which was located by my friend Stefano Greco in an obscure Italian library, and the Sphinx portion of which, translated by us into English, is published here as appendix 4. By the time Salt was able to draw the inscription some weeks or months after its excavation (it could not yet be read, because hieroglyphics had not yet been deciphered), well over a third and nearly a half of the inscription had vanished. Since then, even more has gone, so only about half remains. The new account that Stefano and I have found explains that the inscription was peeled off by the superstitious inhabitants of the neighboring village of Nazlet el-Samman, chiefly women believing it could help them have babies if they had fragments in their homes, presumably under their beds to aid conception. This drawing is found in *Operations Carried On at the Pyramids of Gizeh in 1837* by Colonel Howard Vyse and John S. Perring, London, 1842, third appendix volume, plate opposite page 110. (*Collection of Robert Temple*)

Figure 2.10. A computer-enhanced reproduction of a drawing by Robert Hay done in 1827, showing the rear of the Sphinx free of sand and largely exposed at that date. The original drawing is exceedingly faint and is preserved in the Papers of the Robert Hay Expedition to Egypt, 1826–1838, in the British Library Manuscripts Collection (Add. Ms. 29,812, folio 67 recto). The Old Kingdom blocks are clearly drawn at the base, and thirteen rows of them are shown. The three human figures on top of the Sphinx's back are standing near the point of descent leading to the chamber beneath the Sphinx, which was entered in 1817 by Caviglia and in previous centuries by earlier travelers, whose accounts are gathered here. (*Courtesy of the British Library; computer enhancement by Michael Lee*)

been his motivation? Was he just an ignorant lout? Perhaps he thought of these things as blemishes, and, having exposed the Sphinx to view, he wanted to tidy it up and plug the holes, to render its appearance more beautiful. If he thought of the Sphinx primarily as a magnificent monument that he had helped reveal to the eyes of mortals for the first time since antiquity, he might have been impatient of "imperfections" such as openings, passages, and so forth, which would have meant nothing to him, as he was not an archaeologist. It may simply be that in a pompous sort of way he was just a silly fool. Count de Forbin evidently thought so.

But how do we know that Caviglia really entered the chamber beneath the Sphinx? This was discovered by an early English Egyptologist named Charles H. Cottrell, who seems to have published nothing of his own, but who translated a huge work by Baron Bunsen on the antiquities of Egypt, entitled *Egypt's Place in Universal History*.[34]

In 1855, the French archaeologist Auguste Mariette related the story, which was reported in a French periodical of that time:

> In 1833 an English Egyptologist, Mr. [Charles H.] Cottrell, to whom one owes the translation of the work of Monsieur [Christian Carl Josias Freiherr von] Bunsen on Egypt [*Egypt's Place in Universal History*], found in Florence among the papers of Caviglia, who undertook the first of the extensive excavations around the colossus [the Sphinx], the plan of two chambers discovered behind the Sphinx, and which contained hieroglyphic texts. Monsieur [Samuel] Birch had the thought that if one succeeded in rediscovering these two chambers, the inscriptions in question would reveal the origin of the gigantic statue. Monsieur le Duc de Luynes [Louis-Charles d'Albert, Duc de Luynes], alerted to this fact by Monsieur [Vicomte Emmanuel] de Rougé, wished, with his well known liberality, to help our compatriot [Mariette is referred to here] to pursue this curious quest, and furnished him with the funds necessary for the excavation. This act of generosity was soon followed by an allocation of funds from the French government, and Monsieur Mariette came to clear the Sphinx, which he found to be only a natural rock of which the art of the ancient Egyptians had, so to speak, finished the shapes in order to make the statue of a god. That god is Horus, and the temple where he was worshipped has been rediscovered to the southeast of the colossus [the "colossus" is the Sphinx; this temple is now called the Valley Temple]. It is an enormous square enclosure comprising a crowd of rooms with galleries made of gigantic blocks of alabaster and granite. This edifice, completely devoid of hieroglyphic inscriptions, like most of the monuments dating from the most ancient pharaohs, dates, according to all probability, from the fourth dynasty.

The Egyptians had sculpted the head of the Sphinx and filled up the large natural hollows and moulded the shapes with masonry. This colossus is found at the bottom of a sort of pit of which the lateral walls are twenty metres away from each of its sides. *Monsieur Mariette admits that in antiquity the water of the Nile could have entered this pit.* [My italics, as this is also my own idea, at which I arrived entirely independently, and which is discussed at length later in this book, in chapter 6, which I wrote before I discovered the report about Mariette, which is inserted here.] Later the Greeks had built the steps discovered by Caviglia for going down into the pit. Against the right side of the Sphinx the traveller had found a huge Osiris statue made of twenty eight pieces, reckoned to be the number of pieces into which the body of Osiris had been cut according to the Egyptian myth. [This statue seems to be otherwise unknown, and may have stood on one of the two "cupolas" beside the Sphinx on the southern side, in which case it was probably of New Kingdom, Saite, or Ptolemaic date.]

The Sphinx has been measured in all of its dimensions. Its height is 19.7 metres. In the back and across the hindquarters of the statue, Monsieur Mariette recognized the vertical shaft, the existence of which had previously been pointed out by Vansleb [Johann Wansleben] and [Richard] Pococke, who thought that one could penetrate further down from there into existing chambers, according to their supposition, inside the colossus. This shaft, explored with care, presented at its bottom a roughly hewn room, which was in reality just a natural fissure enlarged by the hands of man. In this room lay some fragments of wood which gave off a strong smell of resin when burnt, which led one to believe that the wood came from a sarcophagus.

One had supposed that in antiquity the Sphinx was entirely painted red, but nothing indicates that this had been so. Only the face was once covered in this colour after the reign of Ramesses the Great [sic; Rameses II], for the beard of the colossus represents an act of worship in the time of that pharaoh, over which the red had been applied.

The Greek inscriptions found near the stairs of the Sphinx tell us that this colossus bore the name of Harmakhis, the significance of which has still not been discovered.

The excavations of the Great Sphinx did not lessen the honour due to the intelligence and to the devotion of Monsieur Mariette in his magnificent discovery of the Serapeum [at Saqqara]. We need to return to this archaeological event before recapturing, as we will be doing in one of the forthcoming issues, the analysis of the works of the Academy since our last survey.[35]

So now we know not only of Caviglia's excavation and study of the shaft and chamber but of Mariette's as well. Caviglia is said to have done plans of two chambers beneath the Sphinx, and we must suppose that the second one was the hollow at the bottom of the rump tunnel, since Mariette speaks of only one chamber at the bottom of the vertical shaft. As there are certainly no hieroglyphic inscriptions in the hollow of the rump tunnel, the hieroglyphic inscriptions referred to must have been inscribed on the walls of the chamber at the bottom of the vertical shaft. This would seem to indicate a date that must be later than the Fourth Dynasty, and hence not contemporary with Chephren. In fact, there is every reason to believe that this vertical shaft is what archaeologists call an "intruded grave," thrust down into an ancient monument at a much later time. But it must have been the grave of a late pharaoh, since no one less than a pharaoh would have dared to give himself a grave under such a prominent monument as the Sphinx. Perhaps it was indeed the pharaoh known to the Greeks as Amasis, so the report of Pliny that the Sphinx was his grave would actually be correct. Amasis was a late pharaoh who reigned 570–526 BC during the Twenty-sixth Dynasty, which is known as the Saite Period. This was a period when there was a great preoccupation with and reverence for the most ancient monuments, a social and cultural tendency known as "archaizing," rather like the European Romantic movement, when picturesque Greek and Roman ruins were idealized. Amasis is just the sort of late pharaoh who would have intruded his own grave into the Sphinx. So it may well be that the vertical shaft and chamber below were cut in 525 BC, and that the vertical shaft was placed at the precise spot where a much earlier top entrance to the rump tunnel had existed. If this was the case, the burial was probably not cut more sensibly in the base of the Sphinx because that base was still covered with sand. Indeed, since the Persians conquered Egypt shortly after the death of Amasis, and they pillaged and despoiled much of Egypt when they did so, it is highly likely that any such grave of Amasis would have been entered and robbed within a generation of his death. On the other hand, of course, the shaft and chamber may well have been much older, and the mention of the name of Amasis by Pliny may be entirely erroneous and misleading. If we could get into the chamber again, we could doubtless read the hieroglyphic inscriptions, and then we would probably know whose tomb it was. Or, there is one more alternative possibility: if Caviglia's missing papers could be located at Florence or elsewhere, he may well have copied down some of the inscriptions in his notes accompanying the plans.

My friend Stefano Greco and I have searched for these papers in Italy for more than a year. We did some searching when we were together in Florence in early 2007 but were unsuccessful. Stefano has continued the search, but so far with no success. He did, however, discover a rare book, which seems to be the only surviving copy in the world, as no other is known anywhere. It is a forgotten booklet written by an Italian friend of Caviglia's named Annibale Brandi, identified by his initials "A.B.," and privately published by him in Livorno in 1823. This booklet is entitled *Descrizione compendiosa delle piramidi di Giza in Egitto (Compendious Description of the Pyramids of Giza in Egypt)*. Most of it is devoted to describing Caviglia's astonishing work and findings inside the Great Pyramid, of which he cleared the entire Descending Passage of rubbish (several hundred feet of it!), entered the subterranean chamber for the first time since antiquity, and cleared it, and also descended the "well shaft" by dangling 175 feet on a rope. Caviglia was a determined and intrepid man! At the end of the booklet is an account of Caviglia's work at the Sphinx, which Brandi calls "the Andro-Sphinx" because of its having the head of a man. Although this previously unknown account is interesting, it does not mention the chamber beneath the Sphinx. Presumably it was entered by Caviglia only after this particular friend had returned to Italy, or otherwise Caviglia might have sworn his friend to secrecy about the subterranean chamber beneath the Sphinx. Stefano has translated the latter portion of this booklet that refers to the Sphinx, and it is published here as appendix 4. This text contains the shocking information that the entire text of the Dream Stela was intact at the time that it was excavated by Caviglia. Today, the bottom half of the inscription is lost, and most of that was lost (but for a few fragments, now gone) by the time Henry Salt carefully copied down what was left. Salt's drawing is shown in figure 3.7, and that contains much more than survives today. The inference to be drawn from this is that after the departure of Caviglia from Egypt, the most severe damage was inflicted on the Dream Stela intentionally, and the bottom half of the text was obliterated by someone wishing to destroy it, perhaps for religious reasons, as a text relating to an "idol." Salt probably made his careful drawing of what was left because he was afraid the whole text might at any moment be defaced (as indeed more of it was), so he wanted to record what remained to preserve the information for posterity, even though he could not read it. (We must remember that at this time no one could yet read hieroglyphics, so no one had any idea what the Dream Stela's text said.)

In 2007, at the same time that Stefano and I were searching for Caviglia's notes in Italy and unexpectedly discovering the sole surviving copy of Brandi's privately printed booklet in Italian, the British Museum published a booklet containing a discovery of its own, entitled *The Sphinx Revealed: A Forgotten Record of Pioneering Excavations*.[36] Five years earlier, in the spring of 2002, the Egyptian Department of the British Museum had to move its offices, and after they settled into their new location, the personnel (presumably the two scholars Patricia Usick and Deborah Manley, the authors of the published booklet) noticed a couple of interesting old bound books sitting around. One contained a manuscript and the other contained its accompanying drawings. These had been in the department for at least 175 years, and no one had paid any attention to them, except that someone in the nineteenth century had taken great care to preserve them and have them carefully bound and even gilt, and had seen to it that they were cataloged. (This may well have been Sir Edward Wallis Budge, the Victorian head of the department, who was a very serious and devoted scholar.) The two authors tactfully refer to the shameful ignoring of this material for nearly two centuries by saying that it had "never been studied in depth and many of the illustrations appeared to be otherwise unknown." That is presumably a way of avoiding criticizing their past and present colleagues too harshly, and avoiding making professional enemies. (Academics have to behave like this all the time in self-protection, for there is no sphere of human activity more vicious than the academic world.) The history of these volumes shows the dangers of sole copies of important material languishing in the private offices of museums where no one has access to them but the staff. Usick and Manley clearly saw the need to take action, and I hope they are not hated too much by their colleagues for daring to do so. But it now means that the rest of us, who are mere lowly uninitiated folk who are not allowed into the inner sanctum of the Egyptian Department, can read what they have been hiding away since at least 1827. If the material had been deposited in the British Library's Manuscript Collection where it belonged, it would probably have been seen and studied by many scholars long ago.

Fortunately, the British Museum Press agreed to publish this important material, although the illustrations are so poorly reproduced that they all look as if they are viewed through a layer of mud. They are, how shall I say it, a kind of dirty dark gray. Clearly, the press does not realize that we are living in the twenty-first century, when there are such things as modern printing facilities. There is no excuse for the scans that were used being printed in such an appalling and semivisible condition. It is really very difficult to make out the detail in many of these drawings.

The text and drawings are those of none other than Henry Salt! They are entitled, on a manuscript title page bound in front of them, *Memoir on Pyramids and Sphinx by H. Salt, Esqr.* and dated on the title page 1821. This is the manuscript record that Salt intended for official publication in London of the excavation of the Sphinx by Caviglia, and it superseded the interim publication based on his notes in the *Quarterly Review* in 1818 (see endnote 22 in chapter 1). But it was never printed until now, although it needs to be stressed that some of its contents were word for word the same as material that had appeared in the *Quarterly*

Review, so not all of it is new. Salt sent it from Egypt; he died six years later, and nobody did anything to bring it out. Two of his colleagues in London went through it and made a lot of textual editing changes, most of them unhelpful and in a style far inferior to Salt's own. (These changes have been carefully included in the British Museum publication by use of italics, because Usick and Manley have been very conscientious and done an excellent, scholarly job.) And then nothing happened and the whole thing sat around in the department's office and was ignored until 2002.

The frontispiece of the British Museum publication is a portrait drawing of Caviglia "in 1827, drawn by H. Salt from life," which is preserved in the Bodleian Library. I was not previously aware of the existence of this drawing, strangely preserved by an archive acquired by the National Trust and deposited in the Bodleian. The archive is that of the manuscripts of Sir Gardner Wilkinson (1797–1875), which were finally cataloged and opened to public access for the first time in Oxford in 2001. In that case, it took a mere 126 years for the material to be made available, which greatly undercuts the British Museum's 175-year availability rate. Clearly, Egyptological resources move exceedingly rapidly when judged by the standard of the ages, and in comparison to the time elapsed since the Fourth Dynasty. Indeed, one might justly and reliably say that Egyptological material is most definitely made public at a speed more rapid than the movement of the tectonic plates of the Earth, whatever skeptics might think.

It is unfortunate that the portrait of Caviglia as reproduced by the British Museum Press looks as if someone had just turned the lights out, and it is being made out dimly by some light leaking in from the next room.

The account by Salt also does not mention the chamber beneath the Sphinx. I am convinced that Caviglia had reservations about Salt, who intruded on his work and joined him by offering some funding, and that Caviglia did not reveal all of his activities to him. The newly published account contains comments by Salt about Caviglia's determination to find a "door" in the Sphinx, however.[37] Although Salt points out that Caviglia employed as many as one hundred laborers daily,[38] he also points out that some of Caviglia's activities "were carried on by a single individual [i.e., himself], attended occasionally only by one soldier."[39] This reveals that Caviglia did a lot of things entirely alone and could easily keep things to himself if he wished. He never seems to have been fully in Salt's confidence, and the only part of the Sphinx work that was fully and completely open to inspection was in front of the Sphinx. But even there, where the entry to the subterranean chamber seen in figure 1.29 must unquestionably have been exposed, since clearance was made to bedrock and it could not have been missed, not a word appeared in any of Salt's reports about its existence. This leads to only two possible conclusions: either Caviglia found it and covered it up to keep it secret or Salt did know of it but chose to keep it secret himself. The latter seems more likely, as Count de Forbin was most likely referring to this chamber in front of the Sphinx when he made his accusations that Salt was blocking up passages and openings so that no one could investigate them. If we could find the missing Caviglia papers, we could probably find Caviglia's own report on this chamber, in addition to his description of the burial chamber at the haunches that Cottrell discovered in those papers in 1833.

Later in this book, the newly published Salt material will be mentioned again, because it includes the original drawing he made, the one engraved for the *Quarterly Review,* of a carved inscription (long since destroyed) that was found by Caviglia on the middle toe of the left paw of the Sphinx.[40] This reveals some information that will later be seen to be of the greatest possible interest to us in trying to determine what the Sphinx actually was and why it was created. But that is for a later stage of our quest, and is to be found in chapter 6.

In 1853, Mariette had earlier written to the French Egyptologist Viscount Emmanuel de Rougé, mentioning the subterranean chamber beneath the haunches of the Sphinx as follows: "The Egyptians remedied these faults [holes in the rock] by covering the entire body of the monument with two layers of masonry. The first, which touches the rock, was intended to fill up the considerable cavities which occurred in the stone. These cavities are numerous; I came across one at the commencement of the thigh, into which I penetrated along with several people. It is without doubt the one which Father Vansleb [Wansleben] took to be a mortuary chamber."[41]

These notices by Mariette were not the last time the vertical shaft and the burial chamber beneath the Sphinx were mentioned in print. The next occasion was in 1897, in an extraordinary article by the distinguished archaeologist Ludwig Borchardt, who for decades was the director of the German Institute in Cairo. I have carefully translated this entire article and reproduce it in full in appendix 2, not because of its mention of the shaft and chamber, but because I am convinced that Borchardt's unusual theory about the dating of the Sphinx has an unexpected relevance, as I explain at length in chapter 4. Borchardt's theory has been dismissed until now, but I believe it needs to be resurrected, because it is "true" in a way he never imagined. But for the moment we are concerned only with his comments on the vertical shaft and the subterranean chamber. The article to which I refer is a rare one entitled (in translation) "Concerning the Age of the Sphinx at Giza," and it appeared in an obscure German scholarly journal.[42] I have been extremely fortunate to obtain an original offprint of this article, which few people alive today have ever seen, and which seems to be largely unknown in Egyptological circles today.

The main purpose of Borchardt's article was to discuss the age of the Sphinx, and the vertical shaft and subterranean chamber are mentioned only as part of a list of features contributing to an argument. The first mention is as follows: "The occurrence of two vertical shafts on the back of the Sphinx, one of which ends in a burial chamber, in which coffin boards have been found. From this we can infer the earlier existence of a mastaba on the back of the Sphinx."[43]

This interpretation of a mastaba (burial edifice) having preceded the carving of the Sphinx, which then incorporated it, is part of Borchardt's argument about the true age of the Sphinx. He then makes further remarks elaborating on this notion, in the context of his belief that the Sphinx was carved by order of Pharaoh Amenemhet III of the Middle Kingdom, who reigned from 1818 to 1773 BC:

> One could imagine the history of the Sphinx in general, mixed with some guesses, in the following manner:
>
> The Sphinx was hacked out of the bedrock, perhaps by Amenemhet III, by destroying one of the mastabas standing on a hill, which now constitutes the back of the Sphinx. And partly by building it up with ashlar blocks. It shows the king in the shape of a prostrate lion with a human head—in front of the chest with a divine image, perhaps of Harmachis or Khepra. When later the monument was largely buried, then Thutmosis IV had it cleared for the first time. In the stela celebrating this fact we find already the mixing of the meaning of the image of the Sphinx itself with the divine image in front of his chest. Perhaps it was then that the braided divine beard was added to the image. The Sphinx was partially freed from the sand in the nineteenth Dynasty.
>
> In a later time, the Sphinx was surrounded by a high brick wall in order to protect him from the drifting sand. From the east, a large staircase led down to the small chapel in front of the divine image in front of the chest. All these means of protection have not helped a lot. In this century it was necessary to dig him out again repeatedly, last in 1883, and actually it would be necessary again today.[44]

Later in this book we shall see why Borchardt's strange theory about the Sphinx having been carved in the time of Pharaoh Amenemhet III should be looked at more carefully. The reason is rather unexpected but may be crucially important. However, it is not surprising that Borchardt's article has lapsed into total obscurity today, since there is probably no one alive who could possibly accept the bizarre notion that the Sphinx was carved as recently as 1773 BC. I am far from being a general champion of Ludwig Borchardt, however important much of his work may have been. He was undoubtedly arrogant and pompous to an extraordinary

Figure 2.11. In the New Kingdom, a pharaoh offers a miniature "sphinx" (as conceived at that time) to the god Khonsu in the Temple of Khonsu at Karnak. At this period, Khonsu was the god of the moon, and as such measured the passage of time. In earlier eras, this had been a function of Thoth. (*Photo by Robert Temple*)

degree. He was also wrong about many things. But one of the greatest of ironies is that what people might be forgiven for thinking of as his greatest folly, namely the suggestion that the Sphinx dates from 1773 BC, which appears wholly absurd on the face of it, probably conceals an amazing truth, which I will explain fully in chapter 4. Borchardt's bold and meticulous analysis of certain evidence that led him to his strange conclusion must be examined very carefully indeed. But for the moment, it bears little relevance to what we are considering here.

It is interesting, though, that in the pursuit of his notion, Borchardt considered the vertical shaft and subterranean chamber sufficiently important that he was prepared to view them as primary features, and the surrounding Sphinx itself as secondary in origin! And he must have inspected what he could of the evidence very carefully indeed. Probably the shaft and chamber were again filled with sand in his time. But as we see quite clearly in the photos in figures 1.31 to 1.34, a gigantic crack had opened in the Sphinx at the point of the shaft, and the rear haunches look as if they were about to detach from the body entirely. This would have enabled anybody in Borchardt's time to form a very clear idea of the importance of this vertical shaft, which had been so prominent that it had effectively split the body of the exposed sculpture. And doubtless it was the clearance of the Sphinx from its surrounding sand and Caviglia's further clearing of the shaft and subterranean chamber(s) that precipitated the splitting away of the haunches, since all support, both internal and external, had been removed. Any damage caused by the previously mentioned Turkish Defterdar would then have been worsened by exposure and the loss of support of the surrounding sand. When Baraize filled this entire section with cement in 1926, he may have thought of himself as heroically "restoring" and saving a disintegrating monument from potential collapse.

By the time the great Egyptian archaeologist Selim Hassan came along, in the mid-1930s, and carried out the final and complete clearance of the Sphinx and total excavation of its pit and surroundings, all possibility of exploring and studying the vertical shaft and the subterranean chamber(s) had been destroyed by Baraize ten years before. Hassan was thus able to discover nothing about them. But this does not mean that he was unaware of them. Indeed, he is the last person to mention them in print, as recently as 1953. That no one has noticed that he did so is perhaps the most puzzling of all the lapses of students of the Sphinx, or perhaps I should say it is the most prominent of many acts of mass blindness and refusal to see, which I call consensus blindness, a psychological condition with its origin in animal behavior (humans being animals, however much they try to deny it, and most of their activities forming a subdivision of animal behavior). I have discussed consensus blindness at length in my earlier book, *The Crystal Sun* (2000). The belief that putting evidence in front of people's eyes will lead to recognition and

Figure 2.12. This is the south side of the Sphinx's haunch area. All the stones along the foot are from the modern restoration of the monument. The upper tip of the tail has disappeared and three courses of modern stone have been cut and added to it. In the center, the upper half of the body consists of material added by Baraize in 1926 to fill the crack that had formed at the point of the intruded vertical shaft leading to the tomb chamber directly below, as described by numerous people who entered it in earlier times. We can be confident that this filled-in vertical shaft wasn't contemporary with the carving of the Sphinx, because the tomb chamber beneath the Sphinx was covered in hieroglyphics, which was not a practice that existed prior to the Fifth Dynasty. (*Photo by Robert Temple*)

acknowledgment is naive and false. People see what they want to see, not what they are shown. That is part of the definition of the human species.

Hassan gives a great deal of attention to Ludwig Borchardt's article about the age of the Sphinx, and he even translates part of it into English (although his translation contains some unfortunate errors, because his German was not good enough; and in any case, Borchardt wrote in a difficult and old-fashioned style of the nineteenth century). Hassan spells *Amenemhet* in the form *Amenemhat,* which is an equally acceptable spelling. (Egyptian vowels were not explicitly written, and versions of words and names rendered into European languages often vary in this way as a result of changing fashions and personal preference.) Hassan naturally dismisses Borchardt's theory about this pharaoh's association with the Sphinx, and he does so in the strongest possible language:

> Under the title "*Ueber das Alter des Sphinx bei Gizeh,*" Borchardt has indulged in an astonishing flight of fancy! . . . It seems to me that Borchardt had gone to a great deal of trouble to prove a theory that is altogether wrong from the beginning to the end; that is if he is not having a joke with the scientific world, and indulging in a little "leg-pulling" at our expense. . . . If Borchardt was really serious about this article, then I think that of all the theories that he ever put into writing, he must have bitterly regretted having published this one![45]

Figure 2.13. A photo of the Sphinx taken in the 1930s, during the final clearance of the monument by Selim Hassan. Railway lines for carrying away the debris are in the foreground. The face has been "restored" with modern cement filling all the gashes and holes, including the large gash over the left eye (see figures 1.16, 1.17, 1.21, and 6.4 to 6.6). The lappets, or side flaps, of the *nemes* headdress have been extended down to shoulder level on both sides by clearly visible modern concrete; the original stone of the lappets, which had been a bit raggedy (see figures 1.5 to 1.7; 1.20 and 1.22 as they appeard before), has been chipped away and made level for the addition of the concrete. Today the striking difference of color between the modern concrete and the old stone is no longer so obvious. This photo must have been a "proud portrait photo" taken of the just completed restoration of the face at the request of Selim Hassan, during the first day or two while the concrete was still drying and was thus still very pale. Scaffolding is in place on the northern side of the Sphinx and at the top of the back. A workmen's gangway has been made along the northern side halfway up, apparently of cement. Considerable amounts of restoration stone and cement seem to have been added later on to the northern side after this photo was taken, as this photo shows (although it is in shadow) that the northern side was extremely worn away, and the Sphinx was there narrow-bodied in a way that it is not today. In fact, the shape is more like that of a dog, receding prominently inward at the side. As for the gap at the commencement of the haunches, where the old vertical shaft to the subterranean chamber existed (as in figure 1.31, taken in 1921), we can see that it has been completely filled. Baraize plugged it with cement in 1926. Certainly, no film star was ever more botoxed or had more face-lifts than the poor Sphinx has had "cement jobs." (*Collection of Robert Temple*)

Figure 2.14. A photo from 1936, showing Selim Hassan's excavations in progress at the Sphinx. (*Collection of Robert Temple*)

Figure 2.15. This snapshot was taken by a British tourist in 1936, during the excavation and restoration of the Sphinx by Selim Hassan. This is the only known photo showing the rear of the Sphinx during this period. It shows the fantastic extent of the erosion of the natural stone of the Sphinx's rump, and reveals that Hassan was collecting fallen blocks of stone and "reconstructing" the rump with them to such a depth that the rump as we see it today protrudes by perhaps as much as 10 feet from the actual underlying stone itself. At the top of the ladder at the rear in this photo is a platform made of replaced stones big enough for at least a dozen people to stand on! Nowhere in his excavation report does Hassan mention that he did anything like this. To the left in the photo are the modern walls constructed by Baraize in 1926 to hold back the sand on the north side. Although he later demolished these, at this stage in his work Hassan was using them to anchor his planking gangways for his workmen to get across to the body of the Sphinx. It is believed that no other photographic evidence of any of this work exists, and this has never been published before. In the distance, it can be seen that the Sphinx Temple has not yet been excavated. (*Collection of Robert Temple*)

Figure 2.16. A snapshot taken by a tourist in 1936, during Selim Hassan's work on the Sphinx. The severely eroded stone of the uncovered rump is visible here from the side. As for the haunch area where the intruded shaft was, we can clearly see that Hassan erected special scaffolding to attend to that precise area. He must have found it necessary to add further filling and patching to Baraize's efforts of ten years before to fill in the broken-off haunch and smooth out the surface of the monument, restoring it to look like a single piece of sculpture again. The scaffolding erected in the front of the Sphinx has a platform used by masons to smear modern cement over the surface of the entire neck of the Sphinx. (*Collection of Robert Temple*)

Below: Figure 2.17. Here is the scaffolding platform used for smearing the modern cement onto the Sphinx's neck in 1936. At left, we see Selim Hassan's southern gangway descending from the Chephren Causeway into the Sphinx Pit on that side. (*Collection of Robert Temple*)

Figure 2.18. An engraving of the Sphinx from the nineteenth century. The prominent crack in the rear, by which one could descend to the chamber beneath, is highlighted here. (*Collection of Robert Temple*)

Within the extensive quotes from Borchardt, Hassan includes the description of the "two vertical shafts in the back of the Sphinx, one of which ends in a tomb chamber, and contained coffin boards."[46]

With this explicit information included in the most recent and definitive excavation report on the Sphinx by its modern excavator, why has no one noticed or commented on it? Hassan certainly does not dismiss this information in the way he dismisses the theory of the Sphinx's association with Amenemhet III. It is there for all to see.

And so this brings us up to a time that is more or less modern; 1953 is not all that long ago. There are still people alive who knew Hassan. Between a third and half of the world's present population must have been alive in 1953. It is not an inaccessible era, lost in the mists of time.

And yet all the "experts" on the Sphinx are in total ignorance of every piece of evidence that I have just presented, knowing nothing of a total of 281 years of discussion of the vertical shaft and subterranean chamber beneath the haunches of the Sphinx. The blindness to this question reminds me of the mass blindness to all evidence of ancient optical technology, which I reported at such length in *The Crystal Sun*.[47] In that book I described my discovery of more than 450 ancient optical artifacts and lenses, and published photos of many of them. Evidence of the use of magnifying aids goes back to 3300 BC in predynastic Egypt! And yet all "experts" in the world were ignorant of this. They thought there were no optical artifacts at all. And this was despite the fact that many ancient lenses are prominently on display in museums around the world. The evidence is all around us, and can readily be seen in Athens, Cairo, London, and elsewhere, by any tourist. But no one could *see* it, despite the fact that it was in front of them. This was because they were convinced it could not exist. Physical evidence, even hundreds of items of it, is useless when people have no mental faculties to allow them to register it. It may register on the optic nerve, it may be perceived by the retina, but the mind is a blank. No impression is made. This case history of what I have named "consensus blindness" is most alarming; it shows that humanity is a strange species indeed, in which massive amounts of evidence may be thrust under the noses of us humans and be totally ignored. We are a stubborn lot. We just refuse to see what we are convinced cannot be seen. It is really the reverse of "The Emperor's New Clothes," the fable in which people see what isn't there. The real problems of humanity lie in the opposite direction, in *not* seeing what *is* there. And we have a classic case of this now, in the refusal to register in their minds what many Egyptologists and others must have read, namely that there was once a vertical shaft in the Sphinx that led to a subterranean chamber beneath the haunches. By some weird unspoken consensus, everyone has agreed *not to know this.*

So where do we stand? We know precisely where the vertical shaft was. We have exact measurements of its location. We know the exact dimensions of the opening. We know the nature of the chamber. We know that it contained an ancient burial. We know that the walls were inscribed with hieroglyphics. Not only could these reveal whose burial was in the chamber, but presumably some pieces of the coffin boards are still in the chamber and could be carbon-dated.

It is possible that the cement that Baraize smeared into the crack in the haunches and stuffed into those portions of the shaft that were accessible has not filled the chamber. There must have been a great deal of sand filling the chamber and much of the shaft, and this would have protected the rock from damage caused by the cement. The chamber could thus be reopened. Probably the whole chamber and much of the shaft itself are intact underneath the restoration of Baraize. The evidence that I have presented is overwhelming. There is no doubt that crucial information about the Sphinx could be recovered if we could reopen the shaft and chamber somehow. But how could we do it without damaging the Sphinx? The Sphinx is a proud symbol of the modern nation of Egypt. It has been laboriously restored in recent years and is one of the main tourist attractions of Egypt. Although the authorities did not hesitate to cover it with scaffolding for years, and equally do not hesitate to shut major sites like the interior of the Great Pyramid for a year or more at a time for restoration, the question arises: Would

Pyramid and Sphinx of Gizeh

Figure 2.19. This postcard, mailed from Port Said to Germany in 1929, shows the Sphinx at a crucial transitional stage. Baraize has obviously finished his clearance in 1926, but has not yet erected his scaffolding or commenced his violent "restoration." The deep crack of the detached rump and the crack near the front of the body are evident. There is also a crack in the middle of the body that can be seen here. Old restoration stones, presumably of New Kingdom (post–Thutmose IV), Ptolemaic, and Roman date, have fallen off the side of the Sphinx and are temporarily piled up close beside it. These were later cemented back into place by Baraize, though he obviously had to guess at their placing, since he was drawing them from a heap. The ravaged core of the Sphinx's side may be seen here in a largely bare state, though along the lower half more ancient repair blocks (presumably of Old Kingdom date) of larger size can be made out, which are still adhering and are of superior workmanship. This shows that older repair blocks from previous epochs underlie many of the historical repair blocks visible on the surface of the Sphinx's body today, many of which in turn are covered by recent ones. This observation agrees with the clear "double-skin" of restoration shown on the Sphinx's rump in figure 5.14 on page 210. When trying to estimate the original width and contours of the Sphinx's sides, we must remember that two or even three later skins exist for most of the surface, along with cement in-fillings and countless "patches," and that all these have been shaped according to the opinions of the restorers, creating contours that met with their approval at various epochs. (*Collection of Robert Temple*)

anyone be prepared to try to enter the shaft and chamber now that the Sphinx is meant to be completely perfect and fully restored? If they aren't prepared to break through Baraize's cement at the upper end of the ascending rump tunnel, which could be done from inside without anybody seeing anything, will they be willing to undertake more drastic investigation on the outside? There are more than archaeological considerations involved. This is really a political and prestige issue. The Sphinx is a political symbol today, representing the glory of the nation.

It is also a nice little earner for the tourist business. And Egypt certainly needs its tourists as it struggles economically.

But on the other hand, the Egyptian authorities have to weigh the advantages of making a discovery of a truly sensational nature. They know enough about international publicity to realize that if they were to open and study and photograph a chamber beneath the Sphinx and decipher and publish the hieroglyphic inscriptions on its walls, and possibly even date a coffin board, they would cause so much excitement that the result could easily be a doubling or even a trebling of the number of foreign tourists suddenly rushing to Giza, and the Egyptian economy could benefit by many tens of millions of extra dollars per year.

So what will they do?

Finally, I must mention again that in more recent times, there has been some scientific survey evidence carried out to try to find underground passages and chambers beneath the Sphinx. The work that has taken place commenced in the 1970s.

Figure 2.20. Here I am standing in front of a paw of the Sphinx, but you would never know it, because the myriad of tiny limestone blocks behind me are all brand-new. This type of "restoration" of the Sphinx was done not for archaeological purposes but to render a national monument fit for viewing by millions of tourists, as customers of the Egyptian economy and as "consumers" of the Sphinx. There is certainly no reason to believe that this restoration of the forelegs and paws of the Sphinx accurately reflects their original appearance, or that the earlier restoration of the forelegs and paws by the Romans (who also used small limestone blocks) was accurate either. In this photo I am wearing my badge as a delegate to the Eighth International Congress of Egyptologists, which took place in Cairo in 2000, at which time I made one of my visits to the Sphinx Pit. (*Photo by Olivia Temple*)

Figure 2.21. I took this view of the Sphinx's head from its feet, shortly after sunrise. It shows several features very clearly that are not readily visible to tourists, who are not allowed this close except with special permission. The lappets, or side flaps, of the headdress have been "reconstituted" since the 1930s. Blocks of concrete have been placed under them, so that at a distance it looks as if they are complete and extend all the way to the shoulders. In the old photos shown in figures 1.5 to 1.7, 1.16, 1.17, and 1.20 to 1.22, it is very clear that until this was done, the lappets were in tatters and the bottoms of them no longer existed at all. Another feature clearly shown here is that the neck has been entirely reconstituted by "reconstruction" in the most barbaric and primitive fashion. It now consists merely of layer upon layer of modern cement smeared roughly, and not even smoothly, to give some kind of approximate impression of a neck, which is not shaped with any care. The nose was broken off by a Muslim fanatic in the tenth century, not shot off by Napoleon's soldiers as the false story goes. You can see that various fissures in the face (which are clearly visible in the old photos in figures 1.16, 1.17, and 1.21) have been filled in with modern cement. The other repairs may be seen very clearly by comparing this photo with figure 1.22. From the evidence, it is clear that the Sphinx today is an absolute mess, a botched job of appallingly bad reconstruction, such that the grand monument has been turned into a kind of Disneyland parody of itself. I hope that one day a restoration of the Sphinx can take place that will lend the dignity and taste to the monument that these ugly disfigurements have gone so far to destroy. However, it will not be easy, because the modern cement and concrete are hard and the native stone is fragile. (*Photo by Robert Temple*)

Figure 2.22. This is a close-up of limestone repair blocks on the Sphinx, which are generally believed to date from the Old Kingdom. (The pale one at top left is a modern replacement block.) I should point out certain details about these blocks. One is that several of the blocks are cut with interlock niches to grip blocks higher up and to one side, as we see with two successive blocks at bottom left in the photo, for instance; they are not cut as simple rectangles but can grip above with their little niches. This technique was often used with large blocks during the Old Kingdom (as can be seen in many places in the adjoining Valley Temple) and indicates a definite finesse in building techniques. Some of the blocks, especially at the bottom of the photo, have negligible mortar and fit together extremely tightly, as one would expect of Old Kingdom blocks. To have achieved this while covering a curved surface at the same time is a considerable feat and shows superior skill, skill that did not exist after the Old Kingdom. On the other hand, the higher courses of stone shown here have substantial mortar, which has clearly been inserted later on. I believe that the blocks in the upper half of the photo have all been retrieved and relaid after having fallen to the ground. This may have taken place at any time from the Middle Kingdom to Roman times. The mortar appears to be so crude that it has probably also been repointed, possibly even by Baraize or Selim Hassan as recently as the 1920s or 1930s. The point of all this is that large portions of the rear of the Sphinx are still covered in these superior blocks of apparent Old Kingdom origin, and they were obviously placed there to cover erosion of the stone body of the Sphinx. But if this is the case, how can the Sphinx have been carved in the Old Kingdom? There is a clear contradiction here: the Sphinx is said to have been carved on the orders of either Cheops or Chephren, of the Fourth Dynasty of the Old Kingdom, and yet repair blocks dating from about that time seem to survive on the Sphinx. How is that? Do you normally repair something that you have just made? The Inventory Stela (see figures 3.5 to 3.8 on pages 134–36) excavated at Giza states that Cheops *repaired* the Sphinx. Although the Inventory Stela is a late stela that does not date from the Old Kingdom, some have suggested that portions of it repeat an older text from an earlier inscription. The popular idea that the Sphinx is thousands of years older than Cheops is absurd and cannot possibly be true (and I show in this book in chapter 6 why the "ancient rain" theory is false), but it is possible that the Sphinx is older than the time of Cheops by as much as several centuries. And that poses even more difficult problems for the origin of Egyptian high civilization, because then we are dealing with a real problem rather than a fantasy problem, and reality is always tougher to handle than fantasy. The idea that the Sphinx is of immense and fantastic antiquity is as remote and unreal as a hedge fund, whereas the fact that the Sphinx was repaired at the same time that it was supposed to have been carved is as real and difficult to handle as your own personal bank account. (*Photo by Robert Temple*)

Figure 2.23. A close-up view of the left lappet of the headdress of the Sphinx. The bottom half of the lappet consists of a complex series of small restoration blocks, with a thin layer of slabs over them, followed by modern concrete up to the level of the original top half of the lappet. The effect from a distance is to make the lappet appear to be complete. (*Photo by Robert Temple*)

Opposite top: Figure 2.24. This photo of the Sphinx's right hind paw shows clearly how artificial it is and reveals the many layers of repair blocks. The pale small blocks are the new ones, made of freshly cut limestone and placed there in recent years to create a coherent tourist attraction that "looks right" from a distance. The protruding element behind the paw is the Sphinx's tail, which, as can be seen, consists now entirely of reconstruction blocks dating from different periods (the pale ones being the recent ones). To the right of the tail, and in the center of the photo above the paw, is the former giant crack in the Sphinx's body that can be seen so clearly in the 1921 photo shown in figure 1.31, before it was filled. In 1926, Baraize filled the crack by pouring in tons of cement and then covered over the cement with small limestone blocks (see at the top of this photo in the central portion). Below those, just above the paw, are a few courses of what appear to be older repair blocks, and to the left of them recent ones that are almost white, which have been stuffed in where some holes had begun to reappear since the 1920s. Those blocks to the left of the tail in this photo, which are large and worn, are thought to date from the Old Kingdom repairs. The small dark blocks at top right in this photo are probably Roman.

Opposite bottom: Figure 2.25. The Sphinx as seen from the roof of the Valley Temple, with the Great Pyramid in the distance. At the Sphinx's feet is the modern wooden ramp that has been constructed to lead select visitors into the Sphinx Pit (it is closed to normal tourists). The long legs and the paws are entirely a work of restoration, small modern limestone blocks having supplemented the Roman ones. Even two thousand years ago, the legs and paws were so worn away that they had to be entirely rebuilt. The outer casing of the rear paw has been similarly reconstructed by modern blocks. The main purpose of the Sphinx today is to act as a national monument and to service the tourist industry. I have never seen a photo of the Sphinx from this viewpoint published before, since no one is normally allowed onto the roof of the Valley Temple. (*Photo by Robert Temple*)

Figure 2.26. A brooding Sphinx. (*Photo by Robert Temple*)

Figure 2.27. A photo of the Sphinx taken from inside the Sphinx Temple, which is closed to tourists. The remains of the uraeus (insignia of a royal serpent rearing its head) on the forehead of the Sphinx is seen particularly clearly from here, whereas it is usually hard to see it properly. The west wall of the Sphinx Temple, which faced the feet of the Sphinx, formed an eastern barrier for the water in the Sphinx moat during the Old Kingdom period. By no later than 2000 BC, the Sphinx Temple was entirely buried in sand and forgotten and was only discovered unexpectedly in the 1930s by Selim Hassan. (*Photo by Robert Temple*)

Figure 2.28. This rear right foot of the Sphinx is heavily restored by small, modern limestone blocks to make the monument presentable for tourists. (*Photo by Robert Temple*)

Figure 2.29. The filled-in waist on the right (southern) side of the Sphinx. The top half of the Sphinx's body seen in this photo is the original carved stone figure, deeply eroded in a series of horizontal stripes, whereas the bottom half is composed entirely of reconstruction blocks from different periods. These have had the effect of filling in the waist of the Sphinx, which was once narrow, thus disguising the doglike appearance and making the body appear to be more massive and leonine. At the left of the photo, the angle of the light on the tail enables us to see clearly that this portion of the tail at least is made entirely of blocks, and does not contain any carved stone core at all. The tail may therefore not be an original feature of the Sphinx but could have been added at a later period as part of a "lionizing" process. In any case, if there were an original tail, what we have now is largely or wholly a replacement, or "tail transplant." (*Photo by Robert Temple*)

Figure 2.30. At dusk, when the glare of the sun has subsided, a clearer view is possible of the contrasting materials that now make up the outer surface of the "restored" Sphinx. Here we see that the elbow of the Sphinx is entirely covered in small modern limestone restoration blocks. The chest is the original weathered bedrock. The bottom half of the headdress down to the neck is of modern blocks and concrete, smeared with modern cement. (*Photo by Robert Temple*)

Results of these first studies were published in 1977 in a booklet entitled *Applications of Modern Sensing Techniques to Egyptology.*[48] In this booklet, the authors write that preliminary work in 1974 showed that the use of radar was ineffective in searching for underground chambers and tunnels: "The fact that radar cannot answer these questions was discouraging to us after our 1974 work; however, the present results using acoustic methods and resistivity [measurement of resistance to the flow of electricity] methods reopen many possibilities for further, efficient surveying of Giza."[49]

They then published a very brief summary of attempts to search for underground chambers and tunnels in the Sphinx precinct. They write that they found "five areas of interest." They believed they detected cavities in front of the forepaws of the Sphinx and also, as quoted in the preceding chapter:

Behind the rear paws (*northwest end*) we ran two traverses . . . . Both traverses indicate an anomaly that could possibly be due to a tunnel aligned northwest to southeast.

Another anomaly exists in the middle of the south side near a square cupola added apparently in Roman times. This anomaly was verified by two overlapping traverses. . . . When the electrodes were moved 2 m away from the previous traverse, the anomaly decreased in value. This is typical of the behavior expected from a vertical shaft. . . . The resistivity anomalies we found around the Sphinx are not defined sufficiently to allow us any absolutely certain conclusions, and we feel that a more detailed survey should be conducted.[50]

These results were certainly suggestive, and at least two of the findings could well have been shafts or tunnels linked or connected to the vertical shaft in the haunches and the chamber beneath it, which of course were unknown to these researchers, an Egyptian physicist named Ali Helmi Moussa and an American physicist named Lambert Dolphin from the Radio Physics Laboratory of the Stanford Research Institute in California.

What is of particular interest is their finding that there appeared to be "an anomaly" that was "behind the rear paws" and that "could possibly be due to a tunnel aligned northwest to southeast." This anomaly falls along a crack in the bedrock that does indeed run northwest to southeast, and that is clearly portrayed in the plan drawn by my friend Professor Lal Gauri, which is reproduced here as figure 1.30 and shows the Sphinx from above looking down. Of this, Lal says: "Dissolution of the limestone by water along the joints has produced cavities. . . . The shaft passing through the middle of the Sphinx as seen from above is one such large cavity. . . . Since these cavities strictly follow the joint patterns [of the limestone bedrock] and are, in most cases, not connected to the surface, it seems that they have been formed by underground water."[51]

The limestone bedrock of the entire Giza Plateau is unquestionably riddled with cavities. However, it should be noted from Lal Gauri's drawing that this particular cavity beneath the Sphinx runs horizontally below the surface straight through the former vertical shaft, Baraize's cement plugging of which may also be seen clearly on Lal's plan as a distinct blob with a dot in the middle. It is as if the bedrock had been cracked at this weak point by some enormous force applied to it, and it may well be that the crack occurred along the joint when the vertical shaft was intruded downward into the bedrock beneath the Sphinx for the construction of the burial chamber, which lay precisely in the path of this extended linear "cavity." Subsequently, the action of water may well have scoured out the crack to form a long hollow space, for once a crack opens in limestone, water is bound to wear it away even further over time. And one of the descriptions of the tomb chamber did mention, as we have seen earlier, that it was an enlarged natural cavity.

A second depiction of the linear crack/cavity is shown in another plan, published by Mark Lehner in the same volume of conference proceedings as the one by Lal Gauri.[52] This drawing is reproduced here in appendix 5 as figure 10 and confirms the drawing of Gauri, although it does not show any cracking on the northwest side of the Sphinx at all, and Lehner seems to have been unaware of it. What Lehner does show is the cracking that runs in a direction southeast from the Sphinx's right rear paw, which Lehner describes as a "Major Fissure."

Thus, we have clear evidence from the plans published by two of the leading experts on the Sphinx that there is a major crack in the bedrock commencing at the point of the former vertical shaft in the haunches of the Sphinx, and this is the same feature reported by Moussa and Lambert in 1977. It is possible that this feature is not merely a crack, fissure, or cavity enlarged by water, but is an actual tunnel leading from the burial chamber. Why not? If they put a chamber down there that was as large as the accounts inform us, then why not a tunnel as well? That our informants do not mention such a tunnel might merely indicate that the tunnel entrance from inside the chamber was concealed, and they did not notice it. Certainly, at the very least, further soundings need to be taken here. If they suggest that the "cavity" is a tunnel, then breaking down into it would lead to the burial chamber without the need for digging out Baraize's cement and going down from the top of the Sphinx's back.

Another thing we need to take seriously is the "cupola" attached to the south side of the Sphinx (see figures 2.31 to 2.33). People just accept this; no one questions it. Why? Is it not the oddest thing imaginable? Ancient sculptures do not normally have cupolas on them, like some kind of huge boil. What on Earth *is* this weird cupola? Why does no one ever challenge it and point out that it is an unacceptable anomaly? Why has no one taken the trouble to find out what is either behind or under it? Could it have been erected with an intention to conceal something or to act as an entrance to something?

Alternatively, it may have been meant to support the mysterious "statue of Osiris in 28 pieces" that was mentioned earlier by Mariette and has now disappeared. We must presume that whoever the people were who built the cupola were not just harmless cupola-lovers who simply went around building stone cupolas for fun and without a reason. So what was the reason? Why has no one ever even thought of investigating it? There is also a mini-cupola, which everyone also just blandly accepts (see figure 2.34). But *what was it?* In fact, there are altogether *four* cupolas!

In 1978, further studies were carried out at the Sphinx to follow up the intriguing results published in 1977. This work was apparently done by Lambert Dolphin, Patti Burns, and John Tanzi of the Stanford Research Institute. However, they never published their results, and in 1999 Lambert Dolphin is reported to have stated, "None of us has been able to locate our logs and printouts," even though "the 1978 resistivity work was much more thorough [than that published

Figure 2.31. This is the larger stone "cupola" or "booth" beside the right elbow of the Sphinx, on the southern side. What is it? No one knows. It seems to date from Roman times and may have been a base for a statue (in which case the top is missing), or a side altar base, or to conceal an entrance to the interior of the Sphinx. There are four of these bizarre protrusions from the side of the Sphinx, none of which has been explained. (*Photo by Robert Temple*)

Figure 2.32. Detail of the larger "south booth" or "south cupola" beside the Sphinx. (*Photo by Robert Temple*)

Figure 2.33. The top section of the large "south booth" beside the Sphinx. This is a very strange thing to be sticking out of the Sphinx, but no one ever mentions it. (*Photo by Robert Temple*)

Figure 2.34. One of the four strange stone boxes protruding from the sides of the Sphinx at the base, presumed to have been constructed during the New Kingdom, perhaps to act as statue bases. This one is the smaller of the two that are on the south side of the Sphinx. The square stones on top at right are modern reconstruction stones, as are the small limestone pieces to the left of the box on the Sphinx's body. No one has any idea as to whether the four boxes sticking out of the sides of the Sphinx at the base might have been constructed to obscure an entrance into the body or to block an entrance to a shaft. Nor has any proper study of the four boxes ever been done, to my knowledge. None of the excavators ever paid much attention to them. It seems extraordinary to me that people just seem to accept the fact that there are four stone boxes protruding from the Sphinx. You would think that archaeologists would be rushing to examine them, study them meticulously, perhaps dismantle at least one and put it back together again (which would not be difficult), just in case there is something hidden inside. But no, nobody does anything. They just sit there and everybody ignores them. No one has even inserted any probes to see if they are hollow, as far as I know. Whoever said that human beings are curious? (*Photo by Robert Temple*)

in 1977]." These comments are published in the book *Secret Chamber* by Robert Bauval and Simon Cox.[53] Bauval and Cox reveal that Lambert Dolphin's work was connected with an organization called the Association for Research and Enlightenment (ARE) in Virginia, which is devoted to researching the prophecies of the psychic Edgar Cayce. Dolphin is also quoted as writing: "Hugh Lynn Cayce [son of Edgar Cayce] was a very gracious sponsor and spent considerable time with us during the time the field work was being done. He mentioned that the Cayce Foundation had less confidence in Edgar Cayce's readings [psychic readings] in archaeology as compared to his medical readings and healing work. Yet ARE had ongoing interest in and around the Sphinx. Ongoing work has in fact continued by Dr Joseph Jahoda."[54]

Apparently, the famous American psychic Edgar Cayce had had a vision while in a trance in 1923 that there were tunnels and chambers under the Sphinx. And that is why his son, the Cayce Foundation, and ARE were endeavoring to find them. Cayce said that this chamber would be what has come to be called "a Hall of Records," containing precious ancient documents about a lost civilization. The Cayce people were strongly supported by their friend of many years, the American Egyptologist Mark Lehner, whose first book, *Egyptian Heritage: Based on the Edgar Cayce Readings,* was a defense of Cayce's theories and psychic readings about the Sphinx and theories of Atlantis that was actually published by ARE.[55] In later work, the Cayce people drilled a hole under the right forepaw of the Sphinx and appear to have found some evidence of a cavity in the rock at that point. But the work was stopped for reasons that are disputed. A strange account of these murky doings has been published in *Secret Chamber,*[56] which is so confused that no matter how many times I read it, I cannot fully comprehend it, so convoluted is the whole issue.

Knowing none of the people concerned, I cannot understand why an organization in America would send a team to study something in Egypt (the expedition of 1978) and then lose the results. Does this strike anyone as odd? We are simply told (assuming the report of Bauval and Cox to be accurate): "None of us has been able to locate our logs and printouts." How many of "us" are there? How many logs, how many printouts, where were they kept? And if there were several of them, how could they *all* vanish when in the apparent custody of "all of us"? I don't get it.

A seismographer named Thomas Dobecki in 1990–1 used some seismic equipment to look for cavities underneath the Sphinx area. He says he confirmed a rectangular cavity measuring 29.5 feet by 39.4 feet under the right paw of the Sphinx.[57] It would be interesting to investigate that further, especially as it could possibly be a further chamber reached from the small chamber between the Sphinx's paws, seen in figure 1.29. As I said earlier, it appears from comments made by Count de Forbin that Henry Salt blocked up a passage leading from the small chamber, and if so, it might well have led to just such a large chamber as the one claimed by Thomas Dobecki. I believe that this was the same location "sensed" by Edgar Cayce. There is no a priori reason whatever why such a chamber should be assumed not to exist, even if it is only one of the natural caverns in the limestone with which the plateau is riddled.

One thing is for sure: none of the researchers of recent decades is aware of any of the material that I have presented in this chapter, so they have all been working in the dark.

There is a chamber, there is a shaft, both of which were discussed for 281 years in a whole series of publications, *but they don't know it!*

3

AN AMAZING SURVIVAL

It seems hardly credible that a story could be accurately passed from mouth to mouth for three thousand years, or seventy-five human generations. Anyone who has played the game of Chinese Whispers knows that messages get distorted incredibly quickly, and often very drastically. Chinese Whispers, for those too addicted to television and computer screens to know what it is like for a group of people to amuse themselves by playing what used to be called a "parlor game" in the days when there was still something called "social life," consists of several people sitting on chairs arranged in a circle, facing one another; the person who starts whispers a message in the ear of the person next to him or her, and this message is repeated around the entire circle of people. Finally, the last person in the circle, who is sitting next to the person who started it all, speaks out loud the message as he or she received it. The results are usually astonishing and bizarre. Suddenly all one's friends, who one assumed were highly intelligent and capable people, strike one as thickheaded or, possibly, perverse. "That wasn't what I said!" one is tempted to shout. The distortions of the message are usually so incredible that everyone has a good laugh at the result, at the same time realizing the extreme fragility of messages, which can be changed beyond recognition after just a few repetitions.

This is called "noise in the system." All messages get distorted. Nothing can be transmitted reliably if it is repeated too often; sometimes it has to be repeated only once to go awry. All of us have had the experience of a friend attributing statements to us that we have never made. Celebrities are frequently misquoted in the press, often on purpose, but sometimes just through garbling. "Noise" interrupting accurate communication even takes place within our own heads. It is called false memory syndrome. Sometimes we get things wrong but don't realize it ourselves, and really *believe* a false message. Or for emotional reasons we may be in denial and unwilling to face a truth, so we distort the message to ourselves. We say: "I never did that," even though we know we did, but by insisting to ourselves that we didn't, we come to believe it. Or we distort what we have said to cast ourselves in a more favorable light.

So when we come across incontrovertible evidence that a tale has been passed down through seventy-five generations and has retained essential accuracy, it is an event in the history of folklore that really deserves to be toasted in champagne. And that is what has happened with the Sphinx.

It was the fifteenth-century Dutch traveler Joos van Ghistele who recorded this fact, although he had no idea of the true significance of what he was recording, because it was only in the nineteenth century that the evidence came to light to prove that his information was accurate.

Here is what van Ghistele set down of the tale told to him about the Sphinx by the local inhabitants of Giza. He was given this information in AD 1482, ten years before Columbus discovered America:

> One day in those [ancient Egyptian] times a man went there to make some sacrifices; he asked of the Idol [the Sphinx] what was going to happen to him, and the head [of the Sphinx] replied to him that he would become King and master of Egypt if he wanted to follow its counsels. Thereupon the man replied that he would follow them and it happened that this man became King of Egypt as he had been told he would by the head. A little while after his coronation he returned to the place where the head was. [The full passage and reference are to be found in part 2.]

Let us keep firmly fixed in our minds that van Ghistele was told this by the locals in AD 1482. No later visitor was told this, and it is likely that van Ghistele arrived at Giza just as this tradition was at last dying out. Perhaps he overlapped with the last generation to remember the tale. But if so, it was a lucky fact that he did. By a hair's breadth the information was preserved just as the candle flickered and died.

What is the significance of this folktale? Of course, it is very clever of the locals to know that people went to offer sacrifices to the Sphinx, since we know from the excavations that have taken place between 1817 and 1970 of the vast amount of evidence that has been uncovered showing that the Sphinx was an object of veneration, to which kings as well as commoners made offerings, from New Kingdom times (circa 1800 BC) through Roman times. But a general tradition like that is not so surprising a thing for the locals to remember, and the end of Roman worship was only about a thousand years prior to van Ghistele's visit, so it was like people at Hastings saying today that William the Conqueror landed there in AD 1066. People at Hastings talking about William the Conqueror is one thing, but it would be quite another if we had the local inhabitants of Wiltshire giving us accurate accounts of what went on at Stonehenge when the trilithons were erected there, and what King So-and-so said and did about it, for that would be more than three thousand years ago, surely too long a time for any folklore to last! Or is it?

This is what is so extraordinary. The people of Giza remembered and accurately recounted a true story about a king named Thutmosis (also known as Thothmes) IV, who lived *three thousand years earlier than Joos van Ghistele's visit.*

"Well," you might say, "someone told them." Or perhaps "they learned it from books." But alas for the skeptical turn of mind, there is no way out. It cannot be avoided that the tale survived accurately for three thousand years by word of mouth, because the stela recording the story was not excavated until 1817 and could not be read until after Champollion deciphered hieroglyphics in 1821.

So it was 339 years after Joos van Ghistele was told the story about the Sphinx before the excavated evidence could even have been read by anyone, even if Champollion had made it the first text for translation, which of course he did not. There were no other records of the story in existence.

The discovery of the story in hieroglyphic form took place in 1817, when Captain Giambattista Caviglia thoroughly excavated the front of the Sphinx and found a large and impressive inscribed stone stela standing in front of the Sphinx's chest, placed there by the pharaoh of the New Kingdom period named Thutmosis (or Thothmes) IV (reigned 1425–1417 BC). Caviglia's excavation of this stela has already been discussed in the previous chapter. The news of Caviglia's discovery was first reported to the world in a trimonthly intellectual news magazine of the time called the *Quarterly Review,* published in London. In volume 19 for the year 1818, an account of the Sphinx excavations appeared in the context of a review of a new book of papers from the collection of Robert Walpole dealing with certain other discoveries in Egypt. The information was forwarded to the *Quarterly Review* from Cairo by Henry Salt, the British consul general in Egypt, whose action in sealing and suppressing some entrances and passages at the Sphinx has already been alluded to.

Captain Caviglia was a very self-effacing character who liked to say modestly that he was merely a sea captain, but he worked harder and more passionately to excavate and discover things in Egypt at that time than any scholar. (Egyptologists as such did not yet exist, so there were no professionals in existence to be jealous of him and try to stop him.) Caviglia seems to have spoken English passably well, as he had sailed under the British flag in a merchant capacity for many years. But he did not write English. He could write letters in French, some of which survive (and one about the Sphinx I have copied from the manuscript and reproduced in full, in translation, in part 2), but his reports were all written in Italian and handed to Henry Salt. Caviglia quaintly called Henry Salt "Enrico," which is the Italian form of Henry. I have looked through these reports, which are preserved in the Manuscripts Collections of the British Library among the Salt Papers. They are written in a very courtly and polite manner characteristic even then of a very old-fashioned type of man. Caviglia was legally entitled under the terms of his agreement with the Egyptian authorities to keep everything that he found in the course of his extensive excavations of the Sphinx, but he very generously retained nothing. He donated everything to the British Museum as a token of thanks to the British people under whose flag he had sailed for so long. This is why the British Museum today has a part of the Sphinx's beard, among countless other things. Unfortunately, most or all of these items have languished in the basement since they reached London 180 years ago. The fragment of the Sphinx's beard has occasionally been a subject of dispute, with people pointing out that it should be returned to the Sphinx, especially as another fragment is in Cairo. But people who say this do not know the facts. The beard was affixed to the Sphinx by the very pharaoh of the New Kingdom whose story we will shortly narrate. It was never part of the original Sphinx, and to "return it to the Sphinx" would be ridiculous. It would make sense to join the two beard fragments, of course, which is another matter. But even when you had done that, there wouldn't be much to see. If you've seen one Egyptian beard, you've seen them all. The Cairo fragments of the Sphinx's beard are pictured in figures 3.1 and 3.2; the latter shows that the fragments that remained in Cairo were smashed, and only portions are left.

Since Caviglia could not write in English, he left the English publication of his exploits to Salt, which is why everything is in the third person, and there is no first-person narrative available in English about what Caviglia actually did. I wish Caviglia's original accounts could be found and then translated from Italian into English and published, as they should form a part of the official printed record of the history of Egyptology. My friend Stefano Greco and I have done this for a previously unknown third-person account of Caviglia's excavations privately printed in Italy at the time by Caviglia's friend Annibale Brandi, of which only one copy appears to survive, and Stefano found it. The section of this booklet dealing with the Sphinx, translated into English, is in appendix 4.

In the *Quarterly Review* account, even Henry Salt is referred to in the third person—"Mr. Salt says"—indicating that someone else took the documents forwarded by Salt and edited them, incorporating comments from Salt's letters, who evidently

FRAGMENTS OF THE BEARD OF THE SPHINX.

Figure 3.1. These are fragments of the Sphinx's beard that were excavated by Giambattista Caviglia in 1817 and drawn by Henry Salt at the time. It can readily be seen that this beard was a New Kingdom addition to the Sphinx and that it bore hieroglyphics and pictures, which was completely different from the style of the Old Kingdom period. The plaited pattern is meant to represent the plaited hair of the beard. The top portions show a New Kingdom pharaoh, doubtless meant to represent Thutmosis IV, kneeling and making an offering. The hieroglyph *ankh* is seen at top left, although it is broken off at the bottom. This portion of the fragmentary inscription, continued in the second fragment, ends in the letter *f*. The third fragment shows what is presumably the pharaoh facing the other way with an offering. To his right are two scepters. The one on the right (with a break in the middle) is known as the *uas* scepter, as can be seen by its forked base, which was used in shadow-measuring. This drawing is found in *Operations Carried On at the Pyramids of Gizeh in 1837* by Colonel Howard Vyse and John S. Perring, London, 1842, third appendix volume. (*Collection of Robert Temple*)

a   Bruchstücke vom Götterbart der Sphinx

Figure 3.2. This is a photo of portions stuck together of what was once the top fragment of the Sphinx's beard; the condition of the fragment before it was further broken by archaeologists is shown in figure 3.1 above. To the right, the kneeling pharaoh making an offering is now lacking his head, which he still possessed in 1817. Many excavated objects suffer further damage after they are found, and this is an example. The German caption says: "Fragments of the divine beard of the Sphinx." This is reproduced from plate 17 of Herbert Ricke's *Der Harmachistempel des Chefren in Giseh* (*The Harmachis Temple of Chephren at Giza*), Wiesbaden, 1970. These fragments are in the Egyptian Museum in Cairo.

stayed in Cairo while this was all being prepared for publication in London.[1]

Figures 3.3 and 3.4 show the engraving published in this report in the *Quarterly Review*,[2] done from a drawing by Henry Salt (or someone commissioned by him), and sent by him to London for reproduction. It shows the layout of the altar and place of worship that existed between the paws of the Sphinx in Roman times, as discovered by Caviglia. In the foreground is a "four-horned" altar. But the Romans and the Ptolemies before them had retained as the central feature, at the very back, the great stela of Thutmosis IV with its inscription and its picture of two sphinxes perched on pedestals, to whom the pharaoh is making offerings. The stela is 14 feet high and is carved in granite. The photo I took of this stela, which is still *in situ* at the Sphinx, is in figure 3.8; figure 3.5 is an older black-and-white full photograph. Salt's drawing of it is reproduced in figure 3.7. These should all be compared.

In the year following the *Quarterly Review* account, an account of Caviglia's work in Egypt was published in Scotland in *The Edinburgh Philosophical Journal*, which contained no illustrations but did have these interesting remarks about the Sphinx:

> The French savants appear to have done nothing more than uncover the back of this stupendous piece of sculpture; and, if they attempted any other excavations, cannot possibly have proceeded far in their work, as the top of the wall, which has now been discovered, is not above [i.e., not more than] three feet below the level of the sand. Mr. Caviglia . . . proceeded, therefore, to carry on his excavations in the front; and, after labouring for the space of nearly four months, with the assistance of from 60 to 100 persons every day, he succeeded in laying open the whole figure to its base.[3]

Here is the description given in the *Quarterly Review* of the scene as it was when excavated:

> On the stone platform in front, and centrally between the outstretched paws of the Sphinx, was found a large block of granite, fourteen foot high, seven broad, and two thick. The face of this stone, which fronted [faced] the east, was highly embellished with sculpture in bas-relief, the subject representing two Sphinxes seated on pedestals, and priests [actually the pharaoh, not priests] holding out offerings, beneath which was a long inscription in hieroglyphics, most beautifully executed; and the whole design was covered at top, and protected, as it were, with the sacred globe, the serpent, and the wings [i.e., a winged solar globe].[4]

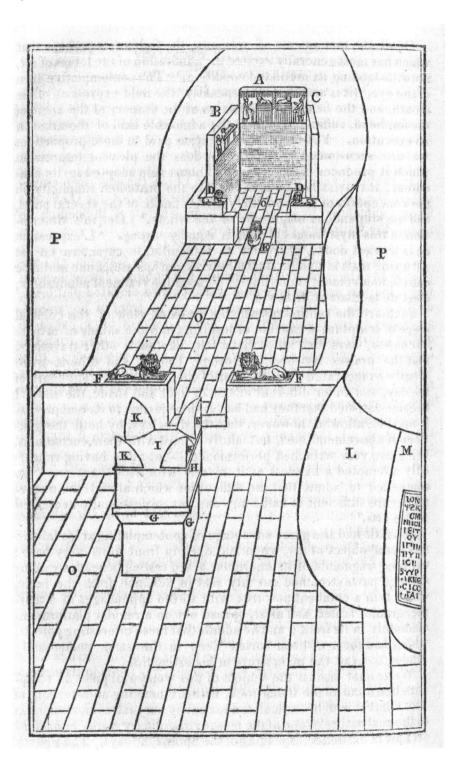

Opposite: Figure 3.3. This engraving was published in the *Quarterly Review*, London, vol. 19, no. 38, April–July 1818, p. 416, based on a drawing sent from Egypt by Henry Salt. It shows the area between the forelegs of the Sphinx, as excavated by Caviglia the previous year. All subsequent illustrations of this scene are copies from this one and not always as accurate. This is what the area between the paws of the Sphinx looked like at the time of the Greeks and Romans, when offerings were burned on the altar to the "god," as the Sphinx was conceived at that time. In the foreground of the engraving is the altar with the four "horns." To either side, designated by the letter "P," are the forelegs of the Sphinx. The Dream Stela, marked "A," is at the back, and still stands *in situ*. (The stelae to either side, marked "B" and "C," have been moved to museums.) The large inscription in Greek at far right, on a toe of the Sphinx, is by Arrian; it is described at length in chapter 6, where the text and translation are also given and the importance of this inscription for our ideas of the true nature of the Sphinx are discussed. This entire area was originally of New Kingdom construction, with the focus on the Dream Stela. The area was altered by the Greeks and Romans, and the altar is probably Greek. The purpose of the area was the worship of the Sphinx as the new deity Harmachis. But this had nothing to do with the original nature and purpose of the Sphinx, which had been long forgotten by the time of the New Kingdom. See figure 3.4 (below) for an explanation of each lettered detail in the drawing. One thing to notice about the drawing is that the Dream Stela's text is shown here as intact. As discussed in the main text, this text was indeed intact when found, but the bottom half was destroyed by the local people. Hieroglyphics had not yet been deciphered, so there was no way anyone could read the text before it was half-destroyed. (*Collection of Robert Temple*)

The annexed sketch will convey to the reader the disposition of the ground, and the objects by which it was occupied, in front of the Sphinx and between its paws, in which

A. Is the granite tablet, 14 feet high, 7 feet wide, and 2 feet thick.
B. The side tablet, still standing.
C. The tablet fallen, which has been sent to the British Museum.
D. Two small Sphinxes, supposed to have stood in these places, fragments of them having been found near.
E. Statue of a lion, of the best Egyptian sculpture.
F. Two lions of ruder sculpture supposed to stand here, being found near the spot.
G. The granite basement of an altar.
H. The upper part of the altar.
I. Top of the altar, bearing the marks of burnt sacrifices.
K. The horns of the altar, one of which was found in its place.
L. The first digit of the Sphinx's paw.
M. The second.
O. The pavement.
PP. Parts of the two fore legs of the Sphinx.

Figure 3.4. Key to figure 3.3.

THE GRANITE STELA OF THOTHMES IV

Figure 3.5. A full view of the front of the Dream Stela of Pharaoh Thutmosis (Thothmes) IV. This is plate XL, following page 140, in Selim Hassan's book *The Great Sphinx and Its Secrets,* Cairo, 1953. A drawing of the full stela is reproduced in figure 3.7, which shows more of the text surviving than is visible here; before this photo was taken, some of it fell off and was lost. Originally, when excavated in 1817, the text was complete, but the local people tore half of it away within months.

Figure 3.6. This stereoview taken between 1926 and 1936 shows the Dream Stela beneath the chin of the Sphinx and the altar area with a man standing just behind it. The two stelae that were found to either side of the Dream Stela when Caviglia made his excavations have been removed to museums. (*Collection of Robert Temple*)

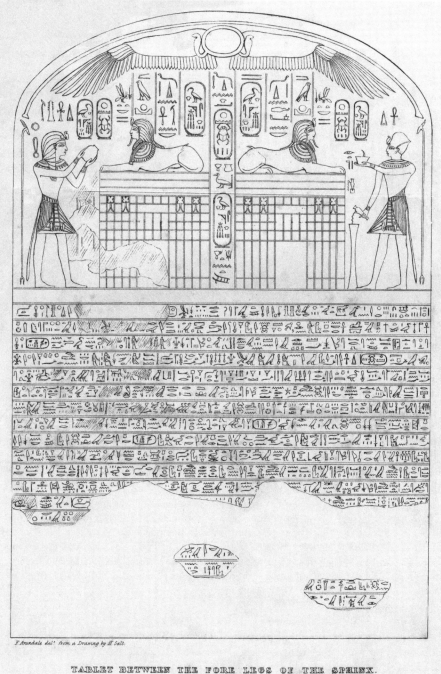

F. Arundale delt. from a Drawing by H. Salt.

TABLET BETWEEN THE FORE LEGS OF THE SPHINX.

Figure 3.7. This is Henry Salt's drawing from late 1817 of what remained of the text of the Dream Stela of the New Kingdom pharaoh Thutmosis (Thothmes) IV, which was found upright beneath the chest of the Sphinx and between its paws when Caviglia carried out his excavations. This drawing is found in *Operations Carried On at the Pyramids of Gizeh in 1837* by Colonel Howard Vyse and John S. Perring, London, 1842, third appendix volume, plate opposite page 110. (*Collection of Robert Temple*)

Figure 3.8. The Dream Stela of the New Kingdom pharaoh Thutmosis IV (reigned 1411–1397 BC), which he erected between the front paws of the Sphinx to celebrate the dream he had about it and to boast of his clearing and restoration of the monument, which had been buried up to its neck in sand until that time. The pharaoh himself is shown twice, once on the left and once on the right, making offerings to a small sphinx on a pedestal, which is a way of representing the Great Sphinx at the same scale with the king for purposes of the stela. (*Photo by Robert Temple*)

The report did not mention that the great stela had been placed there by Pharaoh Thutmosis IV, nor was the story that the stela told recounted, because, as already noted, at that time no one could read a word of it! Hieroglyphics had not yet been deciphered. It would be another four years before Champollion made his very first translations of hieroglyphics, and we do not know exactly when this stela was finally deciphered and actually read, but it would certainly have been some years later.

Here is the key part of the text of the stela, as we can now read it:

Year I, third month of the first season, day 19, under the Majesty of Horus . . . the Son of Ra, Thothmes [Thutmosis] IV, Shining in Diadems. . . . When His Majesty was a stripling, like Horus, the Youth in Khemnis, his beauty was like the Protector of His Father [a title of Horus], he seemed like the God himself. The army rejoiced because of love for him [this is very revealing, since the New Kingdom pharaohs tended to be very militaristic]. . . . Behold, he did a thing which gave him pleasure upon the highlands of the Memphite Nome [a Nome is an administrative district, the district being that of Memphis, and its highlands being the Giza Plateau], upon its southern and northern road shooting at a target with copper bolts [arrows], hunting lions and the small game of the desert, coursing in his chariot, his horses being swifter than the wind, together with two of his followers, while not a soul knew it.

Now, when his hour came for giving rest to his followers, it was always at the Setepet (Sanctuary of Hor-em-akhet [Horus-in-the-Horizon]) [the temple built beside the Sphinx by the slightly earlier pharaoh Amenhotep II, the actual Sphinx Temple itself being then unknown and completely buried in sand], beside Seker [the god Sokar] in Rostaw [this refers to what we today call the Valley Temple of Giza] . . . in the desert . . . the Splendid Place of the Beginning of Time. . . . Now, the very great statue of Kheperi [the rising sun, the name that Thothmes here gives to the Sphinx, which faces due east] rests in this place the great in power, the splendid in strength, upon which the shadow of Ra [the sun] tarries. The quarters of Memphis, and all the cities which are by him come to him, raising their hands for him in praise to his face, bearing oblations for his Ka [his animating principle, one of the Egyptian categories of "spirit"].

One of those days it came to pass that the King's [younger] son Thothmes [who was not heir to the throne] came, coursing [hunting on horseback] at the time of mid-day, and he rested in the shadow of this Great God. Sleep seized him at the hour when the sun was at its zenith [noon], and he found the Majesty of this Revered God speaking with his own mouth, as a father speaks with his son, saying: "Behold thou me, my son, Thothmes. I am thy father, Hor-em-akhet-Kheperi-Ra-Atum [Horus-in-the-Horizon—Rising Sun—Sun God—Creator God]; I will give to thee my Kingdom upon earth at the head of the living [i.e., make you the pharaoh]. Thou shalt wear the White Crown and the Red Crown [the two crowns indicating the pharaoh] upon the Throne of Geb [the god of the Earth; this was the customary phrase to describe the pharaoh's throne], the Hereditary Prince. The land shall be thine, in its length and in its breadth, that which the eye of the All-Lord shines upon. The food of the Two Lands [Upper and Lower Egypt] shall be thine, the great tribute of all countries, the duration of a long period of years. My face is directed to you, my heart is to you; Thou shalt be to me the protector of my affairs, because I am ailing in all my limbs. The sands of the Sanctuary, upon which I am, have reached me; turn to me in order to do what I desire. I know that thou art my son, my protector; behold; I am with thee, I am thy leader."

When he had finished this speech, the King's Son awoke, hearing this . . . [some lost text] . . . he understood the words of the God, he put them in his heart.[5]

This stela is now called by archaeologists the Dream Stela because it bears the inscription recording the pharaoh's dream.

Only after the Dream Stela had been excavated and deciphered did we know the story about the younger son of the king falling asleep at noon in the shade of the Sphinx with his two riding companions and having the dream that if he cleared the Sphinx of sand and paid it honor, it would make him king of Egypt. This story was otherwise unknown. And yet in AD 1482 it was still remembered from ancient times by the local inhabitants of Giza and told to a Dutchman!

As far as I know, this is the only conclusively proven example of an accurate continuity of oral tradition over such a fantastic amount of time. It belongs in the *Guinness Book of Records*.

Since we have had this conclusive and unexpected proof of the validity of some Giza folklore over an otherwise quite unbelievable period of time, we must take the Giza folklore as a whole much more seriously than we would otherwise be inclined to do. We must therefore examine some other claims about the Sphinx that the locals have recounted for centuries, to the amusement of visitors, who have mostly thought it was all fairy tales told to the tourists.

In part 2 of this book I have gathered a massive number of early travelers' accounts of the Sphinx, and anyone who reads through them will see several constantly recurring themes. I intend to examine several of these. But let us start with one that seems to be the most ridiculous of all: the absolute insistence by the locals that there is a direct connection between the Sphinx and the Pyramid of Chephren. Usually this takes the form of insisting that there is an underground tunnel leading from one to the other. Sometimes this tradition varies, and the underground tunnel is said to come out in the well shaft of the Great Pyramid, but that seems to be a variant tale concocted by speculation and the desire to impress European visitors when they began to go down the well shaft. After all, no opening to the Pyramid of Chephren was known until Belzoni found it early in the nineteenth century. So it was difficult when Europeans kept crawling in on their hands and knees over the mounds of sand and bat dung to explore the

Figure 3.9. A late-nineteenth-century photo of the Giza Plateau looking northwest, when the famous centuries-old sycamore tree was still standing, and some palms as well. In the background is the Great Pyramid, and to the right of the sycamore the head of the Sphinx protrudes from the sand in the distance. At this time, there were no tourists, and things were much quieter. This is very much what the Giza Plateau must have been like during the New Kingdom, when the future king Thutmosis IV (who reigned 1425–1417 BC) went hunting on the plateau and fell asleep in the shade of the Sphinx's head and had his famous dream, which he inscribed upon the Dream Stela that still stands between the paws of the Sphinx. The serene timelessness of the Giza Plateau only really ceased after the Second World War, when the international tourist plague commenced. (*Collection of Robert Temple*)

interior of the Great Pyramid and forcing terrified Arabs to hold ropes while they descended the well shaft, from which hordes of huge bats emerged and where candles and lamps went out, to continue to insist that the connection between the Sphinx and the Pyramid of Chephren was so important. It was far easier to speculate that the Great Pyramid's well shaft was the point of connection. And yet there are sufficient occasions when the locals insisted on the connection with the Pyramid of Chephren, into which curious Europeans could not enter, to make it clear that this was the original tradition.

So when I say that I have recently confirmed this folklore tale, the reader may well think that I am claiming to have crawled along a tunnel for the whole distance. But nothing of the kind! In the finest ancient Egyptian tradition, the connection that existed was of a subtle and esoteric nature that until now no one has ever suspected. The locals had obviously been told far in the distant past that such a connection existed, but not understanding its true nature, they assumed that underground tunnels were the answer. This seemed logical, especially since there were plenty of tunnels at the Sphinx that the locals could well imagine once went much farther into the plateau; they also knew that the plateau was riddled with shafts and tombs, and it was by no means illogical of them to presume that anyone who could build something the size of a pyramid could easily dig a tunnel as far as the Sphinx.

To describe the strange connection between the Sphinx and the Pyramid of Chephren I have to refer readers to my earlier book *The Crystal Sun*.[6] In color plate 30 of that book, the reader will see a photo of one of my major discoveries at the Giza Plateau. (I have also reproduced this photo on this book's website, www. sphinxmystery.info.) It is the winter solstice sunset shadow that I discovered cast on the south face of the Great Pyramid by the adjoining Pyramid of Chephren. It had been there once a year for at least 3,500 years but no one had "seen" it until I spotted it in 1998. (It was actually not visible in 2000 because of hazy atmospheric conditions.) I noticed that this shadow had a significant slope. I measured it and discovered that the slope was identical with the slope of the Ascending and Descending Passages inside the same structure. It was therefore a hint on the outside of what was on the inside of the Great Pyramid, but only someone who already knew about such things could ever "see" it. After all, if you didn't know there were passages inside and didn't know their slope, how could you possibly know the significance of the slope of the shadow? If you were an Egyptian architect of the Old Kingdom, you would know the angle, but ordinary folk knew nothing of this. The Egyptians seem to have enjoyed such inside jokes.

Since the publication of *The Crystal Sun*, I have purchased an old photo of the Sphinx with the Great Pyramid in the background, which is reproduced in figure 3.9. This unusual photo, never before published, gives a striking image of the pyramid shadow, though it had not yet risen to its full height (or had declined from it). The photo was obviously taken several days either before or after the actual day of the winter solstice. It is only at the solstice that the shadow achieves the angle that I mentioned. However, this is the only other photo showing the sunset shadow at that time of year that I have ever seen, so I publish it here for the first time. I bought this photo with only the information written on the back that it was taken in 1941 by Frank Freeman, with no explanation as to who Frank Freeman might possibly be. I have done an Internet search, and it is possible that he might have been Professor Frank Nugent Freeman (1880–1961), who was dean of the School

Figure 3.10. This remarkable photo taken in 1941 shows the sunset shadow on the south face of the Great Pyramid, which is cast by the adjoining Pyramid of Chephren. This photo was not taken precisely on the day of the solstice, so the shadow has either not yet culminated or is now in decline (depending on whether this photo was taken before or after the solstice, a detail we do not know), but on the evening of the solstice the shadow becomes the Winter Solstice Sunset Shadow. At that time, its acute angle at the southwest corner of the pyramid measures the same as the angle of slope of both the Ascending and Descending Passages inside the Great Pyramid, a unique angle known as "the golden angle." This was a secret visual code of the Egyptian priests, showing on the outside what was on the inside. The slope of the ascending passage rising out of the Valley Temple beside the Sphinx has the same angle. As for the golden angle of the shadow, it is part of the huge multi-golden-angled complex of the Golden Giza Plan depicted in figure 7.25 and explained at length in chapter 7, pages 366–71. (*Photo by Frank Freeman*)

of Education at the University of California at Berkeley, and whose hobby was photography. However, I bought the photo in Britain, so it is more likely that it was another man. Maybe we will never know who he was. The shadow is cast on the south face of the Great Pyramid by the adjoining Pyramid of Chephren only at sunset near the time of the winter solstice, and the shadow reaches its culmination on that day, when it has the "golden angle," the same angle as the slopes of the Ascending and Descending Passages inside the Great Pyramid. When I use the expression "golden angle" in this book and elsewhere, I invariably mean the angle of 26° 33' 54", and *not* the angle of 137° 30' 27", a related but more complicated angle derived from a formula (360 divided by *phi* squared) to which the name "golden angle" is sometimes applied by certain modern mathematicians. It is unfortunate that there are two angles competing now for the name "the golden angle." As "the golden angle" figures prominently in chapters 7 and 8, it is essential that readers be aware of which angle I mean.

Color plate 31 in *The Crystal Sun* is a photo I took relating to another of my discoveries at Giza. The huge megalithic structure near the Sphinx that we call today the Valley Temple has a narrow sloping passageway leading upward from the interior of the temple and out of the back onto the Chephren Causeway. We can call it the ascending passage of the Valley Temple, since it is on a slope. Of course, if you go back inside, the ascending passage becomes a descending passage, because you have turned around. But there is no doubt that the significance of the passage in terms of cult and ritual was to lead up and out onto the plateau of the sacred necropolis, so ascension was its motif, being also to the Egyptians a metaphor for resurrection. As I describe in *The Crystal Sun*, chapter 9, where I talk about all these things, I measured the slope of this ascending passage, something no one else had ever thought to do. I discovered that it had the same slope as the Ascending Passage and the Descending Passage inside the Great Pyramid, and also of course of the winter solstice sunset shadow on the Great Pyramid. The slope is 26 degrees, 33 minutes, and 54 seconds. It is what I have called the "golden slope." Surely there must be some significance to all this?

Indeed there is. As I explain at some length in *The Crystal Sun*, this particular angle, which we can call the "golden angle," is the precise value of the acute angle of a right-angled "golden triangle" that embodies the golden mean proportion (the ratio of 1 to 1.618). The Danish art historian Else Kielland established with conclusive and absolutely overwhelming evidence and analysis that this angle was the basis for all Egyptian art and architecture. She did this in her monumental work *Geometry in Egyptian Art* (Copenhagen, 1955). Figure 55 in *The Crystal Sun* is taken from her book and demonstrates some of her evidence. Figure 8.2 here is reproduced to help elucidate her ideas. These matters are discussed further in chapter 7.

The King's Chamber inside the Great Pyramid embodies no fewer than eight occurrences of the golden angle, and the coffer in the chamber embodies yet more. Figure 54 in *The Crystal Sun* shows the use of the golden angle and the golden triangle to define the Grand Gallery. I also explain in *The Crystal Sun* that the solstice shadow on the Great Pyramid is truncated by the line running up the middle of the face (which in geometry is called the apothegm); this cuts it at exactly the right point to form a golden triangle, just as the commencement of the Grand Gallery on the inside of the same structure cuts the slope of the Ascending Passage at just the point to make a golden triangle. I also show, in plate 65 of *The Crystal Sun*, the aerial photo that proves that the apothegm of the southern face of the Great Pyramid is marked by a slight indentation made on purpose during the construction that is invisible to the naked eye on the ground and can be seen only from the air. The "formation" of the golden triangle by the solstice shadow could thus be known only by the gods and by the architects.

But we must not go any further into these matters, which I have already discussed at length in another book. My purpose for introducing the material here briefly is to explain my discovery that relates to the Sphinx's connection with the Pyramid of Chephren. On this book's website, www.sphinxmystery.info, I reproduce some of the relevant illustrations from *The Crystal Sun*, as that book is now out of print.

In January 2001 I was allowed access to the Sphinx Temple (the largely ruined structure directly in front of the Sphinx) for the purpose of an archaeological investigation approved by the Egyptian Supreme Council of Antiquities. Normally the Sphinx Temple is kept locked, and few archaeologists have occasion or permission to enter it. It is never entered by tourists.

MEN WORKING IN FRONT OF THE SPHINX TEMPLE

Figure 3.11. A photo from 1936 showing the clearing of the Sphinx Temple from beneath the sand by Selim Hassan. This is plate 32 following page 68 in Hassan's *The Great Sphinx and Its Secrets*, Cairo, 1953. This was the first time the temple had been seen for nearly four thousand years, since circa 2000 BC.

THE WORK IN PROGRESS IN FRONT OF THE SPHINX TEMPLE

Figure 3.12. The mountain of sand behind the men with wagons on rails is what was sitting on top of the Sphinx Temple in 1936, when this clearance by Selim Hassan was undertaken. On top of that sand mountain was, as we can see here, a number of modern tourist shops catering to the visitors to the Sphinx. They all had to be demolished before the sand could be removed from underneath them. This caused an enormous amount of local resentment, as many people lost their livelihoods and businesses. Only after all this was cleared away was it revealed that an entire lost temple lay beneath the buildings and the sand, the Sphinx Temple as we now call it. This photo is plate XXXI, opposite page 68, in Selim Hassan's book *The Great Sphinx and Its Secrets*, Cairo, 1953.

Because I was allowed into the Sphinx Temple and spent considerable time there, I was able to notice many details that are not immediately obvious even to someone fortunate enough to gain access. Most people managing to gain special access would be allowed a quick look-round and then be ushered out again. But I had to linger due to the nature of my work. The floor of the Sphinx Temple may once have been covered with some fine substance. Selim Hassan thinks the floor was once of alabaster, and speaks of "the fine alabaster which paved its magnificent court."[7] There are still large chunks of raw alabaster sitting around inside the temple, which I found rather peculiar, and for which there appears to be no obvious explanation. Egyptian alabaster is different from European alabaster; the former is calcium carbonate, whereas the latter is calcium sulfate. The true mineralogical name of Egyptian alabaster is travertine, and it is a form of limestone. However, the floor of the Sphinx Temple now consists simply of leveled bedrock. My detailed accounts of the Valley Temple and Sphinx Temple may be found in *Egyptian Dawn*, where I also explain the significance of the chunks of raw alabaster.

Figure 6.17 on page 253 is a photo I took of the view of the Sphinx and the Pyramid of Chephren from the floor of the Sphinx Temple. As I gazed at the Pyramid of Chephren from inside the Sphinx Temple, I was suddenly struck by an idea. I took a device called an inclinometer, which we had with us, and took a sighting of the apex of the Pyramid of Chephren. I was able to confirm my hunch: the floor of the Sphinx Temple had been lowered into the bedrock to just the right depth for a sightline from there to the tip of the pyramid to form the golden angle. This angular relationship is shown in figure 3.12. A view of the Sphinx from the top of the Pyramid of Chephren is shown in the photo reproduced as figure 3.14, which was published in 1910.

This means that the slope of the sight line leading upward through the air from the floor of the Sphinx Temple to the apex of the Pyramid of Chephren matches the slope of the ascending passage leading up out of the Valley Temple next door in the same direction, and it forms a golden angle in three-dimensional space! Surely this is an example of the Egyptians carrying their surveying and design planning to extraordinary lengths!

I believe this is the true "direct connection" between the Sphinx and the

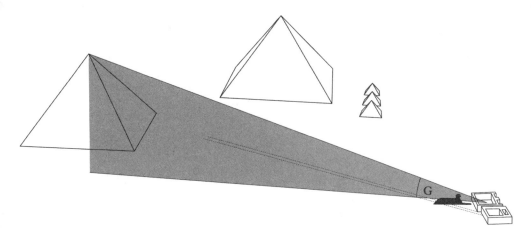

Figure 3.13. A drawing looking northward, showing the Sphinx at right and in front of it the Sphinx Temple, beside which in the foreground is the Valley Temple. In the background are the Great Pyramid and its three mini-pyramids. At the left we see the Pyramid of Chephren. The shaded area is an artist's attempt to show the aerial golden angle that I measured with an inclinometer from the floor of the Sphinx Temple when I took a sighting of the tip of the Pyramid of Chephren. This drawing is not strictly accurate or to scale and is intended to be merely suggestive. The letter G represents "golden angle," as the acute angle of the aerial triangle is a golden angle, and this must have been intentional. The shaded area is shown as going below ground level, because the base of the triangle must be taken to be the horizontal surface of the floor of the Sphinx Temple, not the much higher level of the plateau surface beside the pyramid. (*Drawing by Daud Sutton*)

Opposite: Figure 3.14. This photo, taken by Uvo Hölscher about 1900, was published in 1912. He was standing on top of the Pyramid of Chephren, looking due east. The Chephren Causeway is entirely covered with sand and invisible. The large unexcavated ruin in the foreground is the Funerary Temple of Chephren, which today is fully excavated, and which contains gigantic blocks of stone, some of them weighing more than fifty tons each. Beyond it, slightly to the left of the center of the photo, the head of the Sphinx protrudes from the sand. The Sphinx Temple, still unknown, is entirely buried in a huge mound of sand in front of the Sphinx at this time. The Valley Temple, known and partially excavated, but not yet excavated by Hölscher, is in front of the Sphinx and slightly to the right. The top of it may be seen, but little more, as a dark line protruding from the sand. In the distance, the floodplain of the River Nile extends toward Cairo. In ancient times, the river came right up to the foot of the Sphinx. To the right of the Sphinx, at the edge of the photo, is the huge old sycamore tree that may be seen in the foreground of figure 3.9 taken some decades earlier. This photo was published by Uvo Hölscher in his excavation report of the Valley Temple: Uvo Hölscher, *Das Grabdenkmal des Königs Chephren* (*The Funerary Monument of King Chephren*), vol. 1 of *Veröffentlichungen der Ernst von Sieglin-Expedition* (*Publications of the Ernst von Sieglin Expedition in Egypt*), edited by Georg Steindorff, containing also contributions by Ludwig Borchardt and Georg Steindorff, J. C. Hinrich's Booksellers, Leipzig, 1912. This view is looking *downward* toward the golden angle of the acute angle made at the point below the sand in front of the Sphinx in this photo (i.e., the floor of the Sphinx Temple, which was still unknown and was unexcavated at the date of this photo). Because it is so difficult to get to the top of the Pyramid of Chephren, I know of no other photo like this one in existence.

Pyramid of Chephren. The locals have always known there was one, but they never understood its true nature even in ancient times. And since the Sphinx Temple was buried in sand and totally unknown during the New Kingdom, the vague tradition of this "connection" must go back to Old Kingdom times, which means a survival in folklore for about a third longer than the survival of the story of Thutmosis IV, or an additional thousand years.

Another point to be made is that the hypotenuse (the longest side, which is always opposite the right angle) of a sacred triangle was known in Egypt as "Horus," a fact recorded by Plutarch in his treatise *On Isis and Osiris.* (I have discussed this in *The Crystal Sun,* and I discuss it further in chapters 7 and 8 here.) The sightline leading from the Sphinx Temple to the top of the Pyramid of Chephren was a hypotenuse, and thus a Horus. This could explain why the name Horus was so often associated with the Sphinx even though the Sphinx was not always *identified as* Horus. Also, no other monument in Egypt was called "Horus-in-the-Horizon." But if we consider the geometrical relationship that I have discovered, we realize that if we were to stand on top of the Pyramid of Chephren and look down the sightline, it would disappear into the horizon, and the sightline itself would thus literally be a Horus-in-the-Horizon. I was pleased when I discovered this fact, because I had never accepted the other explanations that various authors had suggested for the meaning and origin of this strange name as applied to the Sphinx.

Now we see even more reason to take the Giza folklore seriously. The folklore is also full of insistence on secret openings, doors, tunnels, and so forth in and around the Sphinx, and insistent also on the Sphinx's use as an oracle with a voice issuing apparently from its mouth. I have already pointed out in chapters 1 and 2 how many openings, doors, tunnels, and so forth are really to be found at the Sphinx, even though most have been sealed off. In part 2 there are numerous accounts of these from early European travelers. We will have more to say about them later. Even when Caviglia was excavating the Sphinx, as we are told in the *Quarterly Review*, "The Arabs . . . told Mr. Caviglia, that the French had discovered a door in the breast of the Sphinx [in 1798, nineteen years before Caviglia's excavations], which opened into its body, and passed through it to the second pyramid." All these things will be discussed further later on and relate also to the section containing the early travelers' accounts.

But let us turn now to another strange feature of the local folklore account of the story of Thutmosis IV, which I did not quote at the beginning of this chapter and have reserved until now. This is the remainder of van Ghistele's account of what the locals told him about that pharaoh, whose name they no longer remembered: "A little while after his coronation he [*the new king*] returned to the place where the head [*the Sphinx*] was, which he decapitated with an axe, saying: 'It's all very well that you have given me counsel so that I can secure Egypt; but from today on, you will not give any more counsel to anyone.' And it is thus that since then the head rests upon the ground up until our own time."

The first thing I want to point out about this part of the tale is that another small detail relating to Thutmosis IV is known to be accurate, namely the passage that says that he returned to the Sphinx "a little while after his coronation." In fact, the Dream Stela is dated in the first year of his reign, whereas one would not normally expect such a prompt tribute. A normal king would get around to it later. So this too reflects an accurate tradition.

But what are we to make of the strange tale, rather amusing in fact, that Thutmosis chopped off the head of the Sphinx and that is why it lies upon the sand? The last part of that is obviously a joke, since all the local accounts of the Sphinx agree that the Sphinx has a buried body, and this account itself states only a few sentences earlier that the Sphinx pleaded with Thutmosis to be cleared from the sand. None of the locals *really believed* that the head of the Sphinx was detached and "lay upon the sand." It was a witticism. But what clearly *was* believed was that the head had somehow been "decapitated" even though it obviously had not really been severed. And although the mutilation of the nose by the fanatical Muslim Sheikh Mohammed had already taken place, this cannot be what the locals were referring to. So what does this strange story really mean?

Figure 3.15. The immense body of the Sphinx has a tiny head that is out of proportion and has been recarved from a much larger head. At right, the rear of the Sphinx Pit shows the horizontal water level that was the general level during the time of its use as a Sphinx Moat. (*Photo by Robert Temple*)

I believe that this tale relates to the recarving of the face of the Sphinx, an action that was of such drastic extent that the Sphinx was effectively decapitated and a face shaped out of a kind of stump. That the head of the Sphinx as we know it today, and as it has been known for many centuries, is far too tiny for the gigantic body has been remarked on by many people. This can be seen easily in figure 3.15 above and figures 4.1 and 4.2. Many people, including some Egyptologists, have suggested that the head was substantially cut down in size and recarved in the image of a pharaoh. What we have not known until now is *which* pharaoh, and when it happened. In the next chapter I answer these questions. It was not Thutmosis but an earlier pharaoh, and I have been able to identify him.

During the New Kingdom, the era of Thutmosis, the Sphinx was honored by a succession of pharaohs, including several before him, and the statue became an object of veneration to which offerings were made (another accurate detail of the folklore). It was apparently during that period that a pharaoh's beard of stone was carved and somehow affixed to the Sphinx's face. See figures 3.16 and 3.17 for evidence of holes bored into the face, to which the beard must have been affixed.

As already mentioned, these holes were found in excavations in the nineteenth century, and part of the beard is in Cairo (fragments that were smashed in the museum, so that only some now remains of what was originally excavated) and part is in London. But this beard was most definitely not an original feature of the Sphinx. It was probably also at this time that the conical hole was bored in the top of the head of the Sphinx and used for the insertion of a pole to support an elaborate headdress. Selim Hassan was proud about filling up this hole in the 1930s: "A hole that existed in the head of the statue was also filled in."[8] This hole was 9 feet deep, with stones at the bottom so that its true depth was never determined, as several of the travelers' accounts in part 2 make clear. Some ill-informed people thought this hole might have been drilled by Howard-Vyse in the nineteenth century, but they are wrong. It was ancient, though probably not original. Pictures of the Sphinx shown on New Kingdom stelae show it with a headdress. An example may be seen in figure 3.18. It is generally also shown with its beard. In other words, the Sphinx was considerably "tarted up," as the British expression goes. It may also have had an ornamental collar thrown around its neck, since some representations show one. And it may have been at this time that the entire statue was painted with a red face and a yellow body. It was only in the twentieth century that the last vestiges of red paint vanished from the surface of the Sphinx's face. Many of the travelers' accounts in part 2 describe the red and yellow color

Figure 3.16. Beneath the left ear of the Sphinx are these two holes, doubtless drilled either during the Middle Kingdom when the face was recarved or during the New Kingdom, at whichever time the Sphinx's beard was affixed. (*Photo by Robert Temple*)

Figure 3.17. Here, the angle of the light enables us to see clearly the holes beneath the right ear of the Sphinx where the beard was affixed in later times. The modern concrete of the 1930s used as an extension of the side lappets of the *nemes* headdress is also clearly visible here, as is the way the bottoms of the stone portions of those lappets were chipped away to be level for the affixing of the modern concrete. (*Photo by Robert Temple*)

Figure 3.18. This stela was excavated by Selim Hassan in 1936 in the Sphinx precinct. This particular stela dates from the reign of King Thutmosis (Thothmes) IV, the pharaoh who cleared the Sphinx of sand and erected the Dream Stela. The solar disk is shown between two feathers of Maat arising from two ram's horns in the Sphinx's headdress. He is smelling three large blue lotus flowers (a symbolic flower; its delicate scent was meant to bestow immortal life). A solar disk with a single wing is seen floating in the air to the left of the headdress, which enables us to date the stela, as this was a short-lived design fashion. The hieroglyphic text below the picture says: "A boon that the King gives, and Hor-em-akhet [Horus-in-the-Horizon, the name given to the Sphinx in the New Kingdom]; (that they may) give him a sweet heart (i.e., contentment) in every place. Made by Inhermes." (Selim Hassan, *Sphinx*, pp. 136–37, figure 32. It is figure 32 also in *Le Sphinx*, opposite p. 86.)

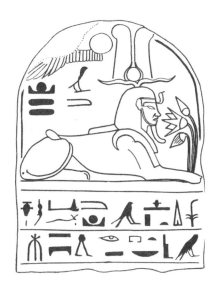

Left: Figure 3.19. This stela, excavated at the Sphinx in 1936 by Selim Hassan, depicts Horus-in-the-Horizon in falcon form. Horus-in-the-Horizon became a name for the Sphinx itself in New Kingdom times, but originally, Horus-in-the-Horizon was the name of the rising sun, who was the revivified and resurrected Osiris, reborn at sunrise in the form of his own son Horus, especially at Giza (for a full account of this mythology and its relevance to Giza, see chapters 7 and 8).

Right: Figure 3.20. A photo of the stela shown in the drawing in figure 3.19, which portrays Horus-in-the-Horizon as a falcon.

of the Sphinx, and by the nineteenth century these accounts speak of traces of it being preserved here and there on the statue.

Several crude pictures of the Sphinx, of New Kingdom date and later, are reproduced in figures 3.21 to 3.23. These depictions were all found carved onto stelae erected in the Sphinx precinct and excavated there between 1817 and 1937. They all show the Sphinx with a beard, all but one of them with the beard clearly held on by a strap to a point below the ear where bored holes may be seen in figures 3.16 and 3.17. All but one show the Sphinx with a fancy headdress protruding from the point where the bored hole in the head is. Since the headdress varies, it may well be that the headdresses were interchangeable, different ones being set upon the Sphinx's head at different times as occasion required. All the depictions also show the Sphinx with a royal uraeus serpent on its brow. One of the depictions (figure 3.21) even shows two pyramids crudely sketched in the background. Since the view is taken from the south, and there is only one pyramid behind the Sphinx from that direction (the Great Pyramid), the two pyramids were clearly meant to be suggestive rather than accurate; they are in any case far too pointed. Not all these pictures of the Sphinx are really meant to represent the one at Giza, because three of them are clearly miniature models of it. But they give the idea, and despite their obvious inaccuracies, we are probably safe in assuming that the

Figure 3.21. A stela excavated by Selim Hassan in 1936 within the Sphinx Moat. Behind the Sphinx at the top, the pyramids of Giza are represented symbolically (there is no attempt at accuracy, as only the Great Pyramid is in that direction). This is the only known ancient representation of the Sphinx in association with a pyramid or pyramids. This is figure 12 opposite page 58 in Selim Hassan's *The Sphinx: Its History in the Light of Recent Excavations,* Cairo, 1949. The text in front of the Sphinx says: "Hor-em-akhet [Horus-in-the-Horizon], the Twice-great God, the Lord of Heaven." Underneath, it says: "Made by the clever scribe, Mentu-her." Two figures are then shown in adoration of the Sphinx, and the text between them reads: "Made by the scribe Ka-Mut-Nekhteu, Justified." The stela was presumably erected at the expense of the two scribes who visited the Sphinx together. The stela probably dates from the New Kingdom. The falcon flying in front of the Sphinx's face is carrying the hieroglyph for "infinity" in his talons, representing Horus as a deity promising eternal life.

Figure 3.22. Selim Hassan excavated this stela in the Sphinx Precinct in 1936. This stela was offered to the Sphinx, under the names of Hul and Hul-Atum, by a foreign visitor named Tutuya. The colors are well preserved on this stela, and the foreigner's hair is still shown as bright red. The foreigner is probably a Canaanite, who has chosen to call the Sphinx "Hul" after the Canaanite god Huron. The stela is believed to date from either the Eighteenth or Nineteenth Dynasty. The Sphinx's headdress here is the white Crown of the South. On the offering table in front of the Sphinx are depicted the conventional offerings to a deity. The Sphinx wears a huge decorative collar. (Hassan, *Sphinx*, pp. 151–52, figure 35. It is also figure 35 in *Le Sphinx*, opposite p. 97.)

Figure 3.23. This stela was excavated by Selim Hassan in 1936 in the Sphinx Precinct. It is dedicated to the Sphinx by an Egyptian prince named Amen-em-Apt, who was a son of King Amenhotep II. He was also the older brother of the later king Thutmosis (Thothmes) IV, who is suspected of having murdered him and of having erased the older brother's name from this stela (though not in all places, so it can still be read). (Selim Hassan, *Sphinx*, pp. 186–97, figure 39. It is also figure 39 in *Le Sphinx*, opposite p. 108.)

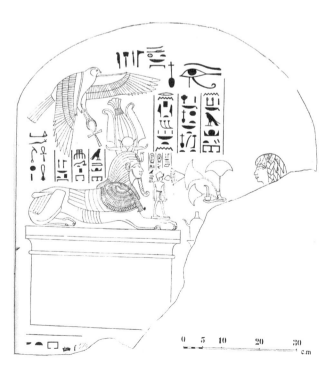

beard and headdress(es) were definitely attached to the Sphinx from the time of the New Kingdom until the Persian Conquest in 525 BC, when they may have been torn down.

Approaching the Sphinx during the New Kingdom, when people like Thutmosis IV were honoring it, one would have seen a very gaudy and unsubtle statue indeed. It would have had a feather on its head at least, if not a wild and waving headdress; a false beard; and probably a bright, thick bejeweled collar round its neck. And its face would have been painted a bilious red that probably resembled the bad makeup of a contemporary streetwalker. Taste had degenerated somewhat during the New Kingdom, when the pharaohs were what I call "the smiting pharaohs," so often shown smiting their enemies, of whom they had plenty. Gone were the calm, tasteful days of the Old Kingdom, when art was more subtle. The geometrical canon was still observed in the New Kingdom, because it was the sacred tradition. But when it came to coloring and showiness, there were often lapses of taste into what can only be called vulgarity. And, frankly, sticking a feather or a crown on the head of the Sphinx can only be described as *frightfully* vulgar.

The last excavator of the Sphinx Temple was the German archaeologist Herbert Ricke, who published his report in 1970.[9]

Now to return to the story of Thutmosis IV decapitating the Sphinx. I believe that the cutting off of the original head and its recarving as a pharaoh's head did indeed take place at some time, and that the story refers to that action. But I am convinced that the recarving of the head of the Sphinx dates from long before the time of Thutmosis IV and was done by a much earlier pharaoh. The story of Thutmosis doing this was thus probably an example of conflation of tradition, where the pharaoh who in popular consciousness was most closely associated with the Sphinx became conflated with the earlier pharaoh who recarved the face (even though the actual names of these two pharaohs were no longer remembered). A lot of discussion has taken place among Egyptologists about the date when the particular type of *nemes* headdress represented on the Sphinx was actually worn by historical pharaohs. Ludwig Borchardt in the nineteenth century was insistent that the date of the headdress and the eye stripes were from the Twelfth Dynasty of the Middle Kingdom, indeed from the precise reign of Pharaoh Ammenemes III (1929–1895 BC).[10] This opinion was ridiculed by various subsequent writers, who pointed out that his argument could not be substantiated from existing statuary and that Borchardt had manipulated various inconvenient facts to accord with his theory.

For instance, Selim Hassan accuses Borchardt of "an astonishing flight of fancy," adding for good measure (as partially quoted earlier):

Figure 3.24. The three pyramids of Giza seen from the air, with the Sphinx near the top right corner to the left of the end of the long causeway. From top downward, the pyramids are: the Great Pyramid, the Pyramid of Chephren, and the Pyramid of Mycerinus. This uncredited photo was reproduced by Herbert Ricke as half of the frontispiece to his book, *Der Harmachistempel des Chefren in Giseh* (*The Temple of Harmachis at Giza*), Wiesbaden, 1972. Ricke reexcavated the Sphinx Temple and decided to call it the Harmachis Temple, which no one else does. His choice of name was most inappropriate because Harmachis, the name given in later times to the Sphinx, was an unknown deity at the time the Sphinx Temple was last visible and in use prior to 2000 BC.

It seems to me that Borchardt had gone to a great deal of trouble to prove a theory that is altogether wrong from the beginning to the end; that is if he is not having a joke with the scientific world, and indulging in a little "leg-pulling" at our expense. Note how he refers to the Sphinx in the feminine gender, and at the same time passes observations upon its beard, and identifies it with the King!

If Borchardt was really serious about this article, then I think that of all the theories that he ever put into writing, he must have bitterly regretted having published this one![11]

I have sat through lectures where Egyptologists have argued about whether the *nemes* headdress of the Sphinx dated from the reign of Cheops or only of Chephren in the Old Kingdom. However, I do not believe that the present face of the Sphinx dates from the Old Kingdom at all. In the next chapter, I shall give the evidence that I believe demonstrates the true date for the face of the Sphinx, and identifies the precise pharaoh whose face it is. This discussion will then answer the question: When was the face "cut down" and recarved? But this evidence alone does not answer the question: What was it cut down *from*? Or, in other words, what was the head of the Sphinx before the particular pharaoh had his own face carved on the stump, or neck, of the original head?

Most people can probably easily accept that the head of the Sphinx was recarved as the face of a pharaoh. Only some people who are very sensitive and touchy about the Cheops-versus-Chephren argument will get highly excited at this. They have a vested interest in insisting that the entire Sphinx was carved either by Cheops (ca. 2589–2566 BC) or by Chephren (ca. 2588–2533 BC) and are prepared to dispute for hours with one another about which of these two actually did it. The fact that there is only a maximum of fifty-six years' difference between the two alternatives does not matter to them; they are engaged in a dispute, and nothing will calm them. I have already said, and will say here again, that it doesn't matter a bit which of the two pharaohs one chooses for having constructed the original Sphinx, as they are so close together. But any student of human disputes will have noticed that what most enrage and envenom people who are arguing with one another are often *small differences*. For some reason to do with human evolution, there seems to be some survival advantage for groups in the fact that small differences are often blown up out of all proportion, which explains why racism is so common, and why skin color (literally a superficial subject) arouses such passions. I suppose that this aspect of animal behavior so commonly seen in humans must have to do with breeding and survival of traits in species. But I prefer to take no part in it.

People who are worried about Cheops versus Chephren will certainly not want to have the interference to their dispute of the suggestion that the face of the Sphinx, which according to them was carved by either Cheops or Chephren (which is what they are disputing), could have been recarved. This would throw their whole argument out of kilter. They can't have that!

In my opinion, the Sphinx may be older than Cheops or Chephren. But, as I shall show in the next chapter, the face as it exists now was recarved by another and later pharaoh who can be precisely identified, and who did not live during the Old Kingdom at all.

In the next chapter, therefore, the true identity of the man whose face is on the Sphinx is revealed, together with all the evidence that makes this identification conclusive. Then, in the chapter after that, we shall consider what the original face of the Sphinx may have been before it was carved into the likeness of that particular pharaoh. And this leads us to a new idea of what the Sphinx itself truly represented. In other words, we then begin to approach the real question that should be concerning us: What *is* the Sphinx?

4
THE FACE OF THE SPHINX

Every tourist who sees the Sphinx can see that the head is too small for the body. Millions of people every year become aware of this at first glance, and they often remark on the oddity of it. The disproportion of the head to the body is very clearly visible in figures 4.1 and 4.2 on pages 159 and 160, where the head appears to be merely a pimple on the vast bulk of the body. It is difficult to get a good photo of the Sphinx that shows this clearly because of the size of the monument and the fact that you cannot get far enough away to get it all into the photo very easily, even with a wide lens. But in figure 3.15 I think I have managed to show this, at the cost of cutting off the paws. Figure 4.1 is also taken from so far away to the north that the disproportion is obvious.

So what are we to make of this problem of the Sphinx's head? The head really does look as if it has been hacked down to a smaller size and recarved out of the stump of a larger neck. Everyone who knows anything whatsoever about Egyptian art and architecture knows that the Egyptians did not customarily build or carve things that were drastically—and in this case, spectacularly—out of proportion. Why go to all the trouble of carving a Sphinx out of the solid rock, sitting prominently as guardian of the Giza Plateau in front of the pyramids, if it is going to look ridiculous because it has a tiny little head on a giant body? Why not carve a smaller body in proportion to the head, if there was only enough stone to make a head that small? That is what one would expect of such careful artists as the Egyptians.

We must remember that this disproportion of the head to the body was not known for a couple of thousand years, from Roman times to the 1930s, because

Figure 4.1. This photo of the entire Sphinx taken from the north, looking south, shows the outrageous disproportion of the present head to the body, something that is entirely against the canons and practice of Egyptian art throughout thousands of years of history. It is impossible that any ancient Egyptian would ever have carved an original statue with such a "pimple" head on such a large body. As is shown in figure 5.11, the present head was recarved out of the neck of a larger original head. The present head was recarved with the face of Pharaoh Amenemhet II of the Middle Kingdom, and although his ego cannot have been of modest proportions itself, out of fairness to him we must admit that there is a very good possibility that the original head had been mutilated, leaving only a neck stump, so that all he had to do was "rehabilitate" the monument in his own image. This would perhaps have seemed an act of piety rather than one of megalomania. (And as the history of the world's religions have proved, the two often go hand in hand.) (The photo is figure 26 in Herbert Ricke's book about his excavations of the Sphinx Temple, which he calls the Harmachis Temple: *Der Harmachistempel des Chefren in Giseh*, in *Beiträge zur Ägyptischen Bauforschung und Altertumskunde*, ed. by Herbert Ricke, Heft 10, Franz Steiner Verlag, Wiesbaden, 1970.)

the body was covered with sand and the disproportion could not be seen. So the issue is therefore a modern issue, an issue dating only from 1926. What people in Roman times thought is no longer our concern; in fact, only one Roman account of the Sphinx survives, by Pliny, and the rest are lost. If anybody at that time thought the head was too small, we have no surviving record of it. And there are no surviving Greek accounts at all.

It doesn't take a lot of imagination to realize that there must have been many megalomaniac pharaohs in Egyptian history, and any number of them would have liked to have his face put onto the Sphinx. The Middle East has had

Figure 4.2. An aerial photo of the Sphinx and the Great Pyramid taken sometime after 1937, probably during the 1940s. The excavations of Selim Hassan, completed by 1937, are finished in this photo. The modern road up to the Great Pyramid has not yet been constructed and is still just a dirt track, seen here as a pale stripe winding up the hill to the right of the Sphinx. This photo is taken from the southeast, looking northwest. It is clear from this photo that far more of the ancient Nile quays in front of the Valley and Sphinx Temples were cleared at this time than they are today, for nowadays those in front of the Sphinx Temple are entirely covered over again. This photo gives a very good view of the Chephren Causeway leading up to the top left corner of the photo, where the Pyramid of Chephren is just out of the shot. The disproportionate size of the Sphinx's head is very obvious from above, being far too small for the body. (*Collection of Robert Temple; photographer unknown*)

some well-known megalomaniac leaders in our time, and one can easily imagine earlier versions of the same type of person. The notorious Saddam Hussein of Iraq "restored" Babylon with bricks all stamped with his name and erected gigantic portraits of himself on every street corner in Baghdad: imagine what he would have done if he could have got his hands on the Sphinx! We should never lose sight of the fact that many kings, emperors, and pharaohs in the history of the world have been equally unpleasant, and have suffered from megalomania. The opportunities for sticking a pharaoh's face on the Sphinx were many, and it is more than likely, in my opinion, that this is precisely what happened.

The question of what the original head of the Sphinx actually was is another matter. Maybe it was an earlier pharaoh, the one who had the Sphinx carved in the first place. Or maybe it was an animal head. Some would say a lion's head. I have an idea about this matter, and I describe it at length in the next chapter, where I suggest it was an animal head and not a pharaoh's head. After all, there is no reason to assume that it had to be an earlier pharaoh's head, since that is a process of reverse reasoning. One cannot logically maintain that because the Sphinx has a pharaoh's head now, it had to have a pharaoh's head before. It could have been anything. Indeed, an animal head is far more logical and reasonable. After all, the human-headed sphinx as a motif in Egyptian art is really something that became popular in the Middle Kingdom only after about 2000 BC and was not a motif of the Old Kingdom, which is the latest possible date when the body of the Sphinx could have been carved, many centuries before the Middle Kingdom began. We must never extrapolate backward and use the criteria of the Middle Kingdom, when human-headed sphinxes became popular, to insist that this must have been the case in the Old Kingdom, when such ideas seem to have been absent.

A small statue of a human-headed sphinx of some kind was found at Abu Ruash, near Giza, and some people have suggested that it might be an Old Kingdom statue, while others have insisted that it is not. (It is shown in figures 4.3, 4.4, 4.5, and 4.6.) This object cannot be dated, since it is merely a statue excavated very long ago, with inadequate excavation reports, somewhere near or on a site that may or may not once have had a pyramid. Its date is just a matter of personal opinion or of guessing, since dating by association cannot be justified in the absence of any real contextual evidence of any kind. It could just as well be a Middle Kingdom statue, or even a New Kingdom one or a Ptolemaic one. It does not constitute evidence because of the impossibility of dating it. And there is no other evidence of human-headed sphinxes in the Old Kingdom, or Pyramid Age. What is more, this mysterious object from Abu Ruash has a female face, not a male one, and this is well known to be a typical late development in the evolution of the sphinx motif in Egyptian art. This point was noted by the historian of Mediterranean iconography (I suppose one would call him an "iconographer," which is a highly specialized corner of the history of art that impinges on archaeology) André Dessenne, in his book *Le Sphinx: Étude Iconographique* (*The Sphinx: An Iconographic Study*), published in 1957.[1] Dessenne was not an

Egyptologist, and Egypt forms only a brief initial portion of his wide-ranging study of the Sphinx motif in the art of many cultures. He surveys the Assyrians, Cypriots, Mitannians, Hittites, Minoans, and Mycenaeans. The Abu Ruash sphinx is the first sphinx that he discusses in his book (the second being the Great Sphinx of Giza), and here is all he says of it:

> It is recumbent. Its face, beardless, is painted yellow, which, following the con-ventions, indicates that it is a woman's head. [Anyone can see that the face is obviously that of a woman; see figures 4.4 and 4.5.] For this reason the features and traits are more feminine and the hair is separated with a middle parting. The headdress has no uraeus.
>
> This sphinx was found during the clearing of Djedefra's pyramid [a gigantic descending tunnel shaft with no roof, at Abu Ruash, where a "pyramid" has often been assumed in an unfinished state, since if it ever existed, it vanished long ago], and for this reason is thought to be contemporaneous to the pyramid's build-ing. It may have belonged to a queen mother of the 4th Dynasty. Djedefra being the predecessor of Khufu [Djedefra was Khufu's (Cheops's) son, so he could not possibly have been the predecessor of his own father, and this shows Dessenne's tenuous grasp of Egyptological matters!] suggests that the sphinx could slightly predate the one at Giza. It is curious that the earliest available evidence for a sphinx presents it with a woman's head. Surely this is pure coincidence. Other than for its head, the sphinx in question presents no major differences with the masculine type, which is the type with which my study is concerned. This makes it difficult to talk about the Abu Ruash Sphinx as a female, since female sphinxes really only appear much later, during the New Kingdom.[2]

Dessenne's lack of logic, and his even more appalling lack of knowledge of the basics of Egyptian chronology, renders most of what he says useless, except for his comment that female sphinxes really begin to appear only during the New Kingdom, a thousand years after the time of Djedefre. Clearly, the fact that Djedefre was the son of Cheops, and not his father, destroys Dessenne's sugges-tion that the Abu Ruash sphinx could be earlier than the Great Sphinx of Giza; at best, it could be from a subsequent generation. Dessenne is even so naive as to complain about this sphinx being female, because his book is only supposed to be about male sphinxes, which "makes it difficult to talk about." Although we are grateful for Dessenne pointing out how anomalous it is for a female sphinx to appear a thousand years earlier than any other, we can disregard the rest of his opinions. If he cannot get his pharaohs straight, then he cannot be expected to get his sphinxes straight either.

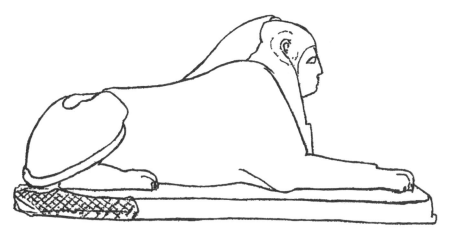

Figure 4.3. This is a drawing of the small limestone statue of a leonine sphinx with a woman's face, which was excavated at Abu Ruash in the nineteenth century and is of unknown date. The body is clearly that of a lion, with a rising massive chest, thick front shoulders, upward-sloping back, and heavy mane. If the Great Sphinx of Giza had been intended to represent a lion's body, it would have looked more like this. This sphinx is also represented in figures 4.4 to 4.6. Since this sphinx is so often mentioned in discussions as possibly being older than the Great Sphinx of Giza, it is important that we be thoroughly familiar with its appearance, for it would therefore constitute conclusive evidence that the Great Sphinx was not a lion. (*Redrawing by Olivia Temple after Bodil Hornemann,* Types of Ancient Egyptian Statuary)

Figure 4.4. The female face of the small leonine sphinx statue excavated at Abu Ruash, date unknown. The headdress resembles that of a modern Muslim woman. (*Photo by Bernard V. Bothmer*)

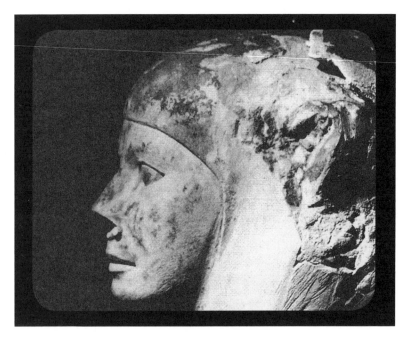

Figure 4.5. A profile view of the female face of the small Abu Ruash leonine statue of a sphinx. (*Photo by Bernard V. Bothmer*)

Figure 4.6. A full view of the small leonine sphinx with a woman's face, carved from limestone, which was excavated at Abu Ruash, date unknown. (*Photo by Bernard V. Bothmer*)

The Abu Ruash statue bears no relation to the Great Sphinx of Giza, since its body is obviously that of a lion, with huge rising shoulders, a massive chest, and a line to its back in profile that rises at a steep upward incline toward the head. The Great Sphinx has none of these features, a point that will be discussed in the next chapter. The bizarre female face, wild eyes, and plain headcloth (which suggests nothing to do with royalty whatsoever) are so atypical of Old Kingdom statuary, and the motif of a woman's face on an animal body being otherwise unknown for another thousand years, we must conclude that this strange statue has nothing to do with the Old Kingdom whatsoever. Why it was found sitting around on the high hill of Abu Ruash is a mystery. But Abu Ruash is an inadequately understood site that puzzles everyone. Frankly, I am inclined to believe that this statue is Ptolemaic, an attempt to represent the Greek sphinx (who was a wild and violent female creature) with whom Oedipus had his famous confrontation near the Greek city of Thebes. Possibly there was a Ptolemaic ritual center at Abu Ruash, where this strange object was produced in its late and hybrid style, combining the Greek and Egyptian sphinx legends in one statue. If the female face had been intended to represent a queen, she would never have been shown with no signs of a regal nature whatever, wearing only a head covering that looks very like a modern Islamic hijab. Certainly, the Abu Ruash statue was dismissed in two sentences by the Egyptologist Christiane Zivie-Coche in her book *Sphinx: History of a Monument,* where she says only: "A small limestone sphinx that some consider to be feminine has been attributed to Radjedef [this is the correct form of the name often given as Djedefre], Chephren's predecessor, who was buried at Abu Rawash [Abu Ruash]. Because of its nemes [headdress], a beautiful quartzite head of this king, now in the Louvre, supposedly belonged to a sphinx. These two early examples are not convincing, however, in part because they are not intact, and in part because there are problems with regard to their date."[3] (Zivie-Coche has written these two sentences in rather a confusing way, since the Abu Ruash statue has no *nemes* headdress, and the *nemes* she is referring to was on a sculpted head supposed to be of Radjedef, which is a completely separate object. It seems truly incredible that just because a detached head with a *nemes* headdress has been found, it is presumed once to have topped a sphinx. The lack of evidence and weakness of the logical inference of whoever made such an assumption—who is not named by Zivie-Coche—is absolutely staggering. This is how false assumptions spread, but it is to the credit of Zivie-Coche that she has rejected them.)

So in this chapter I leave aside for later the question of what was the original head of the Sphinx. What we are concerned with here is: Whose head is on the Sphinx now, and when was it put there?

I believe we can specify exactly whose head is on the Sphinx, and I can give the dates of his reign, so that the question can be answered with complete satisfaction.

Although the Sphinx cannot have been carved later than the Old Kingdom, and indeed it even has some Old Kingdom repair blocks on it, so it must have been carved pretty early, I believe that the head is from the Middle Kingdom.

There are some Egyptologists who strenuously insist that the head of the Sphinx is that of the pharaoh Chephren (Khafre) of the Fourth Dynasty in the Old Kingdom, who reigned approximately 2572–2546 BC. They even try to convince us that the face on the Sphinx resembles that of Chephren, identified statues of whom survive. (Zivie-Coche firmly believes this, as we saw in an earlier chapter.) But it seems to me that any unbiased observer would have to admit that there is no resemblance at all between the two faces. People who say the face on the Sphinx is the face of Chephren are engaging in wishful thinking. They are seeing what they wish to see. Chephren's face is completely different. It is a long, narrow face, which that on the Sphinx is not. The German Egyptologist Rainer Stadelmann has very sensibly denied that the face of the Sphinx is that of Chephren. He says, for instance: "The ears are fundamentally different from those of the statue of Chephren. The ears of the Sphinx are very broad and folded forward, those of Chephren elongated and situated closer to the temples. . . . The overall form of the Sphinx's face is broad, almost square. On the other hand the features of Chephren were long, noticeably narrower, the chin almost pointed."[4]

Stadelmann is absolutely correct in these observations. The face cannot be that of Chephren. Anyone who insists that it is might as well say that Tom Cruise looks like Humphrey Bogart. It just "ain't so." See figure 4.7 for a portrait of Chephren, which, if compared with the face of the Sphinx, is clearly of a different person altogether.

So whose does Stadelmann think the face is, then, if not Chephren's? He speculates that it is of his older brother, Pharaoh Cheops (Khufu), who reigned earlier, approximately 2604–2581 BC. But here we have a problem. Whereas several splendid examples of statues of Chephren survive, only one tiny one of Cheops survives. I had a close look at it in the Cairo Museum, and really it is too small and lacking in detail for us to draw many conclusions about it, except that the face is not a long one like that of Chephren. The little ivory statue is only 3 inches high and 1 inch wide. You could easily hold it in the palm of your hand. There is no reason to believe that it is a serious attempt at portraiture. To use this as a basis to claim a likeness to the face on the Sphinx is hopeless. But for what it is worth, what likeness one can make out from this tiny statue also does not look anything at all like the face on the Sphinx. In figure 4.8 are several views of this only surviving likeness of King Cheops.

Figure 4.7. Pharaoh Chephren, with the divine Horus falcon spreading its wings protectively around his head. This is the top portion of the famous larger-than-life-size statue of Chephren in dark gray diorite stone that was found intact in the well of the Valley Temple, having probably been hidden there by priests to save it from destruction when all his other statues in the temple were smashed to pieces by a rioting mob (thought to be during the First Intermediate Period). The statue is one of the most famous things to see in the Egyptian Museum in Cairo. It may readily be seen that Chephren had a long, thin face that in no way resembles that of the Sphinx of Giza. One of the strangest phenomena of modern Egyptology is that many Egyptologists persist in stating that this is the same as the face on the Sphinx. Draw your own conclusions, psychiatrists! (*The Egyptian Museum, Cairo*)

Figure 4.8. Three views of the head of the tiny ivory statue of King Cheops, the only surviving likeness of him. His face is clearly not that on the Great Sphinx of Giza. (*The Egyptian Museum, Cairo*)

Figure 4.9. This was once a likeness carved in relief of King Cheops, but someone in antiquity who evidently hated him chipped out his face, so we don't know what he really looked like. He is wearing the combined Crown of the North and the South.

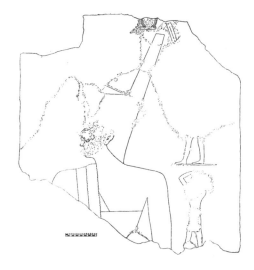

In other words, all attempts to match the face on the Sphinx to Cheops or Chephren are failures. The face is also not that of any other Fourth Dynasty pharaoh whose likeness has survived. For instance, the face of Mycerinus (Menkaure) is also well known, and the face on the Sphinx certainly is not his either. Nor is it that of Pharaoh Radjedef (Djedefre), another pharaoh of that dynasty whose likeness is well known.

I suggest that the whole Old Kingdom should be forgotten when trying to identify the face, and that the face really comes from the Middle Kingdom, hundreds of years later, when I believe the recarving of the head was carried out.

If this were just a matter of my personal speculation, I would certainly never be writing a chapter about it. I might refer to it in passing, express my opinion, and then move on. But it is precisely because I believe that this identification *can* be justified by considerable evidence of a highly specific kind that I am prepared to make an issue of it.

The identification of the period of the face of the Sphinx was, in my opinion, correctly made in 1897 by the famous German Egyptologist Ludwig Borchardt, whose article on this subject I mentioned earlier. I believe Borchardt correctly identified the dynasty, though not the precise pharaoh, for the face of the Sphinx. By a curious coincidence, Borchardt was a predecessor of Stadelmann's. Both are former directors of the German Institute of Archaeology in Cairo. Borchardt's findings were published in a long-forgotten article in an obscure learned journal,[5] and I do not believe anyone in modern times has ever bothered to read it. It is entitled "Concerning the Age of the Sphinx at Giza." I consider this article so important that I have translated it in its entirety; it appears as appendix 2 of this book.

Borchardt wrote his article long before the Sphinx was cleared of sand, when the disproportion of the head to the body was still unknown. In those days, it was possible to stand higher and have a better and closer look at the Sphinx's head. Today one cannot do that. In fact, it is now almost impossible to see, except from old photos such as those in figures 1.21, 1.43, and 1.44, the necessary details of the top of the Sphinx's headcloth. For it is here that the specific clues as to the date and identity of the face are to be found. But in Borchardt's day, these were very clear and easy to see. One had only to stand there and look straight at them.

Those few Egyptologists who may still be aware of Borchardt's article on the Sphinx would be inclined to dismiss it without a thought, due to the fact that in dating and identifying the face as that of a particular Middle Kingdom pharaoh, he made the mistake of insisting that the Sphinx as a whole was carved by that pharaoh, and thus dates from the Middle Kingdom. Now that the Sphinx is cleared, everyone knows that the idea of the Sphinx having been carved as late as the Middle Kingdom is entirely ludicrous, and hence Borchardt's old idea is

Figure 4.10. This glass lantern slide circa 1900 shows the locals clambering all over the head of the still-buried Sphinx. Note the raggedy edges of lappets of the *nemes* headdress, later chipped off and made even by Selim Hassan in the 1930s when he extended them with modern concrete. Why is it that everyone wants to make the Sphinx more beautiful and ends up doing the opposite? (*Collection of Robert Temple*)

dismissed as complete nonsense. No one would even bother to read the article through today, so ridiculous does its conclusion seem. No one but me, that is. For I had a hunch that Borchardt was on to something. And indeed he was! His only mistake was to assume that the entire statue had to be of the same date. It never occurred to him that the head could be a later recarving. But, then, he had not seen the body, which was not yet cleared! It was impossible for him to draw the correct conclusion about the age of a sculpture that was still buried in sand.

One curious feature of the head of the Sphinx is that the pharaoh is wearing a cloth over his head, which Egyptologists call by its ancient name, *nemes* headdress, or *nemes* headcloth. Colloquially, it has even been known as the King's Bonnet. It was worn throughout Egyptian history by pharaohs, and in itself it indicates nothing about date. It appears to have had a sacred character to do with preparation for death (or "eternal life," as the Egyptians would say), as we shall see. But no one knows why it has the peculiar shape that it has, or why it is of folded and starched cloth. The pharaohs had various crowns, which they wore as kings, but the *nemes* is not actually a crown, although it is sometimes called one. The pharaohs wore it in their religious role as opposed to their political role as ruler. It is therefore entirely appropriate that the pharaoh's face on the Sphinx gazes directly east, toward the sun rising on the equinox, in a pious mode, wearing the *nemes* in indication of the pharaoh's reverence for the rising sun god and in expectation of becoming the companion of that god in the afterlife.

The *nemes* is mentioned specifically in some of the ancient texts of the Early Middle Kingdom. In Spell 75 of the Coffin Texts, found on the coffin of an Egyptian of that period named Heqata, the deceased, who has declared his identity with the sky god Shu, boasts: "I have claimed my *nemes*-crowns from the One who is in his cavern. It is the One who is in his cavern who fetched for me my *nemes*-crowns."[6] This clearly stresses the sacred nature of the *nemes*. The translator comments: "It here appears that the *nemes*-crown is a necessary attribute in order to be able to ascend to the sky, and that 'Ruty, who is in his cavern' supplies it."[7]

Ruty, more often spelled Ruti, is the god described as "the One who is in his cavern." This cavern is also known as the House of Ruti, and it was necessary for any dead person to pass through it and collect his *nemes* to put on his head before proceeding to the House of Osiris, which was on an island, where he would be received in death by his "father," the god of the dead, Osiris.[8] And as we shall see later on, Ruti has specific associations with the Sphinx and with Giza. Ruti was an underworld aspect of the sun god himself, in his role of leaving the daytime barque of the sun and entering the nighttime barque of the sun[9] for his journey through the land of the dead, which was often envisaged as lying beneath the plateau of Giza and was imagined as being entered from the precincts of the Sphinx itself.

For the moment, all we need to know is that the *nemes* is a very appropriate covering for the head of the Sphinx, as it indicates religious reverence, and it is necessary for the deceased to put it on before proceeding to the World of the Dead and his eternal life.

The *nemes* seems to have been formed from a single cloth that was starched and folded in pleats, which then hung down over the shoulders. In the case of the Sphinx, the bottom portions of the *nemes* fell off and disappeared in antiquity, as the photos of figures 4.10 to 4.14 show clearly. At the present day, the folds of the *nemes* at the side of the Sphinx's face have continuations downward past the chin that are crude pieces of modern concrete, and which really ought to be removed, as they mar the edifice. They are examples of so-called restoration that are very clumsy and ugly.

Figure 4.11. A stereoview of the Sphinx dated 1896, showing a man standing on the head of the Sphinx. (*Collection of Robert Temple*)

Figure 4.12. This is a photo of the Sphinx from the early nineteenth century. At this time, only the head and back of the Sphinx were visible, and visitors could clamber all over the chest. The wagon on the left in the photo provides a very useful indicator of the scale of distance; it stands about midway along the Sphinx's body. This photo is particularly useful for showing the stripe patterns of the headdress, which were crucial to dating the recarved face. The deep hole between the eyes has long been filled with cement. Here, the extent to which the nose was broken off and the lips damaged, and the right earlobe broken off, can be clearly seen, though much of this is today disguised by restoration work. (*Collection of Robert Temple*)

Figure 4.13. A postcard circa 1890, showing the Sphinx as it was at that time. (*Collection of Robert Temple*)

Figure 4.14. An old postcard circa 1900, showing the deluge of sand that has swallowed up the northern side of the Sphinx. (*Collection of Robert Temple*)

Figure 4.15. A postcard circa 1910, showing the Sphinx nearly as it was prior to 1817, before it was partially excavated in front by Caviglia. (*Collection of Robert Temple*)

Figure 4.16. An old postcard circa 1910, showing the Sphinx nearly swallowed again by sand. (*Collection of Robert Temple*)

Figure 4.17. In this old stereoview of unknown date, the Sphinx is covered again in sand to the top of the chest. I think this photo may be circa 1870, by which time the sand had all blown back again, and the results of Caviglia's excavations were totally obliterated. (*Collection of Robert Temple*)

Figure 4.18. A postcard of the Sphinx from the late 1930s or 1940s, showing the terrible condition of the left paw at that time. The small stones are of Roman date, and many are about to fall off. Even the Romans were desperate to repair the eroded paw, but they did not do a very good job. (*Collection of Robert Temple*)

What Ludwig Borchardt decided to do, which no one else ever seems to have done, was to undertake a scientific investigation into the details of the particular type of *nemes* headcloth worn by the Sphinx. He also took into account that the face of the Sphinx had eye-paint stripes, indicating a particular fashion that must have a specific date. He thought it might be possible to date these features, and he was right!

Borchardt begins by saying that he intends to approach the question of the dating of the Sphinx "from a different direction than has been done heretofore," and he dismisses the supposed evidence from the so-called Dream Stela between the paws of the Sphinx as being unreliable. By this he is referring to the partial appearance in that stela, erected during the New Kingdom, of what some maintain is the name of the pharaoh Chephren, known in Egyptian as Khafre. In fact, this name, if indeed it really is a name at all, has partially peeled off from the stela, so only a single syllable can be made out. As the word was not set inside a royal cartouche (an elliptical line drawn around every royal name by the Egyptians), it cannot possibly have been the name of the pharaoh Khafre, for not to enclose it in a cartouche would have been extraordinarily disrespectful, and another pharaoh would never have done such a thing. The context is also vague, so nothing can really be concluded from it at all. Borchardt also dismisses attempts to analyze the face itself, saying, "the face is so ruined that . . . one can scarcely infer anything from it."

He then says what his method will be:

In what follows, an attempt shall be made to arrive at a date based on details of dress, since for the present that seems to be the only safe way to date Egyptian sculptures, whereas for the treatment of such questions from the purely stylistic point of view there exists up to now neither sorted material nor sufficient preparatory work. We must for the moment content ourselves in the research which confronts us with settling the question solely as a matter of dress, by setting strictly aside all stylistic observations relating to the treatment of the actual portrait, the musculature and so forth, and thus reducing the question to something visibly obvious and tangible—or I might even say—numerical.

This makes a lot of sense, and one wonders why no one ever attempted it before, or, for that matter, why no one has attempted it since. Borchardt then proceeds to use his first method for dating the Sphinx's head:

The first criterion of this kind with which we shall deal concerns the eye-paint stripes which are found projecting from the outer corners of the eyes of

Figure 4.19. A close-up of the Dream Stela of Thutmosis IV. I took this photo of part of the text of the stela to emphasize the careful way in which all royal names in that text were written in cartouches (see the center of the photo), which is the ellipse in which a king's name was always enclosed. This is a crucial point to make, because a now-flaked-off word of the text began with the syllable *khaf*, and many people have tried to insist that this was a reference to the pharaoh Khafre, better known by the Greek form of his name, Chephren. However, everyone admits that this *khaf* was not enclosed in a cartouche, so it cannot possibly have been a reference to Khafre/Chephren, as it would have been impious and insulting to mention that king without enclosing his name in a cartouche such as that seen here in the intact portion of the text. In fact, King Khafre/Chephren is not mentioned in the text at all, nor is King Cheops. The Dream Stela can only be seen properly if you are standing beneath the head of the Sphinx, where only people with special permission are allowed. Normal tourists can barely see the stela in the distance, much less see any detail of it whatsoever. (*Photo by Robert Temple*)

the Sphinx in entirely flat relief and with traces of blue pigment. Regarding these, we should need to apply the law, recently discovered by Herr [Friedrich Wilhelm, Baron] von Bissing, that eye-paint stripes were unknown in the Old Kingdom. That this is so is shown by the following statistics, which unfortunately only refer to what is in the Cairo Museum, but which could hardly be modified by objects from other collections.

The Cairo Museum possesses in its Old Kingdom halls and storage areas over 230 statues and fragments of statues with heads which date from the Old Kingdom [this was in 1897]; none of these have any eye-paint stripes.

He then points out that eye-paint stripes seem to have made their initial appearance during the Sixth Dynasty, which was the last dynasty of the Old Kingdom (2347–2216 BC):

> We have the first appearance of eye-paint stripes during or after the 6th Dynasty, which was the time when all the radical changes in dress and customs appeared, which separate the Middle Kingdom from more ancient times, so that certainly in terms of the history of art, but perhaps also in the political sense, one can properly speak of the Middle Kingdom having begun with the 6th Dynasty.
>
> What we have ascertained from the statues is shown also by the reliefs. Prior to the 6th Dynasty eye-paint stripes cannot be demonstrated anywhere, but thereafter they make their appearance everywhere.

So Borchardt then concludes on the basis of this criterion: "Now, the Great Sphinx has obvious eye-paint stripes. Therefore the time of its creation falls into the period subsequent to the Sixth Dynasty."

It is at this point that most or, to put it more bluntly, all of Borchardt's readers today would fling down his article in dismay, looking on this strange notion as Borchardt's greatest folly, or perhaps they would just laugh. After all, the idea that the Sphinx dated from some time subsequent to the Sixth Dynasty is just so silly that the man must be off his head. But as I have said earlier, we have to remember that Borchardt had never seen the Sphinx. He had seen only part of its head and the top of its back, and this article was published in 1897, nearly three decades before the Sphinx was properly cleared of sand. What Borchardt was doing was making an intensive study of that portion of the Sphinx that was readily visible, namely the head. And he certainly studied it more carefully than anyone before or since.

But if it were only the eye-paint stripes that Borchardt considered, we could always dismiss it by saying maybe he was wrong about that. Maybe there were earlier eye-paint stripes, but we have just lost the evidence. The really convincing part of Borchardt's analysis concerns something else entirely. He decided to look at the pattern of the stripes portrayed on the *nemes* headcloth. It is easy to overlook this detail, as such decoration seems merely gratuitous. And today it is difficult to see these at all, because you cannot get a high enough angle to see the top of the Sphinx's head directly anymore. Also, the sunlight needs to be right to get some contrast, and the glare of the sky can be a problem. The pattern of the stripes is now very difficult indeed to make out from ground level because we are too far below them to get a good look. But in Borchardt's day, it was easy. And thank goodness we have plenty of photos from that time, which record the stripe patterns unmistakably for us, as figures 1.16, 1.21, 1.22, 4.10, 4.12, and 4.18 make clear. After all, in the old days when one was standing at neck level looking the Sphinx directly in the eye; it was hard to miss the stripe patterns.

In evaluating the analysis of Borchardt, we need to consult figures A, B, C, and D, which are reproduced from his article, and which are reproduced in appendix 2 on pages 510 and 511, along with the complete translation of that article. These show different stripe patterns used on *nemes* cloths. C and D show the patterns that actually appear on the Sphinx.

We need to follow Borchardt's analysis rather closely now, and to do so it is best to use his own words:

> Just as this criterion has given us the lower date limit, so we can find the upper limit in the ornaments of the headdress, the so-called King's Bonnet. This decorated piece of cloth lying over the forehead with the uraeus, which is the symbol of the kings, is tied firmly to the forehead with a headband. It frames the face, creating two triangular areas which fall in two pleats on either side of the face down the neck onto the chest. At the back it is gathered together and ends in a plait lying down the back, which is ribbed as well as appearing to be wrapped. The pattern which this scarf shows is in most cases the following: the front folds are, as shown in A, both in frontal view and also in section, folded into horizontal pleats, the piece covering the head, however, is divided into regular alternately sunken and raised stripes (see figure B), which with statues of which the painting is still showing, is depicted in alternating yellow and blue shades.
>
> This King's Bonnet was of course fashion-dependent, and so we can at least in the statues follow different variations through time. From the 18th Dynasty, or perhaps even a little earlier, it becomes fashionable to supply the inside with a vertical smooth hem. Around the 19th Dynasty it becomes common practice to extend the regular division of the stripes of the upper part of the front pleats to the chest by giving up the pleats, and at the same time they now divided the ribbed plait instead into sunken or raised horizontal stripes as well.
>
> The Great Sphinx of Giza also shows yet another pattern in its headdress.
>
> The stripes of that headdress given as sunken are arranged in groups of three stripes each, that is, one wider stripe is always placed between two narrower stripes. Each of the wider stripes has on either side a small accompanying stripe. And this differs from the usual arrangement with stripes of equal width. And therefore we have to examine where and when this anomaly occurs as well.

The following list which shows those kings' statues with the stripes which are grouped in this manner will show this immediately. We must distinguish between two different forms: those with completed groups (figure C) and those where they are only indicated in simple lines (as in figure D). Both types of course belong to the same type; the second is only an abbreviation to the first.

In a footnote, Borchardt makes clear that "we are always only speaking of the stripes on the upper part and the side part of the cloth. The regular pleating of those cloths falling over the chest are not considered here."

Borchardt then gives lists of statues, heads, and busts that were examined. He found six at the museum then at Giza, all from the Twelfth Dynasty of the Middle Kingdom. His friend Heinrich Schaefer, the famous expert on ancient Egyptian art, reported on five more of the same date in the Berlin Museum. In the Louvre, Schaefer found one more; none was found in the British Museum; but two were found in English private collections. These were the collections searched in person. A further search was made in photo collections of other museums, where no further examples were identified. As a result of this search, fifteen clear examples were found to substantiate Borchardt's thesis, and none was found to contradict

Figure 4.20. A portrait of King Sesostris (Senusret) I (1971–1926 BC), the second pharaoh of the Twelfth Dynasty. His face is very different from that on the Great Sphinx of Giza, and the stripe pattern on his *nemes* headdress does not match it either. The Great Sphinx's face is clearly not his.

it. His conclusions were very clear and specific, and on this basis he suggests that there was probably only one pharaoh whose face could possibly be that of the Sphinx, the great and powerful Middle Kingdom pharaoh Amenemhet III of the Twelfth Dynasty (1818–1770 BC):

> The grouped stripes on the King's Bonnet are only found during the 12th Dynasty, perhaps only under Amenemhet III, because those pieces which are precisely dated and which have such an arrangement of stripes are all from his time. And of the others which are only dated generally to the 12th Dynasty it can never be discounted that they also might be images of Amenemhet III. For this more narrow limitation of this fashion of stripes to the time of Amenemhet III speaks as well as the circumstance that the statues of [Pharaoh] Usertsen [now usually called by his other names, Pharaoh Senwosret III and Sesostris III; he was Amenemhet III's father] from Lisht (Giza, Numbers 411–420, Catalogue 1895, Supplement 3, Number 1365, Hall 21) have not grouped but merely regular stripes. But whether or not one wishes to limit the time of the grouped stripings to the reign of Amenemhet III, one thing is for certain: after the 12th Dynasty, this fashion has vanished. The statues of the 13th Dynasty, Sebekhotep (Louvre, Cast G 1, Catalogue S. 332, Berlin) and Sebek-em-sa-f (Giza, Number 386, Catalogue 1895, Number 128, Hall 16), already display the regularly striped King's Bonnet.
>
> So for the dating of the Sphinx at Giza we draw from all of this the following conclusion: Because the headdress of the Sphinx shows the wide stripes with the narrow accompanying stripes, the Sphinx therefore can surely not have been created after the 12th Dynasty. We have now enclosed the origin of the Sphinx within two limits, an upper and a lower.
>
> According to the makeup stripes it is 6th Dynasty or later. According to the stripes on the headdress, it is before the end of the 12th Dynasty. If one wishes to be less cautious, one can add to this perhaps the time of Amenemhet III.

Borchardt cautiously adds: "Finally, if one really wants to, one could even read the type of Amenemhet III's face into the countenance of the Sphinx. But as I have said already in my introduction, this is a rather questionable argument because of the destruction of the features."

In my opinion, Borchardt's calm, reasoned, and logical approach is an absolute model of disinterested forensic analysis, far removed from any desire to prove or retain a theory for reasons of vanity and egotism. Although we shall see that Amenemhet III is probably not the correct pharaoh, there seems to me no question whatsoever that Borchardt is accurate in insisting upon a Twelfth Dynasty

Figure 4.21. A leonine Middle Kingdom sphinx with the face of King Sesostris (Senusret) III (1878–1839 BC). His face is clearly *not* that on the Great Sphinx of Giza. Because this sphinx was later usurped and reused by a pharaoh of the Fifteenth Dynasty, whose members were foreign invaders from the east known as the Hyksos, this sphinx was for a long time known as a Hyksos sphinx, though we now know that they merely stole it and put a new name on it. (*Collection of Robert Temple*)

face for the Sphinx, and that his analysis of the fashion of the headdress, and so on, was absolutely sound.

One of the aspects of the face of Amenemhet III that is particularly striking is his ears. Stadelmann criticized the suggestion that the face of the Sphinx was that of Chephren because he said the ears didn't match. The ears of Amenemhet III match those of the face of the Sphinx precisely! They are large and prominent and have the same conformation. Amenemhet III was also a very strikingly handsome man, and the general shape of his face matches that of the Sphinx, in a way that

Figure 4.22. A statue of the Middle Kingdom pharaoh Amenemhet III when very young. (*Taken from plate 21 of Adolf Erman,* Die Welt am Nil [The World on the Nile], *Leipzig, 1936*)

of Chephren most emphatically does not. A statue of Amenemhet III is shown in figure 4.22. If you hold this up side by side with a photo of the face of the Sphinx, you can see that the ears are the same. And the same stripe pattern is seen in the *nemes* headcloth, of the fat central stripe surrounded on each side by a thin stripe. If you look at works depicting most other pharaohs in *nemes* headcloths, you will not find this pattern, and they certainly occurred throughout Amenemhet III's reign, which lasted approximately 1853–1805 BC. (Officially he reigned for forty-eight years, but it is thought he really reigned for at least fifty.)

After Borchardt's article was published, did anybody take it seriously? Wallis Budge referred to Borchardt's theory without mentioning Borchardt's name in the volume of his *History of Egypt* published in 1902, which dealt with the Middle Kingdom and Amenemhet. He writes: "A theory has recently been propounded which makes the head of the Sphinx at Gizeh [Giza] to represent that of king Amenemhat [Amenemhet] III, 'by whom it may be supposed to have been erected;' but no evidence in support of it has yet been adduced, nor have the old views concerning the Sphinx yet been proved incorrect."[10]

Since the statement "by whom it may be supposed to have been erected" does not appear in Borchardt's article, we must presume that Wallis Budge did not (or perhaps could not, since he evidently did not know German) actually read Borchardt's article itself, but rather relied on a superficial account of it elsewhere, perhaps in a periodical. It may be that Wallis Budge hesitated to mention Borchardt for this very reason, that he was drawing only on a secondary source and felt so unsure of his grasp of the details of Borchardt's argument that he did not wish to criticize him by name. It is also untrue, as we have seen, that "no evidence in support of it has yet been adduced," for Borchardt's article was in fact one long summary of overwhelming evidence; this proves conclusively that Wallis Budge did not (*could not*, for lack of knowledge of the German language) actually have read it.

In 1910, the eleventh edition of the Encyclopaedia Britannica appeared, and in the entry for "sphinx," Borchardt's article was cited. It was due to the fact that I have this edition of the encyclopedia in my home that I learned of the existence of Borchardt's article in the first place. Actually obtaining a copy of Borchardt's article was very difficult, though the hand of fate was at work, since I managed to purchase an offprint of it from a dealer in rare books in Germany. My facility for finding impossibly rare publications was certainly at work here, in what American slang describes as "big time." Translating Borchardt's article with the aid of my German friend Eleonore Reed was a tremendously difficult task for both of us, due to the extreme precision required in elucidating Borchardt's careful physical description of the kind we have already read. (Borchardt's full text in translation can be found as appendix 2.)

The only other reference to Borchardt's article in English that I have ever seen is in the large volume on the Sphinx by Selim Hassan published in 1953 at Cairo.[11] He translates portions of the article into English, although not always correctly, and he does not agree with Borchardt for obvious reasons, having just personally excavated the Sphinx and cleared it of sand, proving beyond doubt that it was far older than the Middle Kingdom. But what never occurred to Hassan was that Borchardt's analysis of the face might be accurate regarding the face alone. In fact, Hassan didn't think of the face as detachable from the body any more than Borchardt thought of the body as detachable from the face. The problem has always been that people cannot separate the two in their minds. They think of the Sphinx as a unity when it probably is not. The "unity" of the Sphinx probably ended in the Twelfth Dynasty, which is about the time when a very egotistical young pharaoh put his own face on the great monument that lay at the feet of the Giza Plateau. However, there is every reason to believe that the original head and face of the Sphinx was badly damaged by that time and beyond hope of repair, so an alternative was not really a bad idea. And let's face it (pun intended): the face of the Sphinx is sufficiently striking that we shouldn't complain. It inspires awe in all who see it, just as the pharaoh who put his face on it presumably hoped it would. Perhaps the extraordinary wide-open eyes are meant to indicate the eager gaze with which the reverent pharaoh peers at the eastern horizon, hoping to catch a glimpse of the sun god, who will rise at any moment. Normally Egyptian statues do not show the eyes opened so wide as this, for portraits tend to show kings in repose. But the face of the Sphinx is not in a state of repose; it is in a state of expectancy, as is appropriate under the circumstances of someone watching for the sunrise.

Who was this Amenemhet III, whose face Borchardt claimed may have been looking down on the rest of us for all these ages? He was a pharaoh particularly noted for immense building projects, for vast irrigation works, and also for an obsession with sphinxes! He lived in a peaceful era, didn't waste time making war on neighbors, and was one of the greatest builders in the entire history of Egypt. He built the famous Labyrinth at Hawara, which is now almost entirely destroyed (see figure 4.25). A few comments about Amenemhet from Wallis Budge's *History of Egypt* gives a good idea of the man. In the histories written by Sir William Flinders Petrie and Erik Hornung, little is said of Amenemhet, so it is necessary to quote from Wallis Budge, who gives him his due credit:

> Amenemhat [his spelling of Amenemhet] III, the son and successor of Usertsen III [now called Senusret III or Sesostris III], was the greatest of all the kings of the XIIth Dynasty. . . . The whole of the energies of this king appear to have been devoted to improving the irrigation system of his country. . . . Amenemhat III found Egypt in a state of great prosperity when he ascended the throne, and as the land had rest [was at peace] during his long reign, he was able to leave his country in a most flourishing condition at his death. Art, sculpture, and architecture flourished under his fostering care, and the remains of his buildings and inscribed monuments testify to the activity which must have prevailed among all classes of handicraftsmen during his reign. . . . The king's activity in building continued throughout the whole of his reign. . . . At [his] time the river level during the inundation was about twenty-six feet higher than it is at the present time [in 1902]. . . . [He] seems to have endeavoured [by annual measurements, which are recorded] to understand the effects upon the agriculture of Egypt caused by inundations of varying heights. . . . The greatest and most useful of all the great works which were undertaken by Amenemhat was the making of Lake Moeris in . . . [the] Fayyum. [The Fayyum is a giant oasis region southwest of Cairo, which has always been heavily populated and agriculturally productive.]. . . The largest circumference of Lake Moeris was about 150 miles; its area was about 750 square miles.[12]

The most amazing building feat of Amenemhet III was the Labyrinth at Hawara in the Fayyum. It seems almost unbelievable that all but a few pieces of stone have now vanished. Wallis Budge says sadly:

> The extent of the area of the Labyrinth is probably marked by the immense bed of chips of fine white limestone which lies to the south of [his] pyramid, and on tracing this bed to its limits, it is found that they cover an area which measures 1000 by 800 feet. The principal part of the pavement to be seen is in the eastern half of the site, and some years ago it covered a tolerable space; but the builders of the railway into the Fayyum discovered the place, and took the stones away to build the line; thus the last remains of the wonderful building disappeared under the process of "civilizing" Egypt.[13]

Figure 4.23 is one of my photos of Amenemhet III's mud-brick pyramid at Hawara, and figures 4.24 and 4.25 are the ones that I took from the top of the pyramid showing part of the remains of the site of the Labyrinth. To appreciate the magnitude of Amenemhet's building operations, one has to read the account of the Labyrinth left by Herodotus, the Greek historian of the fifth century BC, who visited it:

> I have seen this building, and it is beyond my power to describe; it must have cost more in labour and money than all the walls and public works of the Greeks put together. . . . The pyramids, too, are astonishing structures, each one of them equal to many of the most ambitious works of Greece; but the labyrinth surpasses them. . . . The baffling and intricate passages from room to room and from court to court were an endless wonder to me, as we passed from a courtyard into rooms, from rooms into galleries, from galleries into more rooms, and thence into yet more courtyards. The roof of every chamber, courtyard, and gallery is, like the walls, of stone. The walls are covered with carved figures, and each court is exquisitely built of white marble [limestone] and surrounded by a colonnade.[14]

It is extremely irritating to think that the pavement of this monumental construction was stripped away by railway engineers at the end of the nineteenth century and used for something so mundane as laying the bed of a railway track. In fact, this is one reminder that a great deal of the destruction of ancient Egyptian monuments has taken place more recently than we feel comfortable in admitting. Another example of this is the total demolition during the nineteenth century of a beautiful temple on the island of Elephantine. This all goes to prove that oafs are everywhere and active at all times.

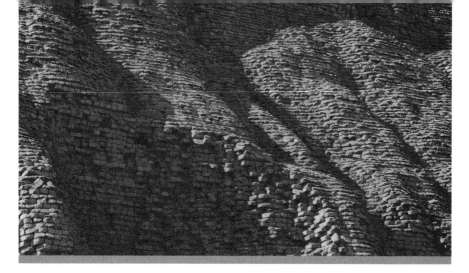

Figure 4.23. This is the strange condition of Amenemhet III's Pyramid at Hawara in the Fayyum today. Unable to build pyramids in stone anymore, the pharaohs of the Middle Kingdom had to use mud bricks instead. Over the millennia, the erosion caused by rainstorms, sun, and wind have turned the once regular pyramid into this wonderful surrealistic work of art, a symphony of light and shade of a kind that the pharaoh never intended. No wonder that Amenemhet II sought to immortalize himself in stone in the only way he could, by carving his face on an older monument, the Sphinx! (*Photo by Robert Temple*)

Figure 4.24. The pathetic remains of the Labyrinth at Hawara in the Fayyum, which was once one of the Wonders of the World, as described by Herodotus. Now, the pockmarks in the sand and a few blocks of stone are all that is left. Even in the nineteenth century, huge portions of the Labyrinth were stripped away and the stone used as sleepers for the Fayyum Railway. If the railway were ever replaced and its stones salvaged, a considerable portion of an ancient monument could be recovered! This photo is taken from above, standing on the remains of the mud-brick Pyramid of Amenemhet, which itself is in no great shape. (*Photo by Robert Temple*)

Figure 4.25. The remains of the Labyrinth at Hawara, seen from the side of the mud-brick Pyramid of Amenemhet III. (*Photo by Robert Temple*)

So if Borchardt were right, we would have the comfort of knowing that the face on the Sphinx is evidently that of one of the greatest pharaohs in the history of Egypt, not just that of a nobody. And the enigmatic expression on the face, made more so by having lost its nose and by its other damage, does bear comparison with the flickering half-smile of Leonardo da Vinci's "Mona Lisa." And like the face of the Mona Lisa, its gender has been questioned. Serious suggestions have been made that the Mona Lisa is really a man dressed as a woman. And for centuries, the Sphinx's face was thought to be that of a woman, as countless early travelers relate. A touch of androgyny always makes a face more intriguing.

One other crucial fact about Amenemhet III is that he was obsessed with sphinxes, and that is certainly appropriate for someone who Borchardt suggests put his own face on the greatest sphinx of them all. There are several surviving small sphinxes that bear the face of Amenemhet III. These are well known to Egyptologists, and it is therefore puzzling that they don't seem to have put two and two together. When some of these sphinxes were originally discovered at the site of the city of Tanis, they were at first thought to date from a later period known as the Hyksos period. But eventually Egyptologists figured out that these statues had been "usurped" by the later Hyksos kings. The process known as "usurpation" was very common in Egyptian history. Lazy builders and sculptors simply plundered previous buildings and works of art and relabeled them. In fact, whole temples could be cannibalized in this way, and often were. One bust of Amenemhet III was usurped by the New Kingdom pharaoh Merenptah, and the lazy sculptor of the later period had the audacity to chip away part of the face to make it look more like Merenptah! As Wallis Budge says, ". . . certain features, e.g., the muscles at the corners of the mouth, were altered by hammering in order to make them to resemble those of the usurper."[15] As for the sphinxes found at Tanis, "We probably see good representations on those of the maker of Lake Moeris and of one of the greatest kings who sat upon the throne of Egypt."[16]

As for his character, perhaps Amenemhet III was a madman and a megalomaniac, and perhaps he was not. It was singularly immodest of anyone to stick his face on the largest sculpture of Egypt, and whoever did it cannot have been without a considerable ego. But so it has always been in the affairs of our species, and so it will doubtless always be: the pushy ones think they are Ra's gift to humankind.

However, it is now possible to narrow down the search for the Sphinx's face even further. Yes, Borchardt was right about the dynasty. But no, he was not right about the actual pharaoh! It was not Amenemhet III after all, but one of his predecessors in the same dynasty, and this fact must have generated Amenemhet III's own obsession with sphinxes. The final piece of the jigsaw has been inadvertently supplied by an Egyptologist named Biri Fay. Dr. Fay published in 1996 a large and impressive book, full of wonderful photographs, entitled *The Louvre Sphinx and Royal Sculpture from the Reign of Amenemhat II*.[17] In this book, which is a truly amazing work of detailed analysis of a large sphinx in the Louvre in Paris (see figures 4.26 and 4.27), Fay discusses the fact that this sphinx bears the face of an earlier Amenemhet, not the one considered by Borchardt. The pharaoh she has in mind is Amenemhet II (reigned 1876–1842 BC), the third king of the Twelfth Dynasty, who reigned for thirty-four years, and who was the great-grandfather of Amenemhet III, who was its sixth king. Amenemhet II shifted his interest back toward the area of Giza, though most of his dynasty showed little interest in the region, preferring the region of the Fayyum farther south, where his father's and grandfather's pyramids were built. He built his own mud-brick pyramid at Dashur, which is not far from Giza. (The art of building pyramids in stone had been lost by this time.) And as we shall see, he seems to have undertaken something at Giza itself that was far more important.

Figure 4.26. A view of the face of Amenemhet II on Sphinx A23 taken at an angle. (*The Louvre, Paris*)

Figure 4.27. The Sphinx A23 as King Amenemhet II, in the Louvre. His name appears in a cartouche on his chest. Note that the patterns of the stripes on his *nemes* headdress are identical to those of the Great Sphinx of Giza and as shown in the drawings in appendix 2, pages 510 and 511. This pattern was used only during the Twelfth Dynasty. (*The Louvre, Paris*)

Amenemhet II seems to have been a restless fellow. He led an expedition to Nubia in search of gold when he was young. During most of his reign, there was a major emphasis on foreign relations, and he strengthened Egypt's presence and reputation in the area now known as Lebanon, particularly at the city of Byblos, which was a traditional Egyptian center. Certainly, Amenemhet II was someone who looked outward and was not content to concern himself with only internal affairs. A considerable number of administrative documents survive from his reign, and also detailed annals of a portion of his reign were discovered carved into some reused stone blocks, one of which was only discovered in 1974. As the Egyptologist Jaromir Malek said: "The text appears to have been transferred to a temple wall from a 'day-book' written on papyri, and is the most detailed example of Egyptian annals (*genut*) known. . . . It will take a while to translate and understand it."[18] That was in 1992, and we are still waiting for the translation and understanding to be published. However, the annals clearly show Amenemhet to have been preoccupied with visiting religious sites and cult centers and demonstrate that he had a fascination with ancient monuments. He described himself as "beloved of Atum" and "given life like Ra eternally." Both descriptions have a potential connection with concepts related to the Sphinx, which was often viewed as having a connection with the creator god Atum, as has already been mentioned and is discussed further later on in this book, and which faced the rising sun of Ra eternally.

As part of her study of the stone sphinx statue in the Louvre, which bears the face of Amenemhet II, Fay does not mention, and shows no knowledge of, Ludwig Borchardt's article that we have just been considering, and which in translation forms appendix 2 of this book. She mentions other books by Borchardt, but it appears that she genuinely did not know that Borchardt had ever written a study of the Great Sphinx. If she had known of it, she might have drawn some rather different conclusions on certain matters. But fortunately *we* know it, so all is well.

The first thing that is evident from Biri Fay's book is that the triple-stripe design found on the *nemes* headdress of the Great Sphinx, which Borchardt had thought was used only at the time of Amenemhet III, was also used by, and apparently even introduced by, Amenemhet II (see figure 4.27). In fact, it prominently appears on the Louvre Sphinx, which is definitely known to bear the face of Amenemhet II. And furthermore, the eye-paint stripes are also there (see figure 4.28). These facts had been unknown to Borchardt.

So it is clear to us (but not to Biri Fay, who did not know of them) that all the arguments Borchardt so carefully marshaled in favor of Amenemhet III also apply to Amenemhet II. However, not for one instant does Biri Fay suspect that

Figure 4.28. A close-up photo of the left eye and eyebrow of the face of Amenemhet II on the Sphinx A23, showing the eye paint and the *nemes* stripes discussed by Ludwig Borchardt in appendix 2. (*The Louvre, Paris*)

Amenemhet II's face might be the face that appears on the Great Sphinx. That is because she believes the conventional opinions and does not even think to challenge them. She accepts what is "known."

Biri Fay not only made a direct comparison between the face of the Louvre Sphinx and the Great Sphinx, *she even published photos of the two faces opposite one another in her book,* stressing their similarities! You might wonder how anyone who went this far could possibly not "see" the point! And yet she did not. Here is what, astonishingly, she actually says:

> Although a stylistic comparison of the Giza and Louvre sphinxes must be restricted to their heads, similarities are profound. Both [kings'] faces are broad and full, and slope downward over the cheekbones (Plates 68 and 69) [her plates mentioned a moment ago]. Each nemes is wide across the wings, set low on the forehead over the brows, and shallow at the crown. On both sculptures, temple folds are rounded as they near the forehead. . . . The pleating pattern found on the nemes of the Louvre sphinx—a fine triple-stripe executed in rounded, raised relief, with a wide stripe and a narrow stripe to each side—is

rare in the Old Kingdom [or absent!], but the treatment is similar on the Giza Sphinx (Plates 68a, 69a). In both cases, the stripes on the wings of the nemes fan upward behind the ears. A broad uraeus hood, with a wide ventral column, appears on both sphinxes (Plates 68–69). . . . The eyes of both sphinxes are strikingly similar. Not only are they large in proportion to the face, but their shapes, with horizontal lower-eye rims and semi-circular upper rims, are closely related. Correspondence between the two works in the eye region extends to the shape and proportion of the wide brows, and broad cosmetic lines (Plates 68–69). Furthermore, in each case, the brows dip slightly at the root of the nose and extend horizontally over the eyes.

Among the most distinctive Louvre sphinx features is the broad mouth; the lips do not meet at the corners, but are instead embraced by a semi-circular muscle at each side. Despite damage suffered by the Giza Sphinx, its width is obvious, and close examination also reveals the muscled treatment of the corners. . . . Comparison of three-quarter views further reinforces the resemblance of the Giza and Louvre sphinxes. . . . The fullness of the face across the cheeks and the slope beneath the eyes above the cheeks is analogous. As in frontal views, the eyes of both sphinxes are closely comparable, with horizontal lower eye rims and upper rims arched to a semi-circle. Furthermore, cosmetic lines embrace the sharp outer canthi [canthus is an anatomical term meaning the angle formed by the meeting of the upper and lower eyelids at either side of the eye], extend horizontally, and flare at the ends similarly on both sphinxes. Even though the ears of Louvre A23 are more damaged than those of the Giza Sphinx, it can be seen that the narrow helix and the antihelix [the helix is the outer rim of the ear and the antihelix is the curved elevation of the cartilage of the ear] branches compare well on both sculptures. Key similarities between the two works raise the question of whether Amenemhat II's sculptors also may have copied the maned shoulder style from the Giza Sphinx.

Plate 69c gives final demonstration of Amenemhat II's dependence on the Giza Sphinx for his own image. Images of both sphinxes laid over one another reveal that the sculptures are almost identical. . . . Amenemhat II used the Giza Sphinx as a model for his own sphinx.[19]

Yes, reader, your optic nerve is not faulty, nor has your retina become detached. No, you have not lost your senses either. What you think you read is actually what you read. Yes, you have just read a meticulous comparison of the identical faces of the Sphinx of Amenemhet II in the Louvre and the Great Sphinx of Giza by an expert analyst: she has gone to great lengths to prove that the two faces are identical, *and yet she does not "see" what this means!*

Figure 4.29. The face of the Sphinx of Giza, as reproduced in Biri Fay's book *The Louvre Sphinx and Royal Sculpture from the Reign of Amenemhat II,* Mainz, 1996, as plate 68a. The photo credit reads "After Uni-Dia Verlag 10049."

Figure 4.30. Amenemhet II's face on Sphinx A23, as seen from below eye level. This approximates more nearly the view of the face of the Sphinx of Giza as we see it today, from below looking up. (*The Louvre, Paris*)

Figure 4.31. Amenemhet II's face on Sphinx A23, seen head-on at eye level, the view that we have not had of the Great Sphinx of Giza since 1936, when it was fully excavated and we could no longer stand at that height. (*The Louvre, Paris*)

Figure 4.32. The face of Amenemhet II can be seen like this nowadays only from inside the Sphinx Temple. In front is the western wall of the Sphinx Temple. (*Photo by Robert Temple*)

Imagine me telling you that I had gone to Buckingham Palace and seen a woman who looked like Queen Elizabeth. I describe to you very carefully how her hair is exactly the same, she speaks like her, has the same expressions, has a lot of little corgi dogs standing round her ankles, has the same regal air, and could be her twin, she is so similar. I then go on to say to you very earnestly, apparently clueless as to any other possibility, that this woman has clearly modeled herself on the queen and made every attempt to resemble her and imitate her, and has even gone so far as to do so in the queen's own palace, and has borrowed the queen's own dogs to make her act of impersonation more convincing. What would you conclude about me?

There are some paranoid schizophrenics who see connections between everything. They think that if a bus passes them on a street corner, it is a "sign." They think that people who have no connection whatsoever resemble one another. But I would postulate an opposite condition: there are some people who are so wholly in the grip of secondhand thinking that all their perceptual abilities, the evidence of their own eyes and ears, are powerless to alert them to anything that challenges conventional reality. Yes, there are actually people in existence who can describe point for point the precise resemblance of the faces of two sphinxes but do not even notice that this means that they *are* the same.

Biri Fay, having proved the identity between the faces of the two sphinxes, then goes on to insist that *Amenemhet II had a face carved for himself on his sphinx statue in the Louvre that would resemble precisely that which was on the Great Sphinx of Giza.*

Sedatives, anyone?

So now we have the answer to whose face is on the Great Sphinx. The face is that of the pharaoh Amenemhet II of the Twelfth Dynasty, who reigned from 1876 to 1842 BC. (And by the way, his ears were the same as his great-grandfather's.)

Now let us consider what the Sphinx was before it became a monument to one pharaoh's vanity. In the next chapter there is a completely different interpretation of the nature and purpose of the monument from any that has ever been advanced (except by myself in a brief preliminary account in 1998).[20]

5
THE SPHINX AS ANUBIS

The first time I went to Egypt and saw the Sphinx with my own eyes, I was deeply shocked. Photos of the Sphinx are misleading in several respects. We have already seen in the previous chapter how hard it is from a photo to get a true impression of the proportion of the head to the body. And when I first saw the Sphinx, the ridiculously tiny head on the huge body was naturally one of the things that most shocked me. But what struck me even more was that the Sphinx did not look at all like a lion. I had always been told the Sphinx had the body of a lion with the head of a man, and I accepted that account as being true, as everyone does, since who are we mere mortals to challenge such a fundamental "truth" that "everybody knows"? It had not even occurred to me that there could be anything wrong with this "truth." But now that I stood there staring at the Sphinx with my own eyes, I failed to see a lion anywhere. No matter how hard I looked, I could not see a lion.

I rubbed my eyes, I examined my conscience, I craned my neck, I stared and stared, thinking that the obvious would soon become apparent to me if I just looked harder. Surely there was a lion there somewhere, as "everyone knows" that there is a lion there. We have all been told that there is a lion there since we were children. There is no one who does not see a lion there. We all know that. *But there was no lion.*

Olivia looked and looked, and there was no lion for her either. But she is rather more cautious than I am, and she wondered if perhaps we lacked some faculty that other people have, an *ability to see lions.* Were we somehow lion-dyslexic? Was this a failing of our own? Had we not consulted properly? Was this somehow our fault? But she has a good eye and notices shapes and forms and recognizes sil-

196

houettes, and her reaction was that this shape was not that of a lion. She thought it looked more like a crouching greyhound.

This was one of those disillusioning moments in life, like realizing that there is no Santa Claus, when all your hopes and dreams are stripped away from you and you are forced to face a hostile reality. There we stood, sadly looking at the Sphinx that "everybody knows" is a lion, and we could see plainly that it was no such thing. We felt very lonely, and I knew that when I eventually came to write about it, I was going to have another one of those tedious and hard battles that I am always having when I try to point out that the emperor has no clothes. Because nobody wants to hear, and everybody tells you to shut up and calls you a trouble-maker. And although I don't care whether I am called names, and just laugh, it does get a bit wearing sometimes, like being in a ferocious gale, so that you are always pulling your scarf tighter to keep out the wind.

Well, there we were, stuck with the reality that wouldn't go away: The Sphinx was *something,* but it certainly wasn't a lion.

So what was it? It had four legs and it was lying on its belly, in a position that is generally called recumbent, or to use a term from heraldry (whose terminology as used in English derives from Norman French after the conquest of England by William the Conqueror, who came from Normandy), *couchant.* In discussing the iconography of the Egyptian gods portrayed as animals, it is common for Egyptologists to refer to a standing animal as "an animal *passant*" and a recumbent animal as "an animal *couchant.*" People who are not familiar with these heraldic words need to have that explained to them. What kind of recumbent beast was the Great Sphinx *couchant,* then? One can't tell much from the paws, because they had been so mangled by restoration work (much of it apparently in Roman times) and covered all over in small stone blocks that they could give no reliable clue as to what type of creature this might be. None of the original carved portion of the paws is any longer visible, so what they looked like originally can be determined only by inference or by guessing.

The thing that struck us as most obvious and most peculiar was that the back of the Sphinx was entirely straight, that is, its spine was absolutely flat. It did not rise anywhere, whether in the rear or in the front. It was *flat.* (This is clearly shown in figures 1.11, 1.33, 1.34, 1.38, 1.39, 2.16, 2.18, 2.19, 2.26, 3.10, 3.15, 4.1, and 5.11.) All Egyptian statues and pictures of lions show the back rising sharply in front, to indicate the massive chest of a lion, and generally a mane is also clearly shown, as well as muscular haunches. See figures 5.1, 5.2, 5.3, 5.4, 5.5, and 5.6 for examples. But the Sphinx has no massive lion's chest, no rising line of the back to a higher neck, no bulging muscles, and certainly no trace of a mane. Figure 5.5 shows what a real crouching lion looks like, and it is clear to anyone that it has no similarity whatsoever to the Sphinx.

Figure 5.1. The design carved into an ebony tablet, which was found in the tomb of the First Dynasty king Den, who is seen seated on a throne within a shrine at the top center of the picture. At top right, the same king is seen running as part of the Sed Festival for renewing the magical power of his kingship, where he had to prove his vitality and virility by running back and forth within a sacred enclosure during the festival, carrying his royal insigniae and wearing the royal crowns and a ceremonial kilt. Behind the seated king, a Horus falcon stands on a rect-angle called a *serekh,* the upper part of which contains the name of the king, Den, shown by two hieroglyphs (the wavy line is the hieroglyph for the consonant *n*). This is from plate XV of Flinders Petrie's *The Royal Tombs of the First Dynasty,* Part 1, 1900. King Den's tomb contained "a great number of tablets of ivory and ebony . . . twenty tablets are known from this tomb" (Petrie, p. 11). The recumbent lion, whose forepart is depicted at lower left, could not be fur-ther from the conception of the Sphinx of Giza. The lion was always conventionally portrayed, throughout the whole of Egyptian history, as having a massive chest and mane.

Figure 5.2. Detail of the lion seen in figure 5.1.

Figure 5.3. Here are seven examples of how lions were actually depicted by the ancient Egyptians prior to the carving of the Great Sphinx of Giza. These are small ivory carvings of lions that are thought to have been used as gaming pieces. They all date from the First Dynasty, the date of which is generally given as approximately 3050–2850 BC. All Egyptologists believe this to be well before the date of the carving of the Great Sphinx, which is generally attributed to the Fourth Dynasty (thought to have been approximately 2640–2510 BC). In other words, these lions are all at least two hundred years older than the Great Sphinx, if conventionally accepted dates are correct, and some may be four hundred years older. These lions, and others like them that have been recovered from royal graves, are known to have been carved over a span of several centuries. They prove that there was a well-established tradition in Egypt of how lions were to be represented in art. These lions are all zoologically accurate, as Egyptian art always was. Lions have massive chests, their backs rise steadily from their rumps into a thick, maned neck. We all know what lions look like, and so did the Egyptians of the First Dynasty. These ivory figurines prove that anyone who tries to maintain that the Great Sphinx is intended to represent a lion because the earliest Egyptians were naive in their art and showed them like that is wrong. These lions were all excavated beside an early temple at Abydos by Sir William Flinders Petrie in 1902/1903, and published in plate 3 of volume 2 of his book *Abydos, 24th Memoir of the Egypt Exploration Fund*, London, 1903.

Figure 5.4. This is a detail of a carving at the Temple of Amun at Karnak. It shows the traditional form in which a lion's head and forelegs were represented in Egypt, with massive mane, wholly unlike the Sphinx of Giza. (*Photo by Robert Temple*)

Figure 5.5. This limestone votive figure of a lion was excavated between the forelegs of the Sphinx in the Sphinx chapel by Selim Hassan in 1936. It is plate XXIIa (following p. 50; the discovery is described on p. 33) in *The Great Sphinx*, figure 4 (opposite p. 36) in *Sphinx*, and figure 4 (following p. 24) in *Le Sphinx*. This depiction of a lion is so dissimilar to the Giza Sphinx that it shows strikingly how nonleonine the Sphinx's body is according to Egyptian artistic traditions.

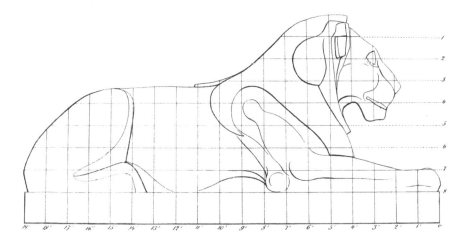

Figure 5.6. This ancient Egyptian drawing of a lion with its accompanying measurements marked off by the artist gives conclusive evidence that lions had a canonic mode of portrayal in Egyptian art, with a sharply rising neck, utterly unlike the shape of the body of the Sphinx, which cannot therefore have been intended to represent a lion. Lion bodies were also squat in contrast to elongated dog and jackal bodies like that of the Sphinx. The drawing also shows how conscious the Egyptians were of correct proportion in representations of animals, and on this basis alone, it is inconceivable that the tiny pimple of a head on the vast body of the Sphinx of Giza could possibly be original. (*Reproduced from Richard Lepsius,* Der wichtingsten Urkunden des Aegyptischen Alterthums, *Leipzig, 1842, Plates (Atlas) Volume.*)

Figure 5.7. The goddess Sekhmet (She of Power), with a solar disk on her head. This statue, covered in sheets of beaten gold, is of New Kingdom date. It is on display in the Egyptian Museum at Cairo. Sekhmet embodied various attributes. On the one hand, she presided over healers and protected women. On the other hand, she could be intensely destructive, especially to the wicked. She embodied the essence of the fiery midday sun, the destructive power of solar rays, and the hot breath of the burning desert, and she acted as a burning Eye of Ra to destroy those who mocked the sun god. It was necessary to keep on the right side of her, for her destructive powers were awesome. She loved Cosmic Order and detested evil and was known as the Lady of Terror, feared by the wicked. She was the special protectress of the pharaoh in battle and was sometimes viewed as his nurse or even as his mother. The pronounced leonine characteristics of the head and neck of Sekhmet are far from what we see on the Sphinx. This statue may have represented a priestess of Sekhmet wearing a Sekhmet head, or it may represent the goddess herself. (*Photo by Robert Temple*)

So why do people call this statue a lion? It has no leonine characteristics at all.

The Sphinx was thought of as having the body of a lion for a very long time indeed, and it was the Egyptians themselves who started this misconception. When the Sphinx was cleared of sand during the New Kingdom by the pharaoh Thutmosis IV, circa 1400 BC, the Egyptians of that time thought they saw a lion. So from then on, it was assumed by many people that the Sphinx was a creature with the body of a lion and the head of man, much as people assume today. This fallacy is thus not a modern one. It has been believed for 3,400 years. But just because something is believed for 3,400 years does not mean that it is correct. For many thousands of years it was believed the sun went around the Earth, and that was not true either.

Many people have commented on the strange fact that there is no mention of the Sphinx in very early times in Egypt. To give a recent example, Mark Lehner has said in *The Complete Pyramids,* "There are no known Old Kingdom texts that refer either to the Sphinx or its temple."[1] But I would say that the reason for this is that people have been looking for the wrong things. Texts referring to a lion with a man's head will not be found, because that is not what the Sphinx was.

This opens up all kinds of possibilities. If the Sphinx was not really a lion with a man's head at all, then of course there would be no Old Kingdom references to such a thing. We have already seen that the man's head was probably a recarving during the Middle Kingdom. So in the Old Kingdom, what we have to do is look for references to *something else* that might be the Sphinx, and which is neither a lion nor an animal statue with a man's head.

We will see that there are numerous references to *something else,* which was a gigantic creature that is sometimes specifically said to be at Giza. But it was not a lion, and it did not have the head of Amenemhet II, who was not born yet!

But before we turn to ancient Egyptian texts, we need to consider what the Sphinx actually is, or should I say *was,* before it had its head recarved. In the previous chapter I said that I believe the Sphinx once had an animal head. But clearly I do not believe it had a lion's head, since I do not believe it was ever meant to represent a lion. Whatever the head was, it needed to be in the correct proportion to the body. So we come to the question: What beast could this be, lying on its belly, guardian of the necropolis of Giza?

The usual guardian of the necropolis in Egyptian tradition was the god Anubis, and he was represented as a dog, or jackal, or jackal/dog. (See figures 5.18 and 5.9.) Anubis is the Greek name of the god called in Egyptian Anpu, but since everyone uses the form Anubis, we shall call him Anubis. In fact, there is no real agreement as to what precise creature Anubis is. Some think that there was a wild dog in those days that looked like this, or the creature may have been a cross between a jackal and a dog. In the thousands of years that have elapsed, it may well be that this precise breed has disappeared. There is a surviving dog today called the pharaoh hound that is close to Anubis in appearance, and the pharaoh hound was long presumed to be descended from those ancient dogs representing Anubis. People who have pharaoh hounds are very enthusiastic about them; there are even pharaoh hound clubs and newsletters and so forth. Anyone curious about them only needs to enter "pharaoh hound" into an Internet search engine. However, in 2004, a study of dog genetics suggested that pharaoh hounds are not related to ancient Egyptian dogs.[2]

The Egyptologist Alberto Bianchi has actually published an article claiming that Anubis was a wild dog, and he says, "The image of the sitting dog as Anubis

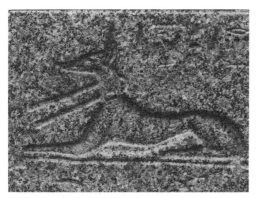

Figure 5.8. A depiction of a crouching (*couchant*) Anubis carved in granite, in a block surviving among the ruins of Memphis. It dates from the period of the New Kingdom and shows Anubis in his characteristic pose. (*Photo by Robert Temple*)

Figure 5.9. This photo of a crouching Anubis resembles what the Sphinx of Giza originally was, although the Sphinx of Giza has a straighter back. However, as an idea of what the Sphinx of Giza originally looked like prior to 2000 BC, this gives a very good impression. This is a wall carving at the Temple of Seti I at Abydos, and therefore dates from the New Kingdom, at least a thousand years later than the time of the carving of the Sphinx of Giza. (*Photo by Robert Temple*)

protects the deceased."[3] He says the position is a natural posture for the wild dog: "As is common with dogs, they adopt when they are resting a characteristic position consisting in projecting their four legs forward, parallel to one another, keeping at the same time an attitude of watchful attention. Surely, the observation of this peculiarity on many occasions, mainly by the people working in the cemeteries, resulted in its being given a transcendent meaning, linking it to the protection of the dead and the burials."[4] Certainly this is the precise position of the Sphinx, which thus conforms exactly with the natural position of the Egyptian wild dog as a guardian.

Bianchi further tells us (I have omitted his many references):

> The jackal is usually considered by some authors as the Anubis canis, but this assumption must be discarded now because of its inconsistency. L. Keimer emphatically denies the existence of the jackal in Egypt. . . . E. Meyer wrote that the Anubis animal was a dog. . . . The Greeks did not know about the existence of the jackal. . . . E. Meyer took from inside a statue of Anubis found in the XVII nome [a geographical district] of Upper Egypt the mummy of a dog. . . . A. Gardiner in his Egyptian Grammar questioned the interpretation of the sitting dog as a jackal in E17. . . . In fact, zoology has established differences in size and skull shape between the archetypal dog and the jackal which can be appreciated with a simple eye inspection.[5]

So we see that many experts have suspected that Anubis was not a jackal at all, but a wild dog. In the discussions that follow, including various quotations from authors, we should keep this in mind, and mentally correct the word *jackal* to *wild dog* when we are considering Anubis.

As I looked at the Sphinx that first time, noting the straight back of the creature and the complete absence of leonine features or characteristics of any kind, I was struck by the fact that I appeared to be staring at a dog. It looked like a dog to me, and it looked like a dog to Olivia. Perhaps this is because we are dog-lovers. However, if we had been cat-lovers, we would have thought no differently. There it sits, crouching on its belly, and it is a dog. And what is more, Anubis was frequently represented in precisely that posture throughout the thousands of years of Egyptian art. Anubis recumbent, or Anubis *couchant,* is one of the most famous of all ancient Egyptian art motifs. A magnificent small statue of the recumbent Anubis was recovered from the tomb of Tutankhamun.

In the countless images of the recumbent Anubis, he lies in precisely the manner of the Sphinx. Anubis always has a long tail, and the Sphinx has one. But because the jackal/dog was a slender creature, he is normally shown with a hollow beneath the lower part of his belly, where his slim form curves upward. However,

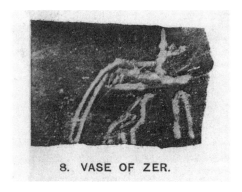

Figure 5.10. This detail of an incised carving in a stone vase found in the tomb of King Zer (Djer) of the First Dynasty shows a recumbent Anubis and demonstrates how unlike a lion the crouching dog was from the earliest depictions in Egyptian art. The straight back resembles the Sphinx.

in the case of the Sphinx, which was carved out of the solid rock, a portrayal of this feature would not have been possible without boring a large hole beneath the haunches and seriously weakening the statue. On the other hand, it is possible that the fissure at the haunches where the shaft had been bored and that is now filled with cement may have shown some sort of Anubis-like indentation, which contributed to the weakening of the stone at that point. If you look at the photo of the Sphinx in figure 1.31, taken before Baraize filled the fissure with modern cement, you can see that the body does seem to narrow somewhat at that point. But it is now difficult to be certain of such a feature, with so much "restoration" having taken place. The colored plotting of repair blocks published by Mark Lehner indicates that the area is now completely covered with repair blocks, with none of the original stone showing, and that many of these date from the 1960s–1970s.[6] Since no one ever seems to have suspected that the Sphinx was Anubis before, it is evident that no one ever gave any thought as to whether any hollowing of the sides existed here originally. But if you look at the plan of the Sphinx from the air, you can see that the body clearly narrows at the haunches on both sides in the manner of Anubis. (See appendix 5.)

Because the Sphinx has definite canine features and no leonine features, the burden of proof is shifted to those who wish to maintain that it is a lion to establish their case. Otherwise we must presume it is a dog. But since there is nothing anyone can bring forward in favor of the Sphinx being a lion but hearsay (i.e., "consensus reality") and the late tradition from New Kingdom times of 1400 BC, when nothing was remembered about the true nature of the Sphinx in Egypt, the case for the Sphinx being a lion is lost. That this has not been recognized for 3,400 years is logically irrelevant: the principles of logic, Occam's razor, and common sense all dovetail in favor of the Sphinx being a dog. The fact is that 3,400 years of "the opinion of the herd" is of no more consequence than a flyspeck when it comes to the determination of the truth. Human beings are notoriously unobservant and

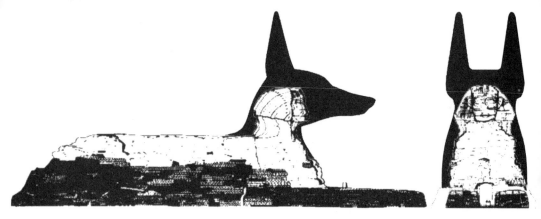

Figure 5.11. At left we see a redrawing of the shape of the Sphinx as it would have appeared in the Old Kingdom, when it was a crouching Anubis. The exact profile and proportions of the Sphinx have been incorporated into the drawing, and the head of Anubis has been added in correct proportion to it. The recarved head of the Sphinx with a pharaoh's face fits within the neck of what I believe to have been the original whole statue. At right is another redrawing of the shape of the Sphinx, this time in full-face view, and once again, the recarved head of the Sphinx with a pharaoh's face fits within the neck of the original statue. (*Drawings by Daud Sutton*)

poor at using their brains, and they tend to allow their thinking to be done for them—second-hand thinking, such as that which is provided for them by numerous churches, religions, political parties, sects, and cults. Humans think in packs, just as wolves run in packs. A human often likes to plug his or her hard disk ("brain") into a network and have all the thinking done remotely. It so much easier.

We have already seen in figures 3.15 and 4.1 the disproportion of the Sphinx's head to its body. Now, in figure 5.11, we see the same side view of the Sphinx with a head of Anubis drawn on top in proportion to the body, and we can see that the existing head fits well within the neck of the dog. We can also see the same in a front view. The side folds of the headdress are well inside the span of the shoulders, whereas for a head in correct proportion, they would be expected to spread widely to either side of the shoulders. From these drawings, it is clear that the existing head could easily have been carved out of the neck of Anubis. And indeed, the proportions are such that in order to do this, a head of approximately the size that we now see would have resulted.

But one question that arises is this: Would anyone have dared to commit such an atrocity as to cut off the head of Anubis? Wouldn't that have been considered an extreme impiety? Doubtless it would, and even the most megalomaniac of pharaohs might have hesitated to do it. We have already seen in chapter 3 that in oral folklore a tradition of the head having been cut down still survives, so it must have made quite an impact on the locals to see this happen, a shock that survived in local lore for millennia. (We should remember that the very locals who said that the head had been cut down had never seen the body, which further confirms the accuracy of their tale, since they themselves were unaware of the disproportion between the head and the body, as they had never actually seen the body.) So what I believe may have happened is that when the Sphinx/Anubis became covered up with sand after the end of the Old Kingdom, in the long, dark days known as the First Intermediate Period, when civilization largely collapsed and there was no law and order and barely any government at all for a century and a half, the head of Anubis must have become damaged. Perhaps it was even vandalized. It must have been easy for a head with a long pointed nose and high pointed ears to be damaged, especially when the sand had risen up to the neck. We know that the stone of the Sphinx is fragile in places, and a large piece of the Sphinx fell off into the Sphinx Pit in the 1990s. If the ears and nose of Anubis were substantially damaged, whether by weakness of the stone or by intention, a reshaping of the head might have been seen as the only sensible course of action to take by the time of the Middle Kingdom. So we must not assume that Amenemhet II was so crazed with egotism that he smashed the face of Anubis. His egotism may have been restricted to putting his own face onto a statue whose original face was so damaged that it had to be replaced with *something*.

We are encouraged to think along these lines by an article published by Zahi Hawass in 1992, in which he writes:

> In my opinion, it seems most likely that the Sphinx was abandoned at the end of the Old Kingdom and then plundered in the First Intermediate Period, ca. 2150–2040 BC. This conclusion is suggested by the evidence of plundering on the Giza Plateau at this time, the scope of which could arguably have also affected the Sphinx. . . . Evidence from the lower temple of Khafra [Chephren; Hawass is referring to the Valley Temple] supports the hypothesis that the monuments on the Giza plateau were viciously destroyed at the end of the Old Kingdom. The temple was certainly robbed, and most of the statuary was smashed, as the many statue fragments in the area testify. The careful burial of the diorite statue of Khafra found in the pit in the antechamber suggests an attempt to protect it from plunderers.
>
> All the cited evidence suggests the monuments of Giza were plundered in the First Intermediate Period. The Sphinx was most likely also abandoned at that time.[7]

I believe that Hawass is absolutely correct in his belief, and that the Sphinx was very seriously damaged and mutilated during this period. The head of Anubis would have been an easy target and was bound to have been vandalized. The ransacking of the adjoining temples, the smashing of all the statues in them, could hardly have taken place while the Sphinx remained untouched.

So we should not condemn Amenemhet II unreservedly for putting his face on the Sphinx, considering that it was probably impossible to restore the head of Anubis correctly.

The so-called Inventory Stela excavated at Giza preserves a tradition of the need for repairs to the Sphinx in the early period, by claiming in its text that Cheops in the Fourth Dynasty *repaired* the Sphinx.[8] (The Inventory Stela may be seen in figure 5.12, and a diagram of its contents may be found as figure 5.13 on page 209.) That claim would indicate the Sphinx being repaired as early as 2500 BC! If the Sphinx needed repair that early, imagine how much more repair it would have needed five centuries later, in Amenemhet II's time. But all Egyptologists get very upset these days when one quotes the Inventory Stela. Although many distinguished Egyptologists of the early twentieth century accepted its evidence and believed that the Sphinx was so old that Cheops had repaired it, today we realize that the Inventory Stela is a much later stela, and its evidence about that point cannot be reliable. But although the stela is clearly of a late date (we think circa 1000 BC) in terms of its carving, that is an insufficient basis for dismissing its text as being of the same age. The texts of the Taharqa edifice (King Taharqa, a Nubian pharaoh of Egypt of the Twenty-fifth Dynasty, ruled 690–664 BC) are also late but are not only accepted by everyone as being copied from texts of much earlier date, but many of them have been proved to be direct quotes from texts also inscribed in a chapel of the earlier pharaoh Rameses III (ruled 1198–1166 BC according to one chronology, or 1183–1151 BC according to another), five hundred years earlier, and who in turn must have obtained them from papyri of a much earlier date still.[9] There are countless examples of texts being recycled throughout the ages in Egypt, and the text of the Inventory Stela is not necessarily entirely a late text just because the stela is late. Things are not as simple as that. But on the other hand, it is not certain that it was Cheops who really restored the Sphinx in the manner described (although there may have been a surviving tradition that Cheops had also restored the Sphinx even earlier), and it was possibly a New Kingdom pharaoh rather than Cheops who is referred to in the text, with the name changed. The main point is that there was a definite tradition of repairs to the Sphinx, which we know in any case to be true, since we have clear proof that Thutmosis (Thothmes) IV cleared and repaired the Sphinx, as we have seen in an earlier chapter and which is recorded in his Dream Stela, a fact accepted by everybody today.

But before we dismiss entirely the idea that the Sphinx was actually repaired by Cheops, let us keep in mind that there are many Old Kingdom repair blocks on the Sphinx, some of which are clearly visible in figures 5.14 and 5.15. These are the only really good repair blocks ever used on the Sphinx, and they have survived for about 4,500 years. All subsequent ones, including modern ones, are

Figure 5.12. A photograph of the famous Inventory Stela, excavated at Giza. This stela includes a text claiming to date from the Old Kingdom, which describes the topography around the Sphinx. The stela itself is much more recent, perhaps from the Twenty-sixth Dynasty (664–525 BC). No one is certain whether the text is authentic and was copied onto this stela or whether it was written at the time of the stela, perhaps garbling some of the information. This photo is plate LV, following page 140, in Selim Hassan's extremely rare excavation report on the Sphinx, *The Great Sphinx and Its Secrets,* Government Press, Cairo, 1953. A diagram of what appears on this stela is shown in figure 5.13 below.

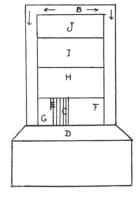

Figure 5.13. This diagram shows the locations on the stela where the different blocks of text and illustrations occur on the Inventory Stela. This is figure 80 on page 113 of Selim Hassan's *The Great Sphinx and Its Secrets,* Cairo, 1953. The stela lists the figures of the gods found by Pharaoh Cheops (Khufu) when he discovered the Temple of Isis at Giza. The Temple of Isis that is known to archaeologists (see figures 1.24, 1.25, and 1.27 on pages 30 and 31) is much later than the time of Cheops, so either there was an earlier Temple of Isis at Giza or this is a late text (perhaps from the seventh century BC) based on garbled information. The inscription along the right edge, beneath the downward-pointing arrow, says: "Live Horus Medjdu, the King of Upper and Lower Egypt, Khufu, given life [i.e., deceased]. He found the House of Isis, Mistress of the Pyramid, beside the House of the Sphinx, on the north-west of the House of Osiris, Lord of Rostau; and he built his pyramid beside the temple of this Goddess." The House of Osiris is thought to be what we now call the Valley Temple at Giza, either before it was usurped by Chephren and filled with statues of himself (if he did usurp it) or otherwise what it became after Chephren's statues were smashed and it reverted to a religious rather than a royal use. The bottom register of the panel then continues: "The Place of the Sphinx, Horemakhet, is on the south of the House of Isis, Mistress of the Pyramid, and on the north of Osiris, Lord of Rostau." This information is so specific that is seems impossible for the House of Osiris of Rostau to be anything other than the Valley Temple of Giza. These texts are so interesting that, whatever their age, we are glad to have them.

Figure 5.14. This photo of part of the southern rump of the Sphinx is what the French might call a *mélange des pierres,* or we could say "a stone cocktail." Just about every kind of patching and reconstruction stone that we could imagine is evident here, the palest ones being the newest. Underneath we see what are believed to be Old Kingdom repair stones. But this raises the question: If it was thought necessary to *repair* the Sphinx in the Old Kingdom, how old really *is* the Sphinx? We see here that later repair stones were laid over the Old Kingdom ones as an entire second skin, and this could have been done anytime during the Middle Kingdom, New Kingdom (after Thutmosis IV cleared the structure of sand), Ptolemaic, or Roman period. The large second-skin repair blocks, especially the long, curving stretched ones, are too sophisticated for Roman repairs and must be earlier, since the Romans used very small stones similar to the modern ones. One wonders just what really is beneath all these stones, and where the carved body is. (*Photo by Robert Temple*)

very inadequate. Who put these on the Sphinx? Maybe it was Cheops after all. It does look like Fourth Dynasty work. So what is the real answer to the age of the Sphinx, if it was *repaired* in the Fourth Dynasty? Some Egyptologists who admit the age of those blocks claim that they were put on the Sphinx at the time of its carving to remedy deficiencies in the rock. But that seems rather a tepid argument, and not particularly convincing. It is more likely, in my opinion, that Anubis was already there at the time of Cheops. But that is merely an opinion, and we shall see what is revealed in the future about the date of the Sphinx. I have worked on an archaeometrical dating project at Giza with the permission of the Egyptian Supreme Council of Antiquities, but as the results are not published yet, I cannot say more at the present time. Some indications of the results at Giza will be given in my next book, *Egyptian Dawn.* They are very surprising, and include dates for the so-called Osiris Shaft beneath the Chephren Causeway, which is 150 feet beneath the surface.

In 2005, Terence Du Quesne, with whom I enjoy a friendly and congenial

Figure 5.15. This is a photo from the right rear of the Sphinx, showing the sweeping tail made mostly of modern blocks. Above it, the superficiality of many of the inlaid modern pale stone patches is clearly visible. The large, dark and weathered blocks may be from the New Kingdom, Saite, or Ptolemaic period. In the upper left of the photo, a strange square area has been patched with small blocks at some time in the past and suggests that a chunk fell out of the Sphinx here at one time. It is behind that area that the internal tunnel extends, so its southern wall must have collapsed and fallen out, possibly during Roman times, and was replaced with the area of small blocks. Just above this square patched area, and extending along most of the rump as visible in this picture, are the oldest repair blocks of all, thought to date from the Old Kingdom. The best patches of the Sphinx were the oldest, and as time went on, the quality of the patches became worse and worse, culminating in the modern ones, which are purely cosmetic, for although the tiny modern stones have been cut with loving care and placed with great precision, the elements are too small to be robust, and they cannot possibly have a long life, but will begin dropping out and falling off within decades at the most. (*Photo by Robert Temple*)

acquaintance, brought out a definitive book on the history of the iconography and inscriptions relating to the god Anubis from the beginnings of Egyptian civilization (what is called the Archaic Period) up to approximately 2000 BC (the date at which the Middle Kingdom began). This book deals not only with Anubis per se, but also with variant forms of Anubis and other jackal deities. It is called *The Jackal Deities of Egypt* and is the product of a lifetime's study of the subject. Like myself and Olivia, Terence is a real dog-lover! We will consider this book as well as earlier publications by Du Quesne a little later on. But there is one subject raised in his new book that I want to mention now, because it has to do with some evidence that hints at a possible existence of the Great Sphinx in the Third Dynasty, considerably earlier than the time of Cheops and Chephren. There is no doubting Chephren's passionate enthusiasm for the Sphinx, and we will be seeing evidence for that later. But it is at least a possibility that Chephren usurped the Sphinx and the Valley Temple, thereby leading us to believe falsely that he was concerned in their actual construction and creation. Usurpation of monuments was practiced by pharaohs throughout Egyptian history, and we must be alert to the possibility—and I call it only a possibility—that Chephren may have done this. Certainly, I do believe that Amenemhet II usurped the Sphinx, as we have already seen in the previous chapter. After all, there is hardly a more extreme form of usurpation than sticking your face onto something!

Du Quesne points out that a boundary stela has been excavated at the site of the Step Pyramid of Zoser, who was the first pharaoh of the Third Dynasty, and that it mentions "Anubis, Foremost of the Secluded Land."[10] The Secluded Land was a name for the necropolis, and in particular that of Giza. Later we will examine the use of this title in connection with Anubis at Giza. I mention this here because of the Third Dynasty evidence, the significance of which will become clearer in the later discussion. Du Quesne has also found at Saqqara in the Third Dynasty an inscription at a priest's tomb that refers to Anubis in the manner that was later to become familiar at Giza: "Foremost of the Secluded Land." The priest's name was Kha-Bau-Sokar, and the inscription describes him as the "Craftsman of Anubis, Foremost of the Secluded Land."[11] There are thus two firm references, as inscriptions on stone, in the Third Dynasty to Anubis in a form that suggests (according to the discussion that is to follow) Anubis as the Great Sphinx at Giza. These references in themselves do not prove anything; they are merely suggestive. However seriously I may take them, everyone is free to dismiss them by saying that the term "Foremost of the Secluded Land" is just a name and means nothing. It will become clear as we go on why I think otherwise.

As for the Inventory Stela that I mentioned a moment ago, we will return to it in the next chapter for information about the locality of the Sphinx, information that derives from a document that cannot be earlier than the Fifth or Sixth Dynasty, because it mentions the god Osiris so prominently. Osiris did not come to real prominence before that time. (Prior to that, his name was not Osiris, which is the Greek form of the name Asar in Egyptian, but Khenti-Amentiu, which means "Foremost of the Westerners," a name also used either for Anubis or for another form of jackal divinity. One might say, therefore, that Osiris was originally a dog!)

But for now, there are some extremely pertinent details about the Sphinx revealed in the Inventory Stela that have never received their due attention. This Inventory Stela was excavated at Giza by Auguste Mariette in the nineteenth century and is now in the Egyptian Museum at Cairo. In referring to the Sphinx, the stela nowhere describes it as having the body of a lion. Its body is not described at all, but by the time this description was written, the Sphinx had a head with a *nemes* headdress. Here is a crucial detail describing what the pharaoh did to it:

"He restored the statue. . . . He made to quarry the hind part of the nemes, which was lacking, gilded stone, and which had a length of 7 ells [3.70 meters]."[12]

This bit of information is of great importance for the question of the present head of the Sphinx having been recarved from the neck of a larger head of Anubis. It suggests either that the neck was not thick enough for the full extent of the pharaoh's headdress to be carved at the back, and that it had to be added separately by a pharaoh when "restoring the statue," or that the job of recarving the neck of Anubis had been left incomplete, and he remedied this. If the present head were the original one, and had been cut from the original solid rock at the same time as the body, the full headdress would have been carved at that time, and would not have had to be added later. It is impossible now to examine these features because in the 1930s, Selim Hassan "restored" the headdress, added the lower portions of the cloth folds, or lappets, in modern concrete, and smeared modern cement around the neck and the rear of the headdress to strengthen and "improve" the structure. But if the rear of the headdress had to be added on in antiquity because it was lacking, it must have been lacking for a reason, and that reason cannot have been an oversight of the original carvers of the Sphinx. They had plenty of stone to work with, and carving the full rear of the headdress would have posed no problem to them. That the pharaoh's head lacked that element indicates clearly that either the back of the original statue's neck had been reached, and there was simply no stone left to carry the headdress any further, or the recarving was left incomplete because it would not normally be seen, so restricted was the access then to the side of the Sphinx. This textual evidence is fairly conclusive, no matter how late it is, or which pharaoh is really being referred to (we may disregard the text's description of him as Cheops). For no matter how late the text is, it is still an ancient Egyptian text, and it still preserves this structural detail. Questions of the date of the text only affect the question of the *date* of the recarving, not the question of the *fact* of the recarving. Furthermore, we can dismiss the possibility of the information being merely fabricated in antiquity, since it is such a bizarre detail for anyone to think of, with no purpose to it, that a motive for inventing it is wholly lacking.

Selim Hassan supports Gaston Maspero in his belief that the Inventory Stela was actually carved by Pharaoh Psusennes I (also known as Pasebakhaenniut I and Pasebehkanu I), of the "Tanite" Twenty-first Dynasty, who reigned 1039–991 BC according to one chronology or 1063–1037 BC according to another. They also both believe that the stela preserves older textual material, though not necessarily of the Old Kingdom date as the stela pretends.[13]

One curious detail relating to the rear of the Sphinx's *nemes* headdress is that a piece of it was found in 1978 by Zahi Hawass. It had fallen into a hole behind the head drilled in the nineteenth century by Howard Vyse. As Mark Lehner comments in a caption in his book *The Complete Pyramids:* "When the cavity created in the back of the Sphinx [behind the head, which as a modern hole I have not bothered to discuss] by Vyse's gunpowder was cleared in 1978 under the direction of Zahi Hawass, it was found to contain not only Vyse's drill hole but also a large chunk of the Sphinx's headdress with its relief-carved pleating."[14]

It is probable that this loose chunk of headdress fell off the Sphinx's head with the force of the blast of the gunpowder that Howard Vyse so foolishly used on the monument, and that it was part of the additional piece added to the head by a pharaoh (whose identity we may consider uncertain, though it is likely that it was Pharaoh Thutmosis IV, of the Dream Stela that was described in chapter 3) as described in the Inventory Stela. It probably constitutes a confirmation of the information preserved in the Inventory Stela, though no one ever seems to have pointed this out before. This in turn encourages us to think that some of the information in the Inventory Stela is more ancient and valuable than it may superficially appear, though it certainly seems to be badly garbled.

With the Sphinx's body, we really have only the choice between a dog and a lion. The body has to represent one or the other, since there is no other beast that can reasonably be suggested. And if anyone were to choose between the two purely on the basis of using his or her own eyes, the choice would have to be for a dog, since the Sphinx looks like a dog and does not look like a lion. Of course, if a person is determined to be conventional, and hates more than anything in life to depart from an accepted notion, that person will never choose a dog. It is really in the end a psychological matter rather than an observational one. On purely observational grounds, anyone would have to agree that the Sphinx has no leonine characteristics but does have canine characteristics and therefore must be a dog.

One of the greatest myths of humanity is that everyone cares about the truth. Many people do not. The idea that everyone does is merely a lie told to children. There are many people who do not give a damn about the truth, because they are too busy thinking about themselves for any exterior factor, particularly an inconvenient truth, to matter. The first question that comes up when faced with an inconvenience is self-interest: Is it to my advantage to admit that the Sphinx is not a lion, or would it make life more uncomfortable for me? The protective mutual construct that people build around themselves and share is something called *consensus reality.* They carry this around with them in the way that astronauts carry oxygen cylinders on their backs when they repair spacecraft in orbit. A person caught without his backpack is in real trouble: if a consensus reality view of something is not ready to hand, he or she may panic. This often happens at concerts and art exhibitions: What reaction is appropriate to something new? Applause?

Jeering? Is it good? Is it bad? Quick, a critic must tell us! The art of political spinning is the art of constructing a consensus reality around political events so that their interpretation is manipulated within a context created by the spinner. It takes advantage of the fact that humans cannot interpret events on their own but require a context; the spinner supplies the context. This excessive timidity of humanity is what enables our species to be routinely manipulated. And as for seeing things, we see only what we are told we can see. The phenomenon of consensus blindness was discussed at length in my earlier book, *The Crystal Sun*, which is basically a huge case history of the phenomenon over the ages.[15] This phenomenon means that people do not see what is in front of them because they believe they should not. They "censor" their optical impressions and rarely trust the evidence of their own eyes. The case of the Sphinx is a classic one of this phenomenon, which can almost be called a defining characteristic of the human race: millions of people have seen the Sphinx since it was cleared of sand, and not one until now has dared to say that it is not what it is said to be, and that it is *not a lion*. But this is just another example of the many cases I give in *The Crystal Sun* of objects on display in museums that have also been seen by millions of people, including countless "experts," but have not really been "seen" at all because they went against a consensus reality and were thus erased from consciousness. Humanity lives not in reality but in a vast collective dream. That is why heretics and original thinkers are always so persecuted, because they threaten the dream. The Sphinx for 3,400 years has been not a reality but rather a collective hallucination.

Anubis was the standard guardian of necropolises, of graves, of the dead. So it makes sense that a gigantic statue of him would have been erected at the entrance to the Giza Plateau. The Sphinx and the two adjoining temples, the Valley Temple and the Sphinx Temple, were at the very point of entry to Giza in ancient times. A quay has been excavated in front of the Valley Temple since the 1930s, which can be walked on by all tourists, and we know that at the time of the annual inundation, the water of the River Nile rose right up to that point and lapped at the entrance to the temples. One could approach by boat, alight, and enter the Land of the Dead. Of course, there has been no annual inundation since the Aswan Dam was constructed. And the course of the Nile has moved very far eastward, away from Giza, since antiquity. But old Victorian photos show the waters of the Nile nearly reaching the Sphinx circa 1900 (see figures in chapter 6), and the many early travelers' reports that I have collected and translated make clear how close one could come to the pyramids by boat in recent centuries. As I mentioned in the previous chapter, it is acknowledged that the Nile inundation rose 26 feet higher in the Middle Kingdom than it did in the nineteenth and early twentieth centuries. And as Richard Pococke recorded after his visit to Giza in the seventeenth century, the Nile at inundation then came to within "half a quarter of a mile [i.e., an eighth of a mile]" of the Sphinx, a distance of only 660 feet, or 201 meters.

This was therefore the appropriate place for Anubis to rest, guarding the entrance to the necropolis. One landed at his feet in a boat and then walked up past the Sphinx on the Chephren Causeway, or by some other route nearby one ascended the slope of the Giza Plateau from this low point. It makes no sense for a gigantic lion to sit there awaiting visitors, because it was Anubis, not a lion, who was the appropriate guardian of the dead. Lions never guarded necropolises in Egypt.

There is fascinating evidence from the Archaic Period in Egypt (the period of the First and Second Dynasties) that huge effigies of Anubis were constructed of perishable materials at least as far back as 2800 BC. This information was collected by the historian of Egyptian architecture Alexander Badawy and published in an article in a journal that Egyptologists normally do not see, *The Journal of the Society of Architectural Historians.*[16] The only reason I was able to discover this important article was that I have been assiduously collecting everything published by Badawy for some years now due to my high opinion of him, and I have purchased portions of the libraries of several distinguished Egyptologists (Henry Fischer, Kent Weeks, etc.). Badawy gave an offprint of this article to one of them and typed the source on top (because this journal did not print it), and it was among a large pile of rare offprints that I have bought from these libraries by people such as Badawy, Hornung, and Lauer, whose work is of particular interest to me. I suspect that only a small circle of Badawy's personal friends and colleagues ever knew that he had published this article in this obscure journal. Fortunately, it came to my hands, as I would never have looked in that journal, of whose existence I was unaware. I reproduce in figures 5.16 and 5.17 the drawings made by Badawy and reproduced in the article. As all who have studied Egyptian funerary architecture know, there was a tendency to represent in stone such items as walls and other structures that were normally constructed either in mud brick or in more perishable materials such as wood, wickerwork, and reeds. This is particularly evident at the funerary complex of King Zoser (Djoser/Djeser) at Saqqara, the center of which is the famous Step Pyramid. Stone was conceived of in religious terms as a kind of "freezing for eternity" of things that would otherwise perish. In the article just mentioned, Badawy discusses this practice as it applied to sacred shrines in both Egypt and India.

He discusses and illustrates the brushwood huts of a hill tribe of India called the Todas, who live in the Nilgiri hills of southern India. He points out

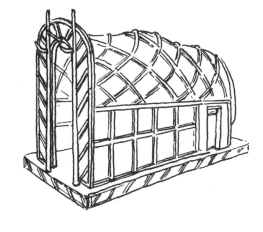

Figure 5.16. This is Alexander Badawy's perspective drawing of the Anubis hut, based on a flat view from the side of it carved in a First Dynasty depiction.

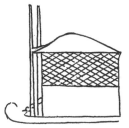

Figure 5.17. Depictions of Anubis huts from ivory labels found in First Dynasty royal tombs.

that these huts have been reproduced in stone as Buddhist and Hindu chaitya-halls (places of worship) commencing in the third and second centuries BC. It is a freak coincidence that the Toda tribe, a throwback to remote antiquity in many ways, still builds these huts of brushwood and lives in them today. By what to me is an even stranger coincidence, I myself noticed this independently as long ago as 1963, as a teenager. I entered university very young, and from the age of eighteen, all my courses were at the postgraduate level. The language I was studying then was Sanskrit, and I naturally pursued Indian studies along with that.

In connection with my Indian studies, I developed a particular interest in the Toda tribe. I wrote two dissertations about the Todas of modest length when I was eighteen and nineteen, in one of which I pointed out that their huts had been reproduced in stone in just the way Badawy describes. I was entirely unaware of

Figure 5.18. This is the earliest published depiction of a typical Toda hut, from the Nilgiri hills in South India. It was published in Captain Henry Harkness, *A Description of a Singular Aboriginal Race Inhabiting the Summit of the Neilgherry Hills, or Blue Mountains of Coimbatoor, in the Southern Peninsula of India,* London, 1832, opposite page 5. The hut is in the foreground at left. It is not unlike the Anubis huts seen in figures 5.16 and 5.17. (*Collection of Robert Temple*)

the existence of Badawy at that time or that he had noticed this himself four years earlier. We both noticed this strange thing entirely independently. No wonder I collect papers by Badawy, as our minds obviously work in the same way. But I have only discovered our mutual observation about the Toda huts now in connection with Anubis in Egypt, which is such an unlikely way to come across it. What a strange world of crisscrossing mental threads we live in!

Badawy wrote the following about the Anubis shrines in ancient Egypt:

It needs no emphasis that symbolism played a predominant role in the religious and funerary architecture of all peoples in antiquity, and still does today. However, symbolic elements of architecture belong to an advanced stage in the development of representation. A much more primary stage is the one where the actual deity is represented architecturally as a structure formed according to his shape. This shape could be conceptual to suggest cosmic elements; for instance, the world itself as in the stupa of India, and the stretch of the horizon where the sun rises between two mountains as in the pylon of Egypt. It could also be simply realistic when it imitates the shape of an animal by which a deity is represented. Such a zoomorphic architecture may be exemplified in the so-called shrine of Anubis in Egypt.

Drawings from the Archaic Period in Egypt (2800 B.C.) represent an edicule ["little house"], probably religious or funerary, characterized by an irregular upper outline (figure 5.17). Structurally it can be described as having an irregular vault with a high arched doorway on the façade and springing from a lower vertical wall set on a shallow platform (figure 5.16). The plan is rectangular, and the possibility of its having an apsidal end is not to be excluded. The style of the representations and their date suggest that light materials such as reeds were used for the frame, and wickerwork for the walls. The structure unmistakably resembles that of a crouching animal, even to the pendent tail. I have presumed, on the grounds of a comparative study with early religious texts, that it could represent Anubis, the god of the dead, in the shape of a jackal crouching on a base. . . . The type does not seem ever to have been translated into stone architecture. The ideological concept is that of the embodiment of a god into his zoomorphic shrine, much the same as that of the cult object of Min into his edicule.[17]

The same subject was referred to in passing, though in not such a way as to draw one's attention, in Badawy's classic work, *A History of Egyptian Architecture*. In volume 1 of that work, Badawy reproduces one of the Archaic drawings and says: "A series of Ist dynasty seals represent a peculiar hut, shown in front elevation with side-elevation rabated. Certain examples (from the tomb of 'Aha') convey clearly the resemblance of a crouching animal, which could be identified with the desert-hound of Anubis."[18]

In other words, we have evidence in the form of pictures on seal carvings dating from the reign of King Āha, the second king of the First Dynasty, that in his day huge images of a crouching Anubis were constructed of perishable materials. Badawy ruefully observes, "The type does not seem ever to have been translated into stone architecture," and clearly expected that it should have been. What could be clearer? The Great Sphinx of Giza was that "translation into stone" of the huge Anubis shrines of the First Dynasty. The Sphinx as Anubis thus has an impeccable pedigree, going back to the very origins of high civilization in Egypt, as proved by images surviving from that time.

There is also evidence from excavations near the Sphinx to substantiate the view that the Sphinx was Anubis. In his excavations in the 1930s, Selim Hassan found a Fifth Dynasty inscription near the Sphinx that mentions Anubis, which would still have been intact at that time, but not any of the names that in later ages became fashionable for the statue, such as Hu and Horakhty. In the second line of the hieroglyphs is the figure of the recumbent Anubis. The inscription was left by a priest named Hotep, and it mentions both Anubis and the hybrid god Ptah-Sokar-Osiris, who originally was simply Sokar, the underground god of Rostau beside the Sphinx. Anubis is mentioned twice, first by his own name and then by one of his titles (Imyut), which is the name of his symbol: "A boon which the King gives, and Anubis, who is upon his Mountain [Hill], Imyut, Lord of the Land [the "Land" is the necropolis]."[19] The king referred to is the king whom Hotep served during his lifetime, King Neferirkare (also called Kakai) of the Fifth Dynasty (who reigned 2473–2463 BC according to one chronology or 2483–2463 BC according to another). Hassan notes: "Now, the name of this King appearing in this place, coupled with the fact that the Tomb of Ra-wer, the most famous and favourite official of King Nefer-ir-ka-Ra, is situated only a stone's throw away, seems to suggest some connection between that King and the Sphinx, or its locality. Perhaps he also carried out some work around the Sphinx."[20] But the main point for us about the inscription at this early date is that Anubis is mentioned twice in a manner that implies his obvious connection with the place, whereas none of the references typical of later New Kingdom times when the body of the Sphinx was thought to be a lion is to be found.

If we search the ancient Egyptian literature for references, we find countless ones about Anubis as guardian of the dead. The Pyramid Texts of the Old Kingdom and the Coffin Texts of the Middle Kingdom are full of references to him. Some of these are associated with descriptions of the edifices and features of that region of Giza known as either Busiris or Rostau. Busiris (in Egyptian, Djedu) was a name attached to two separate places in ancient Egypt, a town in the Delta and, as Pliny makes explicitly clear, the settlement immediately adjacent to the Sphinx Precinct that has now become the modern village of Nazlet el-Samman. Rostau is the name of the immediate precinct at Giza that was particularly sacred to the underworld god Sokar (who later became absorbed into a joint god called Sokar-Ptah-Osiris). As I explain later, in chapter 7, Rostau (which has many variant spellings, such as Rosetau, Rosetawe, etc.) appears to refer to the immediate vicinity of the Sphinx and the Valley and Sphinx Temples. The Dream Stela, the Inventory Stela, an inscription of the Saite king Psamtik II, and other sources all make clear that Rostau includes or is immediately adjacent to the Sphinx enclosure.

Hence it is of no small importance to our thesis of Anubis as the Sphinx to realize that a frequent title of Anubis was Lord of Rostau. If the Sphinx was

Anubis, and was at Rostau, then to substantiate our case we need to find some ancient references to an Anubis at Rostau. And that is exactly what we find aplenty. The Egyptological scholar Terence Du Quesne has gathered many references to Anubis as Lord of Rostau in ancient inscriptions and wall carvings; he lists no less than ten published sources for these, which include many examples of the title.[21] Certainly, a giant statue of Anubis crouching at Rostau is precisely what one would be tempted to call "Lord of Rostau." After the Fifth Dynasty, the title Lord of Rostau began to be applied to Osiris, whereas previously the only joint claimant to the title was the underworld god Sokar, who actually resided beneath the earth at that point. Sokar and Osiris became merged into one another as Sokar-Osiris after the Fifth Dynasty. And as if that weren't enough, the neighboring god Ptah of Memphis was brought into the mix as well, so the Egyptians ended up with a trinity called Sokar-Ptah-Osiris, who then became the new Lord of Rostau. But certainly in the beginning it was only Sokar and Anubis who were Lords of Rostau: Sokar because he lived underground at that spot and Anubis because he crouched on the surface as the site's guardian. And we have plentiful textual evidence as well as inscriptions.

In the Coffin Text Spell 241, Anubis is mentioned in the same breath as Rostau; the deceased, who identifies himself with Osiris, is speaking: "I am Osiris and I have come to Rosetau in order to know the secret of the Dat [Duat; netherworld], to which Anubis has been initiated."[22]

Particular attention has also been drawn to this passage by Terence Du Quesne, who has written several further studies of Anubis and the jackal. His 1991 book *Jackal at the Shaman's Gate* bears the subtitle "A Study of Anubis, Lord of Ro-Setawe" (Rostau).[23] In this book he speaks of "the gate, called by the Egyptians Ro-Setawe" and quotes a Middle Kingdom text referring to it and specifying that Anubis is to be found there:

In the *Book of the One in the Netherworld,* there exists a strange corridor, the "land of Sokar," between the chambers of the third and fourth hours of the night, through which the justified soul must travel in order to reach the dawn. Its explanatory text is unequivocal:

The secret ways of Ro-Setawe
The gate of the gods
Only one whose voice is heard
May pass them . . .
The secret way to which (only) Anubis has access
In order to conceal the body of Osiris.

Anubis, god of embalmment and reviver of the original Osiris, conceals the body of the justified person, who is identified with Osiris, in order to breathe life back into it. Here is the bridge between death and rebirth. . . . Two passages in the *Coffin Texts* are similarly explicit:

> *I have come . . . to enter the secret gateway*
> *By which Anubis is initiated.*
> *I have come to Ro-Setawe*
> *In order to know the Mysteries of the Netherworld*
> *Into which Anubis is initiated.*

It should be understood that the divine king identifies himself with Anubis as all justified souls [*those good people who are worthy to live eternally, and escape annihilation*] do with Osiris later in Egyptian history. . . . Anubis is often given the title Lord of Ro-Setawe [Rostau]. One spell in the *Coffin Texts* is entitled "Invocation for Entering the Gate of the Netherworld" and has the justified person declaring: "I have come in order to enter the gateway that is protected by Anubis." . . . One of Anubis's most appropriate attributions is "Master of Secrets" . . . and the pharaoh Cheops in later times himself received the epithet of "Master of Secrets in Ro-Setawe." . . . The local deity of Memphis is Sokar, whose name survives in "Saqqara." From early times Sokar is "lord of Ro-Setawe," an epithet also given to Anubis. . . . In many representations, the Anubis jackal is shown couchant on a funerary chest or box known as the "sacred casket." . . . This is in his capacity as "Master of Secrets." This container may be seen as a kind of Pandora's box which is the symbolic entrance-way to Ro-Setawe.[24]

We can see that there are many passages in ancient Egyptian texts that locate Anubis at Rostau (which Du Quesne prefers to spell Ro-Setawe, both variant spellings being technically correct), which is at Giza and is believed to be that part of Giza where the Sphinx is found. The problem noted earlier that there are "no references" to the Sphinx in the ancient Egyptian literature is immediately remedied if we assume that the Sphinx was a giant statue of Anubis, for then we are positively deluged with references in ancient Egyptian literature. And one of the passages just quoted actually describes the gate at Rostau as being *protected by Anubis.*

Anubis is often described in the texts as "presiding over the Pure Land," which means the necropolis, and which is one of the names of the Giza Plateau. The Gate of Geb (the Earth god), or the Doors of Geb, was located at Rostau, at the feet of Giza. In the Pyramid Text Utterance 437, we read of Anubis "on his baldachin" at the Doors of Geb. "Baldachin" is the translation often given by Egyptologists to the Egyptian word for the strange shrine on top of which Anubis is usually portrayed stretched out on his belly. Anubis is seen crouching on top of it in figure 5.9. This is what Du Quesne perhaps more sensibly calls a funerary chest. Since *baldachin* is not a word any of us uses in daily conversation, I thought I ought to quote its definition as given in the *Shorter Oxford English Dictionary:* "A structure in the form of a canopy, either borne on columns, suspended from the roof, or projecting from the wall, placed above an altar, throne, or doorway."[25]

From this we may see that "baldachin" is not entirely satisfactory as a translation for a solid structure, but as the Egyptologists insist on using it, we need to know its meaning if we are to understand their translations as they relate to Anubis.

In the Pyramid Texts Utterance 437, we read of the risen soul: "You arise as Anubis who is on the baldachin."[26]

This appears to refer to the resurrected deceased still recumbent on his death-couch, as we see so often in the depictions of Osiris. The recumbent Anubis is therefore to be taken as symbolic of the prostrate but yet living dead. In fact, the god of Rostau, Sokar, is often depicted lying on a bier, perhaps in imitation of the recumbent Anubis. I reproduce an ancient depiction of this eerie scene in figure 8.38, where Sokar is replaced by his successor, Osiris.

Anubis is further described in the same text as "Anubis who presides over the Pure Land," in other words, the necropolis. In Pyramid Text Utterance 581, instead of "the Pure Land," it is "the Sacred Land" over which Anubis presides.[27] These are alternative ways of describing the necropolis. Another form that we have already encountered is "the Secluded Land." These "Lands" are all the same. And one inevitably wonders, if Anubis is "presiding" over the necropolis, how is he doing so? In other words, is he present? Is he represented? To crouch as guardian at the entrance to the necropolis is indeed to "preside" over it.

A description is also given in Utterance 437 of the dramatic events that the risen soul encounters at Rostau, where the gates or Doors of Geb are to be found: "The earth speaks: The doors of the earth-god are opened for you, the doors of Geb are thrown open for you, you come forth at the voice of Anubis, he makes a spirit of you."[28]

If perhaps the gigantic statue of Anubis, now known as the Sphinx, is what is referred to here, perhaps he did "speak" and deliver pronouncements when he was Anubis, just as verbal tradition maintained in much later centuries that the Sphinx, by then with a pharaoh's head, often did. For the tradition is persistent that the Sphinx "spoke," and a speaking tube, tunnel, or simply a projected voice might well have been employed by the priests in the earliest times. Thus there may well have been a physical "voice of Anubis" at ceremonies.

The ancient descriptions of a *couchant* Anubis are so incredibly precise, in fact, that Pyramid Text Utterance 659 describes a recumbent Anubis as being *beside a causeway*. And as we know, the Sphinx is indeed beside what we now call the Causeway of Chephren: "You have descended as a jackal of Upper Egypt [a description of the type of jackal, not of its location in this text, which suggests that these wild dogs came from there], as Anubis on his baldachin. May you stand up at the causeway [as Geb] who presides."[29]

Pyramid Text 677 has an intriguing description of the recumbent Anubis: "O King, your shape is hidden like that of Anubis on his belly; receive your jackal-face and raise yourself, stand up."[30]

"Receive your jackal-face" refers to the common practice of the donning of a jackal mask (see figure 5.19). Many of the jackal-headed figures seen in Egyptian wall carvings are of priests with jackal masks and are not intended to represent Anubis himself. A very clear depiction of a priest wearing a jackal mask is known from the Temple of Denderah, where in an instance of "transparency of depiction," the priest is shown with his own face and superimposed over his face is the head of Anubis (with his eye holes being in Anubis's neck). A clay mask of Anubis with eye holes in the neck is actually preserved in the Hildesheim Museum in Germany and was tried on by Arelene Wolinski, who said "it fitted comfortably over her head and rested on her shoulders and back. The two holes in the jackal's neck turned out to be just at the right spot for eye holes, thus confirming the accuracy of the Denderah relief."[31] An older animal mask dating from the Middle Kingdom also survives, "in the form of a grotesque lion's head, and was found at Kahun . . . This object shows signs of wear, indicating that it was in frequent use." This was discussed by Terence Du Quesne in his lengthy article about ritual Egyptian masks published in 2001, which culminates with his description of getting a modern puppet maker to fabricate an Anubis mask, of which he says that "the process of creating the mask took the equivalent of about five weeks of full-time work." Du Quesne says the mask weighed about 1.1 kg and "adds about 45 cm to one's height," and the effort was very successful at replicating a usable Anubis mask as depicted in ancient Egyptian art.[32]

The strange feature of the Pyramid Text's description of the recumbent Anubis that has just been quoted is the comment that his shape is "hidden." What can this mean? I believe this is a specific reference to the Sphinx, but to make clear how it applies to the Sphinx, I need to move on to the next idea about what the Sphinx was originally like, which is in the next chapter. There we shall see that

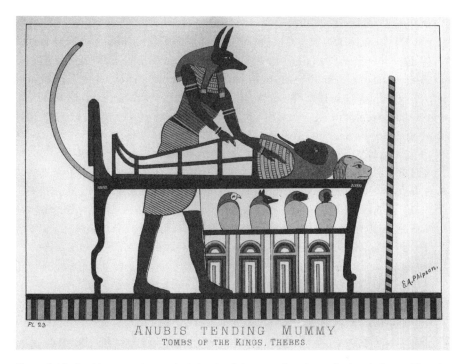

ANUBIS TENDING MUMMY
TOMBS OF THE KINGS, THEBES

Figure 5.19. Anubis not only guarded the dead; he was also the god of embalming. Here he is seen ministering to the king's mummy. Beneath the lion-footed table on which the royal mummy rests are the four jars containing the viscera of the deceased pharaoh. These are discussed in chapter 6, where their part in a ceremony beside Jackal Lake is discussed. This illustration appeared in Villiers Stuart, *Nile Gleanings*, John Murray, London, 1879, plate 23, opposite page 194.

part of the body of Anubis may well have been obscured and "hidden" during the Old Kingdom, in a way that once again accords with much textual evidence.

The book by Du Quesne, *The Jackal Divinities of Egypt,* presents a large amount of crucial information about Anubis at Giza, and what is revealed by this is most remarkable and highly relevant to our subject. There was certainly something of an obsession with extra-large Anubis figures at Giza during the Fourth Dynasty, which is the dynasty of Cheops and Chephren.

Du Quesne calls attention to a considerable number of hieroglyphic inscriptions from Giza during the Fourth Dynasty that contain giant pictures of Anubis. These large Anubis pictures completely dwarf the surrounding hieroglyphics, while acting as a hieroglyphic sign simultaneously with being illustrative. As far as I know, this phenomenon has not otherwise occurred in Egyptian hieroglyphic inscriptions either before or since that time. It is therefore highly important, and so far has had no explanation other than whimsy. Here are the comments Du

Quesne makes about the four Giza tomb inscriptions, which he designates III.A7, III.A8, III.A9, and III.A10: "showing couchant jackal . . . depicted very large," "with disproportionately large representations of couchant jackal," "large isolated figure of couchant jackal, facing right," and "disproportionately large representations of couchant jackal."[33] These Anubis figures really do dwarf everything else. I reproduce examples in figures 5.20 to 5.23. Du Quesne says of these huge jackals in the midst of normal inscriptions:

> L. Holden associates [a jackal statue found at Giza] with a small genre of tomb reliefs of the period which show, in the offering formula, greatly enlarged jackal figures. . . . The earliest . . . has the jackal many times larger than the accompanying signs. . . . In a few cases, similarly enlarged jackals are encountered on sarcophagus lids of the period. . . . These early Anubis representations in the formula of offerings have some intriguing features. They seem to originate in Giza, in the family of the great pyramid-building kings of Dynasty IV . . . the eldest son of Cheops, . . . his son and vizier . . . his daughter . . . [and] Chephren's queen. We may assume that the size of the Anubis figures was designed to emphasize the importance of the god in protecting the tombs' royal occupants in the netherworld. Such images might also have reinforced the kings' funerary cult.[34]

So we have "supersized" images of Anubis in these royal tomb inscriptions dwarfing everything that is near it or around it. It is wholly out of character for Egyptian art for there to be such outlandish "supersized" Anubises. The Egyptians were fanatical about keeping everything in correct proportion. So why were these images of Anubis enlarged to such gigantic size in a way that no other god in the entire history of Egypt ever was? Reinforcing a funerary cult is not a good enough explanation. Neither is protecting the royals in the netherworld. That would not explain the giant Anubises. The Egyptians just didn't do things like that. Furthermore, we cannot even assume propaganda as a purpose, since these were tomb inscriptions, which few people would ever see. So what was the purpose? What if the giant Anubises were intended to represent a giant Anubis that actually existed? Wouldn't that make sense? What if they were actual pictures of the largest Anubis in Egypt, the Great Sphinx of Giza?

Five of the most impressive of the supersized Anubises were found in three of the most prominent of the tombs (mastabas) of the Eastern Cemetery at Giza. Both of them are in the "front row" just east of the three little pyramids known as "queens' pyramids" that stand immediately southeast of the Great Pyramid. Some people like to have "front-row seats" at the theater. But these are "front-row

Figure 5.20. Drawing (left) of the inscription on the northern doorjamb (right) of the tomb chapel of Prince Khafkhufu I at Giza. (*From Dunham Dows and William Kelly Simpson,* The Mastabas of Kawab, Khafkhufu I and II, *Boston, 1978*)

Figure 5.21. Drawing (left) of the inscription on the southern doorjamb (right) of the tomb chapel of Prince Khafkhufu I at Giza. (*From Dows and Simpson,* Kawab and Khafkhufu)

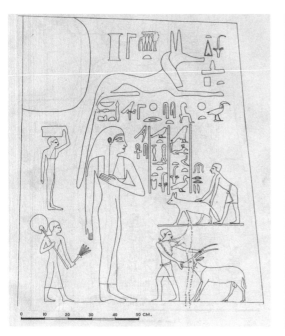

Figure 5.22. Drawing (left) of the northern doorjamb (right) of the tomb chapel of Queen Mersyankh III at Giza. (*From William Kelly Simpson*, The Mastaba of Queen Merysankh III, *Boston, 1974*)

Figure 5.23. Drawing (left) of the southern doorjamb (right) of the tomb chapel of Queen Mersyankh III, wife of King Chephren, in her mastaba at Giza. (*From Simpson,* Merysankh III)

tombs," sure to be of use when you are dead! (That way, do you get to see the gods better?) The first of the front-row tombs for us to consider is that of Prince Khafkhufu, a younger son of Cheops (Khufu). Khafkhufu was Controller of the Palace, Sole Companion to the King, and Priest of the Souls of Nekhen (the "souls of the south"). He was given one of the most important mastaba (aboveground) tombs at Giza. Here is how William Kelly Simpson describes it: "The mastaba of Khafkhufu I and his wife is one of the two great double mastabas in the row nearest the great pyramid in the eastern cemetery, situated south of the pyramid causeway and east of the three queens' pyramids."[35]

Supersized Anubises were carved on the two opposite entrance jambs of the southern chapel of this mastaba tomb. On top of them, at one time, had stood part of the Temple of Isis, which was built at a later epoch. These two Anubises are shown in figures 5.20 and 5.21. Beneath both is a king's name in an ellipsoidal cartouche: that king is Cheops (Khufu), the father of the prince and reputed builder of the Great Pyramid at whose foot this tomb stands. These huge Anubises function as a hieroglyph in each inscription, but at the same time stand out as the prime pictorial element. The inscription of the northern picture says: "A boon which Anubis, foremost of the necropolis, gives, (namely) a good old age before the great god (for) the king's son Khafkhufu." The southern inscription says: "A boon which Anubis, he who is in W[et], [this archaic place name, also spelled Ut, has among its meanings "hole," as well as being the second half of Imiut, a title of Anubis and the name of his fetish symbol, the whole of which name could be taken to have the meaning of "the inside of the hole," thus possibly being a reference to the Sphinx Pit: Anubis being "in Wet" thus potentially meaning Anubis being "in the Pit"] gives, (namely) power and nobility before the great god (for) the king's son Khafkhufu."[36]

These huge pictures of Anubis were thus incorporated into inscriptions that called upon Anubis to grant the soul of Khafkhufu power, nobility, and "a good old age" in the afterlife. Anubis was to grant these things to the prince through his position as Foremost of the Necropolis, that is, the chief deity of Giza. The inference that Anubis as the Sphinx was the chief presiding deity referred to is hard to resist, as is the supposition that the pictures were meant to refer to his giant statue nearby.

The eldest brother of Khafkhufu also had at least one giant Anubis in his tomb, which can be seen in figure 5.24. He may have had more, but his tomb has been greatly destroyed. This was Prince Kawab, who should have become pharaoh after the death of Cheops, but as he died just before becoming king, his other brother Djedefre (also known as Rededef, or Radjedef, who, it has been suggested, may have murdered Kawab to secure the succession for himself) became pharaoh

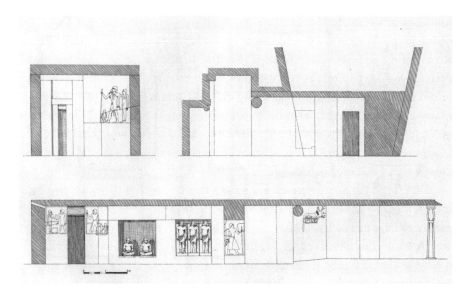

Figure 5.24. Plan and section of the tomb of Prince Kawab at Giza. In the bottom half, to the right of center at the top of the wall beside which the granite sarcophagus (not shown) of the prince would have rested, is one of the inscriptions with a supersized Anubis. (*From Dows and Simpson,* Kawab and Khafkhufu)

instead (though he built no pyramid at Giza), and Djedefre was in turn succeeded by Chephren. Simpson decribes Prince Kawab's mastaba tomb as follows: "Prince Kawab, the eldest son of Cheops, was buried in the large double mastaba on the east side of the pyramid of Cheops in the first row of mastabas nearest the pyramid, just south of the pyramid causeway and east of the northernmost of the three queens' pyramids. By its position it is singled out as the pre-eminent mastaba in the eastern cemetery."[37]

Three surviving inscriptions showing the supersized Anubis were carved just above Prince Kawab's granite sarcophagus and read:

(1) A boon which the king gives and Anubis, foremost of the divine booth, a burial in the necropolis as a possessor of a well provided state before the great god, officiant of Anubis, priest of Selket, Kawab; (2) a boon which the king gives and Anubis, foremost of the divine booth, a burial in the necropolis in the western cemetery [this is an interesting detail, because it shows that what we call the Eastern Cemetery because it is east of the Great Pyramid was called by the Old Kingdom Egyptians the western cemetery because it was west of the Sphinx], having grown gracefully old, the king's son of his body, Kawab; (3) king's eldest son of his body, officiant of Anubis, Kawab.[38]

It is interesting to learn that the eldest son of Cheops and crown prince held as his chief position "Officiant [Chief Priest] of Anubis." One might well wonder what this could possibly mean, and how such duties could conceivably be carried out, since there was no temple of Anubis or even any known cult center of Anubis where one could officiate as a priest. All these problems dissolve when one realizes that Anubis was just a few minutes' walk down the hill, and was the Sphinx. In fact, the ceremonies at which the eldest son of the deceased pharaoh was required to preside after his father's death took place at the Sphinx, and are described in the next chapter, from texts found among the Pyramid Texts of the succeeding dynasty. (I should mention in passing that it has been suggested that Kawab and Chephren were really the same person, and that the tomb of Kawab was built for Chephren before he became king, after which he changed his name. However, this is only speculation, and is also very confusing to us.)

The other front-row mastaba to consider is that of Queen Mersyankh III, who was the granddaughter of Cheops, some say the widow of her uncle Prince Kawab, definitely the daughter of her aunt and sister-in-law, who was wife of King Djedefre (or Rededef/Radjedef), niece and sister-in-law of King Djedefre, and queen of her brother-in-law and uncle, King Chephren. She was also Priestess of Thoth, to whom she was not related. (That's a joke, just in case you are too dazed by all these incestuous relationships to realize it.) The two supersized Anubises in this queen's tomb were carved as part of inscriptions in the northern and southern jambs of the entrance to the tomb chapel, which is the best-preserved tomb chapel in the entire Eastern Cemetery (or as she would have said, the western cemetery). They are shown in figures 5.20 to 5.23. On the north doorjamb, the inscription reads: "A boon [a gift] which the king gives and Anubis foremost of the divine booth to a spirit who is noble in the sight of the great god, lord of the desert. Beholder of Horus and Seth, King's daughter, greatly praised, King's wife, Mersyankh."

On the southern doorjamb, the inscription reads:

A boon which the king gives and Anubis, he who is in Wet, lord of the necropolis, to a spirit who is noble in the sight of the great god, lord of the necropolis. Beholder of Horus and Seth, great favourite, companion of Horus beloved of him, follower of Horus, King's wife, King's daughter, Mersyankh.[39]

We should note that Anubis is called twice not only the Lord of the Necropolis here but also Lord of the Desert, and once again is referred to as "the great god." The eternal gifts are given to the deceased in these inscriptions jointly by the pharaoh and by Anubis. The inference that the Sphinx as Anubis is being referred to

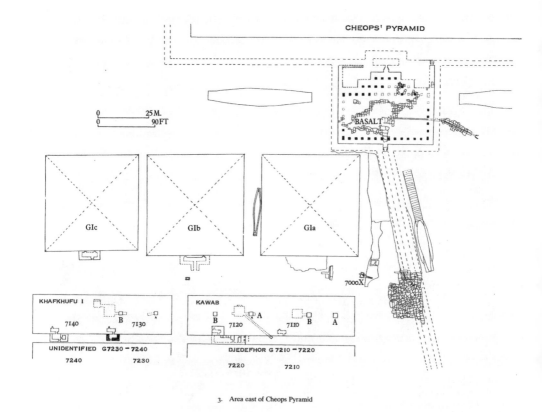

3.   Area east of Cheops Pyramid

Figure 5.25. The mastabas of Prince Khafkhufu (left) and Prince Kawab (right) are shown here on this plan from William Kelly Simpson, at the bottom of the picture. Above them are the three mini-pyramids known as the queens' pyramids. At the top of the picture is the southeast corner of the Great Pyramid of Cheops. The strange oblong shapes are boat pits, where wooden boats were once buried for use in sailing the celestial seas of the other world. At the foot of the Great Pyramid was the Funerary Temple of Cheops, now entirely gone except for part of its magnificent and beautiful basalt floor. Leading down from the site of the Funerary Temple we see the commencement of the now vanished Cheops Causeway, with a long boat pit beside it. It bends at an angle to the north, whereas the Chephren Causeway bends at an angle to the south. The strangest feature of the Cheops Causeway is that it went to the edge of the cliff and plunged off it and then continued below! Part of its further course may be seen in the old plan in figure 6.12 on page 248, drawn before houses crept up to the edge of the Giza Plateau. We now know that this Cheops Causeway culminated in the Valley Temple of Cheops, on top of the ruins of which at the moment sits a private house. Since the man who lives there is a prominent resident of Nazlet el-Samman whom no one wishes to offend, nothing has been done about gently suggesting to him that he might go house hunting. It is hard to imagine what could be more important currently than excavating the Valley Temple of the man who is supposed to have built the Great Pyramid, but then c'est la vie égyptienne. (Figure 3 in Willam Kelly Simpson, The Mastabas of Kawab and Khafkhufu I and II, Boston, 1978)

becomes increasingly strong. As I have already mentioned, the supersized Anubis functions also as a hieroglyph in the inscriptions. Where it does so is in the actual appearance of the name Anubis in each of the inscriptions quoted in translation above. In other words, what the inscriptions really say is, to take one example: "A boon which the king gives and [supersized picture of Anubis] foremost . . ." and so forth. Anubis is not spelled out; it is shown by the giant picture. What all the inscriptions might therefore be saying is that the boons are given by the king and by the Sphinx, understood to be the supersized statue of Anubis presiding over the desert necropolis, or, as we might lightheartedly call him, Anubis Magnus.

Anubis was especially honored by Fourth Dynasty pharaohs in another way as well. In the ruined Valley Temple of Mycerinus (the pharaoh whose name has been attached to the smallest of the three Giza pyramids), archaeologists found the remains of a green statue of Anubis, said to be made of "green basalt" (whatever that is!) or otherwise of green "diorite" (whatever that is!), though I suspect that, as usual, the Egyptologists, who generally know little about mineralogy, have given a wrong identification of the stone, or should I say two wrong identifications. It is probably a stone called by the Egyptians *bekhen* and is a graywhacke, or mudstone, containing chlorite, which makes it look green. This statue was of an Anubis *couchant,* in other words, a miniature replica of what I believe to have been the original form of the Great Sphinx of Giza. This statue was a foot high and nearly 2 feet long. It is preserved in the Boston Museum of Fine Arts. Du Quesne says it "is probably the earliest extant example of a figure of the Anubis jackal in its canonical form. . . . Perhaps the earliest three-dimensional jackal figure extant."[40] I would suggest that, in addition, it is possibly the only surviving three-dimensional replica of the original form of the Sphinx. It is not complete, but enough of it survives for us to be certain that it represents the standard form of the recumbent jackal lying on its belly with its paws stretched out in front of it.

There are many mentions of Anubis in inscriptions in tombs at Giza besides the royal ones of the Fourth Dynasty that were given above.[41] These tend to use more or less the same formulas, describing Anubis as Lord of the Necropolis who gives a boon to the deceased and so forth. However, there is no need to survey the whole of the tomb inscriptions of the Giza Plateau, as the point has been sufficiently made. See figure 5.26.

Another feature of Anubis that is continually mentioned throughout Egyptian history is that he is associated with a hill or mountain. This hill or mountain is never specified precisely, and one gets the impression that we are meant to be familiar with the reference without any need for explanation. Anubis is often called "Anubis on his hill" or "Anubis on his mountain." Most Egyptologists use

Figure 5.26. This fragment of a stone carving shows a portion of an inscription featuring a recumbent Anubis lying on his belly in the same position as the Sphinx. The inscription shows the hieroglyph *hotep* beneath Anubis (whose Egyptian name was Anpu) so that the reference is to the personal name Anpu-hotep, meaning Anubis Is at Peace, which was used by high priests of the period between the First and Third Dynasties, a period prior to the conventional date of carving of the Great Sphinx. The fragment was excavated in the season 1922–1923 at the site of Abu Ruash, a hill that overlooks Giza, by French archaeologists. It was found at the entrance to the underground site, hypogeum H-9. It is plate XVIII, number 4, in M. F. Bisson de la Roque, *Rapport sur les fouilles d'Abou Roasch (1922–1923)*, in *Fouilles de l'Institut Français d'Archéologie Orientale de Caire (Années 1921–1923)*, Cairo, 1924. See also the text discussion of the find on page 62 of that volume. (*Collection of Robert Temple*)

the translation "hill" instead of "mountain," as it is not thought that an actual high mountain is intended, and there is no evidence of any kind to associate Anubis with a real mountain. Strangely enough, in the earliest texts, namely the Pyramid Texts, this epithet does not occur. Because so little has been written about Anubis, it seems that no one has searched the Pyramid Text references to Anubis before now to check this. It is rather odd that this description of "Anubis on his hill," which is so common for thousands of years afterward, is absent from the earliest texts, which are nevertheless full of references to Anubis, generally describing him as being recumbent, presiding over the Pure Land or the Sacred Land, and being "on his baldachin." It is as if at the time of the Fourth Dynasty, as well as in the Pyramid Texts (Fifth and Sixth Dynasties, circa 2500–2200 BC), there was no need to mention that Anubis was associated with a hill, but merely to stress his position as guardian of the necropolis. Later, it seemed important to associate Anubis with a hill. And I believe that this was because the center of gravity of the pharaoh's court had moved away from Memphis, so that it was necessary to call to mind the fact—previously unavoidable and known to all who mattered—that Anubis was to be found at the Giza Plateau, the plateau being, of course, a hill. For those who had moved away from Memphis, it was just as well for them to remember that Anubis guarded the entry to the most famous hill in Egypt. When everyone was living beside it, it was merely called the necropolis, that is, the Pure Land or the Sacred Land. But when people were no longer beside it, it was recalled to mind as *the hill.*

"Anubis on his hill" therefore became, I believe, the standard way of referring to the Great Sphinx of Giza. The phrase seems to have occurred for the first time in the Fifth and Sixth Dynasties, after the Pyramid Age and as the Old Kingdom was drawing to an end.[42] The Egyptian expression "he who is on his hill" is *tepi-djuf.* Du Quesne suggests that this title "has no direct funerary associations, and is usually taken to refer to the natural desert habitat of the jackal, and to the rugged terrain of the necropolis." I would say that this is near to the truth, for the "hill" is clearly the Giza Plateau, which is indeed rugged and a desert, and, above all, is a hill. I believe that "Anubis on his hill" is synonymous with "the Sphinx of Giza." In fact, the word *dju* (hill) also means necropolis, as does *tep-dju.* And a *tepi-dju* is also a "necropolis official." Therefore, the very same words that mean "he who is on his hill" also mean "necropolis official" or "necropolis head." The epithet "he who is on his hill," as applied to Anubis, therefore always had the double meaning of "he who is at the head of the necropolis," that is, at Giza. It seems clear that only the Sphinx can be referred to.

In the Middle Kingdom (2119–1793 BC according to one chronology; circa 2000–circa 1750 BC according to another), the texts known as the Coffin Texts are found in coffins of the period. They were not intended to be read by anyone but the deceased and the gods, as they were inside the coffins in the form of protective spells. But they reveal much mythological and religious lore, and some of it is derived from the earlier Pyramid Texts. In Spell 825, a Spell for Entering the Netherworld, we are specifically told by the deceased that he has entered its "gate which is under the care of Anubis."[43] Since the gate to the netherworld was at Rostau, the expression that the gate was "under the care of Anubis" is another interesting reference that appears to apply to the physical presence of Anubis as official guardian of Rostau at Giza.

In Spell 629, Anubis is described as being in Djedu (i.e., Busiris, now Nazlet el-Samman), which is where Rostau is situated (Rostau being a more restricted portion or precinct of Djedu). He is also there called Lord of the Desert, which is unusually specific, in that his "Land" is generally called, by a religious euphemism, either the Pure Land or the Sacred Land, but here the scribe slips and specifies that it is in the desert, as Giza indeed is.[44] Djedu and Rostau are mentioned together in Spell 314, where the "secret thing" and the "mysteries" of the god Osiris (origi-nally those of the god Sokar) are given the specific physical description of being in "the deep place in Rostau," obviously a reference to a deep underground location there.[45] Although many ancient texts refer to underground caverns and chambers and tunnels at Rostau, it is rare to find a more physically specific description refer-ring to "the deep place." There can hardly be any doubt, from the many textual references, that Rostau contains vast underground constructions, many being expanded natural cavities in the limestone.

I shall have much more to say about this in the future, as the underground complex at Rostau, near the Sphinx, is a subject concerning which discussion has only just begun, and it goes far beyond the scope of this book, the limited pur-pose of which is to establish the truth about the Sphinx as a preliminary step to carrying forward the discussion of what else was really going on at Giza in the period before the Fifth Dynasty. Much of the further discussion is found in my next book, *Egyptian Dawn*. However, a partial indication of that subject is also found in the next chapter, which re-creates one of the most important ceremonial purposes of Giza in the early days, before the true tradition decayed and became merely a memory. It is necessary to establish this crucial ceremonial tradition clearly for the record, since until it is grasped, further discussion of Giza can-not proceed. After all, the Sphinx stands guard over the necropolis not only in a physical sense but in an intellectual sense as well: failure to comprehend its true purpose blocks all further progress by the inquirer, and the problem of the Sphinx thus acts as a guardian and an obstacle to understanding anything else stemming from that period. You have to grapple with the Sphinx first and solve its riddle, just as Oedipus did in Greek myth, before you can avoid being devoured and can go on to *enter the true city*.

6

SPHINX ISLAND

During the 1990s, the general public in many parts of the world was subjected to a massive wave of publicity and marketing relating to the Sphinx. This was principally generated by the books and TV documentaries of three popular writers who agreed about one thing: the Sphinx was at least 12,500 years old because there was evidence of water erosion in the Sphinx Pit, and this must have been caused by "ancient rain" circa 10,000 BC, when Egypt was believed to have had a different climate than it has today. Although I agree that there is evidence of water erosion in the Sphinx Pit, I reject these ideas, believing this can be explained in a new way. Through constant and insistent repetition, like some sort of hypnotic mantra, by means of books, conferences, and television, the idea that the Sphinx is at least 12,500 years old seems to have hardened into a kind of dogma to such an extent that among "alternative" audiences, anyone who does not accept it can even be presumed to be part of an orthodox conspiracy to suppress the truth.

By a strange quirk of fate, I became directly involved in this odd story of the "ancient rain" theory of the Sphinx at a very early stage. The observation that there appeared to be water erosion on the Sphinx itself (no mention was made of the Sphinx Pit) was first made by the Egyptological scholar Schwaller de Lubicz in a book published in French in 1961, where it was mentioned only in passing as an enigmatic feature. The book was called *Le Roi de la théocracie pharaonique* (*The King of Pharaonic Theocracy*). An English translation was eventually published in 1982 under the title *Sacred Science: The King of Pharaonic Theocracy*.[1] In this book, Schwaller de Lubicz mentions, in the midst of a general discussion of the Sphinx, "that Sphinx whose leonine body, except for the head, shows indisputable signs of aquatic erosion." He added a footnote that stated further: "It is maintained that this erosion was wrought by desert sands, but the entire body of the Sphinx is protected from all desert winds coming from the West, the only winds that could effect erosion. Only the head protrudes from this hollow, and it shows no signs of erosion."[2]

Indeed, the neck used to show extreme signs of erosion (see figures 6.1, 6.2, and 6.3, and figure 6.6 on page 242) until it was strengthened in modern times by cement and concrete. As Zahi Hawass, secretary general of the Supreme Council of Antiquities of Egypt, has said: "Baraize restored the head with cement, for at that time it was deemed necessary for the protection of the head. . . . The cement restoration of the head is not good and obscures the impressiveness of the Sphinx. Therefore, one suggests that Baraize's restoration of the head be reversed."[3] At the moment, the head is relatively free of signs of erosion, which is partially due to the fact that it was recarved by Pharaoh Amenemhat II and is thus much younger than the rest of the exterior of the Sphinx, and also because the stone of that part of the Sphinx is much stronger, as it comes from a stronger stratum of the natural rock. Also, the face of the Sphinx that we now see is not the face that was seen in, say, 1900. In figures 6.4, 6.5, and 6.6, photos taken in the 1870s and 1880s, a huge gash can be seen in the upper left side of the Sphinx's face. This is one of many blemishes filled in with cement by Baraize in the 1920s, when he took as much care over the Sphinx's face as a plastic surgeon might with a modern film actress. The only thing the Sphinx hasn't had by now is Botox. But Schwaller de Lubicz's point certainly merits investigation.

Apparently the first person to take Schwaller de Lubicz's comments seriously and to investigate them further was an American, John Anthony West, in the late 1970s. This is when I unexpectedly became involved. Between 1978 and 1980, my friend Randall Fitzgerald and I jointly edited a magazine dealing with the frontiers of science and knowledge called *Second Look*. We worked very happily together as editors and had a model collaboration; we never had any disagreement that I can remember, so the recollections are very pleasant. Our interests did not wholly coincide, as Randy was keen on some things that did not particularly interest me, and I was more interested in advanced theories in physics. We published the first popular articles anywhere on such subjects as twistor theory and the multiple-universes interpretation of quantum mechanics (which I wrote jointly with Roger Penrose and David Deutsch, respectively). Suddenly, out of the blue, one of our readers submitted an unsolicited article about ancient Egypt. His name was John Anthony West, and the article was entitled "Metaphysics by Design: Harmony and Proportion in Ancient Egypt." I enthusiastically agreed to publish this article because I thought such things needed airing, the article was fascinating, and the matters it discussed were of the greatest possible interest, although I disagreed with West's ideas of Atlantis and his notion that the Sphinx was more than 12,500 years old. However, as editors, we made it our policy not to

Figure 6.1. This photo dating from circa 1860–80 shows the extreme neck erosion of the Sphinx before it was "restored." (*Collection of Robert Temple*)

Figure 6.2. This photo, taken probably in the 1920s, shows the neck erosion of the Sphinx and the curiously pathetic attempt to fill holes in the right (southern) side of the Sphinx with stone blocks. They may have been covering an entrance into the Sphinx's body near one of the southern cupolas, or these blocks may merely be filling unsightly hollows. However, they were clearly intended to cover something, whether cosmetically or otherwise. This evidence should be taken into consideration when trying to decide whether the cupolas block an entrance to the body of the Sphinx. (*Collection of Robert Temple*)

Figure 6.3. This photo of a European soldier on a camel, probably in the 1920s, shows the same neck erosion and stone blocks on the southern flank of the Sphinx as we saw in figure 6.2; the photos were probably taken on the same day as part of this man's tourist visit. (*Collection of Robert Temple*)

allow personal disagreements with the opinions of authors to influence our decisions about publishing their ideas. The article duly appeared in our issue for June 1979.[4] Some months later, West brought out a book carrying his arguments much further, entitled *Serpent in the Sky*.[5] By this chain of events, without agreeing with him, Randall and I thus became the first publishers of West's ideas that the Sphinx was of immense antiquity, far older than the archaeological record could possibly justify. Schwaller's observation about water erosion is a fundamental one that needed attention, and who is to say that anyone would ever have called vociferous attention to it if West had not done so? When I first met West in the 1990s, he said he had forgotten about the article he did for our magazine and that he had no copy of it, so I was able to send him one for his files.

Figure 6.4. A photo taken of the Sphinx in 1893 by Emil Brugsch, showing the gash in the Sphinx's left forehead. (*Collection of Robert Temple*)

Figure 6.5. A photo of the Sphinx by G. Sarolides, probably from the 1870s. The altar where offerings were made sits in front of the chapel between the paws. This photo shows clearly the huge gash in the Sphinx's left forehead and the stump of the left lappet of the headdress. The original caption, written by hand, says: "The Sphinx. An emblem of sovereign power—intellect joined with strength. It is not known when or by whom it was erected, it was in existence when Cheops some 3000 years BC reared the Great Pyramid. Its body is in the natural rock and measures 140 feet in length. Its paws 50 feet in length, are built up of huge hewn stones. The head is carved out of the solid rock and measures 30 feet from brow to chin, and 14 feet across. From a sanctuary between the lion like paws, sacrifices were offered to the divinity it was supposed to represent." (*Collection of Robert Temple*)

Figure 6.6. A glass lantern slide circa 1880, showing the gash in the Sphinx's left forehead and the stump of the left lappet of the headdress. (*Collection of Robert Temple*)

The other two popular writers who have campaigned for the idea that the Sphinx is of immense antiquity are Graham Hancock and Robert Bauval, authors jointly and separately of various books on the subject. I know Graham slightly, and Robert rather well, although we have lost touch these days. We all mutually accept the fact that we are in disagreement about the extreme antiquity of the Sphinx.

In principle, it is understandable that these three authors have been driven to what I consider an extreme and untenable position with regard to the age of the Sphinx, because they take seriously the apparent signs of water erosion in the Sphinx Pit. And since Egypt is not known for heavy rainfall today, they have concluded that such water erosion must have been caused at a time when there was much heavier rainfall in Egypt than there is now. This superficially *seems* reasonable, although I do not believe it really is. They propose a date of about 10,000 BC for this heavy rainfall, which may or may not be justifiable. We come across conflicting claims about the climate so long ago, but I have not personally made a particular study of the ancient climate. I was never convinced by this argument from the very beginning for the simple reason that there is just no archaeological record at all for any important civilization during approximately seven thousand years of the time postulated between the "ancient rain" and the apparent beginnings of high civilization in Egypt. Whereas I am the first person to agree that there are curious anomalies about these beginnings, I cannot take seriously the suggestion that the beginnings were separated from any other signs of activity by seven thousand years of nothing. And trying to invoke the hypothesis of Atlantis seems a desperate measure, since Atlantis is a *speculation*. In other words, the logic seems weak and the evidence fragile. One idea often suggested by Robert Bauval is that the Sphinx was a lion statue that was somehow associated with the constellation of Leo rising at the spring equinox at an extremely early date. Since there is no evidence whatsoever that the constellation known to us as Leo was associated with a lion prior to the very last centuries BC in Egypt (when Babylonian influence crept in), and certainly not at some immensely remote era before that, this does not seem a feasible hypothesis. It is simply not an Egyptian tradition prior to the Ptolemaic Period.

There is plenty of evidence, as we shall see, for an alternative explanation of the signs that appear to indicate water erosion in the Sphinx Pit. And as we shall see later on, what I have to suggest is not incompatible with objections to the flowing-water erosion theories raised by Professor Lal Gauri, who has made the most intensive geological study of the Sphinx of anyone in history, is one of the world's leading experts on limestone and its erosion processes, and strongly believes the "ancient rain" theory to be completely wrong, and I certainly agree with him.

One thing that has gone awry in the discussions of the ancient-rain theory of the Sphinx is that Egyptologists have been so horrified by this rain-erosion theory that they have attempted to counter it by denying that there are any signs of water erosion in the Sphinx Pit at all. This is a severe tactical error and merely makes members of the general public believe that the Egyptologists are being silly or stupid, or perhaps worse. The apparent evidence of water erosion is so blatantly obvious to anyone that for someone supposedly knowledgeable wholly to deny it looks disingenuous. In fact, my criticisms of "consensus reality" in the last chapter cannot apply to the signs of water erosion, for Schwaller de Lubicz has already challenged this consensus reality and pointed out that those particular new clothes of the emperor were missing. It is to the credit of West, Hancock, and Bauval that they so passionately seconded this, even if their reasoning from that point on was doubtful. But Egyptologists are making a big mistake in taking refuge in their bunkers. They should not feed the ancient-rain theory speculations by uninformed opposition or contempt alone. What we now have is a situation where neither side is right, and the arguments that have raged between them for years are all spurious and a waste of everyone's time.

So how does one resolve this situation in a reasonable way? I think the starting point is to take seriously the possibility of water erosion in the Sphinx Pit. It certainly looks as if there was a great deal of it in very ancient times. Then one has to think: How can this have been caused, if not by "ancient rain"? Certainly, as we shall see later, exposed subterranean water-erosion channels in the limestone (which is rich in such caves) were revealed by the excavation of the Sphinx Pit, and these geologically ancient channels have been further eroded since exposure. Partially this has been by natural processes that involve dew in microscopic pores, cold temperatures at night and hot ones during the day, even occasional rainstorms, and so forth. But I believe a substantial standing body of water was near at hand to increase the sources of moisture in the air, so that the processes were caused not just by dew and a rare rain shower. And furthermore, I shall describe later very specific causes for vertical scouring of the Sphinx Pit walls by water that has nothing whatsoever to do with rainfall. But first let us establish the central answer to the riddle:

I believe that the Sphinx Pit was once a moat filled with water, and that the Sphinx was an island.

The first objection that anyone might raise to this suggestion is that the Sphinx Pit is open at the east end and enclosed by cliff faces on only three sides (north, south, and west). So how could it have been a moat? However, it was on the east side that the water from the inundation of the Nile was to be found, from which the water to fill the moat must have come. We have already encountered quays in front of the Valley Temple and heard the evidence that in ancient times the water of the Nile lapped at the foot of the Sphinx Temple and the Valley Temple and may well have overflowed into them on occasion. (It was only 660 feet away, even as recently as the seventeenth century, during the inundation.) I believe it is highly possible that the floor of the Sphinx Temple was annually flooded and was intended to be, as I shall explain further a little later on. Although not visible to the naked eye today, additional ancient quays have been excavated directly in front of the Sphinx Temple. They are shown in the early aerial photograph in figure 6.8, before they were covered over again with windblown sand.

THE TWO GREAT PYRAMIDS AT THE TIME OF THE INUNDATION.

Figure 6.7. A Victorian engraving of the pyramids of Giza at the time of the inundation. (*Collection of Robert Temple*)

Figure 6.8. This late-nineteenth-century photo shows the Giza pyramids in relation to the low-water level of a branch of the Nile. The people are on an extended mud bank. At inundation, the water rose nearly to the level of the trees growing along the artificial bank of the Pyramid Road, which is at far right. During the Old Kingdom, the Nile was much farther toward the pyramids and rose much higher than in the nineteenth century, lapping at the door of the Sphinx Temple (not visible here, to left of photo, where the plateau slopes down). (*Collection of Robert Temple*)

Figure 6.9. This photo is from a glass lantern slide taken circa 1900 or earlier from the Giza Plateau at the foot of the Great Pyramid, looking back toward distant Cairo. Victorian visitors are arriving as tourists. In the background is the long road leading into Cairo, which runs across a completely empty floodplain. In those days, before the construction of the Aswan Dam, the annual inundation of the Nile spread across this plain and lapped at the foot of the Giza Plateau. In the long, thin strip on the horizon, Cairo is faintly seen. Today, the floodplain has dried out completely and has been built upon. Cairo now extends from the distant horizon seen here all the way to the pyramids, and the main Pyramids Road, built on top of the trackway seen here, is now an artery of crazy traffic surrounded by modern buildings inhabited by millions of people. The population of Cairo, which at the time of this photo did not exceed six million, is now unquantifiable; estimates vary between fifteen and thirty million, depending on how many drifters, vagabonds, and homeless one counts, whether the estimated two million squatters in the City of the Dead are included, and so forth. The only thing that is certain about modern Cairo is that there are too many people, and since Egyptians believe it is a good thing to have as many children as possible, the population is exploding. (*Collection of Robert Temple*)

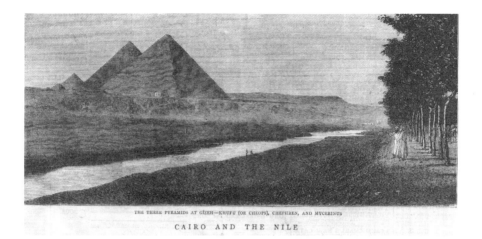

THE THREE PYRAMIDS AT GÍZEH—KHUFU (OR CHEOPS), CHEPHREN, AND MYCERINUS

CAIRO AND THE NILE

Figure 6.10. This is how the Giza Plateau appeared toward the end of the nineteenth century as seen from the tree-lined road leading from Cairo to the pyramids (on right). The Nile is low at this point, as it is not inundation time. (*Collection of Robert Temple*)

Figure 6.11. This French photo from the late nineteenth century shows the pyramids on the Giza Plateau in the background, from the banks of a part of the Nile when it is at a low level. It resembles figure 6.10; the road leading to the pyramids from Cairo is out of sight to the right, where the land to the left is the floodplain seen in figure 6.9, which would be covered by water during the annual inundation. (*Collection of Robert Temple*)

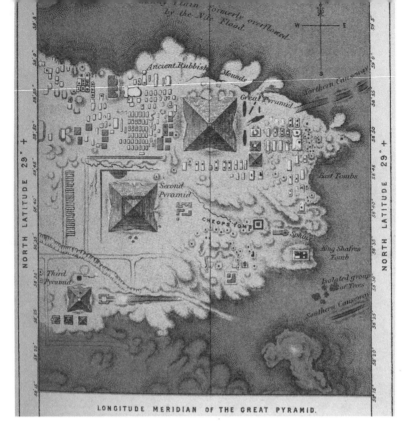

Figure 6.12. Charles Piazzi-Smyth's plan of the Giza (he spells it "Jeezah") Plateau, the pyramids, and the Sphinx, reproduced from his book *Our Inheritance in the Great Pyramid,* London, 1874 (folding plate III). Piazzi-Smyth's main purpose was to discuss the geodetic siting of the Great Pyramid and its longitudinal north–south meridian line, which bisects it, as shown here. However, for our purposes in connection with the Sphinx, this plan's usefulness is for showing in graphic color the Old Kingdom Nile floodplain (represented as brown). It shows that the Sphinx lies near the edge of this floodplain, at the right of the tan area. The word "Sphinx" is written in front of it, on top of the mound that concealed the still undiscovered Sphinx Temple. The structure we now call the Valley Temple is labeled here "King Shafre's [Khafre's] Tomb." The "Southern Causeway" is the top of a massive megalithic wall known today as the Wall of the Crow, which may well have had the double function at that time of acting as a causeway during the inundation period. The Chephren Causeway was still unknown at this time and is not depicted. The square called "Cheops Tomb" is what is today called Campbell's Tomb, and we have no idea who was buried in it; it is slightly north of the Chephren Causeway and is not open to the public, having a deep and dangerous open shaft. The "Northern Causeway" is the Cheops Causeway, now obliterated by housing. At this time, an extension of it into the floodplain area was still used, as it had been for millennia, as a genuine transport causeway across the flooded plain. Its use for that purpose is described in many of the early travelers' reports. This part of the Cheops Causeway was not only maintained by the reigning Mameluks and Turks but probably also extended by them, so no one knows where the authentic Cheops Causeway really ended and where its more recent extension, dating perhaps from the Middle Ages, commenced. In any case, none of it past the plateau's edge can be traced today, so we will never know. Because Piazzi-Smyth was an astronomer, his cardinal points as indicated on this plan are to true north and south rather than magnetic compass directions, in contrast to so many plans by archaeologists who do not even know the difference between geographical north and magnetic north. (*Collection of Robert Temple*)

Figure 6.13. This old photo, probably dating from between 1860 and 1890, has a handwritten inscription on the back: "View of the Pyramids after the Nile has receded." The view is an unusual one, taken from the southwest, with the Pyramid of Mycerinus and its three tiny satellite pyramids in the foreground and the Pyramid of Chephren in the background on the left. (The Great Pyramid is obscured and cannot be seen behind the Pyramid of Chephren from this angle.) The reference to the receding of the Nile is, of course, to its receding after the annual inundation (which no longer happens because of the Aswan Dam). The photographer's comment seems to imply that during the nineteenth century, the Nile at the inundation sometimes extended up to this southwest corner of the Giza pyramid field. I have come across other evidence that suggests that the inundation water did indeed swirl around to this location. In fact, the satellite photo seen in figure 6.22 shows walls and structures near the Pyramid of Mycerinus that I think may have been connected with a facility for unloading stones and building materials from barges. I believe this was the "tradesmen's entrance" to the Giza Plateau. (*Collection of Robert Temple*)

Below: Figure 6.14. A view from the Sphinx Temple looking westward along the south side of the Sphinx's body with the Chephren Causeway on the left and the Pyramid of Chephren in the distance. The edge of the Sphinx Pit shows evidence of a continuous horizontal watermark from when it was filled with water as the Sphinx Moat, and that was the level of the water surface. As for the body of the Sphinx, on the right, this angle of light enables us to see clearly the smearing of the body with modern cement, like icing spread on a cake. The top portions of the Sphinx body visible here are the actual carved rock (in a highly eroded state), whereas the lower portions are reconstituted of repair blocks, and the smeared cement has been used to fill in the holes in both. (*Photo by Robert Temple*)

Opposite: Figure 6.15. This is one of the spectacular aerial photos taken in 1992 from a low-flying aircraft by Marilyn Bridges and published in her large-format book *Egypt: Antiquities from Above* (Bulfinch Press, New York and London, 1996). This photo reveals many crucial features of the Sphinx and its surroundings, which are not so easily visible in any other view. The prominent road on the right is the modern access road to the pyramids for tourist buses that enter the Giza Plateau from the village to the east of the Sphinx, known in Arabic as Nazlet el-Samman but called Busiris in ancient Greek and Djedu in ancient Egyptian. The Sphinx Temple is visible at the foot of the Sphinx; as discussed previously, it was covered in sand and completely forgotten from circa 2000 BC until the 1930s. The temple to the left of it is called the Valley Temple and is connected by the Chephren Causeway to the Pyramid of Chephren, higher up the hill. The Valley Temple is partially open to tourists, whereas the Sphinx Temple is not. The little square temple to the right of the Sphinx, built at an angle, is a small and not very interesting New Kingdom edifice honoring the Sphinx. It was built in ignorance of the existence of the Sphinx Temple, which was covered in sand by then. The square black hole in the sandy area behind the Sphinx is the shaft grave known as Campbell's Tomb.

I would like to call attention to the tiny size of the Sphinx's head (seen also clearly in the horizontal wide-angle photo I took for figure 3.15). Also visible in this view is the tapered waist of the original carved figure, which is typical of a dog but not of a lion. The paws of the Sphinx, front and back, are essentially artificial, having been heavily reconstructed in Greek and Roman times and further reconstructed in modern times, so their leonine appearance is not authentic or original. The nature of the Sphinx Pit, in Old Kingdom times the Sphinx Moat, is dramatically obvious here. The wall of the Sphinx Temple on the side facing the Sphinx (the temple's western wall) was the barrier to the water in the moat. The water was led into the moat through the channel between the two temples, here seen in deep shadow, and the sluices to retain the water were at its western end (see my photos of the traces of those sluices in figures 6.31 to 6.42). The water of the Nile at the period of the annual inundation during the Old Kingdom (the Pyramid Age) lapped at the feet of the two temples, where there were quays, which have been partially excavated. Raising the water from that level to the level of the slightly higher Sphinx Moat was not a problem (see figures 6.23 to 6.27). The Sphinx Moat in the Old Kingdom was the sacred lake known in the Pyramid Texts as Jackal Lake, because the crouching Anubis sat in the middle of it. It also had other names and honorific titles such as Lake of Fire, Canal of the God, Canal of Anubis, Winding Waterway, Lake of Cool Water, and Lake of Life. The four sacred jars containing the internal organs of each deceased pharaoh in Old Kingdom times were ceremonially washed in the waters of Jackal Lake after his death, before they and his mummy were placed in his tomb. Every year, possibly in connection with the annual Festival of Sokar (see figure 7.22 on page 358), the pharaoh made a ceremonial journey around the statue of Anubis in a little boat; the remnants of a tiny landing stage for this ceremony appear to survive in the center of the west wall of the Sphinx Temple. Another place of descent into the Sphinx Moat seems to have been at the northeast corner of the Valley Temple (see figures 6.41 and 6.42). The dredging of the Sphinx Moat, which would have been a drastic necessity several times a year because of the problem of the windblown sand, must have taken place at several points, one of which is the vertical crevice in the bedrock on the left side of the Sphinx Pit in this photo, in the center (shown also in figure 6.57, where Olivia is seen climbing up it). The vertical fissures in the bedrock due to water erosion, mistakenly imagined by some modern writers as being due to impossibly prehistoric ancient rain, were caused by the repeated dredging over several centuries, which resulted in vast torrents of water pouring back down into the moat after each dredging effort. The greatest amount of sand would have accumulated at the west end of the Sphinx Moat (supported by modern archaeological evidence discussed on pages 285–88), and the shelf left in the Sphinx Pit there seems to have served as the primary service access for the maintenance of the moat. The ancient name for the immediate area around the Sphinx, and in particular for the Valley Temple,

was Rostau (or Rosetau). There are reasons to believe that the Valley Temple was originally a Temple of Sokar (later called a Temple of Osiris, by the time Osiris had largely replaced Sokar in religious mythology), the original lord of the underworld, but that Pharaoh Chephren, who may have had ego problems, turned it into a shrine for himself and filled it full of his own statues. We are deeply indebted to Marilyn Bridges for the immense trouble she went to in her struggles to get permission to take her invaluable aerial photos of ancient Egyptian monuments. (*Photo copyright © 1992 by Marilyn Bridges*)

Mark Lehner describes these quays that cannot at present be seen:

> A quay or revetment in front of the Sphinx Temple was revealed by drillings, as much as 16 m (52 ft) deep. It probably continues south in front of the valley temple, from which point ramps lead to the two doors of the temple. . . . In 1995 Zahi Hawass recleared the area, revealing that the ramps cross over tunnels framed within mudbrick walls that formed a narrow corridor or canal running north–south. In front of the Sphinx Temple the canal runs into a drain leading northeast, probably to the quay buried below the modern tourist plaza.[6]

We must keep in mind also that the means of keeping water trapped in the Sphinx Moat on the east side was by means of the west wall of the Sphinx Temple. This rose up very high (see figures 6.16 to 6.18, 6.20, 6.50, and 6.56). Let us stop for a moment and think of just how bizarre it was for there to be this temple wall immediately in front of the Sphinx's face. There is no passage or doorway leading to the Sphinx from the Sphinx Temple. The Sphinx Temple sits directly in front of the Sphinx, and yet *you could not get to the Sphinx from the Sphinx Temple!*

If you think the Sphinx Temple was built for the purpose of worshipping the Sphinx, then you have to explain why there was no connecting passage or doorway between the two. The Sphinx was boxed in and blocked off and could not be approached from the building in front of it. Why would anybody do this? Apart from that, the Sphinx Temple blocked the view of the Sphinx so that no one could see the Sphinx properly from the front. Imagine someone building a wall in front of the "Mona Lisa" in the Louvre, so that visitors to the museum could see the painting only if they brought along a portable ladder to stand on.

Since we are faced with the indubitable fact that this monstrous obstruction exists directly in front of the Sphinx, the only logical explanation is that this was done on purpose for a very good reason. I suggest that the Sphinx Temple's west wall was the fourth wall of the Sphinx Moat. I am convinced that the Sphinx Temple's purpose of obstructing the view was really to obstruct the outflow of the water in the moat, which had been brought in from the Nile at the time of the river's rise at the annual inundation.

In 1739, Richard Pococke visited Giza and stated that at the inundation, the Nile rose to a point in that year that was only 660 feet from the Sphinx itself.[7] That is a distance of 220 yards (201 meters), which is only half the extent of a single circuit of an American high school track, the conventional circuit of which is

Figure 6.16. Looking up at the face of the Sphinx from the floor of the Sphinx Temple at its western end. The walls here are carved out of the solid bedrock, with limestone blocks added above. This western wall would have acted as a massive barrier to the outflow of any water from the Sphinx Moat during the Old Kingdom. (*Photo by Robert Temple*)

Figure 6.17. The Sphinx seen head-on from inside the Sphinx Temple. What remains of the massive limestone west wall of the temple rises well above what would have been the water level of the Sphinx Moat when it was still in use. On the far side of the wall, just in front of the Sphinx (but today obscured by a spot-light installation), there are slight remains of a limestone platform where the pharaoh probably once stood alone for a ceremony, having disembarked from a small boat, as there were steps leading down on either side of this platform. (*Photo by Robert Temple*)

Figure 6.18. This view inside the Sphinx Temple shows the truly extraordinary erosion patterns visible on some of the stones. One has to remember that from about 2000 BC, this temple was entirely covered by sand, until it was rediscovered and excavated in 1936. All this erosion therefore had to take place before 2000 BC. If you go past the eroded stone at left and turn left, you are standing inside the northwest "magazine," which is a word used by archaeologists to refer to a storage space or room, seen in figure 6.19. I believe that with the inundation of the Nile during the Old Kingdom, the entire interior of the Sphinx Temple may well have been flooded for at least three months of the year. The two western magazines, which I believe held boats, would have had considerable water standing in them during that part of the year. (*Photo by Robert Temple*)

Figure 6.19. The Sphinx Temple has various strange design features. At the western end, there is a pair of these seemingly inexplicable chambers of a kind that tend to be called "magazines," that is, they are assumed to have been storage rooms of some kind. This is the magazine in the northwest corner of the temple. The western wall of the temple is on the right. A twin of this chamber is in the southwest corner of the temple. Anyone's guess is as good as another's, but my guess about these two chambers is that they were used for the storage of boats, which were lifted out, passed over the wall to the right, and set down in the water of the Sphinx Moat for special ceremonies. The floor design suggests something of this sort, since it seems obvious that something was stored here that was long and narrow and had its bottom along the center, and the stone walkway surrounding the chamber on three sides suggests a means of access by foot to the sides and far end of something long and narrow. What could that be besides a boat? For those who refuse to accept the idea of a Sphinx Moat, the chambers could still have contained long boats nevertheless, since we know that sacred barques were carried in procession at Giza during the Festival of Sokar. I therefore suggest that the northwest and southwest magazines were storage chambers for long ceremonial boats, whether sacred barques that never touched water or real boats to be lifted over the wall and placed into the moat. (*Photo by Robert Temple*)

Left: Figure 6.20. The Sphinx seen from within the Sphinx Temple at its eastern end. (*Photo by Robert Temple*)

Right: Figure 6.21. This is the western end of the North Trench, which lies along the northern wall of the Sphinx Temple and is padlocked with an iron gate at the eastern end to keep tourists out. At the western end, the bottom half terminates in solid bedrock, as seen here with a man standing on it. The wall to the right is also solid bedrock, being the cliff face of the plateau. Olivia stands looking down at me from the top, in the center. The woman whose head is showing at the top right of the photo is the Egyptian antiquities inspector. The two men in the photo are Greek friends. That this passage ends in a bedrock barrier shows that it could not have served as a water channel in the same way as the channel between the two temples at the southern wall of this temple. This passage was made necessary by the construction of the Sphinx Temple, since otherwise its northern wall would have been laid flat up against a cliff. Some of the limestone blocks in the northern wall are gigantic and must weigh in excess of forty tons. The wooden walkway at the top is part of the modern access to the Sphinx Pit. The small New Kingdom temple of Amenhotep II (see figures 7.3 to 7.5) stands nearby, and the stones lying on top of the bedrock in the center may have been part of its New Kingdom foundations, though I do not believe the details of the stones and rubble at this point have been studied or recorded; and as they are now entirely covered by the wooden access ramp, I could not study them properly. But I suspect the disorderly stones and rubble that constitute the top level must have been added at the time the modern ramp was constructed. (*Photo by Robert Temple*)

a quarter of a mile, or 440 yards. It is only 10 percent more than twice the length of the 100-yard dash in American track events, which can be run in approximately ten or eleven seconds by a sprinter. Consequently, if we ignore the sandy surface and assume a firm surface, a sprinter in 1739 could have run from the Sphinx to the Nile in about 25 seconds at the time of the annual inundation. And that was after the Nile had moved considerably to the east, whereas it is known to have been much closer to the Sphinx in Old Kingdom times, and as previously men-

Opposite: Figure 6.22. This is a NASA satellite photo of the Giza Plateau, supplied to me by my friend Simon Cox, to whom I am very grateful. Many strange features and buried structures invisible on the ground to the naked eye can be seen through the sand in this photo, particularly unexcavated walls around the precincts of the Pyramid of Mycerinus (top). Also, this photo shows that the row of tomb chambers behind (to the west of) the Pyramid of Chephren are not oriented north–south, as they seem to be when viewed casually at ground level. The Causeway of Mycerinus may be seen shooting off to the left and being lost in the sand. The Chephren Causeway, emanating from the Pyramid of Chephren in the center of the photo, shoots off to the left and ends at the Valley Temple, passing the Sphinx, which is below it in the photo. (The temple directly in front of the Sphinx is the Sphinx Temple.) The Great Pyramid is at the bottom, and in this view from above we can see that the west face (at right) has a line running down the middle, which is known as its apothegm, a slight indentation invisible from ground level; we can see also the track of the now demolished Cheops Causeway shooting downward and to the left, terminating at the cliff edge, although it once continued farther in the floodplain below, but is now built over. The town at the left in the photo is the vast, sprawling, and growing Nazlet el-Samman, which clearly wishes to gobble up Giza. In Greek and Roman times it was called Busiris, by the Napoleonic Expedition it was called Bousyr, in ancient Egyptian times it was called Djedu. The steepness of the escarpment rising from the floodplain to the plateau is best seen below the Great Pyramid, where the slope is a sharp one. The rectangular nodule beside the Great Pyramid, above it in the photo, is the modern structure built to house the ancient boat that was excavated from a boat pit and is now a museum. The three squares to the left of the Great Pyramid are known as the Queen's Pyramids. The snaking form threading through the middle of the photo is the modern road; it ends in an oval open area at the extreme left. If you look closely at the bottom (northern) edge of the Chephren Causeway in this photo, about halfway between the Sphinx and the pyramid you will see a crescent-shaped hole just peeking out and extending beneath it: that is the entrance to the so-called Osiris Shaft at Giza. To the left is a square black hole: that is the shaft leading to what is called "Campbell's Tomb." Neither of these subterranean features is accessible to the public, or indeed to most archaeologists either. If you look at the area containing trees in the top left-hand corner, that is the modern Arab cemetery. Just to the left of it you can see a long wall shooting out to the left, which is called "The Wall of the Crow," which functioned as a causeway during the times of inundation. Above it in the sand is the area of the ancient workers' village. This photo shows how the inundation waters once swirled round from just in front of the Sphinx Temple in an arc to the area southward and eastward (south is top, just above the Pyramid of Mycerinus). Even until the twentieth century, floodwaters sometimes reached this far. The buried structures above and to the left of the Pyramid of Mycerinus may perhaps be the remains of a landing stage for barges during the inundation, for the transport of materials. The strange round shape at far right center is a stage where operas and events are staged for the public. (*Photo courtesy of National Aeronautics and Space Agency, USA*)

tioned, the level was 26 feet higher during the Middle Kingdom than it was in the eighteenth and nineteenth centuries.

Since a massive amount of water was ready at hand for filling the Sphinx Moat in Old Kingdom times, a point agreed on by all Egyptologists today, why not take the further step of assuming that it was actually done (see figure 6.18)? To raise the water that small amount was a relatively simple task with even the most primitive water-raising devices, such as the swape, or well-sweep, technically known as the counterbalanced bailing bucket, which is known to have been used

in Old Kingdom Egypt.[8] (Its name in Arabic is *shādūf.* See figure 6.26.) For such a large volume of water, several of these of considerable size would probably have been used, and for weeks on end. But this posed no engineering difficulty even for a primitive people and certainly none to a people capable of building the pyramids! All that was needed for this task were time and plenty of laborers. Swapes were often used in large numbers simultaneously in Egypt:

> Batteries of swapes raising water in successive levels are often seen in Babylonian and ancient Egyptian representations, described in Arabic MSS. [etc.] ... A later development was to elongate the bucket's spout into a flume ... this being linked parallel with a counterweighted beam above, and so arranged that it automatically empties itself into the receiving channel on an upward motion. ... This was really a combination of the ancient swape with another device, the *mote,* consisting only of a scoop-shaped piece of wood suspended at its centre from a kind of a light derrick and used simply to scoop up the water. ... In India the operation of the device is assisted by a moving counterpoise, i.e. by men who walk back and forth along the upper beam. ... This is true also of the large *shādūfs* both in Egypt and in India. The *shādūf* will service a lift of from 4 to 10 feet [i.e., raise the water that high], and while the flume-beamed swape will not lift more than about 3 feet it will carry much larger amounts of water at each stroke.[9]

Figure 6.23. A simple water-raising device in use in ancient Egypt in an engraving of an ancient drawing from Adolf Erman, *Die Welt am Nil (The World on the Nile),* Leipzig, 1936, figure 2, in the section "Land and People." The caption merely says "Bucket in ancient times." This is apparently of New Kingdom date.

Figure 6.24. It took only two men and a bucket to move a significant amount of water at a single site in traditional Egypt. All they had to do was keep going. (*Collection of Robert Temple*)

Batteries of swapes would have been quite sufficient to raise the water the small distance to fill the Sphinx Moat (see figures 6.26 and 6.27). The water-raising machinery may have been more advanced than swapes, but the study of ancient Egyptian engineering, as far as I am aware, is too undeveloped for me to discover whether in Old Kingdom times the more efficient machines known as norias (see figure 6.25) or those known as pot chain-pumps (*sāqīyas*) or "camel-wheels" (*daulābs*), later ubiquitous in Egypt, may have been known and used.[10] Whether the water-raising was accomplished in the slower and more elementary manner with swapes does not really matter, since there was no shortage of labor to accomplish this tedious process, and in engineering terms it was simply a brute-force method applied to an incredibly simple requirement, which the most primitive people could have managed easily. Raising water to fill the Sphinx Moat was, compared to building even a small pyramid or excavating a deep shaft, mere child's play.

We have other evidence that this sort of thing was routine in ancient Egypt. The Greek geographer Strabo (64 BC–AD 25) recorded in his *Geography* that a Roman encampment near the site of what is today Cairo received its water supply

WATER-WHEEL ON THE NILE.

Figure 6.25. This is a noria water wheel, used for lifting quantities of water out of the Nile for irrigation purposes up until modern times. Although the noria did not yet exist in Old Kingdom times, as far as we know, it represents a successor to the *shadouf* system, which did exist then (see figures 6.26 and 6.27). At all times throughout history, the Egyptians have employed massive numbers of water-raising machines and shifted huge quantities of water. They were hydraulic engineers on a grand scale. (*Collection of Robert Temple*)

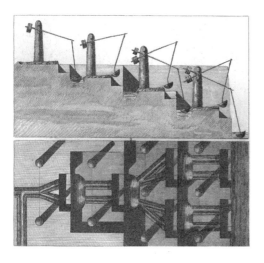

Figure 6.26. These engravings from the Napoleonic *Description de l'Égypte* (1809) show the details of the traditional Egyptian water-raising system known as *shadouf* in Arabic. With such a simple system, the entire Sphinx Moat could easily have been filled by Nile water, since manpower was essentially unlimited, and these devices could have been worked around the clock. The traces of sluices to control the water when it rose to the correct level are seen in figures 6.31 to 6.42, which I took just days before the evidence was covered over by modern "restoration" work on the northern foundations and base of the Valley Temple at Giza. (*Collection of Robert Temple*)

Figure 6.27. A view of a traditional *shadouf* water-raising system in operation circa 1798–1801, as portrayed in the Napoleonic *Description de l'Égypte*. This shows how only a dozen men at a time are needed to raise enough water from the Nile level of Old Kingdom times to the level of the Sphinx Moat. *(Collection of Robert Temple)*

from the Nile by a system of wheels and screws operated by 150 men, which raised the water and transported it along a ridge.[11] The passage reads:

> In sailing up the river [the Nile] we meet with Babylon, a strong fortress, built by some Babylonians who had taken refuge there, and had obtained a permission from the kings to establish a settlement in that place. [This is incorrect, but was believed at that time. The name Babylon in Egypt has a different origin, and a tower of this "Fortress of Babylon," or at least a more modern tower on the site of an even older one, now serves as the entrance to the Coptic Museum in Old Cairo.] At present it is an encampment for one of the three [Roman] legions which garrison Egypt. There is a mountainous ridge, which extends from the encampment as far as the Nile. At this ridge are wheels and screws, by which water is raised from the river, and one hundred and fifty prisoners are [thus] employed. The pyramids on the other side [of the Nile] at Memphis may be clearly discerned from this place, for they are not far off.[12]

For holding the water within the Sphinx Moat, all that was necessary was the western stone wall of the Sphinx Temple and a strong sluice gate in the passage between the Sphinx and Valley Temples. The water must have been led into the Sphinx Moat along this passage that separates the Valley Temple from the Sphinx Temple (see figures 6.28 to 6.30), and that connects the area to the east of the temples, where the Nile water was, and the Sphinx Moat directly. As we shall see in a moment, I have discovered and photographed evidence there of ancient sluice gates.

Opposite top: Figure 6.28. This is probably the most accurate ground plan of the Sphinx Temple ever published. This remarkable labor of love was accomplished by the German archaeologist Herbert Ricke, based on his excavations and surveys. He did not use the usual term Sphinx Temple for the building but called it the Harmachis Temple, after the god Harmachis (a late name for the statue of the Sphinx after it was deified). However, it is too confusing to have two names for the same temple, so we use the more usual name of Sphinx Temple, which all the English-speaking archaeologists use. This is the temple, closed to the public, that sits directly in front of the Sphinx, whose front paws and the pavement in front of them can be seen at the top of this drawing. Near the center of the (west) wall at the top of this temple plan, directly in front of the Sphinx and opposite the space between its paws, are two steps. I believe these to be the remnants of the place of descent of the pharaoh into his boat to sail around Sphinx Island, as described in the main text. It was probably also the place where the four jars containing the pharaoh's internal organs were ceremonially washed in the lake after his death, also as described in the main text. The main advantage of this plan for us, however, is the clear depiction it gives of the passageway between the two temples (shown here as a white corridor between the two dark buildings, at the left of the plan). This is the passage through which the flow of Nile water was regulated by means of sluices (traces of which are seen in figures 6.33 to 6.38) into and out of the Sphinx Moat. At the top left of the plan, the Chephren Causeway commences and abuts the northwest corner of the Valley Temple (the dark structure whose northern wall is shown at the far left of the plan). The photos in figures 6.37, 6.39, and 6.40 show the swirling water patterns in the stone at this point, caused by the rushing water when the sluices were opened and closed, and figure 6.42 shows the remains of the stone stairs descending at this point into the sluiceway for purposes of maintenance and operation of the sluices. This passageway has now been so thoroughly restored with new stone blocks (see figures 6.31 and 6.32 for this work in progress) that all traces of its original surface, together with evidence of the sluices, have been obliterated, so my photos are the only record that remains of the true purpose of this passage and the means by which the ingress and egress of water were controlled and regulated. The North Trench shown to the right of the Sphinx Temple, which I have carefully explored (literally after jumping about 30 feet down into it), never went through to the Sphinx Moat, and the original rock of the plateau blocks it completely at its western end, though that is not particularly clear here. The North Trench therefore had nothing to do with regulating the water flow but was required to give space for the workers to construct the temple, as the north wall of this passage is a solid rock cliff, shown here in dark shading. (*The illustration is Plan 1, the folding plan at the back, of Herbert Ricke,* Der Harmachistempel des Chefren in Giseh (The Harmachis Temple of Chephren at Giza), *in the series* Beiträge zur Ägyptischen Bauforschung und Altertumskunde, *Vol. 10; see notes to main text.*)

Opposite bottom: Figure 6.29. Looking from the water channel between the temples toward the modern gate across the entrance into the Sphinx Moat. On the right is the southeast corner of the Sphinx Temple. (*Photo by Robert Temple*)

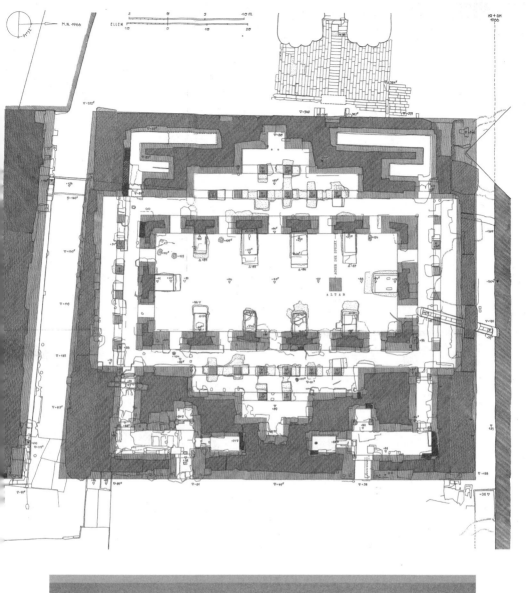

Figure 6.30. This view from the top of the north wall of the Valley Temple shows clearly how the Sphinx Moat ran directly out and into the northwestern corner of the Valley Temple, circumventing the Sphinx Temple, which acted as the moat's eastern barrier. Indeed, from this viewpoint we can appreciate how the strange angle of the southern wall of the Sphinx Moat had a clear purpose, which was precisely to lead the water around the Sphinx Temple and into the narrow channel where the sluice gate was, which regulated the level. The remains of the Sphinx Temple are on the bottom right of this photo. The barred metal barrier closes off this narrow access today so that people who are admitted into the Sphinx Pit cannot wander down between the two temples. (*Photo by Robert Temple*)

Figure 6.34 is a photo I took (as a result of my special access to the site) of the northwest corner of the Valley Temple, showing what appear to be long lines of water erosion along the base, following the entire line of the passage that would have led to the Nile in ancient times. I photographed all this evidence at the very last minute in 2001. The scaffolding was for the restoration of the wall, already well under way at the time, whereby new stone was laid over the

Figure 6.31. The north wall of the Valley Temple undergoing restoration. Modern pieces of limestone have been cut and inserted into holes; cement has been smeared all along depressions to even them out. All traces of anomalies are being erased. This is despite the fact that tourists never come here and never will. The horizontal lines showing ancient water erosion run along the lower wall at a level above the base blocks. (*Photo by Robert Temple*)

Figure 6.32. The eastern end of the north wall of the Valley Temple during restoration. We see piles of modern blocks of stone lined up to be placed and cemented against the base of the temple wall, which will forever obscure its true features and render impossible any closer reconstruction of what was going on here in the Old Kingdom. The Sphinx Temple is to the left of this photo and cannot be seen here. (*Photo by Robert Temple*)

Figure 6.33. This photo is taken looking due west, from the floor of the water channel between the two temples. To the upper right is the iron gate sealing off access to the Sphinx Moat. The limestone directly ahead at the end is natural limestone bedrock. The stone on the left is the north wall of the Valley Temple. Immediately to the left are two ancient bolt holes. The long, dark, vertical pole is part of some modern iron scaffolding erected for the process of "restoring" this wall—in other words, destroying all the ancient evidence in the interests of tidying up, filling in, and smoothing out, which is precisely the mentality that turned the Sphinx into something worse than a Botoxed movie star, resembling Lenin's corpse more than an ancient monument. The horizontal erosion lines on the Valley Temple's wall show clearly that the water level was kept constant during the inundation period up to the level of the Sphinx Moat's bedrock floor. These standing-water lines indicate very clearly that the channel was never dry during that portion of the year. The thin path of stones laid along the channel and leading toward the ancient stairs is a modern pathway for workers. The lumpy stone at lower right is the remains of a platform, with indentations for sluices and mechanisms at its base. Only the single stone seen protruding at the center right is part of the south wall of the Sphinx Temple. (*Photo by Robert Temple*)

original surface, wholly effaced all these ancient indications of water erosion and destroyed all such evidence forever. No one can ever take my photos again! (See figures 6.31 and 6.32.) Unexplained holes as well as larger indentations are seen in the original stones, which indicate that in some previous era wooden, brick, metal, or detachable stone fixtures were inserted into them. Figures 6.33 to 6.38 show evidence of carved indentations and depressions in the stone of the north wall of the Valley Temple that appear to be slots for sluice-gate mechanisms. There are also bolt holes drilled into the wall, apparently for fastening the sluices with metal bolts.

Figure 6.34. In the foreground, the steps descend into the passage between the Sphinx and Valley Temples, with the Valley Temple's north wall on the right. Just beyond the steps are the two indentations carved out of the rock that appear to be connected with the use of a bolt. Beyond them is the long vertical slot carved out of the rock, possibly in connection with a thick sluice gate. The protruding limestone blocks along the bottom of the passage on the right exist only here, from the steps to the other side of the apparent sluice-gate depression. They may thus have been required only in association with a sluice gate at this point. The scaffolding at left was being used at the time these photos were taken to restore this wall, thereby obscuring its ancient features forever. I believe the long horizontal striations along the base of this wall are from water erosion. The water was generally kept standing at that level during inundation time, and the thick sluice gate would have commenced only above that level (at the base of the carved depression) to regulate and retard inflow and outflow higher than this level to keep the moat level stable. There would have been a great deal of water pressure against this sluice gate, which effectively held back the entire Sphinx Moat contents. This would explain its extraordinary thickness. It is possible that the carved depression may have been for a sliding stone counterweight. It is a tragedy that the clumsy restoration of this wall has obliterated so much evidence that might have been examined more closely. (*Photo by Robert Temple*)

Figure 6.35. The northwest corner of the base of the Valley Temple. The cubicle at the far corner of the base of the temple is at extreme right. Steps lead down into the passage running between the Sphinx and Valley Temples. We see clear traces here of indentations and depressions cut into the base of the Valley Temple, which seem to be evidence of a sluice at this point to control the inward and outward flow of Sphinx Moat water. Just above the bottom step is what appears to be the receptacle hole for a bolt carved out of the rock. A carved slot for what may have been part of a thick sluice gate is in the upper central portion of the photo. (*Photo by Robert Temple*)

Opposite top: Figure 6.36. This photo shows particularly well the indentations cut into the left side of the base of the eroded stone platform at the right of the photo and, at the left, the Valley Temple's north wall for the various sluice mechanisms, counterweights, bolts, and barriers to control the water flow into and out of the Sphinx Moat during the inundation period. The south wall of the Sphinx Temple is out of view to the right. The cubicle cut out of the bedrock is out of view to the left at the end of the Valley Temple's wall; it may be seen in figures 6.37, 6.41, and 6.42. The horizontal water erosion marks in the lower portion of the wall of the Valley Temple are here very clear, resembling those that continue along the bottom of the Sphinx Moat beyond. It should be remembered that the Valley Temple wall is made of limestone blocks, which is why its watermarks are perfectly horizontal, whereas the wall of the Sphinx Moat is solid bedrock, which is why its eroded strata follow the softer layers of limestone in the bedrock and are not precisely horizontal, although the causes for the two sets of watermarks are the same, namely standing water over periods of centuries. (*Photo by Robert Temple*)

Right: Figure 6.37. Detail of the base of the Valley Temple wall at the northwestern corner. On the extreme right is the base of the cubicle and at bottom left are the steps. The possible bolt holes are in the center of the photo, and the possible sluice-gate depression is beyond. The strange protrusion of limestone blocks at the base of the wall is seen here from above, already smeared over on top by modern cement. (*Photo by Robert Temple*)

Left: Figure 6.38. A closer view of the apparent bolt slot and sluice-gate slot in the base of the northwestern corner of the Valley Temple. Modern cement is smeared into the base wall here, running from the top of the second step along the photo, as part of a clumsy restoration of the structure. (*Photo by Robert Temple*)

The water-erosion features of this wall are now a thing of the past, and I believe that my photos of them may be the only ones in existence, due to the fact that this area has been sealed off from visitors for the best part of living memory. Certainly the interpretation that I would give to my set of photos is that they suggest that a body of standing water sat in the channel for centuries, sometimes higher and sometimes lower, and as it led toward the Sphinx Moat, it was the channel by which the water in that moat was regulated during the Old Kingdom. We have to remember that these features were buried under sand during the New Kingdom and were only cleared in 1936 for the first time in approximately four thousand years. Therefore, all these strange carved and drilled features in the stone must date from some time prior to 2000 BC.

The water erosion certainly has not occurred since 1936, so it must therefore have occurred in the Old Kingdom, during the period circa 2500–2200 BC. This photographic and physical evidence should therefore be accepted until such time as anyone can produce any alternative explanation for it. Personally, I have to admit that my powers of imagination cannot summon up any alternative but to accept that Nile water stood here, was let in and out here, and from here was carried through to the Sphinx Moat. Some of the curious niches, indentations, and holes in the rock and stone seen at this location may have been connected with the operation of the water-raising equipment, counterweights for raising and lowering devices, sluice gates, and other details of the managing of the water. Certainly there must have been some purpose associated with these many anomalies, some of which were definitely carved out of the stone and rock with great care in Old Kingdom times. Alas, most of these also must have been covered up now by the restoration stones, and not only are my photos probably the only record of them, but I was not in time to photograph them all, as the restoration was well under way. There is no record at all of the others that must have existed. Even before the restoration stones were applied, modern stone had earlier been inserted into some gaps and cement had been pushed into holes to render them level and smooth, as my photos also show. There is thus no photographic record of the pristine evidence in its entirety.

At the very point where the channel between the two temples spills directly into the Sphinx Moat, a clear swirling pattern in the rock is visible, as recorded in my photos in figures 6.37, 6.39, and 6.40, which seems to indicate repeated rushing of water from the channel into the moat when a sluice was raised. The water must therefore have been raised into the narrow channel, and when it had reached a certain level, a sluice was lifted so that the water thus raised could pour into the moat. A full engineering study of all these possibilities should be undertaken by hydraulic engineers. To study the subject properly, they should build a

Figure 6.39. This view shows the swirling pattern in the rock where the water entered from the channel and then passed to the right into the open Sphinx Moat. The horizontal lines in the Sphinx Moat wall beyond the iron gate show how the standing water ate away at the softer veins in the natural limestone; this created the successive indentations, which are approximately horizontal to the bedrock. It is important to stress that they are not waterlines as such, but are erosion lines in the softer veins caused by the water. The veins are not precisely parallel to the bedrock surface because the limestone table is slightly tilted downward to the east. (*Photo by Robert Temple*)

Figure 6.40. Only if one is given special access to the Sphinx and Valley Temples can one get this view of the continuation of the Sphinx Pit around its southeast corner, where the continuity of the water-erosion patterns is clearly visible. The Sphinx Pit leads up and to the right beyond the metal gate. (The base of the Pyramid of Chephren is at top right.) Around this corner and behind the photographer, a channel leads down between the two temples, different aspects of which are shown in the succession of plates documenting these features, some of which have subsequently been covered over by restoration work. I do not believe any other set of photos of these crucial features has ever been taken. (*Photo by Robert Temple*)

scale model of the moat and inlet, calculate the variations of the hydraulic pressures and flows due to the reduction in scale (of the model), and then calculate and plot the hydraulic phenomena. This should then be illustrated by computer graphics showing the water in motion. This would make a very good project for the new Cairo Archaeological Museum at Giza, to demonstrate to tourists how the Sphinx Moat worked in its original state as an ingenious example of ancient hydraulic engineering.

I have looked carefully through the published excavation accounts of Selim Hassan from the 1930s. He is the man who finally cleared the entire Sphinx Pit, which he called the Sphinx Amphitheater, down to the bedrock. I wanted to discover whether there was any evidence that he had encountered a mud-brick wall on the east side of the moat that might have retained the moat water as an additional barrier placed westward of the Sphinx Temple's west wall. He certainly cleared many mud-brick structures and walls from the Sphinx Pit! But my attempts to discover specific evidence on the east side met with frustration because so much work had been done there by his predecessors, most of which was undocumented, in the careless and lazy way archaeologists had in those days. The east end of the Sphinx Pit in front of the Sphinx was largely cleared by Caviglia in 1817 (but the sand returned), partially by Mariette in 1853, partially by Maspero in 1886, again by Baraize in the 1920s, and finally by Hassan in the 1930s. However, Hassan expressed a great deal of frustration at a wall that Baraize had actually himself constructed in front of the Sphinx, and which Hassan had to demolish before he could proceed. Hassan writes: "We commenced our season's work on October 4, 1936, at a spot lying close to the northern and eastern walls which M. Baraize had built, and which we were forced to demolish before we could get down to our task of excavating."[13]

He adds further:

In 1925 M. Baraize was entrusted by the Antiquities Department to carry out excavations there [at the Sphinx] on their behalf. M. Baraize certainly freed the statue from all sides, but instead of clearing the sand away altogether, he erected huge barrage-like walls to hold it back, the demolition of which was one of our most laborious tasks when it became necessary to remove them in 1936–1937. I believe M. Baraize had taken his inspiration from the monuments of the Old Kingdom and built for eternity.[14]

The photo of the eastern wall built by Baraize in front of the Sphinx and published by Hassan (reproduced here as figure 6.43) shows a massive structure resembling a fortress, as if Baraize were expecting an attack on the Sphinx from the east by a heavy artillery division.[15]

Figure 6.41. This is the strange cubicle and base carved out of the bedrock at the northwestern corner of the Valley Temple. The base of the temple itself is a continuation of the same bedrock. See figure 6.42 for further detail. (*Photo by Robert Temple*)

Figure 6.42. Detail of the cubicle and step at the base of the northwestern corner of the Valley Temple. The electricians for the *son et lumière* show have laid their cables across it. The two granite pieces roughly jammed in recent years onto the top, in front of modern masonry, rest upon the original initial step downward from the end of the causeway, which constitutes the top of this cubicle. It is clear from this first step that this corner cubicle was a way to go down, either into water or onto steps that led into the passage between the two temples. Such a narrow and obscure descent as this can have been intended only for very restricted access (not unlike that of today!) and certainly would have been inadequate for a procession. This descent was not noticed or mentioned by the excavator Uvo Hölscher in the only book ever published about the Valley Temple, a book I know intimately, since I have co-translated most of it from the German. Nor was it noticed or mentioned by Selim Hassan or Herbert Ricke in their books on the Sphinx and the Sphinx Temple. In fact, no one seems ever to have noticed it before! Can this have been the mooring point for a small boat that made its way around the corner and into the Sphinx Moat? (*Photo by Robert Temple*)

FIG. 10.—THE EASTERN PROTECTIVE WALL
BUILT BY M. BARAIZE

Figure 6.43. Selim Hassan published this photo in his own excavation report to show the "huge barrage-like walls" built in 1926 by Baraize to hold back the sand so that it did not reengulf the Sphinx. The massive constructions are shown in the upper half of the photo. Hassan and his team had the unenviable task of getting rid of these walls. Often it is more difficult to clear away modern structures than ancient ones! (*From* Excavations at Giza, 1936–1937, *volume VIII*)

The pity is that Baraize's monstrous wall was built on top of the very place where an ancient mud-brick wall would have had to stand to retain water in the Sphinx Moat. In constructing his own wall, and leveling the foundation for it, Baraize would inevitably have destroyed all trace of any ancient mud-brick wall. If anything had survived, it would then have been cleared by Hassan when he got rid of Baraize's wall, for Baraize's wall was too solid and vast to be removed delicately, and an actual assault on it was necessary! So we see that five modern excavators have had a go at the point where the east wall of any moat would have stood. One of them built heavily upon it and the others relentlessly cleared everything to bedrock. No chance of any traces surviving all that! But even in ancient times, activity on that spot was intense. The area was open to the public during Ptolemaic and Roman times, having been entirely cleared by them; this area was the forecourt for the worship of the Sphinx as an idol. The great steps descending to the Sphinx directly over this spot may be seen in figures 6.44 to 6.48. Of the steps, Charles Irby, who visited the Sphinx at the time of the Caviglia excavations and knew Henry Salt, quotes what Salt said to him about the impact they were supposed to make on ancient visitors:

> I must beg you [the reader] to imagine yourself fronting the face of the sphinx, at a considerable distance, and nearly on a level with the lower part of the face, and also with the ground adjoining the animal [he refers to the mountains of sand on all sides that have now been cleared away]. As you advance, you find at some distance from the paws, a flight of steps which lead some depth below the paws to the base of the temple [he means the space with the altar, then called "the temple," as the Sphinx Temple itself was still unknown]. Mr. Salt is of opinion that this descent by steps was meant to impress the beholder (after having first viewed the sphinx at a distance on a level) with a more imposing idea of its grandeur, when he views the beast in its full magnitude from below.[16]

And even before Ptolemaic and Roman times, the area was cleared by the New Kingdom pharaoh Thutmosis IV when he erected his Dream Stela between the Sphinx's paws (see figure 3.3). So over the past 3,400 years, there have been at least seven serious attempts to clear the area east of the Sphinx, where any extra retaining wall for a moat would have stood in the Old Kingdom period.

The irony of all this is that it was Selim Hassan who in 1936 finally cleared the Sphinx Temple, which was farther east. Its existence was unknown even in the New Kingdom, when it was totally buried in sand and forgotten. This subject is discussed more fully in *Egyptian Dawn,* which includes an account of important discoveries made by myself and a colleague within the Sphinx Temple, to which we were given special access by the Egyptian Supreme Council of Antiquities.

Another crucial fact about the Sphinx Moat is that from the earliest times in the Old Kingdom, much of the rainwater from the east slope of the Giza Plateau was fed into it by a prominent drainage channel. This is remarkable evidence in favor of the existence of a moat being recharged with as much as possible of the rainwater and flash-flood water from the occasional downpours that even today Giza experiences once in a while, and that were more common in Old Kingdom times, when the climate was milder. The existence of this drain has been constantly mentioned by Zahi Hawass in recent years in the context of his friendly dispute with Rainer Stadelmann as to who carved the Sphinx, Pharaoh Cheops or Pharaoh Chephren.

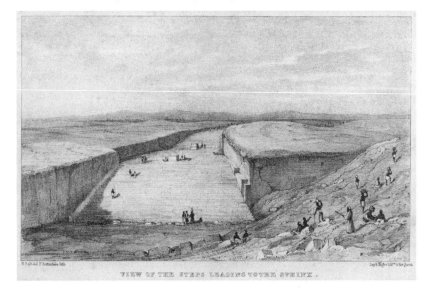

VIEW OF THE STEPS LEADING TO THE SPHINX.

Figure 6.44. This is the only surviving image that shows us the full grandeur of the gigantic stairway leading down to the Sphinx in Roman times to enable the public to come and worship the Sphinx as an idol, and pray to it and make offerings. This drawing, by Henry Salt, shows us the view as seen from the Sphinx itself, with Cairo invisible in the distant background, and the Mokkatam Hills beyond it at the horizon. This drawing was made in 1817, when Caviglia was clearing the Sphinx (men carrying away sand in baskets on their heads are at right). The Sphinx Temple was still unknown at this time and is actually underneath the stairway. The large rectangular mound at the right of the stairway, covered in a hill of sand, covers the right half of the Sphinx Temple (as still seen in figure 6.50, the aerial photo taken in 1926) and the Valley Temple, the latter of which was more or less known to be some kind of covered ancient structure but was not excavated or explored yet. The entire stairway seen here was demolished, and not a stone of it remains, because of the need to excavate the Sphinx Temple beneath. Although it cannot be seen clearly here, to the left of this stairway in this view, along its northern edge at the front, the stairway did not continue to the cliff face, but there was a horizontal passage leading to something underneath, possibly a passage heading northward and descending to a small subterranean chamber. This was never explored. In figure 6.47, which is a ground plan of the stairs and paws of the Sphinx as measured and drawn by Henry Salt, this horizontal side passage is clearly shown, culminating in a left turn marked by Salt "supposed door" and leading to an unknown destination. Since Salt measured the location of this door so carefully, it should be possible to identify that location precisely today by doing measurements on the ground. No one has ever done this, but it is clear that the location is above the northwest corner of the Sphinx Temple, and it may mean that one small section of that structure was known and reached by a shaft at this time. This accords with the findings of myself and my colleague Professor Ioannis Liritzis, in our official dating investigation of the Sphinx Temple, that a small section of the Sphinx Temple just inside the eastern wall was accessible by shaft during late times. Thus, two small ancient exploratory shafts seem to have reached the Sphinx Temple many centuries after its burial by sand around 2000 BC, resulting in intruded material at one location, though the one we investigated was extremely small and restricted to a tiny area, and the one suggested by Salt's drawings was probably similar. Precise measurements on the ground could give us the location for Salt's "supposed door," and then it would be possible to identify which tiny section of the subterranean structure may have been accessible to the Ptolemies and the Romans and perhaps used as a chamber or crypt in connection with Sphinx ceremonies. This drawing comes from *Operations Carried On at the Pyramids of Gizeh in 1837* by Colonel Howard Vyse and John S. Perring, London, 1842, third appendix volume, plate opposite page 113. (*Collection of Robert Temple*)

Figure 6.45. A photo of the Roman steps leading down to the Sphinx (which is behind the camera), taken prior to 1936 and published by Herbert Ricke in *Der Harmachistempel des Chefren in Giseh* (*The Harmachis Temple of Chephren at Giza*), in *Beiträge zur Ägyptischen Bauforschung und Altertumskunde,* ed. by Herbert Ricke, volume 10, Wiesbaden, 1970. The main steps are on the right. Behind and beneath the minor flight of steps on the left was a passage that was never fully explored. All these steps are now entirely demolished.

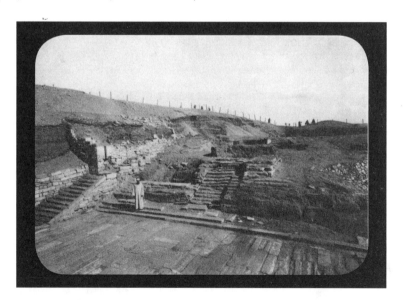

Figure 6.46. After the broad Roman steps down to the Sphinx from the east had been removed (see figures 6.44 and 6.45), these older steps were found underneath. Uncredited photo reproduced in Herbert Ricke's *Der Harmachistempel* (1972), plate 4b. These too have been removed, and no trace remains of any of the steps.

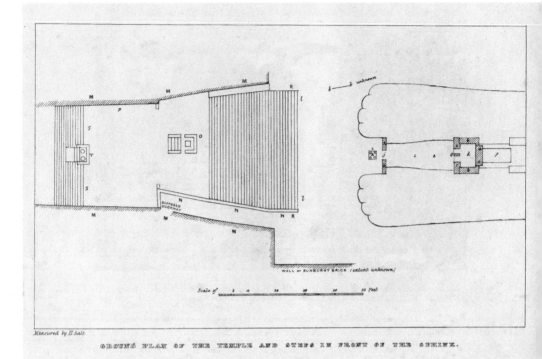

Measured by H Salt.

GROUND PLAN OF THE TEMPLE AND STEPS IN FRONT OF THE SPHINX.

Figure 6.47. This is Henry Salt's carefully measured ground plan drawing of the front paws of the Sphinx (at right) with the altar and stelae between them, facing the now vanished stairway leading down to the Sphinx and dating from Roman times. Salt's view of this stairway, with my extensive caption explaining it, is shown in figure 6.44. The stairway was dismantled and demolished entirely when the Sphinx Temple beneath it was excavated, and not a stone of it now remains. The sections of stairs were separated by platforms containing altars, which explains the curious rectangular structures in the plan. At the bottom of this plan's drawing of the stairs, along the north edge of the bottom of those stairs, was an indented horizontal passage (marked "N") leading to a "supposed doorway" heading north, which was never explored. This probably led to a ladder or small stairway leading to a crypt excavated by a narrow shaft in the northwest corner of the Sphinx Temple, where a chamber may have been used by officiants of ceremonies connected with the worship of the Sphinx at this time.

My colleague Professor Ioannis Liritzis and I discovered a similar small area elsewhere in the Sphinx Temple against the interior of the eastern wall, which had been penetrated by a later shaft, where intruded material had been left. There is no doubt, however, that the existence of the Sphinx Temple as a structure remained unknown in antiquity after 2000 BC, despite these two apparent shafts reaching tiny portions of it, which must have appeared to be remnants of tombs and were not comprehended as being parts of a temple. (I do not believe the one we found was still accessible by the time of the Ptolemies and the Romans.) This drawing is found in *Operations Carried On at the Pyramids of Gizeh in 1837* by Colonel Howard Vyse and John S. Perring, London, 1842, third appendix volume, plate opposite page 110. (*Collection of Robert Temple*)

Figure 6.48. The plan of the descent of the Roman steps toward the Sphinx, whose front paws are at the bottom of the picture. This is the plan as published by Herbert Ricke, who took it from Henry Salt's drawing as published in 1818. Directly beneath the Roman steps was the still undiscovered Sphinx Temple. At left, there is a small opening, and the German word *Tor* followed by a question mark; *tor* means "door."

Below: Figure 6.49. This is the corner inside the eastern end of the Sphinx Temple where an intruded shaft led down to the floor level. The dating results obtained by my colleague Professor Ioannis Liritzis confirmed that this location had been reached by a late intruded shaft. The Sphinx Temple is discussed at length in my book *Egyptian Dawn*. (*Photo by Robert Temple*)

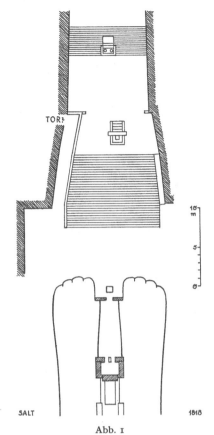

Abb. 1
Plan der römischen Treppe, von SALT 1818

Figure 6.50. This is an aerial photo of the Sphinx taken by the British Royal Air Force on September 28, 1926 (as we know from the information on the back). This image has never been published, as far as I know. This is probably the best photographic evidence to survive of the gigantic barrage walls constructed by Baraize earlier in this same year to hold back the engulfing sand. As can be seen here, his major effort was to prevent the sand from pouring in from the north (on the right in this photo) and the east (the foreground in this photo), since the southern portion of the Sphinx Pit had been completely cleared by him and the portion of the Chephren Causeway beside it had also been cleared. It is remarkable that at this late date, the remainder of the Chephren Causeway was completely covered by sand and was invisible. This photo provides graphic evidence that the Sphinx Temple in front of the Sphinx was still completely unknown, covered in a vast hill of sand. Above and behind the Sphinx Pit, which has been cleared to the bedrock at the back, Baraize has erected strong walls to stop the sand pouring in from the west. All these overwhelming perils of sand were not eliminated until 1936, when Selim Hassan, with hundreds of laborers and railway tracks (see figures 3.11 and 3.12), finally carried it all away in one of the most Herculean clearance efforts in the history of world archaeology. At that time, in clearing the mountain of sand seen here in the foreground, he discovered and cleared the Sphinx Temple underneath, which had been lost beneath the sand and forgotten no later than 2000 BC (which was the end of the Old Kingdom period). This is one of the most historically important photos ever taken of the Sphinx, and I bought it from a dealer for only £2.99. Sometimes in life one gets a bargain. (*Collection of Robert Temple*)

Figure 6.51. "*Before.*" This drawing shows the Sphinx and the Valley Temple as they were known prior to 1936, and the excavation by Selim Hassan that revealed the entire Sphinx Temple in the empty space shown here in front of the Sphinx, which had been covered by a mountain of sand for four thousand years. Compare with figure 6.52 adjoining, which shows the view "*After.*" This drawing is figure 2 on page 5 of Herbert Ricke's *Der Harmachistempel des Chefren in Giseh,* Wiesbaden, 1972.

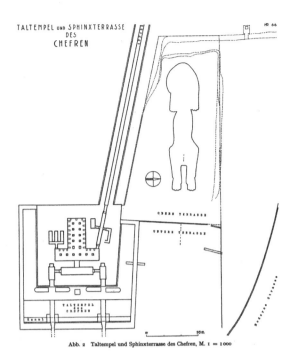

Figure 6.52. "*After.*" This drawing shows the Sphinx with the Sphinx Temple in front of it, as excavated in 1936 and unknown prior to that. This drawing is figure 8 on page 19 in Herbert Ricke's book *Der Harmachistempel.*

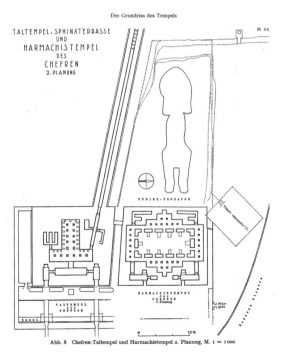

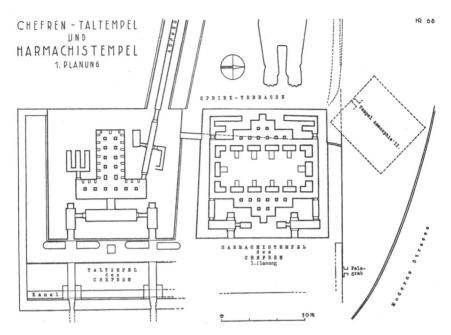

Figure 6.53. This plan from Herbert Ricke's excavation report (in German) of the Sphinx Temple (which he calls the Harmachis Temple) shows very clearly the bedrock barrier at the top of the North Trench, at the right of the Sphinx Temple (seen in figure 6.21). It also gives an accurate location for the small New Kingdom Temple of Amenhotep II, seen in figures 7.3 to 7.5. Although that small temple gives the superficial appearance of having been plunked down more or less at random, in reality it was placed in visual relation to the Great Pyramid, as demonstrated by the photo in figure 7.3. The paws of the Sphinx are at top right. The building on the left is the Valley Temple, and the structures shown in front of it are its quays. The quays of the Sphinx Temple, visible in the old photo in figure 4.2, have been covered over again with sand, and Ricke was unable to draw them because his excavations did not extend that far. *Taltempel* is the German word for Valley Temple. By *Sphinx-Terrasse,* Ricke means the Sphinx Pit, which he calls a terrace.

Figure 6.54. The central court of the Sphinx Temple, seen from the north and looking directly south. The north wall of the Valley Temple rises beyond in the background. Reproduced from Herbert Ricke, *Der Harmachistempel,* Wiesbaden, 1970, in which it is plate 14a.

Figure 6.55. A view of the southeast corner of the Sphinx Temple as seen from the roof of the Valley Temple. Along the bottom of the photo, in deep shade, is the conduit for the water that led into the Sphinx Moat (toward the left) from the Nile inundation floods that would have reached to the place where the people are walking. (*Photo by Robert Temple*)

Figure 6.56. This photo, which I took inside the Sphinx Temple, shows two granite blocks (the slightly pink blocks lying on the bedrock) lying loose and abandoned, left perhaps from some lost part of the structure. The two blocks are far from any obvious construction made of granite. There is no ready explanation for their presence in the midst of this limestone edifice. The one in front was presumably left there subsequent to Selim Hassan's excavation. Ricke does not comment on these anomalous blocks, although he carried out subsequent excavations at this site. The Giza structures have many such anomalies and few convincing explanations. (*Photo by Robert Temple*)

As I described earlier in this book, at the 2000 Congress of Egyptologists in Cairo, Stadelmann was giving his paper about the Sphinx having been carved by Cheops (we have already seen in chapter 4 that Stadelmann dismissed the possibility that the face of the Sphinx could possibly be Chephren's), when Hawass got up from the audience, took the microphone from Stadelmann, and said it was impossible that the Sphinx could have been carved by Cheops. Hawass pointed out that there was a prominent rainwater drain connected with the Chephren Causeway that emptied directly into the Sphinx Pit. The implication was that Chephren would never have constructed such a drain and allowed rainwater to pour into the Sphinx Pit if Cheops had already dug out the pit and carved the Sphinx. It would have been too impolite and an insult to allow wastewater to desecrate the site. Therefore, the Sphinx cannot possibly have been carved before the time of Chephren. Of course, that leaves the embarrassing question of why Chephren would want to desecrate his own site! But presumably it would be more polite to do that than to desecrate an existing site, and it would be his own business.

The drainage channel leading into the Sphinx Moat is about 6 feet wide and 4.5 feet deep, so it was a major construction intended to bring considerable amounts of water down into the moat. It was eventually blocked at some later stage by pieces of granite. It is described by Paul Jordan (who prefers to call Chephren by his Egyptian name of Khafre) as follows:

> The Khafre causeway was equipped with drainage channels which are interesting to us now because they indicate that rainwater run-off was an essential provision of the pyramid complex. We are accustomed to think of Egypt as a very dry place, but even today, in times that are drier still than were the days of the Old Kingdom, rains can sometimes come and cause considerable damage in a context where they are not routinely expected. Evidently the monuments of the Giza necropolis needed precautions against rain. On the north side of the Khafre causeway, there is a ditch (2 m. wide and 1.5 m. deep) that forms a demarcation line between the pyramid complexes of Khufu [Cheops] and Khafre. This rock-cut ditch was large enough to channel a great deal of rainwater when heavy rains occurred. It is cut into by the corner of the Sphinx enclosure, and—were it not blocked at this point with pieces of granite—would allow water to pour in quantity into the basin out of which the Sphinx body was carved.[17]

Jordan does not mention that if rainwater still poured down the plateau today at the rate it obviously did in the past, the blockage by the pieces of granite would cause a real mess, with the water being diverted all over the place. The drain was probably blocked either during the New Kingdom or during Ptolemaic/Roman times, at both of which eras the Sphinx Moat was open and needed to be kept dry for religious observances at the feet of the statue. By these times, the climate must already have become considerably drier. It is obvious that the granite blocks are not original, since no one would build a long channel all the way down the side of the causeway (which is made of limestone blocks) only to render it ineffective for its purpose at the very end, causing all the work of its construction to be wasted. At some later date, somebody wanted to stop the water pouring into the moat, whereas originally the purpose to divert water from the plateau into the moat is entirely obvious.

Far from being of importance only in the Cheops-versus-Chephren controversy (which may be irrelevant anyway), the rainwater drain that leads directly into the Sphinx Moat makes it clear that from at least the time of Chephren in the Fourth Dynasty, the recharging of the moat with as much fresh water as possible was considered to be such a high priority that vast trouble and expense were lavished on the construction of a long stone drain leading into it from high up on the Giza Plateau. It seems not so much an act of desecration of a monument as a technique for keeping the moat full, draining into the moat whatever rainwater might be available during the period of the year when the Nile inundation had receded.

And this brings us to the subject of the upkeep of the moat generally, which will in turn explain much that is strange about the apparent signs of severe water erosion in the Sphinx Moat, many of which are vertical. If we look at my photo in figures 6.57 and 6.58, we can see these vertical fissures that appear to have been scoured out of the rock walls of the Sphinx pit by water cascading downward. It is not strange that West, Bauval, and Hancock have drawn the conclusion that these vertical scourings must have been caused by vast torrents of rain pouring down the slopes in remote antiquity when there was supposed to have been a rainy environment in Egypt, prior to 10,000 BC. (This rainy environment may or may not have existed and is disputed.) After all, what else could have caused them?

Let us think about the problems of maintaining a sphinx moat. There you are with your huge moat on the edge of the desert, and what are your problems going to be? What was it that happened so repeatedly to the Sphinx over the millennia? It was always getting covered with sand. And that is the problem for your moat! Sand! (Technically speaking, *sand* is only a casual term; what you find at Giza is really fine desert dust rather than the coarse sand grains that are familiar to us from beaches.) So what do you have to do, over and over again? You have to *dredge the moat*. And to do that, you are continually dredging at the sides, hauling up the sand from the bottom of the moat and letting all the excess water pour back into the moat in powerful torrents. You are, in fact, creating artificially and

Figure 6.57. Olivia climbing up the vertical crevasse in the south wall of the Sphinx Pit, which I believe was gouged by centuries' worth of water pouring down from dredging operations in the continual battle to dredge the windblown sand out of the Sphinx Moat during Old Kingdom times. (See the crevasses also in figure 6.58 below.) (*Photo by Robert Temple*)

Below: Figure 6.58. To the left is the rear of the Sphinx, in the center is the Sphinx Moat on the southern side, and to the right is the southern cliff wall of the Sphinx Moat. The horizontal erosion along the sides of the cliff in the veins where the limestone was weaker was caused by water lying in the moat for centuries during the Old Kingdom. The separate vertical erosion would have been caused by water pouring down the sides during the process of dredging the windblown sand out of the moat on countless occasions over the same period. (*Photo by Robert Temple*)

in intensive form the same coursing of water down the sides of the moat that is postulated for the "ancient rain" theory. But you don't need rain, you need only sand, because the sand blowing into the moat with the wind is sufficient cause to motivate your dredging and your scouring of the sides of the pit with descending cascades of water, over and over again until the rock is gouged out in just the way that we see now.

You don't need those extra seven thousand years, you don't need Atlantis, you don't need theories about prehistoric climate changes: all you need is sand blowing in the wind, a ditch full of water, and some men with some basic dredging equipment.

Now we can appreciate also the differing patterns of erosion. The vertical fissures in the sides of the Sphinx Moat are from water coursing downward both from dredging and, of course, from rainwater and flash-flood water. (Flash floods may seem anomalous to people who have visited only briefly as tourists, but they are common in Egypt, and in the Valley of the Kings many tombs such as that of Rameses II have largely been destroyed by them. The Old Kingdom dam at Wadi Garawi, east of the Nile, which I have studied intensively and which I will discuss in a future book, was destroyed by an enormous flash flood, and that gigantic dam was of truly enormous strength and bulk.) But there are other patterns: we have already seen that there was standing water in the passage between the Sphinx and Valley Temples, which was of course horizontal. And on the body of the Sphinx itself, there are no great vertical scourings such as there are on the walls of the pit, but rather there are horizontal patterns of erosion, as one would expect on a giant statue sitting in the middle of a moat and constituting an island. The chest and sides of the Sphinx are so prominently scoured horizontally with what appear to be multiple water levels (see figures 2.16, 2.19, 2.25, 2.26, and 2.29 to 2.31), like those along the base of the Valley Temple's north wall, that I am frankly amazed that no one has ever previously pointed out that the statue seems to have sat for long periods in water whose level varied. These horizontal streaks, where the stone has so clearly been eroded in a perfectly horizontal manner (which cannot be as a result of wind!) at multiple levels, are some of the most prominent features of the Sphinx. But even the ancient-rain theorists have never called attention to these patterns. Geologist Robert Schoch published a book entitled *Voices of the Rocks* in 1999 supporting John Anthony West's thesis. This book contains a disappointing chapter about Schoch's study of the Sphinx. In it, he actually says that "vertical crevices" are "well developed and prominent on the body of the Sphinx and within the Sphinx enclosure."[18] Certainly they are prominent on the walls of the Sphinx Moat, but not on the body of the Sphinx, which is marked instead by *horizontal* crevices so prominent that they cry out for attention. Schoch, however, does not mention these features at all! His book lacks sufficient references. It is a pity, because he does have some interesting ideas, and I agree with him about some things. For instance, he is convinced that the head of the Sphinx has been recarved:

> From the first time I saw the Great Sphinx, and particularly after I was allowed to inspect the head firsthand and up close, I have been convinced that the Sphinx's current head isn't the original. Relatively recent tool and chisel marks, as well as the appearance of the stone itself, indicate that the current head is a recarving from an original (which may have represented an animal rather than a human). This recarving hypothesis also helps explain the head's obviously small size in relation to the body, a disruption of proportion unusual in Egyptian monuments.[19]

I certainly agree with all this most heartily, though Schoch then suggests that the head is that of Pharaoh Khafre (Chephren), which it does not resemble in any way, as we have already seen. But Schoch also correctly criticizes a particularly silly passage about the Sphinx by the Egyptologist Mark Lehner, "who used a computer program to reconstruct the appearance of the undamaged Sphinx and felt that the face 'came alive' when he gave it Khafre's features. In other words, when Lehner made the Sphinx look the way he thought it should, then it looked the way he thought it should. Such reasoning is, of course, circular."[20] And this is not the only folly of Mark Lehner's, for his insistence that a straight line can be drawn joining the southeast corners of the three main pyramids of Giza is demonstrably false, as anyone standing at the southeast corner of the Great Pyramid and looking back at the others can instantly see. Lehner's bizarre drawing of this phantom line may be found in his book *The Complete Pyramids*,[21] where a "back sight" is drawn, as if a conclusive observation had been made with a theodolite. In his comments, Lehner calls this "the Giza diagonal line."[22] I do urge anyone who visits Giza to go and stand at the southeast corner of the Great Pyramid and look back at the smallest of the three pyramids, the Mycerinus (Menkaure) Pyramid. He will see that the southeast corner of the Chephren (Khafre) Pyramid is significantly set back and does not fall on this alignment at all. "The Giza diagonal line" does not exist! It does not exist any more than the face of Chephren on the Sphinx exists.

Another interesting revelation in Schoch's book is that an Egyptologist from Chicago, Frank J. Yurco, has the same idea that I have about the Sphinx having sat in a moat, although we formulated our ideas separately, and I have never read anything of Yurco's or even seen any publication of his. Schoch disputes Yurco's ideas, although he does grant that the Nile water would have reached the Sphinx "at least on occasion."[23] One reason he advances for dismissing the idea of a Sphinx

Moat is that there would be "greater wear" on the paws than is found. But that is an entirely unconvincing statement, for the paws are well known to be wholly covered in reconstruction blocks and were rebuilt in this way in Roman times for the obvious reason that they *were* so extraordinarily worn away! Schoch does not give any references to Yurco's publications, which is unfortunate, so I have never been able to find them or to consult them.

There is one other major point in Schoch's book that should be mentioned. He says that he determined through his geological investigations of the Sphinx Pit that there was deeper erosion to the north, south, and east of the Sphinx in the floor of the moat than there is to the west.[24] This discovery substantiates the hypothesis of a moat fed from the east by the Nile. The west end of the Sphinx Moat on the side of the pyramids would have been spared the onrush of the incoming waters and would have eroded less, since the Sphinx itself would have acted as a barrier to protect that end of the moat from water surging in. Also, as the water would have been far more stagnant at that dead end of the moat, sand blowing into the moat would have been less stirred up and would have tended to remain stationary there, thus providing a surface cover. Dredging could never have removed all the sand from the moat, and some would always have settled back. The sand falling back into the west end would have been "dead," in the sense of never moving or shifting around. The wash from the incoming water as it came in from the east would swish extra sand toward the back, western end, where it would tend to collect to a greater depth than elsewhere, and thus the sand there would always have been much deeper than in the north, south, and east portions of the moat. Bottom erosion would therefore *have to be* less at the west end of the moat. Schoch's discovery thus provides a major geological support for the Sphinx Moat hypothesis.

The two differing patterns of apparent water erosion in the Sphinx Moat are thus found in the two different places where one would expect them and differ in the ways that one would also expect. If we had huge vertical scourings on the Sphinx itself such as we have on the walls of its moat, there would be a problem. But everything accords with the simple explanation that in Old Kingdom times the Sphinx was an island sitting in the middle of a moat with its back and head sticking out of the water. This can explain the ancient reference in the previous chapter to the body of Anubis at Giza being "concealed" as he lies in his crouching position. We might also find echoes of this situation in Utterance 213 of the Pyramid Texts, where we are told: "Your arms are Atum, your shoulders are Atum, your belly is Atum, your back is Atum, your hinder-parts are Atum, your legs are Atum, your face is Anubis."[25]

Atum was the creator god of the Egyptians, who emerged from the watery abyss and chaos of the primeval waters as an island. He manifested himself as an "Island of Fire" in the midst of the water on the occasion of the first sunrise and "emerges from the Akhet [horizon]."[26] This accords with the facts that the Sphinx faces due east on the equinox, facing the sunrise, and that the later name of the Sphinx was Horemakhet, or Horus-of-the-Horizon, and was thus associated with the *akhet,* or horizon, that was first manifested in the initial sunrise of the creator god himself. (A great deal more discussion of this subject is found in the next two chapters.) The crouching guardian of the necropolis, Anubis, thus also represented Atum, and faced the sunrise of the first creation, manifesting himself as the primeval Island of Fire in the midst of the Lake of Fire, of which we hear so much in the Pyramid and Coffin Texts as a central feature of the netherworld.

We have definite proof that the Sphinx was associated with Atum from the Dream Stela, which gives the name of the Sphinx in New Kingdom times as Hor-em-akhet-Kheperi-Ra-Atum. (Hor-em-akhet means Horus-in-the-Horizon, referring to the eastern horizon of sunrise. Kheperi is the name of the rising sun, portrayed as a scarab beetle; and Ra is the name of the sun god in general.) Furthermore, in the *Book of the Dead,* Atum is specifically called "the Master of the Lake" (chapter 3, line 2).

Having considered the work of Robert Schoch, we must now take note of the far more elaborate studies of the Sphinx geology by Lal Gauri, who is coauthor of a definitive book entitled *Carbonate Stone,*[27] of which limestone is, of course, the main kind. He is an emeritus professor of an American university at which I was also an adjunct (part-time "visiting") professor from 1999 to 2002. In 1995, Lal and two colleagues published an article in the journal *Geoarchaeology* rebutting the ideas of West and Schoch about a Sphinx going back far beyond the Old Kingdom times in Egypt. The article was entitled "Geologic Weathering and Its Implications on the Age of the Sphinx."[28] Lal and his colleagues pointed out that the assertion by West and Schoch that the weathering of the Sphinx and its pit was extremely ancient was groundless, and that there was no need for frequent and heavy rain to have caused the erosion that we see. However, excluding rain is not the same as excluding water! (Everyone admits *some* rain, but not enough.) They then explain complex details of how erosion takes place in limestone rocks, concerning microscopic pores and so on. Dew (still common at Giza) enters into these at night, temperature differentials work away at the delicate stone, and it flakes and erodes. These processes are still taking place today, as they clearly demonstrate. They also point out that the Giza Plateau is riddled with small caves caused by water flowing through the rock over geologic eons, and then when the Sphinx Pit was excavated, many of these were exposed and the patterns caused by water erosion revealed, having been there all the time underneath the surface. As they put it in conclusion: "The deep channels in the walls of the Sphinx ditch, which [West and Schoch] consider as having been formed by the running water [of "ancient rain"], are actually caves, formed by the underground water in geologic antiquity."[29]

There is no doubt that this is true. But being true is one thing and being the whole truth is another. Lal and his colleagues acknowledge that further erosion of these exposed underground watercourses and caves then took place. But they think this was caused entirely by dew. My proposal in this context is simple: there was plenty more water vapor at hand for these microscopic erosion processes that arose from the Sphinx Moat, and furthermore, there were the vertical scouring effects of the dredging, as I have explained, and the horizontal processes of the varying moat level itself, which rose and fell from time to time over the course of the centuries of the Old Kingdom during which it existed.

Lal and a colleague give a more elaborate account of the Sphinx issue in the book *Carbonate Stone,* which appeared four years later, in 1999. In this book, much more detail and many more illustrations are available. It is, in fact, a classic source that anyone interested in this subject must consult. I shall not attempt to summarize the complex material presented in *Carbonate Stone,* much of which is concerned with the highly technical details of pore size in the rock and what the implications of this are for erosion and durability. Lal was, after all, part of the team who worked (together with Mark Lehner and Zahi Hawass) on the great Sphinx Conservation Project. In this book Lal and his colleague repeat:

> The evidence used by the authors of the new theory [West and Schoch's "ancient rain" theory] is based upon interpretation of geomorphological features and seismic data. We show in this chapter that deep channels in the walls of the Sphinx ditch that they consider as having been formed by running water are actually caves formed by the underground water in geologic antiquity. . . . Thus, they misinterpreted the geological features that are the basis of their theory.[30]

I think we must accept these conclusions and realize that rain is not the answer. It is helpful also to know that the microscopic erosion processes within the stone, explained in such detail by Lal and his colleagues in their publications, have gone on continuously from antiquity to the present. However, all the conclusions reached by Lal and his colleagues are by no means incompatible with the Sphinx Moat. Indeed, the existence of a moat provides the additional moisture needed to bring forward the normal microscopic erosion processes within a reasonable time frame. The vertical scouring caused by dredging would have accentuated the preexisting vertical fissures caused by the underground water, which, although they may already have been there to some extent, would have been deepened. And the horizontal erosion patterns on the Sphinx, which owe nothing to descending water of any kind, were caused not only by moat levels rising and falling, but by the microscopic erosion processes greatly accentuated by genuine soaking in a moat, its withdrawal when the level sank, and its repetition when the level rose, with the weakening effect on the stone that would have resulted. (There would have been a problem of "rising damp," or moisture oozing upward, within the Sphinx body in addition to extra microscopic erosion processes.) In other words, all the arguments put forward by Lal Gauri to counteract the ancient-rain theory are wholly compatible with and mutually strengthening to the Sphinx Moat hypothesis.

And at this point we should turn to the Greek historian Herodotus (fifth century BC), who reports fascinating though highly garbled traditions that further substantiate the idea of an island surrounded by water at Giza:

> Chephren also built a pyramid, of a less size than his brother's [Cheops]. I have myself measured it. It has no underground chambers [these were unknown then, but are known today, having been discovered first by the Arabs and then rediscovered by Giovanni Belzoni[31]], nor is it entered like the other [the Great Pyramid] by a canal from the Nile, but the river comes in through a built passage and encircles an island, in which, they say, Cheops himself lies.[32]

We have already not only encountered the tradition that a king lies buried beneath the Sphinx (as mentioned by the Roman author Pliny and in countless subsequent accounts by Arabs and travelers' reports), but we have seen that there was a shaft leading to a burial chamber and extending right down through the body of Sphinx, into which many people have entered, and of which we even have the dimensions, although it was destroyed by Émile Baraize's "restoration" of the Sphinx in the 1920s. I have fully described this in an earlier chapter. Since there is nowhere else on the surface of the Giza Plateau where an island could be said to exist, we must presume that Herodotus's very late account is a garbled tradition of the Sphinx Island, which indeed was fed by water from the Nile, which "comes in through a built passage and encircles an island." Much of what Herodotus wrote about Egypt was lifted from an earlier author named Hecataeus of Miletus, born 549 BC (not to be confused with the better-known but much later author Hecataeus of Abdera, who also wrote about Egypt). Therefore, the account given by Herodotus may have been garbled by him from an earlier account by Hecataeus, to which scribal errors may also have contributed, since the standard of copying of manuscripts at that early date could easily have resulted in a copy of Hecataeus's work, which already contained many serious scribal errors, coming to Herodotus's hands; we need not attribute them to Herodotus personally. Furthermore, because the Sphinx is beside the Valley Temple of Chephren, the association of the Pyramid of Chephren with the Sphinx Island is a natural garbling of the true association of the Valley Temple of Chephren with the Sphinx Island. But this is not the only relevant passage from Herodotus, for he also wrote that the Egyptians claimed the following with regard to the Great Pyramid:

> They worked in gangs of a hundred thousand men, each gang for three months. For ten years the people were afflicted in making the road [causeway] whereon the stones were dragged, the making of which road was to my thinking a task but a little lighter than the building of the [Great] Pyramid, for the road is five furlongs long and ten fathoms broad, and raised at its highest to a height of eight fathoms, and it is all of stone polished and carved with figures. The ten years aforesaid went to the making of this road and of the underground chambers on the hill whereon the pyramids stand [i.e., the Giza Plateau]; these the king meant to be burial-places for himself, and encompassed them with water, bringing in a channel from the Nile.[33]

This is yet another garbled later tradition, in which confused memories from the past are distorted. The reference seems to be to the Chephren Causeway, or otherwise to the now destroyed Cheops Causeway, or perhaps a conflation of the two. In any case, the Chephren Causeway runs directly to a monument at "the hill whereon the pyramids stand," said to be a burial place of a king, which does indeed seem to have been encompassed with water brought "in a channel from the Nile." In other words, this describes perfectly the Sphinx Island at the very beginning of that great causeway, the rainwater from which even poured directly into the Sphinx's moat.

It is not often noticed either by Egyptologists or by classical scholars that Herodotus does not actually say that the underground chambers to which he refers have anything whatsoever to do with any of the pyramids. He says instead something quite different: that the chambers are inside the *hill*. It happens to be the same hill, or plateau, on which the pyramids also stand. In other words, he is describing underground chambers of the Giza Plateau itself, and definitely *not* underground chambers of a pyramid. The distinction seems to have eluded everyone. This overt ancient evidence *against* the pyramid-tomb theory is ignored by all Egyptologists, and it would not suit many of them to be forced to take note of it, since it opposes their favorite theory.

As we know, the Giza Plateau is riddled with underground chambers everywhere. So the question we have to ask is: Where in the Giza Plateau, associated with underground chambers and near a giant causeway, can we find an island into which the water of the Nile has been admitted by a channel?

The answer is that there is only one such place: Sphinx Island.

It has often been a subject of speculation why Herodotus never mentions the Sphinx. In his day, it was probably covered by sand up to its neck. It was cleared only some centuries later under the Ptolemies, and the clearance nearly a thousand years earlier in the New Kingdom by Thutmosis IV was long forgotten, its effects long vanished. It generally took twenty years or less (before the total clearance in 1936) for the Sphinx to be covered over in sand, and enough time had elapsed by the time of Herodotus for the Sphinx to have been covered nearly one hundred times. It is difficult to see the Sphinx from the pyramids, especially if it is only a head protruding from the sand, and Herodotus probably was not taken down to its site. This assumes that the accounts of Herodotus are really firsthand accounts, which has been passionately disputed both in ancient times and today, with some classical scholars believing that Herodotus pinched most of his material from earlier authors, so the omission of an account of the Sphinx might merely be a sign of his laziness in copying! The Sphinx Temple at that time was definitely covered entirely and forgotten. We do not know how much of the Valley Temple would have been visible then—probably very little or none at all. So there was not much to attract attention from a distance. The simple fact is that at the time of Herodotus, or even the time of Hecataeus, there was no good reason to exert oneself in the heat by walking down the hill, as there were no temples to be seen there, the Sphinx had not yet been cleared, and there was only with difficulty a view of some stone object sticking up out of the sand in the distance, which could not be identified even as the back of a head. Herodotus makes it clear with both descriptions he has given of islands surrounded by Nile water at Giza that he is drawing on Egyptian accounts, for he specifically says: "Thus far I have recorded what the Egyptians themselves say. Now . . . I will add thereto something of what I myself have seen."[34]

And he then goes on to discuss other things. But another interesting detail of what Herodotus has told us about the Great Pyramid is that Cheops specifically did *not* intend to have himself buried inside but rather in a chamber elsewhere beneath Giza and, according to one tradition, beneath the island surrounded by Nile water. So this is clear evidence against the theory that the Great Pyramid was designed as Cheops's tomb. As I have already said, it is difficult to understand on any logical basis why no Egyptologist seems ever to have noticed this explicit evidence from antiquity *against* the prevailing theory that Cheops built the Great

Pyramid as his own tomb. Once again, we encounter a "consensus blindness" situation, where everybody seems to be determined not to see something that is right there in front of his eyes.

When considering these things, it is just as well to take notice of the specific words of the Egyptologist Wallis Budge, who gave a long description of the underworld at Rostau (which he spelled Re-Stau) in describing the Egyptian books dealing with the sun god's journey through the underworld at night. When the sun god's boat comes to the fourth gate, the sun god has to dismount and go across the sands of Giza on a new boat that is dragged; the sun god then

> . . . has entered the kingdom of Seker [his spelling of Sokar], who is probably the oldest of all the gods of the dead in Egypt. . . . The main corridor is called Re-Stau. . . . An inscription . . . tells us that it is the road by which the body of Seker enters and that his form is neither seen nor perceived; hence it is clear that the road by which [the sun god] passed through this Division was supposed to be high up above the dominions of Seker, and that he never saw that god at all. . . . The hidden gods who march in front of the boat [of the sun god as it is dragged over the sand] are few in number, and the names of many of them are unfamiliar; some of them are connected with Osiris, and all of them are under the control of Anpu, or Anubis, and perform some act which helps the boat along.[35]

As I have mentioned already, Anpu is the Egyptian name, which we write in the Greek manner as Anubis.

Once again we have the clearest statement that Anubis was presiding in some sense over all these events at Rostau, which encourages us to think that Anubis as the Great Sphinx is being specifically referred to once again.

We can now begin to look at the many references in the ancient Pyramid Texts, Coffin Texts, and others that appear to refer to the Sphinx Moat. We can start with the Pyramid Texts because they are the earliest. And indeed, the earliest of the Pyramid Texts are those that are inscribed on the interior walls of the Fifth Dynasty Pyramid of King Unas (reigned circa 2375–2345 BC).

I once had the wonderful opportunity of sitting for six hours inside this small pyramid, surrounded by the magical texts. There are hundreds of stars painted all over the ceiling. The texts cover all the walls and almost smother the interior, as if all the words that wished to be uttered were clamoring, almost as if they were raising their hands and entreating to be heard, a thousand voices whispering urgently at once: "Listen to me! Listen to me! Not to *him!* To *me!*" The name of King Unas is everywhere, in its royal cartouche with the beautiful hieroglyph of the long-eared hare. This was the first time that a pyramid's interior had been inscribed with any texts at all. And suddenly they are all there, like an infestation, and the desperate need to glorify the immortality and resurrection of the king is deafening, overwhelming, insistent: "He will live forever! He will live forever!" The king will rise to the sky, he will become Horus, he will become this god, he will become that god, he will be glorified, he will surpass all the gods. One wonders what suddenly possessed the Egyptians at this period to burst into this riotous affirmation of the eternal life of their dead king. The pyramid is pocket-sized, as they could not build them properly anymore and their civilization was in decline. It has been suggested that the explosion of texts inside the Fifth and Sixth Dynasty pyramids, starting with this one, was a psychological compensation for the fact that the pyramids were so small, just as a small person can have a big temper or enormous ego by way of compensation for his size (such as Napoleon). But despite the tiny size of the pyramid, sitting inside it was a profound experience of timelessness, of the silence of eternity, of the brooding mantras that were intoned from the walls with the long vanished voices of the priests who had recited them here as they slowly led the burial ceremony into this vault where the king's mummified remains would rest, awaiting the fulfillment of his "sure and certain hope of resurrection," to use the words of the King James Bible. The pyramid is closed to visitors, except by special permission, to preserve these very texts on the walls, which elbows and hands and breath could damage. Already the paint on them has faded. But their voice has not faded; it has indeed been regained after 4,350 years. And the pharaoh thus indeed lives on, through these voices, though his remains were plundered and scattered in distant antiquity and the huge and heavy sarcophagus lies open, empty, and desecrated in the silent room where I sat and brooded on his lost world.

In these earliest surviving religious texts from Egypt, we find a fairly clear description of Anubis presiding or "ruling" over Giza, which is called "the Western height." In Egyptian religious and mythological terminology, the realm of the dead is often called "the West," and the dead are "the Westerners." Osiris, as god of the dead, for instance, "presides over the Westerners." The earliest deity who presided over the Westerners was Khentiamentiu, which means Foremost of the Westerners. He was a jackal, and in fact he was Anubis. By the Fifth Dynasty his identity had begun to become combined with the god Asar (Osiris in Greek), husband of Isis. This terminology occurs hundreds of times, and was standard, in the same way that Christians often refer to Jesus as "the Savior" without actually saying his name, and sometimes call him "the Lamb of God." All religions have certain standard epithets like these that they use over and over again to show reverence and as a kind of shorthand among themselves. There is also a habit in most religions to avoid directly mentioning the name of a divinity too often, as it might be considered as acting too familiar and even irreverently. For instance, Christian priests, when speaking of Jesus in their sermons, very often refer to him as "our Savior," using that or other epithets more often than they actually say the name Jesus or the name Christ. (Baptist ministers are much less restrained and seem to compete to see who can mention the name of Jesus most often within a given period.) More formal epithets such as "Lamb of God" are reserved for hymns, services, and ceremonies. For instance, in the Anglican Church, just before communion, the priest holds aloft the host and says to the congregation as he welcomes them to come forward: "Behold the Lamb of God!" He does not say, "Look, everybody, here's Jesus!" because that would show less dignity. Similarly, one would not address Queen Elizabeth of England as "Liz." So we have to keep in mind that the ancient Egyptians were similar in their use of formalisms and epithets, and that such works as the Pyramid Texts were formal invocations and spells in which the names of divinities had to be varied in a flowery manner for the correct degree of reverence to be shown. Osiris in his underground chamber was "ruler of the Westerners," but Anubis specifically "rules over the Western height":

> *Thoth, hurry! Announce to the gods of the West and to their*
>   *spirits:*
> *He comes indeed, this [King] Unas, an Imperishable Spirit,*
> *decked like Anubis on the neck, who rules over the Western*
>   *height.*[36]

This is a very specific allusion to Anubis as the presence who is acknowledged to be "ruling" over Giza, which is the only part of "the West" in ancient Egyptian lore that can be said also to be a "height." (Twice in the Pyramid Texts and many times in later ones Anubis is referred to as Anubis of the Hill or Anubis of the Height.) As for him being "decked . . . on the neck," it is highly likely that the Sphinx had rich hangings around its neck not only when it had its present form (when these hangings are actually depicted in New Kingdom stelae, so that there is ancient pictorial evidence of their existence; see figures 3.21 to 3.23 for examples of the Sphinx bedecked with a neck hanging), but also when the Sphinx was Anubis. The reference to this decorative aspect of Anubis is a further confirmation that an actual statue is being referred to in this text. It would be presumptuous to describe a god as "decked . . . on the neck," but acceptable to describe a statue of the god in that way.

The Pyramid Texts and subsequent ones are full of references to one of the major features of the netherworld at Rostau, the Jackal Lake. I believe that the Jackal

Lake, which also had other names, was what the Old Kingdom Egyptians appropriately used as their name for the Sphinx Moat. In fact, like all the sacred entities and places in Egyptian lore, the Jackal Lake also has various epithets. It is also called the Lake of Fire, often within the same passage as its formal name of Jackal Lake or Lake of the Jackal. Other names for it appear to be the Canal of the God, the Canal of Anubis, the Winding Waterway (presumably because if you go along it on a boat, you circumnavigate the island of the Sphinx), the Lake of Life, the Lake of Cool Water, Broad Lake, the Lake of Rushes, the Field of Rushes, and, most often of all, simply the Lake of the Netherworld (or Lake of the Duat, Duat being the netherworld). As for its connection with rushes, it is highly likely that rushes grew in part of the Sphinx Moat in antiquity (most likely the dead western end where the sand/dust tended to accumulate), just as they do today at the west end of the winding waterway of the ancient Osiris temple, the Osireion, at Abydos.

A mysterious ancient text known as *The Book of Caverns* describes the netherworld and gives intriguing references to Anubis. Although in its surviving copies this text occurs rather late, appearing for the first time in the reign of King Seti I of the New Kingdom and repeated again on the walls of the Valley of the Kings tomb of King Rameses VI, its contents seem rather archaic compared to some other texts of this kind. The book, copied from the walls of two ancient monuments, was translated into English by Alexandre Piankoff, who says of it: "The whole suggests a gigantic papyrus which has been unrolled the length of the walls."[37] In fact, all the netherworld books inscribed on walls were copied from papyri originally, so they are all older than the dates of their appearance in tombs. Figure 6.39 reproduces a previously unknown engraving dating from 1837 of the sarcophagus of King Seti I (died circa 1278 BC), which is now in London, and which bears such a netherworld text on it; this picture has not been reproduced since its original publication, and, as it is unknown to Egyptologists, I thought I should put it into circulation for everyone to see.

I suspect that the original "gigantic" papyrus from which *The Book of Caverns* was copied was considerably older than its initial use by this same King Seti I, and that it embodies much more archaic lore than many similar texts of the New Kingdom tombs. I asked Professor Erik Hornung about the relative dates, and he believes the illustrations of *The Book of Caverns,* "being richer in iconographic fantasy (which reached its climax in the twenty first dynasty)" and also containing a view of the mythical serpent Apopis, which was no longer entirely that of an evil creature, meant that the book was not as archaic as I thought. I certainly accept his views on the iconography. But I believe that some of the text precedes that iconography and is extraordinarily archaic, drawn from a far earlier text. On the other hand, if one looks at the netherworld text known as *The Book of Gates,*

THE BELZONI SARCOPHAGUS, IN THE SOANE MUSEUM.

Figure 6.59. The sarcophagus of King Seti I of Egypt (died circa 1278 BC), which was acquired in the eighteenth century by Sir John Soane and is still on display in the Soane Museum (his house, preserved as it was at his death, now open to the public) in Lincolns Inn Fields in Holborn, London, a few minutes' walk from Dickens's Old Curiosity Shop, which still stands. This engraving was published in 1837 in a periodical of the time. Netherworld scenes are depicted on the sarcophagus, accompanied by texts describing the events and phenomena to be encountered there. (*Collection of Robert Temple*)

one is struck by the actual text itself having become too fantastic and baroque, a jumble or improvisation, in fact, and wholly lacking the archaic qualities that so strike me in *The Book of Caverns.*

The Book of Caverns recounts a series of caverns of the netherworld and seems to be based very much at Rostau. There are several suggestive references to Anubis as the presiding presence. At one point, Osiris is described as having "set him [Anubis] in his place without his being able to leave, having been established in the West."[38]

This is a very strange way to describe Anubis. It certainly seems to describe a prominent statue, as what else could possibly be meant by being stuck in place and not able to leave? Furthermore, the same text also describes "those who are between his arms." Although Anubis was the master embalmer, corpses being embalmed are not actually held in the arms of the embalmer, and though one certainly cannot insist on it (as it could be just an exaggerated reference to his work as an embalmer), the reference seems to me to be to something quite different. It sounds strangely like the worshipping of the Sphinx at the altar between its arms that went on for centuries and may refer to an earlier stage of this worship in the Middle Kingdom, by which time the moat was dry. It is probable that the moat was filled with water only during the Old Kingdom, and by the time of the Middle Kingdom it had become a dry ditch containing a great deal of sand, which eventually overwhelmed it, so it was only cleared again by Pharaoh Thutmosis (Thothmes) IV as recorded on his Dream Stela centuries later.

This same text of *The Book of Caverns* refers to Anubis four more times in a manner that describes his presiding presence at Giza. The sun god Re (Ra) addresses a cavern of the netherworld, referring to the secret image of the god Sokar, "whose image is great, created by the Netherworld, engendered by the Silent Region, he whose image is unknown, unique mystery hidden from the inhabitants of his cavern. O Behold, I pass near you, I have placed Anubis as your guardian, I give you light."[39]

This is a clear reference to Rostau and to Anubis being "placed as guardian" there. Later, the sun god Re again speaks to "the Cavern of the Forms of Osiris," which is well known to be a feature of Rostau, and enumerates many features of Anubis, referred to repeatedly as "Power of the West." At the end of this litany of praise for Anubis, Re says: "O Anubis, O Anubis! Behold, I pass Anubis, when I pass through those who are in Exalted Earth [the necropolis]. I pass through the mysterious Netherworld."[40]

This indicates that to enter the netherworld at Rostau, it was necessary to pass Anubis, who stood guard at its gate, another suggestion of the presence of Anubis as a statue there.

Further on in the text, in speaking of the dead, we are told, "Their bodies pass by while Anubis is the guard."[41] And Re again speaks to a netherworld cavern where two goddesses lie buried, once again presumably at Rostau: "O the two great and powerful goddesses whose mysterious coffins are guarded. It is Anubis who guards them . . . as well as the Head of Re—mystery of He (who is Lord) of Forms."[42]

The Lord of Forms is Osiris, who lies buried at Rostau, and is here identified with the Head of Re, which appears when the sun rises over the horizon. The information about the two goddesses lying buried in a cavern at Rostau is unfamiliar and is probably a stray survival of an early and largely lost tradition predating the Osiris cult concerning the cobra goddess of the north and the vulture goddess of the south, who were so prominent as a pair in the Archaic Period. (It was, after all, Sokar who was the original Lord of Forms, and he became merged with Osiris and essentially replaced by him in the Fifth Dynasty.) The goddesses Isis and Nephthys

Figure 6.60. This aerial view from a balloon, looking northeast, shows the position of the pyramids of Giza and the Sphinx in relation to distant Cairo in 1882. Cairo, as can be seen, was at that time entirely on the other side of the Nile, whereas today it has crept up to the base of the Giza Plateau itself. This view highlights the position that the Sphinx held as the "guardian of the entrance to the Necropolis of Giza," literally crouching at the entrance. The head of the unexcavated Sphinx may be seen, with the word SPHINX written below it. Due to the foreshortening effect of the aerial perspective, the Pyramid of Chephren (with part of its limestone cap intact) here appears larger than the Great Pyramid beyond it, though in reality the Great Pyramid is slightly the larger of the two. The cluster of small pyramids on the right are the Pyramid of Mycerinus and its satellite pyramids; the two small ones that appear to be to the right of the Pyramid of Chephren are two of three small satellite pyramids that actually sit in front of the Great Pyramid (the third being invisible in this view). Not having flown in either a balloon or an aircraft above Giza, I cannot say how accurate this view is, or whether the distortions are due entirely to perspective or to the artist's imaginative powers, or both. (*Collection of Robert Temple*)

are constantly shown as a pair on post–Old Kingdom sarcophagi, enfolding the dead pharaoh in their protective winged arms, and they probably perpetuate this motif that we find in this text. (See figure 6.40.) However, I suspect they are not the original form of what is intended here. In my opinion, further research and study are necessary to elucidate this curious reference to the "two goddesses" being buried at Rostau and comprehend what is meant by "their mysterious forms." I am not at all content to let this matter rest, but I do not yet have a sufficient lead to feel that I have the thread in my hand. One thing that occurs to me at this early stage of my thinking on the matter is that this same place, the Door of Geb (the primeval Earth god) at Rostau, was meant to be guarded by a double-headed lion named Ruti, and this beast with two heads may well be the "mysterious form" concealing the truth about the two goddesses, each goddess being secretly represented by one of the heads of Ruti. (Another name for Ruti is Aker: see figure 1.49 on page 66.) That mention of those two goddesses is otherwise suppressed in the surviving texts about this place must be a very important clue in itself; they may represent some deeper mystery that was not supposed to be discussed. Another thing that occurs to me is that there are two temples, not one, immediately next to each other at that precise spot. Could the double-temple architectural motif be a hint at the double-headed lion motif, and in turn an esoteric reference to the two great goddesses? Why so much twinning? Unfortunately, this is mythological terrain that remains untrodden and approaches more closely than usual to the underlying mysteries that the Egyptians took such pains to conceal. It is very difficult to know what the name Aker means because there is no other form of it in Egyptian other than the plural form that refers merely to the serpents of Aker. It may be a foreign loan word. Alternatively, it may be connected with the verb *ak,* which means to bend (as in bending one's knees) or to bow. Those are the only Egyptian words spelled *ak,* and although there are words spelled *akh,* they use a different consonant, and I would hesitate to suggest any linguistic connection. Really, Aker is in my opinion a puzzling name. The name Ruti is not at all puzzling, because it is merely the dual form of Ru, which means lion; Ruti thus means the double-lion or the two lions. One may therefore safely conclude that Ruti is a descriptive epithet of Aker, rather than an actual separate name or a different entity.

There is a strange reference to an "Earth lion" in Book XI of the Sumerian/Babylonian/Assyrian Epic of Gilgamesh. A subterranean serpent leaps up from a deep well in the form of an "Earth lion" and steals from Gilgamesh the herb of immortality just as he is about to eat it and achieve eternal life. In my translation of the epic, published under the original title *He Who Saw Everything,* I called attention to this anomaly in a footnote: "Some esoteric meaning is probably intended, which is not clear."[43] It is not impossible that this "Earth lion" may have some connection with Aker/Ruti of the Egyptians, but I mention this only as a vague and tentative possibility for those who are interested in the occasional points of commonality that seem to appear in Egyptian and Sumerian/Babylonian mythology and religion, which is a subject far from the purposes of this book and which I cannot discuss any further here.

Turning now to earlier texts, Utterance 512 of the Pyramid Texts describes the deceased soul meeting Anubis, apparently at Rostau, since Anubis is there

Figure 6.61. This magnificent and beautiful engraving was published in the Napoleonic series of volumes *Description de l'Égypte* in 1809. It is a copy of an ancient Egyptian temple wall carving, site unknown (possibly no longer in existence), and shows the sister-goddesses Isis and Nephthys with their angel wings outstretched protectively around the sacred symbol of the god Osiris (husband of Isis), who is seen here as a mummy holding crossed royal and divine insigniae across his chest, with his head replaced by his sacred symbol of the Djed Pillar, surmounted by two plumes with a solar disk in the middle. Usually, in pictures of Isis and Nephthys on coffin lids, the goddesses are identified by their respective names in hieroglyphs above their heads, but that is not the case here. There is an unresolved enigma about whether Isis and Nephthys are intended to be identified with the "two great and powerful goddesses with mysterious coffins and mysterious forms" said to be buried at Rostau, the underworld situated beneath the Sphinx and its two temples. The Pyramid Texts suppressed these references, but they survived in ancient texts copied from a lost papyrus and painted on the walls of the tomb of King Rameses VI at the Valley of the Kings. Anyone who wonders how deities, who are supposed to be immortal, can also be dead or even buried need only remember that Jesus "died and was buried and rose again," as we are told by the Bible. This was meant to emphasize to us that resurrection and immortal life involve the necessity of what we call death, when we leave the illusory world of matter and return home to the eternal world of the spirit (if only temporarily, as some maintain). In order to enter that world, we first have to "die" in the flesh. "Dead" gods and goddesses were surprisingly common in the ancient world. The ancients of various cultures also tended to believe in degrees of immortality, such that, for instance, angels might "fall" and gods like Cronus, the father of Zeus, could be imprisoned in sleep as if dead. Immortality is not as simple as you might think, nor is eternity necessarily absolute in all traditions. After all, even in our daily lives we all say to one another: "I will always love you," or "I will love you forever," or "I will never forget," despite our statements being literally impossible. Everyone, even in religion, is entitled to exaggerate in order to make a point from time to time. (*Collection of Robert Temple*)

with Geb the Earth god; they are generally described as a pair only at Rostau. Then the deceased is urged to bathe in the Jackal Lake, which is here also called the Lake of the Netherworld. The words of Utterance 512 are:

> My father has remade his heart, the other [the original physical heart] having
> been removed for him [it has been removed from his corpse in the process of

embalming] because it objected to his ascending to the sky [rising to rebirth] when he had waded in the waters of the Winding Waterway.

Anubis comes and meets you! And Geb gives you his hand, O my father, (even) he who guards the earth and rules the spirits. I weep deeply, O my father.

Oho! Raise yourself, my father, receive these your four pleasant *nemeset* jars [which contain the corpse's entrails]; bathe in the Jackal Lake, be cleansed in the Lake of the Netherworld, be purified. . . . Run your course, row over your waterway like Rē [the sun god] on the banks of the sky. O my father, raise yourself, go in your spirit-state.[44]

The Sphinx Moat seems to have been navigated on reed floats and in small boats in religious ceremonies concerning death that involved bathing and rituals of purification. Perhaps the bodies of deceased kings were even bathed in the Jackal Lake prior to their embalming. There are numerous hints of this kind. Or perhaps this was done symbolically with a substitute, as suggested in Utterance 268: "This [deceased] King washes himself when Rē appears [when the sun rises]. . . . Horus accepts him beside him, he purifies this King in the Jackal Lake, he cleanses this King's double in the Lake of the Netherworld."[45]

In Utterance 301 we again read: "Cleanse the King, make the King bright in this your Jackal-Lake, O Jackal [Anubis is addressed here], in which you cleansed the gods."[46]

The cleansing that took place in the Jackal Lake may not have involved an actual corpse, but may rather have involved the four jars used for the king's entrails. It seems these were really carried to the Jackal Lake, and possibly the contents were removed and washed in the lake. The cleansing was said to be carried out by a goddess of whom we know little, Kebehut, who is specifically described as being the daughter of Anubis,[47] and who was a "celestial serpent" with the face of a jackal. (Wallis Budge used an older transliteration of her name, calling her Qebhut.[48]) It may be that Kebehut was a special priestess, known as Daughter of Anubis, who carried out the funeral ablution and censing ceremony ("censing" refers to the process of fumigating something or someone with incense from a swinging incense holder called a censer), and that she also represented the goddess Nephthys. In Utterance 515 we are told that Kebehut holds the four jars, removes the dead king's heart, and washes it in the lake, and the deceased king says, "The heart of the great god [Osiris] was refreshed on that day of awakening [the entombment of the corpse of Osiris, who became god of the dead], and she refreshes therewith my heart for me for life; she cleanses me, she censes me. I receive my meal [offerings]."[49]

Kebehut appears again in Utterance 674, where "she refreshes your heart in your body in the house of her father Anubis. Be purified . . . the spirits . . . shall grasp your hand."[50]

It seems that the entrails, apart from possibly the heart, were not actually removed from the four jars, but that the four jars were dipped into the lake and filled with water so that the entrails were washed within their jars. This process is described in Utterance 666: "O King . . . take this purification of yours, these four . . . jars of yours which are filled full from the Canal of the God [Anubis], cleanse yourself with them as a god and go forth thence."[51]

It seems that a purification at the Jackal Lake was a necessary part of the ritual for the dead king during the Old Kingdom. Anubis presided over all of this, as Utterance 676 makes clear: ". . . Anubis who presides over the God's [Osiris/Sokar's] Booth [which was at Rostau] has commanded that you be purified with your eight *nemeset* jars and your eight *āabt* jars which came forth from the Castle of the God [a temple, presumably what we now call the Valley Temple, which appears to have been dedicated originally to Sokar but later to Osiris]. You are indeed god-like."[52]

This same utterance places these events specifically at the Sphinx precinct: "You have your water, you have your flood, you have your efflux [the translation "sap" used by Renouf is probably better] which issued from Osiris [a process that is always described as being at Rostau, underground]. . . . This cold water of yours, O Osiris, is what is in Busiris."[53]

Busiris, as we remember, is the particular region of Giza where the Sphinx is found, and its Egyptian name was Djedu, an Egyptian word that means ghosts. (Although there was a city named Busiris in the Delta, the occurrence of the name Busiris or Djedu in an Egyptian religious text is always a reference to the Busiris at Giza, which may originally have had that name transferred to it by association with the Delta city in predynastic or early Old Kingdom times. Pliny is our source for the definite information that Busiris was the Greek name of the village beside the Sphinx.)

During the reign of Amenemhet II of the Middle Kingdom, whose face I believe now to be on the Sphinx, a story called "The Tale of the Two Brothers" was written. The washing of the pharaoh's heart in the Sphinx Moat, or Jackal Lake, before the great statue of Anubis, seems to be echoed in the story, in which Anubis himself places the heart of Bata in a bowl of cool water to resuscitate him.[54]

A causeway is also mentioned as being beside the Jackal Lake, as we are told in Utterance 690, where Kebehut, the Celestial Serpent, washes the dead king: "O King, your sister the Celestial Serpent has cleansed you upon the causeway in the meadow, you having appeared to them as a jackal. . . . May you govern the spirits, may you control the Imperishable Stars."[55]

This may well be a specific reference to the Chephren Causeway, which runs into the Sphinx Moat. We have previously encountered mention of a causeway beside Anubis in another Pyramid Text.

The Pyramid Texts contain many more relevant references, but there is no need to consider them all. Some references from the Coffin Texts are useful, however.

Coffin Text Spell 551 suggests that a ceremony may have existed in which the Sphinx Island was circumnavigated four times on a reed float or in a small boat. The text, which is merely suggestive, has the deceased say: "I have come to you, my father Rē. . . . I have gone round the watery Chaos four times, . . . I have bathed in the Lakes of the Netherworld, I have washed in the Lakes of the Jackals, I have [sailed in] the bark. . . . Going aboard the bark of Rē."[56]

In Spells 33 and 35, we read of the Lake of the Jackal being called the Place of Ferrying: "Welcome, O you whom Osiris has sent. . . . I will cause him to be pure in the Lake of the Jackal among the blessed ones. . . . I will cause him to enter into the Place of Ferrying among the blessed ones."[57]

The deceased bathing in the Jackal Lake is mentioned again in Spell 255: "Promoting a man's double in the Realm of the Dead. Water is upon me, I appear as Rē; water is on my hands. . . . Nephthys has nursed me in the Jackal Lake, I am loosed in the Lakes of Peace, . . . acclamation is made to me by the lords of the West."[58]

The location of the Jackal Lake at Busiris/Djedu, that is, the Sphinx precinct, is specified in Spell 292, where the deceased says: "There is opened to me the sacred place at the Lake of Jackals. O you who are over eternity, who are in your windings, prepare a path for me. . . . O you who are in Djedu. . . . It is I who eat the [word missing] which is in Djedu."[59]

A terrifying aspect of Anubis presiding over a lake is given in Spell 335, Part II, where the deceased begs Atum to "save me from that god . . . whose face is that of a hound. . . . It is he who is in charge of the interior [or island?] of the Lake of Fire, who swallows shades, who snatches hearts."[60]

This image is elaborated later in the same spell: "O Atum . . . save me from that god . . . whose face is that of a hound. . . . It is he who is warden of the windings of the Lake of Fire. . . . As for this god whose face is that of a hound . . . his name is 'swallower of myriads.'"[61]

Here we have the further detail that the lake winds around, an evident description of it encircling its island. Spell 336 repeats this detail.[62]

A group of Coffin Text spells, numbers 1165–1185, relate to Rostau,[63] to a winding or bending waterway, and to a presiding deity of the waterway who is known both as Khepri (Khepera), the rising sun whose name was part of the name of the Great Sphinx in New Kingdom times, and Dog-face (an epithet of Anubis). Spell 1185 specifically refers to "the ways by water which belong to Rostau." The waterway is also called the Lake of Fire, one of the alternative names of the Jackal Lake, and Lustral Basin, because of the purificatory bathing of the deceased's organs that took place in it. As for Anubis, whose giant size is here referred to: "His name is Dog-face, whose shape is big."[64]

There is not much of interest in the late texts of the *Book of the Dead,* but there are some interesting references in the Netherworld Texts of the New Kingdom, so many of which derive from Middle Kingdom material, as we have seen already with the *Book of Caverns.* The texts inscribed on the shrines found in the tomb of King Tutankhamun appear to refer to the Sphinx Island in the middle of Jackal Lake as "the Island of Baba" in the netherworld;[65] they have clear associations with Coffin Text Spell 335, and they add further:

> O Re-Atum, Lord of the Great Palace, king of all the gods, save thou the King . . . from the arm of this god whose face is that of a dog . . . guardian of the winding of the Island of Fire, who swallows corpses. . . . The Swallower of Millions is his name, he is in the Lake of Wen [Opening]. As to the Lake of Fire, it is between Neref [a strange name, see below; it was on the southern side] and Shenit [sister]. . . . Baba is his name. [The name Baba is another puzzling one. Bābā means to drink, or, apparently, to get drunk on blood, but nothing else.] He is the guardian of the winding of the Lake of the West.[66]

The name Broad Lake is used to describe the abode of Osiris-Sokar, another reference to the lake at Rostau.[67] And the cleansing of the heart in the waters of Rostau is twice referred to in a curious way. One of the many epithets known to be used of Osiris at Rostau is Weary Heart. The Tutankhamun texts tell us that the deceased claims: "I am enduring in Busiris . . . the holes are being opened to wash Weary Heart, the mystery of Mysteries in Ro-Setau [Rostau]," a passage that occurs twice. And a third passage says: "I am enduring in Busiris . . . I open the holes to wash Weary Heart, I hide the Mysteries in Ro-Setau."[68] These may simply be references to the washing of the deceased king's heart in a jar in the Sphinx Moat, or they may refer to the letting of water from the moat through some holes down into the subterranean precincts as an ablution intended for the remains of Osiris. Probably it refers to the former, a rite that we have already encountered. This Tutankhamun material, therefore, derives from Old Kingdom times because of the similarity to the vastly older sources, the Pyramid Texts. The Tutankhamun texts also speak of the mysterious presence brooding over the

Jackal Lake by saying: "I know the name of this god, it is He who is on his Lake."[69]

The strange name Neref given above as part of the topography of Rostau occurs in the Tutankhamun texts again in the variant form of Nareref, where it is defined as "the Southern Gate of the Mound of Osiris," which is described as being "opposite the lake of the just," thus again clearly mentioning the existence of the lake at Rostau. However, the translator Piankoff is not absolutely certain that *lake* is the correct word, and in a footnote he says an island may really be intended, within a lake. Neref, or Nareref, was transliterated as Naarrutf by Wallis Budge in an earlier era and means "the place where nothing grows."

Osiris is described by Isis in one of the Tutankhamun texts as emerging from the netherworld, presumably again at Rostau, at "the House of the Lake,"[70] which is presumably one of the old epithets of either the Sphinx Temple or the Valley Temple. And the topography of Rostau is again referred to as a "city on the water": "Thou travelest in thy barge in this city on the water. He rows in this field close to the body of Osiris. . . . He [the king] lands at these mysterious castles [presumably the two adjoining temples] which contain the image of Osiris. This God calls above these mysterious castles. . . . The majesty of this god establishes this city in the Netherworld for these gods."[71]

These many references in the shrine texts of Tutankhamun are very archaic. But by and large, memory of the long-vanished Jackal Lake had faded by the time of most of the New Kingdom texts, and even the archaic tradition mentioning it as a sacred feature in the tradition seemed to have no point any longer to the priests. Whereas the Papyrus of Nisti-ta-Nebet-Taui speaks of "Anubis, the Great God Imyut [the sacred symbol of Anubis], Lord of the Holy Land, He at the Head of the Necropolis,"[72] thus giving a correct impression of the great statue of Anubis seated at the entrance to the Giza Plateau even though it no longer existed in its original form, all reference to the presence of water has disappeared.

I should mention in passing that the hieroglyphic depiction of the name of Rostau features coils of rope. I regard these as images of the long ropes used to lower heavy stone sarcophagi down shafts into their subterranean abodes.

When I was working with my wife and a colleague in the Sphinx Temple, Olivia and I both had the same subjective impression. We felt as if we were walking around in an area that for some part of its history had been submerged in water. It has a kind of "underwater" look and feel about it. Of course, this is just a personal feeling, but I thought it worth mentioning, as so few people have ever set foot inside the Sphinx Temple, which has been closed to visitors for much, or perhaps all, of the time since it was cleared in the 1930s. I think it is at least possible that the Sphinx Temple was partially flooded on an intentional basis during the Old Kingdom when the Sphinx Moat existed. This state may have existed only during the inundation months. Looking at the twisting and turning ways inside the structure (see figure 6.15 for a photo from above), I can imagine a ceremony accomplished in small boats or on reed floats that made their way along the interior corridors and bends of the temple on water. In itself, there is nothing improbable about this. And perhaps the reference above to the "city on the water" at Rostau refers to this state of affairs, with the "castles" of the city being the Sphinx and Valley Temples. Perhaps the large "well" in the center of the entrance to the Valley Temple was really a drain, to help drain away the floodwaters from that temple after the inundation receded. It is easier to think of the "well" as such a drain than as a genuine well, with the Nile at least lapping at its doorway and in danger of plunging down it and polluting any true well water. It was this "well" into which the famous huge seated statue of Chephren with the falcon wrapping its wings around his head (now proudly displayed in the Egyptian Museum at Cairo) was thrust in a time of turmoil, thought to be the First Intermediate Period. The priests who presumably wished to save this statue from destruction may have found it convenient to thrust it down a drain that was still full of dirty drainage water, where it could not be seen, rather than into a clear well, where it would have been visible during the plundering of the temple.

One of the traditional names of the god Osiris was Water of Renewal, followed strangely by a determinative sign of a vase. (A determinative sign is a hieroglyph at the end of a word or name that is read not as a letter or syllable but as an indicator of the meaning of a word, such as for instance drawing a picture of a goddess after a name to indicate that the name is that of a goddess; the sign thus determines the nature of the name or word.) This name occurs in the Pyramid Texts inscribed on the walls of the Pyramid of King Pepi I and even survives in the *Book of the Dead.* I believe this refers to the use of the vase containing the heart, which was washed in the moat, bathing in the water symbolizing an act of renewal and rebirth. It was Renouf who made a special point of commenting on this epithet of Osiris in the notes to his early translation of the *Book of the Dead.*[73] Once one is aware of the ritual of the bathing of the deceased king's heart and other internal organs in their four jars in the Sphinx Moat, many hitherto obscure passages in the Pyramid Texts become clear, such as the one in Utterance 509: "My entrails have been washed by Anubis."[74]

Such passages are no longer seen merely as general descriptions of the embalming process carried out symbolically by Anubis, but as a specific ritual carried out in the presence of the giant statue of Anubis in his Jackal Lake.

Opposite: Figure 6.62. This is an imagined reconstruction of the interior of the Valley Temple of Giza. We see here the transverse hall, which runs north to south, at the eastern end of the structure. Here it is called by the name of the Pillared Hall (*Pfeilersaal* in German). A row of statues of King Chephren is envisaged here, sitting in the tranquil and eternal deathly gloom of faint light filtering in through narrow slits in the roof. The pillars are of solid granite, massive blocks weighing tens of tons each. The floor is of white Egyptian alabaster, called travertine. This is a very evocative view drawn by A. Bollacher and based on the reconstruction by Uvo Hölscher, who excavated the structure fully for the first time. It was published as plate 5 in Hölscher's book, *Das Grabdenkmal des Königs Chephren* (*The Funerary Monument of King Chephren*), Leipzig, 1912. Fragments of many Chephren statues have been found in the vicinity, and one large whole one is preserved in the Egyptian Museum at Cairo. It was thrown down a well beneath the temple, probably by priests who hid it there in a time of turmoil to preserve it. The Old Kingdom period of Egypt came to an end with the Sixth Dynasty, when terrible droughts and flood and plagues devastated the country for about 150 years, between approximately 2150 BC and 2000 BC. During this period, social order broke down and mobs rampaged around the Giza Plateau smashing everything, including the statues of Chephren envisaged here. It was at that time that I believe severe damage was done to the original head of the Sphinx, so the recarving that we see today was done from a kind of stump of the natural head. The period when civilization and the rule of law and order returned to Egypt about 2000 BC is the period that we call the Middle Kingdom. The period of turmoil between the Old Kingdom and the Middle Kingdom is known to archaeologists as the First Intermediate Period. (There was a second intermediate period, which separated the Middle Kingdom from the New Kingdom.)

Figure 6.63. A photo of the Sphinx taken at a specific moment in 1936, after Selim Hassan had reconstructed the lappets of the headdress, after he had removed the scaffolding around the head, but before he had erected scaffolding around the main body of the Sphinx to smear more cement over the body cracks that Baraize had largely filled up with cement ten years earlier. In the foreground is the fully excavated Valley Temple. (*Collection of Robert Temple*)

Figure 6.64. A photo circa 1890, showing the Sphinx behind the Valley Temple, only the interior of which was so far excavated. The Great Pyramid is behind. (*Collection of Robert Temple*)

Figure 6.65. This nineteenth-century French engraving shows how Auguste Mariette excavated only the interior, but did not clear the exterior, of the Valley Temple at Giza during the years 1853–60. It is in the foreground, and at that time was called the Sphinx Temple, because the true Sphinx Temple had not yet been discovered. The head of the Sphinx is seen behind, and in the background is the Great Pyramid. (*Collection of Robert Temple*)

Figure 6.66. An old glass-slide photo circa 1870/1880 showing the Sphinx in front of the Great Pyramid, and in the foreground the excavated interior of the Valley Temple, which was cleared during a seven-year period between 1853 and 1860 by Auguste Mariette. (At that time it was called the Sphinx Temple, because the true Sphinx Temple in front of the Sphinx was still covered by sand and was not discovered until the 1930s.) (*Collection of Robert Temple*)

Figure 6.67. This old photo by Bonfils, probably dating from the 1890s, shows the Valley Temple sanding over subsequent to 1870, when its interior had been excavated by Mariette. Walls made of small stones closely hug the west wall (at rear in photo) and the north wall (right in photo). The Valley Temple during the period from the New Kingdom onward acted as a kind of sand-filled megalithic foundation for inferior structures of small stones and mud brick, which even in this photo have not been fully cleared away. It was only when Uvo Hölscher finally excavated the Valley Temple in its entirety and cleared its outer walls that all these later rubbishy structures were removed; his report was published in German in 1912. (*Collection of Robert Temple*)

Figure 6.68. Yet another view of the foundation wall of small stones (foreground) built into the eastern end of the Valley Temple's roof. (*Collection of Robert Temple*)

Figure 6.69. Another view of the foundation wall of small stones that was built into the eastern end of the Valley Temple roof. (*Collection of Robert Temple*)

Figure 6.70. This is how the Valley Temple looked about 1870, after the excavations of Auguste Mariette. The interior had been excavated, but the exterior was essentially uncleared. Furthermore, the eastern face of the structure was covered over with this crudely constructed wall of small stones, which extends also about halfway along the top of the southern wall of the temple and then bends inward as well. The wall was actually a crude stone foundation of a building that stood for centuries on top of the Valley Temple's eastern half. Obviously, no trace of this crude foundation wall survives today. I have placed a highly enlarged version of this photo on my dedicated website supplementary to this book (www.sphinxmystery.info) so that archaeologists can study the fine detail, as the photo has extremely high definition and depth of field and yields a great deal of detailed information about what the site was like prior to the excavations of Uvo Hölscher. (*Collection of Robert Temple*)

Figure 6.71. This old Victorian glass slide gives a tinted view of the Sphinx seen from the southeast corner of the Valley Temple, at a time when only the interior of the Valley Temple had yet been cleared, and the sand still stood around about it. This was one of the most popular vantage points for photos of the Sphinx taken at that time. (*Collection of Robert Temple*)

Sometimes the topography is muddled, or at least the religious lore is, and the goddess Isis intrudes onto the scene. The mythological context can be altered and expressed in terms of Isis and her son Horus, as in Utterance 510 of the Pyramid Texts:

> I travel the Winding Waterway . . . because I am pure, the son of a pure one, and I am purified with these four *nemeset*-jars [for the internal organs] of mine which are filled to the brim from the Canal of the God in Iseion [sanctuary of Isis, rather than Osiris, in this context], which possesses the breath of Isis the Great, and Isis the Great dries me as Horus.
>
> "Let him come, for he is pure": so says the priest of Rē concerning me to the door-keeper of the firmament [these are probably actual words of the ritual], and he announces me to those four gods [the gods of the four *nemeset*-jars, who were "sons of Horus" or "followers of Horus"] who are upon the Canal of Kenzet.[75]

Kenzet, or Kenset, was another of those names that referred to both a real place (in this case in the very far south, the so-called First Nome district) and a mythological locality. It means the Land Beyond. But there is no need to pursue further all these myriad epithets, their use, and their history in Egyptian tradition at this time.

One could go on gathering up all these confused threads, or scattered limbs, indefinitely. But the essence of the situation is clear. There was a sacred Lake of the Netherworld called Jackal Lake, which had many other names and fancy descriptions, presided over by Anubis, and it was "winding" and also called a "canal of the god." It was at Rostau in Giza. It is mentioned in the ancient texts over many centuries, repeatedly. It was the scene of a sacred ritual of the washing of the internal organs of the deceased king in the four jars that contained them, which were submerged into the water at the edge of the lake, as an act of purification to facilitate his resurrection. I suggest that this was all real, not mythological, and that in Old Kingdom times it took place in the Sphinx Moat, which surrounded the great statue of Anubis, which I choose therefore to call Sphinx Island.

Finally, we come to the most specific evidence of all that the Great Sphinx was once an island. This evidence has been discovered by excavation within the Sphinx Pit itself. In 1817, when Giambattista Caviglia cleared the front of the Sphinx, he cleared its paws of sand for the first time since the collapse of the Roman Empire. And there he found an inscription in Greek carved prominently on the middle toe of the Sphinx's left paw. The inscription was carved with official sanction in the year AD 166, during the reign of the emperor Marcus Aurelius, to commemorate the Roman restoration of the retaining walls that surrounded the Sphinx.[76] It was signed "Arrianos," and it refers to the Sphinx as being an "island (made) of a rock."[77] When this inscription was found, it was wondered whether the Arrian whose name appears at the bottom of the Greek verse might possibly be the same Arrian as the famous historian of that name, who wrote the life of Alexander the Great called *Anabasis of Alexander.* (The Greek word *anabasis* means journey upward, and it was the title the earlier Greek historian Xenophon had given to a famous work of history that he wrote. Arrian was often called in his lifetime the second Xenophon. He paid homage to the original Xenophon by imitating the title of his most famous work.) Although Arrian was a Greek who wrote in Greek, he lived at the time of the Roman Empire, and his honorary Roman name was Flavius Arrianus. He was a personal friend and protégé of the Roman emperor Hadrian (who died AD 138). They met during Hadrian's visit to Athens in AD 126, and Hadrian then took him back to Rome with him and gave him his honorary Roman name personally (Flavius being a forename that could be used only by royal decree), eventually appointing him to be consul of Rome (the highest office under the emperor). Prior to the consulship, in 132 Hadrian had appointed Arrian to be governor of the Roman province of Cappadocia in Asia Minor, where Arrian showed unexpected military prowess and repelled a major barbarian invasion by a fierce and warlike nomadic people called the Alans. Arrian had started life as a peaceful philosopher. He had been a pupil of the famous Stoic philosopher Epictetus (who died circa AD 135), whose chief disciple he was. He published many books of Stoic philosophy based on the discourses of Epictetus and also compiled the famous *Manual* (*Enchiridion* in Greek) of Epictetus's teachings, which is still popular and highly relevant today. Epictetus was like the earlier Socrates in that he wrote nothing. All the works that we have today by Epictetus, which are extensive, were actually written down and systematized by Arrian as a record of his teachings. One of the first seventeenth-century books I ever bought as a young man, and still one of my most precious for both intrinsic worth and sentimental reasons, is George Stanhope's 1694 translation of the Commentary on Epictetus's *Manual* by the Neoplatonic philosopher Simplicius.[78] I pored over this work when I was in my twenties and in my phase of intensively studying both Stoic philosophy and Neoplatonism. As Simplicius says (in seventeenth-century English, in which important nouns were capitalized, as they are today in modern German):

> The principal Design of this book (if Men would but suffer themselves to be wrought upon by it, and not think it sufficient to give him the Hearing only, but let it seriously affect their Minds, and would reduce [transform] what they read into Practice) is, To set our Souls as Free, as when their Great Father and Creator first gave them to us, to disengage them from all those slavish Fears

and confounding Troubles, and other Corruptions of Humane Nature, which are wont to subdue and tyrannize over them.

It is called an *Enchiridion,* or Manual, because all Persons, who are desirous to live as they ought, should be perfect in this Book, and have it always ready at hand: A Book of as constant and necessary use as the Sword (which commonly went by this name, and from whence the Metaphor seems to be taken) is to a Soldier.

The Discourses are lively and moving; and all but the Stupid and Sottish must needs be affected with them.[79]

Clearly, I had no desire to be among the stupid and sottish, so I took the book very much to heart, absorbing at a very early age the crucial distinction it made between "what is in our power" and "what is not in our power," which has enabled me to regard countless vicissitudes of life with a greater degree of equanimity than would otherwise have been possible. I cannot recommend the insights of the work highly enough. Arrian, who had such experience of war, both as a commander who repelled the barbarians and as a magnificent historian of Alexander the Great and his military conquests, clearly gave the *Manual* its particular title on purpose, having very much in mind the soldier's sword as the analogy, as Simplicius points out. One is tempted to hear Arrian humming something like: "Onward Stoic Soldiers, Marching unto War, with the Enchiridion Going on Before." Certainly, the Christian concept of "the Church militant" owes something to this.

There was no other famous Arrian in antiquity. And so, when one speculates on who would have the prestige and authority to inscribe his words on the toe of the Sphinx on the occasion of a great public and official Roman ceremony, one unhesitatingly concludes that it could only have been the historian Arrian, who was one of the highest-ranking retired dignitaries in the entire Roman Empire. Another point to keep in mind is that the inscription was in Greek (Arrian's native language), although the official occasion was a Roman one. One can safely conclude that only someone as famous as Arrian would have been allowed to inscribe something in Greek rather than in Latin to celebrate a Roman state occasion.

Arrian was presumably visiting Egypt and would have been invited to compose a celebratory verse as a courtesy by the Roman governor of Egypt at that time. I think we may safely conclude, therefore, that the verses cut into the toe of the Sphinx were written by the famous historian Arrian. By that time, he had been retired from political activities for twenty-eight years and had returned to his hometown of Nicomedia in Bithynia (Asia Minor) and his main residence, though he must have visited Rome and other parts of the empire from time to time. In Nicomedia, he is known to have become a priest of Ceres and Proserpine.

Proserpine was a goddess of the underworld, known in Greek as Persephone.[80] Arrian would therefore have had a particular and specific interest in underworld deities in Egypt, as he was a priest of a Greek underworld deity himself. He would thus have been fascinated by Giza as the most famous necropolis of Egypt. As an expert historian with an encyclopedic knowledge of the past, the content of his verses would have special importance, especially with regard to historical tradition and detail. Everything suggests, therefore, that Arrian the historian wrote the verses on the toe of the Sphinx. And to us, these verses are very important. The inscription no longer survives, as the paws of the Sphinx have been covered entirely with modern "restoration stones." Curse the "restoration"! It obliterates everything! But in 1817, shortly after it was discovered, the inscription was copied down very carefully. In ancient times, Greek was written entirely in capital letters, as lowercase letters had not yet been devised. So we have an engraving of the original inscription in capital Greek letters (reproduced here in figure 6.51), a rendering of it in lowercase (shown in figure 6.52), a translation of it into Latin, and a translation of it into English. All these were published together in the *Quarterly Review*, volume 19, for April and December of 1818, in London in 1819. There are three English translations of this crucial inscription in existence. Here is the English translation of the verses in modern prose as published by Selim Hassan, and possibly adapted or translated by his assistant, Omm Sety (Dorothy Eady): "Thy formidable form is the work of the Immortal Gods. In order to spare the

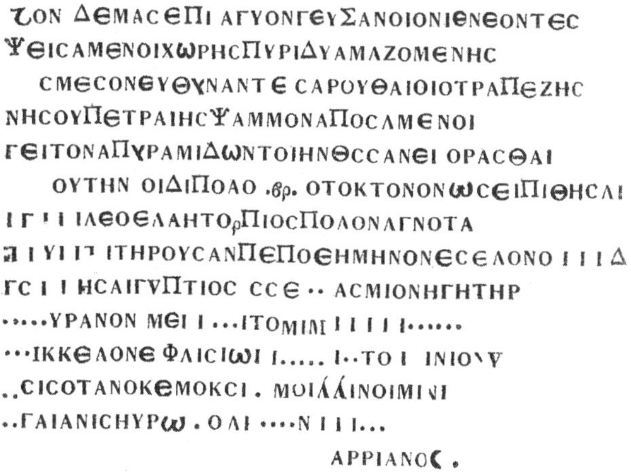

ΖΟΝ ΔΕΜΑΣΕΠΙ ΑΓΥΟΝΓΕΥΣΑΝΟΙΟΝΙΕΝΘΟΝΤΕΣ
ΨΘΙΣΑΜΕΝΟΙΧΩΡΗΣΠΥΡΙΔΥΑΜΑΖΟΜΕΝΗΣ
ΣΜΕΣΟΝΘΥΘΥΝΑΝΤΕ ΣΑΡΟΥΘΑΙΟΙΟΤΡΑΠΕΖΗΣ
ΝΗΣΟΥΠΕΤΡΑΙΗΣΨΑΜΜΟΝΑΠΟΣΑΜΕΝΟΙ
ΓΕΙΤΟΝΑΠΥΡΑΜΙΔΩΝΤΟΙΗΝΘΣΣΑΝΘΙ ΟΡΑΣΘΑΙ
OYTHN ΟΙΔΙΠΟΑΟ .βρ. ΟΤΟΚΤΟΝΟΝΩΣΕΙΠΙΘΗΣΛΙ
Ι Γ ʹ Ι ΙΛΘΟΘΛΛΗΤΟρΠΙΟΣΠΟΛΟΝΑΓΝΟΤΑ
Ͻ Ι ΥΙ Ι˥ ΙΤΗΡΟΥΣΑΝΠΕΠΟΘΗΜΗΝΟΝΕΣΕΛΟΝΟ Ι Ι ΙΔ
ΓΣ Ι Ι ΗΣΑΙΓΥΠΤΙΟΣ ΣΣΘ ·· ΑΣΜΙΟΝΗΓΗΤΗΡ
·····ΥΡΑΝΟΝ ΜΘΙ Ι ···ΙΤΟΜΙΝΙ Ι Ι Ι Ι·······
···ΙΚΚΕΛΟΝΘ ΦΛΙΣΙΩΙ Ι..... Ι··ΤΟ Ι ΙΝΙΟΝΥ
..ΣΙΣΟΤΑΝΟΚΕΜΟΚΣΙ. ΜΟΙΛΛΙΝΟΙΜΙΝΙ
..ΓΑΙΑΝΙΣΗΥΡΩ . Ο ΛΙ ····Ν Ι Ι Ι...

                    ΑΡΡΙΑΝΟϹ .

Figure 6.72. This is the Greek inscription on the left paw of the Sphinx, dating from the official Roman commemorative ceremony of AD 166, as it was published in 1819 in the *Quarterly Review*. The copy was apparently made by Henry Salt in 1817 at the time of Caviglia's excavation.

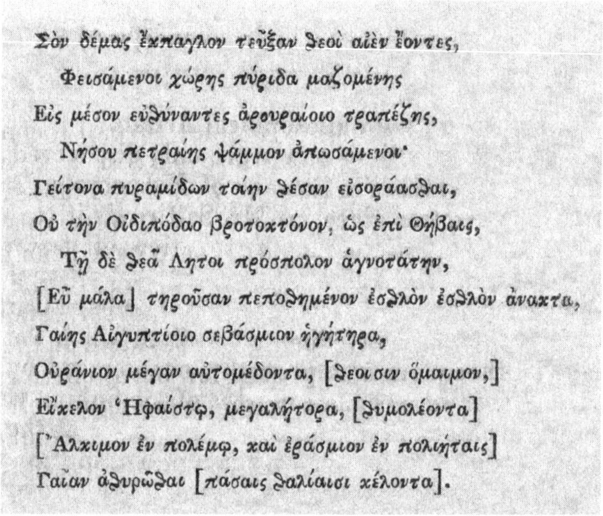

Σὸν δέμας ἔκπαγλον τεῦξαν θεοὶ αἰὲν ἐόντες,

Φεισάμενοι χώρης πύριδα μαζομένης

Εἰς μέσον εὐθύναντες ἀρουραίοιο τραπέζης,

Νήσου πετραίης ψάμμον ἀπωσάμενοι·

Γείτονα πυραμίδων τοίην θέσαν εἰσοράασθαι,

Οὐ τὴν Οἰδιπόδαο βροτοκτόνον, ὡς ἐπὶ Θήβαις,

Τῇ δὲ θεᾷ Λητοῖ πρόσπολον ἁγνοτάτην,

[Εὖ μάλα] τηροῦσαν πεποθημένον ἐσθλὸν ἐσθλὸν ἄνακτα,

Γαίης Αἰγυπτίοιο σεβάσμιον ἡγήτηρα,

Οὐράνιον μέγαν αὐτομέδοντα, [θεοῖσιν ὅμαιμον,]

Εἴκελον Ἡφαίστῳ, μεγαλήτορα [θυμολέοντα]

['Άλκιμον ἐν πολέμῳ, καὶ ἐράσμιον ἐν πολιήταις]

Γαῖαν ἀθυρῶσαι [πάσαις θαλίαισι κέλοντα].

Figure 6.73. This is the transcription of the Sphinx inscription into lowercase Greek such as is used by modern scholars, published in the *Quarterly Review* in 1819. This transcription and effort to fill in the gaps was done by a classicist named Dr. Young. The first two words in line four speak of the Sphinx as an "island of a rock."

level, harvest-bearing land, they placed you in the midst of your cavity, as a rocky island, from which they had driven back the sand. They placed you as a neighbour to the Pyramids, for our beholding; not like the Sphinx of Thebes, slain by Oedipus, but as a sacred servant of the divine Leto, who vigilantly guards the good, lamented Osiris, the Sacred Guide of the Land of Egypt."[81]

It is necessary to point out that the reference to the Greek goddess Leto is merely a polite reference to the region in which the Sphinx lies. The name given to it in Greek by the Ptolemies was the Letopolitan Nome (a *nome* being an administrative district). The Sphinx is thus called a "servant of Leto" only because the Sphinx sits in the administrative district named after Leto. This is a flowery bit of "officialese," because it is a formal state occasion.

Here is the earlier translation by Dr. Young into rhyming verse, which was published 1819, where Leto is called by her Latin name of Latona:

> *Thy form stupendous here the gods have placed,*
> *Sparing each spot of harvest-bearing land;*
> *And with this mighty work of art have graced*
> *A rocky isle, encumber'd once with sand;*
> *And near the pyramids have bid thee stand:*

Not that fierce Sphinx that Thebes erewhile laid waste,
But great Latona's servant mild and bland;
Watching that prince beloved who fills the throne
Of Egypt's plains, and calls the Nile his own.
That heavenly monarch [who his foes defies],
Like Vulcan powerful [and Pallas wise].

ARRIAN[82]

It is a pity that the bottom lines of the inscription were not preserved properly, although Arrian's signature at the bottom is perfectly clear (see figure 6.50 for the reproduction of the original inscription, where ARRIANOS, the Greek form of Arrian, is written as ARRIANOC, because the final *s* tended to be written like that in inscriptions in those days). Dr. Young has not hesitated to fill in some missing bits in square brackets and otherwise, reading understandably *ouranon* where the initial *o* is lacking and only *–uranon* survives (hence the appearance of "heavenly" in his tenth line of verse), but he has not attempted to reconstruct the last two lines at all, even though fragments can be seen. He also omits the name of Oedipus. The last line appears to mention either *gaia,* "the Earth," or Gaia, the Earth goddess of the Greeks, but interpreting the orthography of ancient Greek inscriptions is a highly specialized skill that I lack entirely. The way the words run together and are not separated in these ancient texts is maddening and reminds me of the nightmare of my youthful days in dealing with this phenomenon as a student of Sanskrit (though in Sanskrit, the letters perversely "melt" and change into a new form when run together, as if designed to drive a student truly insane with frustration). However, on a have-a-go basis, I would say that I do not see the name of Thebes in the inscription following the mention of Oedipus in this inscription as published in 1819, or the mention of Osiris by name in the inscription either. However, the "island (made) of a rock" is very much there, at the beginning of line four, followed by *psammon,* the word for sand.

The Greek inscription was published again later, after some tidying up by a Reverend Coleridge of Eton, who was a classicist. This appeared in the appendix volume of *Operations Carried On at the Pyramids of Gizeh* by Colonel Howard Vyse and John Perring, London, 1842.[83] I reproduce this rather different version of the Greek inscription as figure 6.74. In this version, we can see that the name of Greek Thebes does indeed appear (as the last word of line six), whereas the word had been incorrectly transcribed in the version printed in 1819, with the *b* being written as a sigma, so Thebes could not be made out. In this version, the name of Osiris does also appear at the end of line eight (OCEIRIN). Here is

the translation done by Coleridge (who added "The Salutation of" in the last
line himself):

> *The ever-living gods built thy . . . form,*
> *Sparing the ground producing corn.*
> *Having raised thee in the midst of the arable land,*
> *Having driven back the sand from the rocky island;*
> *A neighbour of the Pyramids they placed thee;*
> *(A line seems wanting) . . . such to behold,*
> *Not the slayer of Oedipus, as at Thebes,*
> *But the goddess Latona, a most pure attendant,*
> *protecting the regretted good Osiris*
> *the revered governor of Egypt,*
> *heavenly, great,*
> *like to Vulcan,*
> *the earth.*

THE SALUTATION OF ARRIAN[84]

Figure 6.74. This is a second attempt to publish the inscription on the left paw of the Sphinx, an
"improved version" prepared by the Reverend Coleridge of Eton. In this version, many of the
words are clearer than in the version printed in 1819 and shown in figure 6.72. The name of
Arrian, author of the verses, may be seen at the bottom (in Greek the letter that looks like a P
is really an R). The name of Thebes is the last six letters of line six. The name of Osiris is the
last seven letters of line eight. The first two words in line four speak of the Sphinx as an "island
of a rock." This was published by Colonel Howard Vyse in 1842. Some of the inscription seems
to have been lost since the excavation in 1817, possibly because the surface of the stone peeled,
but other words are now clearer than in the previously published version.

If we examine what is said in this inscription, despite its incomplete state, we find that we are told (a) that the Sphinx is placed in a cavity, by which is meant the Sphinx Pit (although this does not come across in Coleridge's translation); (b) that the Sphinx is an island made of a rock; (c) that the sand has been driven back from the pit and from the Sphinx (held back by the retaining walls, which this inscription commemorates); (d) that the Sphinx is a neighbor of the pyramids; and (e) that the Sphinx stands guard over "the good, lamented," or "regretted good," Osiris.

What is important to us is that the Sphinx is described as an island made of a rock. The Greek adjective describing the island is *petraios*. This is a word that has the meaning "of a rock." It is not strictly accurate to translate it as "rocky," as if one were referring to lots of rocks, although the word was used that way sometimes. But there were other related words such as *petrinos* that were more commonly used to mean "rocky." This particular word was presumably chosen because it was recognized that the Sphinx was a *single* rock. And as this single rock was purposefully described in AD 166 on a state occasion by the scholarly historian Arrian as being "an island," I rest my case.

7

THE SPHINX AND THE
GIZA PLAN

The mysterious plan of the Plateau of Giza will be described later on in this chapter, and is illustrated in figure 7.25 on page 367. It is one of the most fantastic survivals of ancient Egypt, in some ways more remarkable than the monuments themselves, since it actually embodies them within a larger scheme so complex and ingenious that it reminds me of a modern computer program run amok. And it is a plan not only in two dimensions, but in three as well. We shall see that the Sphinx and the Giza pyramids have a precise and direct relation with one another, a relation so specific that the monuments mutually determine one another's positions on the plateau. They form a unified complex. There are numerous correlations, and one may be seen in figure 7.2, which is a detail of the intriguing figure 7.1 and shows the Sphinx from the top of the Great Pyramid. If we look from that point, a line seems to cross the Sphinx's head and become a diagonal through the Valley Temple from its northwestern corner to its southeastern corner, perhaps touching the northwest corner of the Sphinx Temple in the process. I have chosen not to represent this in figure 7.25, which details what I call the Golden Giza Plan, because if this line is intentional and not fortuitous, it appears to represent a correlation that is additional to the "system" of the golden angles, which it is my main purpose to make clear to readers.

It is the Golden Giza Plan in figure 7.25 that proves the main Giza monuments were constructed to a unified plan. The size, position, and general shape of the Sphinx are determined by sighting lines (or "rays," as I like to call them) from the pyramids, which all are generated by the use of a single angle, the sacred angle on which the whole of ancient Egyptian art and sacred and royal architecture were based for religious reasons.

Figure 7.1. A stereoview photo from the top of the Great Pyramid, looking southeast toward the Sphinx, which is in the top right corner, unfortunately covered in shade from a passing cloud. See the detail of it in figure 7.2. In this photo, one gets an impression of the dizzying height of the pyramid, more than 500 feet up in the air with the birds. No place for a person with vertigo! This photo was probably taken in the late 1930s, as the excavated Sphinx Temple is at the feet of the Sphinx. The modern access road to the plateau had not yet been constructed and is still just a dirt track. (*Collection of Robert Temple*)

Figure 7.2. This detail of the previous photo shows how the center of the head of the Sphinx is in line with the diagonal joining the northwest and southeast corners of the Valley Temple, as seen from the top of the Great Pyramid. (*Collection of Robert Temple*)

But before we come to that, we must consider some ancient Egyptian texts that seem to describe some of the mysteries and design of Giza. The ultimate answers to the mysteries of the geometrical plan of Giza are deeply connected with the most bizarre complex of mythological concepts dealing with death and resurrection.

And at the most fundamental level, this all emanated from a single idea: the profound conviction that the universe was based on what the Egyptians called Maāt, or Cosmic Order. Most people think that the Egyptian religious beliefs were spread across many gods and were diffuse and unfocused as a result. It is true that they had many gods, but they had only one Cosmic Order. In that sense, they were more profoundly monotheist than any people since. Ultimately, what they really worshipped was One Principle, with their many gods arranged like so many flowers around its altar of perfection. However, we shall see what comes out of a closer examination of why anyone would construct anything quite so weird as the Giza necropolis; and for the first time for thousands of years, its geometrical plan will become as plain as it was to those who constructed it in the first place.

There are some very strange ancient texts indeed that we must now consider. These are of a different category than the Pyramid Texts from Saqqara that we examined in the chapter on the Sphinx as Anubis. These texts are preserved both in the form of papyri and as sacred Coffin Texts of the Middle Kingdom, and as wall texts in royal tombs of the New Kingdom. The texts were considered so special that they were supposed to be used only by the deceased kings, although a few nobles did so also. Although the wall texts are known only from the period of the New Kingdom, commencing with the Eighteenth Dynasty (circa 1540 BC), they are believed by Egyptologists to be very much older and to have been "recycled" in the New Kingdom. They are thought to date from the Old Kingdom, the Pyramid Age, circa 2700–2200 BC, when Giza was central to the concerns of all the priests and scribes of Egypt. By the time of the New Kingdom, when the capital of Egypt was at Thebes in the south (a town now called Luxor), Giza was no longer central to Egyptian civilization, pharaohs were not building their tombs there, and certainly they were not building any pyramids there. The pharaohs by that time were all being buried in the famous Valley of the Kings across the river from Thebes (Luxor). As we know from the inscription on the Dream Stela erected in front of the Sphinx by the New Kingdom pharaoh Thutmosis (Thothmes) IV, who excavated the Sphinx at Giza as a result of his dream, until then Giza had been a place where one went hunting on horseback and dozed in the shade afforded by the head of the Sphinx, as that and the top of the back were the only portions of that monument that still protruded from the sand. (I assume the top of the back was visible, for otherwise Thutmosis would not have known that the body was buried by sand, as there would have been no evidence of a body's existence.) Giza was essentially deserted. The New Kingdom pharaohs erected a few pathetic little temples there (less impressive, I must say, than many eighteenth-century English garden monuments and decorative mock temples in places such as Buckinghamshire) to show their reverence for the ancient sacred

Figure 7.3. This interior doorway of the small New Kingdom Temple of Amenhotep II at the northeastern corner of the Sphinx Pit has been constructed in such a way that it is in perfect alignment with the Great Pyramid, whose apex is aligned with the center of the doorway and lintel. The view is toward the northwest. The wall beyond the temple, where some people are, is the foundation and border wall of the modern access road from Nazlet el-Samman to the pyramids. It was constructed some timeafter the Second World War. The siting of this temple in such an obvious way to align with the apex of the Great Pyramid reminds us of the relationship of the apex of the Pyramid of Chephren with the floor of the Sphinx Temple (that sight line is at the golden angle, as measured with an inclinometer), and also the general Giza Plan, as it specifies the precise size and location of the Sphinx with relation to the two main pyramids, as described in the text. (*Photo by Robert Temple*)

place, but otherwise Giza was of little concern to them (see figures 7.3 to 7.5). This changed to a certain extent after the Sphinx was cleared and it became the center of a minor cult, with an altar for offerings to the spirit of the Sphinx. No one remembered that it had once been Anubis. It was accepted at face value, as a monument with a pharaoh's face (no one would have remembered which one) and an animal body that from that time onward came to be thought of as a lion. In other words, people of the new Kingdom were as ignorant of the body being that of a dog as modern people are.

The New Kingdom pharaohs could not manage to build pyramids anymore

Figure 7.4. A photo, facing southwest, of the author standing in the doorway of the small New Kingdom Temple of Amenhotep II, overlooking the northeastern portion of the Sphinx. The center of the lintel of the doorway is aligned with the center of the Sphinx's forehead at the top of its head, which was one of the artistic canonical measuring points in traditional Egyptian art. (*Photo by Olivia Temple*)

Figure 7.5. This photo taken in 1951 by Selim Hassan shows the small New Kingdom Temple of Amenhotep II situated in front of the Sphinx, at an angle and to the left. The temple was excavated by Hassan in the mid-1930s. Since this photo was taken, the authorities have raised some of the fallen stones and reconstructed much of the structure, which was not particularly difficult to do, I suspect. This photo was reproduced very poorly in Hassan's book, *The Great Sphinx and Its Secrets,* Cairo, 1953, as figure 34 on page 47. However, I bought the original print from a dealer and have therefore been able to reproduce it at last with proper definition in a digital scan and by modern printing. (*Collection of Robert Temple*)

through loss of the techniques and skills of their predecessors, and they put their efforts into temples and obelisks instead. The Pyramid Age had well and truly passed. Therefore, when pharaohs and nobles of that time used sacred texts referring to Giza and its lore, these were drawn from papyri that preserved the texts from an earlier era. Egyptian religious practice was always highly conservative, and texts were recycled over the centuries. This is true in modern Christianity as well. In church, people still say the Lord's Prayer, which was a prayer said to have been spoken by Jeschu (more commonly known by the Latin form of his name as Jesus) the Nazarene two thousand years ago. No one feels uncomfortable about this. Although new translations have been made, no one says: "This prayer is no good, it's too old, let's throw it out and get a new one." It retains its validity, its importance, and its relevance even in the twenty-first century. Of course, it has been expanded since the time of Jesus. It now says at the end: "For thine is the Kingdom, the power, and the glory, forever and ever, Amen." Jesus never said any of that. His original prayer ended with the words: ". . . and deliver us from evil." Clerics cannot resist tinkering and trying to improve things. Sometimes the Lord's Prayer is said without the extra bits, in its pure form, but there seems to be no pattern determining when it will be said in its pure form and when it will be said in its expanded form. Jews do not complain when rabbis read the Torah, which is hundreds of years older than the Lord's Prayer. Muslims do not complain when someone reads from the Koran, even though it was written in the seventh century. What Hindu has ever complained about his priests, the brahmins, reciting passages from their earliest sacred texts, the Vedas, which are 3,500 years old, even though they are in Sanskrit, a language that only a handful of scholars can any longer understand? (I studied Sanskrit at university, and I can assure you that it is one of the most difficult subjects of study you can possibly imagine, and no wonder no one can understand it anymore, as it has the most complicated grammar of any language in the history of the world. It was by far the most difficult thing I ever had to learn.) So it should not surprise us, therefore, based on what we know of modern religions, to discover that the New Kingdom Egyptians were also using texts that were many hundreds of years old, or even as much as 1,200 years old. After all, most of these texts were not nearly as old for them as the Lord's Prayer is for us now, and were less than half the age the Torah is today. But also, as with the Lord's Prayer, they could not resist tinkering sometimes, and adding some bits. People are always fidgeting, tinkering and fiddling with things if only out of nerves.

There are many surviving ancient Egyptian texts dealing with the afterlife and the netherworld, the best known being the so-called *Book of the Dead*. However, this name *Book of the Dead* is unfortunate, since it is not a real title. It is merely a survival of the name given to a variety of afterlife spells written on papyri that were found in coffins by grave robbers. When the robbers came across these writings, which of course they were unable to read, they merely referred to them collectively as "books of the dead," that is, books belonging to the dead men and women whose mummies they were robbing. The *Book of the Dead* was thus never a book, and there are many different collections of chapters and spells gathered together in different combinations that have come to be known under this general designation. Some portions of this material did have a kind of unity to them; for instance, the title of one genuinely ancient part of the material was *The Book of Coming Forth by Day.* (This refers to the resurrection of the dead.) But one should keep in mind that there is no actual Egyptian *Book of the Dead* as such. This is quite different from the situation in Tibet, where there is another work called *The Book of the Dead* (first committed to writing in the eighth century AD), which is a unified text about the experiences of the deceased soul, together with instructions to be shouted into the ear of the dead person to help him or her navigate the difficult realms of the afterlife.[1] Needless to say, there is absolutely no direct connection of any kind between the Tibetan *Book of the Dead* and the Egyptian texts grouped under the misnomer *The Book of the Dead.* However, the title "Book of the Dead" is considered so evocative and is at the same time so simple and so easily grasped that many members of the public who know little more than the title are inclined to think they know what it is, which merely adds to the confusion. The title has the illusory sense of completeness of a well-edited television sound bite and can lead people astray just as easily.

There are some portions of the *Book of the Dead* material that appear to refer to Giza. But the most important texts about Giza are two sections of the earliest actual "book" of the underworld, which is now known as *The Book of the Am-Duat,* or *The Book of What Is in the Netherworld.* This was not its original title. In the text itself, its original title is given as *Book of the Hidden Chamber.*[2]

Since hidden chambers are an important theme for us, and the subject of an entire earlier chapter of this book, the title is certainly intriguing. I am inclined to view the *Book of the Am-Duat* as a work of the New Kingdom into which has been inserted a section, which is based on an ancient papyrus of the Old Kingdom that the later priests still possessed and decided to incorporate, although it didn't really fit. Many scholars have thought this, so it is not a new idea. There is a clear discontinuity in the text. For most of the *Book of the Am-Duat,* the sun is traveling across water in his boat at night through different gates and regions of the underworld, where he encounters a variety of gods and monsters. Each of the twelve regions of the underworld is called an "hour," and they are passed through in succession. However, the fourth and fifth hours are quite unlike the other hours, so much so that the sun god even has to leave his boat and travel across sand. It is at this point that he is in the realm of the hawk-headed god Sokar, also spelled

Sokaris or Seker. And there seems to be agreement among the authorities that this refers to the necropolis of Giza.

I think *Book of the Hidden Chamber* is probably the original title of the earlier work that contained these two chapters, especially as the section of the fourth and fifth hours refers to hidden chambers. There are various depictions of hidden chambers in the ancient netherworld illustrations, and one of the best is from the left wall of Sarcophagus Hall I in the tomb of Rameses VI (see figure 7.7). The Hidden Chamber was generally inhabited by the deceased Osiris awaiting resurrection. Sometimes it was inhabited by the god of the resurrectable aspects of the netherworld, Sokar, which may go back to the earlier tradition before Osiris became amalgamated with Sokar. (Sokar had no connection with the damned, who were given over to torture and eventual destruction in the Place of Annihilation, tasks that were the jobs of others.) I suspect that the title *Book of the Hidden Chamber* later came to be applied to the New Kingdom Am-Duat book as a whole, carried over from the earlier text of the two chapters that were preserved in something approaching their original form.

The weird contents of this section of the fourth and fifth hours must be studied with some attention, as certain clues seem to be found there that may assist us in considering the Giza Plateau. It should be noted also that a clear illustration of a pyramid is to be found in this section (see figures 7.6 and 7.7).

Wallis Budge as long ago as 1904 realized that the fourth and fifth hours were an insertion into the larger book and once consisted of a self-contained underworld of their own. In *The Gods of the Egyptians,* he wrote: "The domain of Seker [Budge always spells Sokar in the form Seker], although reduced to two hours which have been inserted in their proper geographical position in the [Underworld], certainly at one time formed a complete hell, and . . . the rising of the sun was the final event which took place in it."[3]

This domain of Sokar, identified with Giza, was also known as Rostau. But like all Egyptian names, Rostau can be spelled in various ways, as we have already seen earlier in this book. Budge spells it Re-stau. It was also occasionally called Restatet. Some Egyptologists prefer Rosetau and others use the form Ro-Setawe. This name, which we shall continue to spell Rostau, seems to refer specifically to the underground region at Giza. But it was also by extension sometimes the ancient name for the Giza Plateau as a whole (as separate from Djedu, later known in Greek as Busiris, which was the adjoining village to the east). The translated meaning of the name is Mouth of the Passages[4] or, in other words, Entrance to the Passages. And the passages meant are, obviously, the secret passages of the Giza Plateau, both those underground and, by extension, those concealed within the pyramids.

Figure 7.6. This carving of the god Sokar is found on a wall in the most mysterious and esoteric of all the underground crypts beneath the Temple of Denderah in Upper Egypt, where strange rituals or initiations are believed to have taken place. The crypt is known as Chamber C of the North Crypts. Sokar's name in hieroglyphics is in the small rectangle beside his head. See the drawing of this wall in figure 8.25 on page 418. Sokar was often portrayed as a hawk or a mummified hawk (not to be confused with the god Horus, who was also portrayed as a hawk, but never mummified). Sokar presided over the world of the dead and was an entirely subterranean divinity who never came to the surface. The modern name of Saqqara derives from the name Sokar, because of its many subterranean passages and chambers and its proximity to Giza. Sokar's actual home was said to be at Rostau, or Rosetau, which was described as being at the foot of the Giza Plateau, at the same location as the Sphinx, just west of the village that in Greek times was called Busiris but is today called Nazlet el-Samman. It was there that Sokar had a temple of his own, believed to be what is today called the Valley Temple of Chephren, a huge, gloomy structure made of megalithic blocks of granite. Sokar was the Old Kingdom's underground god and was intimately associated with the dog Anubis, who was the surface guardian of the necropolis and of the dead. They were the predecessors of the later god Osiris, who from the time of the Fifth and Sixth Dynasties usurped both their functions and became the King of the Underworld. From then on, the humanized Sokar, under the name of Osiris, could be successively identified with every dead king, who after death was said to "become an Osiris." A mummiform version of Sokar carried in a sacred barque is shown in figure 7.22, an engraving from circa 1798 of a carving that is now believed to have been lost or destroyed. In the Old Kingdom, there was an annual Festival of Sokar at Giza, when this image of Sokar sitting in a celestial boat was carried around by the priests as part of an itinerant celebration. (*Photo by Robert Temple*)

Figure 7.7. This evocative depiction of a hidden chamber in the netherworld shows a chamber with two stories. On the top story, Osiris is standing as a mummy, wearing the crown of Upper Egypt. In front of him, his own *ba* (spiritual force), called in the text "the Soul of Osiris in the West," is worshipping him and standing on a mound, while the Earth god Geb arises from a mound behind him, also in a posture of adoration. In the lower story, the god Anubis and another figure, probably the Earth god Geb, but called in the text "the One over the Mysteries," preside over a chest called in the text "the mysterious chest." This chest contains the secret of secrets, the thing most carefully guarded of all, and no one is allowed to know what it is. To the right and left of the bottom story are kneeling figures of the evil dead, their hands bound behind their backs in the posture of captives, who have been decapitated as the first stage of their annihilation. To the right and left of the hidden chamber are vertical Nehep serpents standing on their tails, signifying resurrection. The caldrons being held aloft on either side in the top register hold, on the left, hearts, and on the right, a mixture of hearts and upside-down soul-shadows (all the dead were believed to enter the netherworld upside down). The hearts and soul-shadows are pouring from the streams of blood of upside-down decapitated corpses who are being lowered from the sky. (*From Alexandre Piankoff,* The Tomb of Rameses VI, *Pantheon Books, New York, 1954, figure 110 on p. 357*)

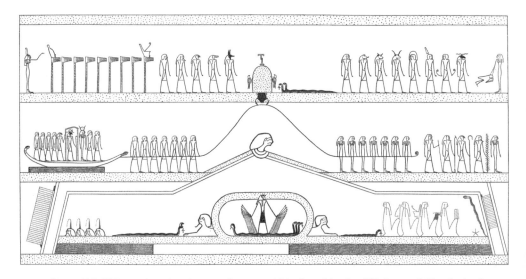

Figure 7.8. This section-view image of a pyramid is found in the fifth hour of *The Book of the Hidden Chamber*. Directly beneath it, the subterranean god Sokar with his falcon head is seen rising, opening a pair of wings, from the body of a serpent within an ellipse of sand. In the text he is called "the Great God who opens his two wings, He of the Dappled Plumage. . . . What he does is to guard his image." The text describes the sandy ellipse as "the mysterious cavern of Sokaris, He Who Is on His Sand." It is also known as the Cavern of the Hidden One. To either side of Sokar are the two heads of Aker, an underworld guardian deity. To the far right, a Nehep serpent leaps up above a star, indicating resurrection. The tip of the pyramid is a human head facing east, which is to the right in this picture. Above this head, the solar barge, known as Life of Power, is being towed across the sand by a rope that passes through the hands of Khepri, the beetle who assists the rising of the sun (see also the discussion of Khepri in the text). The text states: "The towrope which you have brought, the towrope is lifted by Khepri that he may help Re, that he may make straight the mysterious ways of Re, Horus of the Horizon." As the sun god passes the cavern of Sokar, the sun calls out to him: "Guard this thy image, O Sokaris, He who hides the mystery. I call thee, my words to thee are thy illumination, thou rejoicest hearing them." The substitution of a human head for the pyramidion tip of the pyramid is highly suggestive, indicating that the pyramids of Giza may have been conceived of as expectantly awaiting the rising sun to give his flash from their sheets of gold. The head is also a hieroglyph, meaning *tep*, which not surprisingly has the basic meaning of "head," but also means "the top." The visual pun suggests that the top of a pyramid may have been known to the ancient Egyptians as its head. A photo of the same scene in the Tomb of Rameses VI is seen in figure 7.9. (*From Alexandre Piankoff,* The Tomb of Rameses VI, *Pantheon Books, New York, 1954, figure 78 on p. 261*)

I believe that there were also other "passages," laid out on "the sand of Sokar," namely the sand of the Giza Plateau itself, and that these were the invisible "rays" of the geometrical design shown in figure 7.25. However, our discussion of the rays and their significance comes later.

The Book of the Hidden Chamber (for that is how I intend to refer to it from

Figure 7.9. This is plate 86 from volume II: *Plates,* of Alexandre Piankoff and N. Rambova, *The Tomb of Ramesses VI,* Bollingen Series XL.1 (New York: Pantheon Books, 1954), photos by L. F. Husson. This image is from the left wall of Corridor G in the tomb and illustrates the fifth division of the ancient text called *The Book of What Is in the Netherworld.* The introductory text states:

> This Great God [the Sun] is towed along the right ways of the netherworld on the upper half of the mysterious Cavern of Sokaris, He on His Sand, invisible and imperceptible—to make the mysterious arrangements in the land which carries this divine flesh. . . . The name of the Gate of this City is Stop of the Gods. The name of the Cavern of this god is the Hidden One. . . . It is done according to the plan which is drawn in the hidden region of the Netherworld in the South of the Hidden Chamber. He who knows it, his soul will be at peace, he will rest as Sokaris rests. (Translation by Piankoff in his volume I, p. 262)

In the center, a pyramidal mound is portrayed, topped by a head, above which the scarab beetle is rising, symbolizing the rising sun. Beneath the pyramid, in his subterranean elliptical chamber called the Hidden One, the god of the dead, Sokaris, rises, with his wings of resurrection expanding to either side of him. His cavern is guarded on either side by Aker, the double-headed protector deity of the netherworld, with face and paws facing each way. The text says of the mound that it is the "Flesh of Sokaris, He on His Sand" and then adds: "The image is like this in thick darkness. The egg which belongs to this god is lighted up by the eyes in the heads of this Great God [Aker], his flesh shines, the legs are inside in coils. The Great God keeps guard over this image. The noise is heard in the egg, after the Great God has passed by it, like the sound of roaring in the sky during a storm" (p. 267, Piankoff). In the middle register, various gods are towing the rope of the solar barque, dragging it across the sands of Giza, for that is the location of the secret chamber of Sokaris, which was said to be beside the Sphinx at Rostau. (*Photo copyright © 1954 by the Bollingen Foundation*)

now on, as this is its true ancient title) commences its description of Giza with a picture of a descending passage beside which stands the goddess Neith wearing the Crown of the North. (The crown, the goddess, and North all have the same name in Egyptian, *net*. Neith is the Greek form of the name used by scholars, just as they generally call Khafre by the Greek form of his name, Chephren, etc.) It seems reasonable to assume, therefore, that this picture refers symbolically to a northern entrance. Because the three main pyramids at Giza all have descending passages with northern entrances, and since the description is meant to be of Giza, it does not seem to be stretching a point to conclude that at least the commencement of the strange illustrations of "the passages of Rostau" in *The Book of the Hidden Chamber* begin with that simplest of things, the entrance to a major pyramid. Presumably the Great Pyramid was intended. It is most unlikely to be a coincidence that the entrance to Rostau is shown in the papyri and the wall paintings to be "northern," when it was the north faces of all the main pyramids at Giza that "led into Rostau."

Figure 8.6 on page 389 is a photo I took of this entrance scene as it was painted on the walls of the Tomb of Rameses III in the Valley of the Kings. I don't believe the Rameses III version has ever been reproduced before, and it does not appear in any of the relevant books. Nor does Erik Hornung in his survey of Egyptian netherworld literature mention more than in passing the existence of a Rameses III version of *The Book of the Hidden Chamber*.[5] This Rameses III version is a particularly vivid painting, as you can see.

Once we get past the entrance, however, things start to go awry with the tomb paintings and the papyri, and we quickly realize that however many interesting and even authentic details may be shown or hinted at in these pictures of the passages of Rostau, we do not by any means have a map or a straightforward plot of the existing structures and passages. Some curious features can be interpreted as accurate, still others are merely suggestive. But there is no attempt whatsoever to present a physically reliable depiction. It is doubtful if, by the time of the New Kingdom, anyone had the faintest idea of what really lay beneath the Giza Plateau or within the major pyramids. And it is not improbable that the ancient text, when it was reprocessed for inclusion in the New Kingdom text, had many of its truly ancient details removed by the unsuspecting adapters, and that tinkerings and adjustments were made to fit the passages of sandy Rostau into the underworld journey of the sun god, which otherwise took place over water.

A Netherworld Text that is Middle Kingdom in date, *The Book of the Two Ways,* also preserves some interesting information about Rostau, which it mentions frequently. This text is preserved only as paintings inside a few Eleventh and Twelfth Dynasty wooden coffins excavated at a single site, El-Bersheh in Middle Egypt. If these graves had not been found and the coffins excavated, we would not have the text at all. A complete translation was done by Alexandre Piankoff and published in 1974.[6] Piankoff prefers the spelling Rosetau, which is therefore how the name appears in the quotations that I take from his translation.

The pictures painted in the coffins depicting Rostau are very crude compared to those illustrating *The Book of the Hidden Chamber.* But both agree in having the journey into the netherworld commence with a simple descending passage. In the case of *The Book of the Two Ways,* however, there is no goddess with the Crown of the North or any other indication of a cardinal point. The figure awaiting the unwary person entering the passage is a strange human-headed beast with no legs and a single arm holding a very large and threatening knife. The hieroglyphics state that the name of this creature is Voice-of-Misery, and he is the guardian of the entrance, which is known as the Gate of Darkness. As for the entrance passageway itself, we are told of it: "This way [leads] to the cities of Those-Who-Live-on-the Baboons (?) [the baboon was the symbol of the god Thoth, but baboons were also guardians of the netherworld's Lake of Fire and are frequently depicted sitting around it in illustrations accompanying *Book of the Dead* texts] . . . the cities of the Roaring Knives. This is its way from below. Do not go by it."[7]

In front of the entrance to Rostau is the text that says:

I have passed by the roads of Rosetau by water and on land; these roads are those of Osiris; they are in the sky. If a man knows the Spell for going down into them, he will be like a god directed by the followers of Thoth. He will indeed go down to every heaven to which he desires to descend. But if he knows not this Spell for passing on these roads, he will fall a prey to the tribunal of the dead, his destiny being that of one who has nothing, and is without (his) justification eternally.[8]

Although the surface of Giza is now as dry as a bone, in the times of the Egyptian Old Kingdom and possibly the Middle Kingdom as well (until perhaps as late as 2200 or even 2000 BC), a harbor lapped against the eastern walls of the Sphinx Temple and the Valley Temple, as I have already explained at length. It is doubtful that this harbor contained water all year long, but it certainly did during the period of the inundation of the Nile. And as I have already explained in detail, I believe that the Sphinx during these times sat in a deep moat of water that was fed from the adjoining harbor. After the water of the inundation receded, the water was trapped in the Sphinx Moat by the sluices, although as the months wore on, it would have become increasingly stagnant and lower in level from evaporation in the heat, hence the need for the previously mentioned drain to bring water from any rain that might occur down into the moat. During the New Kingdom, the pharaohs

Figure 7.10. This is a photo I took at the bottom of the Osiris Shaft at Giza, approximately 150 feet below the surface, in the third level. The shaft is entered beneath the Chephren Causeway. The central portion of the third level is an "Osiris Island" containing a sarcophagus. It is surrounded by this canal cut out of the bedrock and filled with water. This particular section of the canal is west of the central island. The southern wall of the chamber is at the rear of the photo. The water is covered with an opaque scum but is clear underneath if that is brushed aside. The Osiris Island at the bottom of this shaft portrays the same mythological setting as does the Osireion at Abydos in Upper Egypt. Speculations that this island and canal are of Saite date are false, and the true date is much earlier. (*Photo by Robert Temple*)

of that period landscaped and adapted the area for their small and unimpressive temples. There is still to this day a great deal of water underneath the Giza Plateau, as I have seen with my own eyes and photographed in the so-called Tomb of Osiris in the deep shaft beneath the Chephren Causeway, a site that I have studied in great detail, and my report concerning which can be found in *Egyptian Dawn*. In that book, my photo shows the miniature Osiris Island surrounded by a channel of water, with a sarcophagus in the middle (symbolic of a "tomb of Osiris"), more than 150 feet below the surface, which is reached by a succession of three shafts. Figure 7.10 shows the canal and water in the bottom level of the Osiris shaft.

There is even water inside the Great Pyramid, for the "grotto" of the "well shaft" in that structure seems to be continually wet, even though there is strangely no water to be found at much lower levels, and not a drop is to be found within the Subterranean Chamber, the lowest point of all. We should keep all these things in mind when we read the ancient texts such as the above about the "roads by water and on land" at Rostau/Giza. Despite the desert and sandy conditions of Giza, water was always near at hand.

There is a curious part of the coffin pictures (see figure 7.11) showing four successive levels of what appear to be angled stone slabs blocking the way. The accompanying hieroglyphic text appropriately says of them: "Flame. Spell concerning the roads of Rosetau. These ways lead astray in this manner: each one

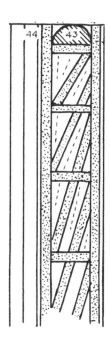

Figure 7.11. This is a detail of a drawing of the illustrated text of *The Book of Two Ways*, preserved on the lid of a coffin of Middle Kingdom date numbered CGC 28083 in the Egyptian Museum at Cairo. The large foldout drawing from which this small detail is taken is at the back of the volume *The Wandering of the Soul: Egyptian Religious Texts and Representations*, vol. 6, by Alexandre Piankoff and Helen Jacquet-Gordon, Bollingen Series XL:6 (Princeton, N.J.: Princeton University Press, 1974). The numbers 43 and 44 appearing at the top of the drawing were added by the modern artist to refer to the Coffin Texts relating to those places (Spells 1072 and 1073, respectively). These texts refer to the "high walls of flint in Rosetau" and "the Kneeling Ones with mysterious faces," which I believe refer to movable slabs that block passages. I believe these slabs may be pictorially represented here, on four successive tunnel levels.

among them meets the next and leads astray. He who knows it will find their roads. They have high walls of flint in Rosetau upon water and upon land."

"Flint" must be a mineralogical mistranslation, though the original Egyptian word is not given and it is not possible for me to give an alternative stone on the basis of what is published; however, Egyptologists are always getting their stones and minerals wrong, as I have many times discovered, working as I have done with stones and minerals in Egypt as part of our official researches there. There are three Egyptian words thought to mean flint, *ār, beshu,* and *desh,* but which is the word used in the text I do not know. Probably it was the mysterious word *desh,* which was specifically said to be black, was connected with magic, and was a "stuff of a decan," meaning a material associated with a division of the sky and the stars of that division. I find it difficult to believe that the real meaning of *desh* is "flint." But then, who am I, a mere mortal, to challenge the all-wise in such matters? Turning to the expert J. R. Harris for enlightenment, I find that all the experts are in confusion where references to "flint" are concerned, and especially regarding the confusing uses of the Egyptian word *desh.* According to Harris, "The textual evidence for *desh* is not very significant, and there are no definite indications of the meaning of the word."[9] The famous Egyptologist Heinrich Brugsch at first throught *desh* meant "flint" and then changed his mind and thought it probably referred instead to limestone or alabaster.[10] That is certainly more appropriate for the "high walls" in Rosetau, although it would mean that they were white rather than black. At the very least, we may be confident that the translation of "flint" for the walls in Rosetau is incorrect, and that some form of stone is referred to.

And immediately adjoining these angled slabs, as may also be seen in figure 7.11, there is an adjoining vertical shaft of which we are told: "The Weary Ones, Kneeling Ones with mysterious faces, who live with the help of their throwing sticks. I am the stout of heart, he whose might is weighty, he who makes his way through the fire. . . . A way is made for me so that I may pass and save Osiris. I am he who sees the unique, who circles about, . . . he for whom a way is made, to whom it is granted to pass. In peace, in peace."[11]

Because there are no figures of men, gods, or animals to be seen in this last section, the "Kneeling Ones with mysterious faces" appear not to be creatures at all, but stones of passages. I believe that these two sections of the picture and their texts refer to concealed entrances to passages such as the famous one inside the Great Pyramid at the junction between the Ascending and Descending Passages. In classical antiquity, the Descending Passage was known, but the roof of this passage contained a slab of limestone that concealed underneath a granite plug, the limestone being mounted on swivel bearings (see figure 7.15), which was flush to the roof but which, if moved or levered in the correct manner, could have been opened to reveal the Ascending Passage. This limestone slab fell off in the ninth century and has now been removed. I discuss this matter and quote a passage from the ancient Greek geographer Strabo about such stones later in this chapter. Even if this swivel stone was known, which is doubtful, the Ascending Passage could not be entered because it was blocked with the three granite plug stones (see figures 7.12 and 7.13). The swivel stone was an angled stone, like the ones in the coffin paintings, and I believe that the expression the "Kneeling Ones" is a general term that refers to such angled stones inside the pyramids. They are in the position of someone kneeling, and also, just like someone kneeling who rises to an erect position, they can be moved to become straight. They do indeed have "mysterious faces," because they are concealed and appear to be normal passage-lining stones. As for "liv[ing] with the help of their throwing sticks," this may be an esoteric allusion to their moving back and forth and returning to their place, just as the ancient Egyptian boomerangs did when used for hunting geese in flight. (Boomerangs are depicted in Old Kingdom tomb paintings, which show them being used in bird-hunting scenes.) "He whose might is weighty" could refer to the huge weight of these concealed and "kneeling" stone slabs that blocked the secret passage entrances. "Circles about" should probably be slightly retranslated to mean "turns about," referring to the movement of the swivel stone on its hinge. And "sees the Unique" may refer to seeing the hidden signs in the passageways that indicate the locations of the blocked passages, just as the intuitive genius Sir William Flinders Petrie discovered the markings in the Descending Passage that

Figure 7.12. This photo shows very clearly the granite plug (top of photo) blocking the entrance to the Ascending Passage of the Great Pyramid from the Descending Passage. The plug is still there because entry to the Ascending Passage is from the forced passage made by al-Mamoun, which was tunneled through the limestone and went around it. This is plate LXVII on page 171 of John and Morton Edgar's *The Great Pyramid Passages and Chambers,* volume I, Glasgow, 1910.

Figure 7.13. A photo of John Edgar, the pyramidologist, suspending a plumb bob at the point in the Descending Passage inside the Great Pyramid at Giza where the lowest of three successive granite plug stones may be seen in the roof, blocking access to the Ascending Passage. The limestone swivel stone that once concealed this granite plug stone from view had already been removed by this time (circa 1909). Edgar's own caption gives further details. This is plate LXVIII on page 172 of John Edgar and Morton Edgar, *The Great Pyramid Passages and Chambers,* volume I, Glasgow, 1910 (the original edition with the best-quality plates). John Edgar died as this book was in press in 1910. His measurements, studies, and above all his unrivaled interior photos (all of which would be impossible today) are extremely valuable. He spared no trouble and expense in obtaining the very finest photography possible at that time for interior views of every passage and chamber of the Great Pyramid.

indicated the existence of the swivel stone of the Great Pyramid. And I have seen such signs myself, which I believe indicate a similar concealed passage that could be reached from the passage that leads to the Queen's Chamber. I discovered these one night when I had the interior of the Great Pyramid all to myself and was able to spend several hours minutely examining it inside without anyone disturbing me. During official opening hours, the crush of tourists is intolerable, and you cannot study anything properly at all.

In this esoteric manner that I have just suggested, genuine physical details of pyramid construction seem to be hinted at. But they appear to be general and not confined to a single edifice such as the Great Pyramid alone, assuming that such blocked passages exist in most or all of the main pyramids. Since an empty concealed passage was discovered in the Pyramid of Meidum as recently as 1999, announced in 2000, and published in 2003,[12] and an analogous concealed passage above the passage leading to the Queen's Chamber in the Great Pyramid almost certainly exists, as many Egyptologists have now concluded, it seems likely that such passages are common, whether they are merely "relieving passages" connected with structural concerns or are genuinely intended to lead somewhere of interest or to contain something of importance.

Another statement in *The Book of Two Ways* that seems reasonably accurate in reference to these phenomena is the statement quoted above about how the roads of Rostau lead astray: "Each one among them meets the next and leads astray." This is an accurate description of what happens inside the Great Pyramid, since the Descending Passage meets the once concealed and blocked entrance to the Ascending Passage but continues to descend and thus "leads astray."

Yet another feature is of interest in the coffin painting from which the detail of figure 7.11 is taken. To the right of the stone slabs we see three horizontal passages directly over one another and separated from each other by stone courses. The text says: "Spell to pass over him [and] those who are below him."[13]

Now that the two horizontal passages with one directly over the other have been discovered inside the Pyramid of Meidum, and bearing in mind the suggested second passage lying directly over the passage leading to the Queen's Chamber inside the Great Pyramid, with of course the Grand Gallery in turn lying over that, we can appreciate that this picture may be an allusion to the structures inside at least two major pyramids. Indeed, it seems that three passages lying above one another do actually exist inside the Great Pyramid, as just described, and if one counts the Descending Passage, three are already known anyway.

Further on in the picture, two horizontal passages are shown lying one above the other. The text above them says: "The roads of Rosetau upon land." And beneath them the text says:

Figure 7.14. The strange Pyramid of Meidum, four hours' drive south of Cairo, which may or may not have partially collapsed in antiquity (not everyone is in agreement as to what really happened to this structure, which is still surrounded by huge mounds of stone and rubble, as seen here). Did someone try to build a pyramid at too steep an angle, causing a disastrous failure in the structure? Inside it a concealed passage was discovered as recently as 1999. It could not be entered but was explored by means of fiber-optic probes. It is parallel to a known passage, and it is believed that a similar concealed parallel passage exists inside the Great Pyramid, running above the familiar passage that leads to the so-called Queen's Chamber. Such passages may be merely what engineers call "relieving passages" for construction purposes, or they may have a different purpose. Alas, too many of the interior features of the pyramids are baffling, and there may well be numerous undiscovered spaces inside them that we have not yet found or may even never find. (*Photo by Robert Temple*)

I have come to establish the things at Abydos, I have opened Rosetau, I have alleviated the suffering of Osiris. I am he . . . who makes his way in the valley. Oh Great One, make a path of light for me, that I may pass. . . . As to these Kneeling Ones, Geb [the primeval god of the Earth] has placed them in Rosetau near his son Osiris out of fear of his brother Seth, lest he might hurt him (?). If any man knows the names of these Kneeling Ones, he will be with Osiris forever, he will never perish.[14]

My suggestion that "the Kneeling Ones" are really angled swivel stones concealing entrances (such as the one known originally to have concealed the entrance to the Great Pyramid itself, seen in figure 7.15) draws support from a further portion of the text, which says: "If any man is seen there alive [in the innermost sanctum of Rostau], he will not perish eternally since he knows the Spell for passing the Kneeling Ones, the keepers of the gates."[15]

This makes it very clear that "the Kneeling Ones" are obstacles sealing the "gates" of the Rostau passages.

Not a great deal is known of the mechanical techniques by which the huge slabs were actually moved on their hinges in the ancient monuments, since although we can see the hinges and we know that such stones existed—and indeed the one at the entrance to the Great Pyramid is even described in the Greek text of Strabo (quoted in a moment) as still being in use and swinging open in Roman times—none survives intact. The one drawn by Flinders Petrie at the Bent Pyramid of Dashur no longer exists either (see figure 7.15, left side of picture). That pyramid at Dashur is extremely unsafe to approach and explore, due to the fact that it has so many of its original casing stones, and they sometimes fall off! For decades it was inaccessible because it was in a closed military zone, and obviously it was not studied during that time. The last time it was studied properly was by the brilliant Egyptian archaeologist Ahmed Fakhry in the days before Nasser came to power and created more military zones. I am very fortunate indeed to have a copy of his extremely rare work in three volumes, *The Monuments of Sneferu at Dashur,* the first volume of which deals entirely with the Bent Pyramid (volume I, Cairo, 1959). There is no mention or depiction of the swivel door in Fakhry's book, and I presume that Flinders Petrie's drawing was entirely a reconstruction.

There must be some swivel doors that are still in place and serving their purpose, but we have simply not discovered them because they are serving their purpose too well and remain successfully disguised! But whether one pushes on a certain spot in a certain manner or perhaps uses some lever or implement (perhaps referred to in the reference to "throwing sticks"?) to make a block of many tons' weight suddenly move on its hinges and open, we do not know. For most of her life at Abydos, Omm Sety, Selim Hassan's assistant, was always going around the Temple of Seti I and pushing here and there on suspicious-looking slabs, hoping to open them and gain entry to the many passages and chambers and crypts that she was certain were concealed both in and under the Temple of Seti I and in the Osireion and the tunnel she believed linked the two, but she never succeeded in finding the right way to shift any of these slabs. Who knows? Perhaps they don't work after all these millennia. Maybe they have become stiff and have "slab arthritis."

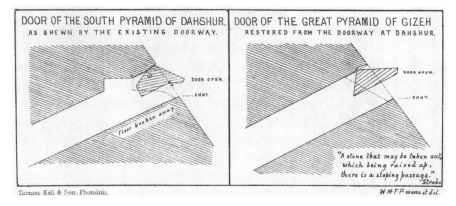

Figure 7.15. These two diagrams were published by Sir William Flinders Petrie as part of plate 11 of the first (and fuller) edition of his book *The Pyramids and Temples of Gizeh,* London, 1883. The diagram on the left shows the swiveling-stone trick door that once led to the passage inside the Bent Pyramid at Dashur, but no longer exists in that pyramid, which retains many of its original casing stones. The diagram on the right shows Petrie's reconstruction of the similar trick swivel door that would originally have led into the Descending Passage of the Great Pyramid, and which was still in use in the first century AD, as recorded by the geographer Strabo. I believe that these secret swivel doors of stone that traditionally concealed the entrances to passages were the "Kneeling Ones" referred to in the Egyptian netherworld texts.

The one famous exception to this, of course, is the swivel slab that she seems to have opened by accident one day when she was stumbling around the temple and in a high fever because she was afflicted with Asian flu, feeling very dizzy and ill, and unexpectedly fell into a treasure room. She recounts this incident in her book.[16] During 1999, an intensive search for this chamber was carried on at the temple in Abydos by an American researcher. Although he did not find the chamber, in 1998 the remnants of a passage inside a wall near the Hall of Barques was found by the Egyptian archaeologist Ahmed El-Sawy, although it contained nothing of interest and does not appear to have been a passage of any major importance; this discovery was announced at the Eighth International Congress of Egyptologists, which I attended in Cairo in the spring of 2000, and was published in 2003.[17] El-Sawy's careful and conscientious work at Abydos was of the greatest possible interest to those who are interested in the Temple of Seti I at Abydos, a structure in which I have already written a detailed report of more than 60,000 words about our work there, which has not yet been published, and which will reveal many unexpected things when it appears. This does not appear in *Egyptian Dawn* because that book does not discuss the New Kingdom period.

If we can begin to decode the esoteric references in some of the ancient texts, we are in a better position to retrieve possibly important information about the monuments. By recognizing that the "Kneeling Ones" are probably swivel slabs blocking passageways, we are already getting somewhere.

The only contemporary description of a "Kneeling One" actually in use is found in the *Geography* of Strabo, a Greek writer who lived during the Roman Empire, first century BC–first century AD. Strabo visited Egypt, and in Book 17 of his lengthy work, he describes visiting the pyramids of Giza. He writes, "At the distance of 40 stadia from Memphis is a brow of a hill, on which are many pyramids, the tombs of the kings. Three of them are considerable. Two of these are reckoned among the seven wonders [of the world]. . . . One pyramid is a little larger than the other. At a moderate height in one of the sides is a stone, which may be taken out; when that is removed, there is an oblique passage [leading] to the tomb."[18]

This proves that in Roman times the Descending Passage and the Subterranean Chamber (thought by the Romans to have been "the tomb," though no one today believes that) were known and regularly entered by tourists, and also clearly indicates that the Ascending Passage, Grand Gallery, and chambers higher up inside the Great Pyramid were entirely unknown at that time, since there is no mention of them at all. The swivel stone that could be "taken out" so that one could enter the Great Pyramid from the northern face is seen in reconstruction in figure 7.15. Figure 7.16 is a nineteenth-century photo of this original entrance where the swivel stone once was; figure 7.17 shows its appearance in 1610. Strabo does not say how one got up the slippery side to this point, but there must have been a stairway or steps made for the visitors. At this time, of course, the casing stones still covered the pyramids, and Strabo even describes those covering the small Pyramid of Mycerinus (Menkaure) as being made of dark granite, but only "nearly as far as the middle," the upper half of that pyramid apparently having been covered with the normal limestone.[19] It is interesting to know that the movable entrance stone of the Great Pyramid still functioned on a regular, presumably daily basis in the first century AD.

There are various scattered references in Greek literature to doors strangely swinging open in temples. In the *Ecclesiastical History* of Sozomen (fifth century AD), we find mention of a curious case of prison doors that "though fastened, opened of their own accord."[20] The inventor Hero of Alexandria (who lived in the first and second centuries AD) in his book *Pneumatics* actually describes a mechanical device that can cause the doors of temples to swing open automatically and is triggered when somebody sacrifices upon an altar.[21] So mysteriously opening doors have been a feature of important sacred structures throughout antiquity.

There is one other possible esoteric reference that could be implied by the expression the "Kneeling Ones." The sides of an acute angle look like kneeling legs. Perhaps the golden angle is being hinted at. To "know the Kneeling Ones"

Figure 7.16. The original entrance to the Great Pyramid, which is on the north face. The casing stones originally covered this, and in Roman times the entry was by a casing stone that was a secret, movable swivel stone, which opened and let people in at this point. Roman tourists loved to enter the Descending Passage by this route and descend all the way to the Subterranean Chamber. The Ascending Passage was unknown to them, and hence also the Grand Gallery and the King's and Queen's Chambers. This old photo was reproduced only in a rare book entitled *Souvenir of Egypt,* published by George Dovas in Cairo (no date). It was given in 1898 to my grandmother by her friend Ebtenago Sehyoun, a Copt, of Kena in Egypt. She was friendly with him and some others of the Copts and had a particular interest in their culture and traditions. Directly above the head of the man sitting in the center of the photo is a strange shape carved in the stone, which Walter Marsham Adams in 1898 clamed was the hieroglyph for "horizon," showing two hills to either side with a dip in the middle, where the rising sun was meant to appear. (*Collection of Robert Temple*)

at Giza could also mean working out a knowledge of the Golden Giza Plan, as shown in figure 7.25. And the phrase in the text above about making "a passage of light" might refer to one of the aerial "rays" at a golden angle, which I discuss later, particularly the one that strikes the tip of the Pyramid of Chephren from the Sphinx at sunrise on the equinox.

The entrance in to the Great Pyramis

Figure 7.17. This engraving appeared in a book by George Sandys, *A Relation of a Journey Begun An. Dom. 1610*, London, 1615. It shows the original entrance to the Great Pyramid as it appeared at that time. (*Collection of Robert Temple*)

We must return now to *The Book of Two Ways*. Where things begin to get really interesting is in the descriptions of what is called "the Mystery of Rostau." There are various references to what appears to be the Great Hall or Chamber underground. Here are the suggestive passages:

Sealed is that thing which is in darkness. A flame is around it; it contains this efflux of Osiris, placed in Rosetau (?). He is hidden since he fell down into it. The descent to him goes over the country of sand. Indeed, what is under him is consecrated in Rosetau. . . . If any man is seen there alive, he will not perish eternally since he knows the Spell for passing the Kneeling Ones, the keepers of the gates. . . . Spell to be in Rosetau. I am the great Name, he who creates his light. I have come to thee, Osiris, I worship thee. He (the deceased) causes thy efflux to permit him to arise. . . . Spell to be in Rosetau, to live on the extra offerings beside Osiris. To proceed in peace; to protect Osiris; to pass by the gates. I am the great Name who creates his light. I have come to thee Osiris. I worship thee. Give me now away, I am purified by thy efflux. I have acted [so that I am the one] who has been exalted by the efflux which flowed out of thee. I have made the name of Rosetau since I fell into it. Salutation to thee, Osiris. Arise! Thou art powerful, thou art strong in life, health and prosperity, thou art powerful in Rosetau, thou art the strong one in Abydos. . . . O this charcoal wall![22] I open my way in Rosetau that I may ease the suffering of Osiris. . . . [I am] he who is allowed to pass by. . . . These are the words of what is inside the [region] of darkness. If any spirit knows this, he will live among the living. A fire is around it which contains this efflux of Osiris. If any man knows this, he will not perish there forever, for he knows that which is in Rosetau, [namely] the Mystery of Rosetau, since he fell there. He who comes down to [this] desert which contains this chest [illustrated in figure 57] is he who carries it in Busiris. [The reference is to the small settlement of Busiris at the foot of the Sphinx of Giza itself, called by the Egyptians Djedu, now known as Nazlet el-Samman, the Greek name of which is recorded by Pliny, who says: "Close by (Memphis) is a village called Busiris, where there are people who are used to climbing these pyramids."[23]] It is the decomposition of Osiris of Rosetau. . . . Grant that I may be brought to thee, O Thoth. I open the Netherworld. . . . The way of Thoth to the House of Truth. . . . I am Thoth, the Lord of Offerings for Osiris, . . . this is for my father Osiris who is on the High Ground. . . . I am the Great Soul of Osiris with whom the gods have ordained him to copulate, who lives on high by day, made by Osiris from the efflux of his flesh, [made] by the seed which came from his phallus, in order to come forth by day that he may copulate with it. . . . For I am the Great Soul of Osiris with whom the gods ordained him to copulate. He lives through it (the soul) on high by day, [the soul] made by Osiris from his efflux which is in his flesh, [made] with his semen which comes out of his phallus, in order to come forth by day that he may copulate with it.[24]

Figure 7.18. This is plate 80 from volume II: *Plates*, of Alexandre Piankoff and N. Rambova, *The Tomb of Ramesses VI*, Bollingen Series XL.1 (New York: Pantheon Books, 1954), photos by L. F. Husson. This image is from the left wall of Corridor G in the tomb and illustrates the fourth division of the ancient text called *The Book of What Is in the Netherworld*. The sun god, with a ram's head, is being towed in his solar barque. The text says: "The towing of this Great God is stopped for a while in this mysterious Cavern of the West whose forms are holy. Taking care of those who are in it with his voice without being seen by them. The name of the Cavern is Life of Forms. . . . The mysterious ways of Ro-setau [Rostau], the sacred roads of the Imhat Necropolis, the hidden gates which are in the earth of Sokaris, He on His Sand. . . . They are like this, the guardians of the Holy Way to the entrance of the West of the netherworld. It is they who keep guard on Anubis . . . Ro-Setau. The mysterious roads of Ro-Setau, the divine portals. He [the sun] does not pass by them, it is only his voice that they hear. The road to enter the body of Sokaris, He on His Sand, a mysterious image invisible and imperceptible. Mysterious road which Anubis enters (leading) to him who hides the body of Osiris" (translation of Piankoff, vol. I, pp. 254–60). (*Photo copyright © 1954 by the Bollingen Foundation*)

To judge from these strange remarks, the ultimate secret of Giza sounds like a chamber full of the semen of Osiris! (The world's oldest sperm bank?) Or perhaps the semen is contained in a chest in that chamber. One wonders whether this might perhaps even be a reference to the coffer of the King's Chamber in the Great Pyramid. It is possible that the reference in the text quoted above to "the High Ground" is to the Giza Plateau, which is indeed high ground above Memphis. But it is not only the semen of Osiris that appears to be hidden at Giza; it is also the "efflux" or "decomposition" of Osiris that is meant to be concealed there. And there are other references in the ancient texts to this efflux of

Figure 7.19. "O thou charcoal wall!" This quotation from the ancient Egyptian netherworld text *The Book of Two Ways*, which describes the obstacles and secrets concealed at Rosetau, may refer to the unexpected inclusion of a charcoal-colored basalt block in the midst of red granite blocks, such as this one at the Valley Temple of Giza, which is the traditional site of Rosetau. Not only does such a basalt block resemble a charcoal wall, but it was probably intended as a sign or signal to the initiated regarding the location of something. Since the text refers to a charcoal wall in connection with discussion of the "Kneeling Ones," which I have already explained as swivel stones that block concealed passages (see figure 7.15), a stone such as this might have acted either as a swivel stone or as an indicator of a swivel stone, or of some other concealed secret, behind or beneath. To find things that the Old Kingdom Egyptians concealed, you have to think like an Old Kingdom Egyptian; it is useless to insist on thinking like a modern person. This is why only a few modern archaeologists, such as Sir William Flinders Petrie, have ever been able to find what the ancient Egyptians had hidden. The subterranean temple, the Osireion, at Abydos, was discovered only because Petrie noticed a slight dip in the sand and his intuition told him to dig there. An Egyptologist who does not have a highly developed intuitive sense, or does not listen to it, will never be a discoverer. (*Photo by Robert Temple*)

decomposition of Osiris and its concealment. What could this mean? We should keep in mind that there is an analogy to this concept in Christianity. "The body and blood of Christ" are continually spoken of in a sacramental and evocative context, and often the blood becomes "the water and the blood," or the mixture of two fluids. In the Anglican/Episcopal Church, one of the hymns frequently sung by the congregation contains a line about "the water and the blood which from thee forever flow." I used to ask what this meant when I was a boy, and I met with puzzled reactions. One suggestion was that because the priests mix water with the wine for communion purposes, *those* were "the water and the blood," as it is well known that the wine represents the blood of Christ, and devout people believe that through a magical and divine process that takes place during the mass, the wine is literally transformed into the blood of Christ, and that people who drink it really do drink Christ's blood itself, not just a substitute. This is what is called "taking communion." To suggest that priests add water to the wine because they don't want to become drunk at mass is not a satisfactory explanation for the words of the hymn and the theological concept behind them. There is no doubt whatsoever that there was some vague concept of "the water and the blood" both streaming as an efflux from Christ on the cross, as a result of the spear wounding him in his side, the "water" presumably being the bodily fluid known as lymph. I mention these strange, obscure, and somewhat necrophilic Christian theological details only because they offer such a tantalizing analogy to the "efflux" of Osiris, who also died and rose again "in sure and certain hope of resurrection," as the Christians say.

The Egyptian word that is generally translated as "efflux" is *redju*. Technically, it is the fluid of decomposition oozing from the corpse. (In the extreme heat of Egypt, this would have occurred rapidly.) It was similar to but distinct from what the Egyptians called *fedet,* which is the sweat of the corpse, since *redju* comes from the interior of the corpse, whereas *fedet* is produced on the exterior. However, *redju* had more profound associations. The word is thought to come from the Egyptian verb *redi,* "to give," so that *redju* literally means "that which is given." It was occasionally said to be responsible for the rise of the Nile and the inundation. It seems to have been conceived of as a kind of fluid emanating from the Earth at the source of the Nile, which created the life-giving Nile.[25] The Nile may thus have been imagined as an internal secretion or seminal emission of the Earth. However, since efflux from the earlier god Sokar, god of the resurrectable Earth, was also viewed as the source of the Nile, that was probably the original tradition prior to the Fifth Dynasty, before Osiris became amalgamated with Sokar as Sokar-Osiris.[26] Plutarch specifically writes of the Egyptians: "They call not only the Nile but all moisture generally the efflux of Osiris." The Greek word used by Plutarch for "efflux" is *aporroē,* which means "a flowing off, stream, efflux, emanation."[27]

In one Coffin Text, we are told that *redju* was the substance out of which the *ba*-spirit or *ba*-power was formed: "For I am this great *ba* of Osiris . . . which Osiris had made from the fluid of his corpse, coming from his body."[28] (This reminds us of the Victorian medium's concept of "ectoplasm.") However, in a resurrected body, there is a fine line between the efflux of decay and the efflux of seed ejaculated from the reinvigorated phallus. Both are interior secretions. There are many sacred depictions of Isis fluttering as a *ba* over the corpse of her husband, Osiris, and settling down on his erect phallus to become impregnated with her son Horus. There was a special verb in Egyptian, *sab,* which meant "to flow out" or "to flow away," that was used to describe the "flowing away," "streaming," or "flowing out" of the *redju*. Clearly, we have here a concept not too remote from that of "emission," as of sperm. There are at least two Coffin Text spells that associate the "flowing away of the *redju*" with Anubis and claim that the emitted *redju* was actually called by the name of "jackal."[29] The name "leopard" (*sab*) was sometimes applied as a pun on the verb *sab*. This may have been connected with the high priest of Sokar wearing a leopard skin during the Festival of Sokar. What is clear in all of this is that there are many levels of meaning, and that everything related to the decomposition of the body after death was, in a society obsessed with mummification, also associated somehow with its opposite. The Egyptians were always saying that the decomposition products were "hidden," and especially hidden at Rostau. What, therefore, could we really expect to find in a chamber beneath Giza one day? An interesting survey of the concepts of *redju* was published in 2006 by Andreas Winkler in an article entitled "The Efflux That Issued from Osiris."[30] Winkler mentions that *redju* has a restorative function, signified in ritual as a libation, connected with the reassembling of the scattered limbs of Osiris and "that *redju* is positive for the deceased when the theme of reconstitution dominates . . ." (I have according to my practice in this book rendered *redju* wholly in English letters here, not in the linguistic symbols used by Winkler, which I have eschewed throughout this book because they are incomprehensible to the general reader.) Because I have elsewhere, in a still unpublished work, finally solved the mystery of what was really meant by "the limbs of Osiris," that interpretation opens a new perspective on the concept of what was ultimately meant by *redju,* but a full explanation must await some future occasion, as it is a lengthy discussion that relies on some complex physical evidence concerning an Egyptian site that affords the "key" to the mystery and its associated secret ritual.

If we ever find and open such a chamber, we should be prepared possibly to find not a grand Hall of Records as many well-wishers imagine, but perhaps a repository of some strange ceremonial fluid, even possibly one containing dangerous substances. The "efflux of Osiris" might be something unpleasant and harmful. There is other evidence suggestive of this, but a discussion of this subject leads us too far astray from our main subject. On the other hand, the "efflux of Osiris" might be "hidden" in its corresponding opposite form, gold. As Zandee says, in quoting one of the Pyramid Texts: "The body of the dead is of gold like that of a god and so it consists of imperishable material. 'Rise on your bones of bronze and on your limbs of gold, for this body of yours belongs to a god. It does not perish. It does not decompose, it does not consume.'"[31] By not consuming, they mean not eating. If you don't eat, you cannot decay. So perhaps there is a secret chamber beneath Giza that contains the "efflux of Osiris" changed into a gigantic mass

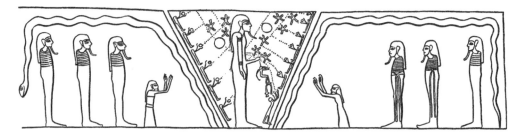

Figure 7.20. In the Tomb of Rameses VI, the central figure has no name. In the Tomb of Rameses IX, another representation of him gives him the name "the One who hides the hours." In fact, this central figure represents the creator god (in this case, Osiris, though originally the creator god was called either Atum or Ptah, depending on whether you were at Heliopolis or Memphis) creating the universe with his sperm by an act of masturbation. In this representation from the tomb of the earlier pharaoh, the scene is not as clear as it is in the Tomb of Ramesses IX, which was beautifully engraved in *Description de l'Égypte*, Paris, 1809, an engraving I have in my collection and have published with my article "The Prehistory of Panspermia: Astrophysical or Metaphysical?" in *International Journal of Astrobiology*, 6 (2), pp. 169–180 (2007). (This article discusses ancient theories resembling those of "panspermia," the process by which life spreads throughout the universe by means of tiny seeds, ideas that were held by several ancient cultures such as the Egyptians, the earliest Hindus of India, and the Greek philosopher Anaxagoras.) The picture shows the youthful god Horus being created by a dribble of sperm from the erect phallus of Osiris (here Horus is seen as a dangling infant just below the tip of the phallus). The trails of sperm are seen throughout the sky, passing between various stars of the cosmos and a number of recumbent receiving parties, who are taking divine disks of light into their hands from the trails of sperm. The creator god stands triumphant atop the defeated body of the serpent Apophis, evil retarder of progress, of life, and of resurrection. The reference to the creator god as "the One who hides the hours" refers to the fact that he created the hours, and time itself, when he created the universe, but the secrets of time and the hours are so esoteric that he hides them from the profane, so that they are known only to the highest level of priests. This image represents an amalgamation of an extremely ancient concept of the creation of the entire cosmos with the conception of the rising of the giant Osiris at the horizon, and indeed, it is likely that these were ideas that were always thought of as one during the New Kingdom period. This is figure 95 on page 339 of volume I, Alexandre Piankoff and N. Rambova, *The Tomb of Ramesses VI*, Bollingen Series 40:1 (New York: Pantheon Books, 1954), 2 vols.

of gold. Perhaps this is the true origin of alchemy, where the "essence of gold" can bring eternal life. Alchemy, especially the alchemy of the ancient world (both Western and Chinese), is a subject that I have studied in a certain amount of depth. I referred to this in passing in my book *The Genius of China* (for instance, in pointing out that gunpowder was discovered by Chinese alchemists), and I have written a large portion of a still unfinished novel on the subject of alchemy, which elucidates many unusual aspects of the subject. Clearly, I cannot discuss such things here, as it would be too great a distraction from our main concerns. However, I am not alone in being convinced that many alchemical processes and traditions originated in Egypt. As recently as 2004, an article appeared in the periodical *Discussions in Egyptology* by Daniel Burnham entitled "Explorations into the Alchemical Idiom of the Pyramid Texts,"[32] referring to the earlier work by Jack Lindsay (*The Origins of Alchemy in Greco-Roman Egypt,* 1970), and attempting to explain these matters more fully. Unfortunately, we cannot pursue this discussion, and once again I am forced to touch on the fascinating subject of alchemy only in passing. One must always keep in mind, however, that the "death" of Osiris and his "resurrection," the "essence of gold," golden statues, and all such symbolical matters may conceal allusions to alchemical concepts and practices. It is highly likely that the Philosopher's Stone is originally an Egyptian concept, and that "turning things into stone" for funeral monuments may be associated with this idea. But we must move on.

We are assured that if we can gain access to this hidden shrine, we will "live forever." (Careful! "Living forever," to an ancient Egyptian, tended to mean eternal life after death!) And this brings us back to *The Book of the Hidden Chamber,* which has more specific things to say about the mystery of Rostau. This book survives in two versions, the "long" and the "short." But the short version is not simply an abbreviation of the long version; it actually gives a slightly different emphasis to certain things and uses some different textual passages that do not occur in the long version. The only publication of the short version in English was by Budge. In this translation the name Rostau is given in two variations: Re-Statet and Re-Sethau. Here are some of the intriguing remarks that we find there (Budge capitalizes some names):

> Whosoever knoweth this representation of the hidden roads of RE-STATET [Rostau], and the holy paths of the AMMEHET, and the secret doors which are in the Land of SEKER [Sokar], the god who is upon his sand, shall be in the condition of him that eateth the bread-cakes which are [made] for the mouth of the LIVING gods in the Temple of Tem [Atum].
>
> Whosoever knoweth this shall be in the condition of him that is *maāt* [Cosmic Order, absolute truth] on the ways, and he shall journey over the roads of RE-SETHAU, and he shall see the representations of the AMMEHET [a name for the underworld]. . . . This great god [the sun god at night] is towed along over the ways of Maāt of the Tuat [underworld] through the upper half of this secret Circle of the god SEKER [Sokar], who is upon his sand, and he neither looketh upon nor gazeth at the secret figure of the earth which containeth the flesh of this god. . . . AMENT [the West] is the name of the Circle of this god, [and in it are] the secret path of Amentet [a name for the most secret and hidden part of the underworld], and the doors of the hidden palace,

and the holy place of the LAND OF SEKER [with his] flesh, and [his] members, [and his] body, in the divine form which they had at first.

BAIU-AMU-TUAT [the spirits who are in the underworld] is the name of the gods who are in [this] Circle. Their forms (*aru*) who are in their hour, and their secret shapes (*kheperu*) neither know, nor look upon, nor see this image (or, similitude) of SEKER (or, the hawk) himself.

Whosoever shall make these representations according to the image which is in writing in the hidden places of the Tuat, at the south of the Hidden Palace, and whosoever shall know them shall be at peace, and his soul shall unite itself to the offerings of SEKER, and the goddess KHEMIT shall not hack his body in pieces, and he shall go on his way towards her in peace.[33]

One detail not to be overlooked in this "short form" of the *Book of the Hidden Chamber* is that the great chamber of mysteries concealed in the Land of Sokar at Giza is here apparently described as being "south of the Hidden Palace." This crucial geographical information does not occur in the "long form" of the same book. This is yet further evidence that these sections were incorporated from some more ancient common text, for otherwise how would the short version contain things that are not in the long version? The short version was obviously a different abridgment of the original source, not an abbreviation of the long version.

What does this mean, "south of the Hidden Palace"? The Hidden Palace might be an appropriate way of referring to the Great Pyramid, as it is the grandest structure to be seen at Giza. In the seventh hour of the same book, there is a reference to "the similitudes which are in writing at the northern side of the Hidden Palace in the Tuat,"[34] so these references may be to the northern and southern faces of the Great Pyramid. And what does it really mean when this ancient text says that an initiate should make copies of the pictures relating to Giza, such as the ones hidden north of the Hidden Palace?[35]

Another point we should notice is that in this text it is not the flesh of Osiris that is said to be beneath Giza. Here it clearly says that the buried flesh is the flesh of *Sokar*. At Giza, Sokar was the original god, and Osiris was a form of him that came later. Margaret Murray stresses this when she tells us: "Osiris Sokar . . . the anthropomorphic god of the dead, as identified both with Ptah and with the hawk-headed Sokar; the three together forming the triple god, Ptah-Sokar-Osiris. The dominion of Sokar is given in the 4th and 5th divisions of the 'Book of Am Duat,' but M. Jequier shows that the dominion of Sokar was originally quite distinct from that of Osiris, and that the two have been incorporated together in the 'Book of Am Duat' by later theologians."[36]

Figure 7.21. The name of the god Osiris, surviving in superb condition on a wall of the temple of Seti I at Abydos. The seated figure of a god on the right is what is called in hieroglyphics a "determinative" sign, which indicates that the name is that of a god. The actual name in Egyptian is generally transliterated as Asar (which is the origin of the Greek form, Osiris). It is symbolized by the two hieroglyphs of an eye and the strange shape on the left, which is thought by Egyptologists to represent a throne. In fact, I do not believe the sign on the left actually represents a throne at all, but something else entirely. I believe it is a specific section of a sacred rectangle, and that it is related both to the archaic sacred rectangular enclosures of the early pharaohs and to certain arcane geometrical conceptions. A vertical line drawn through the pupil of the eye makes a golden angle with a line drawn from the pupil to the tip of the bottom "step" of the rectangle segment. (*Photo by Robert Temple*)

However, the substitution of Osiris for Sokar, which we found so completely done in the Middle Kingdom text, *The Book of the Two Ways,* that we considered a moment ago, was incompletely done in the New Kingdom text of the short form of *The Book of the Hidden Chamber.* Using the fundamental logic of textual analysis, we do not need to be geniuses to conclude that the short form of *The Book of the Hidden Chamber* preserves an earlier and unamended form of the tradition, and is thus an earlier text than *The Book of the Two Ways.* But since *The Book of the Two Ways* dates from the Middle Kingdom and *The Book of the Hidden Chamber* dates from the much later New Kingdom, there is only one conclusion that can be drawn here: the "later" text is later only in that it survives from later editions, but it is really earlier. In other words, we have conclusive textual proof that at least the section dealing with Rostau/Giza of *The Book of the Hidden Chamber* is earlier than the Eleventh Dynasty of the Middle Kingdom (1987–1938 BC) from which *The Book of the Two Ways* is known to survive. Since the material must predate 2000 BC and the Middle Kingdom, and since it cannot possibly have come from the First Intermediate Period (2180–1987 BC) before that, due to the total collapse of Egyptian civilization at that time of social chaos, it must therefore predate 2200 BC and be of Old Kingdom date. This places it no later than the Sixth Dynasty and the Pyramid Texts and means that it is equal in age to those oldest-known Egyptian religious texts. However, I have

Figure 7.22. Here the priests of Sokar, the original lord of the underworld (whose position was later taken by Osiris), are seen carrying the Sokar barque in procession at Giza during the annual Sokar Festival, when they made a circuit with it of the sacred areas near the Sphinx. The strange object with a bird's head sitting in the middle of the barque is a fetish that represents Sokar, in the form of a mummified hawk, with his head protruding from the mummy wrappings. The third priest from the left is wearing an animal skin (which we know from other depictions to be a leopard skin, though the spots are not visible in this picture) over his shoulder, and the medallion suspended on his chest shows that he is the chief priest of the group, while the priest behind him appears to be his deputy and carries a sacred wand or scepter. The two main priests in the center are not sharing in the actual bearing of the load, which is borne by the four groups of four junior priests, suggesting that as sixteen men were needed to carry it, the boat must be heavier than it appears. The exact nature of the Sokar fetish is not known, and the huge mummified portion may have contained something secret and concealed beneath the wrappings. My theory about this fetish is that a solid gold statue of Sokar was concealed inside, making the barque extremely heavy. This gold statue would have been the central cult statue of the god, normally kept in the inner sanctum of the temple. When carried outside once a year, it had to be concealed from the eyes of the profane, and it also could not be exposed to the light of the sun, because Sokar was known never to emerge from his perpetual darkness. The small Sokar-head on top of the fetish serves merely to identify the fetish so that people can realize that the true Sokar is concealed inside the mummy wrappings, in keeping with his nature. This engraving of a temple carving was published in 1809 in *Description de l'Égypte,* before the decipherment of hieroglyphics, but care was taken to engrave correctly the two hieroglyphs in front of the chief priest, which read SEM. This specifically identifies the chief priest in the picture as a Sem priest, and that means that we have here a picture of the high priest of Ptah from the Temple of Ptah at nearby Memphis, in his role as head mortuary priest, or Sem priest, of Sokar. Ptah and Sokar were merged as a joint divinity at Giza. Later the divinity was called Ptah-Sokar-Osiris and became a sacred trinity. The location of this temple carving is unknown, and it has possibly perished since this drawing of it was made prior to 1809. It is possible that it was carved on one of the walls of the Temple of Ptah but was among the vast amount of stone carried away from Memphis and Giza for use in the construction of mosques and palaces in Cairo during the nineteenth century. (*Collection of Robert Temple*)

taken a rather conservative approach to tracking the date of the text. One distinguished German Egyptologist, H. Altenmüller, hasn't bothered with such niceties, and says without a blush that he thinks the text comes from the Fourth or Fifth Dynasties (2640–2360 BC)![37]

Thus, whatever this section dealing with the fourth and fifth hours of the underworld contains, it is truly ancient and has a claim on our attention as possibly containing accurate details relating to some of the mysteries of Giza.

Let us therefore look even more closely at the intriguing short form of *The Book of the Hidden Chamber*. The text specifically refers to "the secret figure of the earth" being on the surface at Giza, above the hidden chamber of Sokar. This reminds us of the many interpretations of the measurements of the Great Pyramid as representing the precise size of our globe. This text could reasonably be claimed as near-contemporary evidence, dating at least from the Old Kingdom, of a description of a major structure on the surface at Giza that was considered to represent the secret figure of the Earth, and therefore to substantiate with textual evidence all the physical evidence that has been so fully brought forward by those who insist that the Great Pyramid is indeed a secret figure of the Earth.

The first to propose this extraordinary hypothesis was the French scholar Edmé-François Jomard, who accompanied Napoleon to Egypt in 1798. Jomard was concerned with the height of the Great Pyramid, and he calculated the height of the apothegm (the central line going up the middle of any of the sides) as being 184.722 meters. This was the "slant height" of the pyramid, which by means of trigonometry could help calculate the vertical height. Here is how Peter Tompkins, in *Secrets of the Great Pyramid,* describes what happened next:

> Jomard remembered that according to Diodorus Siculus and Strabo, the apothegm of the Pyramid was supposed to be one stadium long. He also knew that an Olympic stadium of 600 Greek feet—from which our modern sports stadium is derived—was a basic unit of land measure in the ancient world, one which was said to be related to the size of the earth. . . . Searching further through the trunks full of classics which the savants had brought to Egypt, Jomard found that the stadium of the Alexandrine Greeks [in Egypt] . . . had been the equivalent of 185.5 meters—which was within a meter of what he had found for the apothegm.
>
> To reinforce the point, Jomard discovered that the distance between the Egyptian localities as measured by Napoleon's surveyors also coincided with the classical distances between these localities computed in stadia, if the stadium was taken to be 185 meters.

Finally, Jomard learnt from his perusal of the classics that a stadium of 600 feet was considered to be 1/600 of a geographical degree.

Jomard calculated that a geographical degree at the mean latitude of Egypt was 110,827.68 meters. Dividing this figure by 600 resulted in a measure of 184.712 meters. This was within 10 centimeters of his value for the apothegm.

Could the Egyptians, Jomard wondered, have been capable of working out their basic units of measure—such as the stadium, the cubit, and the foot—from the size of the earth and then built this into the Pyramid?

To reinforce this exciting hypothesis Jomard found that several Greek authors reported that the perimeter of the base of the Pyramid was intended to measure half a minute of longitude. In other words, 480 times the base of the Pyramid was equal to a geographical degree.

Jomard took the 110,827-meter degree and divided it by 480. The result was 230.8 meters, or again within 10 centimeters of his measured length of the base [of the Great Pyramid]. . . . To the end, Jomard remained convinced that the builders of the Pyramid had the necessary astronomical know-how to measure a geographical degree and thus the true circumference of the earth, and had developed an advanced science of geography and geodesy which they had immortalized in the geometry of the Great Pyramid. . . . Jomard's classically indoctrinated colleagues could not stomach the idea that their cherished Greeks might not be the founders of geometry; so the pursuit was dropped.[38]

There are obviously more details to this than I have given, but we do not need the full mathematical account to get the idea. Jomard's hypothesis was not at all outrageous, really, for it had a good pedigree in statements made by various ancient authors. It did not just come out of his head, but was forced upon him by his work. And Jomard was not tainted at all with "Bible mania," as so many of the English authors who wrote about the Great Pyramid were. For some reason, the French were much more sane and did not drag their religious fantasies into their Egyptian studies in the way that the English and the Scots, and many religious Americans, repeatedly did.

The next scholar to consider seriously the theory that the Great Pyramid represented the northern hemisphere of the Earth in symbolic form was John Taylor, in his fascinating book *The Great Pyramid: Why Was It Built? And Who Built It?* published in 1859. It took me a very long time to obtain a copy of this book, as it is so rare. Taylor's book is really very thought provoking. One of his curious discoveries, it turns out, can be interpreted only on the basis of something I published in my own book *The Crystal Sun* 141 years later, in 2000.[39] By that time, alas, it was too late to inform Taylor! But he discovered the very strange fact that two prominent ancient Egyptian units of measurement differed from each other by the tiny amount of 1.01. He was justly puzzled by this. In *The Crystal Sun* I explain that the precise number that we write in our modern decimal notation as 1.0136 (but that the Egyptians expressed as a fraction) was "the greatest secret of the ancient Egyptians," well known to them from its connections with both musical theory and the calendar, and so it is not at all surprising that the same number was embodied in their system of sacred measurements (although as I did not yet have Taylor's book, I was unable to mention it in *The Crystal Sun*). I have returned to this subject of measurements in my book *Egyptian Dawn*. But in the meantime, to retain the thread of our thoughts, I want to show how Taylor conceived of the Great Pyramid as what the ancient text calls "a secret figure of the earth":

The angle of the casing-stones being 51° 50' . . . . What reason, it may be asked, can be assigned for the founders of the Great Pyramid giving it this precise angle, and not rather making each face an equilateral triangle? The only one we can suggest is, that they knew the Earth was a sphere; that they had measured off a portion of one of its great circles; and by observing the motion of the heavenly bodies over the earth's surface, had ascertained its circumference, and were now desirous of leaving behind them a record of that circumference as correct and imperishable as it was possible for them to construct. They assumed the Earth to be a perfect sphere; and as they knew that the radius of a circle must bear a certain proportion to its circumference, they then built a Pyramid of such a height in proportion to its base, that its perpendicular would be equal to the radius of a circle equal in circumference to the perimeter of the base. To effect this they would make each face of the Pyramid present a certain ascertained angle with reference to its base (supposing a vertical section made of it), which angle would be that of 51° 51' 14," if modern science were employed in determining it. . . . Now the actual angle of the casing-stones was found to be 51° 50.' Can any proof be more conclusive than this, that the reason we have assigned for the construction of the Great Pyramid was the true reason which influenced its founders? How the thought occurred to them we cannot tell; but a more proper monument for this purpose could not have been devised than a vast Pyramid with a square base, the vertical height of which Pyramid should be the radius of a sphere in its circumference equal to the perimeter of that base. It was impossible to build a hemisphere of so large a size. In the form of a Pyramid, all those truths might be declared which they had taken so much pains to learn; and in that form the structure would be less liable to injury from time, neglect, or wantonness, than in any other.[40]

If Taylor had known that the short form of *The Book of the Hidden Chamber* dating from the Pyramid Age had mentioned a structure at Giza that was called "the secret figure of the earth," he would have jumped for joy, for this was precisely what he had decided the Great Pyramid really was. Those who are determined to believe that the Great Pyramid was built as a pharaoh's tomb can still retain their belief and at the same time admit that the Great Pyramid was also a "secret figure of the earth," since the two intentions are not in any way incompatible with one another. After all, a pharaoh can be buried in a pyramid that either is or is not a "secret figure of the earth," as the symbolic message of the structure would not interfere with his eternal rest. I personally do not accept the theory that the Great Pyramid was ever built to be a tomb and have already called attention to the fact that Herodotus specifically stated that it was not one. It may have been intended as a dummy tomb or a symbolic tomb, but I am certain that it was never a real tomb. I do not believe the empty sarcopohagus in the King's Chamber ever held a corpse. One of the curious things about that sarcophagus is that it is too large to fit through the door, so it can never have been carried in. In *The Crystal Sun* I discuss numerous strange aspects of the King's Chamber, which I will not repeat here.

In *Secrets of the Great Pyramid,* Peter Tompkins also gives prominent attention to John Taylor's pioneering work, although he was unaware that the book was published in 1859 and knew only a subsequent edition of 1864. Tompkins's account, as usual, is very amusing:

> Taylor then discovered that if he divided the perimeter of the Pyramid by twice its height, it gave him a quotient of 3.144, remarkably close to the value of π, which is computed as 3.14159+. In other words, the height of the Pyramid appeared to be in relation to the perimeter of its base as the radius of a circle is to its circumference.
>
> This seemed to Taylor far too extraordinary to attribute to chance, and he deduced that the Pyramid might have been specifically intended by its builders to incorporate the incommensurable value of π. If so, this was a demonstration of the advanced knowledge of the builders. . . . Searching for a reason for such a π proportion in the Pyramid, Taylor concluded that the perimeter might have been intended to represent the circumference of the earth at the equator while the height represented the distance from the earth's center to the pole.
>
> Perhaps Jomard had been right: perhaps the ancient designers *had* measured the length of a geographical degree, multiplied it by 360° for the circumference of the globe, and by the π relation had deduced the polar radius of the earth,

immortalizing their knowledge by making the circumference to scale with the perimeter and the radius to scale with the height of the Pyramid.

Taylor underlined his thesis: "It was *to make a record of the measure of the Earth* that it was built."[41]

In other words, it was what *The Book of the Hidden Chamber* calls *a secret figure of the earth.*

Having now dealt with this subject by way of an introduction to some of the more ambitious measurements and designs that may possibly be incorporated into the various structures of the Giza Plateau, it is time to explore the interrelationships of those structures in space, and specifically those that affect the Sphinx. My next book, *Egyptian Dawn,* contains extensive discussion of the pyramids themselves, but Sphinx matters are dealt with in this book. In *The Crystal Sun,* I already put forward the evidence that the Pyramid of Chephren was built where it was, and to the size it was, for a very important reason, and as part of a larger plan linked to that of the Great Pyramid. The photo in figure 3.10 on page 141 of this book shows the shadow cast by that pyramid onto the south face of the Great Pyramid at sunset near the time of the winter solstice, similar to one I published in *The Crystal Sun,* and I have already discussed in *The Crystal Sun* its significance in terms of the placing of the Pyramid of Chrephren on the plateau. What about the Sphinx? Are there any determining factors in terms of the other monuments on the Giza Plateau that might be held to specify both its position and its size? As it happens, there are.

In chapter 3, I described my discovery, by means of a scientific instrument called an inclinometer, when I took a sighting through the instrument of the tip of the Pyramid of Chephren while I was standing on the floor of the Sphinx Temple. By reading the information given by the inclinometer, I discovered that the line of sight made the unique sacred angle of the Egyptians of 26° 33' 54" (which we call the golden angle, as it is the only angle produced in the only triangle, the "golden triangle," that can be constructed by means of the Golden Section) with the base of the temple. I could not be as precise as measuring the 54 seconds, but it was clear that the golden angle was intended. This did not surprise me, because I had already discussed the golden angle at such length in my earlier book *The Crystal Sun,* where, as I have already mentioned, I published a photograph (and another is now published here as I just said) showing that angle being cast as a shadow onto the south face of the Great Pyramid at sunset on the winter solstice (a shadow cast by the nearby Pyramid of Chephren). This was the largest and most dramatic physical indicator of the importance of a solstice in the whole of the ancient world. It is shown in figure 3.9, and I have

Figure 7.23. This is the ascending passage that leads out of the back (west end) of the Valley Temple at Giza, onto the Chephren Causeway, in the direction of the Pyramid of Chephren. Its floor is of Egyptian alabaster and its walls are of red granite. I measured the angle of its slope and found that it was the golden angle, identical to the slopes of both the Ascending and Descending Passages inside the Great Pyramid. I was the first person to notice this golden angle in the Valley Temple. Because golden triangles (a golden triangle as I use the term being a right triangle with a golden angle as its acute angle opposite the altitude) were so important at Giza, I am certain that there is a subterranean crypt beneath this passage, which has probably been sealed since Old Kingdom times. That is because when they have a golden slope, the Egyptians always have a golden triangle as well, with that slope constituting the triangle's hypotenuse. And when an enclosed space falls below that slope, there tends to be a chamber, because it is a sacred spot. The so-called Grand Gallery inside the Great Pyramid is the hypotenuse of a golden triangle which defines the location of the so-called Queen's Chamber, with the passage leading to it as one of the sides of the triangle and the chamber itself being situated at the base of the right angle (see figure 54 in my book *The Crystal Sun*). I believe that the probability of there *not* being an important chamber beneath the doorway at the top of this ascending passage is zero. (*Photo by Robert Temple*)

Figure 7.24. This photo is taken from the top of the Valley Temple looking up toward the Pyramid of Chephren along the limestone Chephren Causeway. As can be seen, the causeway is at an odd angle (not the golden angle) to the pyramid, and also to the temple, and no one has ever explained why. The ascending passage arising out of the Valley Temple and leading to the back doorway that opens onto this causeway (see figure 7.23) is on a slope that *is* the golden angle, identical to the slope of the Ascending and Descending Passages inside the Great Pyramid. The line of sight that passes through the air from the top of the Pyramid of Chephren to the floor of the Sphinx Temple is also at the golden angle (as I measured with an engineer's device called an inclinometer), as shown in figure 3.13 on page 145. The shadow cast by the Pyramid of Chephren at sunset of the winter solstice upon the south face of the Great Pyramid also forms a golden triangle, with its hypotenuse forming the golden angle (see figure 3.10, and also plate 30 in my book *The Crystal Sun*). The exact position and size of the Sphinx are also determined in relation to the two main pyramids by multiple golden angles, as shown in figure 7.25 on page 367. All three of these key monuments had to be placed exactly where they are and had to be exactly the sizes they are as part of a unified conception based on geometric principles. (*Photo by Robert Temple*)

reproduced again the color photo from that book on this book's website. My discovery was of particular importance because it is the same angle of inclination of both the Ascending and Descending Passages inside the Great Pyramid, thus hinting on the outside at what lay on the inside. This is the kind of mysterious behavior that so delighted the ancient Egyptian priests. I also reported in that book my discovery that the ascending passage that leads out of the Valley Temple onto the Chephren Causeway was inclined at the same golden angle (see figure 7.23). That passage is what I call a golden slope, which is the name I give to a slope that rises or descends at a golden angle to the horizontal plane. (Both the Ascending Passage and the Descending Passage of the Great Pyramid are therefore what I call golden slopes.)

In *Egyptian Dawn* I give a large number of new discoveries concerning the unified design concept of the Great Pyamid's interior structure. Many of these discoveries have nothing whatsoever to do with the Golden Section, and are straightforward design criteria of a remarkable kind that no one had ever noticed before. There is a second category of design criteria, however, that is wholly connected with the Golden Section. The categories appear to be separate, as if one was superimposed upon the other, thus offering two separate "stand-alone" levels of discoverability to the investigator, one that gives the impression of having been designed to be "idiot-proof" for the most basic investigator to find and one at a higher level of difficulty. I felt as if I was decoding two separate levels of design information, and doubtless there is more to find! Someone really clever now needs to come along and figure out the rest of it, such as what it all means and what it was for!

One reason for bringing the Great Pyramid into the discussion in this chapter is to lay the basis for revealing a hitherto-unnoticed connection between the precise location of the Sphinx and that wonderful structure the Great Pyramid, for the Sphinx's size, general shape, and location are all determined directly by its relationship to the Great Pyramid, as we will now see, and as is made clear in figure 7.25. No one has ever noticed this before, because it is not at all obvious.

In figure 7.25 I reproduce part of the official Egyptian government geodetic survey map of the Giza Plateau, of the sort that in Britain is called "an ordnance survey map," which may be presumed to be as accurate as any other map of the Giza Plateau in existence. It is certainly more reliable than any of the plans prepared by archaeologists, which I have found are often misleading and lacking in accuracy.

I have overlaid across the map in figure 7.25 various lines connecting key points of monuments on the Giza Plateau, and where the golden angle recurs frequently. It is in fact a dominant motif of the entire Giza Plateau Plan.

We can see that the size of the Sphinx is determined first of all by three rays emanating at an identical angle, the "golden angle," from three separate key points of the Great Pyramid and striking it at its own defining points, namely front, midpoint, and rear. The first of these emanates from the northeast corner of the Great Pyramid. This makes a golden angle with the north–south meridian that defines the east face of the Great Pyramid, and it shoots off toward the Sphinx and strikes the northeast tip of that monument, which is the left tip of its left paw. In other words, this ray connects the northeast corners of both monuments with a line drawn at the golden angle to a north–south meridian at either point.

The second defining ray emanates from the midpoint of the base of the Great

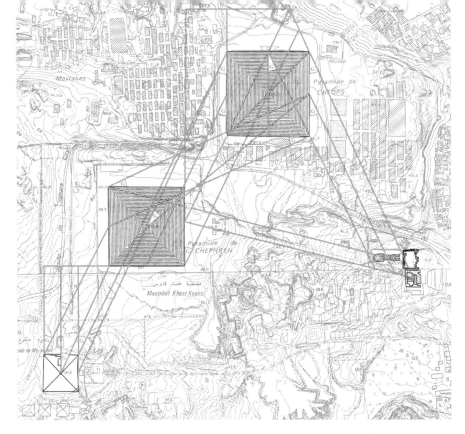

Figure 7.25. This is the Golden Giza Plan, which I worked out laboriously and with the greatest of difficulty. To achieve accuracy, it was necessary for me to work out these geometrical relationships using the official Egyptian government survey map, which is the black-and-white basis for this two-color diagram. The golden lines show what I have chosen to call the "rays" connecting the four key monuments. All of these rays share the same angle, the golden angle of 26° 33' 54", which is the acute angle occurring in a golden triangle, a right triangle formed on the basis of the Golden Section. The ancient Egyptians were clearly obsessed with the golden angle and embodied it superstitiously in all of their sacred art and architecture. (*Drawing of the rays by Daud Sutton from my sketch, copyright by Robert Temple*)

Pyramid's eastern face. It strikes the midpoint of the Sphinx. This ray also makes a golden angle with the north–south meridian at either point.

The third defining ray emanates from the midpoint of the base of the Great Pyramid's northern face. It strikes the southwestern tip of the Sphinx's rump. This ray also makes a golden angle with the north–south meridian at either point.

These three defining rays fix the size and position of the Sphinx. A further defining ray emanates from the Pyramid of Chephren. A ray from the northwest corner of that pyramid parallel with the Chephren Causeway shoots through the midpoint of the Sphinx. (The midpoint of the Sphinx is thus an intersection point of two rays shooting from key points of the two separate pyramids. The latter ray also makes a golden angle, which is described in a moment.) The northwest corner of the Pyramid of Chephren is linked to the midpoint of the base of the Great Pyramid on its eastern face (a point from which a ray is emitted defining the Sphinx's midpoint by a golden angle, as already mentioned), by a further golden angle, this time one made with the east–west line defining the northern face of the Pyramid of Chephren.

The midpoint of the Sphinx is thus one vertex of a triangle, the other two vertices of which are the northwestern corner of the Pyramid of Chephren and the midpoint of the eastern baseline of the Great Pyramid. Each of these vertices is connected by a previous relationship based upon rays of golden angles.

In other words, there is a kind of interlocking grid of these rays whereby they seem to confirm each other by repeating the same golden angle each time. The ray emanating from the midpoint of the base of the northern face of the Great Pyramid also passes through the southeastern corner of that pyramid on its way to strike the Sphinx's rump at its southeastern tip.

If we look at figure 7.25, we can see that the midpoint of the base of the northern face of the Great Pyramid also shoots a ray toward the Pyramid of Chephren, which strikes it at the point where the southern edge of the Chephren Causeway, which I call the *base* of the Causeway, would strike that pyramid if continued. And this ray then makes a golden angle with the north–south meridian defining the base of the eastern face of the Pyramid of Chephren, yet another confirmation of an interlocking Golden Grid.

But there is something even more remarkable about this midpoint of the base of the northern face of the Great Pyramid: the two rays just described cross the southwestern and southeastern corners of the Great Pyramid, respectively, and in doing so they create a superimposed triangle upon the plan of the Great Pyramid that has as its vertex at the northern face a double golden angle (i.e., an angle that if bisected yields two golden angles). In other words, the rays both make golden angles at the vertex with the north–south meridian bisecting the Great Pyramid. No one has ever noticed before that the size and the distance of the base of the Great Pyramid are just right to do this. The same would apply to rays generated at any of the four midpoints: each would generate two golden angles with rays striking the appropriate corners of the pyramid. I have not bothered to show these on the Golden Giza Plan of figure 7.25, because it complicates the design too much with details that do not concern the Sphinx, however important they may be with regard to the Great Pyramid itself. However, the two descending rays from the midpoint of the base of the northern face show clearly what the other three midpoints also generate with their own pairs of rays, which are omitted from this particular diagram to avoid confusing the reader with too much information.

A large number of other golden angle rays exist that connect the four main monuments of Giza: the three main pyramids and the Sphinx. These demonstrate conclusively that the Giza complex was conceived as a unity and that the sizes and positions of the four monuments are rigidly determined by these sighting rays based upon what I call a Golden Giza Plan. In addition to this, we must remember that there is the golden-angled ray that actually shoots through the air from the floor of the Sphinx Temple, which strikes the peak of the Pyramid of Chephren, as already described in a previous chapter, discovered by me using a device called an inclinometer. And just to set the scene appropriately, we ascend on a golden slope rising at the golden angle up the ascending passageway of the Valley Temple to enter upon the Chephren Causeway and approach the plateau. Truly, Giza is golden!

Now we will look at some of the other golden rays of Giza, in order to explore further the rigidity and inflexibility of this geometrical structure created by some ancient designer or designers who was/were obsessed with golden angles. The three main pyramids at Giza are mutually fixed in their sizes and positions by a complex set of golden rays, as is shown in figure 7.25.

Another golden angle is the one made by the ray shooting from the southeast corner of the Pyramid of Chephren to the tip of the Great Pyramid. It makes a golden angle with the north–south meridian defining the base of the east face of the Pyramid of Chephren.

Yet another golden angle exists between the north–south meridian bisecting the Mycerinus Pyramid and a ray shooting from the tip of that pyramid to the southwest corner of the Pyramid of Chephren.

Another golden angle appears when we shoot a ray from the northwest corner of the Pyramid of Chephren to the midpoint of the base of the east face of the Great Pyramid. This line makes a golden angle with the east–west line defining the base of the north face of the Pyramid of Chephren.

There are two more rays at golden angles connecting key points on the Great Pyramid with the tip of the Pyramid of Chephren (which was at a golden angle to the floor of the Sphinx Temple, as I have already described). If we shoot a ray from the northwest corner of the Great Pyramid to the tip of the Pyramid of Chephren, it makes a golden angle with the north–south meridian defining the base of the west face of the Great Pyramid. And if we then shoot a ray from the tip of the Pyramid of Chephren to the midpoint of the base of the east face of the Great Pyramid, we discover that it makes a golden angle with the line I have just mentioned.

Yet another golden angle occurs if we shoot a ray from the southeast corner of the Great Pyramid to the midpoint of the base of the west face of the Pyramid of Chephren. It makes a golden angle with the east–west line defining the base of the south face of the Great Pyramid.

Another ray shooting from the northwest corner of the Pyramid of Mycerinus to the midpoint of the base of the west face of the Pyramid of Chephren makes a golden angle with the north–south meridian defining the base of the west face of the Pyramid of Mycerinus. (The same line also obviously makes a golden angle with the north–south meridian bisecting the Pyramid of Mycerinus, which it intersects, and which itself is the base of another triangle with a golden angle, as already indicated, and additionally it makes a golden angle with the north–south meridian defining the base of the western face of the Pyramid of Chephren when it strikes it.)

Another ray shooting from the northeast corner of the Pyramid of Mycerinus to the northwest corner of the Great Pyramid makes a golden angle with the north–south meridian defining the base of the east side of the Mycerinus Pyramid. The midpoint of the base of the west face of the Great Pyramid shoots a ray to the midpoint of the base of the south face of the Pyramid of Chephren, which makes a golden angle with the north–south meridian that defines the base of the west face of the Great Pyramid.

A ray shooting from the midpoint of the base of the east face of the Pyramid of Mycerinus to the eastern edge of the tip of the Pyramid of Chephren forms a golden angle with the north–south meridian defining the base of the east face of the Pyramid of Mycerinus. That same ray then continues on to the northwest corner of the Great Pyramid, where it forms a golden angle with the north–south meridian defining the base of the western face of the Great Pyramid.

If we draw a straight line connecting the three key defining points of the Sphinx (northeast tip, midpoint, and southwest tip) and continue it slightly to the southwest so that it touches the southern edge of the Chephren Causeway (which I call the *base* of the Causeway), we see that it makes a golden angle with the base of the Causeway. It also makes a golden angle with the ray shooting from the northwest corner of the Pyramid of Chephren to the midpoint of the Sphinx.

A line drawn from the point where the Chephren Causeway's base, if extended, would strike the Pyramid of Chephren makes a golden angle with the north–south meridian defining the base of the east face of the Pyramid of Chephren when it shoots off to strike the midpoint of the base of the northern face of the Great Pyramid, passing across the southeast corner of the Great Pyramid as it does so.

We can thus see that the Chephren Causeway, which runs at a rather odd angle of about 14° to the horizontal (east–west line), is actually linked to the Sphinx by two golden angles and to the Pyramid of Chephren and Great Pyramid by one golden angle, so it is not as haphazard as it might superficially seem.

The following key points of the Giza pyramids are thus found to be mutually defined by a bewildering multiplicity of rays, or sighting lines, shooting out at golden angles:

- Great Pyramid: all four corners, the top, and three midpoints
- Pyramid of Chephren: all four corners, the top, and two midpoints
- Pyramid of Mycerinus: two corners, the top, and one midpoint

The decrease in number of salient midpoints in the progression 3, 2, 1 matches the degree of hierarchical size of each pyramid in the group.

We must not forget that the Great Pyramid itself is full of golden angles and golden triangles and golden sections. I have described them at some length in *The Crystal Sun.* The commencement of the Grand Gallery inside the Great Pyramid is, for instance, determined by a golden triangle. The Ascending Passage and the Descending Passage inside the Great Pyramid are both golden slopes, each at the golden angle of 26° 33' 54" to the horizontal plane. It was Petrie who specified this, for the interior slopes of the Great Pyramid are often given as slightly different than the golden angle value. A fuller discussion of this apears in *Egyptian Dawn,* with extensive detail and references and translations of key German texts that are unknown to English-speaking scholars. The fact that the Descending Passage was at this angle was first discovered in the nineteenth century by Henry Crichton Agnew (born 1797), whose largely forgotten work at Giza is discussed in *Egyptian Dawn.* The King's Chamber has multiple golden angles determining its size and shape. As I have already published diagrams elsewhere showing all of these things, I will not discuss them again here. However, for a full understanding of the golden angles of Giza, it is necessary to have a copy of *The Crystal Sun.* In addition to these, there are the eight golden angles manifested on the plan of the Great Pyramid by triangles described a few moments ago, only one of which is actually shown in figure 7.25 (the triangle drawn between the southwest and southeast corners of the pyramid and the midpoint of the base of the northern face).

You do not have to be particularly astute to see that the ancient Egyptians were clearly obsessed with golden angles to an extent that is mind-boggling to us today. It is as if they had gone mad. How could anybody who was not an obsessive–compulsive personality construct a design for the Giza Plateau such as this? All these monuments that had never before been recognized by us as having any coherent design connection with one another are seen really to be interrelated by a crazy array of rays shooting out at golden angles in every direction, which constitute a vast secret pattern that can be seen and plotted only on an official government geodetic survey map. It is such a crisscrossing spider's web that the concealed structure is hard to grasp. We have to remember that all these many rays are determined by *one identical angle,* repeated over and over again.

The question arises: *How did the ancient Egyptians do this?*

We may not know how, but it is easier to understand why. So we will now turn to that easier question, though in doing so things will become far weirder than fiction, so hold on to your *nemes* headdresses as we take off!

Before we can really comprehend what was going on at Giza, we have to stop to think for a moment: What was the golden angle? And how can you find it? After all, as it is not a whole angle but is 26 degrees plus slightly more than half a degree more, how did the Egyptians know about it in the first place? Were they really that sophisticated? I think a moment's reflection on the last question will permit anyone to answer a resounding "Yes!" Anyone who can build the Great Pyramid can certainly work out an angle in geometry!

As I explain later, the distinguished Egyptian historian of ancient Egyptian architecture, Professor Alexander Badawy, found incontrovertible proof that the Egyptians used a series of numbers that we call the Fibonacci series in constructing their sacred temples. To prove this, he studied more than fifty ancient structures and measured them very carefully. The successive numbers in this series, as they get larger and larger, converge on a fraction (expressed by us as a decimal, 0.618, which is the decimal portion of 1.618, which is a universal natural constant also called *phi*) that expresses the golden section (which then gives the golden angle) in numerical form. (I call the decimal portion the "golden particle.") All you have to do then is to apply the number to a geometrical line, and you have the golden section without the need to construct it geometrically. It is handed to you on a plate by the number series, a number series that we know they used. You do not even have to be a geometer to get the golden section! However, the Egyptians were also expert geometers, so they probably knew about both the number-series method and at least one of the geometrical methods.

One way to approach the problem of the golden angle is to go back to Euclid (a Greek who flourished 323–283 BC and lived at Alexandria in Egypt). He gives the method for cutting a line in the golden section in a rather ingenious and unusual way. This is found in Book Six of his *Elements*. Book Five of the *Elements* is concerned with defining and explaining what ratios and proportions actually are. In Greek, a ratio was a *logos* and a proportion was an *analogon,* which was a contraction of *ana logon,* meaning "in proportion." (I have recently registered a website called www. inproportion.org, which will be devoted to "sacred" geometry, by the way. Check it out.) This fifth book of Euclid is actually suspected of having been written by a distinguished Greek predecessor, Eudoxus, and Euclid merely incorporated it into his compendium, as there was little or nothing that needed to be added or touched up. Definition 3 of Book Five states: "A ratio is a sort of relation in respect of size between two magnitudes of the same kind."[42] Definition 6 states: "Let magnitudes which have the same ratio be called proportional."[43] This may all sound very simple and obvious, but the Greeks were very thorough, and they did not believe in writing books about things unless they first defined what they were talking about.

Book Six then moves on to what concerns us. What we call the golden section was not called that then; it was merely called "the section." But Euclid discusses it in a more fundamental manner still, and calls it "the extreme and mean ratio." Definition 3 of Book Six states: "A straight line is said to have been cut in extreme and mean ratio [*akron kai meson logon*] when, as the whole line is to the greater segment, so is the greater to the less."[44] Bearing in mind the second definition we saw from Book Five, we can realize that this comparison of two ratios means that we are dealing with a *proportion*. Hence we tend to call it today "the golden mean proportion," though that is modern language adopted during the nineteenth century, not Euclid's language. (In the Renaissance, it was called "the divine proportion.")

The demonstration of how to find the golden mean proportion is then given by Euclid in Book Six, Proposition 30, which is called: "To cut a given finite straight line in extreme and mean ratio."[45] Euclid then proceeds to go about it, draws a figure, and so on, in his usual way. What is so intriguing about the way he does this is that he does not follow the more modern methods at all, but approaches the matter in the manner of a man who thinks entirely differently from moderns. His method is incredibly simple when you read it, though how anyone discovered it in the first place is baffling, so one must presume mere trial and error. To summarize, what it amounts to is this: draw a square, then draw any parallelogram that shares a corner with that square and is equal to the square in area, and it will of necessity cut the square at a point that is the golden section of the side of the square that is cut. (The details of what a parallelogram is, and of how to make it equal to the square, and so forth, are all things that Euclid has dealt with earlier, so that the student marching his way through the *Elements* always follows a clear cumulative path of definitions and explanations and knows exactly what is going on at every step, like a baby led by the hand who is being taught how to walk.)

By way of illustration of Euclid's method, I reproduce in figure 7.27 the page from one of the most amazing books about geometry ever published, Oliver Byrne's *The First Six Books of the Elements of Euclid,* William Pickering, London, 1847. Because the book is so unusual, I am reproducing its title page also, in figure 7.26. Byrne pioneered a color-coded method of understanding geometry at the remarkably early date of 1847, and this is one of the rarest books on geometry in the world, of which I have been fortunate to obtain a copy. On my website figure 7.26, the method of Euclid for obtaining the golden section, is shown in full color. It would take too long to explain Byrne's system of color-coding, but the diagram on the left of the page shows the result very vividly. Maybe somebody will publish a reprint of this extraordinary book in full one day, as a copy should be in the hands of everyone with a true interest in such things.

Figures 7.28 to 7.30 and 7.32 reproduce diagrams showing more "usual"

Figure 7.26. The title page of Oliver Byrne's innovative color-coded excursion into Euclid's geometry, which attempts to make the geometrical principles clear to people who are uneasy with equations and standard diagrams, by showing what is happening in different colors. Byrne's thinking was that artists would intuitively grasp the geometry if color was used in this way. His book was a monumental step in the history of printing for the mid-nineteenth century. (For a full-color version of this illustration, visit my website.)

THE FIRST SIX BOOKS OF

THE ELEMENTS OF EUCLID

IN WHICH COLOURED DIAGRAMS AND SYMBOLS

ARE USED INSTEAD OF LETTERS FOR THE

GREATER EASE OF LEARNERS

BY OLIVER BYRNE

SURVEYOR OF HER MAJESTY'S SETTLEMENTS IN THE FALKLAND ISLANDS
AND AUTHOR OF NUMEROUS MATHEMATICAL WORKS

LONDON
WILLIAM PICKERING
1847

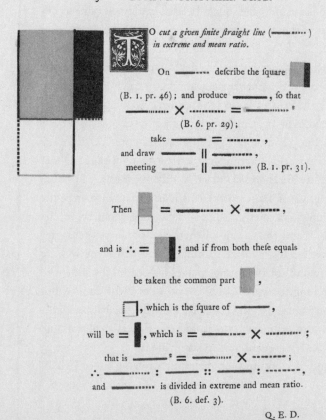

258   *BOOK VI. PROP. XXX. PROB.*

Figure 7.27. Oliver Byrne's depiction in color codes of what happens when you find the golden section of a line (by "cutting it in extreme and mean ratio," as the mathematicians like to express it), according to Euclid, Book Six, Proposition 33. (For a full-color version of this illustration, visit my website.)

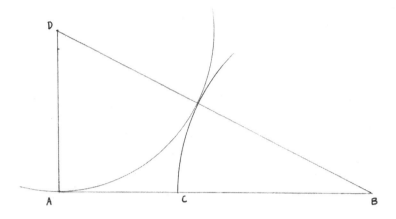

Cut a line A B so that A C : C B is a Golden Section.

(A D is made ½ A B)

Figure 7.28. One method of constructing a golden section on a line. (*Collection of Robert Temple*)

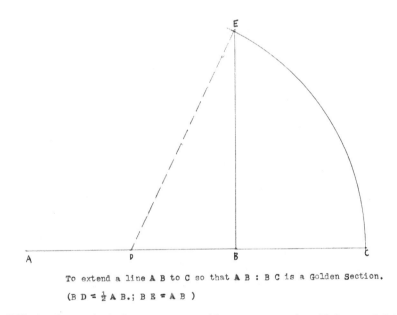

To extend a line A B to C so that A B : B C is a Golden Section.

(B D = ½ A B.; B E = A B)

Figure 7.29. Another method of constructing a golden section on a line. (*Collection of Robert Temple*)

modern methods of determining the golden section. However, it is not necessary for me to go into further detail about these geometrical techniques; I merely wish to indicate them. Serious students of geometry either already know them or can easily find them in standard works of reference.

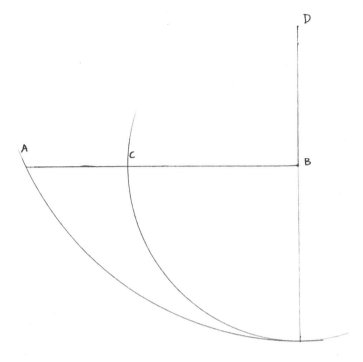

Cut a line A B so that A C : C B is a Golden Section.

(D B is made ½ A B)

Figure 7.30. A third method of constructing a golden section on a line. (*Collection of Robert Temple*)

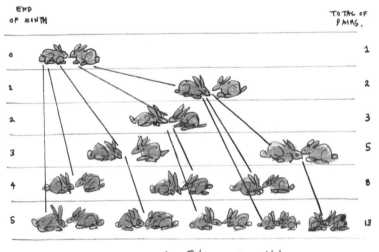

Figure 7.31. A drawing showing how rabbits breed according to the numbers of the Fibonacci series, which are related to the golden section. The Fibonacci-series numbers were used for the layout of ancient Egyptian temples, a fact proved by Professor Alexander Badawy (see page 381). (*Collection of Robert Temple*)

Golden Section, is the name given to an irrational proportion, known at least since Euclid, which has often been thought to possess some aesthetic virtue in itself, some hidden harmonic proportion in tune with the Universe.

It is dipined as a line, which is divided in such a way that the smaller part is to the larger part as the larger is to the whole. AB cut at C, so that CB: AC = AC : AB.

In practice it works out at about 8:13.

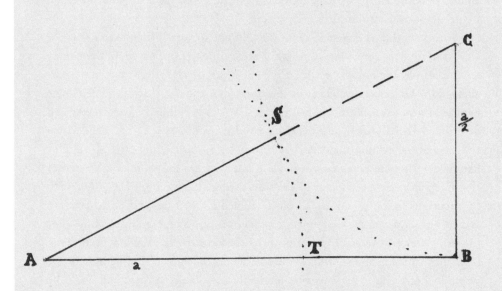

To construct **T**, the point of **C.S.** draw **BC** = a/2 at right angles to **AB**.

The circle with **C** as centre and a/2 as Radius cuts **AC** in **S**;

The circle with **A** as centre and **AS** as Radius cuts **AB** in **T**.

Figure 7.32. Notes and demonstration of the construction of a golden section on a line. (*Collection of Robert Temple*)

I have given all the background that is found in Euclid to establish a more primitive approach to what we call the "golden" section, "golden" angle, "golden" triangle, and so forth, than is usual. Euclid derived his information from the Pythagorean, Aristotelian, and Platonic geometers and systematized their findings in a brilliant manner. His personal affiliation was with the school of Aristotle, though the Platonists like to claim him because they don't want to let him get away. The Pythagoreans in turn got much of their geometrical knowledge from Egypt, which they freely admitted (Pythagoras lived there for some years, and after all, Euclid lived there for most or all of his life also), as well as from the Babylonian traditions. Looking at this from the point of view of Euclid in the fourth century BC, we are actually much closer to seeing it from the point of view of the earlier Egyptians themselves. Although it was the philosopher Thales of Miletus who was the first person to introduce Egyptian geometry to the Greeks, and he was earlier than Pythagoras, that is a detail people generally overlook, and we need not concern ourselves with it here.

So we see that the golden angle is really not so very difficult, and that the golden section that gives rise to it (when we form a triangle based on the golden section) can be obtained as easily as by drawing an overlapping square and a parallelogram! Therefore, let us not be intimidated by the fact that the golden angle has the bizarre value of 26° 33' 54", which seems so—well, so . . . very messy and disturbingly fractional. The Egyptians loved fractions, as they had no decimal system, and they could calculate fractions so fast it was like lightning. (It is a bit like how a Chinese person can calculate faster on an abacus than a Westerner can on an electronic calculator, if they are sitting side by side; I have done such competitions in China myself!) I have dabbled a bit in Egyptian mathematics, and it is a wonderful parallel universe of its own, so strange, so fascinating. (For instance, they had no multiplication or division, as these processes were done instead by addition and subtraction in a very bizarre manner.) But because of the way they did things, fractions were perfectly acceptable to them and could be handled with the greatest of ease and fluency. Thus their manic fixation on the golden angle is not as strange as it seems to us, since its fractional nature was no problem to them.

Let me restate what the golden section is in another way as well. We cut a line at a certain point (the golden section point, which we have found either according to the method of Euclid or by one of the other ways), and that divides it into two shorter lines: one is long and one is short. The long one is called the major and the short one is called the minor. The ratio of the short line (minor) to the long line (major) is the same as the ratio of the long line (major) to the whole line before it was cut; hence the two ratios are what is called "proportional." And this proportion is known now as "the golden mean proportion," but was known to Euclid as "extreme and mean ratio." Leonardo da Vinci was obsessed with the golden section, or divine proportion, as he called it; his famous painting of the Last Supper, for instance, is based on its principles. The millions of people who have read the novel *The Da Vinci Code* will all be familiar with this. Few people realize that the golden section also entered music at the time of Monteverdi, and that Bach was so obsessed by it that he used it as the basis of the composition of all his fugues. Mozart also used the golden section in the composition of his music, as he was a great admirer of Bach. Anyone who wants to know more about that can go to our website, www.brancusiclassics.com, and download the relevant papers by myself and my colleague the pianist and musicologist Stefano Greco.

It is worthwhile keeping firmly in mind that it is not only the ancient Egyptians who were maniacally obsessed with the golden mean proportion, but that such people as Leonardo da Vinci and J. S. Bach were as well. Indeed, so was the twentieth-century architect Le Corbusier, who embodied it in all his buildings just as if he were an ancient Egyptian. (And who can say, perhaps he was one.)

As mentioned briefly already, the golden section is connected with a series of numbers called the Fibonacci series (named after an Italian mathematician of the Renaissance called Leonardo Fibonacci, who discussed those numbers). I do not propose to give a full account of the Fibonacci series, or of Leonardo Fibonacci; that would be a distraction. All you need to know is that the series is a very simple one, where each number in the series is a sum of the two numbers that have gone before: 0, 1, 1, 2, 3, 5, 8, 13, 21, 34, 55, 89, . . . and so on (another name for this is a "summation series"). Know-it-alls of today think this is too complicated for ancient Egyptians. However, it has been conclusively proved by the Egyptian archaeologist Alexander Badawy that it was used in the construction of Egyptian temples throughout history. He studied more than fifty temples, took careful measurements, and published his findings in his brilliant book *Ancient Egyptian Architectural Design*.[46] Badawy is widely recognized as the leading authority on Egyptian architectural design and is also author of a work in three volumes, *A History of Egyptian Architecture*,[47] which is the authoritative work in the field. (The information about the Fibonacci series is not to be found in those volumes, but only in his volume that is specially devoted to the subject, which appeared separately.) I have discussed his findings and especially their application to the temple of Seti I at Abydos in my lengthy account of our work and findings at that temple, which awaits future publication, so I shall not repeat any of it here. Suffice it to say that Badawy established conclusively that the Egyptians not only knew the Fibonacci series, which was based on the golden section (or, alternatively, the golden section derives from the number series, as it can work either way), but also that the Egyptians seem never to have built a temple *without* using it! Those who doubt me can turn directly to Badawy's book for the evidence that he compiled over many years of painstaking research in the field. It takes a long time to visit fifty monuments and measure them in detail, and he could do this only because he was an Egyptian, not just a visiting archaeologist from elsewhere.

I have not made a study of the possible use of the Fibonacci series at Giza. It was exhausting enough discovering all the golden angles and re-creating the forgotten design plan. I leave the Fibonacci aspects to others. I do not have enough time to spend weeks or months at Giza measuring everything the way Badawy did, nor would I be given permission to do so anyway under the present archaeological regime there.

In *Egyptian Dawn,* I carry the geometrical analysis of the Giza Plateau farther. In this book, I have attempted to restrict myself to aspects that have direct relevance to the Sphinx. In the next chapter, we take a "golden flight" into the realms of Egyptian mythology in order to try and group what all this obsession with golden angles was really about. The ancient Egyptians weren't just a lot of idle nerds doing all of this for fun. To them, it was a matter of life and death.

8

THE GOLDEN ANGLE OF RESURRECTION

I explained at great length in *The Crystal Sun* that the brilliant Norwegian architectural historian Else Kielland (niece of the famous Norwegian painter Kitty Kielland) had proved conclusively in her book *Geometry in Egyptian Art*[1] that the golden section was mandated for use in every sacred building and every royal work of art throughout the whole of Egyptian history, even from as early as the First Dynasty. I cannot repeat that discussion here. However, I give one of many examples from her book of her minute analysis even of small royal objects, such as the painted casket from the tomb of Tutankhamun showing the king as a warrior in a chariot. My photo of this casket is in figure 8.1, and in figure 8.2 is a reproduction of Else Kielland's geometrical analysis of its design on the basis of multiple golden sections.

Golden angles, golden sections, golden triangles, and the Fibonacci series of numbers generated from the golden section permeated Egyptian culture for millennia and were a full-fledged priestly obsession for all those thousands of years.

So why did they have to use them all the time? Fine, we know that they *knew about* them, but why the compulsion always to use them?

This is where we enter the ancient Egyptian mind. There was no word for "religion" in the ancient Egyptian language, and also no word for "belief." They did not approach things the way we do at all. They did not have a sacred book in their hand and read from some text that told them how to think. They were not "people of the Book," which is how Christians, Muslims, and Jews are often described. Anyone wishing to understand the ancient Egyptian mentality needs to get as far away as possible from the mind-sets of Christianity, Islam, and Judaism.

Figure 8.1. This decorated chest was found in the tomb of Tutankhamun and is on view in the Egyptian Museum in Cairo. It shows the young Tutankhamun charging in his battle chariot and firing arrows at foes, which it is doubtful that he ever did. Such scenes were traditional for New Kingdom pharaohs, to whom smiting the enemy was part of the state pharaonic cult. Every pharaoh was meant to be the greatest and most fearless warrior in the world. Some pharaohs, such as Thutmosis III, really were ferocious warrior-pharaohs, but the teenaged Tutankhamun was certainly not in that category. There are multiple golden sections used in the construction of this dynamic and powerful design. The geometrical analysis of this image is shown in figure 21, which is taken from Else Kielland's brilliant book, *Geometry in Egyptian Art.* It was Kielland more than anyone else who comprehended the religio-philosophical depth and profundity of the golden section/golden angle obsession of the ancient Egyptians, and from whom I came to understand its true significance for the understanding of their culture. (*Photo by Robert Temple*)

The Egyptians were not doctrinaire, and they did not go to war over dogma. They would have thought the religious wars fought over the last two thousand years were insane, which of course they were. It is much easier to understand the Egyptians if you are familiar with Hinduism, Buddhism, or Taoism. Just as the Taoists' main idea is the *tao* (the Way) and the Buddhists' main idea is enlightenment through *buddhi* (the higher intuitive mind, which transcends the dichotomy of rational and irrational), so the Egyptians' main idea was Maāt, or Cosmic Order. The Egyptians wished always to follow Cosmic Order in the same way the Taoists wished to follow the Way. In both cases, the underlying idea was thought to be

Figure 8.2. This is one of a set of five geometrical analyses by Else Kielland of the Tutankhamun chest in figure 8.1. Unfortunately, Kielland's book, which was published in 1955, has extremely poor-quality illustrations, so reproducing them is difficult. She points out that both the vertical line GG', which crosses the king's elbow, and the vertical line HH', which goes through the horse's nostril and defines the front of its chest, divide the horizontal picture in golden section to the left and to the right. A ray shot down from H' at a golden angle strikes the baseline at O and makes a golden triangle. It is from point U on this line that one can draw two circles delineating the horse: the first, touching the bottom line of the strip (AD), contains the essentials of the horse, touching the top of its head and left foot, and the second and larger circle contains the whole of the horse, touching the top line of the strip (BC) and also the golden dividing line, GG'. From the top left corner of the strip, marked B, a ray shot down at a golden angle strikes the base of the picture at L, forming the golden triangle ABL. If you put your compass point on L, you can draw an arc that touches the center of the chariot wheel at Z. In the four analyses that follow in Kielland's book (which we cannot reproduce here), the unraveling of the geometrical basis of the design is completed, and various other golden angles are discovered within it. Kielland points out that all royal and sacred art was designed using rulers and compasses to exploit the golden angles, which determined the nature of a composition. There were usually multiple golden angles employed even in the smallest design, as a kind of golden spider's web, just as we find in the design for the Giza Plateau. It is clear that Egyptian architects, artists, and craftsmen working on the design of sacred or royal art or architecture were all trained to work like this. The purpose was to honor Maāt, Cosmic Order, and to imitate the sacred design of the cosmos, so that what was below would be the same as what was above.

at the basis of the universal structure of everything. But whereas the Taoist Way was fluid and unstructured, the Egyptian Cosmic Order was highly structured and geometrical, so in that sense, the Egyptians and the Taoists were essentially the opposites of one another. Think of the difference between a young fellow in a T-shirt and a man in a dinner jacket: the first is like the Way and the second is like Cosmic Order. The Egyptians were highly formal. They were more interested in dress codes than the most exclusive American country clubs. Nothing casual was allowed. Furthermore, it was all secret. The public was not admitted to the temples for the majority of ceremonies, for the simple reason that there was no "public" in any sense we would recognize today. The only people who were literate were the priests, scribes, and the royal family, and the royal family were all priests and priestesses anyway, as Egypt was a theocratic state. In the whole of Egypt, therefore, "culture" consisted of only a few thousand people at any one time, in addition to a few thousand more trainees and minor priests backing them up, who had some grasp of the lesser aspects of culture and a great deal of reverence. Everybody else living in Egypt consisted of "the people," who had culture imposed on them from the top down. Self-expression in art consisted of little tweaks here and there where an artist might show a bit of individuality in interpreting some rigidly perfect standard work according to a totally strict canon. What any individual thought or felt was considered to be of no consequence when matters of Cosmic Order were involved. No one, not even the pharaoh, was allowed to be an individuated person in the modern sense. Modern people did not exist, because they had not been invented yet.

People generally assume that the Egyptians had a bewildering array of gods. In fact, those gods were not as firmed up as, say, the Hindu gods. Egyptian gods could blend into one another and frequently did so. No god was safe from being co-opted to become part of another god. They were often as interchangeable as football players, but imagine football players exchanging arms and legs and jockstraps as well, and doing it all on the field in the middle of the game!

All those animal heads were symbolic in a more profound sense than we tend to think of symbolism today. Just because Thoth had the head of an ibis in most pictures, we must not assume for a moment that any Egyptian ever imagined that Thoth *really* had an ibis head. In this sense also, the Egyptians differed greatly from modern people. When Christians show pictures of angels with wings, they tend to believe that angels really do have wings. The first angels with wings were the Egyptian goddesses. I reproduce one in figure 8.3 as an example. No Egyptian truly believed that these goddesses really had wings, whereas many Christians truly believe that their angels do. That, then, gives you a feel for the difference in mental attitude.

Nothing could be further from the ancient Egyptian viewpoint. Doctrines varied as you went from city to city and temple to temple. The pharaoh could perform ceremonies in one tradition at one site and could perfectly happily perform different ceremonies in a different tradition at another site shortly afterward. No

Figure 8.3. "An angel with wings" as portrayed by the ancient Egyptians, in this case Nut, goddess of the night sky. Over the past two thousand years, under the influence of doctrinaire "sacred texts," we have lost much of our capacity for symbolic thought and have developed unnatural habits of attempting to impose a ridiculous precision and specification on images that are meant to be merely suggestive. The Egyptians were not so stupid. The tradition of winged figures like this spread to the Greeks and was particularly prevalent among the Etruscans, thus influencing the Romans. It was from these sources that the highly conventionalized "angels" of Christianity derived.

contradiction was seen in this, because the ossification of religious observance into a single form, fanatically adhered to without variation, was unknown at that time. Attitudes requiring monochrome belief are the psychotic perversions of later literal-minded and decadent cultures.

It is necessary to be aware of this when considering the rich mythological lore, involving several apparently coexisting and even interpenetrating deities, which we will find connected with the golden-angle beliefs. At the same time, we must always keep in mind that beneath the fluid surface there was an immovable and invariant certainty: the all-encompassing Cosmic Order, which was the only thing that really mattered.

The Egyptians were very worried by death, more so than some other cultures. (Buddhists don't worry so much because they know they will be reincarnated.) Resurrection was therefore another of the Egyptians' manic fixations: everything revolved around this obsession. The body, which was called the *khāt*, had to be carefully mummified and preserved as an artifact, not because it would be resurrected itself, but because it acted as a focus for two of the spiritual aspects of the dead person that would survive death. If the *khāt* was interfered with, or if it was interred in a foreign land, this would cause serious trouble and destabilization. The "spiritual double" of the person, or his *ka*, survived, but needed to be near the *khāt*. The "spiritual force" of the person, called his *ba*, also had to come back and flit round the *khāt* from time to time. The *khāt* was thus both necessary and unnecessary at the same time, rather like one of those front rooms in an English working-class home that is never used by the occupants but is reserved for visitors who come once or twice a year.

The *ba* was depicted as a human-headed bird to indicate that it was always flying around and was not constrained by place. Gods could have more than one *ba*, but then they would, wouldn't they? The best thing that could happen to a person after death was to get lucky and become an *ākh*, which meant a glorified spirit who survived in what we today might call heaven. Then you were really okay. But, of course, for that to happen to you, you first had to go to the netherworld and be judged and escape countless ambushing demons who wanted to destroy and annihilate you. So it was all very scary. The Egyptians had a far more nightmarish vision of what we call hell than we do. The terrible things that could happen to you there were beyond our modern imaginings. Another preoccupation of the Egyptians was snakes. Snakes were everywhere. Of course, Egypt was and still is infested with cobras and sand vipers, both of which can kill quickly. It is hard to see a sand viper in the desert; you can step on one without noticing, and that is it. As for cobras, they always turn up just when they are not wanted, but they were especially hazardous in crypts and underground passages and hence troublesome to priests. It was natural for the Egyptians to think that if the surface of the earth was infested with snakes, the netherworld must be more so. After being decapitated, the evil dead then had the indignity of snakes crawling all over them in subterranean snakepits, and the snakes also chewed on them, just to add insult to injury.

There were friendly serpents, however, that were guardians in the netherworld. Presumably on the principle that it takes a snake to guard against a snake, friendly snakes were common because they were needed in such numbers. A massive snake called the Enveloper (Mehen) protected the sun god himself as he made his way through the netherworld every night. The Enveloper wrapped him up as tight as cellophane so he would be fresh in the morning. On the other hand, the most evil of all beings was a giant snake, called in Egyptian Apep and in Greek Apophis. He lived mostly in the netherworld, but he was also in the sky. It was his job to want to destroy everything, to wreck the boat of the sun god so that he could not rise in the morning, and to bring the entire cosmos to destruction. He was the ultimate enemy of Cosmic Order, and one had to struggle against him constantly. The equivalent of Apep in modern terms is Satan, or Samael, who is often thought to have serpentine aspects, specifically lower appendages in the form of snakes instead of legs.

There was, however, one genuine "snake with legs" that was plentiful in ancient Egypt, though it is bordering on extinction there now. I am referring to a North African skink, which is actually a lizard (family Scincidae). There are 1,200 types of skink in the world. But in the Menagerie of the Jardin des Plantes in Paris, Olivia and I were fascinated to observe the type that was once plentiful in Egypt. This type of skink looks so like a snake with legs, just as depicted on some of the Egyptian tomb walls, that Olivia suggested it was precisely what was being depicted in the tombs. (See figure 8.6 for an example.) We stood and watched these skinks for some time, and we noticed that they love to burrow in the sand, leaving only the tip of a tail sticking out. Since these skinks are tunneling creatures who burrow under the sand and stay there for long periods, they must have been seen as having a particular relevance to the netherworld and to the passages of the subterranean tombs constructed by the Egyptians. The Egyptians had not perfected the science of zoological classifications, so it is probable that they did not class skinks as lizards but instead as snakes-with-legs. And as such, the creatures would naturally have seemed to have the most special symbolic significance as denizens of the netherworld.

The third type of netherworld snake in Egyptian mythology is the symbolic snake. These were sometimes shown as the uraeus on the pharaoh's brow, or seen standing vertically on the tips of their tails, like ballet dancers en point. The vertical ones are often called Nehep snakes, from the verb meaning to leap up, which was a euphemism for resurrection, since resurrection was always associated in the Egyptian mind with the leaping of the resurrected sun over the horizon every dawn. These Nehep snakes are common in the netherworld depictions. Figure 8.27 shows one in a crypt of Denderah. It was not imagined that Nehep snakes existed any more than unicorns do, but they were very useful to get ideas across. Nehep also means to leap up early (or get up early, as we would say) to adore the rising sun.[2] Strangely, the Nehep serpent seems somehow to have survived as a motif into the Middle Ages, when it was adopted as the crest of a princely Hungarian family named Bethlen (see figure 8.7, a photo Olivia took of this crest carved in stone at their castle in Transylvania).

Now we come to the main mythological motif connected with the golden angles at Giza. Not surprisingly, it was a resurrection motif. Many people are

Figure 8.4. The mummiform Osiris in his netherworld shrine and the Earth god Geb at right and the netherworld god Sokar (Sokaris) at left are all jointly rising at the horizon, while over them is held by two solar *ba*-spirits the stretched-out length of the evil serpent Apophis, enemy of the sun, whose head has just been severed by a knife. By the slaying of Apophis, victory and resurrection have been achieved, as the sun rises, with the dead Osiris shortly to become transformed into the living Horus. This is figure 127 on page 375 of vol. I, Alexandre Piankoff and N. Rambova, *The Tomb of Ramesses VI*, Bollingen Series vol. XL:I (New York: Pantheon Books, 1954), 2 vols.

Figure 8.5. Here we see yet another view of the giant Osiris rising at the horizon from the netherworld. He is emerging from the coils of the evil serpent Apophis (the Coiled One), showing that life and resurrection are again made possible despite the attempt of Apophis to prevent them. (Apophis was the Egyptian equivalent of Satan.) The two upside-down figures are each called "the gory one" and represent the decapitated spirits of the evil dead who are in the process of being annihilated in the netherworld. This is figure 27 on page 130 of vol.I, Alexandre Piankoff and N. Rambova, *The Tomb of Ramesses VI*, Bollingen Series vol. XL, I (New York: Pantheon Books, 1954), 2 vols.

Figure 8.6. The goddess Neith, wearing the red Crown of the North, stands at left, apparently signifying a northern entrance to a secret passage into the netherworld. The descending passage, which is probably meant to represent the entrance to a pyramid, commences directly over her head. A sarcophagus is depicted as sliding down the passage, though it is shown above the passage so as not to suggest a permanent blockage. (The Egyptians often did this kind of wonky depiction, as perspective realism was not the intention in mythological drawings. Lakes, for instance, were always drawn in plan as if looking down on them from above, even though the figures beside them might be shown in profile as if we were standing beside them. Egyptian sacred art was always a many-viewed totality, and what was being portrayed was never shown only from a single observer's perspective point. The psychology was that the observer was not considered important, which is the precise opposite of the modern Western attitude, which regards the observer as all-important.) This wall painting is in the tomb of Rameses III in the Valley of the Kings, and it has apparently never been reproduced or even discussed before. Such paintings, although of New Kingdom date, derive from images found on old papyri that date from many centuries earlier. Many visual and even textual references to Giza (by this time a largely abandoned necropolis) survive in these New Kingdom pictures, owing to the conservatism of the Egyptian priests and despite the fact that they may have ceased to realize their origin and their original significance. Neith is speaking in a friendly fashion to an enormous netherworld serpent with human legs and a human head, who has a goatee and a skullcap. This is not one of the dangerous and evil serpents of the underworld, such as the horrible demon Apep, but a friendly one who takes his name from the Egyptian word *tep,* which means head. He is called Tepi-sau-medjen, which means "he with a head who guards the way." We can call him Tepi for short. Tepi was a particularly helpful chap to have around because, like many of the benign netherworld denizens, he emitted light, which made it easier to see in the dark passages. This painting in the tomb of Rameses III is a scene from *The Book of the Hidden Chamber,* showing the entrance to the netherworld at Rostau (Giza). It is possible that the artists who painted this in the tomb near Thebes had never seen Giza and had not the slightest idea what was being referred to in the images. The passage in this painting has the number three written in it, and the same number appears beneath Tepi's chin. Neith was an extremely ancient Egyptian deity whose importance goes back to predynastic times. She was said to weave the shrouds for the dead and to protect them. (*Photo by Robert Temple*)

Figure 8.7. This is the heraldic crest of the Hungarian princely family of Bethlen. This particular plaque was erected in the seventeenth century by Prince Alexius de Bethlen at his Transylvanian castle at Kreisch (now called Kris in Romanian). The ancient Egyptian Nehep serpent symbolizing resurrection, the serpent standing on its tail and springing into eternal life, has somehow survived here, having been adopted in the Middle Ages as a family symbol by the Bethlens. In this instance the serpent wears a crown and holds in its mouth an orb surmounted by a cross, symbolizing holy power. Probably this motif survived from antiquity through secret organizations such as the Freemasons. The Bethlens recently reclaimed this half-ruined castle from the Romanian government in restitution for its illegal seizure from them in 1947 by the Communist regime. Unfortunately, the vast library of priceless old books that had been accumulated in this castle for centuries was taken out into the courtyard and burned by the fanatical commissars as decadent bourgeois literature, and not a single volume survived. (*Photo by Olivia Temple*)

familiar with the giant woman arching over certain scenes in Egyptian art, named Nut, who was the goddess of the night sky. She had stars along her body. She swallowed the sun into her mouth every night, and he emerged from her vagina every morning (see figure 8.8). The Egyptians were not shy about discussing and depicting the genital organs and did not consider them rude or shameful; they were rather inclined to flaunt them. Concepts of Puritanism were as alien to the ancient Egyptians as air is to the moon.

Few people realize, however, that Nut was not the only giant figure in Egyptian mythological art. In figures 8.9 and 8.16 to 8.19, we see the giant male deity who was depicted only in netherworld scenes. He was Osiris rising as the sun god Re (also sometimes spelled Ra) at the horizon every morning. He had to be huge, because his feet reached all the way down into the very bottom of the

Figure 8.8. Detail of a painting of the goddess Nut, goddess of the night sky, as portrayed in the tomb of Rameses IX in the Valley of the Kings. (*Photo by Robert Temple*)

Figure 8.9. The giant figure of Ra-Osiris rising from the horizon is here "showing his body" as he rises, having burst forth from the restricted space of the netherworld, where the bodies of the blessed dead are found. The text says of them: "These souls pass after him while their bodies remain in the mounds." This is figure 88 on page 328 of vol. I of Alexandre Piankoff and N. Rambova's *The Tomb of Ramesses VI*, Bollingen Series 40:1 (New York: Pantheon Books, 1954), 2 vols.

netherworld, while as he rose above the horizon, his arms touched the sky. The most interesting and informative study of this giant deity is a book written by John Darnell of Yale and published in 2004 with the rather lengthy title of *The Enigmatic Netherworld Books of the Solar-Osirian Unity*.[3] It is a huge book of 640 pages and is not light reading. It has a price nearly as large as the title. The author also occasionally lapses into German (you have to know that *Normalschrift* means noncryptographic, etc.). Much of it is written for specialists, consisting of lengthy analyses of the cryptographic inscriptions in tombs (because he has to justify to his colleagues his choices of translation), and also the inscriptions on the Second Shrine of beaten gold found in the tomb of Tutankhamun. Anyone who really wants to know about these things needs Darnell's book, and a great deal of time. Because it is inadequately indexed, I found myself forced to memorize rather more of it than I wanted to, because there was no way to refer to many things in it otherwise, as I rarely write notes when I do research. I found it necessary to read Darnell's book many times, because the material is so utterly bizarre that you just have to keep reading it until the bewilderment vanishes. It is like getting used to drinking retsina; you just have to keep at it, and then you like it.

I would have thought it more elegant to call the giant deity "Osiris as the Sun," but Darnell wants to call him Re-Osiris, so who am I to disagree? It is less clumsy than "the Solar-Osirian Unity," a name he also uses. The symbolism is very thick here and involves multiple gods all merging, so you need to keep your head. Explaining what is going on can almost read like a cast list at the theater. First, there is Re, and that is the name of the sun in general, and especially of the daytime sun, whereas his other names are of his specific aspects. For instance, when he is rising, Re is also called Khepri (also sometimes spelled Khepera), which is the name of the scarab beetle, or dung beetle. The symbolism of this is that real dung beetles push spherical balls of dung larger than themselves for long distances over the desert floor. So the Egyptians thought it would be appropriate to adopt this as the symbol of the sun being pushed up over the horizon at dawn. No one imagined that there really was a giant dung beetle doing this; it was all symbolic. In speaking of this, one could also call the sun Re-Khepri, which was another way of saying "the rising sun." In the various depictions in figures 8.10, 8.12, 8.17, 8.37, 8.43, and 8.45, there are Khepri beetles beside the solar disk, and this is what they mean. The setting sun was an aspect of Re called Atum, which was the name of the creator god. Hence the sun was often called Khepri-Re-Atum. That may sound like three gods in one, and it is. But let's not get into arguments about the nature of the Holy Trinity.

As if that weren't enough suns, we also have Osiris as the sun and his son Horus as the sun. In addition, we have not just one *ba* of the sun, but several. The main *ba* of the sun was depicted as a man with a ram's head standing in the middle of the solar disk. But the sun could have extra *ba*s when he needed them. As they represented emanations of the solar force, it is understandable that he did not have to be restricted to one. He also had an eye that roamed around, two eyes that did not roam around but simply gazed, and so forth. But there is no need for us to examine all the things the sun could do: for us, his journey at night and his rising are enough.

What concerns us at Giza are specifically the solar connections of Osiris and Horus. In a sense, Osiris was the netherworld aspect of Re, as he was always represented as a mummy who was king of the netherworld, and so in a sense, when he entered the netherworld, the sun became identified with Osiris in a spiritual manner. Gods are such highly advanced beings that they can become one another sometimes without worrying about it. Then they can separate again with no hard feelings. All this could even take place without the need for sex.

One might wonder how and why the sun would want to become spiritually united with a boring, smelly old mummy. To the Egyptians, however, all important mummies could be revivified. Although one's physical body had to stay behind, the *ba* of one's mummy could be awakened, could fly forth and follow the sun as a member of the divine entourage. In this sense, the Egyptians claimed in their mythological writings that the "deserving dead" were revived and brought back to life by streams of solar light shooting at their foreheads or into their mouths. The sun "spoke light" (in the tomb of Rameses VI we find the statement about the sun that "his speech is light"),[4] and the sun's "word" (an idea that the later Greeks borrowed in their concept of the *Logos*, "the Word," which also passed into Christianity through Egyptian Gnosticism and Neoplatonism) brought resurrection to the dead. See figures 8.38 to 8.41.

So a parallel myth to that of Khepri-Re was the myth of Re-Osiris, and in a sense they were the same, so much so that Khepri was always shown preceding Re-Osiris in the netherworld drawings. We have to keep in mind that gods were not exclusive as far as the Egyptians were concerned, and were not necessarily real either. It would be more correct to say that Khepri was a motive force than that he was any kind of actual god. Khepri was not offended at being relegated to the status of a visual aid, because he did not exist anyway. He was only a pretty picture (if you like beetles).

That leaves us with Re-Osiris. What was he/were they? Here the symbolism gets really thick. The concept of the golden angle becomes part of the symbolism too, although that has not been recognized before. It will become clear to us that the golden angle was viewed by the Egyptians as symbolizing resurrection, and that it represented the transformation of the dead Osiris into his living son Horus in the person of the rising sun. Once we understand that, we can begin to comprehend why Giza was a mass of golden angles. As the ultimate necropolis of the Egyptians, it was important that it be magically replete with the power of resurrection conferred on it by having an invisible pattern on the sand of the resurrection angle endlessly repeated, like a mystical chant that never ends. And the Sphinx was fundamental to this, for as the guardian and watchdog of the necropolis, protecting entry to this magical land of the West, Anubis faced due east and every morning viewed the recurrence of the miraculous phenomenon that the Egyptians called Horus-in-the-Horizon. The most important occasions were, of course, the spring equinox and the autumn equinox, for on those days, the sun rose precisely at the center of the horizon and looked the Sphinx directly in the eyes (both when he was Anubis and when he later became Amenemhet II, for both of them have two eyes, whatever else they may not have in common).

What *was* Horus-in-the-Horizon? It sounds impressive, but was it anything but words? The Egyptian priests were eminently practical people, and they worked out a very precise mythological symbolism and explanation that tied together many of their preconceptions and expressed everything. To understand it, one has to understand their magico-symbolic mode of thought. Just as they might intone prayers every morning to a beetle in the sky without believing there really was a beetle in the sky, they envisaged this giant being standing in the horizon with his feet in hell and his head in heaven and called him Re-Osiris, or Khepri-Re-Atum, or whatever you like. They were not literal-minded. Today, in a culture stripped bare of all magic and symbolism other than that which represents money (a yacht is now a symbol, and so is a Rolex watch), it is difficult for us to imagine how Egyptian priests thought. They did not want to get rich, because there was nothing they could buy. But they did want to live forever. So their priorities were different from ours. They were also fearful that if they became evil, they would not survive, because they were convinced that the evil dead met with the most horrible of fates, culminating in annihilation. They were careful to preserve their purity by washing themselves fastidiously every morning, observing endless ceremonies, washing their statues daily, singing hymns, and generally being good boys. They were always up before dawn because it was a necessary act of politeness and respect for them to welcome the sun's return. They were like butlers greeting the master when he returns home. They avoided various foods that might be taboo, such as certain fish. And among the other things they pursued with the same manic obsession was sacred geometry. It had to be embodied in everything that was sacred. Otherwise, the magic might be lost, a terrible sacrilege might be committed, and Cosmic Order might be defied, which would bring retribution. "Just to be on the safe side," they might say, "we had better add a few more golden angles." So there could never be too many. And Giza is the proof of that mentality.

Now we come to the rising sun as expressed in both mythology and geometry at the same time. If we look at and figures 8.11 to 8.13, which show the same scene, we see one of the most famous of the "leaning pharaohs" in Egyptian art. This is a picture of the deceased pharaoh Rameses IX, who has "become Osiris." All pharaohs when they died "become Osiris" simply by the process of mummification. It was what all the ancient texts said: "He has become Osiris." But since *every* pharaoh was an Osiris, there were rather a lot of Osirises, and it is only in the mode of symbolic thought that you can avoid the clutter of having a lot of look-alikes wandering around the netherworld all claiming to be the same god and getting into fights with one another. Once again, we must realize that the Egyptians did not *really* believe that each pharaoh "[became] Osiris"; what they believed was that each pharaoh became *an* Osiris. This was a symbolic expression. Christians who take communion and eat the bread and drink the wine "partake of Christ" and become one with him. Or at least, that is how they express it. Christians do not take "being one with Christ" literally in the sense that they have *become* Christ; they mean it symbolically and also in the sense of *mystical participation*. Being "one with Christ" is a bit like falling in love: you remain yourself, but you "become one" with the beloved. Similarly, the dead pharaoh "become[s] one with Osiris." I hope that explains it sufficiently.

Now to return to Rameses IX, who has become *an* Osiris. There he is, raising his arms and stretching himself out at a peculiar angle. This drawing occurs on what is called the Enigmatic Wall in his tomb in the Valley of the Kings, on the right as you go down. The entire wall contains strange drawings relating to the netherworld and texts that are written in cryptography. Anyone who was above the rank of junior priest could read cryptographic hieroglyphics, and it may be that the chief reason for using them was to conceal the true meaning of the inscriptions from the tomb painters, who had not been initiated and were not worthy to read what they were painting. In Egyptian cryptography, every sign means something other than what it normally means. Not all cryptography has been deciphered by modern scholars (and there are a few instances of a super-cryptography that cannot be cracked), and they are still arguing about it. However, in most cases, the texts can be read with tolerable reliability. Naturally, the number of people in the world who can actually do this today is remarkably small. You don't get your yachts and Rolexes that way, although in a just and philosophical world, the tycoons would have to hand over their yachts and Rolexes to the people who can read ancient texts, which is more difficult than making money.

The angular pharaoh Rameses IX is a drawing I have already reproduced and discussed in *The Crystal Sun*. But at that time, I carried the discussion only so far. I explained that he was at the golden angle. But now we have to consider what it means for a pharaoh to be at a golden angle, for that is fundamental to an understanding of Giza. This will also bring us to the strange subject of Christ on the cross.

The golden angle occurs at the top of the triangle formed by the leaning pharaoh. The vertical line is in this case the base of a triangle and the pharaoh is the hypotenuse. (A hypotenuse is a right-angled triangle's longest side, which is opposite the right angle.) That is why I call such figures, of which there are many in Egyptian tomb paintings and papyri, "hypotenusal pharaohs" or "hypotenusal

Osirises." Such figures are always hypotenuses of triangles (and if drawn correctly, of golden triangles), even if the other lines are not drawn. In this case, however, the other lines are very clearly drawn. And in the drawing of Rameses IX, just to emphasize the true meaning, the other two sides of the golden triangle are inhabited also by a friendly Nehep (sometimes called Neheher) snake, who, as I explained earlier, symbolizes resurrection. This pharaoh, like all hypotenusal pharaohs, is in the process of being resurrected. If you ever die and want to come back to life, it is very easy. All you have to do is become a hypotenuse.

Another feature of Rameses as a hypotenuse is that he is what is called ithyphallic, that is, he had an erect phallus. It has been largely rubbed out by prudish Victorians, or Copts, or Muslims, or whatever. Many of the phalluses have been hacked off the images in Egyptian temples and tombs because of the hypocrisy of most human societies, which prefer to ignore the existence of the genitals in public while overindulging them in private. So today's computer hackers were once preceded by avid penis hackers.

The Egyptians were very happy incorporating penises and vaginas into their sacred art. They would not have draped a loincloth over the crucified Christ. People of high symbolic rank are often assumed to have transcended the material requirements of ordinary life and not to have genitals, for instance. But as I have already said, the Egyptians were immensely practical. Perhaps they did not need to disguise physical details because they already had enough symbols as it was, without transforming the body into one by stripping it of its genitals.

The obvious procreative power of the erect phallus was a symbol to the Egyptians not only of fecundity, but also of creation itself, and, consequently, of resurrection. If you are a dead pharaoh and you are turning into a hypotenuse, it is only natural that you should get so excited that you have an erection.

Rameses IX was a rather late pharaoh, as the New Kingdom in Egypt was drawing to its close. So his artists got it a bit wrong. They knew he had to be portrayed as a hypotenuse, and that the golden angle must be used, but they put the golden angle at his hands, whereas it is really meant to be at his feet. They had lost the plot by this late period. As we see in our other illustrations, the whole point is that the golden angle generates the image, and it occurs at the feet. As time went on and the traditions were grasped less adequately, many of the priests became alarmed. There is a pathetic hieroglyphic inscription from Roman times, when things really were coming to an end finally and completely, where a priest says in his funerary testament, in desperation: "Set your hearts on what is therein [the texts of the stele]; do not forget the text collection; make copies of it; adhere perfectly to the text."[5]

Darnell quotes this sad example of what happens when things fall apart and the young priests don't listen any more. However, even though things were a

Figure 8.10. A highly aroused hypotenusal Osiris depicted on the Papyrus of Heruben B. We see here the deceased Osiris as a hypotenuse, and directly over his erect phallus we see the beetle Khepri and the globe of the sun, indicating the rising sun, which rises and is reborn from the power of Osiris's fecundity, which is his power of resurrection. A protective Mehen serpent (the Enveloper) constitutes the base and altitude of this triangle, which is crudely drawn. The triangle itself is filled with sand, suggesting the sandy region of the netherworld, which is a reference to Giza. The coded reference of the triangle being on the sand is a way of indicating the many golden triangles "on the sand" that constitute the Giza Golden Plan, though whether this was still consciously understood by the time this papyrus was painted just after the time of the New Kingdom is doubtful. The Papyrus of Heruben B, in the Egyptian Museum in Cairo, is the second of two papyri that once belonged to the Chantress of Amon-Re, Heruben (Resplendent Sky), granddaughter of King Menkheperre of the Twenty-first Dynasty (tenth century BC). A line joining the tip of the penis with the tip of the nose makes a golden angle with the horizontal, as does a line joining the tip of the toe with the bend in the serpent's neck, which is the top of the triangle's altitude. This is a detail from plate 2, a folding plate in volume 2 of *Mythological Papyri: Egyptian Texts and Representations* by Alexandre Piankoff and N. Rambova, Bollingen Series XL:3 (New York: Pantheon Books, 1957).

bit wonky in the design, the picture in the tomb of Rameses IX is very striking. Notice that the beetle Khepri is practically crawling up the pharaoh's nose. This is to remind us that we are talking about the rising sun here, just in case anybody was inclined to forget. Unfortunately, this magnificent image is now behind glass with some rails in the way as well, so a decent photograph has now become impossible. I reproduce my photo through the glass in figure 8.11, which is inadequate, but one cannot really do much better than that nowadays. At the same time, I reproduce an old black-and-white photo from earlier and happier days as figure 8.12.

Because the drawings beside Rameses IX as a hypotenusal pharaoh are so bizarre, I feel that I must take a moment to explain them; otherwise, everyone will be frustrated. I must also repeat what the texts that accompany the pictures say. The cryptographic inscription that goes with the hypotenusal pharaoh states: "This god [Osiris, or Rameses IX as Osiris] is in this fashion: his arm in the height, his feet in the place of destruction."[6]

Figure 8.11. A photo of the hypotenusal pharaoh in the tomb of King Rameses IX. His erect phallus has been chipped away. The image is now behind glass and impossible to photograph properly. (*Photo by Robert Temple*)

Bottom: Figure 8.12. A hypotenusal pharaoh, in this instance, Pharaoh Rameses IX, as portrayed in his tomb in the Valley of the Kings, on the right of the descending passage as you go down. (The painting is now behind glass and partially obscured, so adequate photography is no longer possible.) The mummified pharaoh, who has "become a Horus," forms the hypotenuse (called Horus by the Egyptians, according to Plutarch) of a golden triangle. The golden angle is formed by the vertical and a line that runs from his hand to the back of the pharaoh's heel. In figure 8.37 is another hypotenusal pharaoh preserved in a papyrus, where the golden angle goes the other way, with no arms outstretched and running from his heel to the center of his head. Since the "pharaoh as a Horus," that is, the pharaoh as a hypotenuse, is purely symbolic, it doesn't matter whether the golden angle runs down from his head or up from his feet.

It is a standard formula in all these types of inscriptions to begin by saying "This god/these gods is/are in this fashion . . ." Here, because the text from a papyrus has been correctly copied by the scribes, the description is accurate. Even though the golden angle has been put at the wrong end of the figure, the textual description has the feet in the right place and the arms in the right place. By "the place of destruction" is meant the lowest depths of hell where the evil dead are annihilated, also known as the Place of Annihilation. As Darnell has probably been the first person to observe since antiquity, the Place of Annihilation or Place of Destruction was conceived of as being far below the eastern horizon. (This was necessitated by the fact that Re-Osiris had to have his feet there when he was rising.) And as you may be guessing by now, the hypotenusal pharaoh was meant to be identified with the giant Re-Osiris at the eastern horizon as the sun rises. So, although he was often depicted as a giant standing at the horizon with his feet in the depths of hell, doubtless squashing a lot of the evil dead in the process, the rising Re-Osiris was also represented as a hypotenusal Osiris, or, as Darnell likes to call it, an Osiride figure. In fact, Darnell calls the hypotenusal Rameses IX an Osiride figure, which indeed he is. One way to understand what the scholars are saying is to figure out the terms they use, so one knows what they are referring to. Half the difficulty with scholarly books is that confusing terminology is used, so that ordinary people get lost and cannot follow the argument. As for Egyptological books, they are as incomprehensible to ordinary readers as books on the calculus, due to the fact that they are full of linguistic symbols that spell out the Egyptian words without vowels. These symbols achieve precision and impress fellow scholars, but they exclude readers who are not also Egyptologists, unless they are prepared to learn these symbols. By definition, therefore, Egyptologists are only writing for each other. Since the views of the public do not matter to them, as they are generally interested only in their professional and academic lives, positions, and reputations, they don't care. Thus it is that the public is rarely kept informed, unless an Egyptologist deigns to write a popular book now and then. I have made a point of never using any of those symbols in this book, and sometimes when quoting I have transcribed them into comprehensible familiar letters for the benefit of the reader.

The entire base of the Enigmatic Wall of Rameses IX consists of a row of bound enemies kneeling, with their arms tied behind their backs like prisoners taken in battle. These represent the defeated evil dead, "alluding to the time of the final victory of the sun at the end of the night as the time of the flaming destruction of the damned," as Darnell colorfully expresses it.[7]

The top row of drawings on the Enigmatic row consists of eight circles. The first four are yellow and the second four are red (this cannot be seen in the black-and-white figure 8.13, and there is no color image of the full Enigmatic Wall).

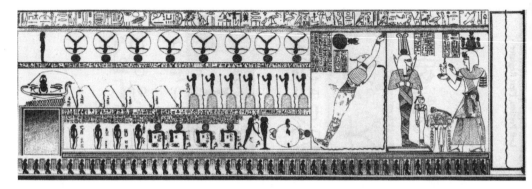

Figure 8.13. This is a drawing of the entire Enigmatic Wall found in the tomb of King Rameses IX in the Valley of the Kings, on the right as you descend into the tomb. The hypotenusal pharaoh in the right third of the wall design is the same as seen in figures 8.11 and 8.12. This image of the whole wall comes from an article by Felix Guilmant, "La Tombeau de Rameses IX" ("The Tomb of Rameses IX"), in *Mémoires de l'Institut Français d'Archéologie Orientale*, Cairo, Volume 15, 1907, p. 63. It is not necessary to comment here on the iconography and importance of this Enigmatic Wall, as the design of the wall and the significance of its elements are analysed in extensive detail in several pages of the main text, commencing on page 400.

They all contain inverted figures of men with their arms and legs spread wide. Solar or stellar disks rest beneath each, indicating their attributes. Darnell believes that the circles represent sources of light, but although the discs containing the men are made of light, they are not emitting light, thus giving the inverted figures a "clothing effect of light," for he says: "Light travels around and hides these figures."[8] Darnell says these plummeting beings are falling stars, "lords of the Netherworld" (*nebu Duat*), "stellar Blessed Dead." (There may also be an implied reference to meteorites, the sacred aspect of which to the Egyptians I discussed at very great length in *The Crystal Sun*. The iron that fell from heaven, often magnetic lodestone, was carefully gathered from the sands of the desert, where it can easily be seen as black stones on the yellow sand, and used for sacred purposes that I have described.) The reason why they are upside down is that everybody who enters the netherworld does so upside down. Part of the struggle in the netherworld is to turn yourself right way up and not remain inverted. The evil dead remain upside down and then have their heads permanently cut off as well. (I say "permanently cut off" because the "justified dead" had their heads handed back to them after their judgment in the netherworld, and the heads were stitched back on for them by Anubis! How many people have dogs like that, who are good with needle and thread?)

One of the strange features of the Great Pyramid is that the Subterranean Chamber beneath it has a smooth ceiling resembling a floor, but the actual floor itself is rough and bumpy and difficult to walk on without twisting an ankle. If the

Figure 8.14. According to ancient Egyptian theology, the dead enter the Other World upside down, as mirror images of themselves on earth. They therefore walk on the ceiling. This photo shows the bizarre Subterranean Chamber beneath the Great Pyramid. No one has ever understood why it has a smooth and flat ceiling, meticulously cut out of the bedrock to be level, but a rough and lumpy floor. The reason is presumably because it represented the netherworld, and the dead entered it upside down, walking on the flat ceiling, and the floor did not matter. We should always remember that the dead also walk on the ceilings of descending passages in Egyptian pyramids and tombs, and we should be alert to signs and indications above our heads, not below our heads, in such passages. (An example is the "black door" in the ceiling of the Descending Passage of the Great Pyramid, seen in figures 7.12 and 7.13 on page 341, which, although obscured originally to the human eye by a limestone slab, would not have been invisible to the dead, who can see through matter. A "black door" of basalt was, I believe, often meant to be a secret sign for the dead. Figure 7.15 on page 351 is a photo of an odd basalt stone in the Valley Temple, for instance, which certainly has mysterious significance of some kind and is definitely not accidental.) This photo was taken in 1909 and shows John Edgar in the center of the photo. Crouching above him is his Egyptian assistant, Judah. All the loose rubble we see here has since been removed, but the floor today remains as lumpy and rough as ever. (This photo is Plate LIII on page 148 of John and Morton Edgar's book, *The Great Pyramid Passages and Chambers*, Glasgow, 1910.)

Subterranean Chamber is taken as representing the netherworld, then of course it would have a smooth ceiling resembling a floor, because the dead are upside down and have to walk on the ceiling.

Beneath the plummeting stellar beings is, first of all at far left, the sun god as

Khepri in his boat, with one of the Eyes of Re on either side of the beetle. He is sailing through the netherworld, with difficulty, trying to avoid getting grounded on the back of the evil satanic serpent Apep, who is shown writhing in his coils beneath the boat. The cryptographic text says: "In this manner does this god travel in his boat, having navigated upon the back of Apep. As soon as he passes by, they loose their arrows. While casting this fire, those on their mounds leap up to (or 'for') him. Those armed with their arrows burn up the enemies of Re, even when he passes by them."

Just to the right of the solar boat, arrows may be seen making golden angles with standing serpents. Darnell thinks these arrows are being fired at the serpents to kill them, but a closer examination of the picture reveals that except for the first, the feathered ends of the arrows are beside the serpents, and the tips are pointing away from them, with dotted lines showing their trajectories from the tail of one to the head of another. These arrows are meant to represent flaming light rays that "cast fire" and "burn up the enemies of Re," but the exact interpretation of the scene is elusive. In Egyptian mythology, however, it was not necessary to have a bow to fire an arrow. Certain netherworld messengers were reputed to shoot fiery arrows directly from their mouths.[9] To their right are seven slaughtering places where evil serpents, enemies of Re, are destroyed. These are slaughtering places represented as mounds of sand. As the text continues: "In this fashion do they exist: the Nehaher snakes which are slaughtered, he making a pause at their slaughtering pit of sand; 'He who hides the mystery, who praises the members which are in it (the *shetau*).'"[10]

Sometimes Nehaher serpents are friendly, but in this text, they are enemies of Re, and Apep himself is called Nehaher. The erect serpents in front of the mounds of sand, on which female executioners stand, have arrows of flaming light penetrating their heads and killing them. These executioners, who are not shown actually firing arrows, are in a posture of adoring the sun while they carry out their job; they are all called *petekhi,* which means "those who lay low the enemy."[11] Although they appear feminine, Darnell believes they are essentially androgynous. Each mound is called an *iat* mound, and is a *shetat* (mysterious place).[12] (The Shetayet is the portion of the netherworld through which the sun moves at night, and is described as mysterious. The name is related to the Egyptian adjective *sheta,* which means hidden.) Two of the arrows flying at the serpents have actually been fired from the solar boat. Darnell points out that in Egyptian, the verb *seti* has two meanings, casting light and firing arrows, and he gives an example from *The Book of the Dead* where a conscious pun on this double meaning occurs.[13] Therefore the firing of arrows in the drawings, either by the sun or on behalf of the sun, really means the shooting of flaming light rays, and the arrows are symbolic of that.

There is a further inscription about this register of the drawing, which says: "In this fashion are they in the Place of Destruction: This god [*the sun*] calls out to them, that they should be high [*leap up*] for him, they being endowed with their *kheperu* [*beetlelike*] manifestations. When this god goes to rest, his disk is in this cavern, and his birth occurs therein. After this great god passes by these goddesses, they stand up; then the complete darkness covers them."[14]

In the third horizontal register, below the serpents and arrows, we have at left what appears to be an empty hidden chamber. Ancient temples tended to have such chambers.

To the right of the hidden chamber, there are four standing goddesses enveloped by protective serpents. Their names are given as "Mother," "she relating to the sarcophagus," "she relating to the Temem Shrine," and "Milk." Each serpent is of a different type, with a different name as well. Farther to the right are four bending figures bearing solar disks on their chests, who are named "The protective one," "(no name given)," "The naked one," and "The pleased one." A text describes this group as follows: "Oh these you four gods who are over these two sides of the sky."[15] Darnell points out that they are hermaphrodites, because although they have names written in the feminine form (and also long hair), they also have phalluses and are ejaculating. In front of each of these bending figures sits a small child, all having the same name: He of the flame. These children represent youthful forms of the rising sun, according to Darnell. And he describes these figures thus: "Each bending, ejaculating figure with a flaming (?) child before it . . . the name of the solar child . . . [could be translated as] the newborn sun."[16] He adds, "The child, the flame, and punishment are all in keeping with a representation of [re-creation] and the eastern horizon, where the sun is reborn, and the damned received their ultimate fiery punishment. The androgynous, bending figures both ejaculate and spit, dots of flame issuing from their mouths and pudenda. These spewing effluvia are a pictorial pun on the verbs *nekh* and *nekhekh*, 'spit' and 'ejaculate' and depict the spitting and ejaculation at creation."[17] (The creator god, when he created the universe from his seed, did so not only by spewing his seed from his erect phallus by means of masturbation, but also by "spitting." "Spitting" was an Egyptian punning euphemism for ejaculating.)

Darnell continues his evocative description:

The spittle of the figures pours down to the left of the figures' heads; in three of the four groups it strikes the ground just to the left of the heads of the scarabs that lie horizontally beneath the bent backs of the figures. In the second group to the left, however, the spittle bends in towards the head of the scarab, an indication that the scarab results from the spittle of the bending figure. In each group the dots of ejaculate flow down to the top of the child's head, an indication that the child results from the semen of the bending figures. . . . The *kheperu*-form of the sun is spat out, and the *mesut*-form is ejaculated. The fiery effluvia of the entities bring forth the sun, and the ejaculate suggests the overflow of Nun [the cosmic ocean], in which the sun is born.[18]

Next, beyond the bending figures, we have a bearded figure leaning forward at a golden angle and presumably being a miniature version of the hypotenusal Osiride pharaoh, though this time facing inward rather than outward. He is holding an upright serpent, who is labeled a Nāu serpent. This is a sacred snake, representing the primeval creative forces, who can lead the dead up to heaven by bringing about a repetition of creation, according to Darnell.[19] Emerging from the head or mouth of the Nāu serpent is a Khepri beetle, symbolizing the birth of the sun. Beneath the Nāu serpent is another flaming child representing the rising sun. Darnell believes that the two sets of four entities in this register refer to the four cardinal points and the four winds, which combine to enable Re to sail in a fair wind toward his rising.[20] Darnell makes no comment regarding the two-faced standing entity who comes next and seems to be female on the left and male on the right. Perhaps this figure is meant to suggest the rising and setting of the sun, or just someone who cannot make up his or her mind. The final drawing in this register is a large solar disk preceded and followed by a Khepri beetle, indicating the solar rising. Inside the disk is a woman. Darnell says of this: "The woman within the disk is the eye of Re, here as mother and daughter; the scarabs emerge from the disk-womb on each side."[21]

Then follows the scene of the hypotenusal pharaoh as Osiris, which we have already considered. The next scene is of the pharaoh in his cultic role of solar priest making offerings to the god Ptah and the goddess Maāt (Cosmic Order), who is shown smaller than Ptah because she was a principle rather than a personality; as this was always understood by everyone, large statues of her never existed, and she was always portrayed as a pervasive but quiet and unobvious presence, sometimes symbolized only by a feather. Ptah is described in this scene as "Ptah, lord of right order, king of the Two Lands, Perfect of face, Who created crafts, One presiding over the great place at rest."[22] This makes it clear that Ptah was the enforcer of the principle of Maāt, and that upholding Cosmic Order was his main job. A very fine image of him can be seen in figure 8.15, which is a photo I took of a magnificent gold statue of Ptah seen in profile.

The final portion of the Engimatic Wall is the vertical panel at the far right showing a resurrection serpent rearing up so high that its head escapes the upper border of the wall decoration entirely, indicating that the dead Osiris has indeed risen and burst through the boundaries of the netherworld.

Figure 8.15. A magnificent small statue of the god Ptah in gold, with a lapis lazuli cap. He is holding a *uas* scepter, which was a sacred scepter used for measuring the calendar and spatial directions (described at length in *The Crystal Sun*). Ptah was the chief god of Memphis, the Old Kingdom capital near Giza. He was merged with the netherworld god Sokar of Giza, and later also with Osiris, to form a trinity known as Ptah-Sokar-Osiris, perhaps the first three-in-one godhead in history. Ptah, however, was always the senior partner of this trinity and was recognized as one of the candidates for creator of the universe. Thoth, god of wisdom and learning, was his son. Ptah had the reputation for being the all-wise intellectual among the gods. There wasn't anything he didn't know or couldn't figure out if he put his mind to it. During the Fifth and Sixth Dynasties, Ptah was unpopular with the pharaohs, and his name was shockingly excluded from the sacred Pyramid Texts inscribed in the pyramids of Saqqara in that period. This is bizarre, considering that his chief temple was just down the road, within walking distance. This hints at some political-religious conflict at the end of the Fourth Dynasty of which we know nothing, due to our lack of historical texts. This statue is in the Egyptian Museum at Cairo. (*Photo by Robert Temple*)

The Enigmatic Wall contains what appear to be no fewer than six golden angles displayed in its figures: four arrows and two hypotenusal mummies. It has been difficult to measure the smaller ones precisely, but they appear to suggest golden angles, whether or not they are exact. In this, a convention appears to have been followed without the artists necessarily appreciating what they were doing, as is indicated by the large Osiris having his golden angle at the top instead of at the bottom.

I hope it was worthwhile giving a full summary of the Enigmatic Wall, so that everyone can appreciate the mythological milieu we are moving in now. The main feature of importance is the large slanting Osiris, who is merely the giant Re-Osiris shown in his hypotenusal form, which manifests the golden angle of resurrection. If we consider the giant Re-Osiris in more detail, we find that he is depicted and described in texts in numerous places. One of the finest pictures of the giant-in-the-horizon is on the beaten gold Second Shrine from the tomb of Tutankhamun, which we see in figures 8.16 to 8.19. I have put descriptions of those scenes in the captions.

The rising of the sun was viewed as a resurrection, and this had direct relevance to every Egyptian, because it was considered a model for his or her own hope of personal resurrection. As Hemingway would have said, *The Sun Also Rises,* although his title was a quotation from the poet John Donne.

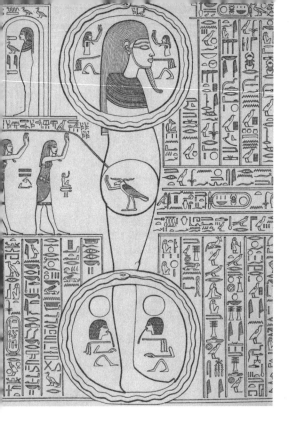

Figure 8.16. This is the giant solar Osiris of the eastern horizon seen in figures 8.17 to 8.19, depicted in beaten gold on the Second Shrine of Tutankhamun. The large encircling serpent swallowing its own tail (called in Greek a *uroboros*) is here called Mehen, which in Egyptian means the Enveloper. The Mehen serpents in general were friendly, protective serpents of the netherworld who wrapped themselves around Osiris and royal mummies to keep them safe. This drawing is taken as a detail from Alexandre Piankoff, *The Shrines of Tut-Ankh-Amon,* Pantheon, New York, 1955, figure 41, opposite page 120.

Below: Figure 8.17. The head of the giant solar Osiris of the eastern horizon, the full figure of which may be seen in figure 8.16. The figure is in beaten gold on the Second Shrine of Tutankhamun at the Egyptian Museum in Cairo. (*Photo by Robert Temple*)

Figure 8.18. This is the middle of the giant solar Osiris of the eastern horizon shown entire in figure 8.16. It is of beaten gold, from the Second Shrine of Tutankhamun. The solar disk fills the belly of the Osiris mummy in the netherworld, and in the center is seen the solar *ba*-bird, representing the spiritual force of the sun, who is about to emerge and be resurrected. The figure to the left is worshipping him as light streams from the solar disk toward him. (*Photo by Robert Temple*)

Figure 8.19. This is the bottom of the image of the giant figure of the solar Osiris shown entire in figure 8.16. The image is in beaten gold on the Second Shrine of Tutankhamun. His feet are in *herit*, the Place of Destruction at the bottom of the netherworld, where the evil dead meet their doom after indescribable agonies. (*Photo by Robert Temple*)

The way in which the sun rises, especially at Giza, was thought of as *at the golden angle*. The sun as an Osiris came alive, transformed himself into a Horus, and did so as a hypotenuse of a triangle formed by the beams of light as they streamed over the horizon. The surface of the Earth was, quite naturally, the base of the triangle. The Egyptian name of the base of a sacred triangle was, as Plutarch informs us, Isis. The altitude was called Osiris. The hypotenuse was called Horus.[23] Although Plutarch is speaking here of the Pythagorean triangle, it is likely that the same terms were used when speaking of any right-angled triangle that had a religious significance. That Osiris was the vertical altitude of the triangle may be associated also with his upright phallus. It is only natural that the joining or "mating" of Isis and Osiris within the triangle would give birth to a hypotenuse: their son, Horus. In fact, Plutarch specifically calls the hypotenuse "their offspring."

In the Pythagorean triangle, where the square of the hypotenuse is equal to the squares of the other two sides (and the Egyptians and Greeks really drew squares on them, and did not merely write algebraic symbols as we do; see the Byrne title page, figure 7.26), it was justified then to speak of the hypotenuse (Horus) as the "resultant" or "child" of the other two sides. In the passage of Plutarch where he gives these names, Plutarch uses the Greek word *apotelesma* to describe Horus as a hypotenuse, which means final completion, event, result. In the three translations that exist in English, Griffiths translates it as "the perfected achievement," Babbitt translates it as "perfected result," and King translates it as "the result."[24] Babbitt and King also call Horus as a hypotenuse the "child" of Isis and Osiris as base and altitude, respectively, and Griffiths uses the expression "offspring."[25] It was considered that the "powers" (i.e., the squares) of Isis and Osiris when combined gave the "power" (i.e., square) of Horus. This is a remarkable mythological expression of a geometrical fact, but it is typical of the way the Egyptian priests thought. Although the golden triangle is not a Pythagorean triangle—in that the sums of the squares of the base and altitude do not equal the square of the hypotenuse—we may assume that the underlying principle of the Pythagorean triangle was a resonant presence in their minds, like the bass accompaniment in music, and that when they spoke of the hypotenuse of the golden triangle formed at the rising of Osiris as a Horus, they still thought of him as the child of Osiris. But in this case, he was more than just the child; he was the resurrected Osiris himself. This concept is illustrated in a drawing from the tomb of Rameses VI in figure 8.9, showing Horus arising from the body of Osiris at dawn, which was the great transfiguration of the sun and by extension of all the blessed dead. From the mummy of Osiris, the child Horus emerged, and this was the essence of resurrection. This was Horus-in-the-Horizon.

The "word" of the rising sun, expressed as light rays, streamed through the air

Figure 8.20. This is a drawing taken from the wall of the Sarcophagus Hall of the tomb of King Rameses VI in the Valley of the Kings near Luxor. Here we see a very explicit resurrection scene where Horus, "the Son of his Father," rises at dawn as the sun (the solar disk is beside his head to make this clear, and the fact that he is still rising and emerging is shown by the fact that he does not yet stand clear) and becomes Horus-in-the-Horizon. He is emerging from the mummified Osiris, who is in his golden-angled form, though here Osiris is actually shown in a *double* golden-angled form, with both his upper body and his legs being hypotenusal. The women standing to either side are the sisters Isis and Nephthys, who guard the sacred egg that contains the scene taking place at the horizon. The ultimate location for this sacred event was at Giza, precisely at Rostau, in front of the Sphinx, from where the resurrected Horus shone as rays of light (the "speech," or *logos*, of the sun) directly upward at the golden angle to strike the gleaming golden tip of the Pyramid of Chephren and give the dawn flash (see text). The wall text says: "This Great God [Osiris] is like this in his egg which is in the Netherworld. Horus comes out of the body of his father, and praises him who has procreated him while the two goddesses join his body. This Great God [Osiris] speaks to him while he sees the rays of his disk." (*Drawing and translated text taken from Alexandre Piankoff,* The Tomb of Ramesses VI, *Bollingen Series 40:1 (New York: Pantheon Books, 1954), figure 116, pp. 364–5)*

as Horus, from the horizon, traveling over the path on the ground called Isis (the base of the triangle), and struck the top of the altitude of that triangle on each of the three Giza pyramids, creating three triangles with acute golden angles. Since the tips of the triangles were pyramidions (mini-pyramidal apexes) thought to have been encased in gold, there would have been brilliant solar flashes on these peaks. These flashes would have taken place in a series of three: first the tip of the Great Pyramid would flash, then the slightly lower tip of the Pyramid of Chephren, and finally the lowest of the three, the tip of the Pyramid of Mycerinus. They gave a three-flash sequence to herald the dawn.

In New Kingdom times (1570–1070 BC), when the Egyptians could no longer construct pyramids, they continued these practices by using gold-tipped obelisks instead. I have discussed this use of obelisks in great detail in *The Crystal Sun,* where I give illustrations and texts. Solar eyes were sometimes depicted on the tips of pyramids even in the New Kingdom, and this is a reference to the earlier practice at Giza, recorded in old papyri that had survived.

The way the sunrise was observed was that the priests would turn their backs

Figure 8.21. A statue covered in gold leaf of a priest wearing a falcon's head to enact the role of Horus. The folded arms beneath the cape are a typical pose of Egyptian priests taking part in ceremonial processions and events, symbolizing secrecy and showing reverence. Such attire may well have been worn by a chief priest observing the sunrise at the time of the equinox at Giza, when Horus-in-the-Horizon appeared. At the moment itself, the priest would have removed his arms from his clothing and held up both hands in a gesture of greeting and prayer. However, as described in the main text, I believe that the priests and celebrants had their backs to the sun just before sunrise, observing the pre-dawn flashes on the east faces of the pyramids (obelisk tips, cased in gold alloy, replaced these in the New Kingdom period), and then turned just in time to see the actual rebirth of the sun, at which point they would have raised their hands in adoration. This statue is in the Egyptian Museum in Cairo. (*Photo by Robert Temple*)

to the eastern horizon and look at the high monument, waiting for the flash, and would then turn and worship the sun in that instant, thus timing their gesture of adoration perfectly, since the sun struck the gold tip first, as it was higher; by the time the priests turned around, the sun would rise at that instant. This was how they achieved their perfect synchronization with the precise moment. To the Egyptians, who were obsessed by ceremonials, this was crucial.

I believe the aerial golden angle that I discovered with the inclinometer from the floor of the Sphinx temple (the horizon) to the tip of the Pyramid of Chephren is a confirmation of this system.

The priests would turn to watch the transformation and resurrection of Osiris, as Horus sprang from the horizon in the form of a stream of light in the sky. To celebrate Cosmic Order, the Pyramid of Chephren was constructed so that it could receive this light at the golden angle, since that was the angle at which "Horus" struck its tip at each equinox. I have not studied the aerial angles of sunrise for the other pyramids or any of the obelisks, and one would have to research the locations from which one would measure the angles. But in the case of the Pyramid of Chephren, it is the Sphinx that determines the angle I found, since the angle is taken from the floor of the Sphinx's Temple. The Sphinx can thus be conceived of as facilitating the golden angle of resurrection by its placement and acting as a conduit for the resurrection by light.

That the light of the sun was conceived of by the Egyptians as the sun speaking, or as his "word," seems to have carried over into the earliest level of Christianity. I show in figure 8.22 one of the strangest early Christian graffito designs. This illustration is taken from a book by the same C. W. King who translated the Plutarch treatise for Bohn's Classical Library that I quoted above as a variant when I gave Plutarch's information about the name for a hypotenuse among the Egyptians. This astounding drawing appears opposite page 90 in King's book *The Gnostics and Their Remains* (1864).[26] The illustration is described by King as "Anubis-Christos." It is the earliest-known depiction of the crucifixion, dating from the late second century AD. It is generally called the Palatine Graffito.[27] It was found drawn on a wall of the Imperial Palace on the Palatine Hill at Rome. There are two accounts of the room where it was found: the first says it was inscribed in a private vaulted cell by a slave who lived there and served one of the early Caesars, and the second says it was inscribed in "a schoolroom," which may actually have been an informal chapel. The name of the man who drew it appears to have been Alexamenos, and he shows himself standing beside the crucified deity with his hand raised in adoration. He appears to be wearing nothing but the short linen garment of someone who has just been baptized or initiated. The inscription in Greek says: "Alexamenos worships the God." King was an expert at analysis of these drawings and stresses that the poorly drawn head definitely represents Anubis and is a jackal head. In other words, the earliest-known drawing of the crucifixion of Christ portrays Christ as Anubis. As time went on, with the many drawings of Anubis that continued to appear on Gnostic gems throughout Roman times, people who had never seen a jackal got the head progressively wrong, and it looked more and more like an ass's or donkey's head. This drawing showing Christ crucified as Anubis suggests a mystic tradition going back directly to the original Giza tradition via the Ptolemaic Netherworld Texts and illustrations, which were themselves drawn from ancient papyri (no longer fully comprehended) dating from the time when the Sphinx was still Anubis, who welcomed the "word" of the sun (*logos,* later meaning "word" in Greek) at his rising. We know that *Logos* was St. John's name for Christ. Just to make the connection with the golden angle more obvious, *logos* also means ratio in Greek, as we have seen. In other words, the "mystery of the cross" is a mystery that goes back to the origins of Egyptian civilization, and Jeschu the Nazarene (better known by the Latin form of his name, Jesus), who spent time in Egypt before his return at the age of thirty to Galilee and Judaea (the original home of his family having been in Galilee at the fishing village of Nahum, known in Latin as Capernaum, which he left as an infant, having been born at Bethlehem in a stable, as the Bible informs us), must undoubtedly, in my opinion, have been deeply learned in Egyptian lore and embodied it in his esoteric teachings. Jesus made himself an actor in a sacred mystery drama, which he lived out in person to enact certain cosmic truths. I believe that some of this drama was directly inspired by Egyptian esotericism that he learned when living at Leontopolis, where there was a Jewish temple larger than that at Jerusalem and where very friendly relations with Egyptian priests and initiates were possible for Jews, because there were no Sadducee fanatics to prevent this happening. The Jews of Egypt were open to many influences, Greek, Egyptian, and Near Eastern, and were not narrow-minded bigots like those to be found in the backwaters of Judaea and Galilee, where intolerance was a mania. The name Jesus of Nazareth is incorrect, because the village of Nazareth did not exist at the time of Jesus. It was founded only about four hundred years later. The historical Jesus was not Jesus of Nazareth at all, but Jesus the Nazarene, describing his affiliation or generic similarity to the vegetarian sect of the Nazarenes, who were opposed to the Sadducees and held to a mystical form of Judaism, rejecting total subservience to the Law of the harsh rabbinical form of the politicians of Jerusalem. When the Roman Church gained control of Christianity with the power of the Roman state behind it, executing all the people whom they called heretics (i.e., opponents) and burning the large number of gospels they didn't like (such as the Gospel of Thomas and the Gospel of Philip, which were recovered at Nag Hammadi in 1947), they altered the texts in the four gospels they chose to retain so as to eradicate the word *Nazarene* (a sect opposed to them, who took their name from *nazara,* "the truth" in Aramaic, although "the truth" in Hebrew is generally called by the name of *emet*), substituting *of Nazareth* for *the Nazarene* and claiming they were correcting a scribal error. That is how the phrase "Jesus of Nazareth" got into the surviving gospels: it was interpolated by censors. They could not strike out "Nazarene" completely, because it was too well known, so they circulated the story that "Nazarene" really meant "man from Nazareth," which it does not, and which in any case was impossible because there was not yet any Nazareth for Jesus to have come from.

But what is the meaning of the crucifixion? This is the remaining piece of the puzzle. The fact is that the crossbar of the cross represents the major of the upright of the cross divided in golden section, and by combining them (whether intersecting or as a top bar does not matter), one was portraying the golden section by a symbol, the cross. Early drawings of crosses often had footbars as well, as this one does, and that was the minor. So the footbar is the minor, the crossbar is the major, and the upright is the sum of the two together. The minor and the major are in a ratio (*logos*). Crucified on the cross is the Logos himself, Christ. And for a sacred figure to be crucified means for that figure to be "nailed to the cross," that

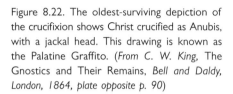

Figure 8.22. The oldest-surviving depiction of the crucifixion shows Christ crucified as Anubis, with a jackal head. This drawing is known as the Palatine Graffito. (*From C. W. King,* The Gnostics and Their Remains, *Bell and Daldy, London, 1864, plate opposite p. 90*)

is, *fixed in correct proportion with the cosmos by means of the divine proportion and sacred ratio, the golden section.* By this means, the sacred figure of a god is "nailed to Maāt" and exemplifies Cosmic Order. Just as Osiris was resurrected as Horus, "the Son of the Father," so too Christ is resurrected as "the Son of his Father," but first both must be crucified, must appear aloft in golden section. *The Logos must be crucified to give the promise of eternal life by his resurrection.* On the basis of such insights, one might create an esoteric and purified Christianity, if people could free themselves from fanatical literalism, which is doubtless expecting too much.

The earliest Christians, presumably the Gnostic ones, wished to make it clear that the symbolism of the crucifixion had its origins in Egypt, in the presence of Anubis. Thus I believe that the distant memory of the Sphinx as Anubis was passed on without people even knowing its significance any more, but due to the conservatism of religious traditions, this lore continued, thousands of years after it had been possible to give it a rational explanation.

It is interesting that the Christian Gnostics were not "people of the Book." There are known to have been more than two hundred gospels freely circulating among the early Christians in those formative days, and it was only after the Roman emperors created a Roman Church that all were burned but four, which were declared canonical by a council of clergy presided over by the emperor, acting as an instrument of state. (The Roman Catholic Church has that name because it was created as an organ of the Roman state. The reason it is so political is that it was created to be political by someone who ruled an empire.) The Gnostics, who were persecuted and burned at the stake by the Catholics, did not want to go around killing people because they held variant opinions. Thus, we may view the intolerant form of Christianity as a perversion created by a Roman emperor, just as the intolerant form of Islam known as Wahhabism or Salafism, which only originated in the eighteenth century, was a perversion adopted and propagated by Saudi kings. In both cases, the original purposes were political. (In the case of the Saudis, they were trying to bolster their legitimacy, because they had seized the "sacred" cities of Mecca and Medina by military force in the 1920s from the Hashemites, who had been the guardians and custodians of those cities for a thousand years. To prove they were worthy in religious terms, they adopted an extreme and insane form of Islam to appear to be more pious than any other Muslims in history, as a means of compensation and as a public relations exercise. Unfortunately, this innovative form of Islam has now, due to propaganda funded by oil money, come to be seen as somehow ancient and authentic, which is one of the greatest lies in history.)

It should be mentioned also that the Jews have never been known to want to convert people, and they try very hard to discourage conversion to Judaism, as friends of mine tell me who have married Jews and attempted to convert. In this respect, they somewhat resemble the first Christians, the Gnostics, who, although wishing to spread the "good news" (*evangelium*, "gospel"), were not going out and beating people over the head or threatening to slit their throats with scimitars to make them accept the "good news." However, whenever religions become aligned with states, persecution commences, and this has happened in Judaism as well. During the time of Jesus the Nazarene, the ruling establishment Jews of Jerusalem were known as the Sadducees. During Jesus's lifetime, the Sadducees are estimated to have executed no less than six thousand Pharisee rabbis who held a different view of Judaism from themselves (but not the same as that of Jesus, whose view was different again), in a ruthless political attempt to seize total control of Judaism and create a state form of the religion based in Jerusalem in which no variation of doctrine would be allowed upon pain of death. However, in Egypt at that time, there were an estimated one million Jews, living at three centers: Alexandria, Leontopolis, and Elephantine Island. Because these Egyptian Jews, who vastly outnumbered the Palestinian Jews, were not caught up in the Sadducean politics of Jerusalem, the Gnostics were stronger in Egypt, and the absorption of Egyptian religious symbols and concepts was greatly facilitated. It is from this background that the crucified Anubis at Rome comes.

In *The Crystal Sun*, I published a color photo (as plate 22) of the sun as represented on the famous astronomical ceiling of the Temple of Denderah. The rays of the sun in that photo are shown as streams of little triangles, as if the sun was spitting triangles, and it makes clear that solar rays were conceived of as specifically triangular phenomena. As I pointed out in that book also, we are told explicitly by the Roman author Pliny that the Egyptians considered their triangular obelisks to be "petrified descending light rays," in which light had been frozen in stone. But I cannot repeat my lengthy account of the optical aspects of obelisks here, as that has already been done in my earlier book, in the context of my discussion of the ancient history of light technology and the use by the ancient Egyptians of crystal lenses, of which I found many examples languishing unappreciated in museums. (I was able to demonstrate that the technology for optical surveying existed in the Fourth Dynasty and prove that optical magnification was used by Egyptian craftsmen for microscopically carving ivory as early as predynastic times, circa 3300 BC.)

According to the French Egyptologist Alexandre Moret, as early as the Pyramid Texts of the Fifth Dynasty, there was a Ray god named Ihhu, "of which the word-sign shows precisely the sun projecting its luminous triangle, divided by a bisector which gives to that triangle a 'pyramidal' appearance." Moret then mentions "the numerous examples where, above all in the paintings of the sarcophagi, the solar disc is depicted projecting some rays which are composed of little triangles packed one on top of the other, from which we have the word sign." He adds that a triangle also figures in the name of Sepedu, god of the Eastern Horizon.[28]

There is a great body of lore of triangles embedded in Egyptian texts and sacred illustrations that has never been investigated properly, because Egyptologists are not geometricians or mathematicians, and also they have not been looking for these things. Above all, the importance of the golden angle and its resultant golden triangle has not been appreciated. Now that we have seen that the Giza Plateau and its main monuments are all interrelated geodetically by multiple interlocking golden angles, all the triangle lore that has always infused the most esoteric aspects of Egyptian religion and design science can be seen to be one of their deepest secrets. We can now appreciate the amazing profundity that geometry had for them. The knowledge of geometry was to them like nuclear science and quantum theory are to us, a way of getting at the heart of matter by elucidating the concealed structures that govern the Cosmic Order. Egyptian religion was, in essence, a sacred science. But what is most surprising of all is that their sacred science was not built on mere superstition and fancy; its fundamentals *are all true.*

What was true in the Age of the Pyramids is true now: golden angles are real, not imagined; the golden section is a universal phenomenon true on all worlds at all times throughout the universe. This is genuine cosmic structure, and it elucidates real Cosmic Order. The number 1.618, which defines the golden section and is called by us *phi,* exists in the most distant galaxies. It is true everywhere, just as *pi* is true everywhere. These are facts from which one cannot "move on." With our mania for the new, we cannot escape the old. The rules of fashion do not apply in geometry. Some things are eternal.

Can it be that the Egyptian civilization lasted for 3,500 years because politicians were not allowed to "move on," and because there was no "media class"?

I mentioned the Temple of Denderah, which contains the most famous and bizarre of all known crypts of ancient Egypt. It is a mystifying and sacred place, which stays with you once you have entered it. Most people we know who have been there have never been able to get it out of their minds and say they keep thinking about it and often even dreaming about it. This is a crypt that celebrates the golden angle as applied to resurrection. The crypt has been discussed by innumerable "alternative authors," though Egyptologists themselves rarely mention it, because they don't know what to say, it is so weird. Some authors have claimed that the strange objects held by figures in the wall carvings represent ancient lightbulbs or other fantastic machines of even more advanced technology, such as ray guns. When Olivia and I first saw these reliefs, we called them "snake aubergines" (aubergines are what Americans call eggplants). They really do look like aubergines, and for gardeners and gastronomes like ourselves, that is what they suggested, rather than lightbulbs. However, they do also look rather like huge aubergine-shaped neon lightbulbs. So what are they? They are shown in figures 8.23 to 8.35. It is worth studying these rather closely, because they relate to our subject, and also because they have become a matter of such sensational interest to readers around the world.

This crypt is in a temple that has many crypts, but this is the only one with these mystifying and puzzling designs (or at least the only one so far discovered, as I suspect there are other crypts at a lower level, and even more at the same level; both of which I believe I have discovered evidence of by detecting either unopened hollow spaces or potentially or formerly movable stones). However, I have never made a proper study of the Temple of Denderah as I have of the Temple of Seti I at Abydos, where I did officially sanctioned work, and of which I have written a comprehensive survey of previous publications, together with a full analysis of published data, and the results of a full and intensive structural investigation and dating study, which awaits publication at some appropriate opportunity and reveals surprising discoveries.

The narrow Denderah crypt with the "snake aubergines" is technically known as Chamber C of South Crypt Number One. The wall carvings and textual inscriptions were first published in 1947 by the great French scholar Émile Chassinat in his massive series of volumes *Le Temple de Dendara,* published in Cairo by the French Institute. The texts and carvings appeared in volume 5, which itself

Figure 8.23. A plate from Chassinat's *Le Temple de Dendara,* volume V, showing the right half of the north wall of the underground "serpent cell" crypt. There is only one serpent cell on this wall, and the netherworld's avenging angel, Uputi, stands before it with his raised knives. Normally he cuts off the heads of the evil dead, but here he stands guard. He wears a monkey skin and has the head of a frog. Because the monkey skin is clearly depicted (see close-up photo in figure 8.33) being worn as a costume, this scene may represent a ritual carried out in the temple, even in this very crypt. If so, the scent of the blue lotus must somehow have been available. The chamber might have been filled with the blossoms at the proper season, or otherwise some method of capturing the scent and the alkaloids in concentrated form may have been used. Since the Egyptians do not appear to have practiced distillation, this may have been done by a process resembling enfleurage or maceration, which are still used at Grasse by the French perfume industry as the only means of capturing the delicate essences of flowers such as violets (the scent of violets does not survive distillation in the way that the more robust attar of roses does, and can never be obtained by that method). The absorption of the active principles of the flowers by a purified fat preserves them indefinitely, provided a natural preservative such as gum benzoin is used to "benzoate it" and prevent it becoming rancid. This fat could then have been burned on a brazier, releasing powerful waves of the scent to provide a deeply scented atmosphere in a closed crypt like this one, into which only a few people can fit. It is possible that the concentrated essence of the blue lotus may have some remarkable property discovered empirically by the ancient Egyptians and unknown to us.

Figure 8.24. A plate from Chassinat's *Le Temple de Dendara,* volume V, showing the left portion of the south wall of the crypt, with one of the two serpent cells issuing from a blue lotus, beneath which crouches a worshipper in prayer. On a plinth at right, one of the sons of Hathor (Ihy or Harsomtus), with a solar disk on his head, supports the serpent cell, with his arms raised in the *ka* position. The serpent representing Resurrection is coming out of the blue lotus, the sacred flower that exhales the scent of immortality. A line drawn from the point where the son of Hathor's left hand supports the end of the serpent cell to the end of the top of the baseline of the central panel at the exact corner of the chamber forms a golden angle with the top of the baseline. The serpent cell and its serpent of Resurrection are thus generated by a golden angle.

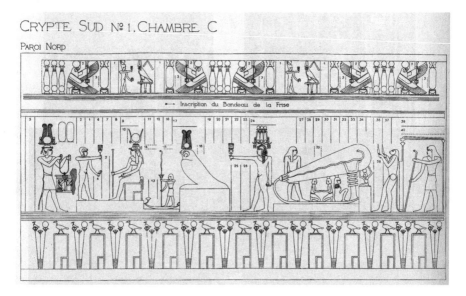

Figure 8.25. The drawing from Chassinat's *Le Temple de Dendara,* volume V, showing the north wall of the "serpent cell" crypt. The solemn figure of the underworld god Sokar sits on a plinth slightly to the left of center, presiding over the scene. My close-up photo of this image is seen in figure 7.6 on page 332, where the hieroglyphic name Sokar is clearly visible beside his head. To the right is the north wall's sole serpent cell, facing which is the netherworld's avenging angel Uputi with his knives (see figure 8.33 for a close-up view of him). Here he is protective, but his normal role is to cut off the heads of the evil dead. (In the German translation of the texts, he is called merely Upu, which was a shorter form of his name.) The enthroned figure at left is the goddess Hathor, with her characteristic headdress. She is receiving an offering from one of her sons, either the younger son, Ihy, or the older one, Harsomtus. Behind her, at a much smaller scale, a man in a netherworld boat, possibly representing the pharaoh, is sailing, holding a staff topped with a blue lotus flower, from which a Nehep serpent symbolizing resurrection is leaping. The figure presenting an offering to Hathor from behind the statue of Sokar is shown as a child of Hathor by his side locks, and is either her older son, Harsomtus, or the pharaoh portrayed as honorary son.

was a double volume. For many years it was impossible to obtain these books, and they could be consulted only in a few specialist libraries. But in 2002, the French Institute reprinted them, and they became freely available to individuals again. Although of course the books are in French, both the hieroglyphic texts (which are not translated) and photographs speak for themselves, the former to Egyptologists of any language and the latter to everybody. As for the texts, they have fairly recently been translated from Egyptian hieroglyphics into both French[29] and German.[30] I can read the German version myself, and for the French version, I am grateful to the young Egyptologist Tessa Dickinson, who is bilingual, for translating the relevant passages into English. I shall be quoting from her

Figure 8.26. The drawing from Chassinat's book *Le Temple de Dendara,* volume V, showing the south wall of the "serpent cell" crypt. Here there are two serpent cells facing one another at left. The enthroned goddess seated at right is Hathor, in her characteristic headdress, and holding a *uas* scepter. An offering is being made to her by one of her two sons, probably the younger one, Ihy, who holds an ankh, symbol of life, in his left hand. The figure making an offering behind the figure of Sokar is probably Hathor's older son, Harsomtus, wearing the joint crowns of Upper and Lower Egypt. Both sons are shown with the side lock, indicating their status as children of the goddess. (It is possible that the "son" with the crown is meant to be the pharaoh, granted honorary sonship in this instance.) The Sokar figure and the Nehep serpent symbolizing resurrection are seen in close-up in figure 8.27.

translation, with a few amendments made by myself. These texts explicitly state what the images are meant to represent.

The reliefs in the crypt show three "snake aubergines" in total, one on the north wall and two on the south wall opposite. What is important about these "snake aubergines" from our point of view is that they are drawn at golden angles to the horizontal. We suspect there must be something strange going on, and there is.

I have given a lot of information about the images in the captions to the photos and drawings, so here I will give a summary account, omitting many of the details of the images, which I leave for the captions, where they may more appropriately be read at the same time as studying the pictures.

I was unable to get far enough back in the narrow crypt to obtain flat images of large sections of wall. These are, however, available in black-and-white photos from the 1940s, lit by professional equipment and exposed by time exposures on tripods, in the Chassinat volume. So my color images taken with a flash need to be supplemented by the Chassinat black-and-white images, which I have reproduced here for comparison. I have also reproduced Chassinat's drawings of the wall designs so that the entire walls can be seen in their total contexts. Otherwise, impressions might be misleading. Mistakes are often made in Egyptology by failing to consider whole contexts of strange phenomena; the main example of that is the Giza Plateau, where the Great Pyramid and the Sphinx have usually been studied in isolation rather than as part of a complex including the other two pyramids as a unified conception (but as we have seen, only by considering them as a whole was it possible for me to discover the Giza Golden Plan).

If we start first with my figure 8.27 below, we can see the netherworld falcon Sokar, and immediately before him is a snake sailing in a netherworld boat, standing on its tail. This is one of the Nehep serpents that we have already encountered and that symbolizes resurrection. We can see that we are in familiar netherworld territory.

In figures 8.25 and 8.26 from Chassinat's book, we can see the entire south wall and the entire north wall represented in drawings. It is impossible for anyone to photograph them in their entirety, as the crypt is too narrow to allow that. In figure 8.26, we can see that the Sokar and Nehep figures that we see in figure 8.27 are in the center of the wall. The left portion of that wall is taken up with two bizarre "snake aubergines." These strange shapes are really "serpent cells," and we shall call them that from now on. If we look at figure 8.28, which is my close-up photo of the right serpent cell, we can see that it issues as an emanation from an upward-curving lotus flower, which is, in fact, the famous blue lotus of the ancient Egyptians, a rare plant that is now verging on extinction and has a flower of a subdued and somewhat pale mauve-blue color. It is a mysterious plant, and

Figure 8.27. At left is the netherworld god Sokar in his falcon form (from the solar disk on his head, two large plumes arise, which are not visible in this photo). To his right is the Nehep serpent standing upright on its tail and sailing in a netherworld boat. It represents resurrection (*Nehep* comes from the Egyptian verb meaning to leap up). This scene is on the south wall of the crypt. (*Photo by Robert Temple*)

Figure 8.28. This is the right serpent cell of the south wall of Chamber C in the Denderah crypts. This close-up photo shows how the cell and the serpent are issuing forth from a lotus flower (in fact, it is the sacred blue lotus of the lotus god Nefertem, which was frequently held to the nose by royal and sacred figures to indicate the breathing in of the essence of immortality). I did not notice this fact, because I persisted in the amusing notion that the serpent cell looked so much like a huge aubergine (eggplant) that I could not get any other image of it into my head. It was Olivia who pointed out to me that this was a lotus flower from which the cell and the serpent were emanating. She is far more visual than I am. It is also the case that the standing figure behind the cell is neither carrying nor supporting the serpent cell, as his hand may be seen not to be touching anything. Instead, this serpent cell is being supported entirely by the Djed pillar with arms, which is shown in figure 8.30. (*Photo by Robert Temple*)

its flower is delicate and eerily beautiful. Although it has a lovely fragrance, that fragrance is very faint, so you really have to smell hard to detect anything other than a vaguely pleasant smell of a singular delicacy. It does not appear to possess any obvious narcotic properties. I wonder if there may have been a variety of blue lotus in ancient times with a more powerful and obvious odor. This is the magical flower that was always being held to the noses of the pharaohs and the gods in sacred art, since its scent represented the breathing in of an essence that could stimulate and provide immortality. Prows of sacred ships, especially netherworld boats, often consisted of these curling lotus stems issuing forth in flowers that bent backward. Superficially, the wall relief shows a man who appears to be carrying the serpent cell, but this close-up view demonstrates that he is not even touching it, and his hand is rigidly and vertically down in the reverential position of a sacred procession. The serpent cell is thus entirely independent of him; he is a mere attendant. A long, thin serpent is issuing out of the blue lotus, inside the serpent cell. Olivia has always thought that the blue lotus contains a so-far-unidentified magic ingredient, possibly an elusive or volatile alkaloid, and maybe even in its stem or bulb.

Figure 8.29 is a close-up of the left serpent cell of the south wall. Here again we see the serpent cell and its interior serpent clearly issuing from the blue lotus flower. In figure 8.30, we can see a close-up of the front end of the right serpent cell of the south wall. A worshipper kneels beneath the serpent cell in a posture of prayer. The serpent cell itself is supported by what is called a Djed pillar, with upraised arms in the position of a *ka* (a kind of soul, the "double" of the deceased person) emanating from the sides of the Djed; this picture of a *ka* may be part of an unrecognized cryptopgraphic inscription, or it may be purely iconographical. Another *ka* emanating from the top of a Djed this time supports the single serpent cell on the north wall, as seen in figure 8.32. Here the *ka* arms penetrate the serpent cell and directly support the serpent within. The Temple of Denderah is sacred to the goddess Hathor, and she may be intended to be the goddess seated in the boat, supporting the serpent cell with her head. (Since her pose is that of a hieroglyph, as are the *ka* and the Djed, a cryptographic statement may be intended here.) This Djed sits on the prow of this particular netherworld boat, whose stern curves around and becomes another blue lotus blossom from which emanates the serpent cell of the north wall, as seen in figure 8.25. In the former photo, figure 8.31, to the right of the Djed a male child crouches on a plinth, with a solar disk above his head and his arms upraised in *ka* position to support the far end of the
· serpent cell. This is one of the two sons of Hathor, either Ihy or Harsomtus. He is shown with the side lock of hair that indicates he has not yet come of age and emphasizes his status as child of the goddess. The serpent, whose head is shown so clearly here, represents the resurrected and emerging life of the risen sun, which has been breathed out by the sacred lotus flower.

The netherworld aspects of these strange pictures are highlighted by the presence on the north wall of the terrifying Uputi, a messenger demon of Osiris and an avenging angel, whose main job was to hunt down the evil dead, like a relentless detective, and chop off their heads as soon as he found them. On the north wall he stands with knives held up in each hand, ready for action, but in protective mode. We can see Uputi in figure 8.33. He wears a monkey skin and has the head of a frog. Uputi's monkey skin is so obviously a costume that we may have

Figure 8.29. This is the left serpent cell of the south wall of Chamber C. Once again, the attendant is not carrying it or touching it. In this case, the lotus flower from which the cell and serpent are emanating curves around, and its stem (to the right of the photo, not visible here) turns into the prow of a nocturnal solar boat. The knees and hands of a praying figure may just be seen at bottom right. (*Photo by Robert Temple*)

Below: Figure 8.30. The Djed pillar, here quaintly portrayed as animate and raising its arms supportively, was sometimes described as the backbone of the god Osiris. It was meant to symbolize stability and correct orientation. It may have had a connection with surveying and the use of angles, concerning which see my discussion of this subject in *The Crystal Sun*. The raised arms also are a hieroglyphic sign for *ka*, which is one of the various types of soul, often called a person's double or the animating principle of a being that survives death. In *The Crystal Sun* I point out that the raised arms may also have been a feature of surveying, when the correct orientation to the cardinal points was being sought for a sacred building and a sighting was being taken, with the person being looked at through the proto-theodolite (using the ancient lenses I have discovered and described) holding up his arms, and something resembling the Djed being a graduated measuring instrument for sighting. It is possible that the textual inscriptions in this crypt contain some supplementary or variant statements using cryptographic writing, in which case the raised arms may actually be read as *ka* and form part of an unrecognized textual statement. I do not believe that anyone has ever considered the inscriptions in this crypt from the point of view of hieroglyphic cryptography. It is not impossible that there may be two separate translations of some of the hieroglyphs in this crypt, the obvious reading and the concealed reading, (*Photo by Robert Temple*)

Figure 8.31. On the right, the god Ihy, son of Hathor, crouching on a rectangular plinth (which, if taken as having its base at the level of the adjoining base on which the goddess sits, is a golden rectangle) and with a solar disk on his head, holds aloft the serpent cell of the emerging life of the rising sun. In the center, support is also given by the Djed pillar (often known as the spine of Osiris) with upraised arms in the form of the symbol for the *ka,* so the cryptographic meaning is probably "the *ka* of Osiris." At left, a goddess sits supporting the serpent cell with her head; she is probably Hathor. She and the *ka* of Osiris are riding in a nocturnal boat, with the Djed at its prow; this boat is made of the stem of the sacred blue lotus of Nefertem. The actual serpent representing the resurrected and emerging life of the risen sun, which has been breathed out by the sacred lotus flower, is directly supported by the raised arms of the *ka* of Osiris, and not merely by its cell. (*Photo by Robert Temple*)

Below: Figure 8.32. The serpent cell of the north wall, issuing from a blue lotus flower that curves out of the keel of the netherworld boat, upon the prow of which sits a Djed pillar that supports the serpent with the serpent cell by means of two upraised *ka* arms. Two worshippers sit beneath the serpent cell facing one another, supporting the serpent cell with their heads, as does the goddess beyond them to the right, who is presumed to be Hathor. (*Photo by Robert Temple*)

Figure 8.33. The central standing figure is Uputi, a netherworld personality with the body of a monkey and the head of a frog. The Uputi demons were the avenging angels of the Egyptians. They were completely harmless to good people who died, but as they had a violent hatred of evil, they relentlessly sought out the evil dead, decapitated them with their sharp knives, and turned their bodies upside down. It was the fate of all evil Egyptians after death to live upside down and decapitated in pits where snakes and vermin crawled all over them and eternally ate away at their heads and bodies, while they suffered a variety of other untold tortures too terrifying to enumerate. The only extended account of the Uputi demons is in J. Zandee's *Death as an Enemy*, Brill, Leiden, 1960, pp. 202–3. The word *uputi* means messenger, and technically, these Uputi demons were the messengers of Osiris and were assistant judges of the dead. Sometimes a Uputi demon would appear to someone about to die as an angel of death. As one spell in the *Book of the Dead* says: "When your messenger comes to fetch you, he finds you prepared. Do not say: I am too young for being taken away." And in a Coffin Text spell, the deceased is advised to say: "Oh savage ones of face, messengers of Osiris, who close the mouths of the spirits over what is in them. You have no power over the closing of this mouth of mine. You do not take away the going of these feet of mine." (*Photo by Robert Temple*)

a depiction of a priestly ritual here, rather than of the netherworld itself. He is standing guard over the north wall's only serpent cell.

Now we come to the true significance of this crypt in terms of what we have been considering about the rising sun at Giza, where the golden angle was discovered to be the angle of resurrection. Here, too, the golden angle is found in a resurrection context. On the south wall, if you draw a straight line connecting the tip of the right serpent head to the upper tip of the lotus flower and then continue it

Figure 8.34. This is the south wall of Chamber C. The serpent cell on the right is being supported by a Djed pillar with arms, and a worshipper is praying beneath it. At far right in the
photo is the rear portion of the large south wall's Sokar falcon on a pedestal. As with the
opposite wall, a line drawn from the edge of the base of the Sokar pedestal forms a golden
angle with one of the serpent heads. In this case, the line touches the tip of the left serpent
head. (On the opposite wall, there is only one serpent cell, and the line from the edge of
the base of the north wall's Sokar falcon touches the tip of the head of that one's serpent.)
The figure in this photo standing between the right serpent cell and Sokar is the pharaoh. The
serpent cell on the left is supported by the god Ihy, who is crowned with a solar disk, sits on
a pedestal, and has the side locks of hair signifying a youth. Ihy was the son of the goddess
Hathor, whose temple this is at Denderah. (*Photo by Robert Temple*)

on to the baseline of the central panel, it forms a golden angle with the horizontal,
so that the serpent of resurrection is seen to be generated by a golden angle. This
is shown in figure 8.34 and can be measured accurately by anyone on top of the
drawing in figure 8.26. Similarly, the left serpent cell is generated by a golden angle
with the horizontal, which can be measured by a line drawn from the point at the
very end of the top of the baseline of the panel at the far left (which is also the corner of the chamber, a fact not made clear in the drawing but seen clearly in figure
8.35), to the precise point where the son of Hathor is supporting the serpent cell
with his left hand. This can also be measured very precisely in figure 8.26, because
it is a drawing that has been done flat-on. The son of Hathor is in this case literally
"upholding the golden angle." Both serpent cells and their serpents on the south
wall are thus generated by golden angles.

Figure 8.35. This photo of the south wall of the crypt shows the two serpent cells pointing toward one another, with kneeling worshippers beneath them, the right one supported by the Djed pillar with arms and the left one supported by one of the sons of Hathor (either the god Ihy or the god Harsomtus) on a pedestal. Both serpent cells and their serpents emanate from blue lotus blossoms, as the breath of resurrection. The two golden angles that generate the two serpent cells are described in the main text and can be measured on figure 8.26. The prow of the nocturnal solar boat beneath the left serpent cell is shown here; it touches the pedestal on which Ihy or Harsomtus crouches (where his left hand supports the end of the serpent cell is a point defining the golden angle with the base). The mortar in the stone wall seems to suggest that there are two small stone blocks beneath the heads of the two serpent cells, which at one time were removable. I am not aware that anyone has ever noticed this or thought of investigating whether they might be removable or lead to something. Perhaps the original excavation records mention something about them. However, in terms of normal construction procedures, it makes no sense at all for these two small blocks to be inserted into the middle of a wall carving, as they disturb the composition. But each is beneath the head of a resurrection serpent, and since resurrection leads somewhere, perhaps these blocks conceal a passage that also leads somewhere. The vertical streak of mortar cutting the right serpent cell, separating two large stone panels, is not unusual, but the two small blocks are definitely suspicious and may well lead to other concealed crypts that could elucidate the strange mysteries of this chamber. I also believe there is another chamber below this one, which has not been entered since antiquity, because I detected by tapping what appeared to be a hollow space beneath the stone at the far end of the crypt from where you descend and go in. Also, in my opinion, an expert at hieroglyphic cryptography needs to examine the inscriptions in this chamber for further or double meanings. Just as golden-angle design construction is not immediately obvious to the untutored eye, so matters may be hinted at in the texts that straightforward translation does not reveal at first attempt. Sometimes in cryptography, figures can double as hieroglyphs, and this may not have been considered yet. (*Photo by Robert Temple*)

On the north wall, the serpent and its serpent cell are also generated by a golden angle with the horizontal, the angle being shown by a line drawn from the bottom right base of Sokar's pedestal to the tip of the serpent's head. This can be measured by anyone on top of the drawing in figure 8.25.

That is all we need to consider here about the Denderah crypt. Because it has understandably become something of a cause célèbre among those intrigued by Egyptian mysteries, it was worthwhile to show that it is part of the same complex of iconography and thought that we find at Giza in association with the Sphinx. The theme is the same: resurrection and emergence from the netherworld by means of the golden angle of resurrection and, in this case, also by the breath of immortality that comes out of the blue lotus.

There is one more amazing physical manifestation and occurrence of the golden angle at Giza, which was discovered by someone in the nineteenth century who did not realize at the time what it was that he really had discovered. This was a very strange discovery of my own, too, to find it buried in the data in his book. Some time ago I managed to obtain a copy of this extremely rare book on the Giza pyramids written by a British engineer named Robert Ballard. He was a chief railway engineer for Queensland, Australia, in the 1880s. In 1882, he published his remarkable book, *The Solution of the Pyramid Problem*.[31] A main theme of the book is that the pyramids of Egypt, which he had studied as he passed through the country as a visitor in 1858 or 1859, made expert surveyors' backsights for measuring and reestablishing the boundaries of the fields of Egypt after the receding of the waters of the inundation of the Nile. "Backsight" is a surveyor's term for a known point of elevation (in this case, the heights of the pyramids, which would have been known) toward which a surveyor looks back in order to calculate his present height where he is standing with his measuring instrument, which is called a theodolite. In *The Crystal Sun* I discuss ancient Egyptian surveying methods and published the photographic evidence to prove that in the Pyramid Age the Egyptians possessed perfectly ground convex crystal lenses to enable them to construct primitive theodolites in order to obtain the extreme precision of alignment of the Giza pyramids, which was possible only by means of optical surveying methods and requires magnifying lenses. Ballard's theory about the backsights is very interesting. His idea first came to him as he rode the train from Alexandria to Cairo and noticed the pyramids shifting their positions relative to one another as he moved. But in the process of later compiling data to support his theory, Ballard traveled extensively on foot in circles around the pyramids of Giza, doing drawings of them from a variety of angles along a complete circuit of 360 degrees. This was easier for him in 1858 than it would be today, because the surrounding area was largely empty. Nor was there yet any smog to interfere with his vision. He stressed that the small Pyramid of Mycerinus needed to be covered in red casing stones, as it partially was (Ballard was unaware that in antiquity the red casing stopped halfway up and became white in the upper half, but this need not affect his argument), to distinguish it from the other two pyramids from certain angles for such sighting purposes. In his book, he printed all his drawings in two colors, with the Pyramid of Mycerinus colored pink, to aid the reader's comprehension. As he circled the Giza pyramids in this way, studying their changing configurations in relation to one another, he was arrested at a particular point by a strange sight. Suddenly, at no angular geographical bearing that appeared to be especially significant to him, a kind of optical illusion presented itself. Taking the apex of the Pyramid of Chephren as north for his sighting purposes, the southwest corner edges of both the Pyramid of Chephren and the Pyramid of Mycerinus appeared to blend into one single edge and to become perfectly aligned with one another along their northeast-to-southwest diagonals.

This is very odd, because as anyone can see from the Golden Giza Plan in figure 7.25, the diagonals of these two pyramids are not really in a direct line with one another at all. If those lines were each carried on toward the southwest, they would be perfectly parallel, but some distance apart. If the two diagonals had been really aligned one behind the other, the merging noticed by Ballard would have been seen from a point that was from true north precisely 45 degrees south of west and 45 degrees west of south, which is the direction both diagonals are pointing from their own separate apexes. However, this is not seen, due to the fact that the diagonals are not in line. It is therefore most extraordinary that the two diagonals *appear to merge* when viewed from an angle all too familiar to us!

The optical illusion then is given of a perfectly triangular chunk being cut out of the southwest corner of the Pyramid of Chephren, with a plug of red stuck in its place into its pale body. (This would have been an even more startling illusion in ancient times, when the casing stones were all in place and their true colors were still bright.) This extraordinary sight is reproduced in figure 8.36, since it is necessary for the colors to be seen for the phenomenon to be fully appreciated. (Bear in mind that Ballard did not realize that the small pyramid was originally only red in its bottom half, so he drew it as wholly red.) Ballard duly made a note of the geographical (not compass) bearing and recorded it as 206° 33' 54.18". He did not see the significance of this angle, and it was assumed to be random. However, he had stumbled on the golden angle without realizing it. The angle just mentioned was viewed from the southwest and is thus 26° 33' 54.18" west of south, which makes a precise golden angle with the north–south meridian passing through the tip of the Pyramid of Chephren. Both the southwest edges of the two merging pyramids as seen along that ray appear to become one. But because the diagonals of the two pyramids are not actually geographically aligned on the Giza Plan, the view recorded by Ballard must be a strange optical illusion whereby two diagonals that are not actually in alignment appear to become so at the precise spot where he stood, which was defined by a golden angle to the north–south meridian. I have not been to Egypt since finding this information in Ballard's book, so I have not been able to take this sighting myself. One does not normally wander southwest of the Pyramid of Mycerinus into the desert unless one goes on horseback or by camel, so this would not normally be seen, even in ancient times. It must presumably have some additional significance yet to be discovered. However, it does not point toward any pyramid farther south, as they are all too far to the east. The line runs toward the Fayyum, but it does not appear to strike anything in particular. This line is deeply puzzling, and perhaps it means nothing outside the Giza Plateau context itself.

This drawing appeared as figure 44 in Ballard's book, one among seven similar drawings on a page, with no special attention being called to it. I had to have a pretty sharp eye to spot this, especially as the angle was given as a bearing, with 180 degrees added to it, so that in a scan for significant angles such as I always carry out when I look at things, it did not jump out and click with my mental "search image" as a number match. I had to excavate it from the data, which is a different and slower, second-order mental process.

This is my last physically demonstrable golden angle at Giza to be presented in this book. Unfortunately for those of us who like answers, it is the most puzzling and bizarre of them all, and it requires a lot of further thought. It has in common with my inclinometer observation from the Sphinx Temple floor the fact that the tip of the Pyramid of Chephren is at the true center of the optical illusion, and that is certainly a crucially important lead in my further detective work. Obviously, I must obtain some photos of this phenomenon from the desert southwest of Giza when I next go to Egypt. My work on the geometrical mysteries of the Giza Plateau has really just begun. Plotting the spider's web of golden angles is just stage one of unraveling a far more complex Giza Plan. Much more is made clear in my book *Egyptian Dawn,* though I doubt that this subject will ever be exhausted. Or at least, I will be exhausted before it is!

Finally, we can gain further insights into the golden angle of resurrection by considering some further ancient illustrations. First, we can see two other hypotenusal pharaoh/Osirises at golden angles that are depicted in papyri in figure 8.10 and 8.37. The first is one I spotted in a glass case in the Egyptian Museum at Cairo (Papyrus 4891), which appears never to have been discussed by anyone as far as I can discover, and the second is depicted in a well-known papyrus called the Papyrus of Heruben, which has been discussed by Egyptologists on various

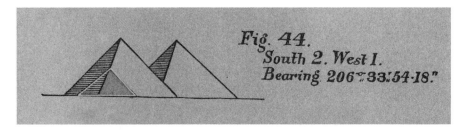

Figure 8.36. This is figure 44 from Robert Ballard's book, *The Solution of the Pyramid Problem or, Pyramid Discoveries with a New Theory as to Their Ancient Use,* John Wiley & Sons, New York, 1882. In his book, the British engineer Ballard walked 360 degrees around the three Giza pyramids (at a time when there were no buildings in the way and no smog), making sketches of the mutual configurations of the three pyramids from a variety of angles and cardinal (not magnetic) bearings. He did this because of his conviction that the pyramids were used as backsights for surveying purposes in ancient Egypt to reestablish boundaries of fields after the inundation waters subsided every year. He made the point that the small Pyramid of Mycerinus had to be a different color (it was partially covered in red granite casing stones instead of white limestone) to differentiate it from the other two. Among the many views Ballard sketched, and for which he meticulously recorded the bearings, was this striking one, where the optical illusion is created of the small Pyramid of Mycerinus (in the left foreground) merging and becoming one with the larger Pyramid of Chephren directly behind it, appearing as a kind of red plug in its corner, with the edges and bases of the two separate pyramids perfectly coinciding so that they look like one pyramid. Ballard duly noted the cardinal bearing of 206° 33' 54.18", or, in other words, by subtracting the 180 degrees from north to south, constituting an angle with the north–south meridian line of 26° 33' 54.18" west of south, which is precisely the golden angle. So Ballard stumbled across another major golden-angle phenomenon at Giza without realizing it, because evidently he did not know the value of the golden angle and did not recognize it. He merely noted the bearing as a matter of routine. I was the one who spotted this in his mass of data.

occasions, and was reproduced by Piankoff. All that needs to be said about these two images is found in the captions to the plates.

We have already seen the remarkable images in beaten gold on the Second Shrine from the tomb of Tutankhamun, reproduced in figures 8.16 to 8.19, of the giant Re-Osiris standing at the eastern horizon with his feet in hell and his head in heaven, and the details are given in the captions.

Figure 8.25 is a photo I took of another portion of the beaten-gold Second Shrine of Tutankhamun. Here we have Osiris portrayed as a prone mummy, lying on his stomach, into whose mouth the "voice of Re" (the *logos*) is pouring as a stream of light. This is yet another form of the hypotenusal Osiris rising in the east at the golden angle. As explained in the caption to the photo, a line drawn from the top of the solar disk through the eye of Osiris, if continued to the base on which he is lying, forms a golden angle with the horizontal plane. This is another clear portrayal of the golden angle of resurrection.

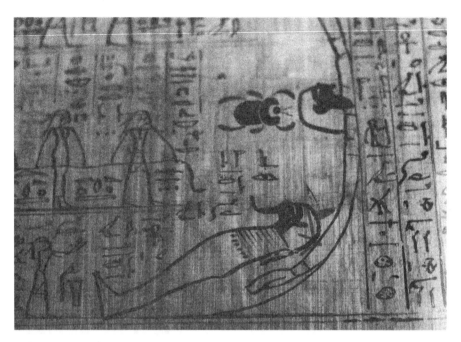

Figure 8.37. This papyrus inside a glass case in the Egyptian Museum in Cairo shows another hypotenusal priest or pharaoh as Osiris. The papyrus is Papyrus J4891, on display in Case 530 in Room 29. Here once again, the mummified pharaoh, identified in his inert state with Osiris, but who through resurrection has "become a Horus," forms the hypotenuse (which was known to the Egyptians, according to Plutarch, as Horus) of a triangle, in this case a golden triangle, such as that projected by a shadow onto the south side of the Great Pyramid at sunset on the winter solstice. (The deceased pharaoh is also affiliated through this means with the mummified god Ptah, who is also "south of his wall," as many inscriptions state.) The angle at the pharaoh's feet, if measured by the line protruding from the top of his head, forms the golden angle. A poor imitation of this portion of the papyrus design from the Twenty-third Dynasty is found in the Papyrus of Djed-Amon-iuf-ankh (the name of a priest of Amun from Thebes, whose funerary papyrus it was), also in the Cairo Museum, and reproduced as Number 27 in Alexandre Piankoff, *Mythological Papyri*, Pantheon Books, New York, 1957. In Piankoff's book, he shows no knowledge of the papyrus in this photo, but as Number 2 he reproduces the Papyrus of Heruben from Cairo, which is shown in figure 8.10, and which contains a very important hypotenusal figure. (*Photo by Robert Temple*)

Another graphic illustration on this shrine of beaten gold of the "call of light" (*logos*) emitted by the sun is found in figures 8.40 and 8.41. The sun as a uraeus serpent spews light into the forehead of a mummy of the blessed dead to reawaken him, and a series of other mummies have rays of light shooting into their foreheads from stars, so they too may be resurrected. In figures 8.46 and 8.47 is another scene from this shrine, in which is depicted Horus emerging from his father, Osiris, in the netherworld preparatory to rising as Horus-in-the-Horizon.

Figure 8.38. A prone mummy figure of Osiris as the sun in the netherworld, into whose mouth the "voice of Re" as a stream of light is pouring from a small solar disk. This is in beaten gold on the Second Shrine of Tutankhamun in the Cairo Museum. Directly beneath the small solar disk is a pair of inverted legs, which means movement in the netherworld (which everybody enters upside down). The outstretched arm of the netherworld solar Osiris is the same as the outstretched arm of the hypotenusal Osiris-as-Horus figure rising at Giza, and like it, this figure forms a golden triangle. A line drawn from the top of the solar disk through the eye of the prone mummy strikes the base on which the mummy lies at a point that creates a golden angle, which is the same golden angle of resurrection that we find at Giza, and the angle on which the entire Giza Plan and positioning of the Sphinx are based. At far right, an upright, friendly Nehaher serpent stands in a rectangular array of vertical light rays, above which a pair of walking legs say "moving." Above them, another solar disk is emitting light. At far left, two androgynous, lion-headed figures have had their corpses resurrected by the light of Re, and they are following him. The arms concealed under the cloaks are a well-known priest's pose, indicating that they are carrying secret things, so these figures probably really represent priests in procession wearing lion heads, who represent those resurrected dead, as part of a ceremony. See also the drawing of this scene in figure 8.39 below. (*Photo by Robert Temple*)

Figure 8.39. A drawing of the scene seen in figure 8.38. Taken from Alexandre Piankoff, *The Shrines of Tut-Ankh-Amon*, Pantheon, New York, 1955, figure 42, opposite page 128.

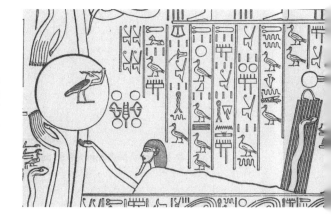

Figure 8.40. This mysterious scene in beaten gold from the Second Shrine of Tutankhamun shows a cobra called the uraeus spouting a stream of light from its mouth. According to one of the creation traditions of the Egyptians, the divine "word" (which became the *logos* of the Greeks and later the *Logos* of the Gospel of John in the Bible, where "In the beginning was the Word . . .") was uttered, and creation came into being as a result. However, what the Greeks and Christians missed in this concept, when they later adopted it, was that the "word" was not meant to be audible, but was in the form of *light*. To the ancient Egyptians, the sun (Re) "spoke light." Here, the "word" or *logos* as a stream of light strikes the forehead of the first of a row of sacred mummies (there are two more to the right, beyond the photo). The uraeus represents Re, the sun, and the stream of light is meant to be the graphical representation of the voice of Re, who had a "fiery call." Each mummy also has a star sending rays of light into his forehead. In front of each mummy is its *ba*, its spiritual force that has survived death. The *ba* was depicted by the Egyptians as a bird with a human head, the bird body symbolizing the ability of the *ba* to flit around wherever it likes, like a bird. Above the head of each *ba* in this picture is a pair of striding legs, to emphasize the mobility of the *ba*. Re is "calling" the *ba*s. Each *ba* is standing on four vertical light rays. As John Darnell says: "The *ba*'s whom Re is said to call appear as though hovering on waves of light before the standing mummies. . . . The *ba*'s, when summoned by Re, enter into the entourage of the sun, following alongside the other *ba*'s already called into the following of Re" (p. 106). The Egyptian cryptographic text that goes with this picture refers to "the light of Re having entered their corpses. When he calls their *ba*'s, they set out after the (other?) *ba*'s. . . . Re calls them, and they come forth from the two caverns (?). . . . When the one who is in his disk calls to you, your *ba*'s ascend towards the one who created you" (pp. 104–5, Darnell). This picture stresses the importance of the call of light uttered by the sun and its ability to waken the dead to resurrection, which was seen in its ultimate form by the rising sun represented by the hypotenusal mummy of the dawn that rose with its feet at the Sphinx and the tips of its hands at the tops of the Giza pyramids. (*Photo by Robert Temple*)

Figure 8.41. This is a drawing of the image seen in figure 8.40. Taken from Alexandre Piankoff, *The Shrines of Tut-Ankh-Amon*, Pantheon, New York, 1955, figure 42, opposite page 128.

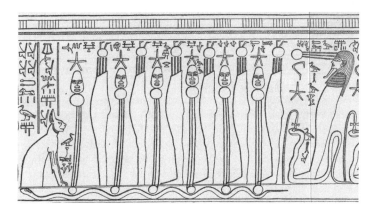

Figure 8.42. This is a drawing of the scene shown in figure 8.43. Taken from Alexandre Piankoff, *The Shrines of Tut-Ankh-Amon*, Pantheon, New York, 1955, figure 42, opposite page 128.

This is another version of the same process that we have seen in figure 8.20 from the tomb of Rameses VI.

Another hypotenusal Osiris appears on this golden shrine at the golden angle (this time vertical rather than horizontal) in the scene depicted in figures 8.43 and 8.44. At the right of this image in figure 8.43 is a leaning Osiris, standing with his feet in a protective Mehen serpent (Enveloper), and with the light of the sun streaming into his forehead to resurrect him. However, the photo does not encompass the entire scene. In figure 8.44, which extends farther to the right

Figure 8.43. An image in beaten gold from the Second Shrine of Tutankhamun. At right, the first of a series of Osirises leaning backward at the golden angle is irradiated by light streaming into his forehead (there are other Osirises to the right of him; see figure 8.44). This light, the "word" of the sun who speaks light, revives Osiris and brings about his resurrection, signified also by his leaning backward at the golden angle of resurrection (the golden angle is between him and the vertical plane). He stands in the protective folds of the Mehen serpent, the Enveloper, who keeps him safe while in the netherworld. At far left, a cat representing the eye of the sun presides over six headless entities. These entities are the blessed dead whose heads, now the property of the sun, will be returned to them because they have been just and are to be spared from annihilation and given eternal life. Individual suns stream light down into the headless torsos, and above each head is a star. The heads of the saved and blessed entities are called "those relating to the pupil of the sun's eye." The sun speaks to these entities: "When he calls to them they live . . . by the breath of his mouth do they receive their heads" (John Darnell's translation). It is the light of the sun that is "the breath of the sun's mouth," since the sun's mode of speech is to emit light. It is this breath that streams as light down into the headless mummies. During the third hour of the night, the heads are returned to the blessed dead, and Anubis ties them back on. See also the drawing of this scene in figure 8.42. (*Photo by Robert Temple*)

in the scene, we see that there is really a series of six hypotenusal Osirises rising from the dead at the golden angle of resurrection. If one draws a line along the beard, face, and forehead of each figure until it reaches a vertical line that is perpendicular to the base of the scene, one gets a golden angle. Further details are given in the captions. No fewer than seven hypotenusal Osirises being resurrected at the golden angle at the eastern horizon—becoming Horus-in-the-Horizon—are shown on this one golden shrine alone.

Also relevant are certain of the wall paintings in the tomb of Rameses VI, of which we have already seen three, the birth of Horus from the mummy of Osiris

Figure 8.44. This scene from the Second Shrine of Tutankhamun shows six Osiris entities rising from the dead at the golden angle from the horizon at Rostau (Giza). Each is protected at its feet by a guardian Mehen serpent. The first Osiris entity is called "he of Mehen." The second is called "born of corpse," the third is called "born of members," the fourth is called "begotten one," the fifth is called "one related to going about," and the sixth is called "leaping of corpse." "Leaping" is from the verb *nehep,* to leap. This verb refers to ascension (which was regarded as leaping) from the netherworld, and there were also *nehep* serpents (see one in figure 8.27) that stood up vertically or leaped up, which were friendly and associated with resurrection. These Osiris entities are the blessed dead, who are being revivified in their mummy state by solar disks beaming light into their foreheads. Soon they will rise above the horizon and be reborn. We know they are being resurrected because their bodies constitute hypotenuses of triangles containing golden angles (which are not drawn in the scene, but which had to be used by the draftsmen in constructing the picture). If one draws a line along the beard, face, and forehead of each figure until it reaches a vertical line perpendicular to the base of the scene, one gets a golden angle; and if the hypotenuse is continued to the baseline, a triangle. These blessed dead are therefore mini-Osirises about to be reborn as Horuses. The text specifically locates this scene at Giza by saying: "You will fly up from Rosetau by day, in exultation every day; you will go about on earth daily" (translation by John Darnell, page 120. Ref. also Darnell plate 10, A Scene 3). Drawing taken from Alexandre Piankoff, *The Shrines of Tut-Ankh-Amon,* Pantheon, New York, 1955, figure 42, opposite page 128.

(figure 8.20), Osiris in his Hidden Chamber (figure 7.7 on page 333), and the Fifth Hour of the Night with Sokar in his cavern beneath a pyramid topped with a human head (figure 7.8). One other may be seen in figure 7.9. Although the captions of all of these give much necessary information, it is important to put these images in their joint perspective. The arduous journey of the sun god in his boat through the netherworld every night, with its perils and vicissitudes, always culminated in his rising successfully in the east, with the aid of the beetle Khepri, who pushed him over the horizon, often into the welcoming outspread arms of Shu, god of air and sky. But when he did emerge, reborn and resurrected, he did so as a resurrected Osiris who had become a Horus-in-the-Horizon, manifesting

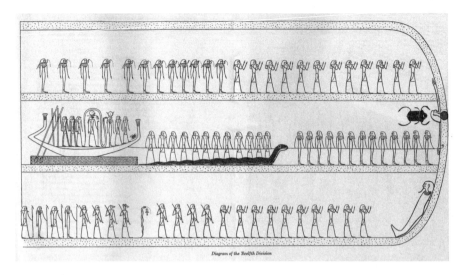

Diagram of the Twelfth Division

Figure 8.45. The final and twelfth hour of the sun's journey through the netherworld, which culminates in the sun's rising at the eastern horizon (at right). In the middle register at the left, the *ba* of the sun is in the last stage of its journey over the water (represented by the wavy lines contained in what looks like a pedestal beneath the boat). The huge serpent in the center of the picture is called the Nau serpent, who is a protective deity. He is described in the text as being 1,300 cubits (2,332 feet) long, and "he moves toward the birth of the god" (i.e., the rising of the sun as Osiris/Horus-in-the-Horizon). It is his job to clear the way for the sun god. Nau also has the meaning of Divine Path, and for some unknown reason, the Nau serpent was associated with the twenty-third day of each lunar month. He is clearly astronomical, but we do not yet fully understand his significance, or what the 1,300 cubits refers to. In the text he is also called the Great Ka, Life of the Gods. The Khepri beetle, symbol of the rising sun, is at the horizon, presiding over the red sun of the dawn, who is being welcomed by the head and outspread arms of Shu, god of the air and sky. The hypotenusal Osiris, who is always associated with resurrection and the revived sun and has now become Horus-in-the-Horizon, is at bottom right, at a golden angle (his head making a golden angle with the vertical plane). Directly in front of the hypotenusal Osiris as Horus is a procession of ten sun worshippers, followed by four priests, behind whom is the Nehep serpent standing on his tail as a symbol of resurrection, spewing a stream of light from his mouth, and with the ankh, symbol of life, beneath his jaw. Twelve sun worshippers form the right side of the procession in the top register. In the middle register, the figures are the towers of the solar boat. (*From Alexandre Piankoff,* The Tomb of Rameses VI, *Pantheon Books, New York, 1954, figure 87, opposite page 312*)

himself at the golden angle of resurrection. In figure 8.45, drawn from a painting in the *Book of the Hidden Chamber* on the walls of the tomb of Rameses VI, we see this culmination of the twelfth and final hour of the night, with the dawn breaking and the hypotenusal Osiris transforming himself into Horus-in-the-Horizon.

The archetypal setting for all of this was at Giza. That was the Place of the Golden Angles, the Place of Resurrection. It was truly Golden Giza, where

Figure 8.46. In the center of this picture in beaten gold from the Second Shrine of Tutankhamun lie two mummies in their sarcophagi. They are both encircled by the protective and friendly netherworld serpent named Tepi, "he with the head," who is always shown with a human head. It is his job to keep the mummies safe and, because he emits light, to provide illumination in the darkness. He is the same human-headed serpent as the one depicted in figure 8.6, a scene from the tomb of Rameses III. The top mummy is labeled "he of the sarcophagus" and represents the dead Osiris wearing the white crown of Upper Egypt; he also represents the corpse of the sun during the night hours when he is in the netherworld. Below him is a mummy believed (on the basis of similar illustrations elsewhere) to be that of the netherworld Horus in the process of emerging from the dead Osiris just prior to the sunrise, when he will be represented as the hypotenuse of the golden triangle who leaps above the horizon and becomes Horus-in-the-Horizon, particularly at Giza. To the right of the encircled mummies is a strange container known as the Chest of Re. It contains secret things. The arms and four hands are a cryptographic inscription that in addition gives a double meaning. Crytographically, the hieroglyphs can be read "chest," but the four hands also stand symbolically for "the limbs of Osiris" that lie concealed in the mysterious chest. Although I have solved the mystery of what the ancient Egyptians were really referring to by their myth of "the limbs of Osiris" and have explained this at length in my study of the Temple of Seti I and the Osireion at Abydos, with physical evidence to make it clear, the explanation is far too lengthy for summary here. Beneath them, and seen more clearly in the accompanying drawn version of this picture in figure 8.47, the ram's head of the netherworld form of the *ba* (spiritual force) of the sun is seen rising out of the earth, which represents the imminent sunrise. When he rises he will be "the great corpse which is in the horizon, the secret divine corpse" (John Darnell, pp. 90–93), who is shown as the hypotenusal mummy rising at Giza. (*Photo by Robert Temple*)

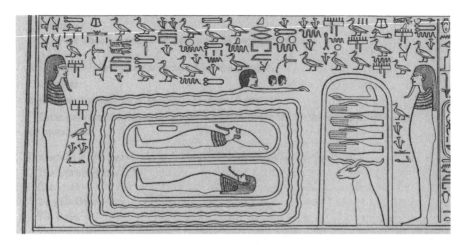

Figure 8.47. This is a drawing of the image seen in figure 8.46. Taken from Alexandre Piankoff, *The Shrines of Tut-Ankh-Amon*, Pantheon, New York, 1955, figure 41, opposite page 120.

Figure 8.48. A magnificent Old Kingdom carving of a solar ram, who has risen from the horizon and is triumphant in the sky. (*Object in the Egyptian Museum at Cairo; photo by Robert Temple*)

eternal life awaited the blessed dead. In this setting, presided over by the guardian Anubis, carved as the largest statue in the world, the resurrected sun flashed on the gold-plated tips of the three Giza pyramids, and the beams of light struck the tip of the Pyramid of Chephren literally at a golden angle through the air. All the key monuments were knitted together tightly by overlapping and interconnecting golden angles in a maze so complex and so unobvious to the uninitiated that it has escaped detection until now, approximately 4,500 years after its pattern was last known, recognized, and understood.

We now know that at Giza there are multiple esoteric connections between the key points of the main structures, which define their size, shape, and location, based on lines drawn by some planner on a map and then carried out on the ground by surveyors and construction engineers.

The location and dimensions of the Sphinx are therefore not accidental. They and the Great Pyramid, the Pyramid of Chephren, and the Pyramid of Mycerinus are all mutually defined. All took their sizes and positions from each other, and all were part of a simultaneous plan. Giza is a unity.

Truly this plan is magnificent and beautiful.

Now perhaps we may at last have a true understanding of the Great Sphinx of Giza. It was originally a gigantic statue of the guardian Anubis, crouching at the entrance to the Giza Plateau. It was an island surrounded by a moat filling the surviving Sphinx Pit, most commonly known in ancient times as the Jackal Lake, which was filled with water from the Nile inundation and was also topped up by water carried down a specially constructed drain to catch any rain that fell higher up the plateau. Sacred ceremonies took place in, on, and around this moat; they are described often in the Pyramid Texts and later texts as well. During the century and a half of chaos, floods, drought, and famine of the terrible time known as the First Intermediate Period, when the government collapsed and mobs ran amok smashing everything in their rage (following the Sixth Dynasty, which was the end of the Old Kingdom period), the head of Anubis must have been drastically mutilated. We know that during this period the statues were smashed in the adjoining Valley Temple, so it stands to reason that rampaging mobs would also smash the head of Anubis at the same time.

When order returned under the Middle Kingdom and the Twelfth Dynasty was established, and an attempt was made to reconstitute Egyptian civilization (though the art of building stone pyramids could never be recovered and was lost forever), the third king of that dynasty took an interest in the mutilated statue of Anubis. That king was Pharaoh Amenemhet II. Because the head of Anubis was ruined beyond repair, he had a new and smaller head carved out of the neck. That head was a human head, and its face was his own. He was clearly not a man who suffered from excessive modesty or lack of feelings of self-worth.

By the time the New Kingdom came along centuries later, after yet another era, known as the Second Intermediate Period, a young son of the king was out hunting on horseback on the deserted Giza Plateau, which was largely abandoned and full of wildlife, and he became tired and looked for some shade in which he might rest. He did so in the shade afforded by the head of Amenemhet II, which was sticking up out of the sand. But of course no one knew that the head was that of Amenemhet II, because no one remembered Amenemhet II any longer, much less what he had looked like. The young man assumed that this was the original head of a gigantic buried statue, traces of the back of which were also visible. This young man fell asleep and had a powerful dream. In the dream, the statue spoke to him and said that if he would clear it of sand and show his piety, the god of that statue would make him king of Egypt. (Being a younger son, this was not expected to happen to him.) We do not know how much truth there is in this story, but it is what the young man ordered to be carved in stone and inscribed on the famous Dream Stela between the Sphinx's paws after he had cleared it of sand. That Dream Stela still survives (see figures 3.3, 3.5, 3.7, and 3.8). And the young man did indeed become king of Egypt, the pharaoh whom we call Thutmosis IV, or Thothmes IV. The Dream Stela may largely have been propaganda intended to legitimize his succession, but that doesn't really matter to us anymore, as he is not around for us to complain about his rule or misrule, whichever was the case.

It never crossed the mind of the future Thutmosis IV that the statue that he cleared of sand was not the original statue in its entirety, and that its head had been remodeled. He strapped a stone royal beard onto the face, drilled a hole in the top of the head into which he inserted a pole with banners, painted the statue in garish colors, hung ornamental collars around its neck, and promoted it as an idol to be visited and worshipped. The altar for doing this was conveniently placed in front of his own dedicatory Dream Stela. Thus, this idol was as much a cult of himself as it was of the spirit of the statue. It was a way of celebrating his pharaohship. He claimed that the body was that of a lion. Even if he noticed that it did not really look like one, he chose to overlook that fact, because the lion was a royal beast, and he *wanted it to be a lion.* So everybody believed in the Emperor's New Clothes, and they still do.

It is amazing how effective propaganda can be.

But what we have needed to recapture is the true purpose, origin, and nature of the Sphinx of Giza. In doing so, we have honored Maāt, Cosmic Order. We can now grasp something that had seemed lost to us forever, the living soul of the Age of Giza. May it bless us in our future endeavors.

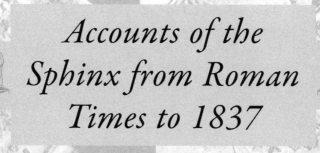

Accounts of the Sphinx from Roman Times to 1837

Section 1

ACCOUNTS OF THE SPHINX FROM ROMAN TIMES TO 1798

The following extracts appear in chronological order and are translated when necessary into English—those from French by Olivia Temple and those from German by myself. The notes in brackets within and following the extracts are by me as well.

PLINY (1ST CENTURY AD)

Natural History, Book 36, Chapter 17

Translated by D. E. Eichholz, Loeb Classical Library series, vol. X
of Pliny, Harvard University Press, USA, 1971

Page 61

In front of them [the pyramids] is the Sphinx, which deserves to be described even more than they, and yet the Egyptians have passed it over in silence. The inhabitants of the region regard it as a deity. They are of the opinion that a King Harmais [corruption of the Greek Harmachis; other texts of Pliny say Amasis] is buried inside it and try to make out that it was brought to the spot: it is in fact carefully fashioned from the native rock. The face of the monstrous creature is painted with ruddle [i.e., painted red] as a sign of reverence. The circumference of the head when measured across the forehead amounts to 102 feet, the length is 243 feet, and the height from the paunch to the top of the asp [uraeus] on its head is 61.5 feet.

[Pliny is the only classical author to mention the Sphinx, apart from the following indirect reference by the Roman poet Lucan. The Sphinx is not mentioned by Herodotus, Diodorus Siculus, Strabo, or any others.]

LUCAN (1ST CENTURY AD)
Pharsalia, Book IX, 156
Translated by H. T. Riley, Bohn's Classical Library, London 1890

Page 344

> Dragged forth from the sepulchres of the pyramids, shall not Amasis and the other kings float for me upon the stream of the Nile? For thee unburied, Magnus [Pompey], let all the sepulchres pay the penalty . . .

[There is general agreement among those few scholars who have noticed this line in Lucan's epic poem about the civil war between Pompey and Julius Caesar that the reference to Amasis is to the tradition in Roman literature at that time that he had been buried at the Sphinx. (There was never any tradition that Amasis had been buried in any of the pyramids themselves.) Riley, the translator, has even added a footnote to this effect (page 344, note 4).]

ABD AL-LATĪF AL- BAGHDĀDI (1220 AD)
Relation de l'Égypte
French translation of "Abd-Allatif" from the Arabic by
Silvestre de Sacy (Paris: Treuttel et Würtz, 1810)

Pages 179–80

> A little more than a bowshot from these pyramids, one sees the colossal figure of a head and a neck, which come out of the ground. This figure is called *Abou'lhaul;* and it is said that the body to which this head belongs is buried under the ground. In judging the dimensions of the body from those of the head, it ought to be 70 cubits or more in length. One sees on the figure a reddish tint and a red varnish, which has a vivid freshness. This figure is very beautiful, and its mouth has an air of grace and beauty. One could say it smiles graciously.
>
> When a perceptive man asked me what excited my admiration most of all the things that I had seen in Egypt, I said to him that it was the precision of

the proportions in the head of the Sphinx. In effect, one remarks between the different parts of this head, for example the nose, the eyes and the ears, the same proportions which one sees in the works of nature. Thus it is that the nose of a child matches its size and it is in proportion with the rest of its body in such a way that if it belonged to the face of a man it would be a deformity. The nose of a man transposed onto the face of a child would disfigure it. It is the same with all the other parts of its head: there aren't any parts of it that should not have a certain shape and certain dimensions to be in proportion with such a figure. And if these proportions are not respected, the figure is spoilt. So it is astonishing that in such a huge figure, the sculptor had been able to conserve the correct proportions of all the parts, while nature does not provide any similar example of such huge size, nor anything that could be compared to it.

[Note: The nose of the Sphinx had not yet been disfigured at this date, and the face was still intact.]

Page 225 (footnote 38 of de Sacy)

I have not discoursed further upon the Sphinx, nor the extensive mutilations that have been inflicted on it since the time of Abd-allatif. One can see these details in the notes and explanations put together by Monsieur [Louis] Langlès in his edition of the Voyage of [Friderik] Norden [see under date 1757, following, the extract from *Travels in Egypt and Nubia* by Friderik Norden; the 1797/98 French editions of Norden's book incorporate these notes referred to by de Sacy, but they were not in the 1757 French edition]: but I cannot refrain from quoting two modern writers whose evidence confirms after six centuries the account of our author: "This monstrous statue is truly colossal, says Monsieur Grobert, . . . it has been painted yellow, and the color has been preserved until today in the parts which are not damaged."

The other passage is even more important in its details, and by the name of the author who is deemed unimpeachable in this subject. This is Monsieur Denon, and he explains thus:

[This passage is translated under "Denon."]

ABD AL-LATĪF AL-BAGHDĀDI (1220)

Modern English translation of above de Sacy passage:
The Eastern Key: Kitāb al-Ifādah wa'l-I'tibār
Translated by Kamal Hafuth Zand and John A.
and Ivy E. Videan (London: Allen and Unwin, 1965)

Pages 123–25

At little more than a bowshot from these pyramids is a colossal figure of a head and neck projecting from the earth. The name of this is *Abu'l haul* (Sphinx) and the body to which the head pertains is said to be buried under the earth. To judge, from [on the basis of] the dimensions of the head, of those of the body, its length must be more than 70 cubits. On the face is a reddish tint, and a red varnish as bright as if freshly applied. The face is remarkably handsome, and the mouth expresses much grace and beauty: one might fancy it smiling gracefully.

A sensible man enquiring of me as to what, of all I had seen in Egypt, had most excited my admiration, I answered: "The nicety of proportion in the head of the Sphinx." In fact, between the different parts of this head, the nose, for example, the eyes, and the ears, the same proportion is remarked as is observed by nature in her works. Thus, the nose of a child is suitable to its stature, and proportioned to the rest of its frame, while if it belonged to the face of a full-grown man it would be reckoned a deformity. The nose of a grown man on the visage of a child would equally be a disfigurement. The same holds good with respect to all the other members. There are none but should have a certain form and dimension in order to bear relation to such and such a face, and where these proportions are not observed, the face is spoiled. Hence the wonder that in a face of such colossal size the sculptor should have been able to preserve the exact proportion of every part, seeing that nature presented him with no model of a similar colossus or any at all comparable.

TAQIYYU 'L-DIN AL-MAQRIZI (1378 OR 1379)

This passage is taken from the French translation in the
Notes of Louis Langlès, *Voyage d'Égypte et de Nubie par Fréderic-Louis [Friderik] Norden,* new edition (Paris: 1798, vol. III), pages 338–39

The blessed Sheikh Mohammed Ssa'im el-Deher, of the Sufi Order from the Monastery of el-Salehhyeh, devised the plan to destroy some of the practices contrary to the law of Allah. We have seen this saintly person go to the pyramids, mutilate the figure of the Sphinx, and dispose of the pieces of it. This figure remains in this state up until today, and since that era the sands inundate the territory of Giza. The inhabitants attribute this scourge [of the sand] to the mutilation of the Sphinx.

BERNHARD VON BREYDENBACH (1483)
Les Saintes pérégrinations de Bernard de Breydenbach, 1483.
Texte et Traduction Annoté, par le Père F. Larrivaz, S. J., *Extraits Relatifs à l'Égypte Suivant l'Édition de 1490* (Cairo: Imprimerie nationale, 1904)

Page 59

Near these pyramids the great idol of Isis [the Sphinx], previously venerated by the Egyptians, is still standing. Beyond, one also sees some vast ancient ruins; previously, the celebrated and mighty capital of Egypt, which had a hundred gates, was also situated there, and it was the birthplace of Saint Maurice and of the Theban Legion.

[Here he confuses Memphis near Giza with the later capital of Thebes in Upper Egypt, which was said to have had "a hundred gates."]

◖ *Voyages en Égypte* ◗

The French Institute of Archaeology at Cairo between 1970 and 1988 published twenty-five volumes (some in several parts) of early travelers' descriptions of Egypt, dating from 1482 to the time of Napoleon. Some volumes contain several travelers' writings. This admirable series is entitled *Voyages en Égypte,* and was published in Paris. Olivia and I have excerpted every description of the Sphinx appearing in these volumes and she then translated them all from French. This was often difficult, as the language was old-fashioned, and many obsolete words occurred. Some of the passages are translations into French from other languages.

JOOS VAN GHISTELE (1482–1483)
Translated from volume 16 of the series *Voyages en Égypte* (1976)

Page 83

Behind these pyramids is found a statue [the Sphinx] of which the head is so large that 4 spans [*brasses*] are insufficient to encompass it. This statue has the appearance of a human being as far as the shoulders, but from there on it reveals the form of a serpent [he could only see the top of the back, which looked like a serpent], of which the tail is a good 50 spans in length. The whole statue is carved from one single piece of rock. In the vicinity people recount that this head had the habit of speaking, at the time of idolatry, after the fashion of other false gods. One day in those times, a man went there to make some sacrifices; he asked of the Idol what was going to happen to him, and the head replied to him that he would become King and master of Egypt if he wanted to follow its counsels. Thereupon, the man replied that he would follow them, and it happened that this man became King of Egypt as he had been told he would by the head. A little while after his coronation, he returned to the place where the head was, which he decapitated with an ax, saying: "It's all very well that you have given me counsel so that I can secure Egypt; but from today on, you will not give any more counsel to anyone." And so it is that since then the head rests upon the ground up until our own time.

[Note: This amazing folklore survival of a true story over the course of three thousand years has been discussed at length in chapter 3.

FELIX FABRI (1483)
Translated from volume 14 of the series *Voyages en Égypte* (1975)

Pages 452–54

The Sphinx of Giza: Idol of Isis?

Near the pyramids we saw a huge stone idol which had the form of a woman, and we had no doubt that it was a monument dedicated to Isis. Daughter of the Greek Prometheus, of a unique beauty, she had been loved and pursued by the adulterous Jupiter. Having fled far away from her father because of the crime perpetrated, and with the assistance of Jupiter, she made her way to Egypt with a naval fleet, and after a series of wars, she submitted to Egypt . . .

Page 455

A Misshapen Rock Near the Sphinx of Giza

Near the idol of Isis, lies a kind of misshapen rock which—it is said—once formed the figure of an ox, of Osiris or of Apis. On the death of Osiris, legend says, his heart emigrated into an ox, which is the reason that the Egyptians worship the ox. As for Isis, his wife, having reassembled the pieces of his cut up body, she deposited them in a wooden ox, re-covered it with bovine skin and left it to the veneration of the people. With the passing of time, the wooden idol rotted and the Egyptians carved an enormous rock and consecrated it to Osiris.

Page 456

A Small Lake with Miraculous Water

On the other side of the pyramids, not far from the Idol of Isis [the Sphinx] there is a small lake, more memorable for its miraculous property than the abundance of its water. Once a year, for one month, its water changes into blood—a fact of which the Saracens attribute to a perpetual reminder of the first wound by which the water and the rivers of Egypt were changed into blood as mentioned in Exodus 7.

[Note: Exodus 7: 17–25, in *The New English Bible* (1970)]:

[Moses said to the Egyptians at the command of the Lord]: ". . . so now the Lord says, 'By this you shall know that I am the Lord.' With this rod that I have in my hand, I shall now strike the Nile and it will be changed into blood. The fish will die and the river will stink, and the Egyptians will be unable to drink water from the Nile." The Lord then told Moses to say to Aaron, "Take your staff and stretch your hand out over the waters of Egypt, its rivers and its streams, and over every pool and cistern, to turn them into blood. There shall be blood throughout the whole of Egypt, blood even in their wooden bowls and jars of stone." So Moses and Aaron did as the Lord had commanded. He lifted up his staff and struck the water of the Nile in the sight of Pharaoh and his courtiers, and all the water was changed into blood. The fish died and the river stank, and the Egyptians could not drink the water from the Nile. There was blood everywhere in Egypt. But the Egyptian magicians did the same thing by their spells; and still Pharaoh remained obstinate, as the Lord had foretold, and did not listen to Moses and Aaron. He turned away, went into his house and dismissed the matter from his mind. Then the Egyptians all dug for drinking water round about the river, because they could not drink from the waters of the Nile itself. This lasted for seven days from the time when the Lord struck the Nile.]

PIERRE BELON DU MANS (1547)
Translated from volume 1 of the series *Voyages en Égypte* (1970)

Page 113a (no modern pagination; pagination derived from the original)

Finally, having come up to the village of Busiris, where the water of the Nile has broken the arches of the stone bridge, it is necessary to go by boat. And after the village of Busiris, there is a long causeway, which goes on to terminate at the desert of the pyramids. [The causeway to which he refers culminated, as one approached the Giza Plateau, in the Cheops Causeway, leading up to the Great Pyramid. In those days it was still intact, and the stones had not yet been carried away or built over. Today, not a stone remains. Old engravings show this causeway intact in the seventeenth century, and portions of it intact well into the nineteenth century.]

[This is the Busiris near the Sphinx, not the Busiris that was in the north of Egypt, in the Delta region. The Gizan Busiris was called Djedu ("ghosts") by the ancient Egyptians.]

Page 113b

Then we came to pass the dike of Busiris, which has been broken in one place, where the water of the Nile has formed a lake (of which the Greeks have taken the occasion to invent the fables of the waters of their Rivers Lethe and Styx: for the embalmed bodies, which were carried to the sepulchre, passed by boat across the said lake, which has completely overflowed and broken the causeway). Those who had ascended well up [the dike] did not have any difficulty in fording across, following the guides, but the others not so high up had to wait for a boat. Nevertheless, some who had stripped their clothes off led the others, mounted, by the halter, enabling them to pass through the water, which was up to their armpits.

Page 115b

Thus we come to the Sphinx or Andro-Sphinx, of which the ancients have spoken so much, which is still entire in the above-mentioned sterile plain with the pyramids. It seems well not to pass it by without saying a little something about it.

Concerning the Great Colossus named by
Herodotus Andro-Sphinx and by Pliny
The Sphinx, Which is a Stone Sculpture in
front of the Pyramids

Having well considered the great stone head, which is adjacent to the water of the Nile a little way below the [level of the] Great Pyramid [a remarkable confirmation, if any were needed, of the points made in chapter 6 of this book], we had occasion to admire the works of the Egyptians. And although Pliny had very much exaggerated the size of the pyramids, nevertheless, he was more reasonable in describing the colossus of the Sphinx, which is to the right of the Great Pyramid towards the east.

We do not want to linger too long on the description of the Sphinx, for truly all that has been depicted and written of this creature, from the Ethiopians to the Egyptians, is fable. . . .

Page 116a

This stone sits on a cubic shape, which is only a large sculpted face looking toward Cairo. Its proportions of face, nose, eyes, mouth, chest, chin, and other parts are so well retained that we cannot deny that it is a very grand creation. It doesn't have any similarity to other sculptures of sphinxes. . . .

Page 116b

But this stone of which we speak is still the greatest marvel, for being massively huge, it has a height of 63 feet. Pliny gave it 143 feet in length. . . . It is the grandeur and sublimity of this colossus that is no less a marvel than a great obelisk. We like to maintain that the Romans never made anything from a huge mass of stone which could compare in sublimity and magnificence to the work of a pyramid, an obelisk, or to the Sphinx of which we speak. . . .

[It must be noted that at this time, as units of measurement, French feet were considerably shorter than English feet, so allowance must be made for this in some of these early accounts. On the other hand, Belon errs in saying that Pliny gave a length of 143 feet for the Sphinx, when it was really given by him as 243 feet, and the Pliny measurements seem to be transposed into English feet rather than French feet. Probably the safest thing to do with all the early accounts is to ignore the many measurements that are given of the Sphinx as being irrelevant, since we now know all the true measurements anyway.]

Page 117a

It remains now that we speak of whence the Sphinx has come to the Egyptians: It is that during the sign of Leo and Virgo [he is unaware that Leo and Virgo did not exist to the ancient Egyptians prior to the third century BC], the Nile inundates the land of Egypt, and the Egyptians, wanting to signify their riches [the crops from the rich soil deposited by this inundation], created a sculpted monster, which is a virgin in front and has the body of a lion, and bears the name of the Sphinx, and because it is something made to please, one thus sees this [image] also in [diverse] sculptures. Witness the above-mentioned great head of the Sphinx. . . .

ANDRÉ THEVET (1552)
Translated from volume 24 of the series *Voyages en Égypte* (1984)

Pages 190–93

Do not expect to see the whole base and foundation of these pyramids, which are in this sandy locality. The sands have covered a good part of them despite the fact that they equal the highest mountains of Egypt in their elevation. [At that time, large mounds of sand-covered rubbish lay against the sides of the pyramids, from the time when they were stripped of their casing stones. Today, all of this has been cleared away.] And this has been seen even more so with the colossi that one calls sphinxes (on account of the monstrous figure and variety that they have), which are beginning to be buried in the piles of sand blown about by the wind.

It is true that I cannot be persuaded, that the colossus which we see there today is not one of these sphinxes which one guesses to be the tomb of some Egyptian king. It represents nothing more than a monster, in that it is made like a man's head, marvelously huge, a body without shape, and of hard stone. . . . Some say that Isis raised the monument after the loss of her friend [Osiris], beating her breast on account of his death. Its head is huge like a tower, being 200 paces broad and about a hundred long. . . . Pliny mistakenly spoke of this Sphinx or Colossus, saying it was more admirable and remarkable than all the pyramids: this comparison is about as true in terms of grandeur and size as would be that of comparing a rat to an elephant. And if he had seen it and studied it as closely as I did, he [Pliny] would not have written such nonsense, unless it was the translator and commentator of my own time [Antoine du Pinet, translator of the French version of Pliny published in Lyon in 1562], who mocks the reader by saying that it has a large head, the wings of a bird, and that the rest of the body resembles a dog. This description is also mistaken in that there are no wings, no body, nor any resemblance at all that I know of, and I have seen it nine times in three years.

[The "wings" mentioned by du Pinet in his marginal note to his translation of Pliny may derive from descriptions of the *nemes* headdress, which has sometimes been called winged because of the folds extending to either side of the head. Thevet points out that since the Sphinx was buried in sand up to its shoulders, it was impossible to say in his and du Pinet's time what its body looked like, and hence it had no discernible resemblance to anything.]

CHRISTOPHER FUERER VON HAIMENDORFF (1565)
Reis-Beschreibung, in Egypten, Arabien, Palästinam, Syrien, etc.
(Nuremberg: 1646)

Pages 59–60

A Large Sphinx Which Was Used for Giving Oracles

In front of the pyramids, in the direction of the city of Cairo, stands a very large Sphinx cut out of the rock, so much covered by wind-blown sand on its lower part that only the head, breast, and back protrude. The head is no less than 53 of my paces [*meiner Schritt*] in circumference [he could walk around it] and similarly also 53 paces tall. An immensely large creature. It has on its right side in its flank a quadrangular hole [*viereckicht Loch,* which could mean either a square or rectangular hole] through which, as we were informed, in olden days one could go inside and could ascend into the head. Inside there the priests spoke, which the Egyptians took for oracles. Nowadays, this hole is mostly collapsed and filled with sand by the wind. [It is unlikely that this is eyewitness evidence that there was an entrance into the Sphinx behind the "cupola," which now sits up against the right side of the Sphinx, since it is difficult to believe that the Sphinx was cleared down to bedrock for it to be seen at this period when, after all, Haimendorff could walk around the head. This reference must therefore be to the same square hole in the Sphinx's back reported by many others, as discussed in chapter 2 of my main text. Because the back was only partially exposed, "its right side" as seen by Haimendorff may have been in the center, structurally speaking, but to the right in terms of what was actually exposed to his view, suggesting that the sand had risen higher at this time on the south side than on the north side, which is the case in many of the old photos in this book. The only other alternative would be to suggest that there had been a partial clearance of the Sphinx in the sixteenth century, though Castela said that in 1600–1601 he could only see a head and shoulders, which is confirmed by Sandys in 1611. The fact that Haimendorff mentions the hole immediately after saying that the Sphinx was "an immensely large creature" suggests that the hole may have been seen only after going a considerable distance along the back to reach it.]

JOHANN HELFFRICH (1565)

Kurzer und Warhafftiger Bericht/ von der Reis aus Venedig nach Ieursalem/von dannen in Aegypten/auff den Berg Sinai, Allcair/ Alexandria/ und Folgends Widerumb gen Venedig

[A Short and True Account of the Journey from Venice to Jerusalem, from thence into Egypt, to Mount Sinai, to al-Cairo, Alexandria, and Afterward Returning to Venice; unpaginated, but organized sequentially by date as in a diary (the year of the journey being 1565)] (Leipzig: 1579)

December 13 [1565; "Den Dreyzehenden December"]

The following day we left early and several of us rode to the place where the pyramids stand. As we approached it, we first encountered a huge standing head cut out of stone, which rose very high, as shown in this figure. [He refers to a crude woodcut opposite, showing a woman's head and torso with two breasts, and hair descending to either side to the extent of the Sphinx's lappets, which is shown protruding from the sand directly below the breasts.]

This head is the height of three men and stands straight up from a neck, it is 8 fathoms [about 50 feet] in circumference, and from ancient times has been called Imago Isidis, that is, the effigy of the goddess Isidis. This Isis of which the image has the name has also been called Io and is a daughter of the King Inachos in Greece, which king in Egypt is called Osiris, where he is her husband. There she is called Isis, who, after she died, was considered a goddess, and this image was set up to honor her. The local inhabitants worship it and honor it as a goddess. They are also in the habit of offering a sacrifice of a goose at the usual time, which offering they call the Isiaca. [The noun spelled in the original, *eine Ganz,* is a sixteenth-century form of *Gans,* "goose."] Concerning this, consult Juvenal, *Satires,* 6: *Si candida iusserit Io,* and recall Lucian's *Dialogues* in three volumes. [No reference is given, so we do not know to which Dialogue by Lucian he is referring. His reference to the Sixth Satire of the Roman poet Juvenal is to lines 526–41, "if the white Io shall so order," Io here being identified with Isis, and a mention by Juvenal that a fat goose was offered to Osiris by a priest dressed as Anubis. Juvenal spoke of Isis giving a command "by the voice of the Goddess herself," presumably referring to the oracular pronouncements issuing from the Sphinx.]

This image [the statue] is entirely hollow on the inside, and one can enter it underground from a distance by means of a narrow passage made of stone, through which one can pass secretly. By means of this passage, the heathen priests entered the head and spoke to the people, making announcements by the babbling of the head, or else the effigy did this by its own means.

Hard by this head are the three pyramids just mentioned. . . .

JEAN PALERNE (1581)
Translated from volume 2 of the series *Voyages en Égypte* (1971)

Page 109

A little to the right of the Great Pyramid is a massive head looking toward Cairo, not a little wonderful, for apart from the fact that it is made from a huge piece of marble lying on its base, in size it has a circumference of around 100 feet, and in height taken from the chin toward the top of the head, some 60 feet. Some people take it to be a monstrosity, having the face of a man and the body of a lion. As regards to the body that it has, it is all eaten away and corroded, appearing nevertheless to have traces of color on the face, with ears of huge proportion; the remains are well enough proportioned.

As has been said, one knows that the Egyptians wished to signify the wealth and fertility of the land that the inundation of the Nile produced, while the sun was in the signs of Leo and Virgo represented by a monster having the front half of a virgin and the back end of a lion: and they called it Sphinx: nevertheless, it had the face of a man, not of a woman.

Other people say that this head served in the past as an oracle. And happy was he who could be buried nearby. This is made apparent by the large number of sepulchres that are round about here . . .

PROSPER ALPIN/ALPINUS (1581–1584)
From his *Histoire Naturelle de L'Égypte*
Translated from volume 20 of the series *Voyages en Égypte* (1979);
the whole work appears in five parts from 1979 to 1980 and
includes volumes 21 and 22 of the series

Part I, page 68:
Chapter VI: "The Pyramids and the Great Colossus Named Sphinx," pages
58–68.

The Sphinx
But last of all we come to that great colossus called Sphinx, near to the first
pyramid and made from an enormous monolith. This massive rock is made of
marble [i.e., limestone. Travelers have often mistaken the nature of Egyptian
stone; also, they have often gotten the descriptions wrong of stones that are
less common in Europe, such as rose granite. The Sphinx is made of limestone,
since it is a rock of the Plateau of Giza recut and finished by man.] It presents
an immense and very large face, looking towards Cairo and sculpted in every
way with great competency. That is to say, its chin, its mouth, its nose, its eyes,
its brow and its ears seem to be cut with a profound knowledge of the art of
sculpture. There does not appear to be in the stone any opening by which one
could go inside, but it is likely, as we have said of it, that one entered into the
colossus from the Great Pyramid nearby. And, since the Sphinx on occasion
gave [oracular] responses, it is likely that inside it contains some empty parts
into which the priests would go in order to be able to reply on its behalf.

Page 60

But now we will talk about what we saw inside the Great Pyramid. For no one,
it seems to me, has properly described the interior. Until 1584, this pyramid
only had one door by which you could enter. But, this past year [1583/1584],
the Bassa [Pasha] Ibrahim, the deputy king of Egypt, urged by curiosity, or
rather by an African sorcerer [or witch doctor], that a valuable treasure was
hidden in the pyramid, ordered that the entrance, which was very narrow and
made access difficult, be enlarged—by cutting into the pyramid so that a man
can now go inside without stooping. The Bassa even, at first, decided to hollow out a shaft inside the pyramid and to fill it with gunpowder to completely
destroy the monument. But he changed his mind at the advice of George
Hemi, now the Illustrious Consul of Venice (for, I say, in doing so he would
have greatly endangered the whole town).

Page 61

But now I speak of the entrance to this pyramid. I have said then, that the pyramid only had a means of entry by a single door, at the base, in the middle of one of the sides. This entrance gave access to nothing important. So, in the stone wall of the pyramid, nearly at the base, in the middle of one side, there is a hole, about 5 paces long, similar to a section of a pyramid with four sides [he is referring to the angled arch above this entrance], with a more spacious opening and larger outside, but narrow and rounded on the inside. At first very large, this opening gets smaller by slow degrees and comes to an end with a long and steep passage. Thus, the opening of this hole, on the interior, becomes narrow and confined, to the point where a man stretched out on the ground on his stomach and crawling like a snake has difficulty entering. [This is the Descending Passage, which at that time was still nearly blocked by sand and rubbish at the bottom.]

Inside (The Interior)
Once inside, one comes across a large space to the right, from which there is a shaft, quite narrow and almost filled with sand and stones. [This is the entrance to the ascending "well shaft," which is found near the bottom of the Descending Passage. The sand and stones were finally cleared from above by Captain Caviglia in 1817.] It is certainly of this well that Pliny himself, among the ancient writers, speaks.

[Pliny speaks of the pyramids more with irony than admiration. He mentions this well: "86 cubits, which, one thinks, received water from a river . . ."]

Page 63

The Well
But we think that we should not pass by in silence another peculiarity which also excites admiration on account of its superiority; it concerns a well which we encountered after our entrance into the pyramid. We found that it was at least 70 paces deep and did not contain any water. And I shall tell you how we were able to verify this.

From a mountain called Liban had come to Egypt the reverend brother Paul Bigi, (*janensis,* as I have heard tell) [indicating his place of origin] from the order of Preaching Friars, a man who was very knowledgeable in all kinds of sciences, specializing in mathematics and mechanics: with the help of bronze clocks, he made a sphere by means of which one could observe with great exactitude all the movements of all the celestial bodies and especially the planets. [Presumably, this was an orrery]. With the same competency, he made in Cairo, for Assan [Hassan], the deputy king of Egypt, a little gold boat which, moved by clockwork, accomplished by itself all the movement essential for navigation. As soon as it was finished he showed it to us: on its own it moved forward, backward, and around; the sails unfolded and folded up again, the anchors were raised, the bronze missiles were automatically fired; one heard the sound of trumpets and all the things that vessels usually do.

Such was the intelligence of this man, that he so closely examined everything with more care than other people. One day, he happened to come with us to look at the pyramids, and once inside the large one [the Great Pyramid] he examined with much care and in great detail what he found there. As a result he came to the idea that the pyramid went deep into the earth before it was raised above the surface, and he suspected that the well had not been made for receiving water but rather to serve as a means of access toward the base of the pyramid.

To verify his hypothesis, he employed some local people, without regard for the expense, so that they could clear the entrance to the pit, filled with earth and stones, and free the passageway [the Descending Passage]. After that, with a long rope introduced into the well, he descended [from the Grand Gallery], with ourselves and some other people for about 70 paces, and with ease, saw that the cavity of the well had, here and there, some jutting stones, like cornices, which made the descent easy and without danger. Once we were about 70 paces down (as we said before), we found two square passages joining again, in the empty space where the well converges, those which we had encountered in the upper parts of the pyramid: one leading to the stone Sphinx and the other to the second pyramid, the one which has no way of entering. [At that time there was no known exterior opening into the Chephren Pyramid; it was opened in 1818 by Belzoni.] We would have got through to these monuments if we had not found the passages obstructed by stones that had fallen and if we had not believed that there were similar subsidences ahead.

Thus, this well had not been hollowed beforehand to provide the necessary water for construction, as [Pierre] Belon had mistakenly believed. It had been constructed to make possible a way to go and see the great stone Sphinx which had been built not far from the pyramid, as well as the second pyramid called Sepulchre of the Queen [Chephren's Pyramid], to which there is no exterior access. This great depth of well is even mentioned by Pliny, who gives it 86 cubits. Relying on his evidence, Paul Bigi wanted to explore even deeper down into it.

Page 67

The Second Pyramid

We come then to the second pyramid [of Chephren], which seems a little smaller than the first, and is a stone's throw away from it. There are no steps that can allow you to go up it on the outside. Furthermore, one sees that all the sides are of smooth marble, perfectly polished, and even until now one cannot find any entrance that gives access from the exterior. Consequently, given that it contains, as all the Egyptians truly believe, the tomb of a king, or, according to the opinion of many, of a queen, one could assume that one could enter into this pyramid from the large one [the Great Pyramid]. It is this that the Rev. Bigi immediately supposed and later told us that he had verified: one entered by the well and through the stone passages dividing at the bottom of the well, which we confirmed with certainty with the aid of a compass, namely that one passage went toward the nearby Sphinx, and one passage went toward this pyramid.

[This is a most extraordinary account. First of all, the Pyramid of Chephren is described as if it had most or all of its casing stones intact as late as 1584. But second, two square passages are said to have been encountered in the well shaft of the Great Pyramid, either at the point of what is called "the grotto" or at the point where the well shaft ends by opening into the Descending Passage, which passages joined one another and led off to the southeast and the southwest, and were blocked with stones and subsidences but were presumed to lead to the Sphinx and the Pyramid of Chephren. There is no knowledge of any such passage entrances today leading from the grotto, but then there are few if any people living who have ever been down the well shaft. This matter clearly requires some further study. Can it be that the entrances to two such passages have been obscured since the sixteenth century and forgotten? Several people explored the well shaft in the nineteenth century and early twentieth century, and they saw nothing of these passages. The grotto area is a small chamber containing much wet sand and gravel, and it is presumably possible that some of this fell across the entrances to some passages. So few people have ever scrutinized this grotto that we cannot be certain whether Alpin's account has any basis in fact. But if he had not encountered two passages, why should he claim that he had? It is at least worth checking out by a close inspection of the well shaft, but then access to the well shaft is now so restricted that even the Giza inspectors have not been down it and regard it as unsafe. Certainly, the well shaft is a claustrophobe's worst nightmare, being exceedingly narrow and extremely deep and requiring one to be lowered on a rope. It is probably more likely that the two passages referred to are portions of the Descending Passage, the one leading to the right heading more or less in the direction of the Pyramid of Chephren (but as we now know, actually leading to the Subterranean Chamber and its strange small tunnel beyond that appears to come to a dead end). It is difficult to imagine, however, that anyone concluded the turning to the left could possibly be heading toward the Sphinx, as surely it must have been clear that it was merely the Descending Passage leading upward to the northern entrance of the pyramid. The use of a compass to determine direction is even more puzzling. Also puzzling is Bigi's wish to go down farther. What made him think he could do that if he had already reached the Descending Passage, where there is no indication that one can go any farther down? Or by "down" did he mean in the direction of what we now know to be the Subterranean Chamber? Since Bigi descended 70 paces, we must presume that by "pace" he meant the Byzantine pace rather than the larger and far earlier Roman pace, and as the Byzantine pace was equal to two and a half feet, this means that he had descended down the well shaft by 175 feet. However, the well shaft is 200 feet long at least. If Bigi really meant 70 feet, then that is the distance to the grotto. At the distance of 170 feet, the well shaft turns farther south before leading the remaining 30 feet down to the intersection with the Descending Passage. Could Bigi possibly be referring to this juncture, which is nearly 70 Byzantine paces down, at which an iron pin also occurs in the rock? Is it possible that at this juncture Bigi discovered an entrance to another passage that has not been noticed since that time because of a stone covering it? In *Egyptian Dawn* I publish a diagram showing the geometrical importance of the point of this juncture to the larger interior design plan of the pyramid, which suggests that it was not at all an arbitrary point, so a concealed passage entrance at that point is by no means inconceivable. I have never been able to gain access to the well shaft to carry out my own close inspections of the kind I would like.]

MICHAEL HEBERER VON BRETTEN (1585–1586)
Translated from volume 18 of the series *Voyages en Égypte* (1976)

Pages 67–68

Not far from the pyramids, one sees a figure called Andro-Sphinx, which the Egyptians made to honor two celestial [zodiacal] signs [Virgo and Leo] which each year brought them all the riches of the Nile. [This refers to the time of the annual inundation and its depositing of the silt.] They made it according to their custom, indicating their beliefs by signs, portraying a Virgin in front and a lion at the rear. From this, one can understand that their greatest riches and their well-being are visible when the sun is in the two signs, that is to say, in the months of July and August, those months [in] which the Nile rises to its maximum, distributing the water over the surrounding land. That is what they wanted to show by these signs and representations.

SEIGNEUR DE VILLAMONT (1590)
Translated from volume 3 of the series *Voyages en Égypte* (1971)

Page 198

[Heading of chapter 13] Full descriptions of the admirable pyramids of Egypt, of the Great Colossus or Idol [the Sphinx], and of the mummies that are in the sandy desert . . .

Page 203

A little distance from the Great Pyramid, and almost adjoining the Nile, is a colossus or head of an idol of a most admirable size: the Campidogle of Rome is nothing compared to it in size. This head is raised on a column [he is referring to the Sphinx's neck; the paws and so forth were then covered in sand] made of a single piece of marble [i.e., limestone]; it is of a height of 92 feet, not including the column [neck] which supports it, and the thickness [*grosseur*] is 60 feet. Pliny gave it the credit of calling it the Sphinx, and said that its face extended 200 feet in width, and the length of its head is 423, which it is not; anyway, it is certainly a head of marvelous size and worthy of being given a marvelous number. It is said that in ancient times it was an oracle that gave responses to the Egyptians for the questions that they asked of it at sunrise.

CHRISTOPHE HARANT OF POLZIC AND
BEZDRUZIC (1598)
Translated from volume 5 of the series *Voyages en Égypte* (1972)

Page 191

The Sphinx
Another thing worthy of admiration and which one finds in these parts is a head whose face resembles a human being and who rests on his neck, facing Cairo. The nose, the eyes, the mouth, the forehead, the cheeks, the ears, and the other elements of the head are cut by the hand of a master, and it is astonishing that all this has remained intact for such a long time. Pliny describes this

head in these measurements: 144 feet [*soulier*, a "shoed foot," slightly larger than a foot (*pied*)] in height, the circumference from the level of the brow and whiskers at the front to the rear is 102 feet. All this is nothing but a single block of marble. It is not only the cutting, but also the transportation of such a stone, that command the admiration of all spectators.

Monsieur de Villamont in book 3 has written that the head is 92 feet high.

According to Pliny, this head had been the tomb of King Amasis, whose body was found in the interior. . . . Others say that this head was an image of the divinity of the Egyptians in the past and that Satan responded [as an oracle] to questions asked at sunrise or sunset. Blaise de Vinegère, in his *Les Images de Plattepeint de Philostrate* [*The Imagines of Philostratus*], says the same thing on that subject, and he adds that those who clamber to the top of the head are struck by misfortune; he cites the example of a Frenchman who, having done this, and led on by curiosity, clambered to the top of the head, and on his return journey to Cairo was thrown to the ground by his horse and killed.

AQUILANTE ROCCHETTA (1599)
Translated from volume 11 of the series *Voyages en Égypte* (1974)

Page 58

(12) At the distance of an arquebus [an old-fashioned rifle] shot from the pyramids, one finds half of a marble statue that, I was told, was made as a certain idol where the pharaohs consulted the oracles; it is a marvelous thing. I did not measure the figure; it is 21 palms [*palmes*] in length. But I quickly left that place for fear of Arab thieves.

HENRY CASTELA (1600–1601 AD)
Translated from volume 11 of the series *Voyages en Égypte* (1974)

Page 181

Prodigious Colossus

I saw a half-figure of a statue, consisting of nothing but a head and shoulders, so excessively and prodigiously large that I could not imagine by whom it was constructed, there being so little means of transporting it in this sandy place. For its shoulders are of such size that according to my measurement they extend up to 80 spans [*brasses*], and from them to the summit of the head, I would say 20 spans. I leave it to those who have never seen the Colossus of

Rhodes whether it could have had any greater bulk. This head is all damaged as a result of its antiquity, rather than by this nation's neglect.

GEORGE SANDYS (1611)

George Sandys, *A Relation of a Journey Begun An. Dom. 1610,* London, 1615, pages 102–103; reprinted later in Samuel Purchas, *Purchas His Pilgrimes* (London: 1625)

Part 2, page 896: "... the Journey of George Sandys in 1610 to the Middle East, including Egypt"

Page 910

The Colossus

Not far off from these the Colossus doth stand, unto the mouth consisting of the natural Rock as if for such a purpose advanced [provided] by Nature: the rest of huge flat stones laid thereon, wrought all together into the form of an Aethiopian woman: and adored heretofore by the countrey people as a rural Deity. Under this, they say, lyeth buried the body of Amasis. [Amasis was a pharaoh of the Twenty-sixth Dynasty, 570–526 BC.] Of shape, lesse monstrous than is Plinies report: who affirmeth, the head to be an hundred and two feet in compass, when the whole is but sixty feet high. The face is something disfigured by time, or by indignation of the Moors, detesting images. The aforesaid Author (together with others) do call it a Sphinx. The upper part of a Sphinx resembled a maide, and the lower a Lion; whereby the Egyptians defigured [represented] the increase of the River, (and consequently of their riches) then rising when the Sun is in Leo and Virgo. This but from the shoulders upward surmounteth the ground [i.e., all that could be seen above ground level at this time was from the shoulders upward], though Pliny give it a belly: which I know not how to reconcile unto the truth, unlesse the sand doe cover the remainder. By a Sphinx the Egyptians in their hieroglyphicks [re]presented an Harlot, having an amiable and alluring face, but withal the tyranny, and rapacity of a Lion: exercised over the poor heart-broken, and voluntarily perishing Lover.

The images of these they also erected before the entrances of their Temples; declaring that secrets of Philosophy, and sacred Mysterie, should be [en]folded in Aenigmaticall expressions, separated from the understanding of the prophane multitude.

WILLIAM LITHGOW (1612)

A Most Delectable and True Discourse of an Admired And Painefull Peregrination from Scotland to the Most Famous Kingdomes in Europe, Asia, and Affricke, 1623 edition (London: 1614)

Page 159

> Betweene the biggest Pyramide, and Nylus [the River Nile], I saw a Colosse, or head of an Idoll, of a wonderful greatnesse; being all of one marble stone, erected on a round rocke: It is of height (not reckoning the Columne) above 815 [this is a typographical error] foote, and of circuite, 68. Pliny gave it the name Sphingo, and reported much more of the bignesse, largenesse, and length of it: but howsoever he erred in his description, yet I resolve my selfe, it is of so great a quantity, that the like thereof (being one intire [*sic*] piece) the world affordeth not [i.e., the like is not to be found elsewhere in the world], and may be reckoned amongst the rarest wonders: Some say, that anciently it was an Oracle, the which so soone as the Sunne arose, would give an answere to the Egyptians, of any thing by them demaunded [i.e., any question they asked].

[Note: The misprint giving 815 feet for the height also appears in the 1614 edition and the modern reprint of 1971. Probably the last digit is accurate, and the 81 was meant to be either a 3 or a 2, giving a height of either 25 feet or 35 feet. By "the column," Lithgow presumably refers to the base of the neck, just visible above the sand, which some people assumed was a column upon which the head rested.]

PIETRO DELLA VALLE (1614)

Les Fameux Voyages de Pietro della Valle, French translation of *Viaggi di Pietro della Valle* (Paris: 1664), 4 vols.

Vol. 1, page 228

> . . . and there nearby I admired a huge head which they call the Sphinx, which is certainly a beautiful piece of stone in the shape that we represent. [Presumably, he refers to an engraving that is not in the French edition.] I cannot remember very well having seen if this rock is natural, from the area, or whether it has been carried there, but the latter is more likely because the country around

there is very level and sandy, and the sand has increased in such a way that the Sphinx is buried there almost up to its shoulders. If it were carried there, the work involved would have been much more considerable than that of the obelisks, because it is so very big, although from its shape and situation, it would undoubtedly have been easier to convey such a thing than to construct the pyramids. At least one does not believe so much of them to be broken [as of the Sphinx]. I was not able to satisfy my curiosity further, because night surprised me, so much so that to get back to the little hamlet several miles away where I wanted to see some other pyramids [at Abusir], I was obliged to walk two or three hours in the dark.

VINCENT STOCHOVE AND GILLES FERMANEL
(1631, JOINT ACCOUNT)
Translated from volume 15 of the series *Voyages en Égypte* (1975)

Pages 80–81

About four hundred steps from here we saw a great colossus called Sphinx; the ancient Egyptians called it the epitome of marvels. It was their principal idol, that which rendered their oracles by means of the devil. Its form is half woman and half bull. The head, with the front of the body, remains still outside the sand, but the rest of it is all covered up. The head, which has the face of a woman, is of two pikestaffs in height, and the rest of the body emerging is entirely cut from one single stone: from it one can judge of its immense size.

ROBERT FAUVEL (1631)
Translated from volume 15 of the series *Voyages en Égypte* (1975)

Footnote on page 81 (MS De Rouen, page 439) [The reference to page 439 is to a page in the manuscript at Rouen. Page 81 is the page in the published book.]

It [the Sphinx] is all made from one piece of stone, hollow inside, having the head of a woman and the rest of the body like that of a cow. One only sees the head and some part of the body; the rest remains hidden under the sand.

HENRY BLUNT (1634 AD)
Translated from volume 13 of the series *Voyages en Égypte* (1974)

Page 44

The Sphinx of Giza

Within two bowshots from there is a rock, about 40 yards in perimeter and about 12 or 14 in height, cut in the form of the head of a man, perhaps that of Memnon, [which is] celebrated for the sound that it emitted at sunrise. [He refers here to the Colossus of Memnon near Thebes, which was noted for this sound, and is not suggesting that the Sphinx did this.] The Egyptians and the Jews who were with us [on this trip] told us that in olden times it had once rendered oracles, and also that it was hollow on top. They had seen several people go in there and come out again at the Pyramid. I immediately thought then of the story of the oracle, and I thought that all the other manifestations had the same cause, rather than the effect of the mist [he is referring to the morning mists, suggested as the cause of the sounds emitted by the Colossus of Memnon at Thebes, and assuming that one explanation for the oracles spoken by the Sphinx might be the same, but he then rejects this in favor of men hiding inside], although this would not be impossible, or even being of demoniacal origin, which would suppose too great a credulity.

[Later it was discovered that the original English text was cataloged in the British Library under the spelling "Blount" rather than "Blunt." Although the British Library does not have the original book *A Voyage into the Levant,* published in London in 1636, there is a modern facsimile reprint of it (Amsterdam and Norwood, New Jersey, 1977). The following is the original English text taken from page 47.]

. . . within two Bowes shoot hereof [from the Great Pyramid], is a Rocke of some fortie yards circumference, and twelve or fourteene high, cut into the forme of a mans head; perhaps Memnons, famous for its sounding at the Sunrise; the Egyptians, and Jewes with us, told us it gave Oracles of old, and also that it was hollow at the top; wherein they had seene some enter, and come out at the Pyramide: then I soone believed the Oracle, and esteeme all the rest to have beene such, rather than either by vapor, though not impossible, or Demoniacke, which require too much credulitie, for me.

GEORG CHRISTOFF VON NEITZSCHITZ (1636)
Translated from volume 13 of the series *Voyages en Égypte* (1974)

Chapter 12, pages 244–45

On My Return Journey to Babylon [Cairo] and of
an Oracle Encountered Enroute

After we had sufficiently examined the pyramids, we continued on our return journey to Babylon. But not far from here we came upon a rock of an extraordinary size, and formed by nature like the head of a man with huge ears, eyes, hair, and a long neck.

In this huge head would have lived, not many years before, an oracle, or divine diabolical spirit, who would reside apparently inside the pyramid described above, in a deep and dark hole through which one would have to pass with much care during the ascent and descent. Then it would return underground into that head, from where would be given counsel and instructions to the pagans on the subjects of which they had enquired. If the divine spirit had the same shape as presented by the head, it would not be astonishing that one would flee from it to a place assigned by it to knowledge and truth. Which is why one cannot ever be too amazed at the complete blindness of some poor people and should thank God for being free and illuminated by the knowledge of the sole true God, a knowledge which procures eternal salvation.

JOHN GREAVES (1637)
Pyramidographia: or, A Description of the Pyramids in Aegypt (London: 1646)
Taken from A. and J. Churchill, *A Collection of Voyages and Travels, etc.* (London: 1732), 4 vols.

Vol. II, page 662

On the east-side of this room [the Queen's Chamber of the Great Pyramid], in the middle of it, there seems to have been a passage leading to some other place. Whether this way the priests went into the hollow of that huge sphinx, as Strabo and Pliny [book 36, chapter 12] term it, or androsphinx, as Herodotus calls such kinds, (being by Pliny's calculation 12 feet in compass about the head, in height 62, in length 143: And by my observation made of one intire [*sic*] stone) which stands not far distant without the Pyramid, southeast of it, or into any other private retirement, I cannot determine; and it may be too this served for no such purpose . . .

JEAN COPPIN (1638–1639 AND 1643–1646)
Translated from volume 4 of the series *Voyages en Égypte* (1971)

Page 186

The Sphinx, or the head that I come to speak of, served as an oracle at Memphis before the coming of Christ, in that the demons spoke effectively from there where the priests went to place themselves in the statue by an underground vault, which it is said leads from the Great Pyramid down to the Colossus. Even though the Egyptians were blinded [misled] by the mistaken [oracular] responses that they received there, they were happy to be buried nearby, and that is the reason why one sees such a large number of sepulchres in that area. What is more surprising is that one is assured that it is bad luck to climb on top of the head, so that all those who out of curiosity climb up onto it soon suffer a great misfortune, even on the same day. I have always taken this sort of thing as a fable, but someone has confirmed to me a recent example of an Italian who soon after he came down from there was killed by his horse. If this opinion be true, it is a great advantage for many people who have difficulty finding their way down from the top of this figure. I don't know if this proves that there is a bad spirit, but nobody can look at it without wanting to climb it.

GABRIEL BRÉMOND (1643–1645)
Translated from volume 12 of the series
Voyages en Égypte (1974)

Page 99

(12) Concerning the Idol of the Sphinx, or Head

This head, or Sphinx as one calls it, is a very beautiful piece of hard stone, well carved; and even though more than half of it is under the sand so that one cannot give a true opinion of the whole of it, it is well proportioned and a very fine work. From close up it looks like a great mass. One believes it to have been carried from a long way off, to be treasured all the more for the difficulty involved. It is hollow inside, and this was how [oracular] responses were uttered by a man hiding within. Only the head, neck, and a little bit of shoulders appear above the sand. The figure represents a young adolescent or a woman.

BALTHAZAR DE MONCONYS (1646–1647)
Translated from volume 8 of the series *Voyages en Égypte* (1973)

Page 63

. . . after that [seeing the second pyramid] we came to the foot of the Idol [the Sphinx], which is 26 feet high and has hair to its chin, which is a part extending 15 feet from the head; from there we went on to the mummies [at Saqqara] . . .

JEAN DE THÉVENOT (1655)
The Travels of Monsieur de Thevenot into the Levant
(London: 1687), 3 vols. in one.
(Translation of *Relation d'un Voyage Fait au Levant*, 3 vols., Paris, 1664–84.)

Vol. I, pages 134–35

Before each of the three Pyramides, the marks [*should be translated* "remains"] of certain square Buildings are still to be seen, which seem to have been so many Temples; and there is a hole at the end of the pretended Temple of the second Pyramide [which is now called the Valley Temple], by which (some think) there was a way down within the Temple to go to [*should be translated* "by which one went down from inside the Temple to go into"] the Idol [the Sphinx], which is a few steps distant from that hole.* The Arabs call this Idol *Abou el haoun,* that is to say, Father of the Pillar, which Pliny calls Sphynx, saying that the People of the Countrey believe King Amasis was buried in it: I am sure they believe no such thing at present, nor so much as know the name of Amasis; and indeed, it is an erroneous belief. Others say, that a King of Aegypt caused this Figure to be made in memory of a certain Rhodope, a Corinthian Woman, with whom he was much in love. It is said, that this Sphynx, so soon as the Sun was up, gave responses to anything it was consulted about; and hence it is that all who go into the Pyramides, fail not to say, that a Priest conveyed himself into that Idol, by the Pit or Well [the so-called well shaft] in the Pyramide which we just now described. But to shew how groundless an Opinion that is, we must know how the Idol is made: It is the Bust of a Body, at some steps distance from the open Pyramide [the Great Pyramid was the only one open at that time], cut out of

---

*[The original French text says: *Devant chacune des trois pyramides se voyent encore des vestiges de certains bastimens quarrez* [obsolete form of the word *carré*], *qui semblent avoir esté autant de Temples, & à la fin du pretendu Temple de la seconde pyramide est un trou, par lequel quelques-uns croyant qu'on descendoit de dedans le Temple pour aller dans l'Idole, qui est eloigné de quelques pas de ce trou.*]

the natural Rock, from which it hath never been separated, though it seem to be of five Stones pieced together one upon another; but, having very attentively considered it, we observed, that that which at first seemed to be seams or joynings [joinings] of the Stones, are only veins in the Rock: this Bust represents the face and breast of a Woman, but it is prodigiously high, being twenty six foot in height, fifteen foot from the ear to the chin, and yet all the proportions [are] exactly observed: Now what probability is there to believe, that every day a man would take the paines, and venture the breaking of his neck, by descending into that Pit, that being at the bottom, he might only have the labour of coming up again, for there is no passage there, as they who have gone down have observed; a passage must have been cut in the Rock then, which would have cost a great deal of Money, and been known of [by] every Body. It were more probable [would be more likely] to think that they entered it by the Hole, which (as I said) is in the pretended Temple of the second Pyramide, or rather by another [hole], which is at the side of that Idol and very near it [i.e., near the head, most of the body being covered by sand]. These two Holes are very narrow, and almost choaked [choked] up with Sand, wherefore we entred not into them, not knowing besides, but that we might meet with Vipers, or other Venemous Beasts in them. But though there had been a way through the Rocks into that Idol, how could the Voice of that feigned Oracle have come out, since there is no hole neither at the Mouth, Nose, Eyes, nor Ears of it?* It may be said, perhaps, that the Voice was uttered by the Crown of the Head, where there is a Hole, into which we endeavoured to have cast some Hooks fastened to Ropes, that I had brought purposely with me, that we might get up, but we cold not compass [achieve] that, because of the height of it; only when we threw up Stones, they rested there. And a Venetian assured me, that he and some others, having got up by means of little Hooks and a Pole, which they brought with them; they found a Hole in the Crown of the Head of it, and having entered therein perceived that it drew narrower and narrower proportionably, as it approached the Breast where it ended. The voice of him that entred then, by the abovementioned Holes, did not come out that way, and therefore it must be concluded, that if any entred it, it must have been by a Ladder in the Nighttime, and that he put himself into the hole that is in the Head, out of which the Voice came.

---

*[The original French text says: . . . il y auroit plus d'apparence de croire qu'on y entrast par le trou que i'ay dit estre dans le pretendu Temple de la second pyramide, ou plustost encor par un autre trou qui est à costé de cét Idole, & fort proche; ces deux trous sont fort estroits, & Presque tout bouchez de sable, c'est pourquoy nous n'y entrasmes point, ne sçachans mesme si nous n'y trouverions point quelques vipers ou autres bestes venimeuses; mais quand après avoir percé les rochers, on seroit venu dans cét Idole, par ou seroit sortie la voix de ce feint Oracle, puis qu'il n'y a point de trou à sa bouche, ny à son nez, ny à ses yeux, ny à ses oreilles?]

EDWARD MELTON (1661)

Eduward Meltons Eengelsch Edelmans, zeldzaame en
Gedenkwardige Zee- en Land-Reizen; door Egypten . . .
(Amsterdam: 1681 and 1702)

Page 51

[Note: This work and author are in all probability spurious. The account of the Sphinx is plagiarized from those of Johann Wansleben and Jean de Thevenot. It is doubtful if any Edward Melton ever existed; although he is described as "an English nobleman," no Edward Melton ever published a word in English, and the name is probably invented. I consulted a seventeenth-century manuscript pedigree of the Melton family in the British Library (MS Egerton 3402, f. 119 verso), and there is no Edward mentioned anywhere in it.]

Description of the Sphinx

We decided to see the Sphinx, which is located to the east of the Pyramids. It has the head and half of the breast of a woman and is of an impressive size. It is 26 feet tall and fifteen feet from chin to ear.

Pliny tells us that the Sphinx is the location of the grave of King Amasis. I like to believe it is a grave, but I am not sure whether it is the grave of King Amasis. It is hard to say, since the original texts are lost.

Some say that the Sphinx is made to look like a certain courtesan named Rhodope. She was considered the prettiest woman of Thrace in her time and admired by the king who is buried in this grave.

We can speak of a grave for certain since the Sphinx is located at a place that used to be a burial ground. Second, it stands close to the Pyramids and the caves, which are nothing but grave-cities. Besides this, it's obvious from the shape that the Sphinx contains a basement as wide as the height of the Sphinx. It also has an entrance. This basement was without doubt used to bury the bodies of dead men.

By the use of a rope ladder that we brought, we climbed all the way up to the head of the Sphinx to see if it was hollow. It was, but it was filled with sand so we could not tell the size of the space inside. We also found that the neck was badly damaged. It looked like the seams couldn't carry the head much longer.

When one looks at this miracle from a little distance, it seems to be made out of five stones. But when you come closer, you find that the lines you first thought were seams turn out to be the veins in the stone.

PÈRE ANTONIUS GONZALES (1665–1666)
Translated from volume 19 of the series *Voyages en Égypte* (2 parts, 1977)

Part 1, pages 144–46
Chapter 14

Description of the Sphinx Idol, of Mummies and of Embalmed Cadavers
Tacitus [*Annals,* 50, 2, chapter 61] wrote that Germanicus saw near the pyramids a stone statue of Memnon, which emitted sound when the rays of the sun touched it or illuminated it [at dawn; this is a confusion, for the famous statue in question, known as the Colossus of Memnon, is near Thebes, not at Giza]. But I have the impression that this statue is that of an old idol, which is one called Sphinx, and which was situated not far from the pyramids, about a quarter of an hour. There today arises a large head or monster, astonishing in its shape and grandeur. On the subject of this monster, Pliny wrote the following (book 36, chapter 12): "In front of the pyramids is found a Sphinx, very admirable indeed, apparently a sylvan god of the locals. It is thought that King Amasis is interred there. The common opinion holds that he was placed there. It is polished, cut from natural rock. The head of this monster has a circumference of 102 feet and a length of 143 feet." I do not wish to judge the height and size of this head, because we had no instruments for measuring them at the time. I only know that the head of this monster is enormous, and that it is called even up until today the idol Sphinx.

Formerly it was the most important idol of the Egyptians, which foretold to them many things that the Devil knew. They took its counsel, and she revealed to them numerous things that took place.

The upper part resembles a man, the lower part is like a bull, one is told by the people of the vicinity. The upper part remains above the sand; the lower part, on the contrary, is entirely covered. If it be true that the rest, or the lower part, is proportionate in size to the upper part, one must consider that it is one of the Seven Wonders of the World, for it seems to be cut from one piece of stone. Some people ask themselves if this stone colossus was cut from a natural rock in situ, or if it had been carried from elsewhere. Plenty of people have wanted to examine it by excavation but they could not because of the sand. Others thought that this monster consisted of nothing more than half a body, for under the neck there is an opening of a stone tunnel which passes across the mountain of sand up to the pyramids, where it ends. Radzivil [Prince Mikolaj Krzystof Radziwill Sierotka (1549–1616)] (1583 AD) believes equally in oracles coming out of the mouth of the Sphinx. [Radziwill's account of his journey to the Middle East in

1582–1584 was originally published in Polish as *Peregrynacia* . . . , unknown date, and then translated first into Latin by Thomas Traterus as *Hierosolymitana peregrinatio* . . . , Brunsberg, Germany, 1601, and later into German by Lorenz von Borkau as *Jungst Geschehene Hierosolymitanische Reyse,* and published in S. Feyerabend's anthology *Reyssbuch dess Heyligen Lands,* 1609. Unfortunately, this information came to light just as this book was going to press, too late for me to consult the German version in the British Library and translate Radziwill's account of the Sphinx into English for inclusion in this book.] For this reason, there are some people who suppose that the priests of this idol went by way of this tunnel into the head. Fuerer (1565 AD) thinks that there is a special channel. [This reference is to Christopher Fuerer von Haimendorff, *Itinerarium Aegypti* . . . (Nuremberg: 1620), also published in German in 1646; 1565 is the date of his journey to Egypt, not the date of publication.] As I said in the preceding chapter, inside the Great Pyramid is a well that seems to open into a tunnel leading toward this head.

But for myself, I believe furthermore that the Devil spoke and replied through this head to fool the poor idolators. For the people told us that if someone had lost a camel, an ox, or a donkey, he would go and burn a little incense in front of this idol, he asked counsel, and after its response he found these missing animals. The Devil knows a lot more than man. *A fortiori,* I have not discovered any openings in the mouth of this head, or any other openings by which the priests could have spoken.

About a hundred paces from there are numerous brick and mortar ruins and extraordinary little hollow chambers in the rock, with some figures and writing in Arabic or Hebrew characters. Some people think that the priests of the idol Sphinx once lived there. Others believe that they were hollowed out by the kings of Egypt and other princes related to them, during the construction of the pyramids, as shelters protected from the sun where they could watch the workmen.

Page 142

Near this chamber [the King's Chamber] another passage opens in the direction eastward, which ends in a second small chamber [this refers to the Queen's Chamber and the passage running southward to it from the bottom of the Grand Gallery] and has a well quite near [the entrance to the well shaft in front of the passage to the Queen's Chamber], wide and deep, with a kind of stairs. One of our soldiers went down there and found a new passage or way, which it seemed to him went down towards the idol Sphinx of which we will speak in the next chapter. As no one had the desire to follow this soldier, and also because our time was running out, he left the well and we departed from the Pyramid together. On leaving, I noticed some passages to the left, but each time one goes there, one always looks at the main things and still has to hurry away.

CORNEILLE LEBRUN (1674)
Cornelis de Bruyn, *Voyage au Levant* (Paris: 1725)

Pages 642–48

Some distance from the largest pyramid on the east side, one sees the Sphinx, famous with the ancients. It is a statue that has been cut from the same rock, representing a woman's head with half of the chest; but just now it is buried up to the neck in sand. On the right hand, the sand is higher than elsewhere to quite a large extent; in a manner that could easily lead one to believe that under this elevation is hidden the rest of the body, which resembles a lion, with its face turned to the right. It is an extraordinarily large mass, but where the proportions can still be seen, even the head alone is 26 feet high, and from the ear to the chin is 14, according to the measurements taken by Monsieur Thévenot. From a distance it seems to be five stones joined together; but when you get closer, you see that what you had taken to be joints of stones are in fact veins in the rock. Pliny states that this colossus was the tomb of the King Amasis, which is not so unbelievable, since it is in a place which was formerly, as we have said, a type of cemetery, and close to the pyramids and the caves that were for that same purpose; but to know whether it was specifically that of King Amasis, is something I cannot assure you of because there is no way it can be proved for certain, all memoirs of that antiquity being lost.

Other people wanted to believe that an Egyptian king had this sphinx built in memory of a certain Rhodope of Corinth with whom he was passionately enamored. Writers have written much about this sphinx. They say, among other things, that she rendered oracles, which was undoubtedly the result of trickery by the priests, who practiced it in nearby subterranean passages. Some people believe that the well that is in the great pyramid could have been used for this. Although one no longer finds any passageway today, perhaps this is because it has been blocked by the caving-in of the earth. Thus one can offer no assurance on this matter. What is certain is that there is no opening there, neither from the mouth, nose, eyes, nor ears; and if the priests had placed here some method of deceit, it would have to have been by means of a hole, with someone climbing up a ladder to the top of the head and descending into the chest, where it [the hole] would end. The Consul, with most of our company, rested in the shade of this great mass while I was occupied with drawing the pyramids, which are nearby. One could easily, upon inspection of the figure, judge the grandeur of this monstrous statue by the proportion one observes between it and people standing roundabout. As for the particular details of the Sphinx in general, I am happy to refer to what Dr. O. [Olfert] Dapper has written of it, and which he had himself borrowed from others. [Much of what is said above is quoted or paraphrased from Thévenot. As for Dapper's book, it appeared under three different titles, twice in 1681 and once in 1688, all published at Nuremberg, but I have been unable to consult it so Dapper's account is missing here.]

He says that when the Egyptians deal with nature, they represent the sphinx in two ways; namely, in the figure of a crouching lion on its belly, or in the form of a type of monster that has the body of a lion and the face of a girl. By the first figure they represent Momphta [presumably he refers to the deity called Hapi], who was one of the Egyptian divinities who lived in all the waters, and who particularly maintained and preserved the causes of the inundation of the Nile; and by the second they represent the same increase of this river. . . . [Much of the omitted text deals with mythology and the overflowing of the Nile, and so forth] . . . They [the Greek authors of fables and mythological tales] had said according to the evidence of Hyginus and some others that the [Greek] Sphinx was a monster born from Typhon and Echidna, that it had the head and the face of a girl, the wings of a bird, and the body of a dog. Or, as Clearchus said of it, the head and hands of a girl, the body of a dog, the tail of a dragon, the claws of a lion, the wings of an eagle. It was, they say, in Boetia on the Mountain Sphincius near Thebes, from where it had the custom to throw passersby from the cliff and propose to them a riddle to which they would have to give the answer. . . .

ELLIS VERYARD (1678)
Translated from volume 23 of the series *Voyages en Égypte* (1981)

Pages 47–48

The Sphinx

Approximately a half mile from the pyramids, we saw an ancient colossus representing the Sphinx, with a face of a woman and a body of an animal. This statue was apparently held in such great veneration by the Egyptians that they gave it first place among their gods. They received from it all their oracles, which the devil pronounced from the mouth of this artificial monster. The body is buried in sand and only the breast and the head are above the ground. Thus one can judge the enormous size of the whole thing from the face, which is 24 feet long. Pliny says that it was the tomb of the King Amasis, but I tend to believe that it was an ornament placed on his sepulchre, for in the rear one finds a subterranean vault hollowed out of the hard rock, which in all likelihood was the tomb.

ELLIS VERYARD (1678; THE ORIGINAL ENGLISH TEXT)
An Account of Divers Choice Remarks . . .
Taken In a Journey through . . . Egypt . . . etc. (London: 1701)

Page 298

About half a Mile from the Pyramids we saw an ancient Colossus representing the Sphinx, with a Woman's face, and the Body of a Beast. This Statue was in so great Veneration amongst the Egyptians heretofore, that they gave it the first place amongst their Gods, and received all their Oracles from it, which the Devil utter'd thro' the Mouth of this artificial Monster. The Body is buried in the Sand, and only the Head and Breast remain above Ground; so that we may judge of the vast bulk of the whole by the Face, which is twenty four foot long. Pliny says it was the Tomb of King Amasis; but I am apt to think it was an Ornament placed on his Sepulchre; for behind it we found a Subterranean Vault cut out in the firm Rock, which in all likelihood was the Tomb.

BENOIT DE MAILLET (1692)
Description de l'Égypte (Paris: 1735)

Pages 221–23

Concerning the Sphinx

Opposite the second pyramid, and exactly to the east is this famous sphinx, of which so many accounts have spoken. It is at least 300 paces away from the pyramid, and from there one can count 200 paces from it up to the spot where the Nile laps at the pyramid plateau. It is a woman's head grafted onto the body of a lion crouching on its belly. This head would probably still be entire if the Mohamedans had not disfigured it. Someone has broken off the nose. The body has been damaged by the passing of years; one sees today only the shape of it, the lower part being buried under the sand. It is a stupendous head, more than 35 paces in circumference on a body that is more than 30 paces long. As several authors have spoken of this colossus, I will content myself with adding to what they have said about it, that although the head has a hole which has been hollowed from above, there is nevertheless, from this void, no connection with the mouth, nor is there any other place on the inside of the figure through which one would have been able to speak, as some people have claimed. I will add that this hole has very little depth and that far from being a communication to the interior of the first pyramid, as some people have falsely imagined, it would be much more natural to believe, if it were true that this artificial tunnel actually exists, that it would lead to the inside of the second pyramid, to which it corresponds so perfectly in its position.

This idol could have had several intended purposes. Perhaps it was not maintained for any specific use, but rather to be admired for its astonishing size. It could have been made from a mountain of stones that were smoothed as proof of those who had removed it, in the same way that today one leaves signs on ground that one has made level. One could even have used it as an auspicious arrangement of the locality, by cutting a figure in the rock which surprises succeeding generations.

Some people say that it was a talisman, others that it was an idol that was adored. What is most likely is that this union of the head of a girl with a body of a lion, so common and ordinary and which we see represented so frequently in Egypt, was a symbol of what happened in that country under the signs of Virgo and Leo. It is in effect in that season, when the sun traverses them, that the Nile overflows and makes Egypt fertile and habitable with its inundation. The kings of Egypt did not believe they could bear better witness to the sun than in their recognition of it as the author of their happiness by consecrating this mysterious figure to him.

Several people have claimed that the sphinx of the pyramids, or at least the head of that prodigious colossus, was composed of several stones placed and well cemented one on the other. What made it possible to have this idea was that in three or four places around this mass one notices, in effect, veins that circle around the head in an almost horizontal way and that these veins seem to contain a kind of mastic of a different color than the stone. For my part, having looked closely at these veins, I am of the persuasion that they are natural to the stone. When one cannot be convinced of it by investigation, when in several places there is no slanting [he is referring to the fact that the rock layers are all tilted and slant slightly at the Sphinx], it would be enough, to ease one's doubt, to take a look at some of the small pyramids not far from this figure that are placed on the level stretch of the same rock. There, one discovers similar veins, which prove manifestly that those observed in the head of the sphinx, like these, are made of nothing more than little bits of stone that are a characteristic of this terrain. I believe that this figure was formerly covered by a temple. The proof I have of this is that the head of the figure is still, today, complete in all parts, where it has not had violence done to it by the hand of man rather than under the chisel. The reddish paint with which it was covered is still there. One notices elsewhere around the colossus a kind of circuit, where the sand under which it is buried stays higher than the rest of it; and I have no doubt that it hides the foundations and the debris of this edifice, which served as the temple to the idol.

On going again from the sphinx back toward the second of the great pyramids, to the front of which, and precisely in the middle, the colossus was placed on the east side, one discovers about 4 paces from the pyramid the remains of another temple, which is almost opposite it. [He is referring to the Funerary Temple of Chephren.] I was surprised that no other traveler that I know of has spoken of this monument, of which for several thousands of years, the intended purpose would not still be in doubt. One finds a similar temple [the Funerary Temple of Mycerinus] opposite the third pyramid and at the same distance from it.

This one is more complete than the first. [These are the funerary temples of Chephren and Mycerinus, which stood at the feet of these two pyramids.]

GIOVANNI FRANCESCO GEMELLI-CARERI (1693)
A Voyage Round the World
Translated from the Italian; the voyage commenced June 1693
Taken from A. and J. Churchill, eds., *A Collection of Voyages and Travels*
(London: 1732), 4 vols., folio

Vol. IV, page 23
[Referring to the "well shaft" in the Great Pyramid]

Between the two ways already mentioned, on the right hand, is a wall, which appears on the ground perpendicularly from the Horizon, making the figure of the Hebrew Lamed [a letter], in which down seventy-seven foot, there is a square window, or inlet to a small cavern cut out of the soft stone that runs westward; the pyramid being built on the hard rock. Down fifteen foot in this cavern, there is an oblique way, cut in the same stone, two foot and four inches in breadth, and two foot and an half in height, descending 123 foot, where it is stopped up with sand and stones. [The sand and stones were finally cleared by Captain Caviglia in 1817.] Those Barbarians say, there was a passage there underground, to the empty head of an idol [the Sphinx], that stood not far from the pyramid. As much of this idol as remains, which is from the shoulders upwards, is twenty six foot in length to the top of the head, and from the ear to the chin fifteen. All this that has been said, will appear the more plainly, by the following cut. [*Cut* is an old-fashioned term for an engraving; he refers to an accompanying engraving of the Great Pyramid in section, which, however, shows the internal passages incorrectly drawn.]

ROBERT HUNTINGTON (1695)
Apparently never published in English. Translated from
volume 23 of the series *Voyages en Égypte* (1981)

Page 167

I would consider it an impiety to forget the Sphinx or statue with a human head. Its bulk is enormous; it is 100 feet in circumference at the level of the shoulders. It is cut from a single stone and faces toward the east.

Page 193

And of this kind of porphyry is the celebrated Sphinx (an enormous head and shoulders, the whole being 110 feet in circumference), still standing near the north pyramid [the Great Pyramid].

[Obviously, the Sphinx is made of limestone, not of porphyry, so Huntington is in error.]

ANTOINE MORISON (1697)
Translated from volume 17 in the series *Voyages en Égypte* (1976).

Page xxiv (editor's introduction)

After the visit to the other pyramids, his excursion ended at the Great Sphinx. He was full of admiration. In supplying the exact dimensions of the monument; he declared that he "pitied Pliny for his exaggerations" (page 166). Meanwhile, without hesitation he claimed that the head of the Sphinx was hollow. This proves that he had only seen the fabulous androcephalic monument either superficially or from afar.

[The editors of Morison appear to be unaware that travelers for centuries had been told that the head of the Sphinx was hollow, and Morison's statement certainly does not prove that he had seen the Sphinx only "superficially or from afar." All it proves is that the same tradition was being repeated to him by the local guides as had been told to visitors for centuries.]

Pages 175–76

About two hundred steps from the Great Pyramid on the east side, one sees the head of a sphinx, whose body is buried in the sand. It seems that the neck of this figure may be 15 feet high, and the head, which is still complete, is of such an extraordinary size that it provided enough shade for eleven people— which we were—to protect us from the extreme heat of the sand, from which we were suffering. As its figure is doubtless proportionate, it would have to be more than 100 feet long, and consequently its size is prodigious. [The length of the excavated Sphinx from the paws to the tail is now known to be 57 meters (187 feet), the height 20 meters (66 feet).] Pliny [book 36, chapter 17] speaks of it with such exaggeration that I feel sorry for him, and I would doubt his accuracy in other things, judging by his credulity in this matter. The head of this sphinx is hollow, that is, according to the priests of these nearby ruins and temples of whom I come to speak. Under cover of night, they would hide in this head and stay there to speak on certain appointed days to the people who had assembled there and who listened to the discourses of these impostors as if they were oracles being pronounced by that idol. What I most admired about this monstrous divinity was the vivacity of its coloring and above all the vermilion of its cheeks, which seemed to have been applied only two years ago, even though it must have been there for more than two thousand years.

[He then mentions collecting petrified wood from the desert, and a Lake Karoun at Giza, which is not the same as Lake Karoun in the Fayyum.]

JOANNES AEGIDIUS VAN EGMOND VAN DER NIJENBURG AND JAN HEYMAN (1709)

Travels through Part of Europe, Asia Minor . . . Egypt . . .
Translated from the Low Dutch (London: 1759), 2 vols.

Vol. II, page 90

After this survey of the first and largest pyramid, we visited the head of the sphinx, and the second and third pyramids. With regard to the former, it is the bust of a woman, with the nose a little mutilated, and is said to have been formed out of one single rock. But I could find no reason for calling it a sphinx, nothing but the head and neck being seen, though the height is full thirty-feet. And it is a question, whether there ever was anything more of this image than what is at present visible; though Pliny, and others, mention a body, and give it a really amazing magnitude, making the circumference of it to be one hundred and two feet. Some later writers have also mentioned a subterraneous passage from the largest Pyramid to this head, which they say is hollow; and that the Pagan priests used to deliver their oracles here. But all this is mere conjecture. . . . About a mile from hence stands the second pyramid. This structure, from the pieces which, in several places, still cover it, appears to have been covered with marble; but hitherto the entrance of it has not been discovered. It is, except on the south-side, well preserved, having neither chasms nor fissures; and from its surface being every where smooth and even, there is no possibility of ascending it.

[This astonishing description of the Chephren Pyramid in 1709 suggests that the limestone casing stones had not yet been stripped from it, and that the story believed today that they were all taken away in the thirteenth century to rebuild Cairo after an earthquake is false. The pyramid seems to have been stripped of its casing stones as recently as the first half of the eighteenth century, if we are to believe this account by Egmond. The entirety of the casing stones is also represented as being intact in a woodcut published in 1579, from a drawing done in 1565, in the book by Johann Helffrich (see above for a translation of the section of his text dealing with the Sphinx). This woodcut shows the casing stones of the Pyramid of Mycerinus intact as well, but the Great Pyramid is shown as entirely stripped of them, and with the pyramidion missing at the apex. It seems therefore that it was solely the casing stones of the Great Pyramid that were stripped away in the thirteenth century, and no others.]

THOMAS SHAW (1721)
Travels, or Observations Relating to Several Parts of Barbary and the Levant
(Oxford: 1738)

Pages 368–69

. . . the catacombs of Sakara [Saqqara], the Sphinx, and the Chambers, that are cut out of the natural rock, on the east and west side of these pyramids, do all of them discover the specific mark and characteristics of the pyramidal stones, and, as far as I could perceive, were not at all to be distinguished from them. The pyramidal stones, therefore, were, in all probability, taken from this neighbourhood; nay perhaps they were those very stones, that had been dug away, to give the Sphinx, and the chambers I have mentioned, their proper views and elevations.

Pages 374–75

Of the Sphinx

Besides what has been already said of the Sphinx, we are to observe, that in July 1721, the sands were so far raised and accumulated about it, that we could only discover the back of it; upon which, over the rump, there was a square hole, about four feet long, and two broad, so closely filled with sand, that we could not lay it open enough to observe, whether it had been originally contrived for the admission of fresh air; or, like the well in the great pyramid, was intended for a stair-case. Upon the head of it there is another hole, of a round figure; which, I was told, for we could not get up to it, is five or six feet deep, and wide enough to receive a well-grown person. The stone, which this part of the head consists of, seems, from the colour, to be adventitious, and different from the rest of the figure, which is all of the same stone, and hewn out of the natural rock. [This is a very sharp observation, for we now know that the head was carved from a stratum of stronger limestone than the body and is indeed harder and "different," quite apart from the fact that also it was cut down and recarved by a later pharaoh in his own image.] It must be left to future travellers to find out, whether these holes served only to transmit a succession of fresh air into the body of the sphinx, or whether they might not have had likewise a communication with the great pyramid, either by the well, or by the cavity or nich [niche] in the wall of the lower chamber [the Subterranean Chamber], that lies upon a level with it. Nay, it may some time appear, that there are chambers also in the two other pyramids [we now know this to be true]; and not only so, but that the eminence likewise, upon which they are both erected, is cut out into cryptae [crypts], narrow passages, and labyrinths, which may, all of them, communicate with the chambers of the priests, the artful contrivers of these adyta; where their initiatory, as well as other mysterious rites and ceremonies, were to be carried on with the greater awe and solemnity.

CHARLES THOMPSON (1733)

Travels through Turkey in Asia, the Holy Land, Egypt, and Other Parts of the World (London: 1754), 2 vols.

Vol. II, pages 143–44

Before I leave this Place [Giza], I must take some Notice of a Colossus, at least the Head of one, which stands about a Quarter of a Mile to the East of the second Pyramid. It is usually call'd a Sphinx, which is a fabulous Monster, having the Head and Breasts of a Woman, the Wings of a Bird, the Claws of a Lion, and the Body like a Dog. This figure, among the Egyptians, was a symbolical Representation of the rising of the Nile in the months of July and August, when the Sun passes through the Signs Leo and Virgo. They likewise made use of it in their Hieroglyphicks to represent a Harlot, intimating the Danger of being captivated by the Charms of a faithless Woman, whom the fond Lover in the End finds as cruel and rapacious as a Lion. Of this Sphinx however, near the Pyramids, there is little to be discern'd but from the Shoulders upwards, being a monstrous Bust of a Woman, all cut out of the solid Rock, and never separated from it; except the upper Part of the Head, which seems to be adventitious [added on]. It is almost thirty Feet high, fifteen feet from the Ear to the Chin, and above thirty feet wide at the lower Part of the Neck or Beginning of the Breast. The sand is so accumulated about it, that one can but just discover the Top of the Back, in which there is a Hole about five Feet long, seventy-five [feet] from the hinder Part of the Neck, and thirty from the Tail. We could not get up to the Top of the Head, but those who have done it report, that there is a round Hole, by which a full-grown Person may descend into it, from whence it is supposed the artful Priests deliver'd their Oracles. Pliny makes mention of this Sphinx, and tells us that it was thought to be the Sepulchre of King Amasis. The Rock is dug away all round the Sphinx to a considerable Distance, and the Stone was undoubtedly employ'd in building the Pyramids, with which some Moderns have supposed it has a subterraneous Communication.

RICHARD POCOCKE (1743)

The Rt. Rev. Richard Pococke, successively bishop of Ossory and of Meath;
A Description of the East and Some Other Countries (London: 1743–1745),
2 vols, folio

[Note: The manuscript of this material is not among the twenty-one volumes of
travel diaries of Pococke, which are preserved in the British Library (Add. MSS.
22,978–22,998), probably because the original manuscript went to the publisher
and was not returned to Pococke afterward. However, some further remarks about
the Sphinx from one of Pococke's letters to his mother are given below.]

From 457.f.8, an edition of 3 vols. (vol. II bound in two parts)
Vol. I, page 46

Directly in front of the second pyramid, about a quarter of a mile to the east
of it, is the famous sphinx H [a reference to his engraving, figure XVI, where
the Sphinx is marked H on a plan of the Giza Plateau] about half a quarter of a
mile from the water when the Nile overflows, being on much lower ground than
the pyramids. Here seems to have been the grand way up to these magnificent
structures. . . . The rock seems to have been dug away all round the sphinx for
a great way, and the stone was doubtless employ'd in building the pyramids, the
sphinx being cut out of the solid rock; for what has been taken by some to be
the joining of the stone, is only veins in the rock. This extraordinary monument
is said to have been the sepulchre of Amasis, tho' I think it is mention'd by none
of the antient authors, except Pliny [book 36, chapter 12; Pococke's footnote
here states: "My account makes the sphinx one hundred and thirty feet long,
that is about seventeen feet more than Pliny. He says it was sixty-three feet high,
probably taking in a plinth that might be cut out under it; so that about thirty-
six feet must be buried in the sand."] I found by the quadrant that it is about
twenty-seven feet high, the neck and head only being above ground; the lower
part of the neck, or the beginning of the breast, is thirty-three feet wide, and it
is twenty feet from the fore part of the neck to the back, and thence to the hole
in the back it is seventy-five feet, the hole being five feet long, from which to the
tail, if I mistake not, it is thirty feet; which something exceeds Pliny's account,
who says that it is a hundred and thirteen feet long. The sand is risen up in such
a manner that the top of the back only is to be seen; some persons have lately
got to the top of the head, where they found a hole, which probably served for
the arts of the priests in uttering oracles; as that in the back might be to descend
to the apartments beneath.

Letter 26 to his mother, dated March 3, 1738 or 1739, from British Library Add. MS. 22,998, f. 67

> I went to the Sphynx the head much worn by time, especially the neck, one just sees the top of the back & either a tail or a thigh in a sitting posture; —the whole by the nicest examination I could make seems to be cut out of the rock; —went into some catacombs & round the second Pyramid. We dined together & returned . . .

CLAUDE LOUIS FOURMONT (1755)
Description Historique et Geographique des Plaines d'Heliopolis et de Memphis (Paris: 1755)

Pages 255–56

> To the east, and more than 300 paces from this pyramid, we visited the Sphinx, whose name among the local people is Abou-Ehoul, which is to say, Powerful Father. In the front it is a head of a woman, resting upon the body of a lion lying on its belly. Someone has broken off its nose; the body has been damaged by the passing of years. Today, one sees only the shape of it, of which the lower part is buried under the sand. Its head is more than 35 feet high. This Sphinx was a symbol of what happened in Egypt under the signs of Leo and Virgo when the Nile overflowed, rendering Egypt fertile and habitable by this inundation.

FRIDERIK NORDEN (1757)
Travels in Egypt and Nubia, by "Frederick Lewis Norden," i.e., Friderik Ludvig Norden, Captain of the Danish Navy, trans. from the [Danish] original and enlarged by Dr. Peter Templeman (London: 1757), 2 vols.

Vol. 1, page 76

> About three hundred paces to the east of the second pyramid, you see the head of the great and famous Sphinx, which I have taken care to delineate. [See plates XLV, XLVI, and XLVII.]
>
> In *Observations on Egypt*, page 46, Doctor [Richard] Pococke observes: "That this Sphynx is cut out of a solid rock. This extraordinary monument is said to have been the sepulchre of AMASIS, though I think it is mentioned by none of the ancient authors, except PLINY, lib. xxxvi, cap. 12. I found by

the quadrant that it is about twenty seven feet high, the neck and head only being above ground; the lower part of the neck, or the beginning of the breast is thirty feet wide, and it is twenty feet from the forepart of the neck to the back; and thence to the hole in the back, it is seventy five feet, the hole being five feet long; from which to the tail, if I mistake it not, it is thirty feet; which something exceeds PLINY's account, who says that it is one hundred and thirteen feet long. The sand is risen up in such a manner, that the top of the back only is seen; some persons have lately got to the top of the head, where they found a hole, which probably served for the arts of the priests in uttering oracles; as that in the back might be to descend to the apartments beneath."

Monsieur [Benoit de] Maillet is of opinion "That the union of the head of a virgin, with the body of a lion, is a symbol of what happens in this country, when the sun is in the signs of Leo and Virgo, and the Nile overflows." The wings were probably added to the Sphynx, as emblematical of the *fuga temporum* [time flying].

Vol. 1, page 73
[Important evidence about water reaching the Sphinx in the eighteenth century]

But when the waters have swollen to their highest pitch, you may go by water from Old Cairo quite to the rock, on which the pyramids are built.

Vol. 1, page 80

After having well considered this first pyramid, you take leave of it, and approach the second, which is very soon dispatched, because it has not been opened. You see there the ruins of a temple, that it has on the east side; and, descending insensibly, you arrive at the Sphinx, whose enormous size attracts your admiration, and at the same time you conceive a sort of indignation at those, who have had the brutality to disfigure strangely its nose.

Vol. 1, page 92 in his section (pages 84–95) "Remarks upon the Pyramidographia of Mr. John Greaves," ref. page 119 of Greaves, edited by Birch

[quote from Greaves]: "On the east side of this room [the Queen's Chamber], in the middle of it [the east wall], there seems to have been a passage leading to some other place. Whether this way the priests went into the hollow of the Sphinx."

This forced and extremely narrow passage subsists still at present, and terminates in a kind of niche. It could never lead to the Sphinx, because it is in the third part of the pyramid, above the horizon.

CARSTEN NIEBUHR (1761)

Captain of Engineers in the Service of the King of Denmark, *Travels through Arabia and Other Countries in the East,* trans. R. Heron (Edinburgh: 1792), 2 vols. [The journey commenced January 1761.]

Vol. 1, page 156

The famous Sphinx is sinking still deeper in the sand; and a great part of the body is already buried. It seems to be formed out of the rock upon which the pyramid stands; a circumstance which confirms my conjecture concerning the place from which the stones for building the pyramids were quarried. I found the chin of the Sphinx to measure ten feet six inches in height; and the whole length of the countenance nearly eighteen feet.

CORNELIUS DE PAUW (1774)

Recherches Philosophiques sur les Égyptiens et les Chinois (Paris: 1774), 2 vols.

Vol. 1, section 4, pages 258–59

Pierius says in the forty-ninth volume of his *Hieroglyphics* that it is very credible that Egyptian sculptors pretended to give to statues a great air of simplicity so as not to draw people into idolatry. Mr Winkelman [Johann Joachim Winckelmann, the famous German art historian] even suspected that there existed in this respect an actual law, which impeded them at all times when it was a question of representing the human figure; meanwhile they were granted liberty without limit with regard to the representation of animals, among which he also counts the Sphinx, all parts of which he scrutinized with much more attention than Belon had done. And one knows that he discovered characteristic marks of both sexes, that is to say those of the lion, and those of the virgin, which were more to the front, toward the chest. This peculiarity, of which no one had been able to guess the reason until now, derived from the mystic doctrine, in which one showed that the divinity is hermaphrodite, letting everyone realize it was self-engendered; and the sphinxes are the emblem of the Divinity, whom the Egyptians never represented in the manner in which Eusebius described a statue of the god Cneph. Also, Mr Jablonski has proved that Eusebius was grossly mistaken in that.

ABBÉ DE BINOS (1777)

Voyage par l'Italie, en Égypte . . . etc. (Paris: 1787), 2 vols.

Vol. 2, page 5
[Letter 53, about the Pyramids]

. . . they [tombs] are about 20 paces from one another, and have at their back a sphinx of which the head is raised more than 20 feet above the sand: the rest of the body, which is said to be more than 100 feet long, is buried in the sand.

CLAUDE-ÉTIENNE SAVARY (1785)

Letters on Egypt, trans. Anonymous, 3rd ed. (London: 1799), 2 vols.

Pages 234–35

Opposite the second [pyramid], eastward, is the enormous sphinx, the whole body of which, as I have said, is buried in the sand, the top of the back only to be seen, which is above a hundred feet long, and is of a single stone, making part of the rock on which the pyramids rest. Its head rises about seven and twenty feet above the sand. Mahomet has taught the Arabs to hold all images of men or animals in detestation; and they have disfigured the face with their arrows and lances. Pliny pretends the body of Amasis was deposited within this sphinx. Many authors believe the well of the grand pyramid ended here, and that the priests came here, at certain times, to deliver their oracles; but these are mere conjectures. (*Note:* They bring the cavity on the top of the head of the sphinx, through which the priests delivered their oracles, as a proof of this opinion; but this cavity is only five feet deep, and neither communicates with the mouth nor the body of the sphinx.)

M. Paw [Cornelius de Pauw, see extract on page 488] (*Recherches Philosophiques sur les Égyptiens et les Chinois*) says, these sphinxes, the body of which is half a virgin, half lion, are images of the deity, whom they represent as a hermaphrodite; which opinion seems not to me more happy than that concerning the sepulchre of Osiris.

[See page 229, where he criticizes the opinion of de Pauw that the Great Pyramid was the Tomb of Osiris and says sarcastically that de Pauw "in his closet sees better than travelers."]

COLONEL COUTELLE (1798)

"Observations sur les Pyramides de Gyzeh," in *Description de l'Égypte* (Paris: 1818)

Vol. 2, pages 52–53

The Sphinx

It is in one of the faults of the Libyan hills, in the area which rises toward the west across the plain, that the Sphinx has been carved; its height is about 13 meters [40 feet] above the actual ground, it remains like a witness and like a mass of stone raised up which has been superficially made to decorate this part of the hill. The rump, scarcely perceptible, seems only traced in the earth, with a length of almost 22 meters [72 feet]; and the side that we wanted to discover in clearing away the sand that the winds had accumulated up to the level of the hill presented no regular shape to us to a depth of approximately 9 or 10 meters [30 feet]: as to the hole which had been noticed on the [top of the] head, it is not deeper than 2 meters 924 mm [9 feet], of a conical and irregular shape.

VIVANT DENON (1798)

Voyages dan la Basse et La Haute Égypte Pendant les Campagnes de Bonaparte, en 1798 et 1799 (London: [although in French], 1807), 2 vols.

Vol. 1, page 98

I didn't have time to examine the Sphinx, which merits being sketched with more scrupulous care, and which has never been done in this manner. Although its proportions are huge, its contours, which have been retained, are supple as well as pure. The expression of the face is sweet, gracious, and tranquil; the character of it is African, but the mouth, of which the lips are thick, has a softness of movement, and both have a truly admirable finesse of execution. It gives the impression of flesh and of life. . . . [The rest of the paragraph is purely an artistic description.]

JOSEPH GROBERT (1798)
Description des Pyramides de Ghize (Paris: 1801)

Pages 31–34

Now we must leave the place far from the pyramids and go down toward the east. One follows the plateau; one passes in front of the meridianal [north] face of [the Pyramid of] Chephren, and one moves off from it as far as one can to the right. One goes down quite a gentle slope to find the Sphinx, almost entirely covered by sand, and of which the projecting head is concealed from the eye by the unevenness of the ground.

[Count Constantin-François de] Volney, the only author worth quoting when you want to recount a sound idea about this region, has rightly observed that the completely Ethiopian profile of the Sphinx bears witness, in an authentic way, that that nation has given the Egyptians its laws, its morals, and its religion. These last are no more than a colony descended from Sennahar and some vast regions that encompass Nubia; they have deteriorated by mixing with the Arabs. The foreigners who can stand the disgusting sight of the Hokheila [evidently, a slave market] where Negroes are sold, will not find much there to resemble the profile of the Sphinx.

This monstrous statue, truly colossal, has been sculpted from a protruding piece of rock on which it sits. It is from a single piece. The quality of the stone perfectly resembles the rock itself, despite being painted yellow, and the color has been conserved up until our day in the places where it has not been damaged. Paintings found in Upper Egypt attest [to] the talent of the Egyptians in composing colors and the influence of the dryness of the climate in preserving them.

The Sphinx is actually very dilapidated, much more than it was in 1738, when [Friderik] Norden drew it. I uncovered enough of its back to measure it. But there should be a very considerable excavation to uncover it entirely. [This finally happened in 1817.] If one climbs onto the head, one sees a hole that is 15 inches in diameter at its widest point, and about 9 feet in depth. The direction is oblique. One sees that the depth has been diminished by stones, which have been thrown down into it. It would be difficult to determine the use of this cavity, unless one presumes some underground passage which this passage leads to, and that the priests hidden in this place delivered their oracles from it. The Sphinx was definitely an idol, and the tutelary divinity of this cemetery. The placement of the surrounding sand makes one suspect that the plain, which is at the foot of the rock to the south, and which is more elevated than the usual flood level of the river, is equally strewn with tombs. A little to the southwest is a tomb where a Turkish hermit lives, a chapel around which several trees have been planted.

Section 2
ACCOUNTS OF
THE SPHINX FROM
1800 TO 1837

WILLIAM HAMILTON (1801)

Remarks on Several Parts of Turkey. Part 1. Aegyptiaca, or,
Some Account of the Antient and Modern State of Egypt
(London: 1809)

Pages 323–24

> Where the causeway [leading from Cairo to Giza] ended, we crossed a larger
> and deeper canal, which we could plainly ascertain to be the line of commu-
> nication still kept up from the Bahhr Jousouf [the ancient Bahr Yusuf Canal,
> which runs west of and parallel to the Nile] along the skirts of the Desert
> under [at the edge of the plateau of] the pyramids, to join the canal of Terram,
> or the Bahhreiré. Herodotus evidently alludes to this navigation, when he
> says that, during the inundation of the Nile, boats coming from Canopus or
> Naucratis [cities on the Mediterranean coast] to Memphis [which is beside
> Giza] skirted along the Desert and the pyramids, in order to avoid the rapid
> currents of the main stream.

Pages 329–30

> A large and strong built causeway [the Causeway of Chephren] has been car-
> ried from the entrances of each of these enclosures [the funerary temples in

front of the Pyramids of Mycerinus and Chephren] to the celebrated sphinx, whose enigmatical meaning still continues to puzzle the antiquaries of Europe, and who has proved during a long lapse of ages the faithful depository of the mysteries which envelop every object round her. The French excavated the body of the lion; which they found uninjured: but the sands of the Desert very soon rendered their labour vain, and the last time I saw the sphinx, the head and neck alone were visible. These have been evidently painted all over, and many characters are to be traced upon the head-dress; but we could not ascertain whether they were the sacred or popular letters of Egypt [i.e., hiero-glyphics or hieratic writing]; some indeed bore a resemblance to the Arabic. It is still a point of dispute among the learned, whether this combination of the human and the lion's form is typical of the rising of the Nile, the summer sol-stice, or the wisdom and power of the deity. Such a personification of human intelligence and brutal force might be the original of the Greek Minerva; and agreeably to this supposition, the sphinx is a very common ornament of this goddess on her statues and on her medals.

JAMES WILSON (1805)

The History of Egypt (Edinburgh: 1805), 3 vols.
[Wilson seems to have been an armchair scholar.]

Vol. 1, pages 93–94

As the sphinx is a monster in shape, so, among the Egyptian ruins, it appears to have been sometimes represented as of a monstrous size. In this situation it appears in the neighbourhood of the largest pyramid of Giza. Conjecture, among its various efforts, has suggested an idea, that secret passages were origi-nally formed between the sphinx and the pyramids, and that the whole of these communicated with secret apartments in the rocks below. But the chambers in the only pyramid which has been examined [the Great Pyramid was then the only one open], are so small in comparison to the mass of the buildings, that there is scarcely room to suppose, that these contrivances had any religious, or highly important, connection with subterranean abodes or apartments in the rock.

[Here he gives a footnote reference to Thomas Shaw's *Travels,* pages 421–22. There is no indication that Wilson ever visited Egypt, and he gives no eyewitness account of the Sphinx.]

EDWARD DANIEL CLARKE (1810 AD)
Travels in Various Countries of Europe, Asia and Africa
(London: 1810–1823), 3 vols.

Vol. 3, part 2 (1814), pages 127–28

PART THE SECOND. Greece, Egypt and the Holy Land

Upon the south-east side is the gigantic statue of the Sphinx, the most colossal piece of sculpture which remains of all the works executed by the Antients. The French have uncovered all the pedestal of this statue, and all the cumbent [recumbent] or leonine parts of the figure; these were before entirely concealed by sand. Instead, however, of answering the expectations raised concerning the work upon which it was supposed to rest, the pedestal proves to be a wretched structure of brick-work, and small pieces of stone, put together like the most insignificant piece of modern masonry, and wholly out of character, both with respect to the prodigious labour bestowed upon the statue itself, and the gigantic appearance of the surrounding objects.

Page 145

We then descended into some of the smaller sepulchres. The walls of these were adorned with hieroglyphics. In some instances, we noticed the traces of antient painting, an art that seems to have been almost coeval with the human race. The most remarkable instance of this kind was discovered by the author in a situation where, of all others, it was least expected, upon the surface of the Sphinx. As we drew near to view this prodigious colossus, a reddish hue was discernible over the whole mass, quite inconsistent with the common colour of the limestone used in building the Pyramids, and of which the Sphinx itself is formed. This induced us to examine more attentively the superficies of the statue: and having succeeded in climbing beneath the right ear of the figure, where the surface had never been broken, nor in any degree composed by the action of the atmosphere, we found, to our very great surprise, that the whole had once been painted of a dingy red or blood colour, like some of the stuccoed walls of the houses in Pompeii and Herculaneum.

[He goes on to give Coptic and Arabic inscriptions that he found on the Sphinx, now vanished.]

THOMAS LEGH, M. P. (1813)
Narrative of a Journey in Egypt (London: 1816)

Page 23

On our descent [from the top of the Great Pyramid] we breakfasted at the base of the Pyramid, and after admiring the graceful outline of the Colossal Sphinx, returned to Cairo, which we reached by two o'clock the same day.

ROBERT RICHARDSON (1817)
Travels along the Mediterranean and Parts Adjacent (London: 1822), 2 vols.

Vol. 1, pages 153–57

. . . we proceeded next morning to take a view of the sphinx. . . . It stands a little to the east of the two last-mentioned pyramids, and on a much lower level. The lower part of this venerable piece of antiquity, which had for ages lain buried under a load of sand, had been a few months before uncovered by the exertions of Captain Caviglia, with the assistance of the two gentlemen before mentioned; at the time, however, that we visited it, the Arabs and the wind had replaced the greater part of the covering, and the lower extremities of the sphinx were equally invisible as before his operations. The breast, shoulders, neck and head, which are those of a human being, remain uncovered, as also the back, which is that of a lion; the neck is very much eroded, and, to a person near, the head seems as if it were too heavy for its support. The head-dress has the appearance of an old-fashioned wig, or periwig, projecting out about the ears, like the hair of the Berberi Arabs: the ears project considerably, the nose is broken, the whole face has been painted red, which is the color assigned to the ancient inhabitants of Egypt, and to all the deities of the country, except Osiris. The features are Nubian, or what, from ancient representations, may be called ancient Egyptian, which is quite different from the Negro feature; the expression is particularly placid and benign, so much so, that the worshipper of the sphinx might hold up his god as superior to all the other gods of wood and stone which the blinded nations worshipt. The whole of it is cut out of the rock, which is calcareous, easily sectile, and abounding in small bivalve shells; and probably the large excavations in front, and on each side of it, furnished part of the stones for the building of the pyramids. There was no opening found in the body of the sphinx, whereby to ascertain whether it is hollow or not. The back is about 120 feet long; the elevation of the head from 30 to 35 feet above the sand; the paws were said to stretch out on the platform in front of it to the distance of 50 feet. Between the paws were found the remains of a trilithic temple, adorned with hieroglyphics. In front of the temple was a granite altar with four horns, one of which remained, and the marks of fire, from the burning of incense, were visible upon it. Several Greek inscriptions were found on the paws of the sphinx, but none of them older than the second century: one of them is signed Arrianus and is merely an address of the poet of that name to the sphinx as the guardian genius of the king of Egypt . . . [a section describing what Caviglia found is omitted here and also below] . . . The Arabs calls the sphinx *abou el hol,* the father of terrors, or *abou el haoun,* the father of the column, which last seems to favour the above supposition [about a column]. . . . Herodotus makes no mention of this enigmatical figure, yet it is completely Egyptian, and from the great disintegration that it has suffered, we can hardly suppose that it did not exist in his time. Pliny, who is the first author that mentions it, merely states its position in front of the pyramids, and that the inhabitants said it was the tomb of king Amasis, and was brought there, which he contradicts, by asserting it to be cut out of the rock; but offers no conjecture of his own as to its use or formation. . . . The countenance of this sphinx, however, was that of a man [contrary to the Greek tradition that a sphinx had the head of a woman]. The red colour does not sufficiently characterize the sex, but the beard, which was found between its paws, leaves little doubt on that subject. The expression of almost all the Egyptian figures is so particularly mild and interesting, that without the accession of the beard, they might all pass for females. This figure was entire in the time of Abdallatif, who describes its graceful appearance and the admirable proportion in the different features of its countenance, of which, he particularly mentions the nose, the eyes, and the ears, and says that they excited his astonishment above every thing that he had seen in Egypt; and Makrisi states, that it was mutilated by Sheik Mohammed, called the faster [meaning "fasting from food"] of his time; the same ravenous animal who mutilated the lions that adorned the bridge at Cairo, and who deserved to be a relation of his savage namesake, who attempted to demolish the pyramids, if he were not the identical animal himself.

CHARLES LEONARD IRBY AND JAMES MANGLES (1817)
Travels in Egypt and Nubia, Syria, and Asia Minor during the Years 1817 & 1818 (London: 1823).
Photographic reprint by Darf Publishers Limited (London: 1985)

Pages 155–58

Wednesday, September 1 [1817]. Our first care now was to shave our beards, which we had allowed to grow from our first departure from Philae, and resume our European costume; we felt as awkward at first at this change of dress, as we did when we first assumed the Arab costume. Mr. [Henry] Salt [the British consul-general in Cairo] received us very civilly. We found that great discoveries had been made at the pyramids and sphinx during our absence; and the first thing that drew our attention was Mr. Salt's elucidative plan of the pyramids, sphinx, and all their interesting environs. As the whole account of the proceedings is going home for publication, I shall only trouble you with a few particulars. On our arrival we found, at Mr. Salt's house, Colonel Stratton, of the Enniskillen dragoons, and Mr. Fuller: these two travellers had come from making the tour of Palestine, having lastly arrived by land from Yaffa and Gaza. They embarked at Constantinople, having first made the tour of Greece. As they had not yet been to the pyramids, we were glad to have an opportunity of accompanying them.

Friday, September 4. We went early in the morning, and Mr. Salt having lent us a copy of his newly made plan, we regularly went over the whole neighbourhood, place after place, according to the plan; we found there was nothing new for us to see, excepting a few of the upper steps fronting the sphinx. Unfortunately for us and all future travellers, they have filled up all the excavations of the sphinx, so that there is not so much to be seen now, as there was previous to our departure, the base having been perfectly cleared on one side, before we started for Upper Egypt. From the several drawings and plans which we have seen, together with the description we have heard, it appears that the indefatigable Captain Caviglia continued his operations till he had cleared all the breast of the animal; that he afterwards pursued his labours till he reached the paws, at fifty feet distance from the body; and here it was, between the two, that he discovered a small temple, views of which are given in this work. I imagine this small edifice was composed of three large, flat stones, like a similar shrine in the possession of Mr. Salt, and that the door was filled up by two smaller pieces of stone on each side of it; these sides have some fine specimens of basso-relievo, and give a fine idea of what the sphinx originally was. A man is depicted as presenting an offering to it; some inscriptions also are interesting, and one of Caracalla has the name of Geta, his brother, erased, as in the Latin inscription at Syene. The lions which were found, together with the tablets, in basso-relievo, have been sent home to the British Museum, where I hope you will see them. The great head of Memnon will please you, and when you contemplate its grandeur, recollect that Thebes has at present the remains of thirty-seven statues of equal dimensions; many greater. Beyond the small temple is an altar. To describe the other parts, I must beg you to imagine yourself fronting the face of the sphinx, at a considerable distance, and nearly on a level with the lower part of the face, and also with the ground adjoining the animal. As you advance, you find at some distance from the paws, a flight of steps which lead some depth below the paws to the base of the temple. Mr. Salt is of opinion that this descent by steps was meant to impress the beholder (after having first viewed the sphinx at a distance on a level) with a more imposing idea of its grandeur, when he views the breast in its full magnitude from below. A wall of sun-burnt brick was on each side of the steps, to prevent the sand from filling up the space. Afterwards we went all over the great pyramid, again descending to the lower chamber, which Captain Caviglia discovered, and also reinspected the well, &c. We could not show them Colonel Davison's chamber, as the Arabs had stolen the rope ladder which was left there. After having slept at the mouth of the great pyramid, we returned to Cairo; the excursion occupied us two days. When we were last at Cairo, a trip to the sphinx used to take two hours; we were now five hours going there, the inundation of the Nile forcing us to go more than double the distance round the edge of the canals. We went in a cangia, or rowing boat, as the canal was quite full.

COUNT DE FORBIN [LOUIS-NICOLAS-PHILIPPE-AUGUSTE COMTE DE FORBIN] (1817–1818)

Travels in Egypt, Being a Continuation of the Travels in the Holy Land, in 1817–18 (Second Part of *Count de Forbin's Eastern Travels,* Part One being *Travels in Syria*), issued, with Explanatory Notes in English (anonymous) as an offprint by the *London Journal of Voyages and Travels,* editor: Benjamin Bensley (London: September 1819)

Page 19

The colossal sphinx still rises thirty-eight feet above the sand that the winds from the desert are accumulating about it. My arrival was too late to avail myself of the labours of M. [Monsieur Henry] Salt. On clearing away about the base of this statue, he had found steps that communicated with the gates of a little temple erected between the feet of the sphinx. An unpardonable egotism led him to block up again objects which call for an active and vigorous investigation, which would throw great light on the history of the arts in ancient days, would bestow éclat on one of the most sublime monumental fictions to be found in ancient Egypt.

JAMES BURTON (1822)
From Burton's original unpublished manuscript in the British Library (MS. Add. 25,619, f. 32)

[Note: The spaces marked by ellipses below are words written in the manuscript in Arabic script, which I have not transcribed.]

Sphinx

The Sphinx is still called Aboo l'hol, a name by which it was known among the natives 650 years ago, and would seem to strengthen the etymology chosen by M. [Louis] Langlès for the word Belheet . . . or Belhoobeh . . . or Belhooyeh . . . which Makreesy [the historian Taqiyyu 'l-Din al-Maqrizi (1364–1442)] and Syotty [the historian Jalalu 'l-Din al-Suyuti (1445–1505), who wrote a history of Old and New Cairo, among other works] give as the *true* one and which it seems according to M. [Silvestre] de Sacy is written thus in different copies and apparently also Belhoot, . . . according to M. Langlès, which he selects and says is compounded of the words . . . eye and . . . terror. The Arab name seems to be a translation of the Egyptian.

The countenance has yet the traces though faint of the red colour with which it was formerly covered, and which 6 or 7 centuries back, was coated with a varnish that then had all the brilliancy of freshness. The colour should certainly never be called *yellow*.

[He then quotes book 1, chapter 4 of Abdallatif about the Sphinx (see page 447) and Denon on the Sphinx (see page 489), and he makes some comments on Denon's artistic remarks, which I omit.]

The statue was mutilated by a bigoted enthusiast [old-fashioned term for a fanatic], Sheckh [Sheikh] Mohammed, about year of the Hegira—? [Burton left a blank for the date.] It was probably when the nose was thus broken that the Asp [uraeus] and headdress were removed. There is little doubt that it carried these ornaments, from the hole now remaining in the top of the head, which the natives have at some time or other enlarged, in the hopes of finding in the interior some hidden treasure. The head however is solid stone, and they soon found their labour useless. I think I remember Mr. [Henry] Salt having told me, that he found in excavating the temple between its paws, part of an asp in bronze. This will have been that placed over the forehead.

The rump was repaired with Mapara [?] stone probably by the Kornans [?]—their repairs were destroyed again by the late Defterdar in order to serve as building materials for one of his palaces.

Moorad Bey [Murad Bey (d. 1801); see his portrait in figure 2.8 on page 92] first uncovered the Sphinx but found nothing—he did not dig deep. The French then did it, and were equally unsuccessful. [Captain J.-B.] Caviglia finally succeeded, and the accompanying notice of the work is copied from the . . . [here the text breaks off].

[The verso side of this manuscript leaf has Burton's copy of Henry Salt's plan of the paws and altar of the Sphinx, with identifying letters and specific descriptions. No succeeding leaf has been bound into this manuscript volume, and the subsequent leaves by Burton change subject.]

JOSEPH MOYLE SHERER (1824)
Scenes and Impressions in Egypt and Italy (London: 1824)

Page 159

The Sphinx disappointed us; as it does generally, I should think: drawings and prints deceive wonderfully; it has neither the size, the majesty, or the sweetness with which it is usually represented.

Pages 149–53

Returning [from Saqqara], we again called on [Captain] Caviglia. Magic had been at work in his little hut: plans and drawings were hung all round, concealing and ornamenting its walls; his books established on shelves and tables . . . He declined returning with us that evening to our boat, but said he would himself accompany us to Saccara [Saqqara] on the morrow, which he did. His wish was to show the interior of that pyramid (the same which the Arabs call the Seat of Pharaoh; and here, perhaps, tradition does not err; but the other pyramids are surely sepulchral) opened by the French, he having founded some opinion on the examination of it, which leads him to suppose, that *none of the pyramids were sepulchres*—I leave him to amuse himself with the difficulty.

He is a kind man, with much enthusiasm about Egyptian antiquities, having exhibited enterprise and perseverance, and fearlessly expended all he could: he is unpretending too, considering his visit to Paris, and the nonsense he heard talked there about Moses and Orpheus, and which, at times, will peep from under his modest avowals, that he is only a sailor [his profession was naval captain], with a strong turn this way, which has made him both labour and read on antiquities. . . . He showed, and with no little pride, a number of the Quarterly Review [volume 19 for 1818], which spoke of his labours with high praise and deserved encouragement. I borrowed the volume . . .

RICHARD MADDEN (1826)

Travels in Turkey, Egypt, Nubia, and Palestine (London: 1833), 2 vols.

Vol. 1, page 257

In the time of Aaron Hill (upwards of one hundred and twenty years ago) there was no entrance into the interior [of the Chephren Pyramid, opened in 1817 by Belzoni]; and when Herodotus was in Egypt [his dates were fifth century BC] it was closed.

Aaron Hill asserts that he found a mummy in the sepulchral chamber of the large Pyramid, covered with hieroglyphics; and that from one of the galleries he made his way under ground to the interior of the great sphinx. This indeed savours of the marvellous [i.e., Madden thinks Aaron Hill made it up, which he certainly did; the publications of Aaron Hill on Egypt are entirely fictitious and were commercially motivated publishing hoaxes].

Pages 260–62

More probably *the use of the Pyramids was connected with the celebration of the mysteries of the Egyptian religion.* The narrow oval apertures in the chambers of the pyramids, into which Caviglia thrust joined reeds eighty feet long, without finding any impediment [these are nowadays called the "ventilation shafts"], we know nothing of, or where they terminate. The secrets of the Egyptian religion, in my opinion, are only to be sought in the interior of the Pyramids. It is vain to look for them in the papyri found either in Thebes or Memphis. Hitherto [prior to 1826] all those which have been found have proved totally devoid of interest. Law processes, votive offerings, narrations of funerals, and title-deeds, are the only subjects of the papyri. Mr. Caviglia, with whom I lived for some months at Mr. Salt's, was strongly of this opinion: his valuable discoveries in the great Pyramid, of the passage of the well [the well shaft, which he was the first to clear of sand and rubble], and of the ruins of temples close to the Pyramids, were published in the Quarterly Review [vol. 19 for 1818]. How much it is to be regretted that commerce alone monopolizes all the enterprise of the affluent, and that no company of scientific men is to be found to invest a capital of five or six thousand pounds in the advancement of science. With such a sum, I believe the real knowledge of the Pyramids might be attained; and so far as regards the religion and learning of the Egyptians, perhaps for the destruction of the Alexandrian library we might be almost compensated.

I would carry on the excavation of the Pyramids both from the upper chamber and the body of the sphinx, in the direction of the base of the pyramid, at about the same monthly expense as Belzoni in 1817; and in the course of a few years, nay months, I am much deceived if nothing should be discovered to redeem the wisdom of the Egyptians from the libel of having constructed a mountain of infamous architecture, like that of the great Pyramid, containing only two insignificant chambers for the accommodation of the corpse of a tyrant.

JAMES WEBSTER (1828)
Travels through the Crimea, Turkey and Egypt; Performed during the Years 1825–1828 (London: 1830), 2 vols.

Vol. 2, page 22

We at length entered the desert, and in a few moments stood before the Sphynx. The ridge of the back is seen rough and time-worn; the head dress is made to project behind so as to counterbalance the chin and face; in front, between the paws, a temple has been discovered, for a drawing of which, see No. 38 of the Quarterly Review. [This engraving is reproduced as figure 3.3 on page 132. The sand has now covered up the temple, and in time the head only of the Sphynx will be visible, as before. Much has been done to prevent this by Mr. Caviglia, who erected a wall around his excavations; but the position of the Sphynx, considerably below the level of the pyramids themselves, heaped up a hundred feet by the sands, renders all attempts of this kind hopeless. No effort can save the excavation from being filled up by the sands.

Page 24

The sands have made irresistible progress in the course of ages. The pyramids were, no doubt, on the bare rock: the body of the Sphynx must have also been uncovered. Now, not only are these encumbered, but the rocks, and all along the edges of the fields below them, are covered with the sands—the tide of an ocean that shall never know reflux!

SIR JOHN GARDNER WILKINSON (1835)
Topography of Thebes, and General View of Egypt (London: 1835)

Page 331

The Sphinx stands nearly opposite the south-east end of the pyramid of Chephren. Between its paws were discovered an altar and some tablets, but no entrance was visible. Pliny says they suppose it the tomb of Amasis; a tradition which arose, no doubt, from the resemblance of the name of the king, by whose order the *rock* was cut into this form, Thothmes IV [1425–1417 BC], to that of the Saite monarch. [There was a king Amasis (570–526 BC) of the Twenty-sixth Dynasty, known as the Saite Period; Wilkinson is proposing that the two became confused in later tradition.] But one author [he refers to the Roman poet Lucan] has gone farther, and given to Amasis the pyramids themselves. The cap of the Sphinx, probably the pshent, has long since been removed; but a cavity in the head attests its former position, and explains the mode in which it was fixed. The mutilated state of the face, and the absence of the nose, have led many to the erroneous conclusion that the features were African; but by taking an accurate sketch of the face, and restoring the Egyptian nose, any one may convince himself that the lips, as well as the rest of the features, perfectly agree with the physiognomy of a Pharaoh; for the reader must be aware that this and all other sphinxes are emblematic representations of Egyptian kings.

[Wilkinson adds in a footnote: "From the name and hieroglyphics on the tablet in front of it, we may conclude it is of Thothmes IV."]

JOHN LLOYD STEPHENS (1835)
Incidents of Travel in Egypt, Arabia Petraea, and the Holy Land (Norman: University of Oklahoma Press, 1970)

Page 38
[In his journey to Giza on December 31, 1835, Stephens noted this about the Sphinx:]

Next to the pyramids, probably as old, and hardly inferior in interest, is the celebrated Sphinx. Notwithstanding the great labours of Caviglia, it is now so covered with sand that it is difficult to realize the bulk of this gigantic monument. Its head, neck, shoulders and breast are still uncovered; its face, though worn and broken, is mild, amiable, and intelligent, seeming, among the tombs around it, like a divinity guarding the dead.

ROCHFORT SCOTT (1837)
Rambles in Egypt and Candia . . . (London: 1837), 2 vols.

Vol. 1, page 242

In the face of the scarped rock, about a quarter of a mile to the south of the great pyramids, is a Hypogean temple, the entrance of which is also decorated with figures and hieroglyphics. The Arab guides were averse to my entering it. . . . The great Sphynx is to the eastward of this temple; no part of it but the head could be seen, the sand drifts so constantly upon it. It stands on a much lower level than the pyramids.

SIR WILLIAM WILDE (1837)
Narrative of a Voyage to Madeira . . . Egypt . . . and Greece
(Dublin: 1840), 2 vols.

Page 393

A line of camels slowly pacing across the dreary waste, on which they [the pyramids] stand, or a Bedawee [Bedouin] careering his horse beside the base, give, by comparison, some faint idea of their [the pyramids'] stupendous size, and an Arab pirouetting his charger on the sphinx* afforded me the desired contrast, at the same time that it showed me what was the magnitude of that emblem of Egyptian reverence and superstition.

*[Wilde adds in a footnote: "The sand has again accumulated so much on the back of the sphinx, that it is easy to ride to the top."]

Appendix One

EXCAVATIONS OF MONSIEUR MARIETTE AT THE GREAT SPHINX

. . . .

AUGUSTE MARIETTE (1855)

TRANSLATED BY OLIVIA TEMPLE

Athenaeum Français: Révue Universelle de la Littérature, de la Science et des Beaux-Arts (Paris: 1855)

Vol. 4, pages 391–92

Learned Societies, Institut de France, Académie des Inscriptions et Belles-Lettres.

EXCAVATIONS OF MONSIEUR MARIETTE AT
THE GREAT SPHINX

We have already announced the important communications made by Monsieur Auguste Mariette of the Academy on the subject of the excavations at the Serapeum of Memphis. Lack of space prevents us from going into this subject in great detail, and especially of speaking about the excavations that have taken place at the Great Sphinx. In 1833 an English Egyptologist, Mr. [Charles H.] Cottrell, to whom one owes the translation of the work of Monsieur Bunsen [Baron Bunsen, i.e. Christian Carl Josias Freiherr von Bunsen] on Egypt [*Egypt's Place in Universal History* (London: 1848), 5 vols.], found in Florence among the papers of Caviglia, who undertook the first of the extensive excavations around the colossus [the Sphinx], the plan of the two chambers discovered behind the Sphinx, which contained hieroglyphic texts. Monsieur [Samuel] Birch had the thought that if one succeeded in rediscovering these two chambers, the inscriptions in question would reveal the origin of the gigantic statue. M. le Duc de Luynes [Louis-Charles d'Albert, duc de Luynes], alerted to this fact by M. [Vicomte Emmanuel] de Rougé, wished, with his well known liberality, to help our compatriot to pursue this curious quest, and furnished him with the funds necessary for the excavation. This act of generosity was soon followed by an allocation of funds from the French government, and Monsieur Mariette came to clear the Sphinx, which he found to be only a natural rock of which the art of the ancient Egyptians had, so to speak, finished the shapes in order to make the statue of a god. That god is Horus, and the temple where he was worshipped has been rediscovered to the southeast of the colossus [Sphinx; this temple is now called the Valley Temple]. It is an enormous square enclosure comprising a crowd of rooms with galleries made of gigantic blocks of alabaster and granite. This edifice, completely devoid of hieroglyphic inscriptions, like most of the monuments dating from the most ancient pharaohs, dates, according to all probability, from the Fourth Dynasty.

The Egyptians had sculpted the head of the Sphinx and filled up the large natural hollows and molded the shapes with masonry. This colossus is found at the bottom of a sort of pit of which the lateral walls are 20 meters [66 feet] away from each of its sides. Monsieur Mariette admits that in antiquity the water of the Nile could have entered this pit. Later, the Greeks had built the steps discovered by Caviglia for going down into the pit. Against the right side of the Sphinx the traveler had found a huge Osiris statue made of 28 pieces, reckoned to be the number of pieces into which the body of Osiris had been cut according to the Egyptian myth.

The Sphinx has been measured in all of its dimensions. Its height is 19.7 meters [64.6 feet]. In the back and across the hindquarters of the statue, Monsieur Mariette recognized the vertical shaft, the existence of which had previously been pointed out by Vansleb [Johann Wansleben] and [Richard] Pococke, who thought that one could penetrate further down from there into existing chambers, according to their supposition, inside the colossus. This shaft, explored with care, presented at its bottom a roughly hewn room, which was in reality just a natural fissure enlarged by the hands of man. In this room lay some fragments of wood that gave off a strong smell of resin when burned, which led one to believe that the wood came from a sarcophagus.

One had supposed that in antiquity the Sphinx was entirely painted red, but nothing indicates that this had been so. Only the face was once covered in this color after the reign of Rameses the Great, for in the time of that pharaoh, the beard of the colossus represents an act of worship over which the red had been applied.

The Greek inscriptions found near the stairs of the Sphinx tell us that this colossus bore the name of Harmakhis, the significance of which has still not been discovered.

The excavations of the Great Sphinx did not lessen the honor due to the intelligence and to the devotion of Monsieur Mariette in his magnificent discovery of the Serapeum [at Saqqara]. We need to return to this archaeological event before recapturing, as we will be doing in one of the forthcoming issues, the analysis of the works of the Academy since our last survey.

Appendix Two

CONCERNING THE
AGE OF THE SPHINX
AT GIZA

· ·

LUDWIG BORCHARDT

TRANSLATED BY ROBERT TEMPLE AND ELEONORE REED

Ludwig Borchardt, Berlin, submitted by Herr Erman
*Sitzungsberichte der Königlich Preussischen Akademie der Wissenschaften zu
Berlin* [Report of the Proceedings of the Royal Prussian Academy of Sciences
at Berlin], Sitzung der philosophisch-historischen Classe [Proceedings of the
Historic-Philosophical Class], vol. 35 (1897)

Pages 752–60

The question concerning the date of origin of the Great Sphinx at Giza,
approached from a different direction than has been done heretofore, shall be
the task of the investigation that follows. The previous investigators have been
guided in their opinions either by the mention of the name Chephren in the
Sphinx stela of Thutmosis IV [the "Dream Stela"], or they have imagined that
they saw some similarities in the type of the countenance of the Sphinx itself,
and have arrived at differing conclusions among themselves. It is precarious,
to say the least, to attempt to maintain the first approach, which concerns the
name of Chephren, since the inscription referred to speaks of nothing more
than a name adjoining a large gap in the surrounding passage of text, possibly completed as Chephren [only half of the name is preserved, and the rest
has flaked off], in combination with some statue. It is not at all clear that the

Sphinx is somehow referred to here. The second approach, which presumes to elicit something from the type of countenance, is even more uncertain; the face is so ruined that unless some other indices can be added to this, one can scarcely infer anything from it.

In what follows an attempt shall be made to arrive at a date based on details of dress, since for the present that seems to be the only safe way to date Egyptian sculptures, whereas for the treatment of such questions from the purely stylistic point of view there exists up to now neither sorted material nor sufficient preparatory work. We must for the moment content ourselves in the research that confronts us with settling the question solely as a matter of dress, by setting strictly aside all stylistic observations relating to the treatment of the actual portrait, the musculature and so forth, and thus reducing the question to something visibly obvious and tangible—or, I might even say, numerical.

The first criterion of this kind with which we shall deal concerns the eye-paint stripes which are found projecting from the outer corners of the eyes of the Sphinx in entirely flat relief and with traces of blue pigment. Regarding these, we should need to apply the law, recently discovered by Herr [Baron] von Bissing, that eye-paint stripes were unknown in the Old Kingdom. That this is so is shown by the following statistics, which unfortunately only refer to what is in the Cairo Museum, but which could hardly be modified by objects from other collections.*

The Cairo Museum possesses in its Old Kingdom halls and storage areas over 230 statues and fragments of statues with heads which date from the Old Kingdom [this was in 1897]; none of these have any eye-paint stripes. In this account the following are not counted:

- Fourteen statues of kings which bear the names of ancient kings are exhibited in the Old Kingdom halls, but on many grounds which would take too long to discuss here, these can in no way be viewed as works of such an early period; further
- Three painted wooden statues (Numbers 289–311, Catalog 1895, page 28, Hall 11, Case A) from Akhmim and Luxor which are placed by mistake in the halls of the Old Kingdom, but are not ascribed to the Old Kingdom, and

---

*The numbers given for the Cairo Collection are those of the new Inventory of the Collection, which is not yet published, but wherever possible, I have given the old numbers as well, to facilitate their consultation in the catalogs which are presently for sale. Wherever there are no old numbers available, then I have at least given the room numbers.

- One torso of a queen (Number 255, Catalog 1895, page 15, Hall 3, Case B) found at Abydos by Mariette, which he affirmed (Mariette, Catalog Number 516) might perhaps be the oldest of Egyptian art, but which contemporary art historians date either as Ptolemaic or Roman.

All of these* show the eye-paint stripes, and so they should, because none of these sculptures belongs to the Old Kingdom.

Only a single statue that can with certainty be dated from truly ancient times shows eye-paint stripes; it is a painted wooden statue found at Meir of a standing naked girl, perhaps a dancer (Number 248, Catalog 1895, Supplement 2, Number 1340b, Hall 2), which is placed together with the contents of the grave of Pepy-n-onh-kem in the same display case, but differs from the works in this grave find, so that the possibility cannot be discounted that it may have been reckoned among these grave goods in error. If we discount this possibility, we have the first appearance of eye-paint stripes during or after the Sixth Dynasty, which was the time when all the radical changes in dress and customs appeared, which separate the Middle Kingdom from more ancient times, so that certainly in terms of the history of art, but perhaps also in the political sense, one can properly speak of the Middle Kingdom having begun with the Sixth Dynasty.

What we have ascertained from the statues is shown also by the reliefs. Prior to the Sixth Dynasty, eye-paint stripes cannot be demonstrated anywhere, but thereafter they make their appearance everywhere: thus, they appear on the *udjat* eyes on the stelas, on coffins, in grave paintings, and even in the [hieroglyphic] sign in the writings.

A single plausible exception is known to me: on the false door of the grave of Schery (Giza, Catalog 1895, Number 13, Hall 1, from Saqqara) one of the women, if one looks really closely, has eye-paint stripes on her eyes, although none of the other figures bears any sign of any. Even though Schery was a priest of the kings Send and Peribsen of the Second Dynasty, the false door does not yield any signs that it also dates from such ancient times. It reminds us rather of the works from the end of the Old Kingdom, especially where the style of the sunken hieroglyphics is concerned. Therefore I believe that, at least until the opposite can be proved, one has to come to the following conclusion: the makeup stripes appear, at least where statues are concerned, at the earliest during the Sixth Dynasty, but become more widespread only during the Middle Kingdom.

---

*For several of statues of named kings, the makeup stripes are not shown in relief. However, they must nevertheless not be counted for statistical purposes.

Now, the Great Sphinx has obvious eye-paint stripes. Therefore the time of its creation falls into the period subsequent to the Sixth Dynasty.

Just as this criterion has given us the lower date limit, so we can find the upper limit in the ornaments of the headdress, the so-called King's Bonnet. This decorated piece of cloth lying over the forehead with the uraeus, which is the symbol of the kings, is tied firmly to the forehead with a headband. It frames the face, creating two triangular areas which fall in two pleats on either side of the face, down the neck, and onto the chest. At the back it is gathered together and ends in a plait lying down the back, which is ribbed as well as appearing to be wrapped. The pattern that this scarf shows is in most cases the following: the front folds are, as shown in A, both in frontal view and also in section, folded into horizontal pleats, the piece covering the head, however, is divided into regular alternately sunken and raised stripes (figure B), which with statues of which the painting is still showing, is depicted in alternating yellow and blue shades.

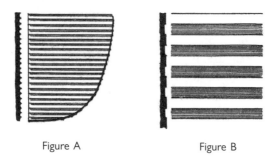

Figure A   Figure B

This King's Bonnet was of course fashion-dependent, and so we can at least in the statues follow different variations through time. From the Eighteenth Dynasty, or perhaps even a little earlier, it becomes fashionable to supply the inside with a vertical smooth hem.* Around the Nineteenth Dynasty, it becomes common practice to extend the regular division of the stripes of the upper part of the front pleats to the chest by giving up the pleats,† and at the same time they now divided the ribbed plait instead into sunken or raised horizontal stripes.

The Great Sphinx of Giza also shows yet another pattern in its headdress. The stripes of that headdress given as sunken are arranged in groups of three stripes each, that is, one wider stripe is always placed between two narrower stripes. Each

---

*For instance, the statue of Horemheb next to Amun at Turin and others. Also, already on the statues of Sebekhotep in Paris (de Rougé, *Notice des mon.*, Numbers 16/17, page 15 ff.).

†For instance, the colossal bust of Ramesses II in London and others.

of the wider stripes has on either side a small accompanying stripe. And this differs from the usual arrangement with stripes of equal width. And therefore we also have to examine where and when this anomaly occurs.

The following list, which shows those kings' statues with the stripes that are grouped in this manner,* will show this immediately. We must distinguish between two different forms: those with completed groups (figure C) and those where they are only indicated in simple lines (as in figure D). Both types of course belong to the same type; the second is only an abbreviation of the first.

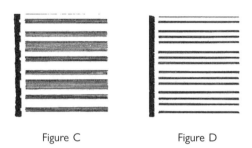

Figure C   Figure D

In the museum at Giza I could make the following observations:

1. Number 384 (Catalog 1895, Number 125, Hall 16). Torso of a statue of the Twelfth Dynasty, usurped and reused by Merenptah-Hetep-her-maat. Cap stripes of type C.
2. Number 385 (Catalog 1895, Number 1370, Hall 16). Statue of Amenemhet III. Stripes of type C.
3. Number 430 (Catalog 1895, Number 226, Court 28). Statue of the Twelfth Dynasty.†
4. Number 432 (Catalog 1895, Number 196, Hall 26). Statue of the Twelfth Dynasty, usurped and reused by Ramesses II. Stripes as in C.
5. Number 481 (Hall 63, Cabinet A). Head of the type of Amenemhet III.‡ Stripes as in C.
6./7. Numbers 482/3 (Hall 63, Cabinet A). Two heads of the type of Amenemhet III. Stripes as in D.

---

*We are always speaking only of the stripes on the upper part and the side part of the cloth. The regular pleating of those cloths falling over the chest are not considered here.
†With 3 and 4, we have another indication of the criteria of the Middle Kingdom, namely the rounding of the front horizontal edge of the seat.
‡See Golenischeff in *Recueil de Travaux* (1893), pages 131 ff.

In the Berlin Museum, at my request Herr Shaefer was so kind as to check through the originals and casts:

8. Number 1121 (Catalog, page 331). Statue of Amenemhet III, usurped and reworked by Merenptah. Stripes as in C. The stripes of the apron show the same pattern.
9. Number 7264 (Catalog, page 24). Statue of the Twelfth Dynasty, usurped and reused by Ramesses II and Merenptah. Stripes as in C.
10. Number 11,348 (Catalog, page 58). Upper part of a statue of the type of Amenemhet III. Stripes as in D.
11./12. G. 388/9. (Catalog, page 331). Casts of the statue of Amenemhet III at St. Petersburg, with reference to this type (see Golenischeff in *Recueil de Travaux,* 1893, plates 1–3). Stripes as in D.

In Paris, where again I owe the material to Herr [Heinrich] Schaefer, we find only one such statue:

13. Number 23 (de Rougé, *Notice des mon.,* page 22). Sphinx of the Twelfth Dynasty of Apophis, later usurped by Merenptah-Hetep-her-maat. Stripes as in C. [Translator's note: This is the Sphinx of Amenemhet II, which is discussed at length in chapter 4 of this book and is identical with the face on the Great Sphinx of Giza. It should be noted that Borchardt had not seen this sphinx A23 personally but had merely received information from Heinrich Schaefer that it had the correct pattern of stripes. Nor was a photo of it supplied to Borchardt, or he would probably have recognized the face instantly.]

In London, where Mr. Griffith has kindly checked through the available material, there seemed to be in the Museum no statues which could be used here as examples.

In England in private ownership we find:

14. Head of the type of Amenemhet III in the Grenfell Collection (Burlington Fine Arts Club, the Art of Ancient Egypt, 1895, photo number 51). Stripes as in D.
15. Head of the type of Amenemhet III, owner unknown (op. cit., photo number 43). Stripes as in D.

Of the other collections, I have checked through the photographs, which are kept in the Berlin Museum, but have not found any further cases of the order of stripes that we are discussing here. So the result of this compilation is clear:

The grouped stripes on the King's Bonnet are only found during the Twelfth Dynasty, perhaps only under Amenemhet III, because those pieces that are precisely dated and that have such an arrangement of stripes are all from his time. And of the others, which are only dated generally to the Twelfth Dynasty, it can never be discounted that they also might be images of Amenemhet III. For this more narrow limitation of this fashion of stripes to the time of Amenemhet III speaks as well as the circumstance that the statues of Usertsen from Lisht (Giza, Numbers 411–20, Catalog 1895, Supplement 3, Number 1365, Hall 21) have not grouped but merely regular stripes [see figure 4.18]. But whether or not one wishes to limit the time of the grouped stripings to the reign of Amenemhet III, one thing is for certain: after the Twelfth Dynasty, this fashion has vanished. The statues of the Thirteenth Dynasty, Sebekhotep (Louvre, Cast G 1, Catalog S. 332, Berlin) and Sebek-em-sa-f (Giza, Number 386, Catalog 1895, Number 128, Hall 16), already display the regularly striped King's Bonnet.

So for the dating of the Sphinx at Giza we draw from all of this the following conclusion: Because the headdress of the Sphinx shows the wide stripes with the narrow accompanying stripes, the Sphinx therefore can surely not have been created after the Twelfth Dynasty.

We have now enclosed the origin of the Sphinx within two limits, an upper and a lower.

According to the makeup stripes, it is Sixth Dynasty or later. According to the stripes on the headdress, it is before the end of the Twelfth Dynasty. If one wishes to be less cautious, one can add to this perhaps the time of Amenemhet III.

For this dating, we can also add some other minor facts to which we do not however wish to attribute too much weight:

- The lack of any mention of the Sphinx in the Old Kingdom, as far as we know from any inscriptions discovered up till now.
- The lack of finds from the Old Kingdom in the immediate vicinity of the Sphinx.
- The occurrence of two vertical shafts on the back of the Sphinx, one of which ends in a burial chamber, in which coffin boards have been found.* From this we can infer the earlier existence of a mastaba on the back of the Sphinx.

---

*See Mariette in *Athenaeum Français* (1855), page 392.

- The original beardlessness of the face,* exactly as Amenemhet was usually depicted.
- The occurrence of a divine image in front of the chest of the Sphinx between its paws, exactly as with the Middle Kingdom sphinx from El Kab (Giza, Number 391, Catalog 1895, Number 139, Hall 16). The traces of this divine image are still clearly visible in front of the chest as a protruding piece of stone.

Finally, if one really wants to, one could even read the type of Amenemhet III's face into the countenance of the Sphinx. But as I have said already in my introduction, this is a rather questionable argument because of the destruction of the features.

One could imagine the history of the Sphinx in general, mixed with some guesses, in the following manner:

The Sphinx was hacked out of the bedrock, perhaps by Amenemhet III, by destroying one of the mastabas standing on a hill, which now constitutes the back of the Sphinx, and partly by building it up with ashlar blocks. It shows the king in the shape of a prostrate lion with a human head—in front of the chest with a divine image, perhaps of Harmachis or Khepra. When later the monument was largely buried, Thutmosis IV had it cleared for the first time. On the stela celebrating this fact we find already the mixing of the meaning of the image of the Sphinx itself with the divine image in front of his chest.† Perhaps it was then that the braided divine beard was added to the image.‡ The Sphinx must have been partially freed from the sand in the Nineteenth Dynasty.§

---

*The beard, which [John] Perring found ([Howard Vyse,] *Operations at Giza,* vol. 3, between pages 108 and 109), is one made out of ashlar afterward cemented onto it, probably in the New Kingdom. It is an added, braided divine beard which the Sphinx only received when he was changed from one of the kings into a god. Herr Sethe has pointed out to me that the Sphinx was viewed erroneously by the Egyptians as an image of Harmachis. Originally, every sphinx was only the depicted king shown as a lion.

†The expression . . . [hieroglyphics] . . . (LD. III 68 Z. 7) could also mean: "The Sphinx with the Khepra," and also on the stela . . . [hieroglyphics] . . . (*op. cit.,* Z. 11) "the sand is rising over me" probably refers only to the divine image in front of the chest, because the back and the head of the Sphinx were probably never covered with sand; however when it talks about . . . [hieroglyphics] . . . (*op. cit.,* Z. 8) "the shadow of this great god," one cannot really see a reference to a king even though it could be inferred according to the words, because one would expect to see the name of that king. So already they here thought of the Sphinx as a god.

‡See the figure LD. III, 68.

§See the stela of Ramesses II. ([John] Perring and [Howard] Vyse, *op. cit.,* vol. 3, page 117).

In a later time, the Sphinx was surrounded by a high brick wall in order to protect him from the drifting sand.* From the east, a large staircase† led down to the small chapel in front of the divine image in front of the chest.

All these means of protection have not helped a great deal.‡ In this century one has had to dig him out again repeatedly, last in 1883, and actually it would be necessary again today.

---

*The east side and the southeast corner of it are today still visible, the west side is given by Mariette (*Mastabas,* page 551). This particular wall could already have existed in the New Kingdom, at least the representation of the Sphinx on the stela of Thutmosis IV (LD. III, 68), where the Sphinx figure is shown to be apparently lying on a building, according to the Egyptian laws of perspective, can also be interpreted in such a way that the Sphinx figure is inside a building open at the top, meaning this particular circular brick wall.

†See [John] Perring and [Howard] Vyse, *op. cit.,* vol. 3, pages 110 and 113.

‡The fact that Herodotus never mentioned the Sphinx, however, is not so much because of it being covered by sand, because the head has never been covered completely, but the reason of its rather hidden location. You can only see the Sphinx from very few vantage points in the necropolis—actually, only from the very closest surrounding.

Appendix Three

SPHINX

· ·

JAMES BURTON (1822)

Taken from Burton's original unpublished manuscript in the British Library: MS. Add. 25,619, f. 32: [Note: The spaces marked by ellipses below are words written in the manuscript in Arabic script, which I have not transcribed.]

✑Sphinx✑

The Sphinx is still called Aboo l'hol, a name by which it was known among the natives 650 years ago, and would seem to strengthen the etymology chosen by M. [Louis] Langlès for the word Belheet . . . or Belhoobeh . . . or Belhooyeh . . . which Makreesy [the historian Taqiyyu 'l-Din al-Maqrizi (1364–1442)] and Syotty [the historian Jalalu 'l-Din al-Suyuti (1445–1505), who wrote a history of Old and New Cairo among other works] give as the *true* one and which it seems according to M. [Silvestre] de Sacy is written thus in different copies and apparently also Belhoot, . . . according to M. Langlès, which he selects and says is compounded of the words . . . eye and . . . terror. The Arab name seems to be a translation of the Egyptian.

The countenance has yet the traces though faint of the red colour with which it was formerly covered, and which 6 or 7 centuries back, was coated with a varnish which then had all the brilliancy of freshness. The colour should certainly never be called *yellow.*

[He then quotes book 1, chapter 4, of Abdallatif about the Sphinx, a passage that we have already printed.]

[He then quotes Denon on the Sphinx, a passage we have already printed, and makes some comments on Denon's artistic remarks, which we omit.]

The statue was mutilated by a bigoted enthusiast [old-fashioned word for a fanatic], Sheckh [Sheikh] Mohammed, about year of the Hegira—? [Burton left a blank for the date.] It was probably when the nose was thus broken that the Asp [uraeus] and head dress were removed. There is little doubt that it carried these ornaments, from the hole now remaining in the top of the head, which the natives have at some time or other enlarged, in the hopes of finding in the interior some hidden treasure. The head however is solid stone, and they soon found their labour useless. I think I remember Mr. [Henry] Salt having told me, that he found in excavating the temple between its paws, part of an asp in bronze. This will have been that placed over the forehead.

The rump was repaired with Mapara [?] stone probably by the Kornans [??]—their repairs were destroyed again by the late Defterdar in order to serve as building materials for one of his palaces.

Moorad Bey [Murad Bey, died 1801; see his portrait in figure 2.8 on page 92] first uncovered the Sphinx but found nothing—he did not dig deep. The French then did it, and were equally unsuccessful. [Captain J.-B.] Caviglia finally succeeded, and the accompanying notice of the work is copied from the [here the text breaks off].

[The *verso* side of this manuscript leaf has Burton's copy of Henry Salt's plan of the paws and altar of the Sphinx, with identifying letters and specific descriptions. No succeeding leaf has been bound into this manuscript volume, and the subsequent leaves by Burton change subject.]

Appendix Four

A DESCRIPTION OF GIAMBATTISTA CAVIGLIA'S EXCAVATION OF THE SPHINX

TRANSLATED BY STEFANO GRECO, WITH NOTES BY ROBERT TEMPLE

Privately published by his friend Annibale Brandi in 1823, from what is believed to be the only surviving copy.
A.B. [Annibale Brandi] *Compendious Description of the Pyramids of Giza in Egypt* (Livorno: Stamperia della Fenice, 1823).

[The final portion of this booklet dealing with the Sphinx is given here.]

Also important are the discoveries made when excavating around the Andro-Sphinx, and concerning the opening of various tombs located in the vicinity of the pyramids, as we will see in the continuation of these memories of mine. The short time that I was at the pyramids and my poor talent don't allow me to give a very exact description. However, assisted by cultivated people's advice, I continue as much as I can to describe what Mr. Caviglia accomplished.

This same Caviglia, after examining the Great Pyramid of Giza and discovering the continuation of the [descending] passage to the length of 280 feet further than was known, with a room at its end [now called "the Subterranean Chamber"], the link between that passage and the well shaft, and the small room of dark granite at the left corner of the tunnel, after cleaning the chambers of rocks and earth, and taking note of the fact that he didn't have any other clues to find new chambers, left the Great Pyramid to look for other antiquities in the vicinity. And these initiatives of his, to say the least, were not fruitless.

In fact, he commenced two separate works at the same time. One was clearing the sand from the body of the Sphinx, and the other was to examine a tomb close to the Great Pyramid. In this he found a statue of stone and various busts, and it is remarkable that in the corridor of the entrance there are some apertures, from which one can see the internal rooms where there were the mummies and their statues, and from these apertures probably the relatives of the deceased could observe the mummies that they were visiting, from time to time.

The Sphinx, which is the custodian of the sacred valley, should rather be called "Andro-Sphinx," i.e., the body of a lion with a human head, which was in fact the Theban Sphinx [he is referring to the Sphinx of Greek mythology, which was near Greek Thebes; he is not referring to Thebes in Egypt], with the beard and with the serpent [uraeus] on its forehead. The head, with an opening in its skull, which is about 7 feet deep, was cleared along with a part of its body to a depth of 30 feet. Caviglia then cleared the rest all the way to the base on the side of the face and from another side [the north side], which is 75 feet high.

The body of this colossus, in order to counteract the rough aspect (because of its delicate condition) of the calcareous rock of which it was sculpted, was embellished with hieroglyphs, which were similar to the ones of the Egyptian doctrines, and it was painted red also on the beard. The red color was sacred to the Egyptians. On the surface of its base they found the head of the serpent [uraeus], even though the rest of it was remaining on the forehead. At the end of the beard there are depicted two persons who are making offerings. Beneath the beard, at the distance of 8 feet, there is a small temple 12 feet tall, 8 feet wide, and 7 feet long.

The innermost wall of this [in front of the Sphinx's chest; he is referring to what we now call the Dream Stela, shown in figures 2.9, 3.3, 3.5, 3.7, 3.8, and 4.19] is a big tablet of red granite, completely full of hieroglyphs very well executed. [The bottom half of the inscription seen by Brandi has now vanished.] In the upper part of this there is a winged snake; a row of hieroglyphs divides the table in the center. From one side and the other inside two temples, there are two Theban Sphinxes to which two persons are making some offerings. The one on the left is offering a vase, and the one on the right side seems to have a hand in the fire, and with his other hand he seems to be pouring some liquid for perfumes. Both have triangular aprons [triangular aprons were worn by the pharaohs, and the "two persons" are two different images of Pharaoh Thothmes IV]; in the first, two serpents form a stair of seven steps, and in the second one the same serpent forms five steps; in the rest of the tablet there are other hieroglyphs and in the bottom part there are two crosses, not of the usual form. [This suggests that the Dream Stela inscription was intact at the time Caviglia excavated it, and that the loss of the bottom half of its inscription was due to damage inflicted on the stela after his sudden departure from Egypt because of a serious case of sunstroke, and that this damage to the lower half of the stela was intentional.]

The two sides [of the temple area] are of limestone and are also full of hieroglyphs. If facing outward from the Andro-Sphinx toward the paws, the scene is one of a normal wall guarded by a lion 2 feet long and made of white marble, about 25 feet away. But if facing the Andro-Sphinx, one can see another wall, 6 feet tall, with a window in the middle, located at the entrance of the small temple. In front of this window there is a base with a small granite column, which covers the hole of the window, and it seems put there specifically to block the view inside the small temple. On this wall there are another lion and a bird, representing the Egyptian Minerva, with some heads of statues. At the end of the paws, they also found a poem referring to the Andro-Sphinx, whose Egyptian mysteries are carved in Greek. [This is the poem by Arrian, inscribed on the middle toe of the left paw, now covered with "restoration blocks," which has been discussed in chapter 6, pages 316–23.] On other stones, also in Greek, there are some dedications to the same Sphinx.

The discovery of this table and of its hieroglyphs has deeply touched the fantasy of the superstitious Egyptian women of the near villages, who come numerous times to touch it and to take some pieces of it, believing it could help their fecundity, even though the Egyptians are already helped very much by the god of the orchards. [Evidently, the bottom half of the inscription of the Dream Stela was destroyed in this way, as it was intact when Caviglia excavated it, but not for long. I do not know what the god of the orchards refers to, but perhaps it is some local fetish image.]

Caviglia descended to an underground tomb, and found a large chamber containing an impressive sarcophagus of granite with its cover, in very good condition. [This is apparently the so-called Osiris Shaft beneath the Causeway of Chephren. Caviglia was the first European to discover it, as James Burton also records in his manuscript record.] He opened another tomb and he found a corridor with some hieroglyphs referring to the arts but mainly to agriculture, which was source of the richness of the nation, with the instrument that is shaped like alpha, which the Greeks have taken as the first element of their alphabet. In another subterranean tomb, he found four corridors. In the first, there still are some hieroglyphs referring to the arts and sciences. The second one is full of the same hieroglyphs, and some sea fights are visible. From here to the left, one can enter the third corridor, which is entirely smooth, and at the right hand, the fourth corridor is also deco-rated with the same hieroglyphs, on the internal wall of which there is a niche in which there probably was a statue, because from both sides of it there are some characters presenting various offerings. On the right side of this corridor there are two more openings, which may lead to other corridors and rooms.

He opened many more tombs, in which he found other rooms, some of them with hieroglyphs; but since they had to enter the greater part of these by descend-ing the shafts, they did not find much, because there was no way to breathe for those who entered.

Caviglia entered and opened a small pyramid, the one in front of the Great Pyramid, on the east side, and there he found rooms and passages that are more comfortable than the ones of the Great Pyramid. After excavating a lot in this one, and after searching in the subterranean passages, he found the space of a lodge which resembles the antrums of Minerva; this space consists of four small caverns, excavated in the calcareous rock. The upper part of the door jamb of the first cavern is the biggest one and has the shape of a cylinder, where there are two eyes sculpted, one being big and the other small with a square on the right and a rectangle on the left; I don't understand what they refer to. In the left wall there are quite-well-preserved hieroglyphs, and above them all a seated statue, in front of which a bended figure which seems to be playing a harp, and further there is a scribe, maybe noting the names of the ones who enter the boat of Charon, which is very well decorated, and they leave to cross the [River] Styx. [This is an attempt to explain the Egyptian pictures in terms of Greek myths.]

In this cave there is the passage to another superior and smaller one, whose door jamb is also cylindrical but with no sculptures. This cave is linked to another one, from which it is possible to enter a small room. From the main cavern it is possible to descend to a deep subway, where probably there was what we would call "the Terrible Hall of Judgement." There is nothing else which is remarkable about these two pyramids, which are in the middle of a large, sandy valley. The small pyramid [of Mycerinus] is not accessible, because so far, nobody has ever suc-ceeded in removing all the stones that surround it, and it seems, as they say, that it is not worthwhile to go to the trouble of trying to find its entrance. The other five pyramids are very far from these, and they are in northern Egypt, but they are not as beautiful as the ones of Giza. The perpendicular height of this Great Pyramid is 462 feet tall, i.e., 70 *tese,* and its sides are 660 feet long, i.e., 110 *tese.*

[Note: *tese* is plural for *tesa,* which was an Italian unit of linear measurement at this time, sometimes also used as a volumetric unit. The unit was borrowed from the French during the Later Middle Ages, the Middle French name being *toise,* from the Late Latin word *tesa,* from the earlier Latin *tensa,* meaning "outstretched arms," via Mediaeval Latin *tensa, teisa* meaning "expanse, extent," and also from Latin *te(n) sa/tensus/tendere,* "to stretch," hence "the stretch, reach, extent, or size of (a road)." The value of this unit varied enormously in nineteenth-century Italy between the value of 1.414 meters at Novara and the value of 2.242 meters at Bardonecchia. (As a volumetric unit, it varied similarly, and was approximately 2 cubic meters.) Brandi is using *tese* in a loose sense, not a precise sense, to mean in the first instance 6.6 feet and in the second instance 6 feet; however, the feet are apparently not English feet but French feet of the nineteenth century, *piedi,* or *piedi* "del Re." Brandi's use of this now obsolete unit of measurement, the *tesa,* and the fact that he contradicts himself in terms of its value in the two instances he gives, means that he is only being approximate. Hence we do not really need to concern ourselves with his mention of *tese,* but just in case there are those who might worry, I have given this survey of the issue, in order to lay it to rest.]

Appendix Five

SCIENTIFIC VISUAL DOCUMENTATION OF THE SPHINX

The following images—"Sphinx Figures"—were all drawn by Mark Lehner or under his supervision, on behalf of an international research project on the Sphinx, and are all from his lengthy report, "Documentation of the Sphinx," in *The First International Symposium on the Great Sphinx, Book of Proceedings*, Cairo, 1992. I have used Lehner's own figure numbering and include his explanatory captions, either in whole or in part, in quotation marks, keeping my own additional comments separate from his so that it is obvious that my opinions are my own and not his. He shares no responsibility for any of my views and, in fact, he holds contrary ones. The Cairo reports of 1992 are hard for people to obtain (I bought mine in Cairo), and I am pleased to give a wider circulation of these illustrations to the general public, as they deserve to be much more widely known than they are at present.

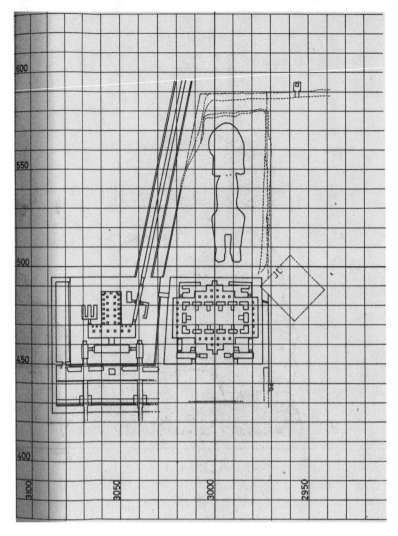

Figure 1. This figure is described by Lehner as "the local Sphinx grid of the ARCE Sphinx Project." (ARCE stands for the American Research Centre in Egypt, with which Lehner is affiliated, as he is an American.) This plan is incomplete for the Valley Temple, some of whose internal features are omitted, though they are perhaps not relevant to a symposium on the Sphinx. I am puzzled by this grid showing the Sphinx facing the western wall of the Sphinx Temple directly. I know that all existing plans do show this, including those of the excavator Herbert Ricke (see figure 6.52), and the evidence of the naked eye certainly suggests the same at ground level. However, I would call your attention to the aerial view of the Sphinx seen in figure 4.2, which appears to offer incontrovertible evidence that the Sphinx is really facing the North Trench, just north of the Sphinx Temple, rather than facing the western wall directly. I don't know whether some bizarre optical illusion is at work here. I am inclined to believe that the optical illusion is the one at ground level and that the aerial photo is the more reliable evidence. I certainly never noticed anything odd at ground level, and so I am not accusing Egyptologists of being dolts, I am just pointing out that we may all be wrong about this. I call for a new and ultra-precise survey to establish the truth about this enigma. Is the Sphinx facing the North Trench, as suggested by the aerial photo, or not? If it is, then this plan and all the other existing plans are in error. There is no use in our burying our heads in the sands of Giza; we must find out the truth about this point, as it may have importance. We absolutely have to know the exact truth about the orientation of the Sphinx.

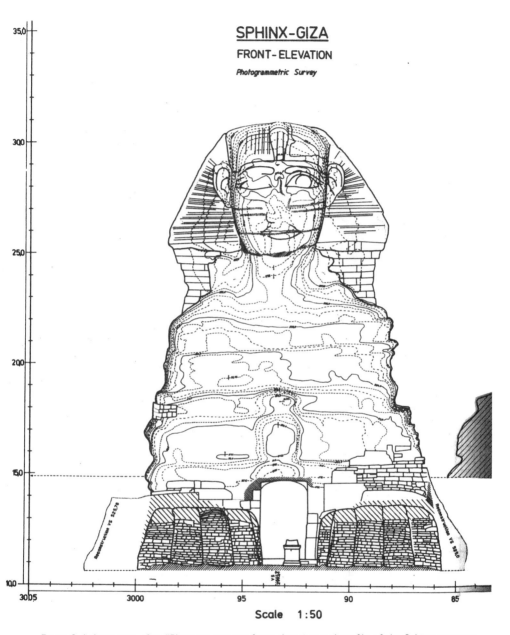

SPHINX-GIZA
FRONT-ELEVATION
Photogrammetric Survey

Scale 1:50

Figure 2. Lehner says of it: "Photogrammetric front elevation and profile of the Sphinx; contour interval is 25 cm. Original drawing is scale 1:50." I think we should note that the altar, though spaced evenly between the paws, is not centered with the Dream Stela, or the sphinx axis. This suggests to me that the Sphinx really is skewed to its left (to the right in this drawing) and is actually facing the North Trench. However, I do not insist upon anything, as we need a proper survey before anyone can be certain of anything regarding this matter.

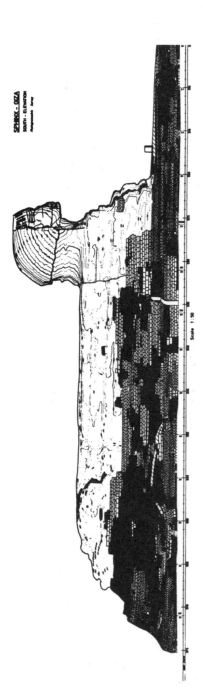

Figure 3. Lehner says: "Photogrammetric south elevation of the Sphinx. Ancient masonry that showed as of September 1979 is shaded. Original drawing is scale 1:50." The tiny head is clearly seen here to be out of proportion with the vast body.

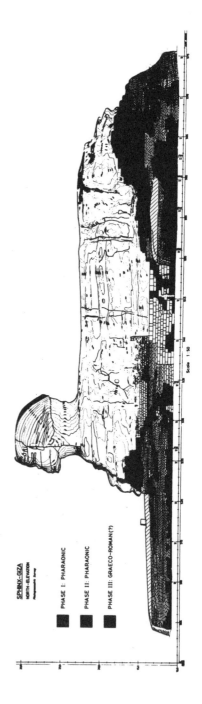

Figure 4. Lehner says: "Photogrammetric north elevation of the Sphinx. Ancient masonry that showed as of September 1979 is shaded. Original drawing is scale 1:50." The entrance blocked up by Baraize in 1926 at the base, just behind the Sphinx's head, is shown here as modern masonry.

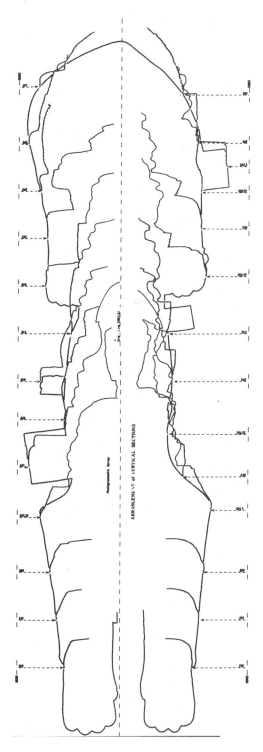

Figure 5. Lehner says: "Photogrammetric profiles of the Sphinx, approximately every 5 m, laid onto the base outline of the Sphinx. Original drawing is scale 1:50." This may look uninteresting, but in fact it is an extremely useful study of the successive profiles, and it has the merit of showing particularly clearly the four strange stone "boxes," two on the north side and two on the south side, that protrude from the Sphinx at the base. No one really knows what they are, although some or all may well have been statue bases. (There is some surviving evidence suggestive of the possibility that a statue of Osiris was erected on one of them.) Of course, some of these bizarre "boxes" may be connected with entries to the interior of the Sphinx. We don't know how old they are, but it is doubtful that any is older than the New Kingdom, and some may even be Roman. They have never been sufficiently studied.

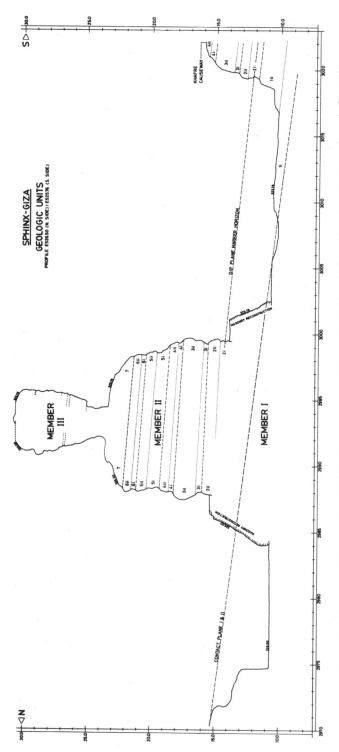

Figure 6. Lehner says: "Profile of the Sphinx face, chest, and sides of the Sphinx ditch with geological units indicated. Original drawing is scale 1:50." The purpose of this drawing is to show the successive geological strata of the limestone from which the Sphinx is carved, all of which are slanting as shown. "Member III," of which the head is carved, is a stronger limestone layer than is "Member II," of which the chest is carved.

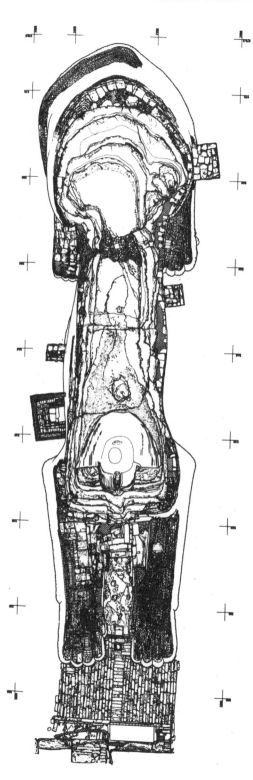

Figure 7. Lehner writes: "Contour map of the Sphinx natural rock core body; contour interval is 10 cm. Original drawing is scale 1:50." This useful plan shows that the altar area between the legs of the Sphinx and its extension eastward are skewed to the south. This may really mean that it is the Sphinx itself that is skewed to the north. Only a more careful survey can tell us. This plan shows how the four strange boxes are made of small stones.

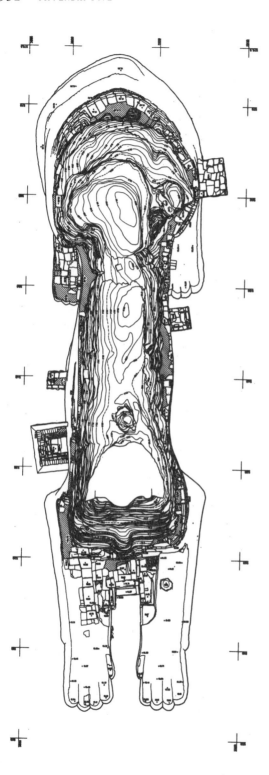

Figure 8 (wrongly described in Lehner's text captions as figure 9). Lehner says: "Form-line master plan of the Sphinx. Original drawing is scale 1:50." (Figures 8 and 9 have their captions mixed up in Lehner's text as published, but that is rectified here.)

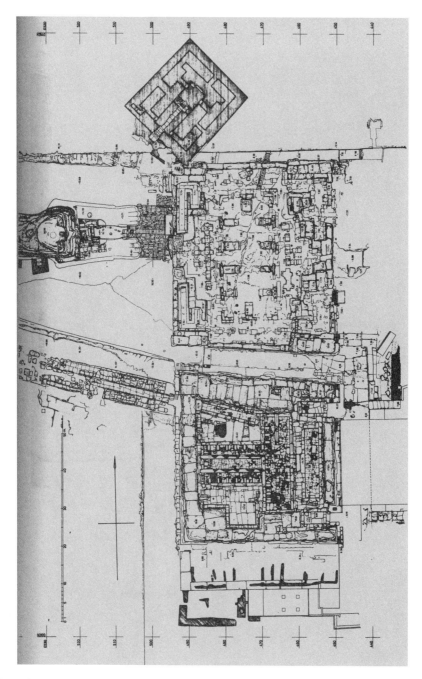

Figure 9 (wrongly described in Lehner's text captions as figure 8). Lehner says: "Detailed map of the temples in front of the Sphinx; Khafre [Chephren] Valley Temple, left; Sphinx Temple, right; Amenhotep II Temple, upper right. Original scale 1:100." The small Amenhotep Temple at far right (see figures 7.3 to 7.5 on pages 327 and 328) dates from the New Kingdom and was built when the existence of the Sphinx Temple beside it was unknown and covered in a mountain of sand. The corridor between the two major temples is well shown here and is discussed at length.

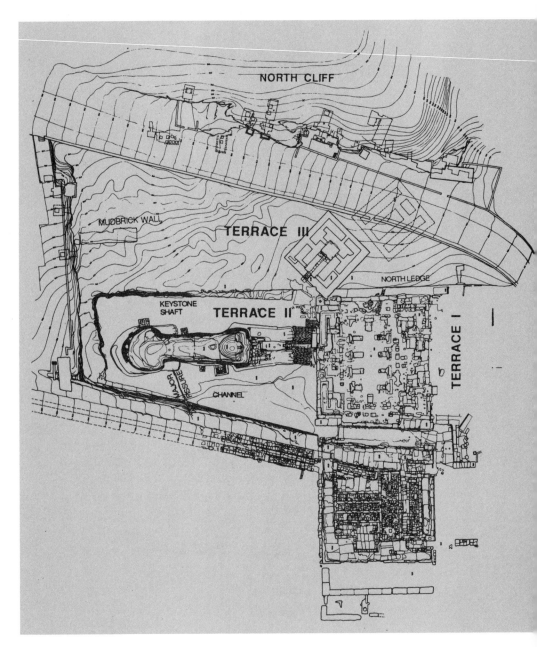

Figure 10. Lehner writes: "Map of Sphinx 'amphitheatre.' Contour interval is 50 cm. Original drawing is scale 1:200."

SPHINX : GEOLOGIC MAP OF ROCK UNITS

Figure 11. Lehner says: "Map of bedrock units: Member I (base), Member II (Sphinx body), and Member III (Sphinx head)." The diagonal crack going across the haunches in the underlying bedrock from northwest to southeast is well shown here, and it crosses the Sphinx at precisely the point where the huge blob of modern cement placed by Baraize in 1926 may be seen. The crack in the bedrock was probably caused by the shock associated with the intrusion of the shaft and construction of the chamber below.

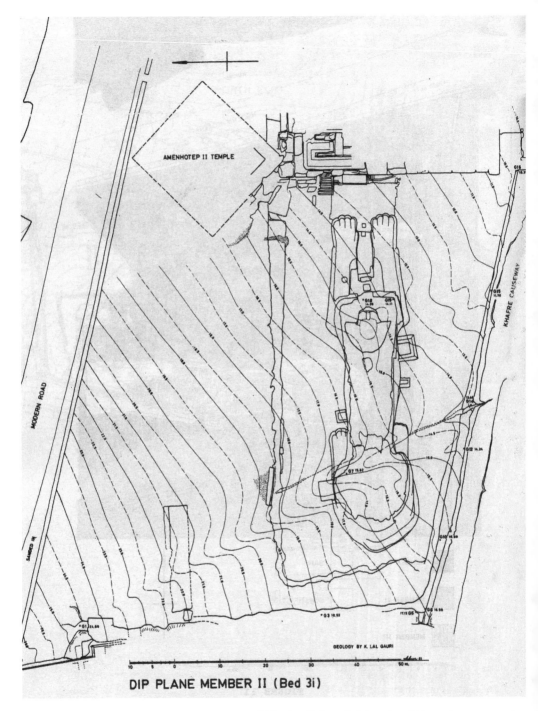

DIP PLANE MEMBER II (Bed 3i)

Figure 12. Lehner says: "Map of dip place of Member II through Sphinx 'amphitheatre'; contour interval is 50 cm."

NOTES

Chapter 1. Sphinx Obsession

1. Imam Marzouk, Amin Hussein, and Ali Gharib, "Underground Structure of Sphinx Area Deduced from Shallow Seismic Refraction Data," in *The First International Symposium on the Great Sphinx, Book of Proceedings* (Cairo: Egyptian Antiquities Organization Press, 1992), 119–28.

2. Ali Helmi Moussa and Lambert T. Dolphin, *Applications of Modern Sensing Techniques to Egyptology* (Menlo Park, Calif.: Stanford Research Institute International, 1977), 31.

3. Ibid., 64–67.

4. Mary Hamilton, *Incubation: Or the Cure of Disease in Pagan Temples and Christian Churches* (London: 1906), 99.

5. Diodorus the Sicilian, *The Historical Library of Diodorus the Sicilian,* translated by G. Booth (London: 1700), book 1, chapter 2, p. 11.

6. *Diodorus Siculus,* translated by C. H. Oldfather (New York: Loeb Classical Library, Harvard University Press, 1933), vol. 1, p. 81 (book 1, 25, 2–6).

7. Zahi Hawass and Mark Lehner, "The Passage Under the Sphinx," in *Hommages à Jean Leclant,* vol. 1 (Paris: Institut Français d'Archéologie Orientale, 1994), 201–216.

8. Zahi Hawass, *The Secrets of the Sphinx: Restoration Past and Present* (Cairo: The American University in Cairo Press, 1998), 13. This booklet is in both English and Arabic, and the English section is only thirty-four pages long. Lal Gauri's work is described in this booklet.

9. Paul Jordan, *Riddles of the Sphinx* (New York: New York University Press, 1998).

10. Johann Helffrich [Johannes Helfricus], *Kurtzer und warhafftiger Bericht, von der Reis aus Venedig nach Hierusalem, von dannen in Aegypten . . .* (*Brief and Genuine Account of a Journey from Venice to Jerusalem, and Thence to Egypt . . .*) (Leipzig, 1579). Reprinted Leipzig, 1589. This work was also reprinted in both 1584 and 1609 in a folio collection of German travelers' accounts of journeys to the Holy Land, edited by S. Feyerabend.

11. Hawass and Lehner, "Passage Under the Sphinx," 201–2.

12. Ibid., 202.

13. K. Kleppisch, *Die Cheopspyramide ein Denkmal mathematischer Erkenntis (The Pyramid of Cheops: A Monument of Mathematical Knowledge)* (Leipzig, 1921).

14. Hawass and Lehner, "Passage Under the Sphinx," 207–8.

15. Ibid., 213–15.

16. Ibid., 215.

17. Christiane Zivie-Coche, *Sphinx! La Père la Terreur: Histoire d'une Statue* (Paris: Éditions Noesis, 1997). English translation by David Lorton, *Sphinx: History of a Monument* (Ithaca, N.Y.: Cornell University Press, 2002).

18. Ibid., 40.

19. Hawass and Lehner, "Passage Under the Sphinx," 215.

20. The famous set of volumes entitled *Description de l'Égypte ou recueil des observations et des recherches qui ont été en Égypte pendant l'expédition de l'armée française (Description of Egypt, or, Collection of the Observations and Researches Which Were Carried Out in Egypt During the Expedition of the French Army)* (Paris, 1816).

21. Howard Vyse, *Operations Carried On at the Pyramids of Gizeh in 1837,* vol. 2B, originally published in London in 1840, ring-bound photographic reprint by ECA Associations, Chesapeake, N.Y., 1990, p. 287, note 1, in the appendix section.

22. James Bonwick, *Pyramid Facts and Fancies* (London, 1877), 106.

23. J. A. St. John, *Egypt and Nubia* (London, 1845), 131–34.

24. Count de Forbin, *The Travels in Egypt: Being a Continuation of the Travels in the Holy Land, in 1817–1818* (London, 1819).

25. *Voyage en Égypte du Père Antonius Gonzales, 1665–1666,* translated from the Dutch and annotated by Charles Libois, French Institute at Cairo, volume XIX (in two parts) of series of *Voyages en Égypte,* part I, p. 145.

26. John Lloyd Stephens, *Incidents of Travel in Egypt, Arabia Petraea, and the Holy Land,* Victor Wolfgang von Hagen, ed. (Norman: University of Oklahoma Press, 1970), 38.

27. Anonymous, "Observations Relating to Some of the Antiquities of Egypt, from the Papers of the Late Mr. Davison. Published in Walpole's Memoirs, 1817." *Quarterly Review* XIX (April and December 1818): 418.

28. Edward Daniel Clarke, *Travels in Various Countries of Europe, Asia and Africa,* vol. III, part the Second (London, 1814), 127–28.

29. William Hamilton, *Remarks on Several Parts of Turkey. Part 1. Aegyptiaca: Or, Account of the Antient and Modern State of Egypt* (London, 1809), 329–30.

30. Selim Hassan, *The Great Sphinx and Its Secrets: Historical Studies in the Light of Recent Excavations* (Cairo, 1953), 223.

31. Sir Peter le Page Renouf, *The Life-Work of Sir Peter le Page Renouf,* vol. 4, *The Book of the Dead: Translation and Commentary* (Paris and Leipzig, 1907), 97.

32. Sir E. A. Wallis Budge, *The Book of the Dead,* 2nd ed. (London, 1928), 173–74.

Chapter 2. The "Secret Chamber" beneath the Sphinx

1. F[ather] Vansleb [Wansleben, Johann Michael], *The Present State of Egypt*, translated by M. D., from the German *Beschreibung von Aegypten* (London, 1678).

2. H. E. G. Paulus, ed., *Sammlung der merkwuerdisten Reisen in den Orient* (Jena, 1794; reprinted 1803).

3. Ibid., 115.

4. Vansleb, *Present State of Egypt,* 88.

5. *The Travels of Monsieur de Thevenot into the Levant* (London, 1687), translation of *Relation d'un voyage fait au Levant* (Paris, 1664–84).

6. Paulus, *Reisen in den Orient,* 208–9. The German text is as follows: "Da er hinterwaerts eine Höhlung unter der Erde hat, deren Breite der Höhe des Kopfs angemessen ist, in welche ich durch eine daselbst befindliche Oefnung hinein sah, und die zu nichts anders gedient haben kann als den Körper eines Todten hineinzustecken."

7. Pietro della Valle, *Les fameux voyages de Pietro della Valle,* vol. 1 (Paris, 1664), p. 228. This work is the French translation of the Italian original, *Viaggi di Pietro della Valle.*

8. Edward Melton, *Zee-en Land-Reizen; door Egypten, West-Indien, Perzien, Turkyen, Oost-Indien* (Amsterdam, 1681 and 1702).

9. Ibid., 1702 ed., 51.

10. Kathleen A. Pickavance, "The Pyramids of Snofru at Dashur: Three Seventeenth-Century Travellers," *Journal of Egyptian Archaeology* 67 (1981): 136–42.

11. Wood, Anthony, *Athenae Oxoniensis* (London, 1721).

12. Ellis Veryard, *An Account of Divers Choice Remarks Taken in a Journey Through Egypt . . .* (London, 1701).

13. Ibid., 298.

14. Guido Pancirollo, *The History of Many Memorable Things Lost, Which Were in Use Among the Ancients: And an Account of Many Excellent Things Found, Now in Use Among the Moderns, Both Natural and Artificial* (London, 1715, and reissued in 1727). I am fortunate to own a copy of this rare book.

15. Ibid., 107.

16. Thomas Shaw, *Travels, or Observations Relating to Several Parts of Barbary and the Levant* (Oxford, 1738).

17. Ibid., 368–69.

18. Ibid., 374–75.

19. Charles Thompson, *Travels Through Turkey in Asia, the Holy Land, Egypt, and Other Parts of the World* (London, 1754).

20. Ibid., vol. 2, 143–44.

21. Richard Pococke, *A Description of the East and Some Other Countries,* 2 vols. (Folio, London, 1743–45).

22. British Library, Add. MSS. 22,978–22,998.

23. Letter 26 to His Mother, dated March 3, 1738/39 [1739 new style, with January 1 being New Year's Day], from the British Library, Add. MS. 22,998, f. 67.

24. Pococke, *Description of the East,* vol. 1, 46.

25. "Frederick Lewis" Norden, *Travels in Egypt and Nubia,* translated from the original and enlarged by Peter Templeman, 2 vols. (Folio, London, 1757).

26. Ibid., vol. 1, p. 80, for Norden's own comments, and p. 76 for the quote from Pococke.

27. Colonel Coutelle, "Observations sur les pyramides de Gyzeh," in *Description de l'Égypte,* vol. 2 (Paris, 1818), 52–53.

28. Joseph Grobert, *Description des pyramides de Ghize* (Paris, 1801), 31–34.

29. Edward Daniel Clarke, *Travels in Various Countries of Europe, Asia and Africa,* 3 vols. (London, 1810–23), "Part the Second. Greece, Egypt, and the Holy Land, Section the Second," vol. III (1814), 127–28. Clarke's further remarks on the Sphinx, which contain an interesting discovery regarding its ancient coloring, are on p. 145.

30. William Hamilton, *Remarks on Several Parts of Turkey. Part 1. Aegyptiaca: Or, Account of the Antient and Modern State of Egypt* (London, 1809), 329–30. Hamilton's last visit seems to have been in 1801, a mere three years after the clearance described by Grobert.

31. British Library, Add. MS. 25,619, f. 32.

32. Anonymous, "Observations Relating to Some of the Antiquities of Egypt, from the Papers of the Late Mr. Davison. Published in Walpole's Memoirs. 1817." A review of the aforesaid publication in *Quarterly Review* 19 (April and December 1818): 418. Henry Salt's expenditures on the clearance of the Sphinx are mentioned on p. 418: "The expenses incurred by all these operations amounted to about 18,000 piastres, a share of which was contributed by Mr. Salt and two or three other gentlemen, who liberally engaged that the disposal of whatever might be discovered should be let wholly to Mr. Caviglia; and he, on his part, generously requested that every thing might be sent to the British Museum, as a testimony of his attachment to that country, under the protection of whose flag he had for many years navigated the ocean." See also *Quarterly Review* 19, no. 38 (July 1818): 391.

33. Ibid., 418.

34. Christian Josias Freiherr [Baron] von Bunsen, *Egypt's Place in Universal History: An Historical Investigation in Five Books,* trans. Charles H. Cottrell (London, 1848).

35. "Excavations of Monsieur Mariette at the Great Sphinx," *Athenaeum Français: Révue universelle de la littérature, de la science et des beaux-arts* 4 (1855): 391–92.

36. Patricia Usick and Deborah Manley, *The Sphinx Revealed: A Forgotten Record of Pioneering Excavations* (British Museum Research Publication Number 164, British Museum Press, London, 2007).

37. Ibid., 63, column a.

38. Ibid., 65, column b.

39. Ibid., 67, column b.

40. Ibid., sketch 41 on p. 42.

41. Auguste Mariette, "Letter to Viscount E. [Emmanuel] de Rougé concerning the Excavations Made in the Vicinity of the Great Sphinx of Giza," in G. Maspero, ed., *Bibliothèque Égyptologique,* vol. 18 (Paris, 1904), 128. Reprinted from the *Athenaeum Français: Révue universelle de la littérature, de la science et des beaux-Arts* 3, no. 4 (Saturday 28 January 1854): 82–84. This and another letter from Mariette were read by E. de Rougé to the Academy of Inscriptions at the meeting of 24 March 1964; compare *Mémoires de l'Académie des Inscriptions,* vol. XX, 1st part, p. 96.

42. Ludwig Borchardt, "Über das Alter des Sphinx bei Giseh" ("Concerning the Age of the Sphinx at Giza"), in *Sitzungsberichte der Königlich Preussischen Akademie der Wissenschafter zu Berlin (Report of the Proceedings of the Royal Prussian Academy of Sciences at Berlin), Sitzung der Philosophisch-Historischen Classe (Proceedings of the Historic-Philosophical Class),* vol. XXXV (1897), 752–60.

43. Ibid., 759.

44. Ibid., 759–60.

45. Selim Hassan, *The Great Sphinx and Its Secrets: Historical Studies in the Light of Recent Excavations,* vol. 8 of his *Excavations at Giza* series, covering the years 1936–37 (Cairo: Government Press, 1953), 158–60.

46. Ibid., 160.

47. Robert Temple, *The Crystal Sun: Rediscovering a Lost Technology of the Ancient World* (London: Century, 2000).

48. Ali Helmi Moussa and Lambert Dolphin, *Applications of Modern Sensing Techniques to Egyptology* (Ain Shams University, Cairo, National Science Foundation, Washington, D.C., and SRI International, Menlo Park, Calif. [it is not clear which is the actual place of publication, and it appears that the booklet was simultaneously published by all three entities]: September 1977).

49. Ibid., 13.

50. Ibid., 64–67.

51. Lal Gauri, "Weathering and Preservation of the Sphinx Limestone," in Feisal A. Esmael, ed., *The First International Symposium on the Great Sphinx: Book of Proceedings* (Cairo, 1992), 46–47.

52. Mark Lehner, "Documentation of the Sphinx," in ibid., figure 10, p. 92.

53. Robert Bauval, *Secret Chamber* (London: Century, 1999). Simon Cox is credited within the book as the author of appendix 4 and thanked in the acknowledgments for "his help in the editorial work," but I understand from Cox that he actually wrote part 1 of the book. I therefore view the book as having two authors.

54. Ibid., 185–86.

55. Mark Lehner, *The Egyptian Heritage* (Virginia Beach, Va.: ARE Press, 1974).

56. Bauval and Cox, *Secret Chamber,* 174–98.

57. Ibid., 202.

Chapter 3. An Amazing Survival

1. Anonymous, "Antiquities of Egypt," *Quarterly Review* 19, no. 38 (July 1818): 391–424. The full title heading of the article is: "Observations Relating to Some of the Antiquities of Egypt, from the Papers of the Late Mr. Davison. Published in [Robert] Walpole's Memoirs." It is important to realize that it is Robert Walpole, not Horace Walpole, whose memoirs are referred to here; Horace Walpole was the more famous author of *Memoirs,* and initially I was confused by this. The Mr. Davison referred to is the discoverer of "Davison's Chamber" in the Great Pyramid. The account about Caviglia's excavations at the Sphinx has nothing whatsoever to do with either Davison or Walpole, and if one were not told, one would have not the slightest idea that they occur in an article purporting to be a review of quite another book in which the Sphinx is not even mentioned. This was the eccentric way in which the *Quarterly Review* occasionally acted as a forum for material only vaguely related to the subject of a "review." The reference for the Walpole/Davison material is: Robert Walpole, *Memoirs Relating to European and Asiatic Turkey, Edited from Manuscript Journals* (London, 1817): pp. xx–xxi and 345–82. The material published by Walpole consisted of extracts from the manuscript diaries of Nathaniel Davison and letters found among his papers, which were made available to Walpole by Davison's widow, who lived at that time at Alnwick, Northumberland, and by Davison's nephew, Dr. Yelloly, of Finsbury Square, London. Davison died in 1809. I am not aware whether the manuscripts of Davison still exist, but I have never come across them. Perhaps somebody should make a search for them. Davison did very important work at the Great Pyramid and elsewhere, and his papers would be of the greatest importance to Egyptology. He counted and measured all the tiers of stone composing the Great Pyramid, and Davison's Chamber above the King's Chamber in the Great Pyramid is named after him, as he was its discoverer.

2. Ibid., 416.

3. Anonymous, "Account of the Recent Discoveries in Egypt Respecting the Sphinx and the Great Pyramid," *The Edinburgh Philosophical Journal* 1 (June to October 1819): 88–96 (the quotation is from p. 95).

4. *Quarterly Review,* "Antiquities of Egypt," 410.

5. Selim Hassan, *The Great Sphinx and Its Secrets: Historical Studies in the Light of Recent Excavations* (Cairo: Government Press, 1953), 92–93. This large book is not the same as Hassan's earlier, smaller, and much briefer book *The Sphinx: Its History in the Light of Recent Excavations* (Cairo: Government Press, 1949). In notes I shall call the former *Great Sphinx* and the latter *Sphinx.* A much better edition of *Sphinx* appeared in French. It was in a larger format with much clearer illustrations. It is Selim Hassan, *Le Sphinx: Son histoire a la lumière des fouilles récente,* Cairo, 1951. We shall call this *Le Sphinx.*

6. Robert Temple, *The Crystal Sun: Rediscovering a Lost Technology of the Ancient World* (London: Century, 2000).

7. Hassan, *Sphinx,* 30.

8. Ibid., 25.

9. Herbert Ricke, ed. and contributor, *Beiträge zur Ägyptischen Bauforschung und Altertumskunde,* Heft [vol.] 10, Wiesbaden, 1970. The illustration is Plan 4, though it is unnumbered. It is unclear whether it is meant to be part of Ricke's portion of this volume, "Der Harmachistempel des Chefren in Giseh," or that written by Siegfried Schott, "Ägyptische Quellen zum Plan des Sphinxtempels." (I should add by way of explanation that although Schott calls the Sphinx Temple the Sphinx Temple, Ricke calls it the Harmachis Temple. These two names are used in the same volume!)

10. Ludwig Borchardt, "Über das Alter des Sphinx bei Giseh" ("Concerning the Age of the Sphinx at Giza"), in *Sitzungsberichte der Preussischen Akademie der Wissenschaften,* vol. 8, Berlin, July 1897.

11. Hassan, *Great Sphinx,* 158–60.

Chapter 4. The Face of the Sphinx

1. André Dessenne, *Le Sphinx: Étude iconographique* (*The Sphinx: An Iconographic Study*) (Paris: Bibliothèque des École Françaises d'Athènes et de Rome, E. de Boccard, 1957).

2. Ibid., 14.

3. Christiane Zivie-Coche, *Sphinx: History of a Monument,* trans. from the French by David Lorton (Ithaca, N.Y.: Cornell University Press, 2002), 5. This small book deals only with Egypt, from the Old Kingdom through to the Greco-Roman period.

4. Rainer Stadelmann, "Royal Tombs from the Age of the Pyramids," a chapter in the profusely illustrated anthology *Egypt: The World of the Pharaohs,* Régine Schulz and Matthias Seidel, eds. (n.l.: Könemann Publishers, n.d.), 75.

5. Ludwig Borchardt, "Über das Alter des Sphinx bei Giseh" ("Concerning the Age of the Sphinx at Giza"), in *Sitzungsberichte der Königlich Preussischen Akademie der Wissenschafter zu Berlin* (*Report of the Proceedings of the Royal Prussian Academy of Sciences at Berlin*), *Sitzung der philosophisch-historischen Classe* (*Proceedings of the Historic-Philosophical Class*) XXXV (1897): 752–60.

6. Harco Olger Willems, *The Coffin of Heqata: A Case Study of the Egyptian Funerary Culture of the Early Middle Kingdom,* thesis for the degree of doctor of letters at the Rijsuniversiteit Groningen, Groningen, Netherlands, 1994, vol. 2, p. 474.

7. Ibid., 484, note bv.

8. A lengthy discussion of these matters, though somewhat confusing, is found in ibid., vol. 1, 262–70.

9. Ibid., vol. 1, 193.

10. E. A. Wallis Budge, *A History of Egypt,* vol. 3, *Egypt Under the Amenemhats and Hyksos,* in the series *Books on Egypt and Chaldaea* (London: Kegan Paul, Trench, Trübner & Co., 1902), 70.

11. Selim Hassan, *The Great Sphinx and Its Secrets: Historical Studies in the Light of Recent Excavations,* vol. 8 of his *Excavations at Giza* series, covering the years 1936–37 (Cairo: Government Press, 1953).

12. Wallis Budge, *History of Egypt,* 43–48.

13. Ibid., 58.

14. Herodotus, *The Histories,* Book II, 149, Aubrey de Sélincourt, trans. (Harmondsworth, Middlesex, U.K.: Penguin Books, 1971), 161.

15. Wallis Budge, *History of Egypt,* 69.

16. Ibid., 71.

17. Biri Fay, *The Louvre Sphinx and Royal Sculpture from the Reign of Amenemhat II* (Mainz, Germany: Verlag Philipp von Zabern, 1996).

18. Jaromir Malek, "The Annals of Amenemhet II," in *Egyptian Archaeology* (2) (1992): 18, Egypt Exploration Society, London.

19. Fay, *Louvre Sphinx,* 54–55.

20. Robert Temple, *The Sirius Mystery,* new expanded edition (London: Century Books, 1998), chapter 1.

Chapter 5. The Sphinx as Anubis

1. Mark Lehner, *The Complete Pyramids* (London: Thames & Hudson, 1997), 128.

2. Roger Highfield, "Genes Prove Hounds Were Never Pharaoh's Best Friend," in the London *Telegraph,* 21 June 2004, reporting a study published in *Science* magazine by a team from the Fred Hutchinson Cancer Research Center of Seattle, Washington.

3. Alberto Bianchi, "On the Presence of the Wild Dog in Ancient Egyptian Iconography," *Discussions in Egyptology* 42 (1998): 10.

4. Ibid., 9.

5. Ibid., 8–9.

6. Lehner, *Complete Pyramids,* 128–29.

7. Zahi Hawass, "History of the Sphinx Conservation," in *Books of Proceedings of the First International Symposium on the Great Sphinx* (Cairo: Egyptian Antiquities Organization Press, 1992), 171–72.

8. Selim Hassan, *The Great Sphinx and Its Secrets: Historical Studies in the Light of Recent Excavations,* vol. 8 of his *Excavations at Giza* series, covering the years 1936–37 (Cairo: Government Press, 1953), 114.

9. Richard A. Parker, Jean Leclant, and Jean-Claude Goyon, *The Edifice of Taharqa by the Sacred Lake of Karnak* (Providence, R.I.: Brown University Press, 1979), ix.

10. Terence Du Quesne, *The Jackal Divinities of Egypt: I, From the Archaic Period to Dynasty X* (London: Da'th Scholarly Services, Darengo Publications, 2005), 43, 102, 108, and the discussion of the title *Khenti-ta-Djeser,* "Foremost of the Secluded Land," on pp. 154–57.

11. Ibid., 220–21.

12. Hassan, *Great Sphinx,* 114.

13. Ibid., 116–17.

14. Lehner, *Complete Pyramids,* 50.

15. Robert Temple, *The Crystal Sun: Rediscovering a Lost Technology of the Ancient World* (London: Century, 2000).

16. Alexander Badawy, "Zoomorphic Shrines in Egypt and India," *The Journal of the Society of Architectural Historians* XVIII, 1 (March 1959): 27–29.

17. Ibid., 27.

18. Alexander Badawy, *A History of Egyptian Architecture,* vol. I (London: Histories & Mysteries of Man Ltd., 1990), 34–35.

19. Hassan, *Great Sphinx,* 60.

20. Ibid., 61.

21. Terence Du Quesne, *Anubis and the Spirits of the West* (Thame, Oxfordshire: Darengo Publications, 1990), 10 and 16, note 34. This publication is remarkably rare, having had a tiny printing, and is absent from most libraries. I am fortunate to have acquired a copy, which greatly astonished Terence when I told him, as he has only one copy of it himself.

22. Harco Olger Willems, *The Coffin of Heqata: A Case Study of the Egyptian Funerary Culture of the Early Middle Kingdom,* thesis for the degree of doctor of letters at the Rijksuniversiteit Groningen, Groningen, Netherlands, 1994, vol. 2, 456.

23. Terence DuQuesne, *Jackal at the Shaman's Gate: A Study of Anubis Lord of Ro-Setawe* (Oxfordshire: Darengo Publications, 1991).

24. Ibid., 9–21.

25. Another meaning of the word is "rich brocade," but that has nothing to do with our concerns here. It was the origin of the structural meaning, because European baldachins were originally made of such brocade.

26. R. O. Faulkner, trans., *The Ancient Egyptian Pyramid Texts* (Oxford: Clarendon Press, 1998), 144.

27. Ibid., 235.

28. Ibid., 144.

29. Ibid., 271.

30. Ibid., 291.

31. Deborah Sweeney, "Egyptian Masks in Motion," *Göttingner Miszellen* 135 (1993): 101–104.

32. Terence Du Quesne, "Concealing and Revealing: The Problem of Ritual Masking in Ancient Egypt," *Discussions in Egyptology* 51 (2001): 5–21.

33. Du Quesne, *Jackal Divinities,* 97–98.

34. Ibid., 90.

35. William Kelly Simpson, *The Mastabas of Kawab, Khafkhufu I and II* (Boston: Museum of Fine Arts, 1978), 9.

36. Ibid., 10.

37. Ibid., 1.
38. Ibid., 6.
39. Dows Dunham and William Kelly Simpson, *The Mastaba of Queen Mersyankh III* (Boston: Museum of Fine Arts, 1974), 8–9.
40. Du Quesne, *Jackal Divinities,* 90, 96.
41. See, for example, Ann Macy Roth, *A Cemetery of Palace Attendants, Giza Mastabas,* vol. 6 (Boston: Museum of Fine Arts, 1995), 35, 89, 103, 126, 130, 137, 146, 164–65.
42. Ibid., 160.
43. R. O. Faulkner, trans., *The Ancient Egyptian Coffin Texts,* vol. 3 (Warminster, England: Aris & Phillips, 1978), 15.
44. Ibid., vol. 2, 212.
45. Ibid., vol. 1, 236.

Chapter 6. Sphinx Island

1. R. A. Schwaller de Lubicz, *Sacred Science: The King of Pharaonic Theocracy,* trans. André and Goldian Vanden Broeck (Rochester, Vt.: Inner Traditions, 1982).
2. Ibid., 96.
3. Zahi Hawass, "History of the Sphinx Conservation," in *The First International Symposium on the Great Sphinx, Book of Proceedings* (Cairo: Egyptian Antiquities Organization Press, 1992), 181.
4. John Anthony West, "Metaphysics by Design: Harmony and Proportion in Ancient Egypt," *Second Look* 1, 8 (June 1979): 2–5.
5. John Anthony West, *Serpent in the Sky: The High Wisdom of Ancient Egypt* (London: Wildwood House, 1979). The American edition was published by Harper & Row in New York. My friend Oliver Caldecott, joint head of Wildwood House, was the person who took the book for England. He had seen the *Second Look* article.
6. Mark Lehner, *The Complete Pyramids* (London: Thames & Hudson, 1997), 126.
7. Richard Pococke, *A Description of the East and Some Other Countries* (Folio, London, 1743–5, vol. 1), 46.
8. Joseph Needham and Ling Wang, *Science and Civlization in China,* vol. 4, part 2, *Mechanical Engineering* (Cambridge, U.K.: Cambridge University Press, 1965, 331–32).
9. Ibid., 331–34, incorporating footnotes c and e on p. 334.
10. Ibid., 352, 356.
11. Jack Finegan, *Hidden Records of the Life of Jesus* (Philadelphia and Boston: Pilgrim Press, 1969), 83. Finegan believes he has identified the ridge. For the Strabo passage, see Strabo, Casaubon 806 (Finegan gives the wrong reference of 86), in *The Geography of Strabo,* translated by Horace Leonard Jones, Loeb Library Series (Cambridge, Mass.: Harvard University Press, 1988), or see next endnote.
12. Strabo, *The Geography,* trans. H. C. Hamilton and W. Falconer, 3 vols. (London: George Bell and Sons, 1881) (book 17, 1, 30; Casaubon 806).

13. Selim Hassan, *The Great Sphinx and Its Secrets: Historical Studies in the Light of Recent Excavations,* vol. 8 of his *Excavations at Giza* series, covering the years 1936–37 (Cairo: Government Press, 1953), 31.

14. Ibid., 29.

15. Ibid., fig. 10.

16. Charles Leonard Irby and James Mangles, *Travels in Egypt and Nubia, Syria, and Asia Minor During the Years 1817 and 1818* (London, 1823); photographic reprint (London: Darf Publishers Limited, 1985), 157–58.

17. Paul Jordan, *Riddles of the Sphinx* (New York: New York University Press, 1998), 14–15.

18. Robert M. Schoch, *Voices of the Rocks: A Scientist Looks at Catastrophes and Ancient Civilizations* (London: Thorsons, 2000), 39. (The book was originally published in New York in 1999.)

19. Ibid., 44.

20. Ibid.

21. Mark Lehner, *The Complete Pyramids* (London: Thames & Hudson, 1997), 107.

22. Ibid., 106.

23. Schoch, *Voices of the Rocks,* 48.

24. Ibid., 40.

25. R. O. Faulkner, trans., *The Ancient Egyptian Pyramid Texts* (Oxford: Clarendon Press, 1998), 40.

26. James P. Allen, *Genesis in Egypt: The Philosophy of Ancient Egyptian Creation Accounts,* Yale Egyptological Studies 2 (New Haven, Conn.: Yale University Press, 1988), 25.

27. K. Lal Gauri and Jayanta K. Bandyopadhyay, *Carbonate Stone: Chemical Behavior, Durability, and Conservation* (New York: John Wiley & Sons, 1999).

28. K. Lal Gauri, John J. Sinai, and Jayanta K. Bandyopadhyay, "Geologic Weathering and Its Implications on the Age of the Sphinx," *Geoarchaeology: An International Journal* 10, no. 2 (1995): 119–33.

29. Ibid., 132.

30. Gauri and Bandyopadhyay, *Carbonate Stone,* 248.

31. For Belzoni's description of his rediscovery and of the Arabic writing he found inside that proved the previous discovery by the Arabs, see the lengthy account in his book *Narrative of the Operations and Recent Discoveries Within the Pyramids, Temples, Tombs, and Excavations, in Egypt and Nubia.* My copy is the second edition, published by John Murray, London, 1821. The first edition appeared the previous year, in 1820. Most of Belzoni's engravings were published in a separate atlas volume, and few of these volumes survive intact, as they have mostly been dismembered and their prints sold off separately by dealers wishing to optimize their profits.

32. Herodotus, *The Persian Wars,* Book II, 127, trans. A. D. Godley, vol. 1 (Boston: Harvard University Press, Loeb Classical Library, 1960), 429–31.

33. Ibid., Book II, 124, vol. 1, 425–27.

34. Ibid., Book II, 147, vol. 1, 455.

35. E. A. Wallis Budge, *The Egyptian Heaven and Hell,* vol. 3 (London: Kegan Paul, 1905), 131–33.

36. Alexandre Piankoff, trans., *The Pyramid of Unas,* Bollingen Series XL:5 (Princeton, N.J.: Princeton University Press, 1968), 63. The quotation is from Utterance 217, line 157.

37. Alexandre Piankoff, *The Tomb of Ramesses VI,* vol. 1, Bollingen Series XL:1 (New York: Pantheon Books, 1954), *Texts,* 47.

38. Ibid., 69.

39. Ibid., 96.

40. Ibid., 105.

41. Ibid., 120.

42. Ibid., 121.

43. Robert Temple, *He Who Saw Everything: A Verse Translation of the Epic of Gilgamesh* (London: Rider, 1991), 130 (the text) and 137 (the footnote).

44. Faulkner, *Pyramid Texts,* 188–89.

45. Ibid., 76–77.

46. Ibid., 91.

47. Ibid., Utterance 515, 190.

48. E. A. Wallis Budge, *Osiris and the Egyptian Resurrection,* vol. 2 (London: Philip Lee Warner, 1911), 323.

49. Ibid.

50. Ibid., 288.

51. Ibid., 277.

52. Ibid., 290.

53. Ibid., 289.

54. Terence Du Quesne, *The Jackal Divinities of Egypt* (London: Darengo Publications, 2005), 411.

55. Ibid., 299.

56. R. O. Faulkner, trans., *The Ancient Egyptian Coffin Texts,* vol. 2 (Warminster, England: Aris & Phillips, 1977), 163.

57. Ibid., vol. 1, 22.

58. Ibid., vol. 1, 196.

59. Ibid., 217.

60. Ibid., 261.

61. Ibid., 265.

62. Ibid., 270.

63. Ibid., vol. 3, 184–89.

64. Ibid., 186, Spell 1171.

65. Alexandre Piankoff, trans., *The Shrines of Tut-Ankh-Amon,* 2 vols., Bollingen Series XL:2 (New York: Pantheon Books, 1955), 32.

66. Ibid., 58.

67. Ibid., 140.

68. Ibid., 60, 97, 137.

69. Ibid., 34.

70. Ibid., 75.

71. Ibid., 87.

72. Alexandre Piankoff, trans., *Mythological Papyri,* vol. 1, Bollingen Series XL:3 (New York: Pantheon Books, 1957), *Texts,* 99.

73. Peter le Page Renouf, *The Life-Work of Sir Peter le Page Renouf,* vol. 4, *The Book of the Dead: Translation and Commentary* (Paris and Leipzig, 1907), 237–38.

74. Faulkner, *Pyramid Texts,* 184.

75. Ibid., 185–86.

76. Hassan, *Great Sphinx,* 123.

77. "Observations relating to some of the Antiquities of Egypt, from the papers of the late Mr. Davison," *Quarterly Review* XIX (April and December, 1818); London, 1819, pp. 391–424. (The reason for two dates with this reference is that the issues of the periodical were for 1818, but the bound edition of them came out in 1819 in volume form.) The original Greek inscription, entirely in capital letters, is faithfully reproduced on p. 411, and the transliteration into lowercase Greek, the Latin translation, and the English translation are all on p. 412. (These were all done by "Dr. Young.")

78. Simplicius, *Epictetus His Morals, with Simplicius His Comment, Made into English from the Greek* by George Stanhope, London, 1694. I bought this book so long ago, from Quaritch's Catalogue 927, which I see from the price written inside and the catalog entry that I clipped and inserted in the book, that it only cost me £10 (although that was a lot then). My copy contains the hand corrections by the translator himself and seems to have been his own personal copy. The leather spine is plain, as he had no need to be told what it was when it was sitting on the shelf beside him. From the nature of Stanhope's corrections, I can see that he must have been irritated by some of the printer's errors, such as mistaking "which" for "when." But in those days, printers did have to struggle to read the handwriting of authors, and that was the cause of many typographical errors. Today, things are different, because so many people under the age of thirty lack the ability to spell correctly due to the collapse in effective teaching methods as a result of the intrusion of crazy political ideas into the educational field, combined with the decline of the print medium in this "I.T. Age," so that even if things are printed out perfectly clearly by the computer, many young people can no longer "read" them, as they simply do not "see" spelling anymore and have no way way of retaining it in their minds, which have not been trained to do so. Also, few young people read enough anymore for standardization of spelling to enter into the memory. And then there are the corrupting influences of abbreviated "texting" by thumb-messaging over handheld devices, so that spelling ends up being dictated by the movement capabilities of the human thumb, in disregard of the obvious fact that

the human thumb is of an inferior status to the human mind, which should be making these decisions. In the twenty-first century, our society is thus reverting to spelling by sound rather than by convention established by the print medium, and has in that sense gone back to the lack of precise spelling characteristic of the seventeenth century. Who says there is such a thing as "cultural progress"? "Decline," on the other hand, requires no proof of its existence.

79. Ibid., 2.

80. See Robert Temple, *Oracles of the Dead* (Rochester, Vt.: Inner Traditions, 2004), for an account of my visit to an underground shrine of Persephone, goddess of the underworld. (This book was entitled *Netherworld* when it was first published in Britain in 2002.) See also the fifty-two-minute television documentary film that I wrote, produced, and presented, entitled *Descent into Hell,* which is shown from time to time on the National Geographic Channel. In one scene, I leave a traditional offering of a bough of mistletoe (brought from England) for Persephone in the very same niche where the fictional hero Aeneas is described as doing so in the *Aeneid* of Virgil. (Virgil was personally familiar with this underground sanctuary known as the Oracle of the Dead, at Baia.)

81. Hassan, *Great Sphinx,* 123. Selim Hassan chose to publish this modern prose version rather than to quote the even more old-fashioned verse translation that was published in 1818.

82. *Quarterly Review,* "Observations," p. 412.

83. Appendix volume (volume 3), plate E on p. 119. The translation is facing on p. 118.

84. Ibid., 118.

Chapter 7. The Sphinx and the Giza Plan

1. This is a subject that I discussed in my earlier book *Open to Suggestion: The Uses and Abuses of Hypnosis* (England: Aquarian Press, 1989), 49–50, in the context of the evidence I presented about how people can still hear when they are in a state of coma or under an anesthetic on the operating table, a phenomenon known as "surgical memory." The sense of hearing is the last to go when you die, and the Tibetans somehow knew this, and realized that shouting into the ears of someone who appears to be dead is not necessarily pointless at all, but may actually be helpful.

2. Erik Hornung, *The Ancient Egyptian Books of the Afterlife,* translated from the German by David Lorton (Ithaca, N.Y.: Cornell University Press, 1999), 32.

3. E. A. Wallis Budge, *The Gods of the Egyptians,* vol. 4 (London: Methuen, 1904), 224.

4. Margaret A. Murray, *The Osireion at Abydos,* Egyptian Research Account, Ninth Year, 1903 (London: Bernard Quaritch, 1904), 15. (This book has also been photographically reprinted by Histories & Mysteries of Man Ltd., London, 1989.)

5. Hornung, *Books of the Afterlife,* 30.

6. Alexandre Piankoff, *The Wandering of the Soul,* completed by Helen Jacquet-Gordon [after Piankoff's death], vol. 6 of Piankoff's series *Egyptian Religious Texts and*

Representations, Bollingen Series 40: 6 (Princeton, N.J.: Princeton University Press, 1974). *The Book of Two Ways* is the first of three ancient Egyptian texts included in this volume.

7. Ibid., 14–17 and foldout plan at back of book.

8. Ibid., 14 and foldout plan at back of book.

9. J. R. Harris, *Lexicographical Studies in Ancient Egyptian Minerals* (Berlin: Akademie-Verlag, 1961), 138.

10. Ibid.

11. Piankoff, *The Wandering of the Soul,* vol. 6, 21 and foldout plan at back of book.

12. I was present at the Eighth International Congress of Egyptologists in Cairo in 2000 when this discovery was announced. The paper was published in 2003: Jean-Yves Verd'hurt and Gilles Dormion, "New Discoveries in the Pyramid of Meidum" in Zahi Hawass, ed., *Egyptology at the Dawn of the Twenty-First Century: Proceedings of the Eighth International Congress of Egyptologists, Cairo, 2000,* vol. 1 (Cairo and New York: American University in Cairo Press, 2003), 541–46.

13. Ibid.

14. Ibid., 22.

15. Ibid., 23.

16. Omm Sety and Hanny El Zeini, *Abydos: Holy City of Ancient Egypt* (Los Angeles, Calif.: L. L. Company, 1981), 176–78.

17. Ahmed El-Sawy, "A New Discovery at the Sety I Temple in Abydos," in Hawass, *Egyptology,* op. cit., vol. 1, 424–31.

18. Strabo, *The Geography,* H. C. Hamilton and W. Falconer, trans., vol. 3 (London: George Bell and Sons, 1881), 249 (Book 17, 1, 33; Causabon 807).

19. Ibid., 250.

20. Sozomen, *Ecclesiastical History,* I, 14, Edward Walford, trans. (London: Bohns Library, 1855), 34.

21. Hero of Alexandria, *Pneumatics,* I, 38–39.

22. This strange expression may conceivably be a reference to a wall or slab of basalt, which, being black, is the color of charcoal. That is just my guess. However, no Egyptologist has ever discovered the name by which basalt was known to the ancient Egyptians. This strange fact is recorded by the leading expert on ancient Egyptian names for stones and minerals, J. R. Harris. He says of basalt: "No name is known." (From Harris, J. R., *Lexicographical Studies in Ancient Egyptian Minerals,* Akademie-Verlag, Berlin, 1961, p. 94.) Basalt largely ceased to be used after the Old Kingdom, but its occurrence in both building and statuary prior to 2200 BC was substantial. The fact that we do not know the ancient name for basalt means that references to it have probably been misunderstood in the texts, where it has doubtless been mentioned but not recognized. Hence, a reference to a "charcoal wall" might, for all we know, actually mean "a basalt wall," or a common word meaning "black substance" might have been used as a general term for both charcoal and basalt. We need always to keep in mind our

ignorance when dealing with matters concerning basalt in ancient Egypt. See figure 4 for an example in the Valley Temple, which is at Rostau.

23. Pliny, *Natural History*, Book XXXVI, 16, 76; D. E. Eichholz, trans., vol. 10 of Pliny (Boston: Loeb Classical Library, Harvard University Press, 1971), 61.

24. Piankoff, *Wandering of the Soul*, 23–36.

25. John Coleman Darnell, *The Enigmatic Netherworld Books of the Solar-Osirian Unity* (Fribourg: Academic Press, 2004), 99.

26. J. Gwyn Griffiths, *Plutarch's de Iside et Osiride* (Cardiff: University of Wales Press, 1970), 436–37; the mention of Sokar is on p. 437. Griffiths adds a curious detail that at the Island of Philae, the *redju* of Osiris that created the Nile was regarding as coming from his left leg. This is doubtless an esoteric reference with an important meaning. If Osiris was regarding as rising in the east at dawn (see discussion of this later in this chapter), then his left leg would be his southern leg. The god Ptah was conventionally described as being "south of his Wall." These references to the cardinal directions are always significant. (See also the later discussion of the shadow on the south face of the Great Pyramid.)

27. Ibid., 172–73 (first sentence of chapter 36 of Plutarch's treatise).

28. J. Zandee, *Death as an Enemy According to Ancient Egyptian Conceptions* (Leiden, The Netherlands: Brill, 1960), 57–58.

29. Ibid., 58–59.

30. Andreas Winkler, "The Efflux That Issued from Osiris," *Göttingr Miszellen* 211 (2006): 125–39.

31. J. Zandee, *Death as an Enemy According to Ancient Egyptian Conceptions* (Leiden, The Netherlands: Brill, 1960), 58.

32. Daniel Burnham, "Explorations into the Alchemical Idiom of the Pyramid Texts," *Discussions in Egyptology* 60 (2004): 11–20.

33. E. A. Wallis Budge, *The Egyptian Heaven and Hell*, vol. 2 (London: Kegan Paul, 1905), 13–17.

34. Ibid., 26.

35. Ibid.

36. Murray, *Osireion at Abydos*, 17.

37. Marshall Clagett, *Ancient Egyptian Science*, vol. 1 (Philadelphia: American Philosophical Society, 1992), 474 and reference on p. 487 to "H. Altenmüller, 'Toten-Literatur,' 22. Jenseitsbücher, Jenseitsführer, *Handbuch der Orientalistik*, Abteilung 1, Vol. 1, Part 2, pp. 70–72," but giving no date. I have not consulted this original reference but took the information from Clagett.

38. Peter Tompkins, *Secrets of the Great Pyramid* (New York: Harper & Row, 1971), 45–48.

39. Robert Temple, *The Crystal Sun: Rediscovering a Lost Technology of the Ancient World* (London: Century, 2000).

40. John Taylor, *The Great Pyramid. Why Was It Built? And Who Built it?* (London: Longman Green, 1859), 19–20.

41. Tompkins, *Secrets of the Great Pyramid,* 70–72.
42. Euclid, *The Thirteen Books of Euclid's Elements,* trans. Thomas Heath, vol. 2 (New York: Dover Publications, 1956, 2nd ed. reprint), 114.
43. Ibid., 188.
44. Ibid., 267.
45. Alexander Badawy, *Ancient Egyptian Architectural Design: A Study of the Harmonic System,* Near Eastern Studies 4 (Berkeley and Los Angeles: University of California Press, 1965).
46. Badawy, *History of Egyptian Architecture,* (Berkeley and Los Angeles: University of California Press, 1968).

Chapter 8. The Golden Angle of Resurrection

1. Else Christie Kielland, *Geometry in Egyptian Art* (London: Tiranti, 1955).
2. John Coleman Darnell, *The Enigmatic Netherworld Books of the Solar-Osirian Unity* (Fribourg: Academic Press, 2004), 297.
3. Ibid.
4. Ibid., 365.
5. Ibid., 477.
6. Ibid., 341.
7. Ibid., 348.
8. Ibid., 276–77.
9. Ibid., 365.
10. Ibid., 286.
11. Ibid., 302–4.
12. Ibid., 291.
13. Ibid., 306–7.
14. Ibid., 309.
15. Ibid., 325.
16. Ibid., 318–19.
17. Ibid, 319–20.
18. Ibid., 320–21.
19. Ibid., 322.
20. Ibid., 325–26.
21. Ibid., 328.
22. Ibid., 357.
23. John Gwyn Griffiths, trans. and ed., *Plutarch, De Iside et Osiride (On Isis and Osiris)* (Cardiff: University of Wales Press, 1970), 209 (chapter 56, 374A, of the text). Because the Griffiths book is unfortunately extremely rare, I give the references to the Bohn and Loeb editions as well: C. W. King., trans., *Plutarch's Morals: Theosophical Essays* (London: George Bell, 1889); absorbed into Bohn's Classical Library with the takeover of Bell by Bohn,

p. 49; Frank Cole Babbitt, trans., vol. 5 of *Plutarch's Moralia* (Cambridge, Mass.: Harvard University Press, 1962), 135.

24. Ibid.

25. Ibid.

26. C. W. King, *The Gnostics and Their Remains* (London: Bell and Daldy, 1864), illustration facing p. 90.

27. There is apparently an extended modern account of this graffito in German by Klaus Parlasca, but I have not been able to find it, as it is published in a book compiled by another German author, and the reference I have is incomplete. Parlasca apparently gives a bibliography to the extensive discussions of this graffito that have been published over many years. Because this graffito is not a main subject of my book, I have cut short my research on it and leave it to others to pursue if they wish.

28. Alexandre Moret, "L'Influence du Décor Solaire sur la Pyramide" ("The Influence of Solar Decoration on the Pyramid"), 623–36, Institut Français d'Archéologie, Cairo, 1934, 29. Sylvie Cauville, *Dendara V–VI Traduction: Les Cryptes du Temple d'Hathor* (*The Crypts of the Temple of Hathor, Translation* [of the Texts of, given in volumes V–VI of the French series, which published the texts in hieroglyphic form]), volume 1, Peeters, Wilsele, Belgium, 2004.

30. Wolfgang Waitkus, *Die Texte in den unteren Krypten des Hathortempels von Dendera, Ihre Aussagen zur Funktion und Bedeutung dieser Räume* (*The Texts in the Subterranean Crypts of the Temple of Hathor at Dendera, Their Evidence as to the Function and Significance of These Chambers*) (Mainz, Germany: Philipp von Zabern, 1997).

31. R. V. Lanzone, *Dizionario di Mitologia Egizia* [*Dictionary of Egyptian Mythology*], reprint by Benjamins, Amsterdam, 1974, vol. 2, pp. 658–66 contains a discussion of Harsomtus, and plates CCXXXIX–CCXXXXI referring to this contain depictions of the reliefs in the crypt, and show all the "snake aubergines." The text is in Italian, with no translation into any other language.

32. Robert Ballard, *The Solution of the Pyramid Problem or, Pyramid Discoveries with a New Theory as to Their Ancient Use* (New York: John Wiley & Sons, 1882).

INDEX

◖◉ Also by Robert Temple ◉◗

The Sirius Mystery
New Scientific Evidence of Alien Contact 5,000 Years Ago

Oracles of the Dead
Ancient Techniques for Predicting the Future

The Genius of China
3,000 Years of Science, Discovery, and Invention

Inner Traditions • Bear & Company
P.O. Box 388
Rochester, VT 05767
1-800-246-8648
www.InnerTraditions.com

Or contact your local bookseller